First published 2014 by
PALGRAVE MACMILLAN

Palgrave Macmillan in the UK is an imprint of Macmillan Publishers Limited, registered in England, company number 785998, of Houndmills, Basingstoke, Hampshire RG21 6XS.

Palgrave Macmillan in the US is a division of St Martin's Press LLC, 175 Fifth Avenue, New York, NY 10010.

Palgrave Macmillan is the global academic imprint of the above companies and has companies and representatives throughout the world.

Palgrave® and Macmillan® are registered trademarks in the United States, the United Kingdom, Europe and other countries.

ISBN   978–1–1373–8862–9

This book is printed on paper suitable for recycling and made from fully managed and sustained forest sources. Logging, pulping and manufacturing processes are expected to conform to the environmental regulations of the country of origin.

A catalogue record for this book is available from the British Library.

A catalog record for this book is available from the Library of Congress.

Typeset by MPS Ltd., Chennai, India.

CUSTOM TEXTBOOK
FOR PEOPLE, WORK AND ORGANISATIONS

PEOPLE, WORK AND ORGANISATION

Compiled for

DAVID SPICER AND HUGH LEE

palgrave
macmillan

CUSTOM TEXTBOOK
FOR PEOPLE, WORK AND ORGANISATIONS

PEOPLE, WORK AND ORGANISATIONS

Compiled for

DAVID SPICER AND HUGH LEE

CONTENTS

LIST OF FIGURES

LIST OF TABLES

SOURCES

This custom publication has been compiled for use in the **University of Bradford.** The chapters included are reproduced from the following works:

Chapter 1 from **KAMEL MELLAHI, KEVIN MORRELL & GEOFFREY WOOD:** *THE ETHICAL BUSINESS 2ND EDITION* © KAMEL MELLAHI, KEVIN MORRELL & GEOFFREY WOOD 2002, 2010

Chapter 2 from **JOHN BRATTON, PETER SAWCHUK, CAROLYN FORSHAW, MILITZA CALLINAN & MARTIN CORBETT:** *WORK AND ORGANIZATIONAL BEHAVIOUR 2ND EDITION* © JOHN BRATTON, PETER SAWCHUK, CAROLYN FORSHAW, MILITZA CALLINAN & MARTIN CORBETT 2007, 2010

Chapter 3 from **JOHN BRATTON, PETER SAWCHUK, CAROLYN FORSHAW, MILITZA CALLINAN & MARTIN CORBETT:** *WORK AND ORGANIZATIONAL BEHAVIOUR 2ND EDITION* © JOHN BRATTON, PETER SAWCHUK, CAROLYN FORSHAW, MILITZA CALLINAN & MARTIN CORBETT 2007, 2010

Chapter 4 from **JOHN BRATTON, PETER SAWCHUK, CAROLYN FORSHAW, MILITZA CALLINAN & MARTIN CORBETT:** *WORK AND ORGANIZATIONAL BEHAVIOUR 2ND EDITION* © JOHN BRATTON, PETER SAWCHUK, CAROLYN FORSHAW, MILITZA CALLINAN & MARTIN CORBETT 2007, 2010

Chapter 5 from **JOHN BRATTON, PETER SAWCHUK, CAROLYN FORSHAW, MILITZA CALLINAN & MARTIN CORBETT:** *WORK AND ORGANIZATIONAL BEHAVIOUR 2ND EDITION* © JOHN BRATTON, PETER SAWCHUK, CAROLYN FORSHAW, MILITZA CALLINAN & MARTIN CORBETT 2007, 2010

Chapter 6 from **JOHN BRATTON, PETER SAWCHUK, CAROLYN FORSHAW, MILITZA CALLINAN & MARTIN CORBETT:** *WORK AND ORGANIZATIONAL BEHAVIOUR 2ND EDITION* © JOHN BRATTON, PETER SAWCHUK, CAROLYN FORSHAW, MILITZA CALLINAN & MARTIN CORBETT 2007, 2010

Chapter 7 from **JOHN BRATTON AND JEFF GOLD:** *HUMAN RESOURCE MANAGEMENT 5TH EDITION* © JOHN BRATTON AND JEFF GOLD 1994, 1999, 2003, 2007, 2012

Chapter 8 from **JOHN BRATTON AND JEFF GOLD:** *HUMAN RESOURCE MANAGEMENT 5TH EDITION* © JOHN BRATTON AND JEFF GOLD 1994, 1999, 2003, 2007, 2012

Chapter 9 from **JOHN BRATTON AND JEFF GOLD:** *HUMAN RESOURCE MANAGEMENT 5TH EDITION* © JOHN BRATTON AND JEFF GOLD 1994, 1999, 2003, 2007, 2012

Chapter 10 from **KAMEL MELLAHI, KEVIN MORRELL & GEOFFREY WOOD:** *THE ETHICAL BUSINESS 2ND EDITION* © KAMEL MELLAHI, KEVIN MORRELL & GEOFFREY WOOD 2002, 2010

Chapter 11 from **JOHN BRATTON, PETER SAWCHUK, CAROLYN FORSHAW, MILITZA CALLINAN & MARTIN CORBETT:** *WORK AND ORGANIZATIONAL BEHAVIOUR 2ND EDITION* © JOHN BRATTON, PETER SAWCHUK, CAROLYN FORSHAW, MILITZA CALLINAN & MARTIN CORBETT 2007, 2010

Chapter 12 from **JOHN BRATTON, PETER SAWCHUK, CAROLYN FORSHAW, MILITZA CALLINAN & MARTIN CORBETT:** *WORK AND ORGANIZATIONAL BEHAVIOUR 2ND EDITION* © JOHN BRATTON, PETER SAWCHUK, CAROLYN FORSHAW, MILITZA CALLINAN & MARTIN CORBETT 2007, 2010

Chapter 13 from **JOHN BRATTON, PETER SAWCHUK, CAROLYN FORSHAW, MILITZA CALLINAN & MARTIN CORBETT:** *WORK AND ORGANIZATIONAL BEHAVIOUR 2ND EDITION* © JOHN BRATTON, PETER SAWCHUK, CAROLYN FORSHAW, MILITZA CALLINAN & MARTIN CORBETT 2007, 2010

Chapter 14 from **MIKE NOON, PAUL BLYTON & KEVIN MORRELL:** *THE REALITIES OF WORK 4TH EDITION* © MIKE NOON, PAUL BLYTON & KEVIN MORRELL 1997, 2002, 2007, 2012

Chapter 15 from **MIKE NOON, PAUL BLYTON & KEVIN MORRELL:** *THE REALITIES OF WORK 4TH EDITION* © MIKE NOON, PAUL BLYTON & KEVIN MORRELL 1997, 2002, 2007, 2012

Chapter 16 from **MIKE NOON, PAUL BLYTON & KEVIN MORRELL:** *THE REALITIES OF WORK 4TH EDITION* © MIKE NOON, PAUL BLYTON & KEVIN MORRELL 1997, 2002, 2007, 2012

Chapter 17 from **PAUL BLYTON & PETER TURNBULL:** *THE DYNAMICS OF EMPLOYEE RELATIONS 3RD EDITION* © PAUL BLYTON & PETER TURNBULL 1994, 1998, 2004

Chapter 18 from **PAUL BLYTON & PETER TURNBULL:** *THE DYNAMICS OF EMPLOYEE RELATIONS 3RD EDITION* © PAUL BLYTON & PETER TURNBULL 1994, 1998, 2004

Chapter 19 from **PAUL BLYTON & PETER TURNBULL:** *THE DYNAMICS OF EMPLOYEE RELATIONS 3RD EDITION* © PAUL BLYTON & PETER TURNBULL 1994, 1998, 2004

INTRODUCTION

OVERVIEW

The module for which this book has been put together, 'People, Work and Organisations', is part of the core first-year programme for all Bradford University School of Management students and is intended to provide an introduction to human behaviour in work and organisations. This module has two complementary aims. Firstly, we are conscious that for some of you, this may be the only 'people' focused module that you will take, if your programmes and interests take you into detailed studies in say Marketing or Accounting and Finance. It is therefore important to us that we provide you with sufficient grounding on the study of the human side of a business for you to see its contribution and relevance as you focus your studies further. Alongside this, it has to act as a foundation for those of you who will develop their studies in this area and undertake modules looking at people, work and organisations in greater depth and detail in subsequent years.

In order to address these two aims, the module has been structured into six blocks of study (see Figure One below). Each of these blocks introduces you to key ideas, from theory and practice, that will help you better understand the organisations (work and otherwise) in which you are involved and the role that you play, alone and in interaction with others, within those organisations. Each block is focused on looking at the human aspect of organisations from a different academic discipline perspective (in other words through different areas of academic study). Across these different subject areas you will gain an appreciation of the different ways we can characterise and understand the nature of work, organisations and the behaviour of people within them.

Alongside introducing you to the study of people and organisations through these blocks, we also want to encourage you to think about some of the ethical and social complexities and responsibilities faced by organisations and their stakeholders. The School and University formally recognise such concerns as central to your learning, in order to enable you to become effective graduates. More personally, we believe that awareness and understanding of the social and ethical challenges you will face throughout your lives and careers will better help you meet these challenges effectively. This centrality is reflected in the placing of 'ethics and sustainability' at the centre of Figure One.

More formally the module aims are:

1 to develop an understanding of some of the key factors that impact upon and influence human behaviour in organisations and the workplace and to address ethical, corporate social responsibility and sustainability issues associated with these factors whilst doing so;

Figure 1 – Blocks of study

2 to develop an awareness of the assumptions and approaches which underpin the differing theoretical perspectives employed for studying people in organisations and the workplace, specifically, the disciplines of Organisational Behaviour (OB), Organisational Psychology (OP) Work Sociology (WS), Employee Relations (ER), Organisational Analysis (OA) and Human Resource Management (HRM) and

3 to enable students to understand their own and others' roles in organisations and the workplace more effectively.

One challenge created by the breadth of the introduction that this module seeks to provide is that no single textbook fits the entire module content that we are asking you to address. For this reason we have compiled this custom textbook, which draws on a number of different, discipline (subject) specialist books to provide you with an overview of the module. As such, it provides a single, reasonably concise source from which to start your reading and offers you a range of perspectives from literature that allow us to capture the module's breadth in a single source. You need to recognise as well that this therefore draws in a number of different original sources so you will find differences in the style and approach adopted across the chapters. Please also recognise that this book is just the starting point for your reading. We would encourage you to read further and more deeply in the modules areas to advance your understanding and the module handbook will provide further guidance on reading to help you with this.

In addition, lecturers and tutors will extend the material provided here through other examples and case studies, drawing on both their experience as practitioners working in organisations and through their own research and that of other academics working across these fields. This is particularly significant for those of you studying this module at Bradford's partnership institutions across the globe. The module, this book and the texts that it draws from could be criticised, as much management thinking can be, for the dominance of a North American and Western European perspective. Whilst there are reasons for this, 'modern' management thinking and business education have their roots in these cultures, we are at least mindful that this bias exists. To students studying outside the UK, we know that you also have your own excellent and experienced lecturers and tutors who will be able to help you take, critique and apply these ideas for your own cultural and geographical contexts.

As the module seeks to introduce you to six distinct, but linked (see Figure One), areas of study, the remainder of this short introductory chapter is given over to providing a very brief introduction to each of these areas. As part of this we highlight which chapters in this book are linked to each of these blocks. The module handbook will provide you with specific details of how chapters map onto teaching on a week-by-week, session-by-session basis.

ORGANISATIONAL BEHAVIOUR

The field of organisational behaviour (OB) spans several levels of analysis from the macro, or organisational, level through department or group (midi) level to the individual (micro) level. At the macro level OB is concerned, for example, with how the structure, culture, management systems and control mechanisms of organisations influence behaviour (this overlaps to a degree with organisational analysis which will form the basis of a later block); at the department/group level interest focuses upon leadership, small group behaviour, communication patterns, inter-group conflict, power and politics, whereas at the micro level individual matters such as motivation, work performance and work stress form the foci of interest.

The block aims to demonstrate how findings from research into OB can help people to work more effectively in organisations and to manage better the many different 'people issues' that arise at work, focusing at the individual/micro level of analysis. Decisions and actions about managing people issues in organisations are, of course, influenced by many factors, including culture, ideology, personal values, individual, group and organisational goals. Chapter 2 below will give you an introduction to OB as a field of study, whilst Chapters 3 and 4 introduce two specific areas for study at the 'micro' level in OB. These are Motivation and Job Satisfaction (Chapter 3) and Groups and Team Working (Chapter 4).

ORGANISATIONAL PSYCHOLOGY

Psychology is concerned with understanding the minds of individuals and has been described as 'the science of mental life' (Miller, 1966). Organisational Psychology is concerned with the application of psychological understanding, trying to better understand the behaviour thoughts and emotions within the work/organisational context and thereby better understand the interface between and individual and the organisations with which they engage. The aim of organisational (or work) psychologists is to try to better understand the complexity of human behaviour in organizations (though many contend with the extent to which such understanding is achievable) and to explain and predict individual behaviours, thoughts and emotions in work and organisational contexts. There are evident ethical issues in this goal that we will address as the study block progresses.

Again we will begin by outlining Organisational Psychology as a field for studying the chapter for this will be available through your module website on Blackboard, before looking at two specific areas of study in Psychology of particular relevance to the study of human behaviour in organisation, Personality (Chapter 5) and Perception (Chapter 6).

HUMAN RESOURCE MANAGEMENT

'People are our most important asset' is one of the most overused phrases in modern business. In essence, everything we study in this module is about developing a better understanding of the people side of an organisation. It seems logical therefore to include a block focused on introducing the formal people management discipline, Human Resource Management (HRM). Academically, this describes the range of strategies and processes utilised to achieve competitive advantage by matching the needs of the organisation with the potential of employees. Practically, HRM is that part of the organization that seeks to manage and maximise people's work contributions.

This block seeks to introduce HRM and explore the complexities surrounding its contribution to organisations. Much has been made of the suggestion that organisations are looking to gain and maintain employee commitment, rather than mere compliance to rules and operating procedures. Effective HRM is seen by many as being critical here. In this block we introduce the role and contribution of HRM in organisations today (see Chapter 7), and we will then go on to look at two key areas of this contribution: employee resourcing (recruitment and selection, Chapter 8) and performance management and development (Chapter 9).

ORGANISATIONAL ANALYSIS

Organisational Analysis is concerned with understanding and influencing the nature of an organisation, its structure, systems, functions, culture and capabilities which all combine to influence its efficiency, outputs and performance. In essence it is about understanding and ultimately being able to manage the contexts within which people work and in many respects is an extension of the ideas and principles first introduced in Organisational Behaviour. In fact, Organisational Analysis might be argued to be a subset or extension of Organisational Behaviour, and certainly, ideas addressed in this block (organisational structure, organisational culture, power and politics) are covered in most mainstream Organisational Behaviour textbooks. What is significant however is the shift in perspective this represents; in focusing on Organisational Analysis we are moving to the organisation itself as the fundamental unit of our analysis (rather than the focus on individuals that dominated in the Organisational Behaviour block).

The content of this block is addressed in Chapters 11 to 13 below. Chapter 11 covers issues of organisational structure and design, Chapter 12 looks at organisational culture, and power and politics are covered in Chapter 13.

WORK SOCIOLOGY

Work Sociology (or alternatively the Sociology of Work) covers those aspects of work where working overlaps with our social lives. This means we have to think about things like the way the nature of work itself has changed and continues to change over time. We might think about what constitutes work and who it is that does it. Is work an activity separate from life as the phrase work/life balance might suggest or are the two things inextricably integrated?

In this particular block we will consider three elements of the many areas of sociological study in organisations that we could consider. First we will look at the transformation of work from pre-industrial times, through the industrial age and up to the present, post-industrial age (see Chapter 14). Next, we will look in more detail at the central industrial phase by exploring 'Fordism' as a concept and the principles of 'Scientific Management' associated with this perspective (Chapter 15). Finally we will think about the place of skills (what might once have been called 'crafts') that we need to do our work and whether these have been increasing or decreasing in recent decades (Chapter 16).

EMPLOYEE RELATIONS

Employee Relations is the aspect of the studies of people in organisations that is concerned with a focused understanding of the nature of the workplace from an employee's perspective and is linked with an understanding and exploration of the role and contribution of Trade Unions. Its study has a long tradition in the UK and the US, focusing on understanding the nature of the workplace and work relations and centring on fundamental debates between unitarist, pluralist and radical perspectives on work relations. Historically known as Industrial Relations, Employee Relations is the more typical term used today given the changed nature of workplaces and the growth of non-industrial employment.

This block will introduce employee relations as a discipline and will look at some fundamental aspects of the employment relationship, specifically collective bargaining and participation and involvement. Chapters 17 to 19 cover these areas. Chapter 17 introduces employee relations as a discipline, Chapter 18 looks at collective bargaining, and participation and involvement are discussed in Chapter 19.

ETHICS AND CORPORATE SOCIAL RESPONSIBILITY

As indicated above, and at the centre of Figure One, we also aim to introduce you to ethical and social aspects of business and working life. These are not really topics that can be studied in isolation. They represent themes and concerns will return to through the module. Nonetheless, two lectures will be given over to introducing these perspectives, and chapters which link to these are included below. We will start off the module by considering the role of ethics and morals in the workplace, and Chapter 1 extends the ideas you will be introduced to in this session. Later in the module we will return to ethical principles to address these at the corporate and institutional level. This will include looking at the much vaunted, debated and criticised notion of corporate social responsibility (addressed through Chapter 10 below).

SUMMARY

This is a book and a module that have been put together with the aim of helping you develop the beginnings of a more critical and nuanced understanding of work, organisations and the roles that we as individuals and those around have in relation to that work and those organisations. This is an understanding which will help you better understand your own strengths and motivations and will influence your ability to work effectively within those organisations in which you become involved.

We hope that by using this book, completing the module and fully participating in lectures and tutorials you will develop critical skills and understanding to help your studies and future careers. These include:

- an understanding of people work and organisations which can be used to solve practical workplace problems and challenges;
- understanding to help effectively address ethical and sustainability concerns with respect to the management of people and organisations and
- improved individual effectiveness, communication skills and effective team-working.

Overall, we hope you find this module and the custom text book useful, engaging, thought provoking and informative. Enjoy your studies.

Dr David Spicer & Dr Hugh Lee
Bradford University School of Management, June 2013

WHAT ARE ETHICS AND MORALS IN THE WORKPLACE?

CHAPTER OBJECTIVES

- To understand what constitutes ethics and the relationship between ethics and specific moral guidelines.
- To introduce the principal philosophical frames of reference and their relevance to ethical practice in the real world.

1.1 INTRODUCTION

Business ethics can mean different things to different people (Jones *et al.*, 2005). Here we want to suggest that it is an attempt to apply the tools and concepts developed by philosophers to distinguish 'right' from 'wrong' and the desirable from the undesirable to the corporate world. Ethics is an applied form of philosophy because it places a greater emphasis on human and organisational behaviour and on action in the world. At their heart, ethical questions include studies of the nature and origin of our concepts of good and bad, the just and the unjust (Lamsa, 1999: 346). These questions have been debated for thousands of years and they are continually contested. 'Business ethics' is a comparatively new development – or at least the phrase 'business ethics' is comparatively new. Essentially it can be thought of as the study of business from an ethical point of view. It is worth saying at the outset that we think it is legitimate to question whether there is a need for a separate term like business ethics at all. In an important sense, 'ethics' should apply equally to life in business as it does to life in general. We even have some sympathy with those who suggest that there is a basic tension between the terms 'business' and 'ethics', and that bringing them together is a mistake. Of course, business decisions have ethical implications, but then so does any sphere of human activity – does the phrase 'business ethics' imply there is a different set of rules for ethical behaviour in business that we otherwise don't have to follow? Is business ethics the 'get-out clause' we look for if we want to continue to profit and compete in the marketplace? We don't think so, but it is true that many of the questions we think of as being at the core of 'business' (how profitable something is, how efficient, how it will survive in the marketplace and so on) involve very different sorts of considerations from basic ethical questions that are related to justice, fairness, and right and wrong. You may already have heard the rather tired phrase that business ethics is a contradiction in terms, an oxymoron. Although it's often said in an intellectually lazy manner – to dismiss, rather than encourage further thought – it does signal a basic challenge that books such as this engage with in different ways. You may also have heard a completely contradictory assertion that is almost as empty – namely, 'good ethics is good business'. That is even less helpful, because it is such a vague generalisation. It becomes a nonsense when we learn how highly profitable companies engage in commercial espionage, union busting, unethical outsourcing and a host of other questionable practices. Or when we consider those legitimate businesses that do exceptionally well from manufacturing products with repugnant consequences, such as tobacco and arms manufacturers. Plenty of illicit organisations do good business precisely because they deal in drug trafficking, people smuggling and counterfeit goods. Where, then, does all this leave business ethics?

In the past few years, there has been a proliferation of courses at business schools which deal with business ethics. Critics have charged that such courses can easily fall into the trap of being seen as little more than a soft and easy option, lacking both theoretical depth and practical nuance (Freeman, 1991: 17). None the less, there is little doubt that there is a rapidly burgeoning body of critical literature on the subject. Alongside this, practical courses have tried to address the challenges of providing worthwhile ethical tools relevant to the rapidly changing business environment of the 2000s. In the first half of this chapter, we explore in general terms what really constitutes ethical behaviour. More specifically, we examine whether there can be any definite and fixed standards about ethical behaviour, or whether moral standards will always change according to different social contexts. This is often referred to as being a debate about ethical relativism. To illustrate, consider two different explanations for how and why we have ethical standards (that is, shared beliefs about what is right and what is wrong). First, some people believe that ideas of right and wrong are social constructs – that is, they are purely and simply the product of whatever society or community created them. If you believe this, or if you believe that what counts as right and wrong depends on the circumstances, then either of those beliefs would put you firmly on the ethical relativist side of the debate. You would feel that ideas about good and bad are relativist because they always need to be understood relative to the context (either the community or the situation): there is no absolute right and wrong. Second, and in contrast to this, some people believe that there are important moral absolutes. An example of one moral absolute might be that 'you must not kill another person whatever the circumstances', or another might be 'you should never discriminate against someone purely on the grounds of their race, whatever the circumstances'. If you believe that this, or something like this, should be a moral principle, that had to be followed without exception, then you are on the anti-relativist (or absolutist) side of the debate.

Deciding on these issues is not by any means easy. You might want to allow some flexibility to determine what is right and wrong if you think life is too simple for moral rules. Some might think, for example, that the state, in protection of its citizens, should give some highly trained and qualified people the right to shoot a person who is a terrorist, if they think this can save other lives. As an individual, you might also feel that you want to respect moral systems from different cultures and traditions, and perhaps allow for the fact that your own opinions about morality may be culturally biased. Those kinds of beliefs seem to commit you to relativism. On the other hand, you might want a guarantee that some of the rights you enjoy as a human being (such as the right to life) should be protected, no matter what. That seems to commit you to absolutism. You might also be unhappy with some of the implications of relativism. For example, if two people disagree completely on a moral issue, a relativist stance would imply that they can both be right (or that neither is wrong). If you disagree, you may discover you are absolutist. At its heart, deciding where to locate yourself in this debate is perhaps less important than continuing to reflect on the basic question that prompts the debate in the first place. Does what is considered 'good' and 'bad' vary greatly from society to society, from business to business or from organisation to organisation, or are there certain broader issues of 'right' and 'wrong' that have a global relevance? In the second half of this chapter we follow up such practical questions, by assessing the extent to which such dilemmas can be resolved through philosophical theory. We outline some of the main schools of philosophical thought that have been applied to understanding business ethics: utilitarianism, deontological ethics, virtue ethics, rights-based approaches and some more contemporary contributions in what are sometimes collectively referred to as postmodern approaches.

As noted in the introduction, there is little doubt that contemporary firms are under considerable pressure – from both consumers and governments – to act (or perhaps at least to be *seen* to act) ethically. However, if they are motivated simply by external pressures, are such actions devoid of moral worth? Should we give credit to businesses for acting ethically, if they are doing it only for selfish motives? Proponents of the different philosophical traditions of utilitarianism, the rights-based approach, deontological and virtue theories, and the more contemporary theorists will differ radically in their responses to this and to other central questions.

1.2   MORAL RELATIVES AND ETHICAL ABSOLUTES

1.2.1   What is ethical conduct?

It may be useful to draw a distinction between ethics and moral codes; the latter are specific and confined to particular sets of social circumstances (Singer, 1995: 2). Ethics can be seen as a more general term, denoting both ethical theories and day-to-day moral beliefs, though many make a more detailed distinction (Beauchamp and Bowie, 1997: 2). Thus moral codes differ greatly from society to society, an example being restrictions on sexual conduct or, for that matter, the use of particularly vulnerable categories of labour, such as children. In contrast, ethics are universal; central to our ideas of what it means to be human are some notions of 'good' and 'evil' and certain social taboos that are common to all societies.

There are problems in trying to decide what counts as ethical conduct. Let us look at the commonplace idea that ethical conduct is partly about putting someone else first. This could be: letting someone cross the road in front of your car or holding a door open for someone; in more dramatic cases, it could be giving blood or donating organs. Such actions are often described as *altruistic* – acting for another's sake (in Latin *alter* = other). Now, some people have suggested that there is no such thing as genuine altruism. Even if we appear to be acting for the good of others, we are only doing so because it is in our own self-interest: we like to feel good about ourselves, act consistently with a favourable self-image and think we are nice people and so on. This theory – that all behaviour is motivated by self-interest – is known as *psychological egoism* (in Latin *ego* = 'I' or 'self'), and it can be summed up by an exam question one of the authors of this book once encountered: 'There are altruistic actions, but there are always egoistic explanations for those actions'. If psychological egoism is true, how can we give credit for ethical conduct? Why should we reward someone who is doing what they want to do in any case and acting in their own interest? This has some quite wide implications. For example, is a bank being 'ethical' if it refuses to lend money to some types of companies (tobacco companies, say). If the same bank advertises an ethical lending policy as part of its business strategy, and makes money doing so, then how is it being ethical?

What makes the question of ethical conduct even more complicated is that even though many agree that altruism is the cornerstone of acting ethically, some people have suggested all individuals *should* try to act solely in their own self-interest. This position of self-ishness is even stronger and is sometimes referred to as *ethical egoism*. It has some wider implications too. For example, some people have suggested that the most efficient way for capitalism to work is for individual firms to pursue their own self-interest. Firms exist to make profits and (provided they act lawfully) by doing that they discharge their social responsibilities. The bank making money through ethical investing could say it is acting ethically simply because it is making money for shareholders. Even if the bank's motives were selfish, it could be said that it had a duty to act selfishly because it needed to offer its own investors a profit.

Self-interest and good ethics often coincide, as it is often in one's interests to act morally or altruistically (Ridley, 1996; Singer, 1995: 3). For example, to our knowledge, all societies have one or another taboo against the arbitrary killing of healthy adults belonging to one's own social unit. However, many societies tolerate some degree of euthanasia (commonly of the very old or the very young) or the slaying of 'outsiders' – those who have for some reason placed themselves beyond the pale of society.

Law is the public's agency for translating morality into specific social guidelines and practices, and specifying punishments (Beauchamp and Bowie, 1997: 4). However, it is often all too easy for firms simply to refer ethical problems to their legal departments, the assumption being that if it is not likely to run into trouble with the law, then an action is ethical (Beauchamp and Bowie, 1997). None the less, the law is not concerned with moral problems *per se*; the fact that an action is legally acceptable does not make it moral. An example cited by Beauchamp and Bowie (1997: 4) is the case of Pacific Lumber, the subject of a hostile takeover by Charles E. Hurwitz. Hurwitz took over the firm, in the teeth of managerial resistance, who feared that he would take a far more ruthless and short-term approach towards the firm's resources, both human and natural. Hurwitz immediately doubled the rate of tree-cutting in the country's largest private redwood forest, to pay off debts incurred in the takeover, an action many critics branded as immoral, though it was perfectly legal (Beauchamp and Bowie, 1997: 5).

It should also be recognised that while it may be very easy to draw ethical boundaries in theory, it is somewhat more difficult to do so in practice. This is partly why debates about relativism and absolutism are often very difficult to resolve. We have just seen that while the killing of fellow humans is generally seen as unethical across societies, in some circumstances it is tolerated or even condoned. Again, most societies value truthfulness; in fact, some degree of truth-telling is necessary for basic social cohesion. However, as Singer (1995: 2) notes, an absolute prohibition on lies may be of little value in specific circumstances. For example, in Nazi-ruled Europe, in response to Gestapo enquiries, it would be surely right to deny it if you had a Jewish family hiding in your house. Similarly, in apartheid South Africa, should managers have co-operated with the authorities in the implementation of the pass laws aimed at restricting the movement (and civil liberties) of African workers? Indeed, hindering the agents of unjust authority wherever possible is surely an ethically commendable stance in life, even if it involves regular deception.

In deciding what constitutes ethical business conduct, it is even more difficult to draw firm distinctions between 'right' and 'wrong'. Perhaps all that can be hoped for is to make people more attuned to recognising moral complexities (Solomon, 1992: 4) and better-equipped to deal with them. This is particularly important in that all business decisions do have an ethical dimension (Solomon, 1992: 4).

Two of the core disciplines of the management sciences – economics and accountancy – are centred on the basic assumption that all social actors (both individuals and groups) are 'utility maximisers' (Bowie, 1991: 29). In other words, in seeking to maximise the material benefits accruing to themselves, these actors are always looking after their own interests (utility can best be understood as the sum of benefits an individual or group may derive from a particular action). However, certain contradictions are inherent in these assumptions, the most obvious being the clash of interests between principals and agents (Bowie, 1991: 29); that is, between the owners of the firm (principals) and their employees (paid agents). This tension is apparent whether the employee is drawn from the highest ranks of senior management, or is the most junior hourly paid worker. While it is possible to argue that the clash between personal and corporate interests can be reconciled, or that any differences that do arise can simply be factored in, in practice, the issue is often neglected (Bowie, 1991: 29). According to Ghoshal (2005) this problem is just one illustration of how the most influential perspectives on business and management come from disciplines whose view of social life is inherently 'gloomy'. The view of people and organisations as utility maximising and self-interested may be useful in modelling behaviour in markets, but it does a poor job of addressing ethical behaviour. In practice, ethical conduct in the business world is likely to involve a casting aside of conventional wisdom and such crude assumptions of self-interested agents. Instead, it will involve taking the interests of others, rather than the firm, or the person of the manager, first (Bowie, 1991: 29).

1.2.2   Why does business ethics matter?

Business ethics became an increasingly fashionable field of study in the 1990s. There is little doubt that, in part, this represented a reaction to the excesses of the 1980s, to the central emphasis on individual financial gain – no matter how that was achieved – and the ostentatious display of wealth that characterised that decade. By the close of the 1980s, a range of factors, from repetitive financial scandals to objective evidence of global environmental damage, underscored the importance of ethical conduct in business (Vinten, 2000). However, as we have already touched upon, and as Solomon (1992) notes, it can be extremely difficult to define what constitutes ethical conduct. An often cited example of the kind of ethical dilemmas confronting managers would be dealing with the problem of downsizing a workforce of dedicated loyal employees as a result of a cost-cutting decision made by superiors (Solomon, 1992). This simple scenario illustrates three sets of competing interests: the principals who presumably wish to minimise labour cost to secure greater revenue (or, more charitably, to ensure the long-term success of the firm); their agents who have to face the fallout of such a decision at the front line, and attempt to manage it; and the redundant employees who have lost their livelihoods and income, and in all likelihood a large part of their identity. More importantly, it also suggests that some ethical problems may well have no solution. Managers in this case may well have to come to terms with the fact that the best they can do in such a scenario is to cause as little further pain as possible.

Given that a firm is legally defined in terms of its stockholders, executives and employees are placed in a morally ambiguous position: both as paid agents entrusted with the task of dealing with competitors and maximising profits. However, as Solomon (1992: 8) notes, competition is just one of a number of relationships that firms have with each other and with members of the wider community. Focusing solely on being competitive can be disastrous for the community and indeed for the underlying co-operation that is necessary for any successful business activity. Indeed, the emphasis on short-term profit maximisation in the closing decades of the twentieth century, characterized by corporate raids and hostile takeovers – in the name of stockholder rights – and the resultant defensive downsizing bloodbaths crippled many firms and injured hundreds of thousands of loyal employees (Solomon, 1992: 8; Lamsa, 1999). Instead, it can be argued that by according greater attention to ethical concerns, the firm can secure its role as a vibrant and creative part of society over the medium and long term (Vinten, 2000).

Solomon (1992: 258) argues that without a sense of community and co-operation there would simply be no firm; indeed, without individual and corporate virtue (virtue being 'goodness' likely to benefit society as a whole), all success would be empty and transient. However, in any less than perfect organisation or society, there is no guarantee as to what virtue theorists would refer to as the 'unity of virtues' (Solomon, 1992: 260). 'Good' conduct is dependent on the context, and different contexts may overlap or they may clash with one another. This problem of the unity of virtues can be seen as another example of the problem of ethical relativism we introduced above. If we accept that context has a very strong influence on what people perceive to be ethical behaviour, it is possible to see how, in some situations, people can become so tied to their jobs, or to their company's way of doing things, that they become incapable of looking beyond the narrow horizons of what their company or their manager defines as ethical. This may explain why a stockholder view of the firm and its responsibilities means that people can become focused on profit, or the 'bottom line', to the detriment of other considerations. One feature of organisational life is that hierarchies can result in people behaving out of character, or with insufficient thought about the ethical implications of their actions. The combination of a focus on the bottom line and unthinking obedience to superiors can be an unhappy one. More recently, however, and particularly in the wake of a number of high-profile corporate scandals, there has been something of a reaction against unethical business practice (Daily et al., 2003; Lamsa, 1999). This reaction encompasses many of the topic areas we introduce in this book. The role of corporations in marketing their products to vulnerable audiences the impact of corporations on the environment, and on working conditions for those in developing countries; the need for ethics in accounting practices and attention to governance mechanisms; discomfort with organisations treating their employees as a disposable commodity or 'human resource'. Some theorists suggest that firms today are more conscious of the importance of taking ethical issues seriously (Solomon, 1992: 261–6). Barry describes how, '[t]he world of global business is marked by a remarkable and growing concern with ethics' (Barry, 2004: 195).

1.2.3   Practice and theory

Despite, or perhaps even because of, this recent flurry of interest, there is a danger that business ethics can simply be deployed as a whitewash, without any real changes in conduct (Freeman, 1991: 12). For example, there is little doubt that *claims* of environmental good conduct can help to sell products; however, there is often little monitoring of environmental claims that can be ambiguous or bogus. Examples of the former could include claims that wood or paper products are from sustainably managed plantations. However, this could conceal the fact that the plantations in question may have been planted in the place of clear-felled tropical forests, or that thirsty alien species of trees may disrupt natural rainfall catchment areas, with negative consequences for human and natural communities downstream. Other claims may simply be bogus: the consumer has little chance of discovering, for example, if tropical hardwood products are indeed from sustainable sources or from the uncontrolled timber 'gold rushes' that are currently taking in place in countries such as Cambodia, Mozambique and Brazil. Similarly, there is a high likelihood that wildlife products – ranging from ivory to skins – may be sourced from international poaching rackets, whatever the vendor's protestations.

Beauchamp and Bowie (1997: 11) argue that there are three basic approaches to studying business ethics: the prescriptive (an attempt to formulate and defend basic moral norms); the descriptive (focusing on describing practices, moral codes and beliefs) and the conceptual study of ethics (involving analysing central ethical terms, such as right, good, justice, virtue in an attempt to distinguish what is moral from what is immoral). Some critics of prescriptive approaches to business ethics argue that rule-setting erodes the freedom of the individual and entails a degree of inflexibility, which means we are insensitive to the particular features of an ethical problem. However, while it is undoubtedly correct to argue that any regulation erodes the freedom of the individual, there is little doubt that a number of practical measures to enforce ethical conduct have been of great benefit to humanity (Beauchamp and Bowie, 1997: 9). For example, the banning of the use of chlorofluorocarbons (CFCs) represents a major step towards undoing damage to the ozone layer.

To proponents of ethical relativism (to recap, these are people who believe that what counts as good or bad varies so greatly from society to society that there can be no ethical universals) moral rules are culturally specific. It follows, then, that any attempt to enforce universal ethical codes represents little more than a form of cultural imperialism (one society imposing its will on another). Some Asian critics of attempts to promote Western democracy have suggested that democracy is neither in the interests of, nor desirable in, certain Far Eastern societies. This viewpoint is most associated with the governments of China and Singapore. However, despite considerable variance in moral rules and what different communities may see as desirable, there is little doubt that the underlying principles of morality are often similar. It is generally recognised, for example, that sometimes the interests of the individual have to be sacrificed for the good of society as a whole. It therefore follows that – at least in some cases – a distinction can be drawn between relativism in terms of judgements about a particular situation and relativism in terms of underlying standards (Beauchamp and Bowie, 1997: 10). In other words, people may differ on how ethical standards may be best met, but certain basic underlying norms may still be common to all societies. A controversial illustration of this may be that some features of family life are often considered cultural universals (for example, taboos on incest and illegitimacy, or male dominance) (Hendrix, 1993). None the less, it should be recognised that moral disagreements are inevitable – by their very nature they provoke disagreement and diverse opinions. Also, they may not always be resolvable, because of, among other things, a lack of information, lack of definitional clarity and selective use of evidence: 'Though there is a sense in which ethical issues in business can, and must, be resolved, this is a very different proposition from suggesting that there will be one, definitive solution "out there" that will be accepted by everyone' (Morrell, 2004: 390).

However, whether one's starting point is ethical relativism or a more universalist approach, there is little doubt that, even outside the basic family unit, certain strictures (or social taboos) underpin ethical conduct within specific social settings. This can be in the form of laws, unwritten rules or various codes of conduct relevant across firms, industries or professions. In academic life, for example, there is a strong taboo against plagiarism. Any false or malicious allegation of plagiarism will irreparably damage a relationship, as any half-competent academic will know. This is an example of a strong universal professional taboo. Sometimes, though, questions relating to ethical behaviour are set down explicitly or codified. In terms of the relationship between the law and ethics, we saw earlier that laws can facilitate ethical behaviour, but they cannot ensure ethical conduct by all individuals, all the time. There is little doubt that a degree of self-policing may be desirable. For many years, a number of professions (such as law and accounting) have upheld sets of professional standards. However, in a rapidly changing global environment, several professions have increasingly battled to maintain professional reputations given the consolidation of the industry. The accounting industry is often singled out in this regard, since conflicts of interest can arise with some of the larger accounting firms who simultaneously offer consultancy and auditing services. In the 1990s, there was a string of high-profile scandals which highlighted specific cases of auditing shortcomings (Daily *et al.*, 2003). The most infamous recent example of this was the case of Enron in the United States (McCall, 2004). The firm's auditors, Arthur Andersen, also offered managerial consulting services to Enron. This situation resulted in senior partners being allegedly complicit in covering up malpractices, leading to the latter's demise, with 'fundamentally unfair and inaccurate portraits' of the management accounts (Jennings, 2004: 1). 'Enron collapsed when the market lost confidence in it ... loss of market confidence was not so much the cause of the collapse as a symptom of the long-term inflated reporting of assets and expected earnings ... compounded by the passive compliance of the auditors' (Morrell and Anderson, 2006: 123). High-profile corporate scandals such as Enron have led critics to argue that the setting of ethical standards is too serious a business to be left to the professions, and that more ethical conduct can only be engendered through both an overhaul of existing legislation and a sea-change in popular attitudes.

There are indeed people who advocate sweeping and systemic change. Goodpaster argues that creeping moral disorder in society can only be checked if the respect for persons is placed at the centre of our notion of corporate community (quoted in Gilbert, 1991: 111). This should be incorporated in the overall strategic vision held by senior management, leavening out the demands of corporate self-interest, profits and the law, to be enacted out through managerial processes (Gilbert, 1991: 111). It can be argued that Goodpaster's vision is a somewhat limited one; a more comprehensive approach to ethics should also incorporate an underlying 'respect for persons' alongside the grand strategic vision. Such an underlying ethos would include the organisational rank-and-file, allowing room for a firm-wide dialogue on values and introspection by non-executives (Gilbert, 1991: 111). From this viewpoint, the modern firm is perceived as an arena, within which interacting individuals have the opportunity to reconcile their relationships. This arena is a forum for the exchange of ideas and a place where different opinions are listened to because of a shared respect and commitment to some underlying ethical values.

1.2.4   What is ethics practice?

Singer rejects the notion of ethical relativism and instead suggests that we should 'do what increases happiness and reduces suffering' (1995: 5). As we shall see, this is a utilitarian stance on ethics. Before we discuss this more fully, it is worth examining his rejection of relativism in more detail. He suggests that ethical relativism can provide a justification for situations that seem to us intrinsically unfair, for example, the use of child labour. Ethical relativists would argue that child labour could be justified if a particular community or society believed that it was the right thing to do. This is a 'global' argument for the rejection of ethical relativism, but there are individual and personal arguments against it as well. For example, self-interested acts should surely be compatible with more broadly based principles if they are to be thought of as ethical (Singer, 1995: 10). This means that there has to be some basic commitment to shared standards, or else we would have chaos, with each person justifying their own choices with reference to the relativist argument that 'there are no absolute rules, so everything and anything is permitted'.

In the end, because it is an applied discipline, ethics should be about deeds, not about sterile philosophical debates. Both Immanuel Kant and Adam Smith repeatedly emphasised that our day-to-day actions should be guided by enlightened self-interest and altruism – a concern for others (Freeman, 1991: 19). It is from this position that many writers – and most other philosophers of ethics – postulate their theories (Freeman, 1991). A central practical concern which many of these theorists share is that we should have a fairer and more just world. Many ethical problems are about trying to redress instances of unfairness and inequity. This inequity can be seen in the way that governments or regimes control power and in the way that goods are unfairly distributed in society. It is also evident in how most people's chances of success are allocated to them at birth, and in the way that, across all nations, power is concentrated in the hands of a few. The desire to promote greater equity does not have to be about such grand or abstract issues, nor does it have to be based on the assumption that all individuals are equal and with equal abilities. Instead, acting ethically should mean that we work on the notion that all individuals should be given fair opportunities to realise themselves to the best of their potential (Singer, 1995: 16–17). A contemporary illustration of this might be in relation to debates about positive discrimination or affirmative action (for example, large organisations may seek to promote women from minority ethnic groups on the grounds that they are under-represented). Some forms of affirmative action can be justified regardless of whether the beneficiaries are of superior, inferior or equal ability to the bulk of the populace and regardless of whether such actions lead to greater profit. In the case of the under-representation of women from minority ethnic groups, we could argue that some organisations are set up in such a way that prejudice is built into their corporate structure. Breaking down such entrenched barriers to equality is an ethical stance that should be pursued irrespective of whether or not there is a 'business case'.

1.3 DIFFERENT PHILOSOPHICAL APPROACHES TO BUSINESS ETHICS

1.3.1 Key perspectives

Bowie (1991: 33) argues that there are two major theories of business ethics: deontology, founded on underlying rules, and utilitarianism, which sees ethical behaviour in terms of desired outcomes. In addition, a further three frames of reference have had increasing influence. The first, virtue ethics, is founded on the philosophies of the ancient world and in particular on the writings of Aristotle and Plato. The second explores ethics from the issue of basic personal rights. The third reference frame (which is really a loose cluster of viewpoints), postmodernism, would blame ethical failings on the Enlightenment's emphasis on rationality and on the pursuit of 'progress' and 'advancement', regardless of the subjective human cost. Beginning with a discussion of deontology and utilitarianism, we shall move on to discuss virtue ethics, rights-based approaches and postmodernism.

1.3.2 Deontology

From the ancient Greek *deon*, meaning duty, deontology has its foundations in the works of Immanuel Kant (1724–1804). In his influential *Practical Reason*, Kant argued that we should 'impose on ourselves the demand that all our actions should be rational in form' (quoted in Burns, 2000b: 28). Kant suggested that there are certain rules of morality that are binding on all rational beings (he was most definitely an anti-relativist). He went on to say that an action is only morally right if you were willing to have everyone act in a similar way in a similar situation (Lamsa, 1999: 347). In other words, 'maxims should be universalized' (Burns, 2000b: 28). What the phrase 'maxims should be universalized' means is that each of us should act as though our choice would become a moral law for everyone else. Though it is sometimes summarised in a trite way as the 'golden rule' or a 'do unto others as you would have them do unto you', Kant's ideas are far stronger than that. He is not simply suggesting we treat others as we would want ourselves to be treated in return. He goes a lot further, by placing an obligation on us that almost requires the actions of a saint. His golden rule is more like, 'behave towards others as if the whole world was watching you, and as if from that moment on the whole world would behave in exactly the same way for the rest of time'. This was something that should be applied to all actions (so it was categorical) and it was a 'must' statement (so it was an imperative). In what was another implication following from his categorical imperative, Kant stated that people must never be treated only as a means, but always as an end in themselves (Lamsa, 1999: 347; Beauchamp and Bowie, 1997: 30). Kantianism has some very powerful and stringent implications. It implies that one should act in an ethical way because it is one's duty, regardless of the consequences (Kitson and Campbell, 1996: 13). Kantianism also lays down obligations that – if followed – are strong enough not be self-defeating, solving the problem of destructive individual 'freeriding' (a problem that, as we have seen, plagues utilitarianism) in the face of co-operative action (Kitson and Campbell, 1996: 15).

Of course, moral problems in the real world are extremely complex. Above all, there is the problem of uncertainty and what really constitutes right and wrong. A decision to downsize the workforce in a company may, for example, be a product of forces beyond the manager's control. It may work out as the best course of action for those staff members who are retained, yet it may also inflict great misery on those who are made redundant (Lamsa, 1999: 347). As Kant argues, human nature is ultimately fallible, and it is impossible to ensure perfect outcomes 'from the warped wood of human nature' (Kant, 2000: 55). Lamsa suggests that one way out of such moral dilemmas is often to behave according to custom, which can provide useful moral benchmarks (1999: 347). The problem with this approach is that any reliance on custom brings us back to a relativist standpoint, when the whole point about Kant is that his rule – the categorical imperative – is universal.

For Kant, people's motives for their actions are critical. People should make the right decisions for the right reasons; if people are honest only because honesty pays, honesty itself is cheapened (Beauchamp and Bowie, 1997: 30). In other words, if a firm acts in an ethical fashion to help it market its goods and services, and hence to enhance its profits, then such actions are devoid of moral worth. Absolute morality is a categorical imperative, with social interaction and civil society being dependent on moral action by all (Kant, quoted in Burns, 2000b: 28). Or, to give another example, managers are not really acting ethically at all, if they are simply prompted to do so out of fear of prosecution or by consumer pressures. This emphasis on motives is an important one. It is not a distinction that would necessarily trouble those in the utilitarian camp; to the latter, any increase in overall happiness, regardless of the rationale underlying the actions that led to this, would be desirable.

Kant believed that actions should respect underlying moral law; a person's motives should reflect a recognition of a duty to act – and that morality provides a rational framework of rules, which constrains and guides people (Beauchamp and Bowie, 1997: 33; Kant, 2000: 54–5). While certainly detailed, Kant's writings are somewhat open-ended and incomplete; contemporary deontologists use Kant's notion of respect for persons as a ground for providing ethical theories of justice and rights, and for distinguishing the desirable from the undesirable (Beauchamp and Bowie, 1997: 33). Even so, it is difficult to overstate the importance that his ideas have had on moral philosophy, and Kant is often considered to be one of the greatest philosophers to have ever lived, in part because of his ideas about ethics.

Ultimately, deontology hinges on a system of rules. This has led critics to argue that deontology is overly inflexible, and that any moral ambiguities may only be resolved by finding ever more complicated or specific rules and by ranking them in a hierarchical way, so that they do not conflict with one another (Singer, 1995: 3). However, empirical research would seem to indicate that many managers do approach ethical decision-making from what is effectively a deontological starting point (Menguc, 1998).

1.3.3 Utilitarianism

Utilitarianism is based on a moral principle (the utility principle), but it is not really founded on moral rules (the means). Instead, it is founded on goals (the ends) (Singer, 1995: 3). The classic utilitarian view sees an action as right if it results in the greatest net utility (happiness) for the most people possible. So, out of a choice of several options, the one that should be pursued is always the one that maximises happiness and minimises pain overall. There are some problems with this view, as we shall see, but the main thing to bear in mind is that utilitarianism is concerned with the consequences of a particular action; hence, it is consequentialist. This is in contrast with those who would try always to follow set principles. A utilitarian would not have a rule of 'you should never lie', for example. To a utilitarian, lying may be commendable in some circumstances (if you refuse to tell a drunk and abusive mother where her baby is, for example), but it may be bad in many others. Utilitarians argue that the 'goodness' of one's actions is to be understood in terms of the consequences; ethical conduct seeks to ensure the 'greatest good for the greatest number' (Lamsa, 1999; Maciver and Page, 1961: 55). This is sometimes referred to as the 'happiness principle' or 'hedonic calculus' for balancing pleasure versus pain, the overall good of any action versus the costs entailed (Solomon, 1992: 90). As John Stuart Mill (1964: 5) argues, the 'utility or greatest happiness principle holds that actions are right ... if they tend to promote happiness, wrong if they tend to produce the reverse of happiness. By happiness I mean pleasure, by unhappiness pain and the privation of pleasure'.

In other words, individuals should seek to act in such a way as to maximise the net social benefits accruing from their actions (Lamsa, 1999: 346); a practice is good or right if it leads to the best possible balance of good consequences over bad ones (Beauchamp and Bowie, 1997: 22). This will entail measuring possible benefits and harm as best one can and then weighing these up (Lamsa, 1999: 346). As noted earlier, utilitarianism has had a profound impact on classical theories of economics (for example, on the writings of Adam Smith), and because of this and because of its applied, practical nature, it has become a perspective held by many business people (Lamsa, 1999: 347). Prominent utilitarian theorists include David Hume (1711–76),

Jeremy Bentham (1748–1832) and J. S. Mill (1806–73). Perhaps the most influential contemporary utilitarian philosopher is the eminent Harvard professor, Peter Singer, who has argued that the practice of genuine utilitarianism involves considerable reflection if the good of society – and the biosphere – is to be maximised. Unlike more conservative writers who make extensive use of utilitarianism – such as Milton Friedman – Singer places a great deal of emphasis in his writings on social good, rather than concentrating exclusively on economic growth.

Thus utilitarianism centres on the assumption that, when faced with a choice, the 'right' thing to do is to try ensure the best possible outcome for the bulk of people affected as long as it does not result in a disproportionate amount of suffering by a minority; nothing is wrong which allows this, and nothing is right which fails to do so. As Mill (1964: 6) argues, 'pleasure and freedom from pain are the only desirable ends'. However, one of the most difficult challenges facing utilitarians is what constitutes happiness. Bentham appears to simply have seen happiness as the avoidance of pain (Kitson and Campbell, 1996: 7). This may be true, but what is sometimes neglected is that Bentham was advocating welfare reform and writing at a time when vast numbers of the population suffered from poor sanitation, hunger and disease. In those settings, the idea that everyone should be happy and free from pain was truly radical. Mill, who was also a remarkable radical, did take some care in identifying different degrees of happiness and in trying to forestall some of the vulgar critics of utilitarianism. He differentiated human happiness from that of animals, for example, and famously wrote 'better to be Socrates dissatisfied than a fool satisfied'. Both these sentiments should have pre-empted some of the more rudimentary criticism of utilitarianism – though the problem of defining happiness still remains. In terms of the business world, and in how utility is most frequently operationalised, modern neo-classical economists tend to refer to expected utility as the key mechanism that drives individual choice. Consumers (and organisations) are thought to behave in such a way that, for each of their choices, they try to maximise utility (Kitson and Campbell, 1996 : 7). This view of consumers as utility maximising is at the root of the most influential models of human behaviour – in what is sometimes understood as the rational choice paradigm. It informs the agency view of the firm with which we opened this chapter, for example. In these models, though, what is crucial is that consumers (and organisations) are understood as being self-interested. The utility they seek to maximise is their own, whether as consumers, citizens, employees, shareholders or organisations competing in the marketplace This is not at the core of utilitarianism though, since that concerns itself with utility for the greatest number. So, to confuse these two accounts – utilitarianism as a moral principle and rational choice as a descriptive or explanatory account of choice – is misleading.

To recap: for utilitarians, the individual is faced with the dilemma of choosing what will benefit those affected by her or his actions the most: the maximisation of good and the minimisation of evil (Beauchamp and Bowie, 1997: 22). Invariably, the individual is confronted with trade-offs. For example, a 'green' energy source such as hydroelectric power may inflict great damage on river systems. Utilitarians also hold on to the key concept of intrinsic good, expressed variously as pleasure/ happiness/utility. The implication of this is that profit *per se* is not intrinsically good, but, if increasing the prosperity of shareholders may contribute to increasing overall happiness of society, then the overall consequences of increased profit may be so (Beauchamp and Bowie, 1997: 23). Of course, if these come at the expense of exploitation, increased inequity or harm to the environment, such costs would need to be offset against the benefits of increased profit. While it is problematic to meas- ure these things on the same terms, the benefit of a genuinely rounded utilitarian perspective is that it should get us to concentrate on costs overall. Part of the problem with environmental pollution is that, historically, companies have not had to factor in fully the cost to the environment. Though they may be forced to pay for catastrophes such as oil spills or chemical leaks, historically they have not been made to pay for costs to less visible by-products of their manufacturing processes (the rise in CO_2, for example).

Although the basic precepts of utilitarianism are relatively simple, they in fact represent the foundation of a sophisticated ethical paradigm. The latter is often ignored by 'vulgar utilitarians', seeking to defend the neo-liberal orthodoxy (in other words, a belief in the beneficial powers of unrestrained free markets). Conversely, utilitarianism can be attacked because it is seen as simply being the basis of this orthodoxy. Utilitarianism is often simply seen as a cost–benefit analysis (Solomon, 1992: 90). Commonly seen as the father of classical economics, Adam Smith is depicted as a defender of the profit motive, independent of moral considerations (see Maciver and Page, 1961: 36–7; Evensky, 2001: 497). Indeed, several prominent proponents of unrestrained free markets, influenced by the works of Milton Friedman (see Friedman, 1997: 57) have argued that at times profoundly amoral approaches to doing business may be desirable (Evensky, 2001: 497). If one is to argue for an amoral approach, this would imply that any consideration of whether something is ethical or unethical is irrelevant. Instead, businesses should act within the law and leave ethics to other kinds of institutions (governments, charities). For example, Albert Carr argues that, in poker, deception and concealment are virtues, as opposed to kindness and open-heartedness, and no one thinks the worse of the poker player for this; the same should be true for the entrepreneur (Bowie, 1997: 97). This is a rather shaky argument (as many arguments from comparison are) since it depends on the legitimacy of the comparison. Poker players do not usually employ other people or risk other people's money or livelihoods – which an entrepreneur will do. One could also argue that murder, violence and the ability to smuggle drugs are virtues for the Mafia, but that does not mean they apply in other businesses (and organised crime is a lot more like a business than is a poker game).

Similarly, Theodore Levitt, a marketing scholar at the Harvard Business School, argues that embellishment and distortion may be desirable attributes in business; consumers do want not only products but also the 'tantalizing imagery' held out through creative advertising and ambitious claims (quoted in Bowie, 1997: 98). However, while claiming to be true to the neo-liberal traditions, such viewpoints represent little more than crude parodies of what Adam Smith really has to say. In *The Theory of Moral Sentiments* Smith stresses the importance of co-operation and trust, and the indispensability of a basic degree of social solidarity. Surprisingly, Smith mentions the concept of the 'invisible hand' – the forces of the market that will ultimately result in equilibrium – only once in his classic work, *The Wealth of Nations* (Solomon, 1992: 86). Indeed, as Solomon (1992: 87) argues, Smith's view was that the individual and firm should strive to be good citizens, contributing to the overall good of society, in an age when innovation was often stifled. Smith saw people as being naturally social and benevolent; justice provided the main pillar of society; our self-interest was constituted within society and 'tied to that system of virtues that makes us good citizens' (Solomon, 1992: 87–9).

Indeed, Smith does not reduce altruism to a kind of ethical egoism that supports utilitarian results. His view is a long way from that of the market-based free-for-all that is sometimes attributed to him. He would reject the view that each person is the best judge of his/her own interests, and that consequently people should look out for themselves – with market mechanisms in some way sorting it all out for the best

(Maciver and Page, 1961: 42–3). Smith really argues (in his own words) that 'society cannot exist unless the laws of justice are tolerably observed, no social intercourse can take place among men who do not generally abstain from injury of another ... Man, it has to be said has a natural love of society, and desires that the union of mankind should be preserved for its own sake, and though he himself was to derive no benefit from it' (quoted in Bowie, 1991). Indeed, it is increasingly recognised that 'a society that only pursues individual self-interest is inherently unstable' (quoted in Bowie, 1991). Unlike many of his later admirers, Smith remained convinced of the importance of society and of the need to take conscious steps to promote a general social good, issues that are echoed in the works of contemporary utilitarian philosophers such as Singer.

Similarly, another early proponent of utilitarianism, J. S. Mill, stressed the importance of virtue and of the general social good, concerned about the prosperity and well-being of society as a whole, arguing that a simple utilitarian happiness calculus (in other words, trying to calculate the possible social good stemming from a particular action) was insufficient to ensure ethical behaviour (Solomon, 1992: 93). As we have seen, utilitarianism is often held up by neo-liberals as 'the business philosophy', the hard-headed, essentially quantitative approach that seeks to balance the material costs and benefits of any action. This has led critics of utilitarianism, such as John Rawls, to charge that utilitarianism legitimates behaviour such as the rich consistently exploiting the poor, as long as the rich are collectively happier than the extent of collective suffering by the less endowed (Solomon, 1992: 91). However, to many utilitarians, the right of the bulk of society to a basic quality of life receives primary importance. It can be argued that the relentless pursuit of individual profit desensitizes business, and has the capacity to eclipse the most basic ethical considerations (Solomon, 1992: 94).

As with most philosophical paradigms, there are considerable divisions in the utilitarian camp as to how the general good of society should be advanced. One such division is between those who can broadly be referred to as 'act' utilitarians and 'rule' utilitarians. The former hold that, in all situations, one should perform acts that lead to the greatest good (Beachamp and Bowie, 1997). In contrast, the latter believe that there should be certain rules governing human conduct that are not expendable, nor subject to changes by the demand of individual circumstances, a possible example being rules aimed at protecting life. It could be argued that the differences between 'rule' utilitarians, in particular, and deontologists is simply one of style; both are committed to some basic rules governing human conduct (Solomon, 1992: 253). However, deontologists are rather more inflexible when it comes to rules; the latter to utilitarians are only valuable if they can be demonstrated to serve a practical purpose (Solomon, 1992: 253). Critics of utilitarianism have often questioned whether happiness can be measured and how the best action may be selected when confronted with a range of alternatives (Beauchamp and Bowie, 1997: 26). Utilitarian responses have included the argument that, in the end, the choice between a number of seemingly equally valid alternatives is one that confronts all ethical theories. Alternatively, it could be suggested that this criticism is a 'pseudo-problem': in the real world, people are capable of making rough and ready comparisons of values on a daily basis (Beauchamp and Bowie, 1997: 27).

A more serious criticism could be that decisions that would be most beneficial to the bulk of members of society – for example, denial of health insurance (or even state health care) for those with HIV/Aids – may inflict a great deal of misery on a few. This scenario would strike many of us as unjust, and indeed countries such as the United Kingdom, which have a universal healthcare system, seem to be based on alternative principles. However, even where there is a universal healthcare system, some rationing of resources has to take place. Agencies responsible for such rationing – such as the National Institute for Health and Clinical Excellence (NICE) in the United Kingdom – use broadly utilitarian principles when deciding whether a particular drug or intervention should be funded by the state. Another example would be where companies use poorly paid subcontracted labour in some production processes. This may be exploitation of the few subcontractors, but it could be beneficial to the firm as a whole (and its shareholders) because it could mean that greater security for those employed in secure contracts in core areas of the firm's business. An example of the latter would be the following, cited by Legge (1996): 'The case that caught my eye was that of a 16-year-old who was paid £30 for a 40-hour week in a garage. When he inquired about compensation for losing the top of a finger at work, he was apparently told he was a "subcontractor".' This seems a horrendous injustice – how could one defend a company that exploits a vulnerable child and then fails to offer adequate compensation following an industrial accident? Cases such as this may strike us as lying beyond the pale and not be justifiable on any grounds. While in law it is likely that there is a definite value given to a person's finger, there may be no excuse for what happened in terms of net utility. We might feel uneasy if faced with a utilitarian formula with 'lost top of finger' on one side apparently being balanced out by 'continued savings with using subcontractors + decreased insurance and liability costs + minimal costs through health and safety practices'. The classic utilitarian response – that all entailed costs must be properly weighted – does not absolve utilitarians from the task of making some very hard choices. However, it is important to note that Mill and others advocate utilitarianism as a principle of last resort, to be used where all other moral frameworks fail to result in an agreed course of action. It is the most important principle, but that does not mean that other moral principles are ignored. Instead, Mill argues at the very beginning of his essay that utilitarianism should be understood as 'the rule for deciding between the various principles *when they conflict*' (emphasis added) (Mill, 1964: 5). This important qualification is ignored almost universally by critics of utilitarianism, but it means that in the case of the injured subcontractor, utilitarianism might never come into the picture because we could all agree that such a situation was deplorable. Given the many ways in which utilitarianism is attacked and vilified, it is hardly surprising that the world's leading living utilitarian thinker, Peter Singer, has had to contend with ongoing, sometimes violent, protests. These have been mounted not only by religious fundamentalists but also by others who find his views on various questions, such as euthanasia, unacceptable for other reasons. As Singer himself concedes, utilitarianism lacks obligations strong enough to produce the outcomes that it calls for – unlike the case of a religious commandment, there is no external power sanctioning or monitoring behaviour. In reality, what may shape the outcome of events and the overall net utility can depend on whether others act selfishly or not (Singer, 1995: 7). In other words, ethical conduct by a few, or even the majority, can be eroded through others 'free-riding'. One example of this can be that companies who want to reduce their operating costs may discharge untreated waste into the environment. If only a few organisations do this, it can prejudice the attempts by other companies to improve the environment.

1.3.4   Virtue ethics

Virtue theories draw on the classic Hellenistic (that is, ancient Greek) tradition to provide some guidelines as to desirable social conduct (Beauchamp and Bowie, 1997: 38). Virtue theory takes into account the nature of the agent making the decision and her/his cultural context (Aristotle, 1952: vi). Moreover, unlike, say, deontology, virtue theory seeks to get away from either rule-making or near-rules. In terms of its emphasis on individual accountability, a key principle within virtue ethics can be traced back to Socrates' admonition 'know yourself', since it emphasises reflection on one's actions and character. A second key feature of virtue ethics is the realisation that action is grounded in a context – a social context, but also a temporal one. To see whether someone is virtuous, it is not enough to look at an individual action but instead to study their life as a whole. Importantly, these two elements (personal responsibility, sense of context) imply a need to transcend traditional or static notions of what is right and wrong, and instead to approach ethical questions from a critical and ever-questioning standpoint (Burns, 2000a: 45–6). No matter how detailed or explicit moral rules are, a virtue theorist would argue that there is always a need to exercise some judgement to decide how they fit a specific case (Kitson and Campbell, 1996: 16).

For Aristotle, moral judgements are learnt and founded on acquired virtues (Aristotle, 1952: v). Virtues are not rules, but rather personal characteristics, tendencies to behave in one way or another and influenced by habit. Aristotle suggested that one thing we should try to do is to avoid extremes and aim for moderation or a 'golden mean' between two vices. For example, he suggests that bravery lies between cowardice and recklessness (there is an element of judgement). There are no teachers of virtue, since it is not something that can be transferred. Instead, virtue is something that has to be in part infused from an entire community, in part learnt through direct experience and in part learnt through reflection of life in works of art. Initially, virtues can be acquired through the process of socialisation, but a mature person will learn to adjust his/her behaviour in the light of that person's experiences of the world and the exercise of reason. Whetstone (2001: 101) attempts to translate this framework into the contemporary world of work:

> The excellent manager overcomes pressures to compromise even newly acquired values, at times even opposing and then changing his or her habitual behaviour. Field research in the Southeast U.S. found that those managers most admired by peers and subordinates had successfully rejected values ingrained in them as youths in the period of racial segregation, adopting new habits of language and behavior toward other races.

The emphasis here on learning and sensitivity to changing contexts is one that Aristotle would have approved. Aristotle includes in his catalogue of virtues, among other things, courage, liberality, a sense of self-worth, gentleness, modesty, justice and wisdom. He argued that all of these were required in order to 'live well' (Kitson and Campbell, 1996: 17). Though they differed quite significantly in their moral philosophy (and on many other things), both Plato and Aristotle argued that the cultivation of virtuous traits of character represents the primary function of morality (Beauchamp and Bowie, 1997: 39). Virtue is not something that springs spontaneously from a social environment, but has to be nurtured (Aristotle, 1952: vi).

On the one hand, it could be suggested that, in the world of modern business – as opposed to classical Greece – this list of virtues is somewhat incomplete and requires supplementation. However, that is to ignore the historical context for the development of this form of ethics. Virtue ethics arose during the time of the first city-state, at the birthplace of modern democracy and in a society whose ideas of trade, statecraft and politics have become the cornerstone of Western civilisation. Many of the struggles Plato and Aristotle discussed are as relevant today as they were 2,500 years ago. A sad truth is that, while our sophistication in technology and invention has grown exponentially in the intervening years, we appear to be still no further developed in terms of our moral sophistication. One could even argue that if latter-day managers based their conduct on Aristotle's list of virtues, this would solve many of the ethical problems facing modern business. To virtue theorists, 'right' actions are those actions taken by a genuinely virtuous person. All ethical actions, whether they are carried out within or outside the business environment, cannot hinge on absolute rules; at some stage, personal characteristics must take over. An important and ever-present question remains, however: how can virtue be achieved? To proponents of this philosophical tradition, expertise in being virtuous is something to be cultivated over a lifetime, with experience and reflection being necessary (Kitson and Campbell, 1996: 17) – people acquire virtues by acting virtuously and establishing habits that lead to good character. Having a virtuous character is something that is neither natural nor unnatural, but something that has to be cultivated (Beauchamp and Bowie, 1997: 38). Whether there is room for such critical reflection in today's 'runaway' world could be disputed, though one could also argue that such reflection could over time enable more efficient decision-making if it were simply an expression of character. To proponents of virtue theories, firms are only ethical if their actions are prompted by a due process of introspection as to what really is 'virtuous'. So, for example, the marketing of 'green' or 'fair trade' products would not constitute a virtuous act if the firm was motivated solely by wanting to pursue a profit rather than by an innate desire to 'be upstanding' or virtuous.

1.3.5 Rights-based approaches

The rights-based approach holds that individuals have certain basic entitlements. Some famous examples (taken from different contexts) are the right to free speech, to freedom of association, the right to form and join trade unions, the right to liberty and the right to vote. It is worth noting initially that there is a difference between universal rights and those that are specific to a given community or society. Even within a single society or nation, the rights may not be extended to all members of that society. For example, in almost all nations the right to vote (also known as suffrage) was extended to women only after a political struggle. In Sweden, this happened comparatively early: women could vote in local elections in 1862 (though they had to wait until 1909 for the right to vote in general elections). However, women have only had the right to vote in certain cantons in Switzerland since 1971 (Heater, 2004). In many countries in the developed world, voting was restricted to those from certain classes and races. This echoed the unhappy situation in ancient Greece, where slaves and women were denied the right to be considered citizens. A final problem with the idea of relying on rights as a guide for ethical action is that even where there is a commitment to those basic rights, they may not necessarily be observed. Wherever someone has a right to something (free speech, liberty and so on) this implies that other members of that society – and the state as a whole – have a reciprocal or corresponding obligation. An individual's right to free speech means that others have a duty not to persecute someone for what they say. An individual right to liberty means that others have a duty not to deprive someone of their liberty.

Some readers may be able to see how the contrast between a situation where we have shared and universal rights and a situation where rights are afforded to an elite or special community, links back to the earlier discussion in the chapter of the difference between ethical relativism and anti-relativism. If you believe that certain rights are inalienable (that is, cannot be transferred or forfeited) and inviolable (cannot be infringed or dishonoured) and furthermore that they are also universal (extend to every person), then you cannot be an ethical relativist. In this vein, some suggest straightforwardly that rights should, wherever possible, be upheld, including life, liberty and a degree of freedom for people to do as they choose (Beauchamp and Bowie, 1997). To advocates of the rights-based approach, utilitarianism does not properly take rights and their non-violation into account (Nozick, 1984: 101). A classic question on this topic is whether it is acceptable to kill one person if that saves the lives of five (or ten, or a hundred, or a thousand) others? The utilitarian would seem committed to accepting the death of an individual (thereby violating their right to life) if this increased overall utility. Perhaps the most notable theorist on the rights-based approach is John Rawls. Writing at a time of civil unrest in America, Rawls was keen to have an alternative to utilitarianism. He could see a world where utility could be maximised, but some people (minority ethnic groups, women, the poor, the disabled, those with severe learning difficulties and others) would still be sorely disadvantaged. Rawls was an advocate of the liberties of the individual (Sandel, 1984: 8). However, Rawls argued that inequalities in society are only justifiable if they can be shown to benefit the position of the worst-off (Rawls, 1984). This was in contrast to the more 'red in tooth and claw' liberalism of writers such as Hayek and Nozick: and before them, Bentham, the founder of utilitarianism. This implies that poverty is not simply a function of inefficiency, incompetence or laziness; it is a social condition that needs to be examined and analysed (Parekh, 1982: 179). Where inequalities are patterned and reproduced, some people are likely to be able to exercise their basic rights more strongly than others. This makes these supposedly basic rights worthless. If there is not the right to equality of opportunity, this compromises the way in which the goods are distributed in society. There will always be some who are unjustly worse off unless there is the right to such equality of opportunity. Rawls advocated various steps designed to bring about a more just society. In *Justice as Fairness*, his final work, Rawls suggested that we could only bring about a just society under the conditions of a form of market socialism, or where a great many members of society owned property (Rawls, 2001). Rawls' approach is a departure from utilitarianism and it is fair to say that it is probably closer to the Kantian notions of enshrining principles or categorical imperatives – where our basic duty is to offer the greatest help to those who are most severely disadvantaged (Lamsa, 1999). What is suggested is that society should be structured so as to minimise violations of rights. In effect, what is suggested is a 'utilitarianism of rights; violations of rights (*to be minimized*) would replace total happiness as the required end state'.

An alternative perspective is as follows. The rights of others determine constraints on actions (because each right implies a reciprocal duty) (Nozick, 1984). In order to have individual liberty it is necessary to reduce to a minimum the interference of the state (Beauchamp and Bowie, 1997). This frame of reference is based on the assumption that individual rights are paramount; the principal function of the state should simply be to ensure that such rights are not infringed. One political conclusion that seems to follow from this position is that we pursue the 'ultraminimalist' state favoured by Friedman and other neo-liberal economists. If we pursue liberty above all else and advocate the barest minimum of intervention by the state, then there will be few constraints on the behaviour of individuals – but also little constraining the behaviour of firms as actors within a market. The same logic that suggests the state should not interfere with individual liberty also seems to imply that the state should impose unnecessary regulation on businesses and instead allow firms to compete in a market that is as free as possible from interference. It is true that there is a distinction between the social, political and economic implications of a commitment to liberty (though, confusingly, they can all be referred to as libertarianism or liberalism). None the less, in the context of business ethics, those who are strong proponents of libertarian approaches tend to suggest that the ethical duties of the firm are also somewhat minimalist. Shareholders may have a right to a fair return on their investment, and employees may have a right that their employment contract be correctly implemented, and so on – but these rights are only defined minimally. If they were defined at length, there would be a reciprocal duty on firms that would restrict their freedom to compete in the marketplace. As long as one plays by the rules of the game (that is, is legally compliant) then businesses have only one responsibility: to make a profit for their shareholders. The rights-based approach provided much of the philosophical underpinnings for the policies of the Thatcher (in the UK) and Reagan (in the USA) governments of the 1980s. Reflecting this, legislation protecting social collectives – such as trade unions – was pared back, though there was an increase in legislation governing the rights of individual employees. None the less, a genuinely rounded, rights-based ethical approach should call for the protection of the interests of individuals against the powers of corporations. For example, the discharge of waste by agricultural enterprises may infringe on the property rights of others downstream (Wetzstein and Centner, 1992). However, the way in which rights are defined in terms of legislation may result in a formal commitment to a rights-based approach that amounts to little in practice. One example – again relating to environmental pollution – is that of recent, ineffectual 'reforms' governing groundwater contamination in the United States (Wetzstein and Centner, 1992).

1.3.6   Postmodern ethics

Critics of postmodernism have argued that this school of thought is fundamentally aethical, representing a fractured and localist rejection of universal standards governing behaviour (Lash and Friedman, 1992: 8). It may be misleading even to suggest that there is a coherent body of ideas we can refer to as a 'postmodern' approach to ethics. Instead, different writers may approach the subject of ethics from different vantage points, and grouping them together may be inappropriate. Postmodernism is perhaps best understood as a way of thinking about the world, and the nature of truth and claims by different communities to truth. It is also a reaction against modernism – an historical period associated with claims to progress and enlightenment based on reason and the application of science. The horrors of the twentieth century showed many that these claims were hollow, as instruments developed by science and reason were deployed in ways too unpleasant to describe. A postmodern perspective involves scrutinising beliefs as to what constitutes reality (also known as ontological beliefs), as well as beliefs about what constitutes knowledge (also known as epistemological beliefs): these underpin claims to a better world.

It is misleading and a contradiction in terms to call postmodernism a theory or to refer to postmodernism as a school. This is because leading writers such as Lyotard, Baudrillard, Derrida and Foucault (each closely associated with postmodernism) all reject the idea (in different ways) that there are theories or truths or schools that are independent of history. The belief that what counts as knowledge, certainty, and even reality, is something local and grounded in a particular community is sometimes expressed as a denial of 'transcendent' truths. For postmodernists, truth is something that is a product of a particular social order (see Figure 1.1). Lyotard (1984) offers a neat, if somewhat cryptic definition of postmodernism as incredulity towards metanarratives.

In other words, postmodernism involves suspicion and mistrust of wide-ranging belief systems (such as Marxism or any religious faith) and scepticism about the claims

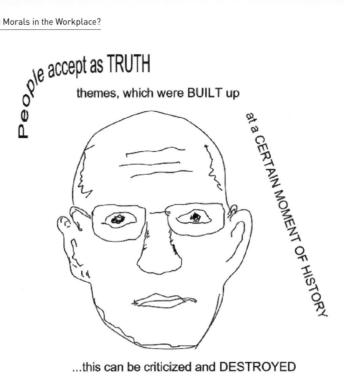

People accept as TRUTH themes, which were BUILT up at a CERTAIN MOMENT OF HISTORY

...this can be criticized and DESTROYED

Figure 1.1 – Michel Foucault – postmodern guru

produced from within social structures (such as bureaucracies, or large, multinational corporations). This scepticism – or incredulity towards metanarratives – goes beyond the claims of political philosophies, religions or organisational forms. It means not only that grand systems or structures are suspect, but that what we take to be true anywhere depends on the social and historical setting (Morrell, 2002). Thus any and all truths are partial and local (including presumably any truths about postmodernism). This would seem to put postmodernists (again, assuming we can refer to them all as one) firmly in the ethical relativist camp. It would certainly be a mistake to suggest that because postmodernism denies transcendent truths, then 'anything goes' for postmodern ethical theorists. Not many people do make such a crass mistake, but relativism remains a problem for postmodernists, as we discuss below. However, it is important to note that some postmodern scholars have provided the most powerful and compelling criticisms of unethical practices.

For example, postmodernism shares with conservative philosophers such as Michael Oakeshott (1983) a fundamental distaste for universal notions of rationality. The rationality metanarrative, to use Lyotard's phrase again, has led to the prioritisation of 'development and progress' irrespective of the human costs involved. Some of the worst atrocities in human history have only been realisable because of technological 'progress', that is, built on the application of reason in science. Moreover, there is often a very narrow interpretation of what rationality means in the context of human behaviour. That narrow interpretation is open to challenge, as we have already discussed, when looking at contemporary economists' explanations of choice. Many of the models used in business to predict both individuals' and firms' behaviour are based on a view of 'rational choice', where rationality is understood as the desire of individual agents to maximise the benefits accruing to themselves. This interpretation is based on an idea of self-interest and it serves to erode the very moral standards that would make other forms of progress (social, philanthropic, ethical) viable and sustainable (Friedman, 1992: 356).

To Baumann (1993), the unprecedented human rights abuses of the twentieth century, coupled with widespread environmental degradation, reflects the limitations of modernist ethical theories. He argues that, whether these theories are utilitarian or deontological, rigid notions of reason or general good have been imposed. These notions take little account of diversity and the real needs of the mass of society at a local level. Postmodernists would argue that the modern work organisation is one setting where self-serving truths evolve that conceal structures of domination and the interests of those in power. An organisation may represent little more than an 'apparatus of capture', a stultifying environment 'overcoding' rationalist norms, repressing individual creativity and expressiveness (Deleuze and Guattari, 1988: 380).

In contrast to the assumption of ultimate social progress that underlies much of the modernist project, postmodernism makes no claims as to the inevitability of a better life. Deleuze and Guattari (1988: 380) assert that it is possible to cast aside the universalistic rationalist codes governing conduct. Individuals or micro-collectives can, and will, continue to seek to escape the oppressive power of the status quo. Instead, they can construct their own, particularistic ethical realities more appropriate to their needs. There are potential problems for postmodernist thinkers that arise from the nature of this approach. Two key ones are *ethical relativism* and *ethical conservatism* (Morrell, 2002). We have discussed the problem of relativism at length in this chapter, but it can be thought of with respect to postmodernism in particular in this way. If we believe that what counts as reality is socially constructed, and that truth is local and partial, then there is no transcendent basis for judgement. How, then, can there be any basis for describing behaviour, an individual or a firm as ethical or unethical? A consequent, related problem is conservatism. Because postmodernism does not offer any scope for transcendent judgements, there is no firm basis for undertaking change. Relatedly, postmodernists may have very little to offer managers seeking guidelines or tools for dealing with ethical dilemmas. Rather, they may argue that contemporary society, and individual work organisations, are inherently repressive environments; none the less, the potential for liberatory action at the grassroots level persists.

1.4 SUMMARY

The field of business ethics seeks to apply the tools of philosophy to understand the day-to-day ethical challenges facing modern work organisations. After highlighting a number of general ethical quandaries, we have explored and highlighted several distinct philosophical traditions that provide insights of relevance to the modern firm. These included discussion of the following: virtue ethics (with its ties to the traditions of ancient Greece and the emergence of the city-state, where context and individual responsibility are key themes); utilitarian ethics (with its emphasis on the utility principle – a consequentialist doctrine that can be treated somewhat simplistically, but where various refinements to the understanding of the term 'happiness' suggest it can lead to sophisticated debate); deontological ethics (Kant's categorical imperative being the clearest and best-known example); rights-based approaches and the reciprocal obligations that follow from rights (libertarianism in politics and the economy) and postmodernist ethics (incredulity to metanarrative through a critique of contemporary social life rather than by imposing explicit ethical guidelines). We suggest that each of the approaches highlighted has some merit in providing practical analytical tools to help in understanding the nature of contemporary ethical dilemmas, be they in terms of core internal managerial functions or relations with the broader community, or, indeed, the natural environment.

DISCUSSION QUESTION

Which ethical perspective, do you think, is most relevant to the world of business? Give reasons for your answer.

REFERENCES

1. Aristotle. 1952. *Politics*. London: Everyman.
2. Arvey, R. D. and Sackett, P. R. 1993. 'Fairness in Selection: Current Developments and Perspectives', in N. Schmitt and W. Borman (eds) *Personnel Selection*. San Francisco, CA: Jossey-Bass.
3. Barry, A. 2004. 'Ethical Capitalism', in W. Larner and W. Walters (eds) *Global Governmentality*. London: Sage, pp. 195–211.
4. Bauman, Z. 1993. *Postmodern Ethics*. Oxford: Blackwell.
5. Baumhart, R. 1961. 'How Ethical Are Businessmen?', *Harvard Business Review*, 38: 6–31.
6. Beauchamp, T. and Bowie, N. 1997. 'Ethical Theory and Business Practice', in T. Beauchamp and N. Bowie (eds), *Ethical Theory and Business*. Upper Saddle River, NJ: Prentice Hall.
7. Bowie, N. 1991. 'Business Ethics as a Discipline: The Search for Legitimacy', in R. Freeman (ed.), *Business Ethics: The State of the Art*. Oxford: Oxford University Press.
9. Bowie, N. 1997. 'New Directions in Corporate Social Responsibility', in T. Beauchamp and N. Bowie (eds), *Ethical Theory and Business*. Upper Saddle River, NJ: Prentice Hall.
10. Burns, R. 2000a. 'Enlightenment', in R. Burns and H. Raymond-Pickard (eds), *Philosophies of History*. Oxford: Blackwell.
11. Burns, R. 2000b. 'On Philosophising History', in R. Burns and H. Raymond-Pickard (eds), *Philosophies of History*. Oxford: Blackwell.
12. Daily, C. M., Dalton, D. R. and Cannella, A. A. 2003. 'Introduction to Special Topic Forum Corporate Governance: Decades of Dialogue and Data', *Academy of Management Review*, 28, 3: 371–82.
13. Deleuze, G. and Guattari, F. 1988. *A Thousand Plateaus*. Minneapolis, Minn.: University of MN Press.
14. Evensky, J. 2001. 'Adam Smith's Lost Legacy', *Southern Economic Journal*, 67, 3: 497–517.
15. Freeman, R. E. 1991. 'Business Ethics as an Academic Discipline', in R. Freeman (ed.), *Business Ethics: The State of the Art*. Oxford: Oxford University Press.
16. Friedman, M. 1997. 'The Social Responsibility of Business Is to Increase Its Profits', in T. Beauchamp and N. Bowie (eds), *Ethical Theory and Business*. Upper Saddle River, NJ: Prentice Hall.
17. Ghoshal, S. 2005. 'Bad Management Theories Are Destroying Good Management Practices', *Academy of Management Learning and Education*. 4, 1, 75–91.
18. Gilbert, R. 1991. 'Respect for Persons, Management Theory and Business Ethics', in R. Freeman (ed.), *Business Ethics: The State of the Art*. Oxford: Oxford University Press.
19. Heater, D. B. 2004. 'Citizenship: The Civic Ideal in World History, Politics and Education', Manchester: Manchester University Press.
20. Hendrix, L. 1993. 'Illegitimacy and Other Purported Family Universals', *Cross-Cultural Research*, 27, 3–4: 212–31.
21. Jennings, M. M. 2004. 'Incorporating Ethics and Professionalism into Accounting Education and Research: A Discussion of the Voids and Advocacy for Training in Seminal Works in Business Ethics'. *Issues in Accounting Education*, 19, 1: 7–26.
22. Jones, C., Parker, M. and ten Bos, R. 2005. *For Business Ethics*. London: Routledge.
23. Kant, I. 2000. 'Progress in History', in R. Burns and H. Raymond-Pickard (eds), *Philosophies of History*. Oxford: Blackwell.
24. Kitson, A. and Campbell, R. 1996. *The Ethical Organization*. London: Macmillan.

25. Lamsa, A-M. 1999. 'Organizational Downsizing – An Ethical versus Managerial Viewpoint', *Leadership and Organizational Development Journal*, 20, 7: 345–53.

26. Lash, S. and Friedman, J. 1992. 'Subjectivity and Modernity's Other', in S. Lash and J. Friedman (eds), *Modernity and Identity*. Oxford: Blackwell.

27. Legge, K. 1996. 'Morality Bound', *People Management*, 2, 25: 34–7.

28. Lyotard, J.-F. 1984. *The Postmodern Condition: A Report on Knowledge*, Manchester: Manchester University Press.

29. Maciver, R. and Page, C. 1961. *Society*. London: Macmillan.

30. McCall, J. J. 2004. 'Assessing American Executive Compensation: A Cautionary Tale for Europeans', *Business Ethics: A European Review*, 13, 4: 243–54.

31. Menguc, B. 1998. 'Organizational Consequences, Marketing Ethics and Salesforce Supervision: Further Empirical Evidence', *Journal of Business Ethics*, 17, 4: 333–52.

32. Mill, J. S. 1964. *Utilitarianism, Liberty and Representative Government*. London: Everyman.

33. Morrell, K. 2002. 'Postmodernism/Postmodernity', in T. Redman and A. Wilkinson (eds), *The Informed Student's Guide to Human Resource Management*. London: Thomson, pp. 199–200.

34. Morrell, K. 2004. 'Socratic Dialogue as a Tool for Teaching Business Ethics', *Journal of Business Ethics*, 53: 325–31.

35. Morell, K. and Anderson, M. 2006. 'Dialogue and Scrutiny in Organisational Ethics', *Business Ethics: A European Review*, 15, 2: 117–29.

36. Nozick, R. 1984. 'Moral Constraints and Communicative Justice', in M. Sandel (ed.), *Liberalism and Its Critics*. Oxford: Basil Blackwell.

37. Oakeshott, M. 1983. *On History and Other Essays*. Oxford: Blackwell.

38. Parekh, B. 1982. *Contemporary Political Thinkers*. Oxford: Martin Robinson.

39. Rawls, J. 1984. 'The Right and Good Contrasted', in M. Sandel (ed.), *Liberalism and Its Critics*. Oxford: Basil Blackwell.

40. Rawls, J. 2001. *Justice as Fairness: A Restatement*. Cambridge, MA: Harvard University Press.

41. Ridley, M. 1996. *The Origins of Virtue: Human Instincts and the Evolution of Cooperation*. London: Penguin.

42. Sandel, M. 1984. 'Introduction', in M. Sandel (ed.), *Liberalism and Its Critics*. Oxford: Basil Blackwell.

43. Singer, P. 1995. *Practical Ethics*. Cambridge: Cambridge University Press.

44. Solomon, R. 1992. *Ethics and Excellence: Co-operation and Integrity in Business*. Oxford: Oxford University Press.

45. Vinten, G. 2000. 'Corporate Governance: The Need to Know', *Industrial and Commercial Training*, 32, 5: 173–8.

46. Wetzstein, M. and Centner, T. 1992. 'Regulating Agricultural Contamination of Groundwater through Strict Liability and Negligence Legislation', *Journal of Environmental Economics and Management*, 22, 1: 1–11.

47. Whetstone, T. 2001. 'How Virtue Fits within Business Ethics', *Journal of Business Ethics*, 33, 2: 101–14.

WHAT IS OB?

CHAPTER OUTLINE

- Introduction
- The meaning of organizational behaviour
- A framework for studying organizational behaviour
- Managing work organizations
- The multidisciplinary nature of organizational behaviour
- Why study organizational behaviour?
- The influence of class, gender, race, ethnicity and disability on organizational behaviour
- Researching organizational behaviour
- Summary and end-of-chapter features
- Chapter case study 1: Managing change at Eastern University
- Chapter case study 2: Tuition reimbursement for studying OB?

CHAPTER OBJECTIVES

After completing this chapter, you should be able to:

- explain work organizations, their basic characteristics and their connections to the wider social context
- define the term 'organizational behaviour'
- appreciate the meanings and complexities behind the words 'management' and 'organization'
- demonstrate an understanding of why behaviour may vary because of an organization's strategy, structure, technology and environment
- identify the key changes occurring in the world and the effect that they are likely to have on organizational behaviour
- describe the contribution to the field of organizational behaviour of three disciplines: psychology, sociology and anthropology
- describe the evolution of organizational behaviour as a field of research and learning, and explain an integrated framework for conceptualizing organizational behaviour
- describe the challenges of conducting research on organizational behaviour

INTRODUCTION

Most mornings, we turn the front door handle of our home and set off to work in formal organizations such as banks, insurance offices, retail stores, garages, schools, universities, hospitals, sports centres, police stations, hotels and factories. In work settings like these, people engage in a host of work-related activities, communicate and interact, and learn with and from each other. For example, members of an organization may operate a computer, serve customers, teach students, diagnose patients, coach athletes, apprehend and arrest criminals, cook meals for guests or build cars. People's behaviour in their workplaces – and indeed the way the workplaces and work processes themselves have been set up – are the result of myriad factors. Partly, they reflect individual preferences or psychologies among those in the workplace. But the full picture is more complex: people are exposed to a multitude of organizational processes and control systems that limit, influence or determine their behaviour in work organizations.

A 'work organization' is a physical and legal structure within which people undertake paid work, and it is the people rather than the organization of course who undertake the relevant behaviours. The work organization is in fact the most obvious symbol of **capitalist modernity**. Its presence affects our economic, cultural, political and ecological environment, providing employment, producing goods, delivering services, lobbying politicians and infecting the ecosystem. Richard Scott observed, 'Ours is an organizational society' (ref. 1, p. 3). We sell our mental or physical skills to organizations, and we buy the goods or services they provide. Our 'experience' of organizations, as employees, customers or stakeholders, may be good, bad or indifferent, and standard approaches to **organizational behaviour** analyse and explain this using a variety of individual, group or organizational processes. Theoretical accounts of organizational behaviour typically centre on how the behaviour of individuals evolves and adapts, how it is shaped by group dynamics and how organizations are structured in different ways. It looks at why organizational controls occur in the way they do, and how organizational processes have an impact on societal and ecological stability or instability. The emphasis is on how organizational behaviour theories underscore management practices and organizational efficiency and effectiveness.

Organizational behaviour is not a subject that can be studied in isolation: organizations and the people who work within them are socially embedded and can be profoundly influenced by contextual processes, as the extraordinary global economic recession that began in 2008–09 attests. Organizations are shedding jobs, and those surviving are 'downsizing'; as people struggle to come to terms with these events, they experience feelings of acute anxiety. As in previous economic recessions, there is evidence that this global economic and financial meltdown has caused a psychological meltdown, an emotional state in which people, whether employed or not, feel extremely vulnerable and afraid for their futures.[2] The term '**psychological climate**' describes the psychological well-being of individuals, organizations and communities and how this may fluctuate over time.[3] We already know that the current downsizing and joblessness is – perhaps not surprisingly – having a damaging effect on the men and women, and their families, who experience it.[4] In concrete terms, it means redundancy, long-term unemployment, foreclosure and homelessness, immense upheaval and dislocation and poverty. In psychological terms, individuals may face feelings of guilt, shame and fear, as well as mental health-related problems. Writing about the 1980–81 economic recession in Britain, this writer characterized its social effects as the 'fear syndrome', which was succinctly expressed by a trade union leader this way: 'We've got three million on the dole, and another 23 million scared to death'.[5]

capitalist modernity: a term used to characterize the stages in the history of social relations dating roughly from the 1780s that is characterized by the constant revolutionizing of production and culture

organizational behaviour: the systematic study of formal organizations and of what people think, feel and do in and around organizations

psychological climate: the psychological well-being of individuals, organizations and communities and how this may fluctuate over time

After 25 years of excess, when deregulation of the financial services industry spurred footloose capitalism, when the bonus culture inspired bankers and fund managers to engage in high-risk behaviour, and now this inequality has grown, there is evidence of a sea change in social attitudes that could lead to reform. Before the global economic recession that started in 2008–09, there was debate about the need for an alternative to so-called 'Anglo-American' capitalism,[6] but this debate has been highlighted by recent events. The Anglo-American model is characterized by low taxation, minimal regulation and a focus on exports. In the midst of the deepest recession for 70 years, prior to the G20 summit on the world financial and economic crisis in London, in 2009, French President Nicolas Sarkozy called for the 'moralization' of the capitalist system, arguing that 'Financial capitalism is a system of irresponsibility and … is amoral'.[7] German Chancellor Angela Merkel advocated the creation of an international 'architecture of institutions'.[8] In addition, British Prime Minister Gordon Brown urged the European Union to work with America to forge a new 'moral' global capitalism, saying, 'Just as globalization has been crossing national boundaries, we now know it has been crossing moral boundaries too.'[9]

weblink
You can read the full text of the April 2009 G20 communiqué at www.g20.org/Documents/final-communique.pdf

As a result of their meeting in 2009, the G20 countries produced an official 'communiqué' outlining their interpretation of events and their plans to ensure a recovery. Potentially, this communiqué is of seminal importance, because it represents a serious intellectual and political challenge to the ideology of Anglo-Saxon neo-liberal capitalism, or market fundamentalism. Probably nothing demonstrates more both the universality and depth of this economic crisis and the profundity of its effects than the new consensus that government is the solution, not the problem, in regulating the financial sector and the economy. Such a seismic shift in both politics and public thinking is likely to change the nature of capitalism, and ultimately the way in which work and people are organized and managed in organizations.[10]

Plate 1 – Graffiti outside the Bank of England sums up public anger about MPs' expenses and bankers' bonuses as job losses and home foreclosures hit unusually high levels in 2009. Responses to the recession and credit crunch may change the nature of capitalism, and ultimately the way work and people are organized and managed in organizations.
Photo: suburbanslice on Flickr

In this chapter, we look at organizational behaviour and explain in particular that it is a multidisciplinary field of study. We emphasize that globalized capitalism has a significant impact on the way in which people undertake paid work and behave in organizations. We explore the process of management through a three-dimensional model to help us understand that any social action by managers and other employees is not isolated from the rest of society but is deeply embedded in it. So, as an introduction to what follows, we will discuss how the social dynamics of class, gender, disability, race and ethnicity underpin contemporary organizational behaviour, before examining the challenges of researching behaviour in workplaces.

THE MEANING OF ORGANIZATIONAL BEHAVIOUR

capitalism: an economic system characterized by private ownership of the means of production, from which personal profits can be derived through market competition and without government intervention

means of production: an analytical construct that contains the forces of production and the relations of production, which, when combined, define the socioeconomic character of a society

This book is about how people in capitalist societies are organized and managed in organizations. **Capitalism** is a system for organizing economic activity. Although capitalist activities and institutions began to develop in Europe from the 1400s, modern capitalism has come to define the immense and largely unregulated expansion of commodity production, the related market and monetary networks and rule of law. The need to maximize profit from the 'rational' organization of work and exchange of goods or the delivery of services, rather than to satisfy the material needs of the producers, is the *leitmotiv* of capitalism. Capitalism creates a qualitatively distinct kind of work organization and society from any of those which preceded it.[11]

Theorizing about work organizations has deep historical roots. Well before the publication of any 'organizational behaviour' textbook, Adam Smith's (1776) *The Wealth of Nations* and Karl Marx's *Das Kapital* (1867) provided seminal accounts of how early factory owners organized and managed people. This current textbook has two broad aims. First, it aims to help the reader understand how people living in the era of mature global capitalism undertake paid work, how they interact with each other in organizations, and how the decisions made by managers affect others. Second, it aims to help the reader learn to influence the processes and shape events within organizations.

What are organizations?

work organization: a deliberately formed social group in which people, technology and resources are deliberately co-coordinated through formalized roles and relationships to achieve a division of labour designed to attain a specific set of objectives efficiently. It is also known as formal organization

society: a large social grouping that shares the same geographical territory and is subject to the same political authority and dominant cultural expectations

sociology: the systematic study of human society and social interaction

A **work organization** is a socially designed unit, or collectivity, that engages in activities to accomplish a goal or set of objectives, has an identifiable boundary and is linked to the external **society**. Work organizations can be distinguished from other social entities or collectivities – such as a family, a clan or tribe, or a complex society – by four common characteristics.

First, when we state that an organization is 'a socially designed unit or collectivity', we mean that one essential property is the presence of a group of people who have something in common, and who deliberately and consciously design a structure and processes. We use the term 'social structure' to refer to those activities, interactions and relationships that take on a regular pattern.

Some form of hierarchy exists in organizations. There are standard methods of doing things, norms, communications and control techniques that are coordinated and repeated every day. Organizations are made up of people, and they form relationships with each other and perform tasks that help attain the organization's goals. In **sociology**, we refer to this as the 'formal social structure'. Many aspects of the formal social structure are explicitly defined in organizational charts, job descriptions and appraisal documents. However, human activities, relationships and interactions emerge in the workplace that are not expressed in charts or written job descriptions.

Plate 2 – Today, our lives revolve around diverse work organizations, universities, banks, hospitals and factories. Work organizations are structures and groups of people organized to achieve goals efficiently. For-profit organizations have financial goals, normally profit maximization. Non-profit work organizations, such as Friends of the Earth, organize their activities around raising public awareness and lobbing politicians and governments to protect the environment and wildlife, and to reduce greenhouse gas emissions.
Source: Nick Tutton

This covers an array of human behaviour including the communication of rumours – the 'grapevine' – destructive or misbehaviour such as the sabotaging of a computer or machine by a disgruntled employee, and trade union action. These activities are referred to as the 'informal social structure'. The formal and informal social structures are the basic building blocks of an organization.

The second common characteristic of organizations is that human activity is directed towards accomplishing 'a goal or set of objectives'. For-profit organizations have financial goals – specific targets towards which human action is oriented, normally those of profit maximization. For Bakan, the modern for-profit organization is a 'pathological institution' that strives for profit and power and primarily exists 'to pursue, relentlessly and without exception, its self-interest, regardless of the often harmful consequences it might cause to others' (ref. 12, pp. 1–2). This means that making money is the first priority for for-profit businesses. They survive by minimizing their costs in any way they can within the law. As Stiglitz explains, the modern multinational corporation avoids paying taxes when possible, and many try to avoid spending on cleaning up the pollution they create, the cost being picked up by the governments in the countries where they operate.[13] Benevolent non-profit organizations have goals such as helping the destitute, educating students, caring for the sick or promoting the arts. In addition, most organizations have survival as a goal.

The third common characteristic is the existence of an 'identifiable boundary' that establishes common membership, distinguishing between the people who are inside and outside the organization. The fourth element of our definition connects the organization to the 'external society' and draws attention to the fact that organizational activities and action influence the environment or larger society. The impacts or 'outcomes' on society may include consumer satisfaction or dissatisfaction, political lobbying, pollution of the ecosystem and other by-products of the organization's activities. In Western capitalist economies, argues Stiglitz, big **corporations** have used their economic muscle to protect themselves from bearing the full social consequences of their actions.[13] Despite the rhetoric about organizations being 'socially responsible', the law 'compels executives to prioritize the interests of their companies and shareholders above all others and forbids them from being socially responsible – at least genuinely so' (ref. 12, p. 35).

corporation: a large-scale organization that has legal powers (such as the ability to enter into contracts and buy and sell property) separate from its individual owner or owners

Multiple types of work organization are possible. Organizations vary in their size, the product or services they offer and their purpose, ownership and management. An organization's size is normally defined in terms of the number of people employed. We are all familiar with very small organizations such as independent newsagents, grocery stores and hotels. Larger organizations include the Ford Motor Company, Lloyds Bank, Google and governments. Organizations can be grouped into four major categories according to their products: *food production and extraction* (for example, farms, forestry and mining organizations), *manufacturing* (for example, apparel, cars and mobile phones), *services* (for example, hairstyling, and train and air transportation) and *information processing* (for example, market research). The growth in the number of people employed in the service and information categories defines the **post-industrial** society.

post-industrial economy: an economy that is based on the provision of services rather than goods

Work organizations can also be categorized into those which operate for profit, and not-for-profit institutions. The purpose of for-profit organizations is to make money, and they are judged primarily by how much money is made or lost: the bottom line. Not-for-profit organizations, such as registered charities, art galleries and most

Plate 3 – Organizations vary in their size, the product or services they offer, their purpose, ownership and management. For example, we are all familiar with a small organization – such as a newsagent, grocery store or independent hotel – operating for profit. At the other end of the spectrum are large organizations, such as Ford Motor Company, and organizations not operating for profit, including charities such as Oxfam. Take a look at this typical English high street. How might a large chain such as Tesco measure its success or failure? And how would this be different from the small independent grocery store just two doors away?
Source: Nick Tutton

hospitals, measure their success or failure not by profit but in some other way. A university, for example, might measure its success by the total number of students graduating or obtaining grants from research bodies.

The primary purpose of an organization is linked to who owns and manages the organization. Many are owned by one person, one family or a small group of people. An individual may own and manage a small business, employing a few other people. Not all businesses are incorporated (that is, are companies), but also many companies are owned by only a few individuals. It is estimated that one-third of US Fortune 500 companies (the top 500 companies in the USA) are family controlled. Privately owned organizations are a large part of the British and North American economy. Private companies may have corporate shares (that is, they are part-owned by other companies), but the shares are not traded publicly on a stock market.

In contrast, publicly held organizations issue shares that are traded freely on a stock market and are owned by a large number of people. These organizations normally pay dividends – a proportion of their profits – to their shareholders. The owners are its principals, and these individuals either manage the activities of the organization themselves or employ agents (the managers) to manage it on their behalf. Privately and publicly owned organizations have the rights, privileges and responsibilities of a 'person' in the eyes of the law. But because a company is not actually a 'person' as such, its director or directors are held responsible for its actions, and directors have been fined and even jailed for crimes committed by 'the organization'.

Now we have reviewed the basic characteristics and types of work organizations, we can look more directly at the meaning and scope of organizational behaviour.

What is organizational behaviour?

As a field of study, organizational behaviour is not easy to define because it is an extremely complex and wide-ranging area that draws upon numerous disciplines, theoretical frameworks and research traditions. Within the organizational behaviour academy, there is a collection of 'conversations' – from individuals with different standpoints on organizational **theories** – each offering a competing theory and interpretation of organizational behaviour.

Standard organizational behaviour textbooks begin with a single definition of the subject, and tend to emphasize the contentious relationship between organizational behaviour and management theory and practice. One popular North American text, for example, explains that organizational behaviour involves the systematic study of the attitudes and behaviours of individuals and groups in organizations, and provides insight about *effectively managing* and changing them' (ref. 14, p. 8, emphasis added).

Organizations are arenas of situated social behaviour (that is, places in which particular kinds of social behaviour take place), which are both explicitly organized by management theory and practices, and fashioned consciously and unconsciously by values, beliefs, a community of practices, gender, ethnicity and national employment relations systems and practices.[15] Organizational behaviour is, in other words, embedded in the wider social, cultural and institutional fabric of society. It is best understood as a series of complex active processes in which people participate, formally and informally, at several levels including the micro, macro and global (Figure 2.1), in ways shaped by organizational roles and power.

A wider, more inclusive definition would recognize the importance of 'social embeddedness', and the external as well as internal forces that affect the behaviour of people in organizations. We can define organizational behaviour as *a multidisciplinary field of inquiry, concerned with the systematic study of formal organizations, the behaviour*

weblink
Within capitalist countries, there are alternative ways of organizing and managing people in workplaces. The best known worker cooperative is probably the Mondragón Movement in Spain. For more information, go to www.iisd.org/50comm/commdb/desc/d13.htm

theory: a set of logically interrelated statements that attempts to describe, explain and (occasionally) predict social events. A general set of propositions that describes interrelationships among several concepts

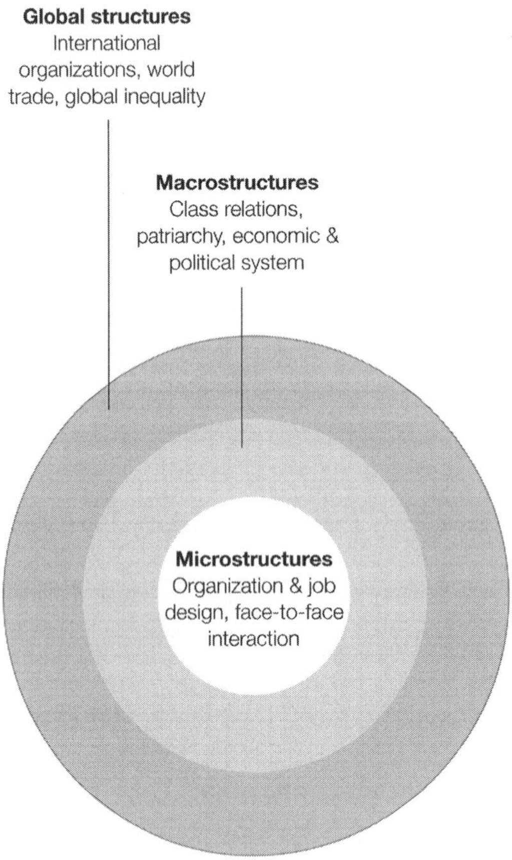

Global structures
International
organizations, world
trade, global inequality

Macrostructures
Class relations,
patriarchy, economic &
political system

Microstructures
Organization & job
design, face-to-face
interaction

Figure 2.1 – The three levels of social structure surrounding the organization

of people within organizations, and important features of the social context, that structures all the activities that occur inside the organization. Workplace behaviour for this purpose includes face-to-face communicating, decision making, ethical practice, leadership style and cooperation over work processes, learning and innovation. Behaviour also includes cognitive behaviour, such as thinking, feeling or perceiving, and values. Furthermore, behaviour includes power struggles, alienation, absenteeism, bullying, racial, ethnic and gender discrimination, sabotage and other forms of misbehaviour, and **conflict** and resistance between managers, as well as between managers and workers.

The organization's **microstructures** and processes must be analysed and explained by reference to events and developments outside it. **Macrostructures**, composed of class relations, cultural, patriarchal, economic and political systems – the external environment – represent the 'macrocosm' or the immediate outer world that affects organizational life and behaviour. *Global structures* composed of international organizations, such as the World Bank, the International Monetary Fund and the International Labour Organization, and patterns of global communications, trade and travel also surround and permeate work organizations.

Micro-, macro- and global structures surround people and influence organizational behaviour. These social structures are also interrelated: they are shaped by each other, and action or change in one stimulates or affects action in the others. Consider, for example, a change in the patterns of global trade and investment. In France, the change might cause the government to amend 'macro' public policy by increasing the

conflict: the process in which one party perceives that its interests are being opposed or negatively affected by another party

microstructures: the patterns of relatively intimate social relations formed during face-to-face interaction

macrostructures: over-arching patterns of social relations that lie outside and above a person's circle of intimates and acquaintances

length of the working week, with politicians claiming that this will improve labour productivity and France's international competitiveness. The change in the macro-structure might in turn generate action inside the organization, the microcosm zone, as workers stop work and take to the streets to protest against the government policy. We can think of these three levels of social structures – global, macro and micro – as concentric circles radiating out from people in the workplace, as shown in Figure 2.1.

The leading American sociologist C. Wright Mills (1916–62) argued that we can only gain a full understanding of human experience when we look beyond individual experiences and locate those experiences within the larger economic, political and social context that structures them. Mills wrote in 1959 that the 'sociological imagination allows us to grasp the interplay of man [sic] and society, of biography and history, of self and world' (ref. 16, p. 4). We agree with Mills here, and suggest that the behaviour of managers, and the agency of individuals and work groups, cannot fully be understood without reference to the outer organizational context. While we focus here primarily on issues related to workplace behaviour in advanced capitalist economies, it is important to remind ourselves that 73 per cent of the world's workers live in developing economies.[17]

The workplaces employing the other 27 per cent of workers are arenas of competing social forces that mirror and generate paradox, tension, misbehaviour, conflict and change. This characterization of the organization as an 'arena' provides a theoretical framework for examining the behaviour of managers and other employees in relation to politics, gender, power and ideology (for early literature on this, see refs 18–20). There are many valid ways of studying organizational behaviour, but by recognizing the interplay between the global, macro and micro social dimensions, we are led to acknowledge the dynamic linkages between external forces on the one hand, and internal management processes and individual and group agency on the other. At the risk of simplification, we illustrate the multifaceted and interdisciplinary nature of organizational behaviour in Figure 2.2.

A FRAMEWORK FOR STUDYING ORGANIZATIONAL BEHAVIOUR

The manifestations of human behaviour provide parameters within which a number of interrelated dimensions can be identified. These collectively control and shape how people and work are organized and managed. In Figure 2.2, we offer a simple integrative or 'open' model for studying organizational behaviour. It is divided into four components.[21] These are:

- environmental forces as external context inputs
- processes for converting the inputs into outputs in a managerial context
- the evaluation of outputs
- a feedback loop that links the processes and external forces with the feedback flowing into the organization, and from the organization into the external context.

The external context: global capitalism

In examining the external context, we shall highlight a few of the 'inputs' that are most crucial for the study of organizational behaviour. This discussion is meant to be illustrative – rather than exhaustive – of how the external context affects organizational processes through, for example, global economic activity, government regulations, technological change, cultural influences and ecological pressures. Globalization underscores the need to examine the organization within its totality,

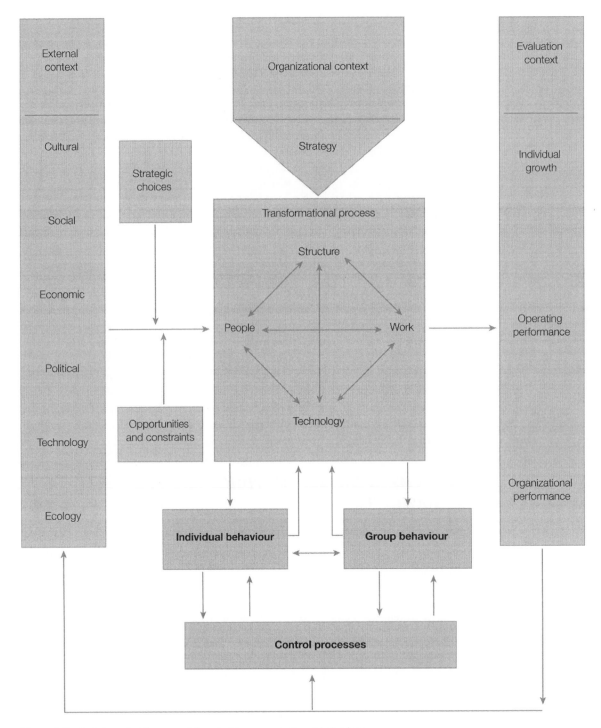

Figure 2.2 – An integrated framework for studying organizational behaviour

the embedded nature of organizational behaviour and the processes by which those with most power respond to the demands of the external context.[22–25] However, globalization itself is a thoroughly contested concept, depending whether it is viewed as primarily an economic, a political or a social phenomenon.

The fact that we live in a globally interconnected world has become a cliché. As part of this interconnected world, the acceleration of the **globalization** of economic activity is one of the defining political economic paradigms of our time. In the early twenty-first century, globalization is arguably about the unfettered pursuit of profit.[26] International management literature gives accounts of how higher profits can be realized by relocating production operations abroad and by economies of scale. Organizations are embedded within their own economic, political, legal and social spheres. Levels of corporate taxation, employment standards and other 'business-friendly' incentives can affect profits. Since capital is portable (that is, it can be employed in different countries), it is possible for global corporations to indulge in an endlessly variable geometry of profit searching.[27] The logic of unfettered globalization, propelled over the twentieth century by cheap oil, means that any labour-intensive, value-added activity is likely to migrate from high-wage to low-wage economies – that is to say, from the rich, developed countries like the USA and Western Europe to the poorer developing countries such as China, Bangladesh and India. For our purpose, as the global recession unfolds, the main issue is how globalization is affecting organizational behaviour.

globalization: when an organization extends its activities to other parts of the world, actively participates in other markets, and competes against organizations located in other countries

stop reflect
How have external environment factors impacted on work organizations that you, or members of your family or your friends, have worked for? How did these external factors influence the behaviour of people in the organization?

Critical insight

By its very nature, globalization implies both a broadening and a deepening. Economic and social phenomena that once affected a particular nation-state or region in the European Union now have broader implications and must of necessity include a greater number of states and powerful actors. The globalization of economic activities has given rise to renewed interest in the actions of 'big business', and more specifically in the managerial behaviour of large work organizations that operate in the global marketplace.

One part of the debate involves assessing the extent to which managerial behaviour is 'disembedded' from the domestic institutional and social contexts that affect management actions. It is argued that any understanding of the impact of globalization on organizational behaviour must recognize that managers and other actors are exposed to multiple and conflicting systematic constraints and opportunities, with no guarantee that the societal effects of the organization's home base will always prevail.

As an introduction to the debate about the effects of organizations being 'embedded' in society, obtain a copy of a book edited by Marc Maurice and Arndt Sorge, Embedding Organizations.[28] Consider its arguments, and ask yourself, does globalization mean that managerial behaviour will be universal? What are the counteracting forces to the implied 'convergence' of work and employment practices?

strategy: the long-term planning and decision-making activities undertaken by managers that are related to meeting organizational goals

organizational structure: the formal reporting relationships, groups, departments and systems of the organization

bureaucracy: an organizational model characterized by a hierarchy of authority, a clear division of labour, explicit rules and procedures, and impersonality in personnel matters

The organizational context

The structure of the organization is formed from the interaction between individuals, groups and organizational controls. Organizational context describes the regular, patterned nature of work-related activities, technology and processes that is repeated day in and day out. There are at least six identifiable variables that impact on the active interplay of people within the structure of the organization: strategy, structure, work, technology, people and control processes.

In an organizational context, **strategy** refers to what senior managers do over time to accomplish an organization's goals. **Structure** is defined as the manner in which an organization divides up its specific work activities and achieves the coordination and control of these activities. The structure of organizations can take many forms. Much debate on changing organizational forms has centred on the argument of whether organizations have shifted from **bureaucratic** forms with highly specialized tasks and a hierarchical authority to post-bureaucratic forms with low specialization and 'flat' authority. Empirical studies suggest that in spite of 'virtual' and 'lean' organizational forms, the majority of organizations still rely on a fundamental division of labour and are rule-bound.

The way people interact within the organization will be strongly influenced by the way the work is designed, for example how tasks are divided into various jobs and the degree of autonomy employees have over their work. **Technology** affects the behaviour of individuals, groups and operating processes. Here we would just note that technology is a multidimensional concept.

By now, it should be obvious that organizational behaviour is concerned with *people*. The study of people's values and behaviours in the workplace, of work organizations, necessitates that we make an important distinction between employees or workers, and employers or their agents, that is, managers. The social relations between these two groups constitute the *employment relationship*. The nature of the employment relationship is an issue of central importance to organizational behaviour. In some workplaces, these relations are supportive, fostering a sense of autonomy and human development. In other workplaces, these relationships are toxic, discouraging learning and putting health-damaging stress on individuals. The differences in work activities, motivation and rewards associated with being either a worker or a manager mean that the individual actors in these two groups more likely perceive and respond to events and social actions in the workplace rather differently. Analyses of workers' and managers' behaviours imply, even if they do not explicitly state, a perspective of the employment relationship.[29]

Within the notion of 'behaviour', we include individual action and *emotion*, whether expressed in an individual capacity or as a member of a work team, and whether it is prompted by global forces or by organizational processes of control. It is *people*, not inanimate organizations or technology, who make organizational processes happen, who produce goods and deliver services through human labour, creativity, learning and effort. People differ on a number of dimensions that are relevant to organizational behaviour. Demographics such as age, education, experience, skills, abilities and learning styles are just a few of the variables that can affect how individuals and groups behave and relate to each other in the workplace.

Understanding the dynamics of the employment relationship and individual behaviour is both complex and fascinating, and requires us to examine the concepts of personality and identity. The dynamics of both are shaped by the psychological contract, that is, what an employee can expect of the organization beyond the formal employment contract (for example, wage or salary, job security or job satisfaction). Employee *misbehaviour* – such things as arson, fraud, lying, pilferage and sabotage – tends to be under-reported, but these 'warts' constitute part of organizational reality.[30] Studies emphasize that gender, class, race, ethnicity and disability make an overwhelming difference to the organizational reality too.[31-35] Thus, the 'people' aspects of our model cannot be examined in isolation. As others have also emphasized, we need to adopt a multidimensional approach to studying organizational behaviour:

> The time-honoured distinctions between three levels of analysis – the individual, the organization, and the environment – are clearly breaking down. The previous certainty of discrete, self-contained individuals, fully informed by their roles in organizations, has been shattered.

(ref. 36, p. 9)

---

technology: the means by which organizations transform inputs into outputs, or rather the mediation of human action. This includes mediation by tools and machines as well as rules, social convention, ideologies and discourses

web link
Visit www.fastcompany.com for some short articles on management strategy. You will also find articles that analyse the strategies of various organizations

Given the general nature of the divergent interests between managers and the managed, our reciprocal model contains *control* processes. Control systems enable managers to accomplish the organization's objectives and to deal with recalcitrant subordinates. Numerous studies suggest that formal organizations are in essence 'structures of control'.[19,37,38] If we accept this premise, the question is, how exactly is this control exercised and by whom, and why is control necessary? Control may be exercised directly by technology or indirectly by peer pressure within groups, or by **organizational culture**, or by an array of human resource management techniques designed to make people's behaviour more predictable and controllable.

organizational culture: the basic pattern of shared assumptions, values and beliefs governing the way employees in an organization think about and act on problems and opportunities

The evaluative context

Organizational processes are not an end in themselves, but are explicitly related to the goals of the over-arching organization. The evaluative context addresses the much-researched question, 'Do certain behaviours actually lead to high-performance organizations?' Issues of individual, operating and financial performance are all involved. But although there is well-documented evidence that a combination of determinate organizational behaviour variables is associated with positive performance outcomes, the association is by no means uncontested. Any serious analysis of the goals of management brings into focus the build-up of internal contradictions and the control of 'strategic tensions'.[39] Among the most challenging are the tensions between maximizing profit or shareholder return and employee security, between organizational control and employee motivation, and between managerial autonomy and social responsibility. The more critical accounts of organizational behaviour expose internal tensions and paradoxes.

MANAGING WORK ORGANIZATIONS

How work is designed and how people behave inside organizations is strongly influenced by management decisions, as well as by what happens outside the boundaries of the organization. The term 'manager' refers to an occupational group that organizes and coordinates, and makes decisions about what work is done, how it is done and by whom. Management is distinguished from 'leadership' by a greater emphasis upon directing others through control systems and a reliance upon hierarchical position, rather than through inspiration, and upon the mobilization of higher employee commitment.

It is important to understand that there is a relationship between economic stability or instability outside, and decision making and behaviour inside, the organization. The external context, the business strategy, structural design and control processes, and the abilities and attitudes of employees, all affect the way the manager performs managerial activities. The manager can adopt a wide array of means to accomplish his or her ends. These may range from common processes such as communicating, motivating and coercing, to complex technologies. Combined, these constitute the manager's repertoire for 'getting things done through people', and each individual manager may be more or less skilled in or disposed towards using a particular process. This section aims to provide a short overview of the nature of management, and to consider how managerial behaviour affects the behaviour of other employees.

The meaning of management

The words 'manage' and 'manager' are derived from the Italian word *maneggiare* – to handle or train horses.[40] Henri Fayol (1841–1925), regarded as the 'father of modern management', provided the classic definition of management as a series of four key activities that managers must continually perform: planning, organizing, directing and controlling (Figure 2.3).

The management cycle presents the job of the manager in a positive way, and to this day all mainstream management textbooks present management as having four central functions: to plan, organize, direct and control – the PODC tradition. For Fayol, *planning* meant to study the future and draw up a plan of action. *Organizing* meant coordinating both the material and the people aspects of the organization. *Directing* refers to ensuring that all efforts focus on a common goal, and *controlling* means that all workplace activities are to be carried out according to specific rules and orders. In Peter Drucker's canonic text, *The Practice of Management*, management is seen as both a function and a social group. The emergence of management as a social group is seen as one of the most significant events in modern history: 'Management expresses basic beliefs of modern Western society' (ref. 41, p. 4).

The process of management

To study behaviour in workplaces, we need to address two related questions: 'What do managers do?' and 'Why do managers do what they do?' The nature of managerial work is an amorphous topic in the literature. Since the mid-twentieth century, studies have offered a comprehensive picture of what managers do. Many are in the Fayolian genre: that is, managerial behaviour is represented as a rational and politically neutral activity. Other studies offer a more complex account, emphasizing the time spent building a reciprocal network of social relationships. Managers' work is typically characterized by brevity, fragmentation and variety.[42,43]

Henry Mintzberg offers a multifaceted concept of managers' work consisting of three sets of behaviours: *interpersonal*, *informational* and *decisional* (Figure 2.4).[43,44] 'Role' here refers to a set of behaviours that individuals are expected to perform because of the position they hold within the organization. Mintzberg usefully distinguished three different interpersonal roles – figurehead, leader and liaison – which arise directly from the manager's formal authority.

By virtue of these interpersonal encounters, with both other managers and non-managers, the manager acts as a 'nerve centre' for the dissemination of information. The manager's three informational roles – monitor of information, disseminator of information and spokesperson – flow from the interpersonal roles. Finally, the interpersonal and informational roles enable the manager to perform four decision-making roles: entrepreneur, disturbance handler, resource allocator and negotiator.

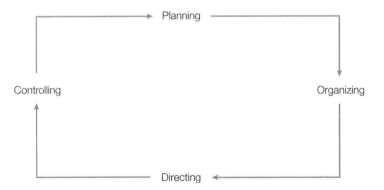

Figure 2.3 – The classic Fayolian management cycle

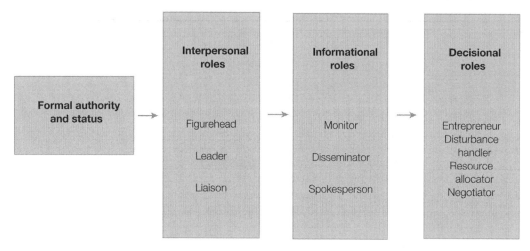

Figure 2.4 – The manager's 10 roles
Source: adapted from Mintzberg (1989/1975)[44]

The extent to which managers perform these functions will depend upon their position in the organization's hierarchy and their specific functional responsibilities. For example, we would expect human resource managers to give relatively more attention to the disturbance-handling and negotiating roles, given the nature of their work.

Unsurprisingly perhaps, studies have found that the relative importance of managerial work varies not only with the respondent's position in the management hierarchy, but also with the level of education of the co-workers. Interestingly too, managerial work in 'creative milieus' may not follow the conventional activities. Evidence shows that, in research-intensive organizations, managers not only coordinate day-to-day work, but, as scientists, play a major role in scaffolding the research project, and 'conventional management practices and managerial concerns come, at best, second'.[45] Despite claims to the contrary, surveys of managerial work exhibit striking parallels with the classic Fayolian management cycle (Table 2.1).[46]

Much of the earlier research reflects an Anglo-American bias. Some more recent studies have challenged the universality of managerial behaviour, and have

Table 2.1 – Summary of managerial work

Acting as a figurehead or leader of an organizational unit

Liaising with other managers

Monitoring, filtering and disseminating information

Allocating resources

Handling conflicts and maintaining workflows

Negotiating with other managers or representatives

Creative and innovative

Planning

Controlling and directing subordinates

Source: adapted from Hales (1986)[46]

emphasized the importance of factoring into the analysis gender and cross-cultural considerations.[47–51] Others suggest that managerial behaviour is 'gendered', while others counter-argue that male and female managers' behaviour is largely determined by structural, control and market imperatives – in other words, there is no such thing as 'female' management behaviour.[35]

An alternative, less flattering picture of managerial behaviour is indicated through studies on workplace bullying and sexual harassment.[52,53] Bullying and harassment in workplaces is not a new phenomenon. Indeed, in the context of profit maximization and managerial control, bullying is part of the management repertoire of getting things done through people, and reflects the significance of the unequal balance of power in workplaces.

An integrated model of management

The different dimensions of manager's work are brought together in the three-dimensional model shown in Figure 2.5. The vertical axis lists activities that answer the first question, 'What do managers do?' The horizontal axis shows the contingencies, and relates to the second question, addressed later in this chapter, 'Why do managers do what they do?' The diagonal axis relates to the third question, 'How do managers do what they do?', topics that are examined throughout this book.

The set of managerial activities is strikingly similar to those found in the classic Fayolian management cycle.[26] The contingencies are those forces and events, both outside and inside the organization, that affect management behaviour, as shown in

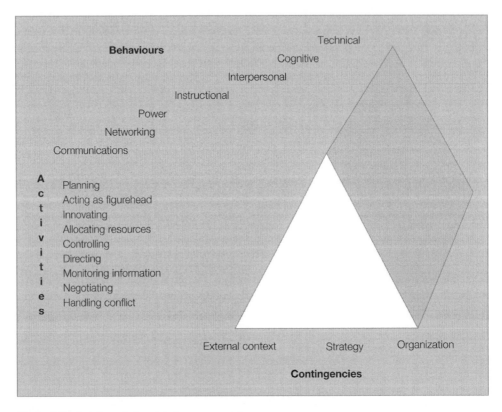

Figure 2.5 – An integrated model of management

Figure 2.2, above. The third dimension, managerial behaviours, lists various means by which managers communicate ideas, gain acceptance of them and motivate others to change in order to implement the ideas. Managers use technical, cognitive and interpersonal processes and skills to accomplish their work. Power is included in the list because it is part of the influence process. Management involves a blend of processes, and individuals will vary in terms of their capacity or inclination to use them, but these processes are ultimately about human interaction and relationships.

The model suggests that management is a multidimensional integrating and controlling activity, which permeates every facet of paid work experience and profoundly shapes the employment relationship and human behaviour. It does not assign values to the relationships and does not claim to be predictive. The model is, however, a useful heuristic device that helps us explore how management functions are translated into means, such as leadership processes, and equally how various contingencies influence behaviour in workplaces.

OB In Focus Climate Change – A Challenge For Us All

Mount Kilimanjaro – the tallest mountain in Africa – has been topped with snow for millennia. But scientists are predicting that its ice cap may have less than a decade left, with ice quantities falling by over 80 per cent in the past 100 years. As our planet warms up, Kilimanjaro's disappearing snow cap aptly illustrates both the climate challenge facing us and the urgency of addressing it.

The 10 hottest years on record have occurred during the past 15 years. Margaret Beckett, formerly British Secretary of State for Environment, Food and Rural Affairs, and Patricia Hewitt, formerly Secretary of State for Trade and Industry, said, 'Climate change is the greatest environmental challenge facing the international community today … It's now widely accepted by most independent scientists that climate change is taking place as a result of human activity releasing greenhouse gases into the atmosphere.'

As the world's economy grows, energy demand will undoubtedly increase. In 2002, the generation of energy and heat accounted for 40 per cent of worldwide carbon dioxide emissions. In China, 80 per cent of the power plants that will be used by 2020 have yet to be built. Climate change is not just an environmental challenge; it is an economic challenge too. It has been estimated that the economic cost of global warming could double to US$150 billion each year in the next 10 years, hitting insurance companies with US$30–40 billion in annual claims.

'We must achieve increased awareness of the need for cleaner, more efficient technology in the short term, and R&D into new technologies in the longer term, but this doesn't remove the need for action now,' said Beckett and Hewitt. G8 members are reported to be already showing leadership, particularly on work towards a hydrogen economy, carbon dioxide capture and storage and renewable technologies. Climate change affects us all today, and will increasingly affect future generations and therefore can not be viewed as a far-off, abstract, future inconvenience. The international community must act decisively now.

THE MULTIDISCIPLINARY NATURE OF ORGANIZATIONAL BEHAVIOUR

Organizational behaviour as a body of knowledge and field of inquiry is multidisciplinary in nature. It draws on theory and research findings from a number of social science disciplines, including psychology, sociology, anthropology and political science.

Psychology

The word 'psychology' literally means 'the science of the mind'. Psychology can be defined as the systematic study of human behaviours and mental processes. (For more information on the development, definition and scope of psychology, see, for

web link
Go to the following sites for information and a list of resources on industrial-organizational psychology and social psychology: www.socialpsychology. org/io.htm; www. socialpsychology.org/

example, refs 54 and 55.) Although we cannot directly observe mental processes (at least in the sense that we cannot readily tie what we can see of brain activity to behaviour of complex kinds), we have concepts for a wide range of them, for instance thinking, imaging and learning. Psychologists concern themselves with studying and attempting to address one key question: 'Why did this individual behave in this way?' The branch of psychology that deals with people in work organizations has been labelled as 'occupational' and 'organizational' psychology. Whichever label is used, 'work' psychology is primarily concerned with developing generalizable models about human behaviour in the workplace, with an emphasis on **social interaction** at the level of the individual, groups or entire organizations, and with testing theoretical predictions against observable facts.

social interaction: the process by which people act toward or respond to other people

Sociology

weblink
Go to the following site for further information and resources related to the sociology of work: www.intute.ac.uk/socialsciences/sociology

Sociology is the systematic study of the pattern of social relationships that develop between human beings, with a particular focus on the analysis of industrialized societies. Sociologists have made their greatest contribution to organizational behaviour through their study of formal organizations. They have explored the relationship between organizational actions and culture, and analysed the effects of macrostructures and global structures in buttressing or undermining organizational structures and processes. Sociology addresses such questions as: 'What is society?' 'Is society made up only of individual people in different types of relationship, or are social groups, such as social classes, more important than individuals?' 'Or is society something which exists over and above individuals?' 'Who exercises power in society, and how does power impact on relations in the workplace?'

Anthropology

Anthropology is the scientific study of humanity. Cultural anthropology, or ethnology, a subdiscipline of the field, is the study of contemporary and historically recent human societies and cultures. Ethnologists are especially enthralled by the great variety of the world's cultures. Multiculturalism as a European and North American phenomenon can be examined and understood from an anthropological perspective, focusing, for example, on concepts of ethnocentrism, cultural relativism and culture shock. **Ethnocentrism** is the tendency for people to view their own culture as superior to all others. In contrast, **cultural relativism** is the appreciation that all cultures have intrinsic worth and should be judged and understood on their own terms. It is an ethical positive which assumes that people should not evaluate other people's customs and mores without understanding them. When workers migrate and encounter cultures that are very different from their own, they may experience a feeling of disorientation, isolation, loneliness and depression. This is called *culture shock*. In terms of organizational behaviour, being aware of ethnocentrism, cultural relativism and culture shock helps you to become a more informed and critical thinker, and a better manager.

ethnocentrism: the tendency to regard one's own culture and group as the standard, and thus superior, whereas all other groups are seen as inferior

cultural relativism: the appreciation that all cultures have intrinsic worth and should be judged and understood on their own terms

Political science

Political science is the study of individual and group behaviour within a political system. The essence of politics involves not only making and executing decisions for society, but also choosing between competing demands in the midst of social conflict. Politics, therefore, might be defined as the struggle for power and the management of conflict. It is often viewed as a junior discipline in terms of its influence on organizational behaviour, but in recent years it has made a significant contribution to the understanding of managerial behaviour, in particular towards the understanding of power and how individuals and groups manipulate power for self-interest. Recognizing the relevant work of psychologists, sociologists, anthropologists and political scientists aids our ability to accurately explain and predict the behaviour of people in organizations. This multidisciplinary framework and the major contributions to the study of organizational behaviour are shown in Table 2.2.

WHY STUDY ORGANIZATIONAL BEHAVIOUR?

At this point, the sceptical reader may be thinking 'I cannot see the practical use of organizational behaviour. I don't see how it helps the manager.' Organizational behaviour is more than just an intellectual exercise – it is an applied social science with practical, everyday management uses. The practical use of organizational behaviour is to make the student and manager more attentive to unexamined common assumptions that may be influencing their decision making. It is best understood as a set of intellectual tools designed to help people predict, explain and influence organizational activities (Figure 2.6).

Both outside and inside the organization, predicting the behaviour of other people is an inherent requirement of everyday life. In other words, we want to be able to say that if X happens, then Y will occur. Our lives are made easier by our ability to predict when people will respond favourably to a request or when workers will

Table 2.2 – Towards a multidisciplinary approach to organizational behaviour

Social science	Contribution		Levels of analysis
Psychology	Personality	Communication	Individual
	Perception	Leadership	
	Learning	Group processes	
	Motivation		
Sociology	Class relations	Control processes	Group organization
	Power	Gendering of work	
	Bureaucracy	Technology processes	
	Conflict		
	Group interaction		
Anthropology	Comparative attitudes	Organizational environment	Group organization
	Comparative beliefs & values	Cross-cultural analysis	
	Organizational culture		
Political science	Conflict	Decision making	Organization
	Power		

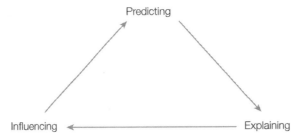

Figure 2.6 – Reasons for studying organizational behaviour

Plate 4 – The ability to understand behaviour in the workplace is a necessary prerequisite for making informed choices and for influencing organizational action.
Source: Getty Images

respond favourably to a new reward system. So-called 'common-sense' predictions of human behaviour are often unreliable. The discipline of organizational behaviour makes generalizations and predictions about behaviour as systematically as possible in the light of available research and theory. Studying organizational behaviour will help you further develop your knowledge of human behaviour, and so help you more accurately predict human behaviour within work organizations.

Although it is important to predict human behaviour, it is also vital to understand and *explain* the behaviour of people in complex organizations. Prediction and explanation are not the same. Accurate prediction usually precedes understanding and explanation. Through observation and experience, we are all capable of predicting the downward direction of an apple when it falls off a tree, but unless we have knowledge of the theory of gravity developed by Isaac Newton (1642–1727), we cannot fully explain *why* the apple falls to the ground. In the work context, organizational behaviour will help us explain (for instance) why individuals are less or more motivated when certain aspects of their job are redesigned, why various aspects of team processes cause misbehaviour and why networks and new forms of organization can have negative effects on performance.

The ability to understand human behaviour is a necessary prerequisite for making informed choices and for influencing organizational actions. According to Chris Grey, 'Theory is a weapon used to bludgeon others into accepting practice' (ref. 56, p. 14). The key question is 'What is *really* happening in workplaces?' There is well-documented evidence demonstrating a positive relationship between certain 'clusters' of organizational practices and behaviours and superior performance. For Jeffrey Pfeffer, for example, the real source of sustainable competitive advantage, he persuasively argues, is derived from 'the culture and capabilities of your organization that derive from how you manage your people' (ref. 57, p. 5). In other words, sustainable development increasingly comes from understanding and managing organizational behaviour.

stop reflect

Can you think of other reasons for studying organizational behaviour?

As we have explained already, work organizations are social structures, designed and created by people who have the capacity to shape and change them. Learning organizational behaviour theory is indispensable because it provides a conceptual 'toolbox' to at best understand and at worst justify social action: it can be characterized as a journey of self-enlightenment. We suggest that studying organizational behaviour is a requirement for active citizenship in advanced capitalist societies that are subject to periodic turbulence and change. We need to go to the root of the nature and tendencies of work organizations, and to exercise our sociological imaginations by presenting options for changing the way they function in society.

THE INFLUENCE OF CLASS, GENDER, RACE, ETHNICITY AND DISABILITY ON ORGANIZATIONAL BEHAVIOUR

Anyone who takes even a cursory look inside a contemporary organization will most likely see a diverse workforce. Although different groups will be segregated into specific jobs, the presence of women and visible minorities will be evident. Together, people of Afro-Caribbean, Bangladeshi, Pakistani, Asian, Chinese and East European origin account for an increasing proportion of the British workforce, and the same is true in many other European Union states and other countries that have expanded their populations through immigration, such as Australia and Canada. Studying diversity is not simply a matter of learning about other people's cultures: it involves discovering how social class, gender, disability, race and ethnicity frame people's life chances and work experience. It may come as a surprise, therefore, to learn that academic journals and most mainstream textbooks in the organizational behaviour field show little interest in social class, gender, disability, race and ethnicity. Why is this? But to frame our discussion at the outset, we suggest that class relationships, for example, are so deeply embedded in capitalist employment relations as to become all but invisible.

We focus on diversity and equity here not because they are an interesting yet benign fact of the modern workplace, but because we consider that the social dynamics of class, gender, race, ethnicity and disability underpin contemporary organizational behaviour. To understand the significance of class, gender, race, ethnicity and disability is to give emphasis to power imbalances, and to put the behaviour of individuals and groups in the organization into a wider social context. However, no book can contain everything: the material we have chosen inevitably not only reflects our personal bias, but is also highly selective. Although we draw mainly from the narrow field of workplace psychology and sociology, we cannot cover everything, even in a cursory fashion.

In every society, inequalities exist between individuals and groups, with some people having more money, wealth, schooling and power than others. Sociologists use the term 'social stratification' to refer to a system by which each society ranks people in a hierarchy. One type of stratification is the class system. A social **class** is defined as a large group of people in a given society who have a similar degree of access to a material resource such as income, wealth or property. The sociological analysis of class has been strongly influenced by the work of Karl Marx (1818–83) and Max Weber (1864–1920). In Marx's view, class is rooted in people's relationship to the means of production – the means by which they gain an economic livelihood. Under industrial capitalism, capitalists exploit workers who sell their productive labour for wages. Marx believed that the relationship generates perpetual social conflict.

class: the relative location of a person or group within a larger society, based on wealth, power, prestige or other valued resources

OB and globalization

Hijab on the job: religion in organizational culture

With the acceleration of the global movement of both workers and organizations, questions have arisen about the some-times uneasy relationship between religion and the workplace. How can an organization accommodate workers' rights to free expression without violating the rights of other workers? What constitutes a reasonable accommodation of religious beliefs, practices and symbols in the workplace? Does the banning of religious symbols from the workplace constitute discrimination? These questions, and organizations' work to address them, have garnered much attention in the media and in legal arenas in recent years.

One of the most public and vigorous debates has been around the right of workers to wear the hijab, a traditional head scarf worn by Muslim women, while at work. This debate garnered international attention in 2004 when France banned the wearing of religious symbols including the hijab, Christian crosses, Sikh turbans and Jewish skullcaps in state schools.

Other countries, such as Britain, have taken different approaches to the incorporation of religious symbols and practices into public and work life. In 2001, for instance, the London Metropolitan Police, 'the Met', determined that female officers would be able to wear the hijab as part of their police uniform. Incorporating the hijab as an optional component of the office police uniform was expected to increase the number of Muslim women interested in joining the force. An article from the Daily Telegraph (McIlroy, 2001) hints at other moves towards the accommodation of religion within workplace culture being considered by the Met:

> Sikh officers are allowed to wear turbans and the Met is also considering whether to let potential recruits from London's 10,000 Rastafarians have dreadlocks. Other changes being discussed include the provision of prayer rooms in police stations, halal food in staff canteens and special washing facilities for Muslim officers.

Although the hijab has been endorsed by London's Met, other countries and organizations have banned the traditional garment in the workplace. For instance, the Philadelphia Police Department in the USA has banned female officers from wearing the hijab on the job, citing the city's policy of religious neutrality (Duffy, 2007). Some organizations, scholars and members of the public have argued that, as a religious symbol, the hijab has no place in secular public organizations. Others point out that religious and cultural symbols and practices, like bank holidays that coincide with Judeo-Christian religious celebrations, are already ingrained in the organizational culture of many public and private workplaces in Western countries. Accommodating workers who wish to wear the hijab, they argue, signals a welcome move toward what religious scholar Douglas Hicks (2003) calls 'respectful pluralism' in workplace culture.

Respectful pluralism is a 'set of ideas for creating a culture that models ... mutual respect amidst diversity' (Hicks, 2003, p. 37). Hicks asserts that religion forms an integral part of many workers' identities, and that the suppression of worker's identities may violate their basic human right to dignity. Under the framework of respectful pluralism, workers should be permitted to incorporate aspects of their religious beliefs in their work life, as long as they do not degrade or coerce others in the organization, or interfere with the productivity of the organization.

The move by the Met to permit officers to wear the hijab as part of their uniform indicates that ideas like respectful pluralism are gaining a foothold, as organizations and their workers exist in an increasingly globalized world.

stop! What do you think about the place of religious and cultural symbols and practices in the workplace? Can you think of any ways in which organizations may unwittingly promote particular religious and cultural beliefs or practices? What is your opinion about the concept of respectful pluralism in the workplace?

Sources and further information

Barrett, D. (2009) 'Christian health workers faces sack over crucifix necklace', *Daily Telegraph*, May 23, 2009. Available at: www.telegraph.co.uk/news/newstopics/religion/5374277/Christian-health-worker-faces-sack-over-crucifix-necklace. html.

BBC News (2006) 'Woman to sue BA over necklace row', October 15, 2006. Available at: http://news.bbc.co.uk/2/hi/uk_news/england/london/6052608.stm.

Duffy, S. (2007) 'Muslim police officer loses suit over headscarf', *Legal Intelligencer*. Available at: www.law.com/jsp/article.jsp?id=900005555748#.

Hicks, D. A. (2003) 'Religion and respectful pluralism in the workplace: a constructive framework', *Journal of Religious Leadership*, 2(1), pp. 23–51.

Knox, K. (2004) 'World: Head scarves in the headlines, but countries take different approaches', Radio Free Europe/Radio Liberty, April 8, 2004. Available at: www.rferl.org/Content/Article/1052223.html.

McIlroy, A. J. (2001) 'Met will let Muslim WPcs wear traditional headscarf', *Daily Telegraph*, June 15, 2001. Available at: www.telegraph.co.uk/search/?queryText=Met+will+let+Muslim+WPcs+wear+traditional+headscarf%92&Search=Search.

National Film Board of Canada (1999) *Under One Sky: Arab Women in North America Talk About the Hijab*. Directed by Jennifer Kawaja.

Note: This feature was written by Gretchen Fox, PhD, Anthropologist, Timberline Natural Resource Group, Canada.

Weber expanded upon Marx's theory of class by arguing that there are internal divisions within each group, based on status, social prestige and power. For Weber, people's position in the class hierarchy derives not from only their ability (or inability) to control the means of production, but also from their 'market position', which is determined by the possession of skills and qualifications. Weber's more complex, multidimensional view of class also led him to believe that a person's market position strongly influences her or his overall **'life chances'**. In the contemporary workplace, class translates into the employment relationship between the employer or agent (manager) and workers. The analysis of this relationship in class terms has been important in allowing us to predict, explain and manage work-based conflict.

Traditionally, studies of organizational behaviour have devoted little attention to the question of gender. **Gender** refers to the attitudes, feelings and behaviours members of a society typically associated with being male or female. Gender is a dimension of social organization, affecting how we interact with others, how we think about our identity, and what social behaviours and roles are expected of men and women in society in general, and the workplace in particular. Gender involves hierarchy, because men and women tend to be found in different social positions, as judged by their access to resources and power.

The feminist movement has produced a body of literature that offers various explanations for gender inequality. Radical feminism, for example, looks for explanations of gender inequality through the analysis of patriarchy: the systematic domination of women by men. From this perspective, men's power characterizes all relationships between the sexes, including those in the public world of organizational activity, and is sustained by the whole of our culture.[34,58,59]

life chances: Weber's term for the extent to which persons have access to important scarce resources such as food, clothing, shelter, education and employment

gender: the culturally and socially constructed differences between females and males found in the meanings, beliefs and practices associated with 'femininity' and 'masculinity'

Gender is embedded in the modern workplace. Organizational structures and hierarchies are characterized by gender segregation, in which women predominantly occupy jobs that are part time, low skilled and low paid, whereas men occupy full-time, high-skilled, high-pay positions and are allowed to climb the corporate ladder to senior management. A career in management is typically viewed as a 'male career'. Some feminists emphasize that patriarchal society confuses sex and gender, deeming appropriate for women only those occupations associated with the feminine personality. So in Western societies, for example, young women are encouraged to enter child care, nursing and elementary school teaching, and discouraged, or even barred, from entering such 'masculine' jobs as mining or working on oil rigs.

The gendering of work and organizations in 'malestream' organizational behaviour textbooks is normally discussed – if at all – in the context of the benefits to the organization (in economic terms) of a 'diverse' workforce. As Fiona Wilson correctly argues, 'women and issues about their work have been considered by many as less important than that of men' (ref. 34, p. 3). In our view, one of the most important consequences of acknowledging the crucial role of gender analysis in organizational behaviour studies is its power to question organizational behaviour research findings and analysis that segregates studies of work behaviour from occupational gender segregation, 'dual-role' work–family issues, the consideration of patriarchal power and issues of gender inequality.

Race and ethnicity are complex sociological concepts to introduce in organizational behaviour. Race can be understood as a socially constructed community composed of people who share biological characteristics that members of a given society consider important. Typically, people in Britain attach more meaning to skin colour and hair texture than, for instance, people in Cuba do. The variety of racial traits found in Britain and the European Union today is the product of European colonialism and subsequent migration, so that genetic traits once common to a single place are now found in all European Union member states.

Whereas the concept of 'race' implies something biological and permanent, 'ethnicity' is purely social in meaning.[60,61] It refers to the shared cultural practices and heritage of a given category of people that set them apart from other members of society. Britain is a multiethnic society in which English is the official language, yet many people speak other languages at home, including Hindi, Punjabi and Mandarin. Ethnic differences are learned, and for many people ethnicity is central to individual identity.

The concepts of race and ethnicity are fundamental to an awareness of racism and discrimination in society and the workplace. Prejudice is an attitude that judges a person on her or his group's real or imagined characteristics. Racism refers to the prejudices held by members of one group towards another based on socially important traits. In Weberian sociology, race appears to have a major influence on life chances. **Discrimination** is a behaviour affecting all minorities in work organizations. Discrimination can be direct or indirect, and takes many forms. Direct discrimination at work involves, but is not limited to, cases whereby individuals of a particular race, ethnic group or sex are treated less favourably than other members of the organization. In the UK, such behaviour is disallowed and is unlawful under the Race Relations Act 1976 (amended in 2000) and the Sex Discrimination Act 1975 (amended in 1986).

Although it is important to assess class, gender and ethno-racial issues in the workplace in order to generate a broad and critical view of organizational behaviour, here we wish to introduce another important under-researched area of inequality and disadvantage in the workplace: disability. Theoretical and empirical organizational

weblink

Go to the following sites for more information and resources on race, ethnicity and human rights in the workplace: www. ethnos.co.uk is the site of a consulting company that researches ethnic minorities in the UK; www.coe. int/t/E/human_rights/ecri/ is the Council of Europe's site on human rights; www.businessweek.com/ magazine/content/01_31/ b3743084.htm gives an article on the subject

discrimination: the actions or practices of dominant group members (or their representatives) that have a harmful impact on the members of a subordinate group

behaviour or sociological research on disability has been extremely limited, as disability has tended to be analysed primarily within a 'medical model'. Disability is viewed as a specialized medical condition requiring the intervention of qualified medical professionals. Disabled people and their families are viewed as passive recipients of care who have no informed opinion and therefore need not be consulted about matters that directly concern them; disabled people's needs are seen as special and different from everyone else's.[62] The common assumptions about disability focus on disabled people's lack of abilities. In the UK, for example, more than 2.4 million people are disabled, and those who are disabled are three times more likely to be unemployed than others. A critical perspective on disability draws to our attention how the capitalist mode of production is itself disabling for some people, and calls for the 'normalization' of disabled individuals as socially valued members of society, and for an end to inequitable treatment in the workplace.[63]

stop reflect

Have you experienced or observed discrimination in the workplace based on class, gender, race or ethnicity, or disability? What form did it take? How did management handle the discrimination?

In our view, the various permutations of relationships at work stemming from the variables of class, gender, race, ethnicity and disability are necessary factors in explaining the social world of work and contemporary organizational behaviour. We do not suggest that this book single-handedly redresses the imbalance in research and writing on these topics, and here we can do little more than skim the surface, but we hope that by adding class, gender, race and ethnicity, and disability to the work behaviour equation, we can encourage more lecturers in organizational behaviour to give major coverage to these important issues, and support more students in asking serious questions about diversity/equity issues.

RESEARCHING ORGANIZATIONAL BEHAVIOUR

It has been said that what you see depends on where you stand, especially when studying organizational life. How researchers approach their study of work and organizations depends on their life experiences and a whole series of assumptions they make about people and society. Although this is acknowledged in most standard textbooks, accounts of organizational behaviour tend to be presented in a sanitized, matter-of-fact-way; as an uncontested field of study devoid of controversy. Yet there are profound differences of opinion among academics about how work and organizations are designed, how people are managed and how they should be studied. Much of the controversy stems from competing theoretical perspectives, which we can define for our purposes as frameworks of interconnected beliefs, values and assumptions that guide thinking and research on the nature of the social world. In organizational behaviour, these rival perspectives or ideologies tend to be reflected in different schools of thought, each of which disseminates its research findings through particular academic journals.[64,65]

Work and Society: Knowledge, evidence and propaganda

How do we produce knowledge about a phenomenon as complex as organizational behaviour? How do we find out what is true and what works in this particular area of human endeavour?

Philosopher Paul Boghossian (2006) offers us one way to think about these difficult questions. Using the subject of the first inhabitants of North America as an example, he offers the following perspective on how we arrive at rational beliefs:

We may not know the facts [about North American's first inhabitants] ... but, having formed an interest in the question, we seek to know. And we have a variety of techniques and methods – observation, logic, inference to the best explanation and so forth, but not tea-leaf reading or crystal ball gazing – that we take to be the only legitimate ways of forming rational beliefs about the subject. These methods – the methods characteristic of what we call 'science' but which also characterize ordinary modes of knowledge-seeking – have led us to the view that the first Americans came from Asia across the Bering Strait. This view may be false, of course, but it is the most reasonable one, given the evidence.

This perspective on knowledge is one version of what Boghossian calls the classical view of knowledge. This classical view typically includes the following set of assumptions:

○ We should have evidence for believing something is true.
○ We should look impartially at all the evidence, not just the evidence that confirms what we already believe to be true.
○ We should acknowledge that our beliefs are fallible.
○ When confronted by new evidence, we should be willing to revise our beliefs about what is true or what works.

The classical view of knowledge offers a powerful way to think about how knowledge about any given thing or process ought to be produced. It serves as an invaluable reference point for those who seek to understand how organizations work, and why people in organizations behave the way they do. So, for example, we could ask whether an organization is attaining its goals and, if it is not, what course of action might enable it to attain its goals. Evidence enters into this investigation at two key points: evidence that supports a claim that the organization's goals are not being met, and evidence that supports the claim that a particular course of action would enable it to attain its goals.

Obviously, the classical model of knowledge, with its emphasis on evidence, is relevant here. But does it follow that the study of organizational behaviour is 'value-free' and is somehow insulated from politics and power? Not necessarily. Researchers need to recognize that an organization's goals may be contested and that the most obvious, official, versions of the organization's goals may not tell the whole story. Moreover, researchers have long recognized the existence of bureaucratic propaganda. Organizations may manipulate evidence to make it appear that official goals are being met.

So it makes sense for students of organizational behaviour to be aware of classical views of truth and evidence. The idea that we should use evidence to determine what is true and what works in the world of organizations is a useful starting point. But politics has a way of infiltrating the world of organizations and the knowledge we produce about organizations. Students should therefore be open to critical views of truth and should recognize that goal conflict, misinformation and manipulation of evidence are not uncommon in the world of organizations.

stop!   Debates over the role of Wal-Mart in society offer an interesting perspective on the issues of propaganda and counter-propaganda. Critics charge that Wal-Mart is guilty of discrimination and, more generally, that it contributes to 'reproletarianization' (a process that turns back the clock on the rights and protections that workers have won over the last century). Wal-Mart has fought back, pointing to the various benefits it has brought to the communities where it is located.

○ Take a moment to assess critically the various positions in this debate, starting with the following resources:
○ www.walmartwatch.com (for a critique of Wal-Mart)
○ www.walmartfacts.com (for a defence of Wal-Mart).
○ If you were researching organizational behaviour in Wal-Mart, what biases might you yourself bring to the subject, and why?

Sources and further information

Boghossian, P. (2006) *Fear of Knowledge: Against Relativism and Constructivism,* Oxford: Oxford University Press.
Gereffi, G. and Christian, M. (2009) 'The impacts of Wal-Mart: the rise and consequences of the world's dominant retailer', *Annual Review of Sociology,* 35, pp. 573–91.
Note: This feature was written by David MacLennan, Assistant Professor at Thompson Rivers University, BC, Canada.

perspective: an overall approach to or viewpoint on some subject

When people ask, 'What's your perspective on this?', they might just as well be asking, 'What is your bias on this?' because each **perspective** reflects a particular bias, based on our life experience, how we see an issue and our vested interests. Thus, perspectives are theoretical 'lenses' or 'road maps' we use to view the social world. When we refer to a perspective on organizational behaviour, we are therefore speaking of an interconnected set of beliefs, values and intentions that legitimize academic and organizational behaviours. Before we continue further with our educational journey in organizational behaviour, it is worth considering two fundamental questions: 'What major perspectives do academics adopt when studying behaviour in work organizations?', and 'To what extent can researchers construct a truly objective account of behaviour in work organizations?'

Major theoretical perspectives on organizational behaviour

Organizational behaviour theorists using one or more theoretical perspectives or 'lenses' offer many different explanations to the question, 'Why do people in organizations do what they do?' At the risk of glossing over a multiplicity of theoretical perspectives that academics identify with and defend with passion, it is possible to identify four competing ideological camps into which many, or most, academics fall. They are the managerialist, the **conflict**, the symbolic-interactionist and the feminist camps. These perspectives or **paradigms** will serve as useful points of reference for understanding the competing views discussed throughout the remainder of the book.

The managerialist perspective

The managerialist perspective is also referred to as the structural-functionalist perspective in sociology, and is adhered to by most studying organizations. Managerialists view organizations as complex systems whose parts work together to promote consensus and stability. They are interested in order, employee commitment and performance issues, with a partisan preference for managers rather than the managed. Although there are variations and tensions, functionalists make a number of core assumptions about the nature of organizational behaviour.

In their view, the question, 'Why do managers do what they do?' is largely explained by the fact that managers serve as 'agents' of owners and investors, and that, as agents, they strive to maximize the efficiency and profits or meet set targets by minimizing the costs of (people or materials or machines) inputs. Managers strive to be rational. That is, they systematically apply various techniques to accomplish some given goal. The organization itself is characterized as a paragon of rational decision making. Managers do what they do because the imperatives of markets or government require that it is done. Those who do not manage in this way are deemed to be 'unsuccessful'. The managerialist perspective, therefore, becomes inseparable from the notion of efficiency and effectiveness. Most functionalist thinking also assumes that work organizations are harmonious bodies, tending towards a state of equilibrium and order. The focus of much of the research endeavour is about finding the 'winning formula' so that more managers can become 'successful' in achieving prescribed goals by successfully shaping the behaviour of other employees.

Within the mainstream functionalist school, there are differences of view. The **contingency** literature focuses largely on the internal authority structure of the organization, and acknowledges that different technologies, depending upon their complexity, strongly explain managerial behaviour and impose different kinds of demands on people and organizations.[66] Contingency theory is helpful for understanding variations in organizational structures and, ultimately, managerial behaviour in the workplace. The *political* perspective focuses upon pressures, constraints and power relationships as causal explanations of managerial behaviour. Rather than presenting an image of managers as simple agents of owners, managers are viewed as having to respond to pressures from various stakeholder groups such as shareholders, suppliers, consumers and employees. The organization is viewed as a coalition of stakeholder groups.[67] The **strategic choice** literature (see Figure 2.2, above) stresses that management is a social process. Accordingly, managerial behaviour is 'bounded' by such factors as cognitive capacity, imperfect information, organizational politics, strategic business decisions, worker resistance and misbehaviour, and managerial

conflict perspective: the sociological approach that views groups in society as engaged in a continuous power struggle for the control of scarce resources

paradigm: a term used to describe a cluster of beliefs that dictates for researchers in a particular discipline what should be studied, how research should be conducted and how the results should be interpreted

contingency approach: the idea that a particular action may have different consequences in different situations

strategic choice: the idea that an organization interacts with its environment rather being totally determined by it

Plate 5 – Information overload can lead to poor decisions and work-related stress.
Source: Getty Images

beliefs, values and philosophies. Common to most variations of the managerialist paradigm is a failure to connect organizational behaviour to the larger dominant political economic paradigm of neo-liberalism.

The critical perspective

The critical perspective views capitalism and work organizations as a system that is both economically exploitative and socially alienating. The workplace here is understood as an arena of inequality, exploitation and structured antagonism that generates conflict. Accordingly, understanding managerial behaviour is related to action to reduce the indeterminacy resulting from the unspecified nature of the employment relationship by exerting control over others. In turn, employee misbehavior and open conflict between employer and employee reflects some level of individual or collective discontent with the employment relationship. Critical analysts argue that managers' attempt to extract the maximum of effort from workers for minimum reward is the primary cause of conflict and employee misbehaviour. As such, critical theorists are interested in power, control, the degradation of work, inequality and conflict, with a partisan preference for the less powerful, the managed rather than the managers. They attempt to discover the ways in which asymmetrical power relations affect the social relations between employers and workers. They also believe, to varying degrees, in a positive role for government in the economy and in the rights of workers to organize into trade unions.

As is the case with the mainstream managerialist perspective, the critical perspective is based on numerous theoretical ideas. Obviously, the starting point is criticism itself, that is, an identification of the limitations, paradoxes, contradictions and ideological functions of the orthodox standpoint.[38] Consequently, organizational behaviour theory and practice can only be understood as something in process and located within a structural setting.

The symbolic-interactionist perspective

The behaviours of managers and other employees interacting in the workplace are the typical social behaviours that catch the attention of symbolic interactionists.

Whereas managerialist and conflict theorists both analyse macro-level patterns of behaviour, the symbolic-interactionist perspective generalizes about everyday forms of individual-level social interaction in order to understand social behaviour.

The European philosopher Georg Simmel (1858–1918) is credited with the development of symbolic interactionism. He was interested in how individuals interact with one another in small groups, and wrote about the 'web of group affiliations' – aspects of social reality that are invisible in macro-sociological analysis. George Herbert Mead (1863–1931) and Charles Cooley (1864–1929) developed Simmel's ideas. Charles Cooley introduced the notion of the 'looking-glass self' that we form by looking into the reactions of people around us. If everyone treats us as intelligent, for instance, we conclude that we are.

Mead focused on the role of communications in human behaviour. He argued that most social interactions revolve around individuals reaching a shared understanding through the use of symbols such as language, non-verbal cues and gestures. The symbolic-interactionist paradigm is captured in Karl Weick's notions of 'enactment' and 'sense-making'.[68] It is argued that a sense of mission, goals and a language are constructed and communicated (or 'enacted') so that employees can make sense of what it is they do, and explain what it is they have accomplished. Employees are embedded in a symbolic context.

The feminist perspective

feminism: the belief that all people – both women and men – are equal and that they should be valued equally and have equal rights

The **feminist** perspective emerged out of criticisms of traditional research, which feminist scholars argued has been mainly concerned with research *on* men *by* men. The feminist perspective involves more than criticizing the use of masculine pronouns and nouns. It is rooted in a critical analysis of society, and draws attention to aspects of organizational life that other perspectives neglect. In part, feminist research has focused on gender differences and how they relate to leadership styles, interpersonal communications, discrimination and inequality of opportunities in paid work. Feminist scholars not only reveal sexual discrimination or the experience of oppression, but often also point to limitations in how other aspects of organizational behaviour are examined and understood.

Which of the four perspectives should a student use when studying workplaces? Each offers unique insights into behaviour in organizations (Table 2.3). We do not aim to privilege a singular perspective, but rather to provide a frame of reference against which readers can learn and develop their own understanding of organizational behaviour. Our view is that organizational behaviour cannot be understood without appreciating that organizations are places where those with power determine what work is done, how it is done and the effects on people by getting work done in a certain way. We think these are really important issues that should be examined and debated in any study of organizational behaviour.

Organizational theorists as researchers

Organizational behaviour theorists do not merely approach their subject from different paradigms; they also make different assumptions about the way in which organizations should be investigated. In addition, they employ varied research methods to build and test organizational behaviour theory. The second question we asked – 'To what extent can academics construct a truly objective account of behaviour in work organizations?' – brings up issues of social ontology (which deals with the nature of being), **epistemology** (the theory of knowledge) and research methodology, which

Table 2.3 – Comparing major perspectives on organizational behaviour

Topic	Managerialist	Conflict	Symbolic-interactionist	Feminist
View of society	Stable Well integrated	Unstable Tension	Dynamic	Inequality
Key concepts	Functions Dysfunctions	Capitalism Power	Symbols Communications	Patriarchy
Primary focus	Management practices Performance	Conflict Control	Sense-making	Gender equality
Prescriptions	Better practices Greater cooperation	Employee ownership and control	Create space Dialogue	Law reforms
Proponents	Emile Durkheim Talcott Parsons	Karl Marx Richard Hyman	George Mead Karl Weick	Mary Wollstonecraft Kate Millett

all affect the conduct of organizational behaviour research. We have no wish to re-route our intellectual journey into an academic quagmire, but you need some sense of these issues in order to appreciate some rather different aspects of the debate about organizational behaviour.

Social **ontology** issues are concerned with whether social entities, such as formal organizations, can and should be considered as objective entities with a reality external to individuals, or whether they can and should be considered as no more than social constructions built up from the perceptions and actions of individuals. These positions are referred to respectively as **objectivism** and **constructionism**. One simple way to think about this distinction is to look at the working of a hospital. In any hospital, there is a hierarchy of authority, a mission statement, a division of labour that assigns people to different jobs, and rules and regulations for doing those jobs. People learn the rules and follow the standardized procedures. The organization represents a social order in that it exerts pressure on members to conform to the rules and regulations.

The 'objectivist' view is that the hospital (as an organization, not as a building) possesses a reality that is external to any individual who occupies it. Individuals come and go, but the organization persists, so it is something that is 'out there' in the social world, and not just something that exists in people's minds.

Constructionism is an ontological position which asserts that social entities such as work organizations are produced or constructed by individuals through their social interaction. The core of the 'constructivist' discourse is that organizational reality does not have an objective existence, but is constructed in the accounts of organizational researchers and others. The constructivist concept of a hospital, for example, is one of a 'social order'. The hospital does not just encompass the formal rules; it is concerned with informal rules and activities as well. For instance, the official rules may state that only a doctor can increase a patient's medication but, unofficially, nurses are routinely given the power to do this. Both these understandings become part of the researcher's construction of the hospital.

The social order of any work organization is characterized as an outcome of agreed-upon patterns of actions among the different social actors involved, and the social order is in a constant state of change because the informal agreements are being

epistemology: a theory of knowledge particularly used to refer to a standpoint on what should pass as acceptable knowledge

ontology: a theory of whether social entities such as organizations can and should be considered as objective entities with a reality external to the specific social actors, or as social constructions built up from the perceptions and behaviour of these actors

objectivism: an *ontological* position which asserts that the meaning of social phenomena has an existence independent of individuals; compare this with *constructionism*

constructionism: the view that researchers actively construct reality on the basis of their understandings, which are mainly culturally fashioned and shared. It contrasts with realism (see below)

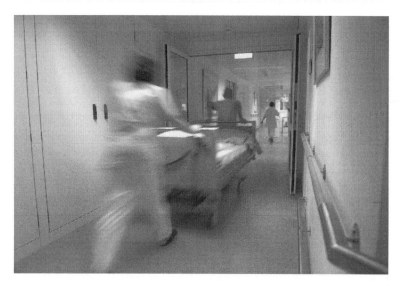

Plate 6 – One simple way to think about the distinction between the objectivist and constuctivist positions is to look at the working of a hospital.
Source: iStockphoto

constantly established, revoked or revised.[69–71] The notion that knowledge and truth are created, rather than objectively discovered by researchers, means that constructionists are more inclined to challenge researchers to re-examine their perspectives, the research process itself and the whole process of the production of knowledge.

An epistemological issue concerns the question of what is (or should be) regarded as acceptable knowledge in the social sciences, for example what forms of knowledge can be collected, and what is to be regarded as 'true' or 'false'. An important issue in this context is whether organizational behaviour can and should be investigated according to the same principles and methods as the physical sciences. The doctrine of **positivism** affirms the importance of modelling social science research on the physical sciences.

The French social theorists Auguste Comte (1798–1857) and Emile Durkheim (1858–1917) were early leaders in embracing positivist approaches to understanding human behaviour. There are five working assumptions that 'positivists' make in approaching their research. First, knowledge is arrived at through the gathering of social facts, which provide the basis for generalizations or laws by which human behaviour operates. Second, the purpose of theory is to generate hypotheses that can be tested, and this allows explanations of laws to be assessed. Third, only phenomena and regularities confirmed by the senses (that is, by, for example, sight or hearing) can genuinely be warranted as knowledge. Fourth, research can and must be conducted in a way that is value-free. And finally, social science must distinguish between 'scientific' statements and normative statements.[72] This means the social science deals with 'what is', not with what 'should be'.

It is a common mistake to equate positivism with the 'scientific'. Many social scientists differ fundamentally over how best to characterize scientific practice. An alternative term to describe the nature of social 'science' practice is **realism**.[73,74] This epistemological position shares two features with positivism: a belief that the social sciences can and should use the same approach to the collection of data and to its analysis, and a commitment to an external reality.

positivism: a view held in quantitative research in which reality exists independently of the perceptions and interpretations of people; a belief that the world can best be understood through scientific inquiry

realism: the idea that a reality exists out there independently of what and how researchers think about it. It contrasts with constructionism

critical realism: a realist
epistemology which
asserts that the study
of human behaviour
should be concerned
with the identification
of the structures that
generate that behaviour
in order to change it

Two forms of realism can be identified. Empirical realism simply asserts that, using appropriate methods, social reality can be understood. **Critical realism** is a philosophy of and for the social sciences. It distinguishes between the social world and people's experience of it, as well as between the real, the actual and the empirical. It maintains that deeper social structures and generative processes lie beneath the surface of observable social structures and patterns. For empirical realists, a social scientist is only able to understand the social world – and so change it – if the structures at work that generate human activity are identified.

An example of the application of both symbolic interactionism and critical realism is the work of Yrjö Engeström on informal workplace learning. Individual and small group learning is understood as an observable social process – the 'tip of the iceberg' – but learning is also embedded in an interlocking human activity system – the 'submerged part of the iceberg' – consisting of a community of practice, rules and division of labour.

interpretivism: the view
held in many qualita-
tive studies that reality
comes from shared
meaning among people
in that environment

The doctrine of **interpretivism** is a contrasting epistemology to positivism. The interpretivists' preference is for an empathetic 'understanding' and interpretation of human behaviour. For them, it is important to examine how people define their situation, how they make sense of their lives, and how their sense of self develops in interaction with other people. The interpretive approach has its intellectual roots in Max Weber's concept of understanding, or *Verstehen* (*Verstehen* being a German word that can be translated as 'human understanding'). In Weber's view, the social scientist should try to imagine how a particular individual perceives social actions, and understand the meaning an individual attaches to a particular event. The symbolic-interactionist perspective attempts to provide an empathetic understanding of how individuals see and interpret the events of their everyday work experiences.

The purpose of this brief discussion of epistemological issues in social research is to point out that, over the last 25 years or so, some organizational theorists have abandoned the application of the canons of physical science – positivism – to the study of human inquiry. The ontological and epistemological issues we outlined above have direct implications for research methodology.

qualitative research:
refers to the gathering
and sorting of informa-
tion through a variety of
techniques, including
interviews, focus groups
and observations, and
inductive theorizing

quantitative research:
refers to research
methods that
emphasize numerical
precision and
deductive theorizing

deductive approach:
research in which
the investigator
begins with a theory
and then collects
information and data
to test the theory

Research methodologies can be broadly classified as either **quantitative** or **qualitative**. Each strategy reflects differences in ontological and epistemological considerations: differences in the types of question asked, the kinds of evidence considered appropriate for answering a question, the degree to which the analysis is done by converting observations to numerical or non-numerical data, and the methods used to process the data.

Quantitative research can be defined as a research strategy that emphasizes numerical data and statistical analyses, and that entails **deductive theorizing**. It incorporates the practices and norms of positivism, is oriented towards aggregated data that compile responses from many respondents so that general patterns are visible (a process called nomothetic analysis), and embodies a view of social reality as a relatively constant, objective reality.

Qualitative research, on the other hand, can be defined as a research strategy that emphasizes non-numerical data, entails inductive theorizing, rejects positivism, is oriented towards case studies (a process called ideographic analysis), and embodies a view of social reality as the product of individual thought.

Figure 2.7 compares the differences between quantitative and qualitative, at least as they have historically been associated with different assumptions. At first glance, the quantitative/qualitative distinction seems to be about whether quantitative researchers employ more 'hard' measurements than qualitative researchers do, but

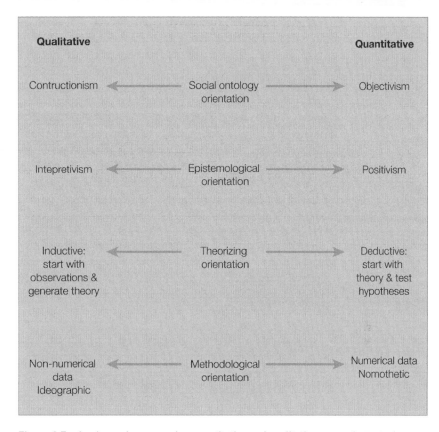

Figure 2.7 – A scheme for comparing quantitative and qualitative research strategies
Source: Burrell and Morgan (1979)[64]

there is in fact much more to it than that. These two approaches affect how social scientists do research, and are fundamental to understanding any inquiry into organizational behaviour.

Drawing on the elements in Figure 2.1 above, you should now be better able to account for the misrepresentation of social reality by researchers. First, researchers make different ontological assumptions that affect how they attempt to investigate and obtain 'knowledge' about organizational behaviour. For example, if a researcher subscribes to the view that organizations are objective social entities that shape individual behaviour, the research endeavour is likely to focus upon an analysis of the formal properties and regularities between the various elements of the organization. Alternatively, if the researcher subscribes to a view that emphasizes the dynamic nature of organizational life, the researcher will focus on the active participation of individuals in reality construction.

Second, the epistemological assumptions that researchers make about the social world affect how they attempt to investigate and obtain 'knowledge' about organizational behaviour. As we have discussed, at the heart of epistemology lie questions such as 'What is the relation between seeing and knowing?' and 'Whose knowledge is produced in surveys and interviews?' For the positivists, the challenge is to discover the laws of human behaviour, and perhaps then predict future social action. The constructivists reject the notion that we can ever have an objective account of the phenomenon under investigation, because all such accounts are 'linguistic reconstructions'.

As we have seen, the constructivist approach recognizes that the researcher and those being researched create the data. Researchers' data do not discover social reality; rather, the 'discovery' arises from the interactive process (between the researcher and the organization) and the political, cultural and structural contexts. Traditionally, the interview, for example, is viewed as an opportunity for knowledge to be transmitted between, for instance, a manager and a researcher. Yet, through the interactional process, the viewed and the viewer are active *makers of meaning*, assembling and modifying their questions and answers in response to the dynamics of the interview. The researcher is not simply a conduit for information, but is in fact deeply implicated in the production of knowledge.[75]

The constructivist approach suggests that what the manager and the situation actually are is a consequence of various accounts and interpretations. From this perspective, managers act as the 'practical authors' of their own identities. Furthermore, some interpretations are more equal than others. For example, one account of British Prime Minister Tony Blair's leadership performance following the September 11, 2001 attack on the World Trade Center in New York might describe it as 'Churchillian eloquence'. Others could interpret his speeches as populist rhetoric. The point here is that if more powerful 'voices' (including the popular press and television news channels) support Blair, 'the Churchillian' view will prevail, and the negative voice will carry little weight. The constructivist conclusion in this case is that what is important is not what the leader (or the organization) is 'really' like, but the processes by which he or she (or it) is perceived and defined as a success or failure. In terms of managerial behaviour, what constitutes a 'good' manager does not rest on an objective evaluation but on criteria generated by the social setting.[76,77]

This does not mean that knowledge is impossible. Rather, it means that the knowledge that is produced on what people in organizations allegedly do cannot be an objective narrative about their workplace activities. We must maintain a healthy scepticism as we read what researchers have to say about organizational behaviour.

Third, there are different research strategies, or general orientations to the conduct of the inquiry. The different research designs – such as questionnaire surveys, interviews and observational studies – may capture distortions of reality. For example, the mail survey (a questionnaire sent out to employees or customers) is favoured by quantitative researchers, but it can at best only provide a 'snapshot' of managerial and employee workplace activities. It cannot hope to provide an accurate picture of the subtleties and dynamics of employment relations, or of how individuals perceive social actions. The sample size may vary considerably, and if small samples of organizational members are surveyed, one or more atypical participants could unduly influence the findings. Case studies and direct observational techniques, favoured by qualitative researchers, often provide 'rich' data on workplace activities but may not capture cognitive processes. For example, a manager or group leader who is captured sitting in his or her office staring through the window could be either reflecting on a long-term plan or simply admiring the spring blossom.

Finally, we should be aware that management is embedded in the social structure and is highly political. This means that it involves power relationships between managers and non-managers, and between managers and other managers. As a result, political issues will rarely be far removed from the research process.[78] Consequently, the data gathered by researchers might not provide a 'reality report' on what managers do inside the organization, but rather reflect the diversity of managers and their need for self-justification, perhaps in connection with complex internal power struggles.

To extend our discussion of the limitations of research methodology a little further, managerial behaviour is most often analysed using 'scientific' or positivist methods,

stop reflect

According to the constructivist approach to knowledge making, language does not transmit truth; instead, it produces what we come to regard as truth. What are your views of the constructivist model? What are the implications of this view for understanding behavioural studies?

but organizational behaviour theorists sometimes quote managers' opinions to the exclusion of other people who are affected by the managers' actions (not least, their subordinates). Interviewing people from a cross-selection of the organization, including lower-level workers and trade union representatives in unionized establishments, is always likely to provide 'nuggets' of information that rarely surface in positivist research, and to suggest different lines of interpretation of human behaviour in the workplace.[79]

CHAPTER SUMMARY

- In this introductory chapter, we have attempted to cover a wide range of complex issues. We have emphasized that external contexts have a significant impact on the way in which individuals and groups work and behave. The external context influences the structure and behaviour of work organizations and, in turn, organizations influence the wider society. The linkage between the external contexts and the search for competitive advantage through employee behaviour is complex. Globalization means that there is a need for a multidimensional approach to the study of behaviour in organizations.

- We have reviewed orthodox treatments of management – as a set of technical competencies, functionally necessary tasks, and universal roles and processes found in any work organization.[41,43,80–82] For the traditionalist, managerial work is regarded as rational, morally and politically neutral, and its history and legitimacy are taken for granted. Alternative accounts of management emphasize that managerial work is embedded in a politically charged arena of structured and contested power relationships.

- To help us deconstruct the many facets of organizational complexity, we have used a three-dimensional management model. This encourages us to go beyond simply describing managerial behaviour, to provide an understanding of the contingencies that explain why managerial policies and behaviour vary in time and space. Managers' behaviour does not follow the famous Fayolian management cycle. They are typically engaged in an assortment of frenetic, habitual, reactive, fragmented activities.

- Organizational behaviour is a complex field of study with no agreed boundaries, and draws from a variety of disciplines including industrial psychology, sociology, anthropology and political science. We have defined it as a multidisciplinary field of inquiry, concerned with the systematic study of formal organizations, the behaviour of people within organizations, and important features of their social context that structure all the activities that occur inside the organization. To draw on the work of American sociologist C. Wright Mills, an 'organizational behaviour imagination' allows us to grasp the interplay of people in organizations and the larger economic, political and social context that structures the behaviour.

- Studying organizational behaviour can help put people in a stronger position to influence and shape the workplace and their own future. Organizational behaviour is very much an applied social science, which provides a conceptual 'toolbox' to help people predict, explain and influence organizational actions.

- We also focused on diversity because we consider the social dynamics of class, gender, race and ethnicity to underpin contemporary organizational behaviour. Understanding the significance of class, gender, race and ethnicity, and disability puts the behaviour of individuals and groups in the organization into a wider social context.

⊙ We identified four major theoretical frameworks or paradigms used by organizational behaviour theorists for the study of behaviour in organizations: the structural-functionalist perspective, the symbolic-interactionist perspective, the conflict perspective and the feminist perspective. The managerialist or structural-functionalist perspective represents 'mainstream' organizational behaviour analysis. It assumes that work behaviour takes place in rationally designed organizations, and is inseparable from the notion of efficiency. The symbolic-interactionist perspective focuses on the microanalysis of small workgroups, and interpersonal interaction in the organization. The critical and feminist perspectives set out to discover the ways in which power, control, gender and legitimacy affect relations between managers, and between managers and non-managers.

⊙ Finally, we discussed two ontological orientations – objectivism and constructionism – and two epistemological orientations – positivism and interpretivism – and outlined how these influence decisions on research methodology. Depending on the researcher's perspective, which reflects a whole series of assumptions about the nature of the social world, organizational behaviour researchers will tend to lean towards either quantitative or qualitative research strategies.

KEY CONCEPTS

class
constructivist approach
employee misbehaviour
employment relationship
gender
management
managerial behaviour
positivist approach
qualitative research
quantitative research
strategic choice
Verstehen

VOCAB CHECKLIST FOR ESL STUDENTS

Anthropology, anthropological, anthropologist
Bureaucracy, bureaucratic, bureaucrat, bureaucratization
Capitalist, capitalism, capitalize
Conflict
Conflict perspective
Constructivism
Critic, critical, criticize
Critical realism
Deductive
Dialectical
Discrimination, discriminate
Economy, economics, economical, economic, economist
Epistemology
Ethics, ethical

Evaluation, evaluative
External
Feminist
Gender
Global
Interactionist
Interpretivism
Life chance
Macro
Manager, management, managerial, manage
Means of production
Micro
Multidisciplinary
Objective
Ontology
Organization, organize, organizational
Organizational behaviour
Organizational culture
Organizational structure
Paradigm
Perspective
Political science
Positivism, positivist
Post-industrial
Proletariat
Psychology, psychological, psychologist
Qualitative
Quantitative
Realism
Social class
Social interaction
Society, social
Sociology, sociologist
Strategy, strategic, strategist
Symbolic, symbolism, symbolize
Technology, technological, technologist
Theory, theoretical, theorist

CHAPTER REVIEW QUESTIONS

1 What is meant by 'organizations' and 'organizational behaviour'?
2 What are capitalism, management and globalization?
3 Self-regulation and laissez-faire are finished, declared France's President Nicolas Sarkozy in 2009. Is this true? Why? If it is true, what are the implications for organizing and managing people at work?
4 Give three reasons for studying organizational behaviour.
5 Some authors state that organizational behaviour relates to the process of a manager's job. What does this mean?
6 Which of the four sociological perspectives do you think best fits your own ideas about human behaviour in work organizations?

7 Why is it important to include gender, race and disability in the study of behaviour at work?

8 If you were asked to conduct research in organizational behaviour, which research approach would you use? Explain your preference.

CHAPTER RESEARCH QUESTIONS

1 Form a study group of three to five people. Each member is to share with the group the number of organizations she or he has a connection with, for example, credit card (bank), driving licence (government agency), student ID card (university) and so forth. Using the Internet and/or newspaper sources, collect examples of the effects of the global economic and financial recession that started in 2008 on the functioning of at least two known organizations. What are the implications of restructuring for organizational behaviour in the next 5 years?

2 Obtain a copy of Stephen Ackroyd's and others (2006) *The Oxford Handbook of Work and Organization*. Read Chapter 3, 'Gender, race, and the restructuring of work' (pp. 74–94). What have been the implications of Anglo-Saxon capitalism for existing configurations of gender and racial inequality?

3 Retrieve and read Ulrich Beck's (2008) article, 'Reframing power in the globalized world', *Organization Studies*, **29**(5), pp. 793–804. Why does the author argue that, in an age of global crisis, the creation of a dense network of transnational interdependencies is what is needed to regain national autonomy? What implications does this have for the development of organizational management?

FURTHER READING

Anonymous (2009) The jobs crisis. *Economist*, March 14, p. 11.

Atkinson, C. (2008) 'An exploration of small firm psychological contracts', *Work, Employment and Society*, **22**(3): 447–65.

Bakan, J. (2004) *The Corporation*, London: Penguin.

Beck, U. (2008) 'Reframing power in the globalized world', *Organization Studies*, **29**(5), pp. 793–804.

Challiol, H. and Mignonac, K. (2005) Relocation decision-making and couple relationships: a quantitative and qualitative study of dual-earner couples. *Journal of Organizational Behaviour*, **26**, 247–74.

Collin, K. (2009) Work-related identity in individual and social learning at work. *Journal of Workplace Learning*, **21**(1/2), pp. 23–35.

Jacoby, S. (2005) *The Embedded Corporation*. Princeton, NJ: Princeton University Press.

Sklair, L. (2002) *Globalization: Capitalism and its Alternatives*. Oxford: Oxford University Press.

Sorge, A. (1997) 'Organization behaviour', pp. 3–21 in A. Sorge and M. Warner (eds), *The IEBM Handbook of Organizational Behavior*, Boston, MA: International Thomson Business Press.

Stiglitz, J. E. (2006) *Making Globalization Work*, New York: Norton.

Thompson, P. and McHugh, D. (2009) 'Studying organizations: an introduction', pp. 3–19 in *Work Organizations* (4th edn), Basingstoke: Palgrave.

Tyler, M. and Wilkinson, A. (2007) 'The tyranny of corporate slenderness: "corporate anorexia" as a metaphor for our age', *Work, Employment and Society*, **21**(3), pp. 537–49.

Weick, K. (2006) 'Faith, evidence, and action: better guesses in an unknowable world', *Organization Studies*, **27**(11), pp. 1723–36.

Wilson, F. M. (2003) *Organizational Behaviour and Gender*, Aldershot: Ashgate.

Wright Mills, C. (1959/2000) *The Sociological Imagination* (40th anniversary edn), New York: Oxford University Press.

Case Study   1

Managing change at Eastern University

Setting

In Canadian universities, it is evident that there is a need for positive change, including in how they manage and lead their employees. Various reports emphasize that they compete not only for government and sponsorship funding, but also for the market share of potential students in the increasingly competitive local, provincial and international arenas. In a university setting, key factors in facing these challenges successfully are cooperative and collaborative relationships between administration and the unions representing the university's workers, including support and faculty employees. Publicly funded universities are under increasing pressure to thrive in an atmosphere of reduced funding and increased competition. Working collaboratively in the same direction can produce a viable enduring future.

Background to the case study

Eastern University College is located in Ontario, Canada, and has approximately 14,000 full-time and part-time students. It was recently granted full university status, enabling the institution to grant its own degrees. In addition, it was expanded to include a comprehensive distance learning programme as an alternative to traditional classroom learning. Resources for new research and developing postgraduate programmes are also planned for the near future. With these fresh opportunities, it was recognized that changes were needed in the institution's strategic direction, including in its management policies and practices.

The university's labour relations were a particular area of focus. Over the years, the university had developed an adversarial and confrontational relationship with the union representing the institution's 300 support workers. In a study undertaken by the administration to identify the drivers or resistors in creating a more positive alliance with the union, it was found that the university's hierarchical and bureaucratic organizational structure was one possible reason for the dysfunctional relationship. Agreements on issues became stalled as administrators were required to take items back to senior managers for their perusal. The union contributed to the delay of reaching resolutions as it referred back to its members for approval on any decisions to be made. In the process, each group sought to protect its own interests. The net result was loyalty to factions, departments, leaders and unions, rather than to the organization as a whole.

Management meeting: preparing for change

Lisa Chang, 28, was the new Assistant Human Resource Manager for Eastern University. Improving student services at the university was a high priority for Chang. Based on feedback from the students' union, one idea she had was to extend access to the computer labs so they would be available for student use 24 hours a day, 7 days a week, except when they were being used by lecturers for teaching.

Chang visited the websites of several universities and downloaded details of their student computer services. She met with the Manager of Facilities, Doug Brown, the Vice-president of Student Services, Dr Susan Allen, and the Head of Campus Security, Paul McGivern. Chang presented her proposal, which included the estimated cost, and was able to resolve the few questions the others had with examples and information acquired from other comparable universities. It was agreed that Chang would present her proposal to the next meeting of the Council of Deans.

The presentation to the deans went flawlessly. Chang was confident that the deans would agree to her proposal. But just as the meeting was to wrap up, the Dean of Arts said, 'Have the union agreed to this?' Alarm bells went off in Chang's head. 'Union?,' she thought. 'Why wouldn't they agree to the new service?' She told the Dean she would discuss it with her boss Peter Webster, Director of Human Resources.

At the next human resources management meeting to discuss the labour relations situation, administrators were reviewing the most recent grievances and potential arbitrations, and the generally poor relationship with the union representing the support staff. Peter Webster, a manager who had several years' experience in dealings with the union, sighed in frustration as he echoed a sentiment of many in the room. 'It seems to be impossible to work together collaboratively with this union. I think we may as well accept it.'

'It doesn't have to be this way,' said Chang, as she handed out copies of her proposed new student service. 'When I talked to one of the stewards last week, he actually expressed the same desire for a more cooperative relationship. That is a sign of positive change already.'

After some discussion on what could be done to build upon this progress, the group asked Lisa Chang to prepare a detailed report for the next meeting outlining the next steps.

Tasks

Working either alone or in a small group, prepare a report drawing on the material from this chapter addressing the following:

1 Thinking about the situation at Eastern University, how effective are Lisa Chang's and Peter Webster's performances in each of Mintzberg's managerial roles?
2 What recommendations would you make to the university's senior management? How would this help?

Sources of additional information

Mintzberg, H. (1990) 'The manager's job: folklore and fact', *Harvard Business Review*, March–April, pp. 163–76.

Kersley, B., Alpin, C., Forth, J. et al. (2006) 'The management of employment relations,' pp. 36–70 in *Inside the Workplace: First Findings from the 2004 Workplace Employment Relations Survey (WERS2004)*, London: Routledge.

Visit www.change-management.com for information on change management.

Note

This case study was written by Dan Haley, Director of Human Resources, School District No. 57, Prince George, BC, Canada.

Case Study   2

Tuition reimbursement for studying OB?

Visit www.palgrave.com/business/brattonob2e to view this case study

WEB-BASED ASSIGNMENT

To help you develop your understanding of the subject, we have developed an activity that requires you to maintain a learning journal or log. A learning journal is a simple and straightforward way to help you integrate content, process, personal thoughts and personal work experience of organizational behaviour. Learning logs operate from the stance that people learn from reflection and through writing.

We suggest you make an entry in your log after each completed week of class time. Properly understood and used, learning journals assist the learning process by becoming a vehicle for understanding the complex nature of human behaviour in the workplace. Visit the website http://olc.spsd.sk.ca/DE/PD/instr/strats/logs for information on the value of learning journals.

Learning journals are concise, objective, factual and impersonal in tone. The following questions could be used to guide you in making thoughtful entries in your learning journal about organizational behaviour:

- What did I learn in class this week?
- What did I find interesting?
- How well does the material connect with my work experience?
- How well does the organizational behaviour material connect with my other management courses?
- What questions do I have for the instructor about what I learned?

Later in the book, we shall be asking you to use your completed learning journal to help evaluate your studies of organizational behaviour.

OB IN FILM

In the film *Working Girl* (1988), Tess McGill (played by Melanie Griffith) is employed as a secretary to Katharine Parker (played by Sigourney Weaver). When her boss breaks her leg in a skiing accident, Tess has an opportunity to implement some of her own ideas for new business ventures. An investment banker, Jack Trainer (played by Harrison Ford), helps Tess to present her proposal to a group of senior business executives. The film humorously illustrates the meaning of gender harassment and organizational politics.

Watch the early scenes in the film. How is Tess treated by her male co-workers? What does the film tell us about the gendering of organizations? When Tess is presenting her proposal, what is her power base, and does this shift in the scenes near the end of the film?

REFERENCES

1. Scott, R. W. (2003) *Organizations: Rational, Natural, and Open Systems*, Upper Saddle River, NJ: Prentice-Hall.
2. Furness, V. (2008) 'Impact of economic downturn on the psychological contract between employer and employee'. Available at: www.employeebenefits.co.uk/item/7912/23/307/3 (accessed February 27, 2009).
3. Williams, D. (2001) 'Power or peace? Trauma, change and psychological climate in national and international affairs'. Available at: www.eoslifework.co.uk/pop1.htm (accessed February 27, 2009).
4. Anderssen, E. (2009) 'Men open up like never before as recession takes its toll', *Globe and Mail*, April 1, p. A1.
5. Todd, R. Quoted in Bratton, J. (1992), *Japanization at Work*, London: Macmillan, p. 70.
6. Sklair, L. (2002) *Globalization: Capitalism and its Alternatives*, Oxford: Oxford University Press.
7. 'New world order to save earth'. Available at: http://timescorrespondence (accessed March 25, 2009).
8. Thaiindian News. Available at: www.thaiindian.com/newsportal/business/ (accessed March 25, 2009).
9. 'PM urges 'moral' global capitalism'. Available at: www.onenewspage.com/news/UK/ (accessed 26 March, 2009).
10. 'Global heroes: a special report on entrepreneurship', *Economist*, March 14, 2009, p. 11.
11. Sayer, D. (1991) *Capitalism and Modernity*, London: Routledge.
12. Bakan, J. (2004) *The Corporation*, London: Penguin.
13. Stiglitz, J. E. (2006) *Making Globalization Work*, New York: Norton.
14. Johns, G. and Saks, A. (2001) *Organizational Behaviour* (5th edn), Toronto: Addison-Wesley.
15. Clegg, S. and Hardy, C. (1999) *Studying Organization: Theory and Method*, Thousand Oaks, CA: Sage.
16. Wright Mills, C. (1959/2000) *The Sociological Imagination* (40th anniv. edn). New York: Oxford University Press.
17. Ghose, A. K., Majid, N. and Ernst, C. (2008) *The Global Employment Challenge*, Geneva: International Labour Organization.
18. Giddens, A. (1979) *Central Problems in Social Theory*, London: Macmillan.
19. Clegg, S. and Dunkerley, D. (1980) *Organization, Class and Control*, London: Routledge & Kegan Paul.
20. Esland, G. and Salaman, G. (1980) *The Politics of Work and Occupations*, Milton Keynes: Open University Press.
21. Nadler, D. A. and Tushman, M. L. (1997) *Competing by Design: The Power of Organizational Architecture*, New York: Oxford University Press.
22. Scholte, J. A. (2005) *Globalization: A Critical Introduction*, Basingstoke: Palgrave Macmillan.
23. Hoogvelt, A. (2001) *Globalization and the Postcolonial World* (2nd edn), Basingstoke: Palgrave.
24. Stiglitz, J. E. (2002) *Globalization and its Discontents*, New York: Norton.

25. Saul, J. R. (2005) *The Collapse of Globalism*, Toronto: Viking.

26. Hertz, N. (2002) *The Silent Takeover: Global Capitalism and the Death of Democracy,* London: Arrow.

27. Castells, M. (2000) 'Information technology and global capitalism', pp. 52–74 in W. Hutton and A. Giddens (eds), *On the Edge: Living with Global Capitalism*, London: Cape.

28. Maurice, M. and Sorge, A. (2000) *Embedding Organizations*, Amsterdam: John Benjamins.

29. Brown, R. K. (1988) 'The employment relationship in sociological theory,' pp. 33–66 in D. Gallie (ed.), *Employment in Britain*, Oxford: Blackwell.

30. Ackroyd, S. and Thompson, P. (1999) *Organizational Misbehaviour*, London: Sage.

31. Alvesson, M. and Due Billing, Y. (1997) *Understanding Gender in Organizations*, London: Sage.

32. Mills, A. and Tancred, P. (eds) (1992) *Gendering Organizational Analysis*, Newbury Park, CA: Sage.

33. Hearn, J., Sheppard, D., Tancred-Sheriff, P. and Rand Burrell, G. (eds) (1989) *The Sexuality of Organization,* London: Sage.

34. Wilson, F. M. (2003) *Organizational Behaviour and Gender*, Farnham: Ashgate.

35. Wajcman, J. (1998) *Managing Like a Man: Women and Men in Corporate Management*, Cambridge: Polity Press/Penn State University Press.

36. Clegg, S., Hardy, C. and Nord, W. (eds) (1999) *Managing Organizations: Current Issues*, Thousand Oaks, CA: Sage.

37. Salaman, G. (1979) *Work Organizations: Resistance and Control*, London: Longman.

38. Thompson, P. and McHugh, D. (2009) *Work Organizations: A Critical Approach* (4th edn), Basingstoke: Palgrave.

39. Boxall, P., Purcell, J. and Wright, P. (eds) (2008) *The Oxford Handbook of Human Resource Management*, Oxford: Oxford University Press.

40. Williams, R. (1983) *Keywords*, New York: Oxford University Press.

41. Drucker, P. (1954/1993) *The Practice of Management*, New York: Harper Collins.

42. Carlson, S. (1951) *Executive Behaviour: A Study of the Workload and Working Methods of Managing Directors*, Stockholm: Stromberg.

43. Mintzberg, H. (1973) *The Nature of Managerial Work*, New York: Harper & Row.

44. Mintzberg, H. (1989) *Mintzberg on Management*, New York: Free Press, p. 16. (Originally sourced from Mintzberg, H. (1975) 'The manager's job: folklore and fact', *Harvard Business Review*, July/August.)

45. Sundgren, M. and Styhre, A. (2006) 'Leadership as de-paradoxification: leading new drug development work at three pharmaceutical companies', *Leadership*, **2**(1), pp. 31–51.

46. Hales, C. (1986) 'What do managers do? A critical review of the evidence', *Journal of Management Studies*, **23**, pp. 88–115.

47. Willmott, H. (1989) 'Images and ideals of managerial work', *Journal of Management Studies*, **21**(3), pp. 349–68.

48. Knights, D. and Willmott, H. (eds) (1986) *Gender and the Labour Process*, Aldershot: Gower.

49. Alvesson, M. and Willmott, H. (1996) *Making Sense of Management: A Critical Introduction*, London: Sage.

50. Stewart, R., Barsoux, J.-L., Kieser, A., Ganter, H. and Walgenbach, P. (1994) *Managing in Britain and Germany*, Basingstoke: Macmillan.

51. Helgesen, S. (1995) *The Female Advantage: Women's Ways of Leadership*, New York: Doubleday.

52. Hoel, H. and Beale, D. (2006) 'Workplace bullying, psychological perspectives and industrial relations: towards a contextualized and interdisciplinary approach', *British Journal of Industrial Relations*, **44**(2), pp. 239–62.

53. Bolton, S. (2005) *Emotion Management in the Workplace*, Basingstoke: Palgrave.

54. Plotnik, R. (2005) *Introduction to Psychology* (7th edn), Belmont, CA.: Thomson/Wadsworth.

56. Carlson, N., Buskist, W., Enzle, M. and Heth, C. (2005) *Psychology* (3rd edn), Toronto: Pearson Education.

56. Grey, C. (2005) *A Very Short, Fairly Interesting and Reasonably Cheap Book about Studying Organizations*, London: Sage.
57. Pfeffer, J. (1998) *The Human Equation: Building Profits by Putting People First*, Boston, MA: Harvard Business School Press.
58. Millett, K. (1985) *Sexual Politics*, London: Virago.
59. Bryson, V. (2003) *Feminist Political Theory* (2nd edn), Basingstoke: Palgrave.
60. Tong, R. P. (1998) *Feminist Thought* (2nd edn), Boulder, CO: Westview Press.
61. Giddens, A. (2001) *Sociology* (4th edn), Cambridge: Polity Press.
62. Camilleri, J. M. (1999) 'Disability: a personal odyssey', *Disability and Society*, **14**(4), pp. 79–93.
63. Oliver, M. (1996) *Understanding Disability*, Basingstoke: Palgrave.
64. Burrell, G. and Morgan, G. (1979) *Sociological Paradigms and Organizational Analysis*, London: Heinemann.
65. Mills, A., Simmons, A. and Helms Mills, J. (2005) *Reading Organizational Theory* (3rd edn), Toronto: Garamond.
66. Woodward, J. (1965) *Industrial Organizations: Theory and Practice*, London: Oxford University Press.
67. Cyert, R. M. and March, J. G. (1963) 'A behaviour theory of organizational objectives', in M. Haire (ed.), *Modern Organizational Theory*, New York: Wiley.
68. Weick, K. E. (1995) *Sensemaking in Organizations*, London: Sage.
69. Palys, T. (2003) *Research Decisions: Quantitative and Qualitative Perspectives* (3rd edn), Scarborough, Ontario: Thompson-Nelson.
70. Neuman, W. L. (2007) *Basics of Social Research* (2nd edn), London: Pearson.
71. Schwandt, T. A. (1994) 'Constructivist, interpretivist approaches to human inquiry', pp. 118–37 in N. K. Denzin and Y. Lincoln (eds), *Handbook of Qualitative Research*, Thousand Oaks, CA: Sage.
72. Bryman, A. and Teevan, J. (2005) *Social Research Methods*, Oxford: Oxford University Press.
73. Bhaskar, R. (1989) *Reclaiming Reality*, London: Verso.
74. Sayer, A. (2000) *Realism and Social Science*, London: Sage.
75. Charmaz, K. (2005) 'Grounded theory: objectivist and constructivist methods', pp. 509–35 in N. Denzin and Y. Lincoln (eds) *Handbook of Qualitative Research* (2nd edn), Thousand Oaks, CA: Sage.
76. Grint, K. (1995) 'The culture of management and the management of culture', pp. 162–88 in *Management: A Sociological Introduction*, Cambridge: Polity Press.
77. Bratton, J., Grint, K. and Nelson, D. (2005) *Organizational Leadership*, Mason, OH: Thomson-South-Western.
78. Easterby-Smith, M., Thorpe, R. and Lowe, A. (1991) *Management Research: An Introduction*, London: Sage.
79. Nichols, quoted in Bratton, J. (1992) *Japanization at Work*, Basingstoke: Macmillan, p. 14.
80. Taylor, F. W. (1911) *The Principles of Scientific Management*, New York: Harper.
81. Fayol, H. (1949) *General and Industrial Management*, London: Pitman.
82. Kotter, J. P. (1982) *The General Managers*, New York: Free Press.

MOTIVATION AND JOB SATISFACTION

CHAPTER OUTLINE

- Introduction
- The nature of work motivation
- Content theories of motivation: workers with needs
- Process theories of motivation: workers with choices
- The sociological analysis of motivation: alienation, culture and self
- Integrating the approaches
- Applying motivation theories
- Summary and end-of-chapter features
- Chapter case study 1 : Equity at FindIT
- Chapter case study 2: Motivation at Norsk Petroleum

CHAPTER OBJECTIVES

After completing this chapter, you should be able to:

- define motivation and explain how motivation reflects the exchange embodied in the employment relationship
- compare and contrast needs-based theories of motivation at work
- describe the expectancy and equity theories of motivation
- discuss the managerial implications of process-based motivation theories
- understand the complexity of motivation at work through sociological insights, including alienation, culture and self-identity

INTRODUCTION

As you interact with other people, travelling on buses and trains, entering offices, banks, hospitals, schools, daycare facilities, shops or university lecture theatres, you might observe that in any group of workers who are performing identical jobs, some do the work better than others. What is it that causes some people to exert much more effort than others in what they do in the workplace?

The observed differences in effect among people doing identical work reflect differences in individual knowledge, skills and abilities, or can reflect differences in the extent to which individuals are prepared to direct their energies. Work-related effort is thus contingent upon two different kinds of variable: the ability and skill of the

motivation: the forces within a person that affect his or her direction, intensity and persistence of voluntary behaviour

organizational commitment: the employee's emotional attachment to, identification with and involvement in a particular organization

stop reflect
Before reading on, you may wish to ask yourself what motivates you. In doing your current or planned paid work, are you motivated primarily by money, or by something else? Go to our website and click on the 'Motivation questionnaire'. Alternatively, go to the website www. myskillsprofile.com/tests. php?test=20 and complete the questionnaire – it should take you about 20 minutes. Consider your response to the questions in the context of your current employment or previous work experience, and of what you have read in this book so far

individual, and his or her **motivation** to make use of personal endowments in the performance of paid work within a given social context.[1]

The issue of motivating workers underscores the nature of the employment relationship. At its most basic, the employment contract represents the exchange of effort or knowledge for pay. This effort–pay contract is, however, typically indeterminate: whereas the contract specifies pay, benefits, hours to be worked and so on, a workers' capacity to work – in Marxist terminology, his or her labour power – is indefinable with regard to the amount of effort and **commitment** the employee will apply to the job. The contract implies that workers are 'free' to decide whether to accept the pay on offer, free to internalize about their work situation and develop positive or negative attitudes toward their employment, and free to seek employment elsewhere.[2] In other words, employees have, as Peter Drucker once wrote, 'control over whether they work, how much and how well' (ref. 3, p. 14).

The indeterminate nature of the typical employment contract makes motivation (working harder) a running theme of management. Managers find themselves in positions of subordination as well as superordination, and, as a result, they themselves also have to be motivated in order to be able to motivate others. Top managers are often mystified on a daily basis by what motivates middle managers and what motivates male and female knowledge workers; in turn, middle managers are frequently mystified by what motivates male and female front-line employees. Why do highly paid managers and knowledge workers resign or not perform as expected? Why do low-paid manual and front-line non-manual workers baulk at resigning even when they receive better job offers? For both managers and some organizational behaviour theorists, the task of discovering what motivates different categories of employee in different work settings is of the same magnitude as finding the Holy Grail.

The mainstream theories of work motivation that emerged during the last century as part of the hoped-for movement to employee commitment and enhanced effort focus on what are called *content theories of motivation* and *process theories of motivation*. Critical theories of motivation are more attentive to the contradictory nature of capitalist employment relations, to power relations, to the meanings men and women attach to paid work and to the ways through which management practices are expressed and reproduced.[4–8] As a result, they tend to emphasize the need for a societal analysis of work motivation. This chapter therefore has two broad aims. The first is to examine the mainstream theories of motivation, the second to provide a more holistic understanding of work motivation by expanding beyond notions of individual needs and cognitive processes to incorporate an awareness of the effects of complex interconnecting levels of domination stemming from class, gender and race relations in society.

THE NATURE OF WORK MOTIVATION

After the Second World War, Western economies invested in education, and people experienced relatively full employment. In this social context, workers' fear of unemployment was no longer an individual or a collective motivation for work performance. If workers became dissatisfied with the effort levels expected by managers, or with another aspect of the job, they could find alternative employment relatively effortlessly. As management guru Peter Drucker wrote, 'fear no longer supplies the motivation for the worker in industrial society' (ref. 3, p. 303). This post-Second World War phenomenon led to an interest in the question, 'What motivates workers to perform effectively?' 'Effectively' meant closing the gap between the workers' potential to work and their willingness to maximize their effort towards the attainment of work objectives.

The indeterminacy of the employment contract is interpreted by both managers and pro-management theorists as the problem of motivation. Management concern with discovering the motivation elixir is a direct response to the constant pressure on management to employ people even more efficiently, thoroughly and rationally.[9] Most of the scholarship is primarily *normative*, directed at providing prescriptions for motivating workers. It tends to emphasize what it is that managers *should* do to ensure that subordinates close the gap between potential and actual performance.

The word 'motivation' comes from the Latin *movere*, 'to move', and work psychologists have traditionally focused on identifying factors that move workers towards accomplishing organizational **goals**. Motivation from a psychological perspective may be defined as a cognitive decision-making process that influences the effort, persistence and direction of voluntary goal-directed behaviour.

The first element in this definition is *'effort'*, which is a measure of intensity that maximizes workers' potential capacity to work in a way that is appropriate to the job. The second characteristic of motivation is *'persistence'*, which refers to the application of effort to work-related tasks that employees display over a time period. The third characteristic of motivation is *'direction'*, which emphasizes that persistent high levels of work-related effort should be channelled in a way that benefits the organization. Whereas effort and persistence refer to the *quantity* of paid manual or knowledge work, direction refers to *quality* of work done.

Intrinsic versus extrinsic motivation

Theorists distinguish between **intrinsic** (inside) and **extrinsic** (outside) motivators. An intrinsic motivator stems from a person's 'internal' desire to do something, and is therefore usually self-applied. Outside the workplace, avid participation in hobbies or sports is typically intrinsically motivated. For example, we may be willing to exert a considerable amount of effort over many months with the aim of climbing a mountain, without any thought of financial reward, because we expect it to provide personal satisfaction: that is, we are intrinsically motivated. In the workplace, pure interest in a project, or a sense of professional accomplishment or positive recognition from our peers, is an example of intrinsic motivators. 'No single phenomenon,' Ryan and Deci argue, 'reflects the positive potential of human nature as much as intrinsic motivation.'[10] Intrinsically motivated people tend to seek out new challenges and explore new ways of doing things and learning. Extrinsic motivators, on the other hand, stem from outside the individual, and are generally applied by others higher in the organization's hierarchy. Extrinsic motivators include such tangible rewards as pay, bonuses and promotion (Figure 3.1).

We should be aware that there is disagreement on these definitions and the relationship between intrinsic and extrinsic motivators, and even more disagreement on whether organizations can categorize all work motivators as precisely as these definitions suggest. For example, an employee might receive a promotion that also results in more interesting and satisfying work and additional pay. Thus, some potential motivators have both intrinsic and extrinsic qualities.[11] It should also be apparent from these examples that intrinsic and extrinsic motivators are strongly influenced by the values, ways of thinking, behaviours and social factors typical of a society. North American and European theories of motivation are embedded in management practices, as such practices offer the means to render workers and their behaviour predictable and measurable.[12]

---

goals: the immediate or ultimate objectives that employees are trying to accomplish from their work effort

intrinsic motivator: a wide range of motivation interventions in the workplace, from inner satisfaction from following some action (such as recognition by an employer or co-workers) to intrinsic pleasures derived from an activity (such as playing a musical instrument for pleasure)

extrinsic motivator: a wide range of external outcomes or rewards to motivate employees, including bonuses or increases in pay

weblink
Visit the following websites: www. higbee-schaffler.co.nz/ Portals/0/Documents/ TOGETHERNESS%20 IN%20PERFORMANCE. pdf for information on team-based rewards; www.berr.gov.uk for data on profit-related pay in Britain (search '2004 employee relations survey') – this site gives a summary of the UK 2004 survey, including a section on work teams; and www. inc.com/guides/hr/20678. html for information on the role of stock options in motivating employees

	Intrinsic	**Extrinsic**
Individual-based	Feeling of self-accomplishment	Pay increase
Organization-based	Professional pride in being a member of a 'socially responsible' company	Profit sharing

Figure 3.1 – Examples of intrinsic and extrinsic motivators

Motivation theories attempt to explain how employee behaviour is initiated and shaped, as well as the different factors that contribute to directing and sustaining that goal-directed behaviour. Models show the variables believed to be important, but remember that these are a simplification of the phenomenon. Bearing in mind this caveat, there is no shortage of theorizing and modelling. Students of management should know that there are no quick solutions for releasing the motivation genie. Next we focus on theories that have been categorized in the literature as *content* and *process* theories of work motivation.

CONTENT THEORIES OF MOTIVATION: WORKERS WITH NEEDS

needs: deficiencies that energize or trigger behaviours to satisfy those needs

Content theories of motivation assume that all workers possess a common set of basic '**needs**'. Five of the better-known need theories are (1) Maslow's hierarchy of needs, (2) McGregor's Theory X and Theory Y, (3) McClelland's 'three learned needs' theory, (4) Alderfer's ERG theory, and (5) Herzberg's 'two-factor' need theory.[13–16]

Maslow's hierarchy of needs

In what is probably the most well known of the content theories, psychologist Abraham Maslow proposed that people have a built-in set of five basic needs, which can be arranged in a hierarchy as shown in Figure 3.2.

needs hierarchy theory: Maslow's motivation theory of five instinctive needs arranged in a hierarchy, whereby people are motivated to fulfil a higher need as a lower one becomes gratified

The so-called lower-level needs in the **needs hierarchy** (the physiological and safety needs) are at first predominant: people's behaviour is directed towards satisfying these needs until they are met, at which point the next higher-order need comes to dominate, and so on. For example, only once an individual's physiological needs for the basic necessities of life – food, water and shelter – are satisfied will that individual focus on the next higher need. Once lower-order needs are addressed, the theory assumes that people direct their behaviours towards satisfying their needs for companionship, love and positive social regard by other people. The progression

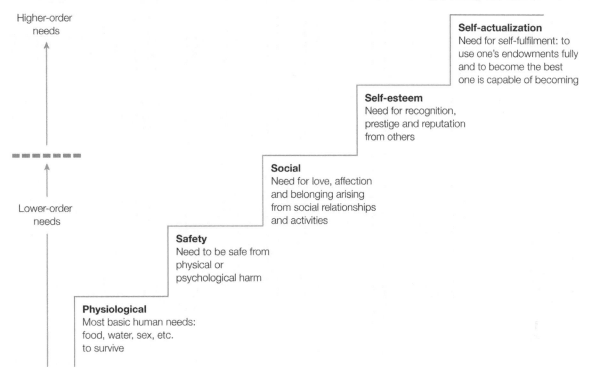

Higher-order needs

Lower-order needs

Self-actualization
Need for self-fulfilment: to use one's endowments fully and to become the best one is capable of becoming

Self-esteem
Need for recognition, prestige and reputation from others

Social
Need for love, affection and belonging arising from social relationships and activities

Safety
Need to be safe from physical or psychological harm

Physiological
Most basic human needs: food, water, sex, etc. to survive

Figure 3.2 – Maslow's hierarchy of needs

self-actualization: a term associated with Maslow's theory of motivation, referring to the desire for personal fulfilment, to become everything that one is capable of becoming

ultimately leads to behavioural change motivated principally by people's need to realize their full potential, which Maslow termed the **self-actualization** need.

According to Maslow, the self-actualization need, which involves people directing their behaviour towards work learning opportunities, is the ultimate motivator, because unlike the other needs it is insatiable. The second key aspect of Maslow's theory is that a satisfied or satiated need is not a motivator of behaviour. Once a person satisfies a need at one level in the hierarchy, the need ceases to motivate him or her. Only the need at the next level up the hierarchy will motivate the person and influence her or his behaviour.

Although it was not originally intended as an explanation of employee motivation, Maslow's needs hierarchy theory has been influential in mainstream management texts. It was seen as offering predictions about what directs behaviour in different contexts. In a context of relatively high unemployment, when jobs are relatively scarce and people do not automatically feel secure about meeting their basic needs, workers are motivated strongly by the need to satisfy their lower-level needs. In contrast, in a context of relatively full employment, when lower-order needs are more easily satisfied, social, self-esteem and self-actualization needs become important motivators in the workplace.

One implication of Maslow's theory is that, if workers are to continue to be motivated once their social needs have been satisfied, managers have to find ways to offer them self-actualization, which implies a focus on the intrinsic aspects of paid work. This might mean reconfiguring work structures and processes to challenge both manual and knowledge workers, and offer them a degree of autonomy. To apply Maslow's theory to the current management practices of organizational re-engineering and outsourcing, it might be feasible to motivate part-time or other 'peripheral' workers by appealing to their lower-order needs, while knowledge-based

Plate 1 – Will a person really focus on satisfying physiological needs before safety needs? Is this construction worker likely to stop to eat or drink before making sure the swinging girder is secured?
Source: iStockphoto

'core' workers are motivated by satisfying their higher-order needs. The prescription offered by Maslow's theory is that managers need to know where their employees are located on the needs hierarchy, and ensure that their lower-order needs are satisfied before appealing to their higher-order needs.

Maslow's needs hierarchy appears to offer common-sense advice to managers, but how valid is this theory of work motivation? One of the major problems with Maslow's theory is that it is extremely difficult to identify which need is predominant at any given time. Without this information, managers cannot confidently redesign the workplace or emphasize work-based learning to appeal to their employees' self-esteem or self-actualization needs, for instance, as these might not in reality be their main motivators.

To take a simple example, is it really true that a person will focus on satisfying physiological needs such as hunger and thirst before he or she attends to matters that threaten his or her security or safety? Does a construction worker have a bite to eat before checking that the scaffolding she is standing on is safe?

The significance of Maslow's work, it is suggested, might lie in its rhetorical value. Tony Watson, for example, offers a scathing critique of Maslow's theory, arguing that it has little scientific validity and that its main role has been as 'a propaganda device: propaganda in a good and humanistic cause, but propaganda nonetheless' (ref. 17, p. 110). Maslow's theory is still worth reviewing, however, because of its influence on the subsequent alternative motivation theories developed by Douglas McGregor, David McClelland and Clayton Alderfer.

McGregor's Theory X and Theory Y

Whereas Maslow focused on defining a hierarchy of needs that influence work-related behaviour, Douglas McGregor, a human psychologist, drew heavily from Maslow to argue that managers need a greater understanding of and attention to employees' needs. McGregor contrasts two opposite theories of employees and management: Theory X and Theory Y. According to McGregor, managers can be classified in terms of how they believe others (and perhaps they themselves) behave towards paid work, and how managers approach the issue of work motivation is strongly influenced by their assumptions about human nature. The two extreme sets of propositions are shown in Table 3.1.

McGregor suggests that underpinning the Theory X propositions is the conventional Tayloristic belief that the average employee is indolent, lacks ambition, dislikes responsibility, is inherently self-centred and is not very bright. These basic assumptions, he suggestions, shape and become embedded in organizational structures, culture and practices. McGregor's Theory Y offers an alternative set of assumptions about the essence of human nature and work motivation.

The problem of motivation lies not in the subordinate, but in the beliefs and resulting behaviour of the manager. Theory Y supports Maslow's higher-level needs by advocating a clear shift towards 'self-control and self-direction', and towards allowing self-esteem and self-actualization needs to be satisfied.[19] Despite the fact that many managers publicly support Theory Y, there may be a significant gap between the rhetoric and the practice, especially during an economic downturn.

stop reflect
Can you think of managers you have encountered who were influenced by these two sets of assumptions about your attitude to work and motives?

McClelland's theory of needs

According to David McClelland's learned needs theory,[15] workers are motivated by the need to satisfy six basic human needs: achievement, power, affiliation, independence, self-esteem and security. In contrast to preceding theories, McClelland argued that these needs are not inherent, but learned from national culture. Employees are said to

Table 3.1 – McGregor's Theory X and Theory Y of motivation

Theory X	Theory Y
1. Management is responsible for organizing the elements of productive enterprise – money, materials, equipment, people – in the interest of economic ends	1. Management is responsible for organizing the elements of productive enterprise – money, materials, equipment, people – in the interest of economic ends
2. With respect to people, this is a process of directing their efforts, motivating them, controlling their actions, modifying their behaviour to fit the needs of the organization	2. People are *not* by nature passive or resistant to organizational needs. They have become so as a result of their experience in organizations
3. Without this active intervention by management, people would be passive – even resistant – to organizational needs. They must therefore be persuaded, rewarded, punished, controlled – their activities must be directed. This is management's task in managing subordinate managers or workers	3. The motivation, the potential for development, the capacity for assuming responsibility, the readiness to direct behaviour towards organizational goals are all present in people. Management does not put them there. It is a responsibility of management to make it possible for people to recognize and develop these human characteristics for themselves
	4. The essential task of management is to arrange organizational conditions and methods of operation so that people can achieve their own goals *best* by directing *their own* efforts toward organizational objectives

Source: McGregor (1957/1970/1966)[18]

accomplish the most when they have a high need for achievement. Employees with a strong need for achievement tend to set goals that are moderately difficult, to seek out feedback on their performance, and to be generally preoccupied with accomplishment.

Unlike Maslow, McClelland did not become preoccupied with specifying a hierarchical relationship between needs. Instead, he argued that employees differ in the extent to which they experience needs for achievement, affiliation and power. McClelland and Burnham addressed the issue of power as the 'great motivator'.[20] They argued that, in practice, managers with a need for power might be more effective motivators than those with a need for achievement. The work of Harrel and Strahl[21] suggests that assessing the strength of these learned needs can be helpful in identifying employees who will respond positively to different types of work context. The advice that follows from this alleged insight is that it might be important for managers to consider the extent to which employees possess these needs, and to design motivational strategies that permit workers to satisfy those needs which are strongest for each individual.

Alderfer's ERG theory

ERG theory: Alderfer's motivation theory of three instructive needs arranged in a hierarchy, in which people progress to the next higher need when a lower one is fulfilled, and regress to a lower need if unable to fulfil a higher one

growth needs: a person's needs for self-esteem through personal achievement, as well as for self-actualization

Clayton Alderfer's **ERG theory** is closely related to Maslow's work. Based upon an alternative set of assumptions, it suggests that employee needs can be divided into three basic categories: existence (E), relatedness (R) and growth (G). Existence needs include nutritional, safety and material requirements. Relatedness needs involve an individual's relationships with family and friends, and colleagues at work. **Growth needs** reflect a desire for personal psychological growth and development.

As can be seen in Figure 3.3, Alderfer's ERG theory is not a major departure from Maslow's theory. Unlike Maslow, however, ERG theory does not assume a progression up a hierarchy. Alderfer suggests that all three levels might be important at the same time, and he believes that it is better to think in terms of a continuum, from existence needs to growth needs, with workers moving along it in either direction. Consequently, if, for example, growth needs are not satisfied, an inner state of frustration regression occurs, causing the person to focus on fulfilling her or his relatedness needs. For example, a supervisor unable to satisfy his or her growth needs by accepting greater responsibility might respond by demanding an increase in pay, thereby satisfying his or her existence needs. Therefore, unsatisfied needs become less rather than more important. This is the opposite of what Maslow assumed.

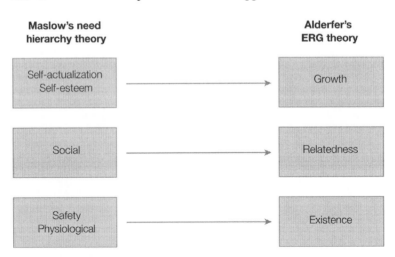

Figure 3.3 – Comparison of Maslow's needs hierarchy and Alderfer's ERG theory

weblink
Go to the following
websites for more
information on motivation
theories: http://academic.
emporia.edu/smithwil/
oofallmg443/eja/tuel.
html; http://www.accel-
team.com/motivation/
index.html for details
on Maslow's hierarchy
of needs; and http://
psychology.about.com/
for links to motivation
theories

Furthermore, ERG theory emphasizes the importance to employees of satisfied needs. Alderfer's work suggests that growth needs are actually more important when satisfied, whereas Maslow argued that, when it is fulfilled, a need becomes less important to an individual. One implication of Alderfer's work is that work designs that satisfy workers' relatedness needs can continue to motivate workers, and that these are not necessarily superseded by growth needs. If this theory is correct, it would make it easier for managers to motivate their employees.

A recent study by Arnolds and Boshoff[22] provides data to support a key hypothesis associated with Alderfer's ERG model. Unlike many conventional studies, it incorporates personality in the motivation conundrum, and is sensitive to potential social factors affecting motivation at work. The study investigates to what extent a personality trait (self-esteem) impacts on the relationship between need satisfactions – as modelled by Alderfer – and the performance intentions of senior managers and white-collar 'front-line' employees in the banking, legal and retail sectors (Figure 3.4).

The model hypothesizes that employee need satisfaction, based upon Alderfer's theory, exerts a positive influence on self-esteem, which in turn exerts a positive influence on work behaviour in the form of job performance intentions (H). Arnolds and Boshoff argue that their data show that self-esteem significantly influences the performance intentions of senior managers, and conclude that 'top managers are primarily motivated by growth needs, in other words, higher order needs' (ref. 22, p. 712). The empirical results suggest that front-line white-collar workers are primarily motivated by the satisfaction of relatedness needs from co-workers, by existence needs and particularly by monetary reward.

Interestingly, and in contrast to Maslow's belief that growth needs do not motivate lower-level workers, Arnolds and Boshoff's sophisticated study suggests that higher-order needs such as growth needs can motivate front-line workers through increasing their self-esteem, 'provided that the motivation strategies directed at these higher-order needs are correctly implemented' (ref. 22, p. 713). The importance of this study is that it provides a plausible explanation, with supporting empirical data, of the relationship between needs satisfaction, an individual personality trait (self-esteem) and job performance intentions. More generally, by differentiating between different categories of employee, the analysis affirms the importance of avoiding the common tendency to generalize about managers' motivation interventions.

stop reflect
How helpful are Maslow's
and Alderfer's theories
in explaining why chief
executives and car
assembly workers might
be predisposed to respond
to different ways of
motivating them to work?

Although Maslow's, McClelland's and Alderfer's needs theories of work motivation have been popularized in mainstream organizational behaviour texts, detractors

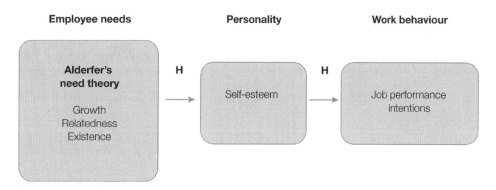

Figure 3.4 – Employee needs, personality and work behaviour
Source: Adapted from Arnolds and Boshoff (2002),[22] p. 702

have identified several important limitations. It is posited that these less than robust theories are conceptually flawed; they do not provide managers with a clear, unambiguous basis for predicting specific workers' behaviour to satisfy a particular need. Recent critics have also pointed out that the needs theories are strongly informed by the Anglo-American cultural paradigm of individualism – other societal cultures might have different hierarchies of needs. Finally, there is an assumption that needs motivate regardless of the age, sex or ethnicity of those involved. As a result, it can be argued that these theories are androcentric and reflect the values of a hierarchical social order.[23–25]

OB in focus Money is the key incentive to work motivation

Most organizational behaviour theorists and behavioural scientists have consistently downplayed the importance of money as a motivator. They prefer to point out the value of challenging jobs, goals and participation in decision making to stir the motivation genie. We argue otherwise here: that money is the crucial incentive to work motivation. As a medium of exchange, it is the vehicle by which employees can purchase the numerous need-satisfying things they desire. Money also performs the function of a scorecard, by which employees assess the value that the organization places on their services and can compare their value with that of others.

For the vast majority of the workers, a regular pay cheque is absolutely necessary in order to meet their basic physiological and safety needs. Money has symbolic value in addition to its **exchange value.** People use pay as the primary outcome against which they compare their inputs to determine whether they are being treated equitably. In addition, expectancy theory attests to the value of money as a motivator. Specifically, if pay is contingent on performance, it will encourage workers to put in high levels of effort. Consistent with expectancy theory, money will motivate to the extent that it is seen as being able to satisfy an individual's personal goals, and reward is perceived as being dependent on performance criteria. The evidence demonstrates that money may not be the only motivator, but it is difficult to argue that it does not motivate!

exchange value: the price at which commodities (including labour) trade on the market

Money doesn't stir the motivation genie!

There is no doubt that money can motivate some people under some conditions, so the issue is not really whether money can motivate. The more relevant question is, does money motivate most employees in the workforce today to higher performance? The answer, some organizational theorists argue, is 'No.' For money to motivate an employee's performance, certain conditions must be met. First, money must be important to the employee. Second, the employee must perceive the money as being a direct reward for performance. Third, the employee must consider the marginal amount of money offered for the performance to be significant. Finally, management must have the discretion to reward high performers with more money.

Since not all these conditions apply in all employment situations, money is not important to all employees. High achievers, for instance, are intrinsically motivated. Money should have little impact on these people. Money is relevant to those individuals with strong lower-order needs, but the lower-order needs of many employees are substantially satisfied. Money would motivate if employees perceived a strong link between performance and rewards in organizations. However, pay increases are far more often determined by levels of skills and experience, the national cost of living index, union–management pay bargaining and the firm's overall financial prospects, than by individual performance. In theory, money might be capable of motivating employees to higher levels of performance, but most managers do not have much discretion to match individual pay with individual performance levels.

Sources: K. O. Doyle (1992) 'Introduction: money and the behavioural sciences', *American Behavioural Scientist*, July, pp. 641–57; S. Caudron (1993) 'Motivation? Money's only no. 2', *Industry Week*, November 15, p. 33; B. Filipczak (1996) 'Can't buy me love', *Training*, January, pp. 29–34.

Herzberg's motivator–hygiene theory

Frederick Herzberg's motivation research was designed to test the concept that a worker has two different needs: the need stemming from a human being's nature to avoid pain from the environment, and the need thought to stem from a unique

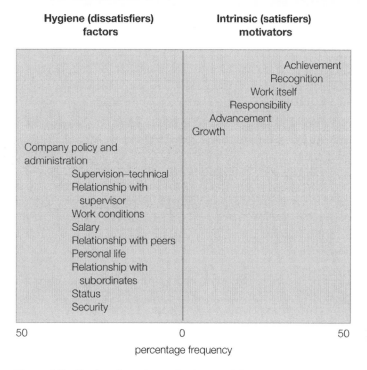

Hygiene (dissatisfiers) factors	Intrinsic (satisfiers) motivators

Achievement
Recognition
Work itself
Responsibility
Advancement
Growth

Company policy and
administration
Supervision–technical
Relationship with
supervisor
Work conditions
Salary
Relationship with peers
Personal life
Relationship with
subordinates
Status
Security

50   0   50

percentage frequency

Figure 3.5 – Herzberg's motivator–hygiene model
Source: Adapted from Hertzberg (2003),[26] p. 90

characteristic to grow psychologically. Samples of workers were asked to describe events that resulted in either a significant increase or a significant decrease in their job satisfaction. After analysing the data, Herzberg found that the factors identified as sources of job satisfaction (called 'satisfiers', and later 'motivators') were different from those identified as sources of dissatisfaction (called 'dissatisfiers' or 'hygiene' factors). The strong *motivators* were achievement, recognition, work itself, responsibility and advancement. The strong *hygiene* factors causing work dissatisfaction were company policy and administration, supervision, salary, interpersonal relations and working conditions at work. Figure 3.5 summarises the major findings of his study.

Herzberg's model predicts that managers can motivate subordinates if they are aware of and incorporate 'motivators' into job design. His motivator–hygiene theory has clear parallels with other content theories of motivation. For example, Herzberg's motivators are similar to Maslow's higher-order needs and Alderfer's growth needs, and his hygiene factors resemble Maslow's lower-order needs, as well as Alderfer's existence and relatedness needs. Empirical studies on the motivator–hygiene theory have had mixed results, but are credited with stimulating research on the association between job design and performance, including the later work of Hackman and Oldham.

PROCESS THEORIES OF MOTIVATION: WORKERS WITH CHOICES

Process theories of motivation focus on how employees make conscious choices that lead to a specific work behaviour; they emphasize the role of an individual's cognitive processes in determining her or his level of work motivation. Organizational leaders using process theories to motivate employees do so by clarifying the link between effort and reward. The three process theories of work motivation examined here are equity theory, expectancy theory and goal-setting theory.

Equity theory

equity theory: the theory that explains how people develop perceptions of fairness in the distribution and exchange of resources

Equity theory is one of the most influential process theories and is best known through a series of studies by J. Stacey Adams, and his colleagues (1963). Its basic premise is that there is one important cognitive process that involves employees comparing what effort other employees are putting into their work and what rewards they receive, with their own experience. This 'social comparison' process results in feelings of equity or inequity, and leads employees to form judgements on the value or 'valence' of a reward or outcome. According to equity theory, employees perceive effort and reward not in absolute but in relative terms, in the form of a ratio:[27]

$$\frac{\text{Outcome (self)}}{\text{Inputs (self)}} : \frac{\text{Outcome (other)}}{\text{Inputs (other)}}$$

When employees perceive others receiving a similar ratio of inputs (such as hours worked, time studying for qualifications and relevant work experience) to outcomes (such as pay, status and promotion) as they receive themselves, they experience equity. When workers perceive an input–outcome ratio that favours other workers in the organization (underpayment) or relevant others (such as workers in a similar company) or themselves (overpayment), they experience inequity, which is assumed to be a sufficiently unpleasant experience to motivate changes in behaviour (Figure 3.6).

One practical application of equity theory is in the area of *reward management*. Managers must be careful to avoid setting pay rates that cause employees to feel underpaid relative to others either in the same workplace (internal equity) or in comparison groups outside the organization (external inequity). It should be noted

	Self	Other
Equity	Outcomes (100) Inputs (100)	Outcomes (100) Inputs (100)
Inequity (under-rewarded)	Outcomes (100) Inputs (100)	Outcomes (150) Inputs (100)
Inequity (over-rewarded)	Outcomes (150) Inputs (100)	Outcomes (100) Inputs (100)

Figure 3.6 – Adams's conditions of equity and inequity

that the reward system is part of a diverse range of interlocking control techniques that contain internal tensions and inconsistencies. For instance, a performance-related reward system might become discredited in the eyes of employees because of perceived 'procedural injustices' caused by subjective and inconsistent appraisals by managers who did not have the skills needed to judge performance fairly. As a result, the employees would experience internal inequity, and instead of the reward system motivating them, their commitment would be weakened.[28] The nature of the internal inequity can generate negative feelings such as anger, which results in reduced employee commitment or even in acts of sabotage in the workplace. Collectively, if the perception of external inequity is strong and is shared by a sufficient number of workers, unionization and strike action can occur. Most recent studies are most conclusive about perceived negative inequity and 'relative deprivation' in conditions of underpayment.[29]

In this context, a classic study by Baldamus of the 'wage–effort exchange'[30] is still relevant to understanding conflict behaviour in the workplace, because it links the notion of external inequity to inherent tensions and workplace conflict. A fuller understanding of this relationship between effort levels or inputs, and rewards or outcomes, is provided by the expectancy theory of motivation.

Expectancy theory

The role of the employee's perception of the link between levels of effort or performance and desirable reward is further reinforced in the **expectancy theory** of work motivation. The theory assumes a rational model of decision making whereby employees assess the costs and benefits of alternative courses of inputs and outcomes, and choose the course with the highest reward.

The first formulations of expectancy theory are found in the work of Kurt Lewin in 1935. The theory was popularized, however, by the work of Vroom, and further developed by Porter and Lawler.[31–34] Psychologist Victor Vroom proposed that work motivation is contingent upon the perception of a link between levels of effort and reward. Perceiving this link is a cognitive process in which employees assess:

- whether there is a connection between effort and their performance, labelled *expectancy*
- the perceived probability that the performance (such as higher productivity) will lead to those valued outcomes (such as higher pay), which is labelled *instrumentality*
- the expected net value of the outcomes that flow from the effort, labelled *valence*.

Expectancy theory, therefore, has three basic parts:

1. the **effort–performance expectancy** (E→P)
2. the **performance–outcome expectancy** (P→O)
3. the attractiveness or valence of the outcomes (V).

According to expectancy theory, work motivation can be calculated if the expectancy, instrumentality and valence values are known. The formula for the calculation is:

$$\text{Effort} = E \sum I \times V$$

where *effort* is the motivation of the employee to exert effort in her or his paid work, E is expectancy, I is the instrumentality of job performance, and V is the valence of an outcome(s). The Σ (capital sigma: the summation sign) indicates that effort is affected by a range of possible work and non-work outcomes that might result from job performance.

Expectancies are probabilities, ranging from 0 to 1, that effort will result in performance. An expectancy of 0.5 means that the person perceives only a 50 per cent

expectancy theory: a motivation theory based on the idea that work effort is directed toward behaviours that people believe will lead to desired outcomes

effort-to-performance (E→P) expectancy: the individual's perceived probability that his or her effort will result in a particular level of performance

performance-to-outcome (P→O) expectancy: the perceived probability that a specific behaviour or performance level will lead to specific outcomes

instrumentality: a term associated with process theories of motivation, referring to an individual's perceived probability that good performance will result in valued outcomes or rewards, measured on a scale from 0 (no chance) to 1 (certainty)

valence: the anticipated satisfaction or dissatisfaction that an individual feels toward an outcome

probability of increased effort leading to increased performance. **Instrumentalities** can range from −1 to +1. An instrumentality of +1 means that performance is certain to lead to the desired outcome. For example, an insurance agent selling a home insurance policy is certain to receive a commission. The instrumentality between the two events is therefore +1. **Valence** is defined to vary between +10 and −10. A large anticipated satisfaction (high positive valence) and large anticipated dissatisfaction (high negative valence) will, when multiplied by associated instrumentalities and performance expectancy, have a large effect on work motivation.

As an example of the operation of expectancy theory, consider an employee – let's call him Joe – who perceives important work-related outcomes to be an increase in pay, promotion, longer vacation time and job-related stress. Figure 3.7 shows his expectancy theory calculations.

Joe has ranked four outcomes on a +10 to −10 scale, and has estimated the probability of increased effort producing each of these outcomes. He sees both positive and negative expected outcomes from increased job effort. He reckons there is only a 60 per cent chance that any increased effort on his part will lead to increased performance.

The motivational force of the job – the effort the individual is willing to expend on it – is calculated by multiplying the expectancy value (0.6) by the products of the instrumentality and valence estimates. Thus:

$$\text{Effort} = (0.6) \times [(0.9)\,(+6) + (0.5)\,(+8) + (0.3)\,(+5) + (0.6)\,(-6)] = 4.38$$

Summing the expectancy theory variables, the overall motivation to exert increased job effort is positive. Therefore, for Joe in this case, the rewards of putting in increased effort outweigh the costs.

To use expectancy theory in an attempt to increase job effort by each employee, a manager can focus on each element of the theory. For example, a manager can aim to increase the employee's perception that her or his expenditure of effort will result in completing the task successfully. The effort–performance expectancy (E→P) for Joe could increase from 60 per cent to 80 per cent, perhaps through additional training. In addition, a manager can help the employee to re-evaluate the performance–outcome expectancy (P→O). For example, the chances of promotion might be higher than is anticipated by the employee. To go back to the example of Joe, his manager might use the experiences of other employees to persuade him to increase his estimated probability of promotion if he does the job successfully from 50 per cent to 90 per cent.

Finally, a manager can attempt to increase the attractiveness of the outcome, the valence (V). Thus, in our example, Joe could perhaps be persuaded that the outcomes from exerting additional effort (a pay increase, a promotion, a longer vacation) would be more important or have more value to him than he had previously thought.

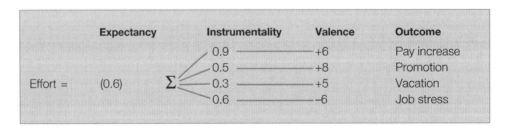

Figure 3.7 – Sample expectancy theory calculations

A development of the expectancy theory of work behaviour is to be found in research by Porter and Lawler.[33–35] In their models, the determinants of each element are incorporated to provide a more comprehensive explanation of both the *what* and the *how* of the work motivation process. The effort–performance expectancy is, for example, moderated by past experiences of similar situations and communications from other people. The assumption here is that what employees learn from past experiences contributes significantly to their effort–performance expectancies. If employees have had a series of past successes at similar work tasks, they will have a strengthened belief in their ability to perform those tasks, and to that extent their effort–performance expectancies will be high. The informal learning – learning that is embedded in work activities – need not be only from personal past experiences. Employees can and do learn from their observations of relevant others in similar situations, and from others communicating their past experiences to their peers. If I see Sally, for instance, succeed at a work task, and she has qualifications and work experience similar to mine, I am more likely to calculate that I too will succeed at that task. This informal learning operates at individual and group level, as well as in the opposite direction.

The performance–outcome expectancy link is contingent upon past experiences, communications from others and the attractiveness of the outcomes. The past experiences determinant refers to the experience in relation to outcomes. Suppose, for example, that a manager introduces a reward system that is performance based, and that her appraisal ratings of her staff are known to be arbitrary. With knowledge of this past experience, it is unlikely that her subordinates will believe that the reward system will be truly performance based in practice. The past experience will influence employees' performance–outcome expectancies for the system. This assessment is, however, considerably affected by another determinant – communications from others – which represents an array of social interactions between employees, and between the supervised (employees) and their supervisors (managers), on a variety of outcomes, both positive and negative.

Work and Society: Finding 'flow' at work

Motivation can be defined as a willingness to expend effort on a particular activity or task. Defined in this way, its importance to the study of organizational behaviour is obvious. Managers want to know what makes employees work hard, and the study of motivation promises to answer this question.

What makes the study of motivation challenging is the fact that prevailing views of motivation have changed dramatically over the last two decades. Following the Second World War, the study of motivation was dominated by behaviourist models. Many readers will be familiar with the behaviourist view that human behaviour is motivated by 'reinforcement contingencies'. Behaviourists maintain that people will expend effort on an activity if they believe they will be rewarded for that effort.

The behaviourist view of motivation has been challenged by new perspectives. One of the most influential of these devotes attention to the emotions and thought processes of individuals engaged in activities of various kinds. Researchers have discovered that, under certain conditions, individuals involved in activities reported experiencing intense feelings of satisfaction and enjoyment. These individuals expended high levels of effort when appropriate, but they were not motivated by the anticipation of a future reward. Their motivation appeared to spring from another source: they were experiencing what has been called 'intrinsic' (as distinct from 'extrinsic') motivation. For these individuals, the act of doing something produced a positive experience that was rewarding in itself.

Pioneering research in this area was conducted by psychologist Mihaly Csikszentmihalyi, who used the word 'flow' to describe the positive experiences of persons fully immersed in the pleasure of various activities. What were the characteristics of the activities typically associated with flow experiences? Crucial to these experiences is the relationship between the challenge associated with a particular activity and the skill a person brings to the activity. In the ideal situation, there is a 'balance between high levels of challenge and high levels of skill' (Csikszentmihalyi and Schneider, 2000, p. 97). Csikszentmihalyi elaborates:

> *Enjoyable experiences are usually described as having a cluster of related subjective dimensions. [In addition to a balance] of challenges and skills, enjoyable experiences provide clarity of goals: knowing what must be done from one moment to the next. Another dimension is immediacy of feedback: a person always knows how well he or she is doing. For instance, if a young boy enjoys fixing a bicycle, it is likely that he will say he knows exactly what he has to do – the chain must be tightened just so – and that he can test as he goes along whether the chain is working as it should. (Csikszentmihalyi and Schneider, p. 97)*

This example has much to tell us about motivation. No doubt the boy fixing the bicycle may be motivated by an anticipated future reward: the opportunity to ride a bicycle with a properly functioning chain. But the fact that he gives the task his full attention, and is willing to expend whatever effort is required, does not depend primarily on this future reward. Because the task carries within it its own reward, the boy is fully engaged in his 'work' and yet is hardly aware of the effort he is expending.

Much of Csikszentmihalyi's work is relevant to a new model of motivation, a model that takes intrinsic motivation as its central idea. This new model of motivation is fascinating, and its implications for work design seem profound. But it is difficult to extract specific lessons for managers. We might begin by asking why, in the contemporary workplace, do so few employees report flow-like experiences? The reasons for this are complex. Some might argue that behaviourist models of human motivation are themselves to blame. Guided by the principles of the behaviourist model, managers have sought to motivate workers using a range of rewards external to the work process.

But the causes for the transformation of work lie deeper. Macrosociologists Chris and Charles Tilly suggest that over the last 300 years there has been a trend towards increased 'time-discipline' in the world of work, defining time-discipline as 'the extent to which other persons decide the disposition of a worker's effort within the working day' (1998, p. 30). It could be argued that as time-discipline increases opportunities for flow-like experiences decrease.

stop!   Is this a valid argument in your view? How do employers justify the need for increased time-discipline? In what ways might the idea of flow lead employers to rethink their emphasis on time-discipline?

Sources and further information

Bakker, A. and Schaufeli W. (2008) 'Positive organizational behavior: engaged employees in flourishing organizations', *Journal of Organizational Behavior*, 29, pp. 147–54.

Csikszentmihalyi, M. (2008) *Flow: The Psychology of Optimal Experience*, New York: Harper Perennial.

Csikszentmihalyi, M. and Schneider, B. (2000) *Becoming Adult: How Teenagers Prepare for the World of Work*, New York: Basic Books.

Tilly, C. and Tilly C. (1998) *Work Under Capitalism*, Boulder, CO: Westview Press.

Note: This feature was written by David MacLennan, Assistant Professor at Thompson Rivers University, BC, Canada.

The valence of the outcomes (*V*) is moderated by the perceived *instrumentality* of the outcome to satisfy needs, and the perceived fairness or equity of the outcome. An outcome that is instrumental in satisfying an important need would have greater valence. Which outcome will an employee use to satisfy which need? Expectancy theorists suggest that it depends on the way the person has been socialized. Research suggests that, for Anglo-American employees at least, pay is most instrumental for satisfying physiological, security and ego-status needs, and not at all instrumental in satisfying social and self-actualization needs.[35]

The findings also explain why pay is important to both low-paid and high-paid employees. To the former, pay is instrumental in satisfying their physiological needs; to the latter, a high monthly pay cheque is instrumental in satisfying their ego-status needs.[36] The value of the outcome is also determined by the perceived equity of the reward. As we discussed earlier, employees compare their own input–reward ratio with the input–reward ratio of relevant others. If the two ratios are perceived

Plate 2 – Expectancy theory can be used to better understand student motivation. It would predict that studying for an examination (effort) is conditioned by its resulting in answering questions in exams correctly.
Source: Getty Images

goal setting: the process of motivating employees and clarifying their role perceptions by establishing performance objectives

role perceptions: a person's beliefs about what behaviours are appropriate or necessary in a particular situation, including the specific tasks that make up the job, their relative importance, and the preferred behaviours to accomplish those tasks

to be equal, equity exists and the reward's valence increases. Thus, the valence of an outcome is affected by employees' perception of its equity, considering their overall effort level relative to the effort level and reward of their co-workers.

By recognizing the importance of informal workplace learning and social comparisons, the Lawler model provides an insightful refinement of expectancy theory. The model enables managers to better understand the complexity of managing people, and in particular, how the elements of work motivation relate to one another in the motivation process.

Goal-setting theory

The theory of **goal setting** assumes that participatory goal setting and communicating accurate information on work performance can be positive motivators for employees. One version of this theory of motivation contains four major assumptions:

1 *Challenging* goals will produce higher performance than less challenging goals.
2 *Specific* challenging goals will produce higher performance than no goals or vague or general goals, such as 'do your best'.
3 Goal setting with *feedback* on goal attainment will produce higher performances than goal setting alone.
4 *Employee participation* in goal setting will produce higher performances than no participation.[37]

management by
objectives: a participative
goal-setting process in
which organizational
objectives are cascaded
down to work units and
individual employees

weblink
Go to the following
websites for more
information on
management
by objectives:
www.1000ventures.
com/business_guide/
mgmt_mbo_main.html;
www.managepro.com/
MBOtoPM.html

stop reflect
What do you think of
this explanation of work
motivation? To what
extent, if at all, can
work be designed to
reduce alienation in the
workplace?

Research conducted in several countries over the years has been consistent in demonstrating that goal-setting techniques do have a positive influence on work motivation.[38,39] The management technique of **management by objectives** is one of the best-known applications of goal-setting theory, and has been extensively used by Anglo-American management. Under management by objectives, a manager sets specific and challenging goals for a specified time period, periodically reviews progress towards goals that have previously been set, and provides feedback on goal accomplishment before setting goals for the next performance time period. In non-unionized workplaces, management by objectives also provides a mechanism for the appraisal of employee performance pay awards.

THE SOCIOLOGICAL ANALYSIS OF MOTIVATION: ALIENATION, CULTURE AND SELF-IDENTITY

Sociologists have developed a very different approach to understanding motivation in the workplace. Using concepts such as alienation, culture, orientation to work and the 'self', they challenge the adequacy of mainstream psychological theories of work motivation. Sociological theories remind us of the complex connection between the patterns of people's lives shaped by the societal configuration of class, gender and race that lie outside the workplace environment, and the pattern of social relations with others inside the work organization. This analysis of motivation also incorporates what critical theorists call 'antagonisms' or 'contradictions' inherent in capitalist employment relations.

Alienation

The problem of alienation as a condition of capitalist modernity is found in many novels. Witness Dr Robyn Penrose, a central character in David Lodge's novel *Nice Work*, set in the early 1980s, condemning the mindless, repetitive work and brutalizing conditions in Vic Wilcox's factory. The concept of alienation was developed by Karl Marx. For most sociologists today, alienation is seen as residing in the social structure of paid work rather than in personality traits. In other words, its causes are rooted in capitalist employment relations, and are *social* rather than psychological.[40,41]

When we refer to alienation in this book, we mean a phenomenon in which people have little or no control over the products or services they produce or offer, the organization of work, and the immediate work process itself. As James Rinehart writes:

> alienation is objective or structural in the sense that it is built into human relationships at the workplace and exists independent of how individuals perceive and evaluate this condition. Alienations can be viewed broadly as a condition of objective powerlessness. (ref. 41, p. 14)

Much of the psychology-based research on work motivation appears entirely indifferent to, possibly even ignorant of, the concept of alienation.[9] For sociologists, a major source of alienated labour is division of labour or specialization. Critical analysts have argued that workers are alienated because the nature of the work progressively wears away their self-esteem, and consequently their commitment to work and the organization.[41] Consistent with need and expectancy theories of motivation, alienating work obstructs higher-level needs and valent outcomes (instrumentalities), causing low commitment and low work motivation.

Critical insight

Few of the early content theories of motivation acknowledge personality, class, gender, race or age as factors influencing work motivation. Few of the popular theories provide empirical data to substantiate their claims. Arnolds and Boshoff state that the impact of personality traits was ignored in earlier studies of motivation, and acknowledge the need to include variables such as age, gender, cultural background and so on in motivation models.

Obtain a copy of Arnolds and Boshoff's article, 'Compensation, esteem valence and job performance: an empirical assessment of Alderfer's ERG theory'.[22] What are the strengths of this approach to investigating work motivation? What would be the advantages and disadvantages of gathering qualitative data from top managers and front-line employees on their views on what motivates them?

Culture

The concept of culture refers to the tangible and intangible aspects of human society including material objects, technology, language, beliefs and values that are shared and learned, rather than inherited, from person to person and from one generation to the next. How does culture determine work motivation? A national culture can shape individual work values and patterns of behaviour in the workplace. The study of organizational culture, which draws upon concepts from sociology, examines the connections between both tangible and intangible aspects of the organization and behaviour in the workplace. Here we can emphasize that it can act as a form of managerial control, prescribing and prohibiting certain activities to shape and reshape worker behaviour in a way that is consistent with top management's expectations.[42,43] A perceptual analysis, however, should remind us that a 'strong' culture that motivates one employee will not necessarily motivate another employee.[44]

Work orientation

work orientation: an attitude towards work that constitutes a broad disposition towards certain kinds of paid work

Work orientation refers to the meaning that individuals give to paid work and the relative importance they assign to work within their lives as a whole. This perspective to understanding workplace behaviour encourages a greater awareness of the connections between work attitudes, values and behaviour patterns, and the structure and culture of society. As mentioned above, people's working and non-working lives are shaped by the societal configuration of class, gender and race that lies outside the workplace, as well as the behaviour of managers and non-managers inside the organization. Interest in individual differences to work orientation has led some researchers to investigate the connection between work motivation and social factors. These social factors include, but are not limited to, class, gender and race.[45]

A classic British study[46] focused on the relationship between work orientation and social class. The researchers argued that if individuals enter an impoverished work situation in the full knowledge that intrinsic rewards are not available, their work motivation is not likely to be significantly influenced by the absence of such rewards. In essence, they suggested that, for a majority of workers in their study, extrinsic rewards – such as pay or what they called the 'cash nexus' – were much more important than intrinsic rewards. The majority of workers, they explained, had decided 'to give more weight to the instrumental at the expense of the expressive aspects of work' (ref. 46, p. 33).

Numerous studies have investigated possible gender-related differences of work orientation, and the determinants of work satisfaction.[23,47–50] Testing the hypothesis

Plate 3 – The task of discovering what motivates different categories of employee in different work settings is of the same magnitude as finding the Holy Grail. For example, what factors motivate each of these men at work?
Source: iStockphoto

that men and women have different expectations from paid work, results show that although women are more likely to enter an impoverished work situation than men, they have lower expectations and hence are as satisfied with their paid employment as men are. When men and women in management positions are compared, it has been found that both have very similar orientations to work.[47] One possible explanation for gender-related work orientation is differences in sex-role socialization. In support of this argument, there is well-documented evidence that women are socialized to pursue occupations reflecting their stereotyped sex-roles, regardless of individual abilities and talent. Studies affirm that women's employment aspirations and choices are frequently far lower than the aspirations of men with comparable ability.[51]

The work orientation approach was seen as an alternative to needs theories of work motivation. It adds support to expectancy theory, in that it emphasizes the need to focus on the expectations that individuals bring to the workplace in order to understand behaviour *inside* the workplace. As others insist, the conundrum of how to motivate workers cannot usefully be considered until we know their needs and expectations relative to their employment.[46] Although the orientation to work thesis is a useful corrective to the psychological universalism of needs and process motivation theories, it is important not to be drawn into a determinism about the possibilities for work motivation.[17] More importantly perhaps, orientations to work are ever-changing and can alter with the particular circumstances in which they become relevant to shaping behaviour. Examples of major change include attitudes to work–life balance, job insecurity arising from global economic recession or precarious employment relationships, and employers' coercion of employees.[17,52–57] The notion of 'dynamic orientations' suggests factors that will motivate the individual can be seen to be embedded in both the social and the individual's psychological contract with the employing organization.[53]

The 'self' at work

The sociological concept of the 'self' informs new theories of work motivation. When we are born, we have no idea that we are separate beings. Through life experiences, we develop a sense of *self*, the perceptual picture we have of ourselves, our view of what kind of person we are. The concept of self is most often held to derive from the influential work of American sociologists George Herbert Mead and Charles Cooley. In Mead's philosophy, the self-identity develops through the process of social interaction with others.

The *self-concept theory* of motivation is derived from the concept of the self-identity as an underlying force that motivates non-calculative-based behaviour in the workplace. The self-concept, the totality of our beliefs and emotions about ourselves, is an inner source of energy that gives direction to our behaviour. As such, the self-concept theory of motivation connects the individual's personality with paid work.[58] The theory is based on a number of assumptions about human nature: (1) people are motivated to retain and enhance their self-esteem and self-worth; (2) they are not only goal oriented but also self-expressive; (3) they are driven to maintain and increase their sense of self-consistency; (5) self-concepts are composed, in part, of social identities; and (5) self-concept behaviours are not necessarily related to specific calculative instrumental goals. So, for example, a person may volunteer to do unpaid work at a shelter for the homeless out of a sense of self-esteem and responsibility. And a young person may choose to enter the family business or to enter a profession because it has since early childhood always been expected of her by significant others and has become an important part of her social identity.

The *whole-self theory* of motivation posits an association between an individual's needs for spirituality and work. It assumes that human beings are motivated by more than financial rewards – by spiritual needs. According to this theory, people are looking for their work to provide deeper significance and self-meaning. So, as one advocate of the theory explained, 'the pressure many of us feel to recognize and respond to the sacred in us must find outlet in the secular workplace'.[59] The whole-self theory is a variant of Maslow's higher-order self-actualization need. The self-concept theory and whole-self theory of motivation imply that employee motivation is less susceptible to managerial initiatives and control. It seems intuitively plausible that there are significant individual differences based on self-concept that strongly influence motivation in the workplace. However, research is needed to support the hypothesis and establish a direct link between self-concept and workplace behaviour.

INTEGRATING THE APPROACHES

The integrated motivation model shown in Figure 3.8 goes beyond notions of individual motivational drive, and takes into account other theories of motivation. It presents a dynamic framework that incorporates into it expectancy theory and some sociological concepts influencing motivation.

The model portrays individual work motivation that is based on the three expectancies – effort-to-performance, instrumentalities and valence – and is also influenced by individual abilities and personality traits (such as self-esteem) (Box 1), by the psychological contract (Box 2), by organizational culture (Box 3), by employee relations (Box 4), by work orientation (Box 5) and by the alienating aspects of work (Box 6). We believe that this integrated model of work motivation has several advantages. It is informed by the work of psychologists and sociologists, incorporates expectancy theories, and emphasizes the importance of complex social processes in shaping individual and group behaviour. For an alternative integrated theory model, see the work of Klein.[60]

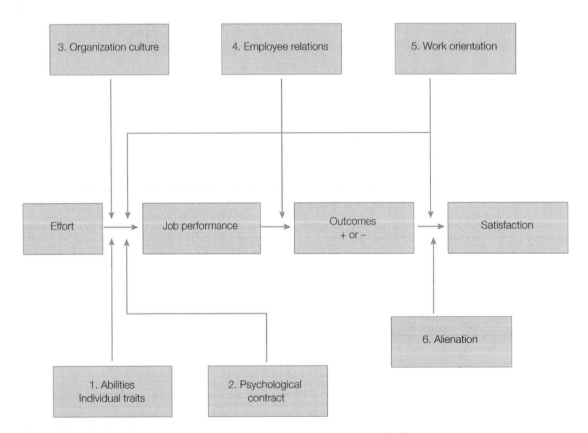

Figure 3.8 – Integrating psychological and sociological approaches to work motivation

APPLYING MOTIVATION THEORIES

Implementing motivational theory successfully in the workplace is challenging, and managers cannot simply transplant one of the theories discussed in this chapter and apply it in its 'pure' form. Every individual is unique and will respond differently to attempts to motivate him or her. What factors motivate a 56-year-old computer engineer? What factors motivate working mothers with young children? What factors motivate Muslin women at work? Managers need to be sensitive to the differences in individual needs and values among the people they manage. They need to avoid viewing their 'employees' as a homogeneous group. People are different in what they need and what they value, and in how they perceive and judge their work situation. For this reason, managers' motivation interventions must take into account the occupation (for example, managers, knowledge workers and first-level employees) and the employees' age, gender, race, ethnicity and disabilities (if any). This is only possible when managers know their employees.

People engage in paid work for many reasons besides the weekly or monthly pay cheque. They work so that they can be with others, gain respect, form an identity and realize their human potential. As an illustration, consider possible motivation interventions for knowledge workers. We said that knowledge work is 'ambiguity intensive' and that knowledge workers are defined in terms of the requirement to share and apply their professional knowledge with others in the organization. Drawing on a study by Horwitz and his colleagues,[61] Table 3.2 shows the most popular, highly effective and least effective motivation interventions for managing knowledge workers.

As column 2 indicates, the most highly effective motivation interventions for knowledge workers included employment practices that allow them the freedom to plan work independently (in other words, autonomy). Although an important

Table 3.2 – Most popular, highly effective, and least effective motivation strategies for knowledge workers

Most popular		Highly effective		Least effective	
Strategy type	Rank	Strategy type	Rank	Strategy type	Rank
Freedom to plan and work independently	1	Freedom to plan work	1	Flexible work practices	1
Regular contact with senior executives	2	Challenging work	2	Large cluster of knowledge workers	2
Incentive bonuses	3	Access to state-of-art technology and products	3	Generous funding for conferences	3
Challenging work	4	Top management support	4	Cash awards for innovations	4
Top management support	5	Ensure fulfilling work	5	Recruit people who fit organizational culture	5

Source: Adapted from Horwitz et al. (2003),[61] pp. 31–2
Note: These rankings are based on the number of responses that were marked as the five most frequently used motivation interventions, and the five most highly effective and ineffective in motivating knowledge workers.

OB and globalization

Dressing for success: control and agency in an offshore office

Many of us are familiar with media images of factory floors and data entry workspaces in places like India, Mexico, China and the Caribbean, where local workers complete low-skilled, low-paying jobs outsourced from large companies headquartered thousands of miles away. These images of self-contained workspaces can give the impression that the work carried out there remains separate from the local social, economic and cultural worlds that exist outside the factory or office doors. A closer look, however, reveals the complex ways in which outsourced work intersects with local lives.

In a study of the impacts of outsourced work on female workers at Data Air, an overseas company operating in Barbados, anthropologist Carla Freeman (2002) notes the ways in which local cultural values associated with womanhood and the middle class were evoked by Data Air managers, and by the company's female staff, to achieve different goals. Managers drew on these values to shape organizational behaviours deemed favourable for a data entry office, namely docility, conformity and attention to detail. The workers, on the other hand, viewed their office-based work as a way to improve their social and gender status in the community. A local observer explained to Freeman (2002, p. 93) how the modern office environment shaped employees' behaviour at work and beyond the office environment:

When you see a group of the young ladies, like the ones from Data Air, you can see that they're much better dressed than the ones from the assembly plant ... They're probably not getting paid much better but their work environment is a cleaner one, a purer one ... the young ladies working in there perceive that they are working in an office and they dress like it and they live like it.

This 'professionalism' – and the behaviours and status that accompanied it – was cultivated at the Data Air office and was valued by both the company and the workers. Through policies such as a dress code, the company was able to manage its image and the behaviours deemed necessary to uphold that image. Likewise, the workers valued the dress code for its role in helping them shape new 'professional' or 'middle-class' identities. One worker explained:

Our policy is governed by a dress code ... We are not a factory. We call ourselves an 'open office' and if you were working in an office, you wouldn't go in a jean skirt or jean pants or short skirts. You would dress as if you were an executive. That's what we expect our persons to do. And we instil that in our people, so by practice and counselling, we have reached the stage where people recognize us for the way we look.

(Freeman 2002, p. 93)

Rather than interpreting the management of foreign workers through policies like a dress code as simply the exercise of institutional power over low-wage workers, Freeman urges us to consider the workers' complicity and participation in the management of organizational behaviour and culture at Data Air. In this instance, the workers themselves recognized policies governing dress and behaviour as resources they could use to exert agency and improve their social and economic positions in local Bajan society. Through this example, we can begin to see the complexities inherent in the flows of capital, labour, culture and power associated with the outsourcing of work.

stop!   Do you think that too much – or too little – emphasis is placed on how one dresses in the workplace? Are there particular types of work where dress matters more than in other types of work? Is there a relationship between dress and behaviour in the workplace? What is it?

Data Air management recognized the high value that Bajan women place on dressing well, and evoked this existing local value to manage workplace behaviour in the service of the company. What issues might arise when organizations doing business overseas capitalize on – and possibly change – local values and behaviours?

Sources and further information

Freeman, C. (1993) 'Designing women: corporate discipline and Barbados's off-shore pink-collar sector', in J. X. Inda and R. Rosaldo (eds), *The Anthropology of Globalization: A Reader*, Malden, MA: Blackwell Publishing.

Freeman, C. (2002) *High Tech and High Heels in the Global Economy: Women, Work, and Pink-Collar Identities in the Caribbean*, Durham, NC: Duke University Press.

Metters, R. and Verma, R.. (2007) 'History of offshoring knowledge services', *Journal of Operations Management*, 26(2), pp. 141–7.

Note: This feature was written by Gretchen Fox, Anthropologist, Timberline Natural Resource Group, Canada.

limitation of the research data is that they are based on employers' perceptions of effectiveness rather than on knowledge workers' views of what motivates them, the results are consistent with other studies surveying knowledge workers themselves.[61] There is a sizeable literature indicating that work motivation strategies need to consider carefully appropriate rewards and job design.

Reward design and motivation

In the context of mobilizing the motivation of employees in order to achieve the organization's objectives, rewards emphasize a core facet of the employment relationship: it constitutes an economic exchange or relationship. The reward is typically a package made up of pay, extended health plans, pension plans, vacation time and so on. Since the early 1980s, a 'new pay' agenda has been imported into UK workplaces moving from pay for time – show up and get paid – to pay for individual or team outputs – show up and perform to a satisfactory standard and get paid, perform to a highly satisfactory standard and cooperate with co-workers and receive more pay.[62] This individualized performance model is undoubtedly associated with the decline of trade union influence, neo-liberal economics and market deregulation, topics too large to examine in detail here. Table 3.3 classifies types of reward and behaviour objectives of the new pay paradigm.

Here, we will be concerned with pay – money paid for work done – as an essential factor in work motivation. The motivational characteristics of pay are controversial, not least because of the fundamental tension between the economic, sociological and psychological theoretical frameworks or perspectives. Orthodox economic theory takes as its starting point the free labour market, which is based on the assumption that individuals are rational economic maximizers. Thus, other things being equal, higher pay will increase the number of people willing to work for the organization, and pay incentives will generate superior performance. Sociological thinking emphasizes that varying amounts of power relationship can be of central importance in determining work motivation. Furthermore, as previously discussed, sociology proposes that gender differences, culture and social inequality have a major influence on work motivation. The major psychological theories focus on the individual employee's perception, needs and expectations.

Table 3.3 – New rewards and behaviour objectives

Type of reward	Examples	Behaviour
Individual rewards	Pay Overtime Performance standard Commission Bonuses Merit Paid leave Benefits	**Time**: maintain work attendance **Outputs**: perform assigned tasks **Competence**: complete tasks without error
Team rewards	Team bonuses	**Cooperation** with co-workers, sharing information and knowledge
Organizational rewards	Profit sharing Share ownership	**Commitment** to culture and goals

We began this book by noting the effects of the global recession on the *psychological climate*. The analysis of the motivational characteristics of pay cannot ignore a whole range of important contextual variables such as economic recession, culture and pay inequality. Evidence from international studies indicates that the perceived importance of pay as a motivator is bound up in the 'cultural clothes of masculinity'.[63–65] On one important aspect of social inequality – economic inequity – the statistics are truly breathtaking. Over the last 25 years in both Britain and North America, it has become socially acceptable for the income gap between rich and poor to widen. In Canada, for example, 99 per cent of working Canadians will work full time throughout 2010 to earn an average income of around $39,000 (£19,500). But by 10.33 am on January 2, 2010, the top 100 CEOs in the country will have already earned that amount. On average, the top 100 CEOs make more than 218 times as much as an average employee working full time for a full year.[66] Global capitalism has widened the gap between executive pay and the rest.

Organizational psychology uses a distinctive range of concepts, and emphasizes individual employees' perceptions, needs and expectations. Pay is considered to be one of the most noticeable employment practices through which the psychological contract can be established, changed, or violated.[67] Pay shapes the psychological contract by signalling to employees the behaviour that the organization values. A violation refers to the feelings of anger, fear, helplessness and betrayal experienced when the employee perceives that a breach of contract has occurred. This may occur when a promise on the nature of the contract turns out to be less favourable (for example, lower payment) than the employee expected, or as a result of job loss when the employee expected long-term security. The nature of the psychological contract means that every employee will put a somewhat different valuation on the pay provided and on the value of their contribution depending on their individual traits and situational circumstances.

The motivational characteristics of pay are multifaceted as a result of the conflict between intrinsic and extrinsic motivators. According to Maslow's and Alderfer's need theories, pay addresses lower-level needs as it can be exchanged for basic necessities of life. Adam's equity theory posits that pay is an important motivator because workers compare their performance and pay with their peers. And pay should prove motivational to the extent that it is highly valent and is clearly tied to performance, according to Vroom's expectancy theory.

So is pay an effective tool to motivate workers? Motivation is the nexus of character and circumstance. This observation takes account of both human perception, needs and expectations in motivation and the fact that human behaviour always happens within a particular time and situation. Empirical research has found that pay is not always an effective motivator as it will only motivate some people at some points in time, whereas with other people and at other times, it will actually demotivate them.

Research by Horwitz and his colleagues highlights the contradictions and controversy over pay–performance systems.[61] Pay contingent upon performance in this case had a detrimental effect on highly paid knowledge workers because, arguably, these individuals considered additional extrinsic rewards to be less important than intrinsic motivators. A study by Benabou and Tirole suggests that, in the short term, an emphasis on pay may act as a stimulus for effort, but in the long term, money may have a detrimental effect by reducing intrinsic motivation.[68] Finally, we can note in this discussion on motivation the role that reward has played in the recent global economic recession. A key contributor to the crisis leading to the pandemic criticism of executive bankers is that, in a 'culture of easy reward', they engaged in excessive risk-taking behaviour in their quest for huge bonuses.[69,70]

Empowerment and job satisfaction

Employment is a social activity, and for many people it is not regarded simply as a means to an end. Jobs are central to the lives of most people, in that they provide identity, status and experienced meaningfulness. The motivation theories discussed in this chapter suggest that the design of work can be the most effective motivator for many employees (see Table 3.2). *Job design* refers to the process of assigning tasks to a job, including the interdependency of those tasks with other jobs. Redesigning work to enlarge the number of tasks performed and allow greater decision making can be effective in motivating the individual employee to superior performance and an enhanced sense of achievement and self-worth. The concept of *empowerment* is one term used to describe motivational job design practices designed to allow employees some 'voice' in group or/and organizational decision making, either in their day-to-day work or through formal managerially driven mechanisms that enlist workers' skills, experience and **creativity**.[71] Empowering job design initiatives are predicated on the social psychology theory that individuals have a cognitive need for self-actualization and self-determination and, as such, can heighten **self-efficacy**. The cognitive concept of self-efficacy or a 'can-do' mentality refers to the beliefs people have about their ability to perform specific situational task(s) successfully.

Contrary to Theory X precepts, higher-level growth needs have been shown to have a significant influence on the self-esteem of first-level employees as well as of higher-level employees (see Figure 3.4, above). As Arnolds and Boshoff put it, 'frontline employees ... also like to make one or more important decisions every day, use a wide range of their abilities and have the opportunity to do challenging things at work' (ref. 22, p. 715). However, although the job design motivation strategy focuses on notions of self-fulfilment, identity and employee perceptions of task characteristics, the way in which two employees view a particular job and perceive an identical task may be quite different depending on such factors as their age, personality and orientation to work, so achieving this is not straightforward.

Gender, for example, influences identity formation among women. Josselson, in her work on identity, found that 'in comparison to men, women orient themselves in more complicated ways, balancing many involvements and aspirations, with connections to others paramount; their identities are thus compounded and more difficult to articulate' (ref. 72, p. 8). Following on from this and the requirement for differentiation between occupational groups, it is insufficient to make objective changes in skill variety, autonomy or other job dimensions. Managers need to also appreciate and monitor how those objective changes influence the perceptions of different employees.

Herzberg's motivator–hygiene theory, described above, supports motivator empowerment strategies to increase job satisfaction. Hackman and Oldham's job characteristic theory[73] identifies five core job characteristics – **skill variety, task identity, task significance,** autonomy and feedback – as critical factors to produce a high job satisfaction. Overall job satisfaction refers to a collection of feelings or emotions that an employee has about her or his job as a whole.

Peter Warr's three-dimensional model (Figure 3.9) portrays the range of emotional responses to paid work.[74] Central to this model is the horizontal pole illustrating emotions of high or low pleasure. In research on job-related well-being, this horizontal pole is traditionally indexed as job satisfaction. The second pole runs between anxiety and comfort. In the top left quadrant, feelings of anxiety combine high mental arousal with low pleasure. The third pole runs from depression to enthusiasm. In the

creativity: the capacity to develop an original product, service or idea that makes a socially recognized contribution

self-efficacy: the beliefs people have about their ability to perform specific situational task(s) successfully

skill variety: the extent to which employees must use different skills and talents to perform tasks in their job

task identity: the degree to which a job requires the completion of a whole or an identifiable piece of work

task significance: the degree to which the job has a substantial impact on the organization and/or larger society

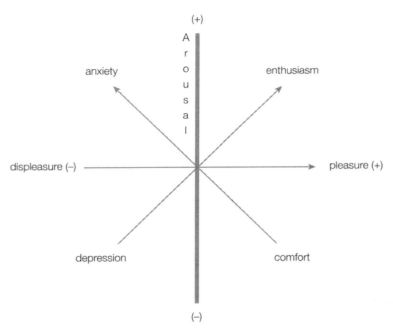

Figure 3.9 – Three poles for the measurement of well-being
Source: Adapted from Warr (2002),[74] p. 3

top right quadrant, feelings of positive motivation combine high mental arousal with enthusiasm. An employee's location on each of the three poles can be determined through a standard questionnaire. This model has been extended with a fourth pole describing feelings of fatigue or vigour.[75]

That job satisfaction is essentially an affective rather than a cognitive response means that the concept is integral to the wider context of emotional labour, job-related stress and psychological well-being. It is important to bear in mind that job satisfaction is not a totally individualistic notion. Employees' accounts of their job satisfaction given to researchers will be influenced by their life experiences and orientation to paid work. Finally, research on job satisfaction has proved mixed results on the correlation between job satisfaction and workplace behaviour.[76,77]

Job satisfaction seems a crude measure for the almost infinitely complex array of social disparities in work-related stress and psychological well-being. A growing consensus points to wider life experiences, in particular the quality of people's social relationships in society. In some workplaces, employment relationships are support-ive, helping individuals deal with life's challenges. In other workplaces, these relation-ships are toxic, putting health-damaging stresses on workers. Here we have identified a number of factors influencing whether employment relationships are supportive or toxic. For example, Warr's research highlights the importance of job designs that foster a sense of autonomy and trust rather than powerlessness and distrust. Recent research by Wilkinson and Pickett,[78] by contrast, suggests that people's health depends on the quality of their social relationships, and the most important determinant of the quality of relationships is the level of inequality. This is not a new idea, but if it is true, the effects of income inequality extend well beyond individual motivation and the work domain.

OB in focus Anxiety and stress in the workplace

It is a well-established that depression is associated with a significant burden of illness and immense costs to organizations. However, anxiety disorders are more common and responsible for at least as much personal suffering, disability and economic loss. Anxiety disorders encompass six main categories: phobias, panic disorder with or without agoraphobia, generalized anxiety disorder, obsessive-compulsive disorder, acute stress disorder and post-traumatic stress disorder. One in four individuals suffers an anxiety disorder sometime in their life and one in 10 is likely to have had an anxiety disorder in the past 12 months.

Workplace stress occurs when we perceive the challenges and demands of work as excessive and don't think we can cope. Anxiety in the workplace is associated with: elevated fatigue; exhaustion; increased stress; irritability; attention or concentration problems; increased worrying and anxious thoughts; emotional and physical symptoms such as moodiness, agitation, restlessness, irritability; muscle tension; abdominal distress; feeling isolated; decreased well-being; as well as behavioural symptoms such as changes in appetite and sleep and nervous habits such as nail biting or pacing.

In order to promote a healthy workplace, employers need to recognize factors contributing to work-related stress and anxiety. Effective managers could provide workshops on various health-related topics, including stress reduction. Attention to individual needs such as role definition, flexible work hours, learning opportunities, advancement and regular feedback on job performance are also essential elements of a healthy workplace.

Source: Extract from 'High cost of anxiety' by Katy Kamkar, psychologist with the Work, Stress and Health Programme at the Centre for Addiction and Mental Health, Toronto, *Canadian HR Reporter*, December 15, 2008, p. 34.

CHAPTER SUMMARY

- This chapter has emphasized the centrality of motivation in the employment relationship. Motivation is the driving force within individuals that affects the direction, intensity and persistence of their work behaviour in the interest of achieving organizational goals.
- We discussed Maslow's famous needs hierarchy. It assumes that when a person's need is not satisfied, that person experiences internal tension or states of deficiency, and this motivates the person to change behaviour to satisfy that need.[79] All the need theories tend to be heavily prescriptive in nature.
- We explained how process theories of work motivation place emphasis on the actual psychological process of motivation. According to the equity theory, perceptions of equity or inequity lead employees to form judgements on the value (or valence) of a reward or outcome. When an employee perceives a reward item to be inequitable, the individual will be dissatisfied, which will result in the individual not finding the outcome attractive; thus, reward will not be an effective motivator.
- Expectancy theory is based on the idea that motivation results from deliberate choices to engage in certain behaviours in order to achieve worthwhile outcomes. Its most important elements are the perception that effort will result in a particular level of performance (E→P), the perception that a specific behaviour will lead to specific outcomes (P→O), and the perceived value of those outcomes, the valences. The attractiveness of work activities (their valence) depends on an employee's individual differences, cultural factors and orientation to work.
- This chapter also suggested that if we are to understand what motivates people, we must go beyond psychological notions of individual needs and cognitive processes. We need to incorporate into any analysis the psychological climate, the culture, the dynamics of employment relations, orientation to work, and the effects of complex interconnecting levels of domination, which stem from the class and gender relations in society.

KEY CONCEPTS

alienation
equity theory
expectancy theory
extrinsic motivator
goal setting
instrumentality
intrinsic motivator
motivation
needs
organizational culture
orientation to work
the self
self-concept theory
valence
whole-self needs

VOCAB CHECKLIST FOR ESL STUDENTS

- Alienation
- Creativity, create, creative
- Equity theory
- Exchange value
- Existence, exist
- Expectancy theory
- Extrinsic motivator
- Goals
- Goal setting
- Growth needs
- Inequity
- Instrumentality
- Intrinsic motivator
- Motivation, motivational motivate
- Needs
- Needs hierarchy theory
- Organizational commitment
- Orientation
- Self-actualization
- Skill variety
- Task identity
- Task significance
- Valence
- Work orientation

CHAPTER REVIEW QUESTIONS

1   To what extent is motivating workers increasingly more or less challenging for managers in the early twenty-first century? Explain your answer.

2 Compare and contrast Maslow's needs hierarchy theory and Alderfer's ERG theory. How are they similar? How are they different? What do both theories imply for managerial practice?

3 Identify two different types of expectancy referred to in the expectancy theory of work motivation. What can a manager do to influence these expectations?

4 What are the limitations of expectancy theory in predicting an employee's work behaviour and performance?

CHAPTER RESEARCH QUESTIONS

1 One way to understand different motivation theories is to interview your peers on what is important to them when choosing a job. Form a diverse study group including, if possible, an international student(s). Discuss the following questions: How important is pay in choosing a job when you graduate? To what extent are needs theories of motivation culturally based? Give examples. Is personal autonomy important to your work motivation? Why? How helpful are self-concept and whole-self theories in thinking about your own choice of job and work motivation?

2 Obtain a copy of *Inside the Workplace: Findings from the 2004 Workplace Employment Relations Survey* (2006). After reading pages 196–201, how important is pay to overall job satisfaction?

3 Read Evert Van de Vliert's (2008) article investigating whether pay is perceived to be more important in poorer countries.[65] After looking at Figure 3.7, 'The international HRM cycle', in this book, what insights does the research provide for managing international rewards?

FURTHER READING

Corby, S., Palmer, S. and Lindop, E. (2009) *Rethinking Reward*, Basingstoke: Palgrave.

Horwitz, F. M., Chan Teng Heng and Quazi, H. A. (2003) 'Finders, keepers? Attracting, motivating and retaining knowledge workers', *Human Resource Management Journal*, **13**(4), pp. 23–44 (see p. 33).

Lawler, E. E., Mohrman, S. and Ledford, G. (1998) *Strategies for High Performance Organizations*, San Francisco: Jossey-Bass.

Pfeffer, J. (1998) *The Human Equation: Building Profits by Putting People First*, Boston, MA: Harvard Business School Press.

Van de Vliert, E., Van Yperen, N. W. and Thierry, H. (2008) 'Are wages more important for employees in poorer countries with harsher climates?', *Journal of Organizational Behavior*, **29**, pp. 79–94.

Chapter case study 1

Equity at FindIT

Setting

FindIT is a US-based company, founded in 1989. In 2009, it has become the leader in publishing print and online directories for local and regional markets in the country. With the realization that their customers were looking to diversify their advertising outside the traditional channel of print, the company recently announced an expansion into the digital media market, including online and mobile platforms. At the same time, senior management began planning to introduce a new job evaluation scheme to simplify the pay structure.

Background to the case

To understand how management's plans affect people's experience of work, it is necessary to recognize the core features of job evaluation. First practised in the 1920s and 1930s, job evaluation is a systematic approach to establishing pay rates. Although variations have existed since its development, one popular method, the point system, attempts to create a more equitable process by ranking jobs based on a number of key factors (each assigned a number of points), such as required education, working conditions and supervision of others. Comparable jobs are grouped into different pay levels, creating a 'hierarchy of jobs': higher rated jobs are paid at the higher pay rates on the hierarchy. Although the actual pay rates are determined by comparing key jobs to the external market, the process of measuring jobs relative to each other within the organization creates a system focused on internal equity.

This approach was suited to the narrow and tightly structured jobs and job descriptions favoured by the classical organizations and unions of the first part of the twentieth century. Later, emerging human relations firms also embraced the method, believing that it established fairness and equity in a pay system. Job evaluation was perceived to minimize subjectivity, favouritism and management bias in the distribution of pay. Despite changing approaches to how work is organized and the increasing complexity of work since then, job evaluation as a means of determining base pay is still widely practised in unionized and government organizations in North America.

With the change in focus, many of FindIT's 600 employees whose work duties had been routine now argued that their jobs had became more complex. Several approached management and asked to have their jobs evaluated under the new system. The company agreed to first evaluate those jobs most directly impacted by the digital media initiative. A small group consisting of management and selected employees helped to gather the job information through worker questionnaires and conducted the evaluations.

The problem

The evaluations took 6 months to complete. When the results were released with the revised job descriptions, a number of employees were shocked to discover that their jobs had been overgraded under the old system, and they would not receive any salary increases, despite the new responsibilities and skills now required in their jobs. Of these employees, 25 per cent left the company, stating that their contributions or personal performances were not recognized. For the rest, there was a distinct drop in their productivity and a rise in absenteeism. Interpersonal conflicts became more common, as employees began to argue over the value of their jobs relative to others. On the shop floor, employees began to share notes on how to influence the evaluation results through the questionnaires they were asked to fill out.

Tasks

Working either alone or in a small group, prepare a report for FindIT's senior management on the employees' reaction to the new job evaluation scheme. Your report should address the following questions:

1 How do equity theory and expectancy theory help to explain the reaction of the employees to the evaluation results?
2 What role should managers play in ensuring the acceptance of a job evaluation system by the organization's employees?
3 What would be the challenges in using job evaluation for today's more complex jobs, such as in research or information technology?

Further reading

Armstrong, M. and Baron, A. (1995) *The Job Evaluation Handbook*, London: CIPD Publishing.

Bratton, J. and Gold, J. (2007) 'Job evaluation', pp. 383–90 in *Human Resource Management: Theory and Practice*, Basingstoke: Palgrave.

Lawler, E. E. (2000) *Rewarding Excellence*, San Francisco: Jossey-Bass.

Note

This case study was written by Lori Rilkoff, MSc, CHRP, Senior Human Resources Manager at the City of Kamloops, and lecturer in HRM at Thompson Rivers University, BC, Canada.

Chapter case study 2

Motivation at Norsk Petroleum

Visit www.palgrave.com/business/brattonob2e to view this case study

WEB-BASED ASSIGNMENT

Form a study group of three to five people, and go to the website of any of the following organizations, or a similar one that interests members of the group:

- Compaq Computers (www.compaq.com)
- Apple (www.apple.com)
- Airbus Industrie (www.airbus.com)
- Walmart (www.walmart.com)
- General Electric (www.ge.com)
- Virgin Airlines (www.virgin.com).

When there, go to the 'Company overview' and the human resource management section of the site, and look at the language, assumptions and espoused values. Evaluate the organization's dominant culture in the light of our discussion in this chapter. Write a report that draws out the common features.

Alternatively, go to the websites of a number of universities, and compare and contrast your own university with others in the UK or abroad. As a guide to your search, ask the following questions: What artefacts are displayed that expresses the institution's culture? (Hint: do departments display the publications of the teaching faculty?) In the advertising material, does the institution emphasize teaching excellence, research or both? What are the President's espoused values? What rituals and ceremonies dramatize the institution's culture? What practices shape the university's culture? (Hint: ask your lecturer what is the most important criterion for promotion – excellence in teaching or the number of articles/books published.) Do the visible artefacts and processes provide a guideline for behaviour at the university? If so, why?

OB IN FILM

The film *Dangerous Minds* (1995) centres on a former US Marine turned teacher, LouAnne Johnson (played by Michelle Pfeiffer). Ms Johnson accepts a teaching position at an inner-city high school and tries to motivate her students. The school principal, however, does not approve of her unorthodox motivation methods.

Watch the scene, starting with a shot of the school hallway, after the principal has reprimanded Johnson for taking students to an amusement park without signed permission. The film raises cognitive and behaviour motivation issues. Ask yourself, what methods does Ms Johnson use to motivate her students? Do the students change their behaviour as a result of her teaching approach? What lessons can be drawn from the film for motivating young workers in the workplace?

REFERENCES

1. Vroom, V. H. and Deci, E. L. (eds) (1970) 'Introduction: an overview of work motivation', pp. 9–19 in *Management and Motivation: Selected Readings*, London: Penguin.

2. Legge, K. (2005) *Human Resource Management: Rhetorics and Realities* (2nd edn), Basingstoke: Palgrave.
3. Drucker, P. (1954/1993) *The Practice of Management*, New York: Harper Collins.
4. Fox, A. (1974) *Beyond Contract, Power, and Trust Relations*, London: Faber & Faber.
5. Friedman, A. (1977) *Industry and Labour: Class Struggle at Work and Monopoly Capitalism*, London: Macmillan.
6. Salaman, G. (1979) *Work Organizations: Resistance and Control*, London: Longman.
7. Clegg, S. and Dunkerley, D. (1980) *Organization, Class and Control*, London: Routledge & Kegan Paul.
8. Thompson, P. (1989) *The Nature of Work* (2nd edn), London: Macmillan.
9. Salaman, G. (1981) *Class and the Corporation*, London: Fontana.
10. Ryan, R. M. and Deci, E. L. (2000) 'Self-determination theory and the facilitation of intrinsic motivation, social development, and well-being', *American Psychologist*, **55**(1), pp. 68–78.
11. Vallerand, R. J. (1997) 'Toward a hierarchical model of intrinsic and extrinsic motivation', *Advances in Experimental Social Psychology*, **29**, pp. 271–360.
12. Townley, B. (1994) *Reframing Human Resource Management: Power, Ethics and the Subject of Work*, London: Sage.
13. Maslow, A. H. (1954) *Motivation and Personality*, New York: Harper.
14. Herzberg, F., Mansner, B. and Snyderman, B. (1959) *The Motivation to Work* (2nd edn), New York: Wiley.
15. McClelland, D. (1961) *The Achieving Society*, Princeton, NJ: Van Nostrand.
16. Alderfer, C. P. (1972) *Existence, Relatedness and Growth*, New York: Free Press.
17. Watson, T. (1986) *Management, Organization and Employment Strategy*, London: Routledge.
18. McGregor, D. (1957/1970), 'The human side of enterprise', pp. 306–19 in V. H. Vroom and E. Deci (eds), *Management and Motivation*, London: Penguin. McGregor, Douglas. Edited by Rob Roy McGregor, Martha McGregor, and Gregory N. Colvard, *Leadership and Motivation: Essays of Douglas McGregor*, figure from essay "The Human Side of Enterprise", © 1966 Massachusetts Institute of Technology, by permission of the MIT Press.
19. Pitsis, T. S. (2008) 'Theory X and Theory Y', pp. 1545–9 in S. R. Clegg and J. Bailey (eds), *The Sage International Encyclopedia of Organizational Studies*, Thousand Oaks, CA: Sage.
20. McClelland, D. C. and Burnham, D. H. (1976) 'Power is the great motivator', *Harvard Business Review*, March–April, pp. 100–10.
21. Harrel, A. M. and Strahl, M. J. (1981) 'A behavioral decision theory approach to measuring McClelland's trichotomy of needs', *Journal of Applied Psychology*, **66**, pp. 242–7.
22. Arnolds, C. and Boshoff, C. (2002) 'Compensation, esteem valence and job performance: an empirical assessment of Alderfer's ERG theory', *International Journal of Human Resource Management*, **13**(4), pp. 697–719.
23. Cullen, D. (1994) 'Feminism, management and self-actualization', *Gender, Work and Organization*, **1**(3), pp. 127–37.
24. Gordon, J. R. and Whelan, K .S. (1998) 'Successful professional women in midlife: how organizations can more effectively understand and respond to the challenges', *Academy of Management Executive*, **12**(1), pp. 8–27.
25. Wajcman, J. (1998) *Managing Like a Man: Women and Men in Corporate Management*, Cambridge: Polity Press/Penn State University Press.
26. Herzberg, F. (2003) 'One more time: how do you motivate employees?', *Harvard Business Review*, **81**(1), pp. 87–96.
27. Adams, J. S. (1965) 'Inequality in social exchange', pp. 267–99 in L. Berkowitz (ed.), *Advances in Experimental Social Psychology*, New York: Academic Press.
28. Bratton, J. and Gold, J. (2007) *Human Resource Management: Theory and Practice* (4th edn), Basingstoke: Palgrave.
29. Feldman, D. C., Leana, C. R. and Bolino, M. C. (2002) 'Underemployment and relative deprivation among re-employed executives', *Journal of Occupational and Organizational Psychology*, **75**(4), pp. 453–88.
30. Baldamus, W. (1961) *Efficiency and Effort*, London: Tavistock.
31. Lewin, K. (1935) *A Dynamic Theory of Personality*, New York: McGraw-Hill.
32. Vroom, V. H. (1964) *Work and Motivation*, New York: Wiley.
33. Porter, L. W. and Lawler, E. E. (1968) *Managerial Attitudes and Performance*, London: Irwin.

34. Lawler, E. E. (1973) *Motivation in Work Organizations*, Monterey, CA: Brooks-Cole.
35. Lawler, E. E. (1971) *Pay and Organizational Effectiveness*, New York: McGraw-Hill.
36. Kanungo, R. and Mendonca, M. (1992) *Compensation: Effective Reward Management*, Toronto: Butterworth.
37. Locke, E. A. (1968) 'Towards a theory of task motivation and incentives', *Organization Behavior and Human Performance*, **3**, pp. 152–89.
38. Tubbs, M. E. (1986) 'Goal-setting: a meta-analytic examination of the empirical evidence', *Journal of Applied Psychology*, **71**, pp. 474–83.
39. Latham, G. P. and Locke, E. A. (1990) *A Theory of Goal Setting and Task Performance*, Englewood Cliffs, NJ: Prentice-Hall.
40. Mandel, E. and Novack, G. (1970) *The Marxist Theory of Alienation*, New York: Pathfinder.
41. Rinehart, J. W. (2006) *The Tyranny of Work: Alienation and the Labour Process* (4th edn), Scarborough, ON: Nelson Thomson.
42. Roddick, A. (1991) *Body and Soul*, New York: Crown.
43. Tichy, N. and Sherman, S. (1993) *Control Your Destiny or Someone Else Will*, New York: Doubleday.
44. Hofstede, G. (1998) 'Organization culture', pp. 237–55 in M. Poole and M. Warner (eds), *The Handbook of Human Resource Management*, London: International Thomson Business Press.
45. Mottaz, C. J. (1985) 'The relative importance of intrinsic and extrinsic rewards as determinants of work satisfaction', *Sociological Quarterly*, **26**(3), pp. 365–85.
46. Goldthorpe, J., Lockwood, D., Bechhofer, R. and Platt, J. (1968) *The Affluent Worker: Industrial Attitudes and Behaviour*, Cambridge: Cambridge University Press.
47. Mottaz, C. J. (1986) 'Gender differences in work satisfaction, work-related rewards and values, and the determinants of work satisfaction', *Human Relations*, **39**(4), pp. 359–78.
48. Murry, M. A. and Atkinson, T. (1981) 'Gender differences in correlates of job satisfaction', *Canadian Journal of Behavioural Sciences*, **13**, pp. 44–52.
49. Metcalfe, D. (1989) 'Water notes dry up', *British Journal of Industrial Relations*, **27**(10), pp. 1–32.
50. Hodson, R. (1999) 'Management citizenship behavior: a new concept and an empirical test', *Social Problems*, **46**(3), pp. 460–78.
51. Wilson, F. M. (2003) *Organizational Behaviour and Gender*, Farnham: Ashgate.
52. Daniel, W. W. (1973) 'Understanding employee behaviour in its context', in J. Child (ed.), *Man and Organization*, London: Allen & Unwin.
53. Rousseau, D. M. (1995) *Psychological Contracts in Organisations: Understanding Written and Unwritten Agreements*, Thousand Oaks, CA: Sage.
54. Kelly, J. (2005) 'Industrial relations approaches to the employment relationship', pp. 48–64 in J. A.-M. Coyle-Shapiro, Shore, L. M., Taylor, M. S. and Tetrick, L. E. (eds), *The Employment Relationship*, Oxford: Oxford University Press.
55. Kersley, B., Alpin, C, Forth, J., Bryson, A., Bewley, H., Dix, G. and Oxenbridge, S. (2005) *Inside the Workplace: First Findings from the 2004 Workplace Employment Relations Survey (WERS 2004)*, London: Department of Trade and Industry.
56. Vosko, L. (2000) *Temporary Work: The Gendered Rise of a Precarious Employment Relationship*, Toronto: University of Toronto Press.
57. Charles, N. and James, E. (2003) 'The gender dimensions of job insecurity in the local labour market', *Work, Employment and Society*, **17**(3), pp. 531–52.
58. Leonard, N. H., Beauvais, L. L. and Scholl, R. W. (1999) 'Work motivation: the incorporation of self-concept-based processes', *Human Relations*, **52**(8), pp. 969–98.
59. Fairholm, G. W. (1996) 'Spiritual leadership: fulfilling whole-self needs at work', *Leadership and Organizational Development*, **17**(5), pp. 11–17.
60. Klein, H. J. (1989) 'An integrated control theory model of work motivation', *Academy of Management Review*, **14**, pp. 150–72.
61. Horwitz, F. M., Chan feng Heng and Quazi, H. A. (2003) 'Finders, keepers? Attracting, motivating and retaining knowledge workers', *Human Resource Management Journal*, **13**(4), pp. 23–44.
62. Corby, S., Palmer, S. and Lindop, E. (2009) *Rethinking Reward*, Basingstoke: Palgrave.
63. Hofstede, G. (1998) *Masculinity and Femininity: The Taboo Dimension of National Cultures*, Thousand Oaks, CA: Sage.

64. Hofstede, G. (2001) *Culture's Consequences: Comparing Values, Behaviors, Institutions, and Organizations across Cultures*, Thousand Oaks, CA: Sage.

65. Van de Vliert, E., Van Yperen, N. and Thierry, H. (2008) 'Are wages more important for employees in poorer countries with harsher climates?', *Journal of Organizational Behavior*, **29**, pp. 79–94.

66. Mackenzie, H. (2007) *The Great CEO Pay Race: Over Before it Begins*, Toronto: Canadian Centre for Policy Alternative.

67. Rousseau, D. M. and Ho, V. T. (2000) 'Psychological contract issues in compensation', pp. 273–310 in S. L. Rynes and B. Gerhart (eds), *Compensation in Organizations: Current Research and Practice*, San Francisco: Jossey-Bass.

68. Benabou, R. and Tirole, J. (2003) 'Intrinsic and extrinsic motivation', *Review of Economic Studies*, **70**(3), pp. 489–520.

69. Perkins, T. (2009) 'Financial watchdog tightens leash on banker pay', *Globe and Mail*, March 6, p. A1.

70. House of Commons Treasury Committee Report (2009) *Banking Crisis: Dealing with the Failure of the UK Banks*, London: Stationery Office.

71. Marchington, M. (2008) 'Employee voice systems,' pp. 231–50 in P. Boxall, J. Purcell and P. Wright (eds), *The Oxford Handbook of Human Resource Management*, Oxford: Oxford University Press.

72. Josselson, R. (1987) *Finding Herself: Pathways to Identity Development in Women*, San Francisco: Jossey-Bass.

73. Hackman, J. and Oldham, G. (1980) *Work Redesign*, Reading, MA: Addison-Wesley.

74. Warr, P. B. (ed.) (2002) *Psychology at Work* (5th edn), London: Penguin.

75. Daniels, K. (2000) 'Measures of five aspects of affective well-being at work', *Human Relations*, **53**, pp. 275–94.

76. Patterson, M. and West, M. (1998) 'People power: the link between job satisfaction and productivity', *Centrepiece*, **3**(3), pp. 2–5.

77. Somers, M. J. (2001) 'Thinking differently: assessing nonlinearities in the relationship between work attitudes and job performance using a Bayesian neutral network', *Journal of Occupational and Organizational Psychology*, **74**(1), pp. 47–62.

77. Wilkinson, R. and Pickett, K. (2009) *The Spirit Level: Why More Equal Societies Almost Always Do Better*, London: Allen Lane.

78. Kanter, R. (1990) 'Motivation theory in industrial and organizational psychology', pp. 75–170 in M. D. Dunnette and L. Hough (eds), *Handbook of Industrial and Organizational Psychology*, Palo Alto, CA: Consulting Psychology Press.

GROUPS AND TEAMWORKING

CHAPTER OUTLINE

- Introduction
- Work groups and work teams
- Group dynamics
- Work teams and management theory
- Work teams: ending bureaucracy and extending employee empowerment?
- Paradox in team-based work systems
- Summary and end-of-chapter features
- Chapter case study 1: Building cars in Brazil
- Chapter case study 2: Teams at Land Rock Alliance Insurance

CHAPTER OBJECTIVES

After completing this chapter, you should be able to:

- distinguish between informal and formal work groups
- explain the current popularity of teams in work organizations
- articulate how group norms and cohesiveness exert influence on individual and group behaviour
- describe and critically evaluate the theories of team development
- explain the pros and cons of using groups to make decisions
- identify the different theoretical perspectives and paradoxes related to work teams

INTRODUCTION

Without doubt, everyone will find him- or herself at some point in life to be a member of a group. You have probably already experienced group membership through participating in a sports team, climbing or caving club, jury service, church, political party or study group. In many organizations, people are called upon to work in groups. Work groups influence the behaviour of their members, often enhancing job satisfaction, promoting learning and increasing individual and unit productivity and more effective decision making.

Work groups are not something invented by management consultants. History shows that they have been part of human social development since ancient times. For thousands of years, men and women lived in small hunting and gathering groups, and later they lived in small farming or fishing groups. It is only in the last 200 years, with the advent of industrial capitalism, that small groups have become the exception rather than the rule.[1] The factory system ushered in a minute division of labour and close direct supervision, which substantially improved labour productivity and profits. By the late twentieth century, however, extensive specialization and hierarchical forms of work organization were identified as a 'problem'.

A host of mainstream management literature proselytized the notion that traditional work organization was an obstacle to innovation and competitiveness.[2–4] Team work as a system of paid work is intended to transcend the alleged problems of inflexibility, poor quality, low employee commitment and motivation associated with traditional work structures. Its increased prevalence in Europe and North America is a recognition by employers that competitive advantage comes from so-called lean organizations, the full utilization of their human capital, and a set or 'bundle' of 'soft' human resource management practices that form part of an integrated high-performance workplace (HPW).[5] In the critical literature, team work and HPW initiatives are a means of increasing work intensification, obtaining higher productivity, increasing workplace stress and controlling workers indirectly through a culture of self-control.[5–9]

If you paused and thought about the questions we asked in the 'Stop and reflect' box above, you should appreciate that understanding groups and teams in work organizations is important for several reasons. Team work has become a significant feature of organizational life. Individuals behave differently when in a work group from how they do when they work independently. Team synergy can potentially transform moribund productivity and improve organizational performance. Finally, understanding group dynamics is seen to be an important aspect of managing (controlling) people more effectively.

This chapter introduces the complex phenomenon of work groups and work teams in organizations. It begins by examining the background, nature and behavioural implications of work groups. We also explore the nature of work groups through the concepts of group norms, cohesiveness and learning. Finally, we go beyond management rhetoric, and present arguments and evidence to suggest that self-managed teams shift the focus away from the hierarchy, and direct and bureaucratic **control** processes, to a culture of self-control.

WORK GROUPS AND WORK TEAMS

What are work groups?

The term 'group' can be used to describe a cluster of individuals watching a hockey game or queuing for a bank teller. When studying the behaviour of groups, it is important to distinguish between a mere cluster of individuals and what organizational theorists call a 'psychological group'. This term is used to describe individuals who perceive themselves to be in a group, who have a shared sense of collective identity, and who relate to each other in a meaningful way. We can define a **work group** as two or more people who are in face-to-face interaction, each aware of their membership in the group, and striving to accomplish assigned work tasks.

The first part of this definition suggests that there must be an opportunity for people to interact socially with each other, that is, to communicate with each other, to behave in each other's presence, and to be affected by the other's behaviour. Over time, group members who regularly interact socially become aware of each other's values, feelings and goals, which then influence their behaviour. Although a work

stop reflect

Before reading on, consider your own experience of group membership. Do people behave differently in groups? You might have experienced working in a study group at college or university. Reflect on your experience, and consider what specific behaviours exhibited during the group sessions were helpful to the group. What specific behaviours exhibited were detrimental to the group? How did the group deal with a member who was constantly late or did not complete his or her assigned work for a group assignment?

control: the collection and analysis of information about all aspect of the work organization and the use of comparisons that are either historical and/or based on benchmarking against another business unit

work group: two or more employees in face-to-face interaction, each aware of their positive interdependence as they endeavour to achieve mutual work-related goals

group can theoretically range from two members to an unspecified upper limit, the need to interact limits the size of the group.

The second part of the definition refers to group members' perceptions of the group itself. Members of the group are able to distinguish who is and who is not in the group, and are aware that an action affecting one member is likely to affect all. This part of the definition helps us to exclude mere clusters of people who are simply individuals who happen to be assembled at the same location at a particular time (such as soccer fans, bank customers or airline travellers). These individuals do not consider themselves a part of any identifiable unit, nor do they relate to one another in any meaningful fashion, despite their close proximity.

On the other hand, a soccer team, an airline crew or a project team at the Bank of Scotland would fulfil the criteria for a work group. In a situation of extreme danger – such as the hijacking of an airline – an aggregate of passengers could be transformed into a group. For example, several passengers on US United Airlines Flight 93, which crashed on September 11, 2001, apparently formed a group that stormed the cockpit to prevent the hijackers from carrying out any further terrorist acts.

The third part of the definition implies that group members have common goals, which they work collectively to accomplish. Six individuals drinking coffee in the company rest area at the same time would not necessarily be considered a group. They do not have common goals, nor are they dependent on the outcome of each other's actions. However, six union shop stewards drinking coffee together regularly to discuss health and safety issues or grievances would be considered a work group.

Groups in organizations can be formal or informal. Organizational decision makers create formal work groups to permit collective action on assigned task(s). In this sense, the rationale for creating work groups can be linked to an organization's competitive strategy. A manufacturing strategy that emphasizes flexibility can result in tasks and responsibilities being reassigned from individual employees and supervisors to a group of employees. This process of dividing up the tasks, assigning responsibility and so on, is called **job design**, and it is through the restructuring of work that formal work groups are created and consciously designed. Managers are interested in ensuring that the behaviour of the formal group is directed toward organizational goals. Not surprisingly, therefore, much of mainstream organizational behaviour research focuses on the dynamics of formal work groups.

In addition to formal work groups, organizations also contain **informal work groups**. Managers do not specifically establish these work-based groups; they emerge from the social interaction of workers. Although an organization employs people for their intellectual capital, unlike with other forms of capital, the organization gets the whole person. People bring their personal needs to the workplace. Organizational behaviour theorists suggest that informal work groups are formed as an outcome of psychological processes: the perception of a shared social identity and to fulfil social needs for affiliation and supportive relationships. A cluster of employees can become an informal work group when members influence others' behaviour and contribute to needs satisfaction. Informal work groups are important in that they can help shape communication flows in the organization.

What are work teams?

The words 'group' and 'team' are often used as substitutes. In the management literature, the word '**team**' is more likely to be used in a normative sense as a special type of group with positive traits.[10] Like a soccer team, it has connotations of collaboration, mutual support and shared skill and decision making.[11] The observation and

job design: the process of assigning tasks to a job, including the interdependency of those tasks with other jobs

informal group: two or more people who form a unifying relationship around personal rather than organizational goals

teams: groups of two or more people who interact and influence each other, are mutually accountable for achieving common objectives, and perceive themselves as a social entity within an organization

implied criticism that 'He is not a team player' or 'This group is not a team' expresses the difference in meaning between 'group' and 'team' in the management lexicon. A mainstream text defines a team as 'a set of interpersonal interactions structured to achieve established goals' (ref. 1, p. 539), and two popular writers define a team as 'a small number of people with complementary skills who are committed to a common purpose, performance goals, and approach for which they hold themselves mutually accountable' (ref. 2, p. 45).

Another variant of 'teams' has become part of current managerial rhetoric – the words **'self-managed work team'** (SMWT). The SMWT, which suggests a new way of organizing work, is not the same as a 'work group': an SMWT is 'a group of employees who are responsible for managing and performing technical tasks that result in a product or service being delivered to an internal or external customer' (ref. 12, p. xiii). The difference between work groups and SMWTs is explained in terms of the degree of interdependency and accountability. The interdependence among SMWT members is typically high, and the accountability for the work focuses primarily on the team as a whole rather than the individual group member. Another distinguishing feature of SMWTs is their longevity: SMWTs are typically an integral part of a redesigned organizational structure, brought together for long-term performance goals.

Work teams can be classified according to their position in the organization's hierarchy and their assigned tasks. Figure 4.1 shows three types of work team most commonly found in organizations. Teams that plan and run things are positioned in the top echelon (senior level) of the organization, teams that monitor things occupy the middle levels, and teams that make things occupy the lower levels of the

self-managed work teams: cross-functional work groups organized around work processes that complete an entire piece of work requiring several interdependent tasks, and that have substantial autonomy over the execution of those tasks

Plate 1 – A self-managed work team allows employees in the core work unit to have sufficient autonomy to manage the work process.
Source: Getty Images

organization. It is important to emphasize, however, that the nature of teams varies considerably among organizations, depending on whether they are engaged in value-added activities in small batches or large batches, or whether they provide financial or other services.

The formal definitions of work teams are not so different from the definition of a formal work group, which might explain why both words are used interchangeably in the organizational behaviour literature. However, the conscious use of the word 'team' is not simply a question of semantics. Mainstream management rhetoric is awash with what Bendix called 'a vocabulary of motivation'.[13] In this instance, communication emphasizes the 'team' (with phrases like 'We must all pull together') and the 'family' (suggesting that employees are brothers and sisters and customers are family guests), using these metaphors to obfuscate the power differentials and conflicting interests between management and workers. Whether employees are organized into a 'work group' or a 'work team', the effectiveness of the work configuration will be the outcome of complex group behaviours and processes, which is the focus of the next section.

GROUP DYNAMICS

group dynamics: the systematic study of human behaviour in groups, including the nature of groups, group development, and the interrelations between individuals and groups, other groups and other elements of formal organizations

Group dynamics is the study of human behaviour in groups.[1] The field studies the nature of groups, group development and the interrelations between individuals and groups. Group dynamics or processes emphasize changes in the pattern of activities, the subjective perceptions of individual group members and their active involvement in group life. Studies on group dynamics by mainstream researchers draw attention to two sets of process that underlie group processes: task-oriented activities and maintenance-oriented activities. Task-oriented activities undertaken by the group are aimed at accomplishing goals or 'getting the job done'. Maintenance-oriented activities, on the other hand, point to the subjective perceptions of group members and their active involvement in keeping acceptable standards of behaviour and a general state of well-being within the group. Conventional wisdom argues that the two processes constantly seek to coexist, and an overemphasis of one realm at the expense of the other leads to discontent and withdrawal. An effective group or team is one that creates a reasonable compromise between both realms.[10,14,15]

Some of the major factors influencing group dynamics are shown in Figure 4.2. The framework does not attempt to offer a theory of group dynamics, nor does it

weblink
www.managementhelp.
org/grp_skll/slf_drct/
slf_drct.htm is an online
library devoted to self-
managed teams. At http://
groups.yahoo.com, people
form their own social
groups to exchange ideas.
Visit the site and see how
'virtual groups' work

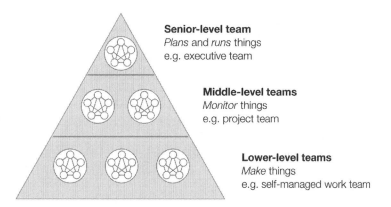

Figure 4.1 – Classification of work teams

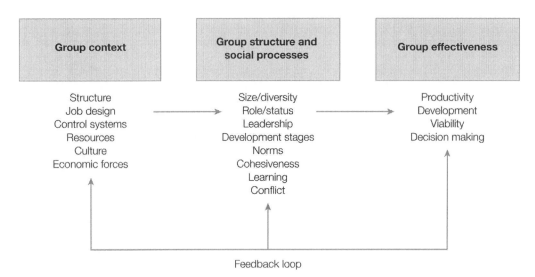

Figure 4.2 – A model of group dynamics

necessarily follow that all elements of the model must, or can, be applied to every work group. We offer it here as a useful heuristic for understanding the complexities of group dynamics. Four major elements are graphically depicted in the model: a context, team structure and processes, group effectiveness, and a feedback loop that links the outcomes back to the other main components. We look at each of the first three elements over the next few pages.

Group context

Although the work group or team is a structure in itself, it is also a subset of a larger structure, the organization. Thus, the work group is constrained to operate within the structure of the organization, and **group context** refers to organizational and job design, organizational control systems, resources and the external political economy and economic forces.

group context: refers to anything from the specific task a work group is engaged in to the broad environmental forces that are present in the minds of group members and may influence them

The implementation of team-based working requires organizational restructuring, by which we mean changing the core dimensions of the organization: its centralization, complexity and formality. Tasks and responsibilities must be designated within and between teams. Task interdependence, which refers to the level of relationship among members in the work activities, can affect group structure, processes and outcomes. Alternative work configurations are typically followed by alternative control systems. For example, when work groups are introduced, the direct supervisory control of employees is typically replaced by a computer-based control of group performance. The adoption of team work is normally contingent on management installing a system to control the redesigned work process.[6]

Resources are another contextual factor affecting group structure and processes. The amount of resources management is willing to commit to teams is directly related to the organizational context. Specifically, the policies and procedures of the organization must provide for sufficient physical (such as computer software), financial and human resources to enable the team to function and complete the task. Inadequate resources, it is argued, will delay group development and have a negative impact on group outcomes.[3]

Group structure

Work groups and teams have a structure that influences the way in which members relate to and interact with one another, and makes it possible to explain individual behaviour within the group. Have you ever noticed that, when people come together in a new group, some listen while others talk? Such differences between group members serve as a basis for the formation of group structure. As differentiation takes place, social relations are formed between members. The stable pattern of relationships among the differentiated elements in the group is called **group structure**.

The group can be differentiated by a number of variables including size, roles, status and leadership. The *size* of the group plays a critical role in how group members interact with one another. The German sociologist Georg Simmel pointed out that increasing the size alters the group's dynamics, since the increased number of relationships results in different interactions.[16] Figure 4.3 shows the incremental impact of group size on relationships. Two individuals form a single relationship; adding a third person results in three relations; a group of seven, however, has 21 relationships. According to Simmel, as groups grow beyond three people, the personal attachments between individuals become looser, and coalitions emerge in which some group members align themselves against other group members. Thus, the more impersonal relationships need additional formal rules and regulations. At the same time, the group's growth allows it to become more stable, because the intensity of the interactions is reduced, and because it becomes better able to withstand the loss of some of its members.

The *composition* or diversity of work groups is another key variable that influences individual behaviour in a group setting. Work group composition can be diverse in terms of gender, ethnicity, age, hierarchical status, performance levels and educational background. Research suggests that group composition is a predictor of members' creative behaviour and the quality of decision making. Gender and hierarchical status diversity tended to decrease a member's creative behaviour, and this

group structure: a stable pattern of social interaction among work group members created by a role structure and group norms

weblink

The notion of diversity and balance in teams is central to Belbin's team role theory. Visit www.belbin.com for more information and www.palgrave.com/business/brattonob2e for an activity on team roles

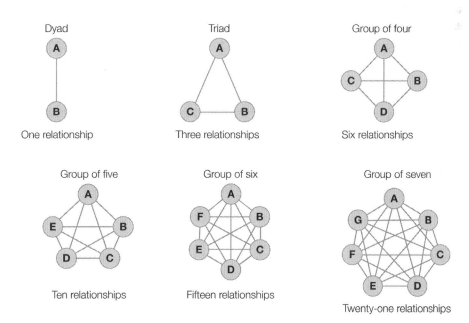

Figure 4.3 – The incremental effects of group size on relationships

negative effect appeared to be particularly strong for women members in a minority and 'low-power' group situation. The group's composition may also impede the shared exchange, discussion and integration of information, with negative effects on decision quality.[17,18]

role: a set of behaviours that people are expected to perform because they hold certain positions in a team and organization

All group members are expected to carry out certain functions. The set of expected behaviours associated with a position within the group constitutes the **role** of the occupant of that position. The role concept helps us understand how a member's behaviour is structured by the prescriptive dictates of the group and/or organization. A team-based culture will influence the roles individuals play within the organization. With HPW forms of organization, a premium is placed on values such as cooperative behaviour with team members, sharing information and expertise with others, and more generally on promoting a social network necessary for effective team performance. Role definition is often used as a diagnostic tool by management consultants to determine causes of poor team performance. Problems of **role ambiguity** – uncertainty on the group member's part about what exactly he or she is supposed to do – and **role conflict** – conflicting requests from more than one source – allegedly have far-reaching negative outcomes on group performance.[3] Role ambiguity and role conflict affect the socialization of new employees into existing work groups.[19]

role ambiguity: uncertainty about job duties, performance expectations, level of authority and other job conditions

role conflict: conflict that occurs when people face competing demands

status: the social ranking of people; the position an individual occupies in society or in a social group or work organization

Status is the relative ranking that a member holds, and indicates the value of that member as perceived by the group. Status is important because it motivates individuals and has consequences for their behaviour. Almost every work group has either a formal or an informal leader, who can influence communications, decision making, learning and similar processes, thereby playing an important part in group's outcomes.

It is necessary, but not sufficient for team efficacy, to have an organizational design strategy that incorporates adequate resources, effective control systems, role clarity and leadership. To be effective, managers and group members must learn to work in the new work structure. The group processes responsible for group development, norms, cohesiveness and learning are extremely important.

Group social processes

group processes: refers to group member actions, communications and decision making

The term **group social processes** refers to the manner in which various aspects of group behaviour are constructed on a continuing basis, and the behaviour that serves to encourage or discourage group learning and to ameliorate or exacerbate group conflict. Understanding group social processes is important in so far as they are often considered to be key predictors of group effectiveness.

Group development

Organizational behaviour theorists typically highlight the importance of understanding the developmental stages that a group must pass through: groups are born, they mature and they die. It is suggested that a group must reach the mature stage before it achieves maximum performance. Of course, it is also acknowledged that not all groups pass through all these stages, and some groups can become fixed in the early stage and remain ineffective and inefficient. A good example of the life-cycle metaphor is Tuckman and Jensen's five-stage cycle of group development model: forming, storming, norming, performing and adjourning (Figure 4.4).[20]

In the *forming* stage, individuals are brought together and there tends to be ambiguity about roles and tasks. Group members are polite as they learn about each other and attempt to establish 'ground rules' for accomplishing the assigned task(s). Dependency on the group leader is said to be high at this stage.

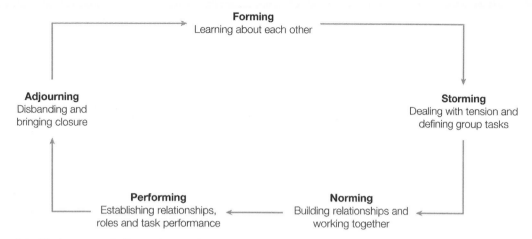

Figure 4.4 – The incremental effects of group size on relationships

In the *storming* stage, individual members become more proactive by taking on specific roles and responsibilities. Members frequently compete for positions in the group, and conflict occurs between individuals, and/or alliances are formed between members. The group leader must be able to facilitate dialogue and handle conflict at this stage.

When group members begin to accept differences of opinion, conform to their roles and cooperate (for instance, sharing information), the group has reached what is called the *norming* stage. As a consensus forms around the group's goals and means of attainment, group cohesion grows.

High productivity is typically achieved at the *performing* stage of group development. A high level of trust in each group member is prevalent at this phase, and there is 'consensual validation' in the sense that members are positively valued for their specific attributes and qualities.

A work group does not exist infinitely. The *adjourning* stage refers to individuals leaving the group and being replaced by others, or to the group's disbandment. Social rituals, such as having a party, often accompany group disbandment.

Tuckman and Jensen's model is based on the premise that a group must go through each stage before being able to move on to the next, and every transition holds the potential risk of regression to an earlier stage. Organizational behaviour theorists taking a managerialist perspective have tended to interpret the five-stage model in terms of levels of performance, with group productivity being higher after the second stage. While this assumption may be correct, what makes a work group effective is more complex than this model acknowledges. Although the model has become entrenched in mainstream organizational behaviour texts and in management training, it has more recently been shown 'to be of little or no assistance in getting teams to perform better' (ref. 3, p. 34).

An earlier critique of Tuckman and Jensen's five-stage model found the phenomenon of 'punctuated equilibrium' to be a more useful concept to explain group development.[21] Specifically, a team does not accomplish a great deal up to about the halfway point to completion (this midpoint occurring regardless of the time-frame involved). At the midpoint, there is an acceleration of activity by members to accomplish their assigned work. In essence, the 'punctuated equilibrium' model characterizes work groups as exhibiting long periods of inertia interspersed with shorter bursts of activity, initiated primarily by their members' awareness of the impending completion deadline. This would suggest, therefore, that not all groups develop in a universal linear fashion.

The research on group development has drawn criticism because much of it has tended to be laboratory-based rather than workplace-based research. For example, old favourites like Tuckman and Jensen's model were developed from work with therapy, laboratory or training groups, not 'real teams in real contexts'. Group development models that predict linear sequential phases have particularly been criticized. As Kline graphically points out:

> Imagine the following situation. The cockpit crew of a 747 boards the plane twenty minutes before take-off. You are seated in seat 117B, and as the airplane rushes down runway nine you hope like hell that this team is past the storming stage of group development. (ref. 3, p. 5)

Kline argues that there is something, personalities aside, about the aircrew that enables them to fly the aircraft safely, even when they have just met one another. These 'contextual variables', she asserts, are powerful tools for understanding group dynamics and group performance.

Although alternative research suggests that every group does not go through all the development stages, Tuckman and Jensen's model can be a useful heuristic for understanding group dynamics and why some groups fail to perform. A group might be ineffective and inefficient because individuals are pulling in different directions, since the goals of the group have not been agreed. Alternatively, individuals might have a tendency to dismiss or ridicule others' thoughts, ideas and feelings, which leads to low trust among the group. For all these reasons, effective group functioning and learning might be hindered. The main conclusion drawn from the group development models presented here is that a team-based organizational structure does not imply an effective and efficient organization. Top managers introducing team-based work structures need to attend to the development of group interactions.

Plate 2 Organizations send their employees to outdoor corporate training centres where they learn to work as teams.
Source: Getty Images

Group norms

Have you ever noticed that professors do not normally criticize other professors? Why? The answer is 'norms'. Groups significantly influence their members' behaviour through the operation of norms. Social norms are a set of expected patterns of behaviour that are established and shared by the group's members. Norms inform members on what they ought and ought not to do under certain situations. A group's norms do not occur in a vacuum: they represent the interaction of historical, social and psychological processes. In the workplace, for example, a new employee joining a group will assess the norms for work effort from how most individuals in the group behave. In turn, members of the group observe the extent to which the new member's behaviour matches the group's norms. Norms develop in work groups around work activities (the means and speed), around attitudes and opinions that should be held by group members regarding the workplace, and around communications, concerning appropriate language.

group norms: the unwritten rules and expectations that specify or shape appropriate human behaviour in a work group or team

The Hawthorne studies[22] highlighted the importance of **group norms** to management theorists. The researchers identified three important norms: no 'rate-busting' (working too hard), no 'chiselling' (working too little) and no 'squealing' (telling the supervisor anything that could undermine the group). Group members who significantly deviated from these norms were subjected to either ridicule or physical punishment. Groups typically enforce norms that:

- facilitate the group's survival
- allow members to express the central values of the group
- reduce embarrassing interpersonal problems for group members – for instance, a ban on discussing religion or politics at work.[23]

Norms are communicated to new employees through a process called 'group socialization', whereby the new member learns the group's principal values and how these values are articulated through norms. Emergent group leaders differ from their peers in that they make more attempts to influence the group and play a role in forming team norms.[24]

Group cohesiveness

cohesiveness: refers to all the positive and negative forces or social pressures that cause individuals to maintain their membership in specific groups

The term **cohesiveness** refers to the complex forces that give rise to the perceptions by members of group identity and attractiveness of group membership. The cohesiveness of a group has a major effect on the behaviour of its members, because higher cohesion amplifies the potency of group norms. A series of experiments conducted by Solomon Asch in 1952 and Stanley Milgram in 1963 suggested that group membership can engender conformity, and also that members are likely to follow the directions of group authority figures, even when it means inflicting pain on another individual. These psychological experiments can be used to help explain the brutalizing acts inflicted on prisoners by both male and female US guards at Abu Ghraib prison.[25]

weblink
For more information on Milgram's classic psychological prison experiment, go to Stanford University's site: www.prisonexp.org

A cohesive group can develop norms that can be a great asset to the organization, for example a norm that prescribes voluntary overtime working when required. Equally, a cohesive group can undermine organizational goals, for example by enforcing conformity to a work effort below what is considered acceptable by managers. Not surprisingly, therefore, sources of group cohesiveness are of considerable interest to mainstream organizational behaviour theorists and managers. For example, a recent study contends that humour can have a positive effect on a variety of group or team processes including group cohesiveness and the management of emotion.[26]

The attractiveness of a group is partly determined by its composition. Members of the group need to get along with each other, which might be difficult if members have very different values, attitudes towards work or interests. Research suggests that behaviour in work groups is shaped by a sex difference in aggressiveness, with male members engaging in more dominating behaviour than female members. Studies have found that, in groups, men talk more frequently, interrupt others and express anger more than women (see ref. 27, especially pp. 181–3). As a result, more men than women are chosen as group leaders. In institutions of learning, the experiences of work groups by women and faculty members from racial and ethnic minorities tend to differ significantly from the experiences of white male group members.[28]

Ensuring diversity in a work group or team is not only an equity matter – a lack of diversity might inhibit some of the benefits of group working. An early study suggests that moderate heterogeneity in a work group balances the requirements of cohesion and productivity.[29] As we will examine in the next section, one notable disadvantage of groups that are *too* cohesive is that their decision-making ability can be impaired by what Janis termed '**groupthink**'.[30] He defined this group phenomenon as a psychological drive for consensus at any cost, which suppresses dissent and the evaluation of alternatives in cohesive decision-making groups.

Group learning

We turn now to another aspect of social interaction within groups and teams: work-based learning. It will be apparent from this review of team theory and practice that expanding workers' skill sets and **empowering** workers to make prescribed decisions has significant implications for learning in the workplace. Rather than learning a narrow set of skills, the need for flexibility and interchangeability necessitates that workers acquire new knowledge and technical skills to perform the new repertoire of tasks. In addition, the experience of 'lived reality' – decision making, trial and error experimentation – and the social relations associated with teams create their own dynamic environment for enhancing informal work-based learning.

If the group or team is going to make its own decisions, control quality and control its own behaviour, members must engage in learning. Adult educators and human resource development theorists have suggested that, in order for a group or team to learn, individual members of the unit must be able to learn: that is, to experiment, reflect on previous action, engage in dialogue, and share and build on their individual knowledge.[31,32] Adopting a culture of learning in the workplace impacts on innovation, employment relations and leadership style.

Group conflict

Work groups do not exist in isolation: they are located within capitalist workplace dynamics and linked by a network of relationships with other groups. Unsurprisingly, with the proliferation of teams in organizations, there is more research on behaviours that serve to ameliorate or exacerbate the effect that group conflict has on their effectiveness. In the critical studies, analysts have highlighted the inevitable tensions between team-based HPW rhetoric and the reality of work intensification and job insecurity.[33] Mainstream research on group conflict is, however, generally limited to investigating how dysfunctional behaviour at individual or group level affects the variance in groups' performance generally. There are many definitions for the term *conflict*. A broad definition describes conflict as 'that behaviour by organization members which is expended in opposition to other members' (ref. 34, p. 411).

groupthink: the tendency of highly cohesive groups to value consensus at the price of decision quality

weblink
For more information on how 'groupthink' can influence decision making, visit www.afirstlook.com; www.abacon.com. Search for 'groupthink'

empowerment: a psychological concept in which people experience more self-determination, meaning, competence and impact regarding their role in the organization

Researchers widely recognize that group conflict is comprised of two dimensions: task and emotional conflict.[35] *Task conflict* refers to disputes over group members' tasks or the extent to which members disagree on the utilization of resources or ideas related to group tasks. *Emotional conflict*, which is also known as relational conflict, is more personal and involves personality clashes within groups and incompatibilities among team members, or the extent to which tension or verbal or non-verbal friction characterizes members' interaction within the group. Exemplars of specific types of behaviour associated with task and emotional conflict are shown in Table 4.1.

Psychological studies confirm the notion that individuals' personalities are part of the contributions that group members make to work groups, and, moreover, a mix of these individuals' personalities plays a key role in how intragroup conflict unfolds. It is well documented how many occupations regard team work and support from team members as 'lifelines' in coping with the various demands of work. For example, nurses and air cabin crew are known to rely upon support from fellow co-workers to help them deal with work-related emotion and difficult situations.[36] Studies on the consequences of members' emotions on team performance show that the team members' shared negative emotion, or what is called 'negative affective tone', is inversely related to team performance.[37] A conceptual framework for linking dysfunctional group behaviour and group effectiveness is shown in Figure 4.5.

The proposed sequence of incidents depicted in the model begins with dysfunctional group behaviour causing an increase in what is labelled groups' 'negative affective tone' – groups' collective shared experience of negative emotions. In turn, it is hypothesized that that greater levels of negative group affective tone tend to reduce group effectiveness. It also proposes that 'display rules' capable of adjusting or varying the expression of negative emotions through verbal and non-verbal (for example, facial or body) cues is critical to groups' goal-directed behaviour and effectiveness. A study by Dunlop and Lee found that dysfunctional behaviour predicted 24 per cent of the variance in groups' performance.[38] With this assertion in mind, the model further proposes that emotion management strategies will mediate the effect of negative group affective tone.[37]

Research findings suggest that how well conflict resolution strategies address a group-level balance between task and emotion management is what yields superior group productivity and viability.[39] On the basis of reported results, when work groups withhold displays of negative emotionality, it seems they are better able to control the detrimental performance implications of dysfunctional behaviour.[37]

Table 4.1 – Task-related and emotion-related behaviours in groups

Task-related behaviours	Emotion-related behaviours
Goal setting	Criticizing
Integrating	Judging
Utilizing resources	Violence
Calculating	Bullying
Compromising	Favouritism
Decision making	Teasing
Evaluating	Sexual harassment

Source: Adapted from Proctor et al. (2009)[90]

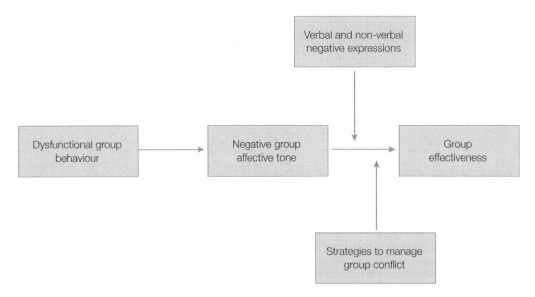

Figure 4.5 – A conceptual framework for examining intragroup conflict
Source: Adapted from Cole, Walter and Bruch (2008),[37] p. 946, itself based on Brown et al (2005),[91] p. 793

Intergroup conflict might also occur. One explanation for intergroup conflict is that when a group is successful, members' self-esteem increases, and conversely when group members' self-esteem is threatened, they are more prone to disparage members of other groups.[40–43] Another alternative explanation contends that intergroup conflict is the result of one group's perceiving another group as a threat to its goal attainment.[1,3,44]

Work and Society: Making it work

With the emergence of the idea of 'positive psychology', there has been a pronounced effort to shift research attention away from its traditional focus on abnormal or problematic patterns of human functioning, and towards the study of optimal functioning and human flourishing. This shift in attention away from the problematic and towards the optimal is evident in many fields of study – from organizational behaviour research to studies of marriage. For example, in a pioneering analysis of marriage dynamics, Frank Fincham and his colleagues argue (2007) that the traditional preoccupation with conflict in marriage must be corrected. Their article focuses on 'naturally occurring marital self-repair processes' and seeks to understand the mechanisms that enable some couples to bounce back from conflict while others separate or continue to live together unhappily.

Does this research on marriages have anything to tell us about group dynamics? Obviously, the differences between small work groups and marriages are fundamental, and there is no need to review those differences here. The question is, are there enough similarities between work groups and marriages to derive some insights into group dynamics from recent research on marriages? You be the judge. Consider the following synopsis of the work of Fincham and his colleagues.

Inspired by the move toward positive psychology, Fincham and his co-investigators set out to identify what distinguishes marriages that endure (or 'bounce back' after trouble) from marriages that fall apart. They found that couples who stay together do not necessarily experience conflict-free relationships. What distinguishes these resilient couples from couples who separate are mechanisms that work to defuse conflict, often without the help of external interventions. One might say that spouses in these resilient couples exhibit capacities for 'self-regulation' and the couples themselves are capable of 'self-repair'.

To understand how this works, Fincham and his colleagues suggest we consider how conflicts unfold in time. An initial disagreement or problematic event will often escalate over time as couples become locked into cyclical patterns of 'tit-for-tat' responding. Resilient couples seem to be able to avoid this pattern. They do so by engaging in two kinds of regulation: they regulate both 'the degree to which a negative partner behaviour elicits a correspondingly negative response' and 'the extent to which negative partner behavior produces a change in the overall view of the relationship' (2007, p. 283). With regard to this second kind of regulation, one can imagine a wife (or husband) coming to the realization: this marriage is not worth saving. Spouses in resilient couples seem to be able to avoid these profound and irreversible changes of heart.

The two kinds of regulation associated with resilient couples are clearly relevant to work groups. Work groups experience internal conflict, and people in work groups become locked into cyclical patterns of 'tit-for-tat' responding. As with couples, the likelihood that members of work groups can resolve their conflicts without resorting to external mediation will depend on their capacity to engage in the kinds of regulation identified by Fincham and his colleagues.

Readers may feel comfortable with the analogy between marriages and work group thus far. But consider the proposed explanation of why some couples more than others are able to engage in effective self-regulation. Fincham and his colleagues offer the following list of factors that they believe enhance a couple's capacity for self-regulation and repair:

> Without methods for changing negative processes over time, or for changing direction once negative interactions begin, even the best marital skills for dealing with conflict may provide couples with insufficient basis for long-term marital satisfaction. The framework [described in this article has] ... the potential to help us understand the impact [on self-regulatory processes] of forgiveness ... commitment ... valuing sacrifice ... and sanctification. (p. 287)

stop!   Fincham and his colleagues associate this list of qualities – forgiveness, commitment, valuing sacrifice and sanctification – with couples who engage in effective self-regulation. Would these same qualities be associated with the optimal functioning of work groups? How would each of the four qualities contribute to higher levels of self-regulation among work group members?

Given its links to organized religion, the idea of sanctification may seem irrelevant to many work groups. Is there a secular version of sanctification that might be relevant to a broader range of work groups?

Sources and further information

Bakkle, A. and Schaufeli, W. (2008) 'Positive organizational behavior: engaged employees in flourishing organizations', *Journal of Organizational Behavior*, 29, pp. 147–54.

Fincham, F., Stanley, S. and Beach, S. (2007) 'Transformative processes in marriage: an analysis of emerging trends', *Journal of Marriage and the Family*, 69, pp. 275–92.

Note: This feature was written by David MacLennan, Assistant Professor at Thompson Rivers University, BC, Canada.

The traditional managerial perspective tends to hold that conflicts between individuals and groups, and between workers and management, are a bad thing. An alternative perspective, the *interactionist theory*, holds that conflicts in work groups are productive and can increase rather than decrease job performance.[45] The view holds that group leaders should encourage an ongoing 'optimum' level of conflict, which allows the group to be self-critical, creative and viable. But notions of 'win–lose' scenarios complicate estimates of what constitutes an 'optimal level' of conflict. It has been suggested, for instance, that the more the intergroup conflict is defined as a 'win–lose' situation, the more predictable are the effects of the conflict on the social relationships within the group and on relations between work groups.[1]

stop reflect

Sociologists maintain that relationships formed in groups shape members' behaviour. Think about your own experience of working in a group. What norms and values did the group exhibit? Did any particular members challenge a particular group norm? If so, how did the other group members respond to the challenge? If they did not, why not?

Group effectiveness

Most group theory examines group effectiveness or outcomes in terms of group performance and group decision making. Since the widespread proliferation of team work, much research has been occupied with investigating the link between work teams and performance. Two aspects of group effectiveness are examined in this section: performance and decision making.

Group performance

Research on group performance has often drawn upon Hackman's normative theory of group effectiveness, where effectiveness consists of (1) productivity, (2) employee development, or the opportunity of the individual team member to learn from her or his experiences within the team as well as from other team members, and (3) team viability, or the degree to which members of the team are able to continue working together in the future.[46] The group literature contends that a combination of high-level cohesion and norms, consistent with organizational objectives, will have a positive effect on team productivity.[47–49] Figure 4.6 illustrates the relationship between group cohesiveness and group performance norms. Improved productivity of employees in SMWTs is said to stem from the fact that the interrelationship between the configuration of job design and employment practices inevitably leads to more intrinsic **job satisfaction**, higher team member commitment and the mobilization of greater discretionary effort from employees.[50,51]

job satisfaction: a person's attitude regarding his or her job and work content

Group decision making

In theory, one advantage of cohesive groups is that, by combining member resources, they make better decisions than those made by a single individual. In mathematical logic, this phenomenon of groups, called synergy, suggests that 2 + 2 is greater than 4. The concept is used extensively in mainstream texts to understand group processes and to justify the implementation of work teams. The general assumption is that moderately cohesive work teams (sufficiently diverse to avoid groupthink), together with better communications and 'enlightened' leadership, are best able to encourage the sharing of information and group learning – which results in superior decision-making outcomes. In terms of group decision making, here we examine some important concepts and empirical research on the decision-making performance of groups.

An important concept that might cause groups not to live up to their decision-making potential is *conformity* for people to change their behaviour to fit the norms of a group or team. It may make sense to follow others' behaviour or judgement when you are inexperienced or when the situation is ambiguous, but just how strongly do group norms influence individual behaviour and decision making when the situation is unmistakable?

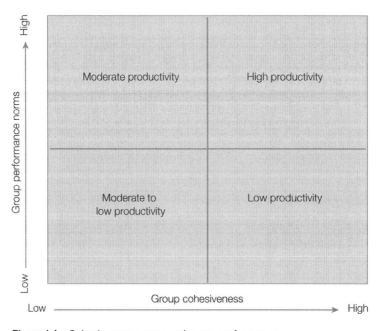

Figure 4.6 – Cohesiveness, norms and group performance

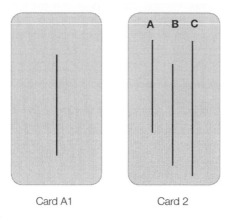

Card A1   Card 2

Figure 4.7 – An example of the cards used in Asch's experiment in group conformity

Research by Solomon Asch and Stanley Milgram provided the answer to this question.[52,53] Asch recruited several groups of students, allegedly to study visual perception. Before the experiment began, he explained to all the students, apart from one student in each group, that the real purpose was to put pressure on the one selected student. Each group of students was asked to estimate the lengths of lines presented on a card. A sample line was shown at the left, and the group was to choose which of the three lines on the right matched it (Figure 4.7). Group members were seated so that the subject answered last. Group pressure did not affect the subjects' perception, but it did affect their behaviour. Initially, as planned, group members made the correct matches (B on Card 2). When, however, Asch's accomplices made incorrect responses, the uninformed subject became uncomfortable, and 76 per cent of the subjects chose to conform by answering incorrectly on at least one trial. The study shows how strong the tendency to conform can be, even when the pressure comes from people we do not know.

In Milgram's controversial study, a researcher explained to male recruits that they would be participating in an experiment on how physical punishment affects adult learning. The learner, actually an accomplice of Milgram's, was seated in a fake electric chair, with electrodes fastened to the wrist and secured by leather straps. In an adjoining room, the subject, playing the role of educator, was seated in front of a replica 'shock generator' with the capacity to administer an electric 'shock' of between 15 and 315 'volts' to the learner. The educator was directed to read aloud pairs of words, and the learner was asked to recall the second word. Whenever the adult learner failed to answer correctly, the educator was instructed to apply an electric shock. Although the educator heard moans and then screams as the level of voltage increased, none of the subjects questioned the experiment. Milgram's research suggests that people are likely to follow the directions of 'legitimate authority figures', even when it means inflicting pain on another individual. To learn about how this classic experiment by Milgram has been related to contemporary events, see ref. 54.

As previously mentioned, Irving Janis's study illustrates how 'experts' can succumb to group pressure.[30] Interestingly, to illustrate the concept of groupthink, Janis analysed the ill-fated attempt by President Kennedy's administrative team to invade Cuba in 1961. He argues that the executive group advising the US President displayed all the symptoms of groupthink: they were convinced of their invulnerability, and 'self-censorship' prevented members from expressing alternative views even when intelligence information did not align with the group's beliefs. There was, according to Janis, an illusion of unanimity, with silence being interpreted as consent. In other words, the pressures for conformity that can arise in a highly cohesive group can cloud members' judgement and the decision-making process. Table 4.2 outlines some symptoms of groupthink.

Obviously, groupthink results in low-quality decisions. More seriously, it has been implicated in the decision processes that led to NASA's fatal launch of the space shuttle Challenger in 2003, and the US and UK invasion of Iraq in 2003. Prior to the invasion, the US official position was that Iraq illegally possessed weapons of mass destruction in violation of UN Security Council Resolution 1441 and had to be disarmed by force. The decision to embark on the Iraq invasion, termed 'Operation Iraqi Freedom' was made by President George W. Bush and a small group of military and intelligence advisers. After investigating the events, which continue to shape the course of twenty-first century history as we write, a US Senate Committee found that the Central Intelligence Agency had dismissed alternative reports, and that the intelligence community as a whole suffered from 'collective group think'.[55] The research by Asch, Milgram and Janis tells us that groups influence the behaviour of their members, altering perceptions of reality and often promoting conformity, which can lead to imperfect and even catastrophic decisions.

The phenomenon of groupthink, therefore, has the potential to undermine the group's ability to appraise alternative choices and make quality decisions. Another phenomenon that has the potential to adversely affect decision making is group polarization. This refers to the tendency of groups to make more extreme decisions than managers and employees working alone. For example, suppose that a board of governors of a college meets to make a decision on the future of a new sports complex for the college. Individual board members might come to the meeting with various degrees of support or opposition to the project. However, by the end of the board meeting, it is highly possible that the board of governors will agree on a more ambitious (that is, a higher financial cost) plan than the average individual had when the board meeting began.

One reason for the more ambitious preference is that individual board members feel less personally responsible for the decision consequences because the entire board of governors makes the decision. Another reason is that board members become comfortable with more extreme positions when they realize that co-members also support the same position. Persuasive arguments favouring the dominant position

Table 4.2 – Symptoms of groupthink

Symptom	Description
Illusion of invulnerability	Group members are arrogant and ignore obvious danger signals
Illusion of morality	Groups decision(s) are not only perceived as sensible, they are also perceived as morally correct
Rationalization	Counter-arguments are rationalized away
Stereotypes of outsiders	Members construct unfavourable stereotypes of those outside the group who are the targets of their decisions
Self-censorship	Members perceive that unanimous support exists for their decisions and action
Mindguard	Individual(s) within the group shield the group from information that goes against its decisions

OB and globalization

Power and culture in work team relations

The globalization of work has opened new opportunities for workers from different cultural backgrounds to work closely with each other – both in person and remotely. Diverse work teams can have positive effects on productivity and problem solving by generating a greater number of innovative ideas and approaches (Earley and Gibson, 2002). Many organizations with overseas operations, however, have also encountered challenges in managing multicultural work teams. These challenges are primarily related to team members' different cultural understandings about their role in the team (and within the larger organization) and how the work should be accomplished.

In an insightful study, Mutabazi and Derr (2003) explore the cultural and historical roots of a breakdown in work team relationships at a Franco-Senegalese organization the authors call Socometal, whose work teams were made up of French expatriates and local Senegalese workers. Mutabazi and Derr concluded that inefficiencies and misunderstandings in these multicultural work teams were, to a great extent, connected with the enduring legacy of colonialism. They explain:

> the problem associated with multiculturalism [on work teams] comes from preexisting attitudes about relations between Africa and the West. This is a deeply-rooted relationship with perceptions distorted by historical consternation. On one side, the West as the dominant partner overemphasizes its own culture, ideals and conceptions of the world … the resulting tendency is to impose this cultural determination upon the party that is considered inferior … [and] this characteristic of multiculturalism becomes embedded in the relationship creating a vicious cycle of misunderstanding. (p. 3)

At Socometal, French managers and work team members did not understand the Senegalese community-based approach to team work, which relies on the circulation of people, goods, services and information through local social and economic networks. Likewise, the Senegalese workers did not understand the approaches of the French expatriate managers and workers, mistaking their focus on top-down decision making and individual competition as an assertion of superiority. The result was the reproduction of colonial power relationships between French and Senegalese workers, and work teams that were 'characterized by indifference toward the values and perspectives of fellow team members … The professional and personal difficulties that [ensued led] to a breakdown of operations' (Mutabazi and Derr, 2003, p. 4).

This case highlights the centrality of power and culture in organizational behaviour. Gibson and Zellmer-Bruhn (2001) remind us that workplaces are culturally situated, and that relationships within organizations are shaped by culturally and historically embedded power relationships. Misunderstandings about work team relationships and responsibilities can be exacerbated in situations where team members make assumptions about their colleagues' capabilities and motivations based on preconceived notions. The potential of multicultural work teams to excel will remain untapped as long as they are managed according to a single cultural paradigm. Effective management approaches in these situations must address cultural misunderstandings and power imbalances head on, and provide enough flexibility to incorporate multiple approaches to team work and decision making into the organization.

stop!   Have you ever worked on a project or a work team with members from different cultural backgrounds? Discuss any culturally based misunderstandings or 'disconnects' that you or your colleagues might have encountered while working on the project. How did you address your differences?

Can you think of any other examples of how historical relationships between nations or cultures could affect organizational behaviour if members of those groups were assigned to the same work team?

Sources and further information

Earley, P. C. and Gibson, C. B. (2002) *Multinational Work Teams: A New Perspective*, Mahwah, NJ: Lawrence Erlbaum Associates.

Gibson, C. B. and Zellmer-Bruhn, M. E. (2001) 'Metaphors and meaning: an intercultural analysis of the concept of teamwork', *Administrative Science Quarterly*, 46(2), pp. 274–303.

Mutabazi, E. and Derr, C. B. (2003) 'The management of multicultural teams: the experience of Afro-Occidental teams', Research Paper 13, *European Entrepreneurial Learning*. Available at: www.em-lyon.com/%5Cressources%5Cge%5Cdo cuments%5Cpublications%5Cwp%5C2003-13.pdf; http://cat.inist.fr/?aModele=afficheN&cpsidt=18098760 (accessed September 22, 2009).

Note: This feature was written by Gretchen Fox, Anthropologist, Timberline Natural Resource Group, Canada.

convince doubtful members and help form a consensus around the most ambitious or extreme option. So persuasion, group support and shifting responsibility explain why groups make more extreme decisions.

Research has repeatedly demonstrated that group decision making is not always superior. In reality, groups sometimes do perform better than the average group member but rarely do better than the best member.[56] One explanation is that even relatively homogeneous groups often fail to exchange their members' unique resources. One key assumption underpinning the enthusiasm for group-based decision making is the expectation to benefit from group members' distributed experiences and informational resources. This point is particularly important with regard to group diversity enhancing the quality of group decisions. Increasingly, diversity is an organizational fact of life, and many work groups are diverse in terms of the characteristics of their membership, bringing together members who may differ in gender, ethnicity, age, disability, hierarchical status, educational background and so forth.

Research on diversity in work teams has shown mixed results regarding the effects of group diversity on team decision making. On the one hand, the processing of decision-relevant information may benefit from a wider pool, variety of perspectives and life experiences in more diverse groups. On the other hand, diversity may actually impede the exchange, discussion and integration of decision-relevant information, with consequential negative effects on decision quality.[18] Others suggest that increasing diversity can have both positive and negative effects on group information processing and decision making contingent on 'individuals' beliefs about diversity'.[57] Thus, educating employees in diverse organizations to value diversity can improve the quality of decisions. Furthermore, the positive effects of diversity might be propagated through several structured group processes that are designed to improve the exchange of group members' unique information and the decision quality. These structured group decision-making processes include brainstorming, the nominal group technique and the stepladder technique.

Clearly, group social processes are complex and contentious, and are strongly influenced by the individual characteristics of team members and by dominant gender, race and power patterns. The wealth of research and interest in work teams over the last decade is related to the changing fashion in US and European management theory on how to compete in conditions of globalized capitalism.

weblink

For examples of team working in European and North American companies, visit: www. honda.com; www.sony. com; http://ptcpartners. com/Team/home. htm; www.dti.gov.uk/ employment/useful-links/ index.html. Search for '2004 employee relations survey'. This site gives a summary of the UK 2004 survey, including a section on work teams

WORK TEAMS AND MANAGEMENT THEORY

The theoretical interest in work groups or teams draws upon human relations, socio-technical and Japanese perspectives on organizational design.[5,6,12,58] Pioneering work on human relations by Roethlisberger and Dickson, Mayo, Maslow and McGregor focused top managers' attention on the importance of social relations within work groups.[22,59–61]

The collaborative research by Roethlisberger, an industrial psychologist from Harvard University, and Dickson, a manager at the Western Electric plant, involved studying the job performance of two groups of front-line workers doing identical work but in separate rooms. Each work group's productivity was carefully monitored. One work group – the study group – experienced ergonomic changes including increasing the intensity of the lighting in the workshop. The study group's productivity increased. The other work group – the control group – experienced no changes in lighting. However, to the astonishment of the researchers, its productivity increased also. Even more mystifying to the researchers, when the level of light intensity was lowered for the study group, the results showed that output continued to go up. After repeated experiments over many years, the researchers began to make connections between social interaction and job performance. In 1939, Roethlisberger and Dickson wrote:

> The study of the bank wiremen showed that their behaviour at work could not be understood without considering the informal organization of the group and the relation of this informal organization to the total social organization of the company. The work activities of the group, together with their satisfactions and dissatisfactions, had to be viewed as manifestations of a complex pattern of interrelations. (ref. 59, pp. 551–2)

After the Second World War, the work of Maslow and McGregor helped US human relations advocates to clarify their perspective, with its focus on the interrelations between workers and the quality of the employment relationship.

In Europe, much of the early research on work teams was conducted within the framework of sociotechnical **systems theory**. This theory developed from work in 1951 on autonomous work teams in the British coal-mining industry under the supervision of Trist and Bamforth. These researchers proposed that 'responsible autonomy' should be granted to primary work groups, and that group members should learn more than one role, so that an interchangeability of tasks would be possible within the group. The flexibility would permit the completion of sub-whole units. The studies showed that the labour process in mining could be better understood in terms of two systems: the technical system – including machinery and equipment – and the social system, including the social relations and interactions among the miners.

Later advocates of the sociotechnical systems approach to organizational design argued that work teams provide a work regime for achieving the 'best match' between technical and social considerations or 'systems'. The term 'best match' is used to describe the relationship between the social and technological systems of the organization, where each is sensitive to the demands of the other.[12]

Attempts to implement the sociotechnical systems approach have included work redesign to 'enrich' jobs. The concept of '**job enrichment**' refers to a number of different processes of **rotating**, **enlarging** and aggregating tasks. It increases the range of tasks, skills and control that workers have over the way they work, either individually or in teams. Job enrichment theory, also known as **job characteristics** theory, was given theoretical prominence by the work of Turner and Lawrence, and Hackman and Oldham.[29,62] As a counter to the thinking underlying Taylorism and Fordism, the job enrichment model has been influential in the design of work teams. It suggests a casual relationship between five core job characteristics and the worker's psychological state. If this relationship is positive, it leads in turn to positive outcomes. The five core job characteristics contained in the model are defined as:

1 *skill variety*: the degree to which the job requires a variety of different activities in carrying out the work, requiring the use of a number of the worker's skills and talents
2 *task identity*: the degree to which the job requires completion of a whole and identifiable piece of work
3 *task significance*: the degree to which the job has a substantial impact on the lives or work of other people

stop reflect
Think about your experience of working in a group. Do Roethlisberger and Dickson's findings resonate with any aspect of your own view on group working? Why?

systems theory: a set of theories based on the assumption that social entities, such as work organizations, can be viewed as if they were self-regulating bodies exploiting resources from their environment (inputs) and transforming the resources (exchanging and processing) to provide goods and services (outputs) in order to survive

job enrichment: employees are given more responsibility for scheduling, coordinating and planning their own work

job rotation: the practice of moving employees from one job to another

job enlargement: increasing the number of tasks employees perform in their jobs

job characteristics model: a job design model that relates the motivational properties of jobs to specific personal and organizational consequences of those properties

stop reflect
Think about your
experience of working in a
group. Do Roethlisberger
and Dickson's findings
resonate with any aspect
of your own view on group
working? Why?

4 *autonomy*: the degree to which the job provides substantial freedom, independence and discretion to the worker in scheduling the work and in determining the procedures to be used in carrying it out

5 *feedback*: the degree to which the worker possesses information on the actual results of her or his performance.

The more that a job possesses the five core job characteristics, the greater the motivating potential of the job (Figure 4.8).

The model also recognizes the importance of learning to achieve motivation and outcome goals. Workers' work-related learning is implicitly linked to the existence of the 'moderators' – knowledge and skills, growth need strength and context satisfaction – contained in the model. The presence of moderators is used to explain why jobs that are theoretically high in motivating potential will not automatically generate high levels of motivation and satisfaction for all workers.

The argument goes that an employee with a low 'growth need' is less likely to experience a positive outcome when her or his work is 'enriched'. Thus, the neo-human relations approach to job design in general, and the job characteristic model in particular, emphasized the fulfilment of social or relatedness needs by recomposing fragmented jobs. In certain circumstances, self-managed teams could provide an alternative to individual job enrichment.

The quality of work and work-related learning in small SMWTs rests on five principles of 'good' job design:

◉ The first principle is *wholeness*: the scope of the job is such that it includes all the tasks to complete a product or process.

◉ The second principle involves individual and group *learning and development*. Opportunities exist to engage in a variety of fulfilling and meaningful tasks,

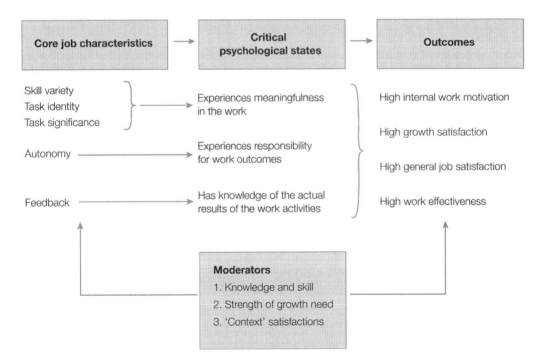

Figure 4.8 – Oldham and Hackman's job characteristics model
Source: Oldham and Hackman (1980)[29]

allowing team members to learn a range of skills within a community of practice, and facilitating job flexibility.[63]

- The third principle relates to *governance and self-regulation*. With the focus on product differentiation and the rise of knowledge-based economies, the imperatives of work do not permit managers to master all the challenges. As a result, they must allow team and project members to assume responsibility for the pace of work, problem solving and quality control.
- The fourth principle involves occupational *wellness and safety*. Work is designed to maintain the safety and wellness of team members and to support a good work–life balance.[64]
- Finally, the fifth principle is *social interaction*. The job design permits interaction, cooperation and reflexivity among team members.

Drawing upon the work of Klein and McKinlay et al.,[65] the principles of 'good' job design are achieved by management interventions in the technical, governance and sociocultural dimensions of work (Figure 4.9).

The horizontal axis in Figure 4.9 represents the functional or technical tasks that are required to produce the product or service. Group working involves combining a number of tasks on the horizontal axis to increase the cycle times and create more complete and hence more meaningful jobs. The technical dimension is then regarded as the central purpose of work teams, and is concerned with the range of tasks undertaken by members, multiskilling and functional flexibility. The vertical axis represents the governance aspects of the labour process, and shows the extent of workers' autonomy on the job. The third axis, the diagonal, represents the sociocultural aspects of work, one of which is the social interaction that takes place in work groups. The sociocultural dimension is perhaps the most interesting as far as organizational behaviour is concerned, since it represents the behaviour or 'normative' considerations – what ought to happen – to secure effective team performance. This dimension of group work recognizes that employees' compliance and cooperation depend upon the complex interplay of social interactions in the group. It should be noted that, in a five-member team, there are 10 relationships (see Figure 4.3, above).

The SMWT represents an *ideal-type* work regime because it restores the craft paradigm by enlarging tasks on the horizontal axis and by giving members greater

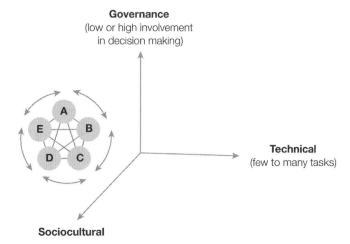

Figure 4.9 – The three dimensions of group work: technical, governance and social

autonomy over how the work is accomplished on the vertical axis: a reversal of Taylorism. The movement along the diagonal axis represents the implications of group working in terms of group norms, group cohesion and organizational culture. The three dimensions of work organization in Figure 4.9 help to illustrate the point that top managers make strategic choices regarding how work is designed, and alternative work structures have an impact on social behaviour and organizational culture.

Critical insight

Workplace observers agree there is evidence that, in organizations that have been successful in devolving decision making to work groups, there have been benefits for management and workers: a 'win–win' situation. Visit www.jobquality.ca and 'High-performance working' at www.cipd.co.uk. Read also Andy Danford et al. (2008), 'Partnership, high-performance work systems and the quality of working life', *New Technology, Work and Employment*, 23(3), pp. 151–66. Who are the prime beneficiaries of team-based working? Do SMWTs reduce workplace stress?

WORK TEAMS: ENDING BUREAUCRACY AND EXTENDING EMPLOYEE EMPOWERMENT?

Whereas groups as social entities go back thousands of years, management interest in work teams is much more recent. From early experiments in sociotechnical job design techniques in the 1970s, teams became the hallmark of postmodern work organizations in the 1990s. Team work has been popularized by mainstream organizational behaviour theorists and management consultants as a panacea for curing inflexible work systems and allegedly inefficient bureaucratic structures, and for enhancing employee higher-order 'growth' and 'relatedness' needs by job enrichment and empowerment.

Motivated by the prospect of connecting the synergy of work teams with corporate goals, managers have focused on teams to help improve organizational performance. In Sweden, the most celebrated example of work teams was introduced at the new Volvo car plant in Uddevalla in 1987. It was reported that the new assembly line avoided the classic problems associated with Fordism.[66] However, in 1992 Volvo closed its Uddevalla factory. For many organizational behaviour researchers, the Swedish plant had become an icon for a European, human-centred and productive organization, and its closure suggested that Taylorist and neo-Taylorist solutions still dominate management thinking in the automobile industry.[67]

In critical accounts of team work, in which group practices are connected to the class power relations in which they are embedded, there is considerable debate over whether or not these regimes constitute a significant departure from Western-style 'high-autonomy' work teams.[5,68] Some argue that the difference lies in the fact that team work utilizes a control orientation that depends upon 'self-control'. Others persuasively argue that self-managed teams create a culture that enhances management control via self-regulation. This insight into group dynamics focuses on the socialization and organization culture, and on the behaviour deemed necessary to make teams work effectively.[69]

The discussion on different group and team concepts highlights the array of definitions, and the need for commentators to define work groups carefully if comparisons are to be made. As mentioned earlier, the reason that so many organizations have 're-engineered' work processes around teams is that managers are looking for improvements in productivity resulting from the positive synergy associated with teams. Thus, the perceived connections between the way work is designed and organizational performance need to be appreciated to understand the current wave of corporate interest in teams.

In standard accounts of team work, such regimes do not necessarily lead to improved organizational performance. People must learn to work in team-based structures: clearly a lesson from sociotechnical theory, which acknowledges the importance of the dialectic relationship between the technical and social aspects of work. In critical accounts of teams, there is deep scepticism. Work teams do not eradicate the three chronic capitalist antagonisms that centre on issues of managerial control: producing goods and services for a global market, which creates uncertainty and pressure to control costs; designing work structures and employee relations systems that maximize shareholder interests; and managerial top-down control over employee behaviour, in contrast to employee autonomy.

Contrary to the management rhetoric, work teams involve elaborate computer information systems developed to support a control-oriented management philosophy.[12] This observation illustrates the work of critical scholars who tend to be interested in understanding the power relations in team design. For example, one study found that while team members had increased their autonomy in performing their work and additional responsibilities, managers had actually increased their control over value-added activities through a computerized production system. This control-oriented approach can be given the name 'computer-controlled autonomy'.[6] Another study offered a scathing account of team working in white-collar work, arguing 'that workers experience forms of team organization as being no less coercive than classically understood Taylorism' (ref. 70, pp. 168–9).

PARADOX IN TEAM-BASED WORK SYSTEMS

How are we to interpret the effects of group membership on employee behaviour? As with the other aspects of organizational behaviour we cover in this text, it depends on the author's approach to the subject. For some, team synergy can be a panacea to bureaucratic ills: 'Teams foster a sense of dignity, self-worth, and a greater commitment to achieving the performance that makes an organization competitive' (ref. 71, p. 10). More critical sociological analysis serves as an antidote to the mainstream assumptions that team work is inherently favourable. The employee commitment implications of team work are not entirely positive. As an empirical reality, working in self-directed teams had no significant effect on employee commitment to the organization, whereas it was associated with higher work-related stress.[72] For others, team work, far from being 'empowering', actually intensifies management control over workers by cultivating a form of self-management through constant peer and self-monitoring.[73] This critical perspective focuses on, among other things, the effect of team ideology and behaviour on the working lives of workers. Whereas the managerialist approach found in most mainstream organizational behaviour texts focuses on the technical and the empowering dimensions of teams and team efficacy, a feature of a critical approach is a focus on the normative dimension of groups and teams, the 'tyranny' arising from team work and paradoxes in team-based work structures.

A paradox involves ambiguity and inconsistency, and both are evident in work group design. A central pillar of team work involves combining a number of tasks on the horizontal axis. This has led many traditional scholars to argue that SMWTs reverse Tayloristic deskilling tendencies by enhancing workers' skills. It is suggested that SMWTs exemplify the re-emergence of the craft model.[74] Critical organizational theorists, however, have challenged the popular logic that SMWTs lead to a more highly skilled workforce. Detractors argue that although they apparently give limited empowerment to workers, they do not necessarily reverse the general 'deskilling' trend, but generate new forms of control that assist management in extracting higher productivity from workers via work intensification as the range of horizontal and vertical tasks expands.[75–80]

Those subscribing to this critique almost invariably draw parallels with Taylorism and Fordism. A number of accounts stress that, with the assistance of microtechnology, re-engineering work into teams is an 'up-dating of Taylor's crusade against custom and practice in which the silicon chip plays an equivalent role in [re-engineering] to that performed by the stop watch in Scientific Management' (ref. 81, p. 96). In other words, it provides a disguised form of intensified managerial control. Others offer more optimistic analyses, in which the outcomes of team working are less deterministic. Whether work teams result in the 'upskilling' or 'deskilling' of workers depends, among other things, on factors such as batch size, managerial choice and negotiation.[6]

Critical organizational theorists have illustrated the paradox in another way. The behavioural dimension of the team work model emphasizes worker empowerment while simultaneously increasing management's control over the labour process. This is achieved using both 'hard' technology (such as computers) and 'social' technology (such as group norms). When decision making is devolved to the team, members begin to think and act like managers, and they internalize company values. In this way, team work influences the attitude and behaviour of the team's members by creating a work culture that reproduces the conditions of employees' own subordination. In other words, team members perceive a moral obligation to increase their level of effort on the job, and 'put in a full day' because of peer group pressure or 'clan control', thereby unwittingly creating a control culture system.[8,9,82–85] Critical studies have found team members' discipline to be more punitive than that of the managers: 'Team members are tougher on fellow workers than management is' (ref. 9, p. 75).

Plate 3 – Team members can perceive a moral obligation to increase their level of effort on a job, and 'put in a full day' (or more) because of peer group pressure, or 'clan control', thereby unwittingly creating a control culture system.
Source: iStockphoto

A 50-year-old male explained how peer group surveillance influenced the behaviour of the team's members like this:

> I think it's a matter of conscience. A person who under the old system might go away for an hour, now he will think twice: Are they [co-workers] going to think they are carrying me because I've been away? ... Because you are a close-knit community in the [team] system. You get niggly remarks: 'Where have you been all morning?' That sort of thing and it gradually works its way in psychologically. (ref. 6, p. 186)

In their account of team learning processes, Kasl and colleagues unwittingly provide further evidence of the control culture generated by work teams.[86] When one particular work team 'failed', some team members left the company, while others worked on 'disheartened'. Moreover:

> The team became the laughing stock of the whole company and the people who weren't involved in it at all, the people who worked on a different floor, would walk right in and say, 'How's logistics, ha ha ha?' They heard about it, it was like this big disaster. (ref. 86, p. 238)

OB in focus Few employees have a 'good' job

Despite the hype about improved quality of work arising from the growth of team working, it is reported that 'only 39 per cent of workers think that their job is "good", according to new research from the Chartered Institute of Personnel and Development (CIPD)'. 'Good' roles are defined as 'exciting but not too stressful', according to a new report from the UK institute, *Reflections on Employee Well-Being and the Psychological Contract.*

The research explored how employees felt about their job and their relationships with managers and colleagues. It concluded that employers should make jobs more appealing and interesting to improve commitment from employees. 'Most jobs can be made interesting or even exciting if they are well managed,' Mike Emmott, CIPD employee relations adviser, said. An interesting and exciting job was one with variety and security, and where the role of the employee was clear. Many workers did not believe that their job had these qualities. A fifth of respondents thought that the demands of their job were unrealistic, and the same proportion found their jobs either very or extremely stressful.

Nic Marks, head of well-being research at the New Economics Foundation and co-author of the report, said that interest and excitement were key elements in the psychological contract between employers and employees. 'If employees don't feel their role is exciting, this will be reflected in underperformance and their lack of commitment and satisfaction,' he said.

Source: adapted from Julie Griffiths, 'Only 39 per cent of employees have a "good" job', *People Management Online*, August 9, 2005.

There is another paradox. The managerial literature views team work as organizational synergy unifying people and thus developing members' capacities through dialogue and learning. Critical reflection in workplace learning literature presumes that if team members can just detect their dysfunctional or inefficient practices, they are free to find more creative and efficient ways of doing and thus improve their performance in the workplace. One mainstream assumption is that all members of the work team are equal. Recent empirical research on multiprofessional team work in the health sector, however, contends that, rather than unifying health professions, team work produces unintended divisive effects.[87] It is argued that power relations and the language used by the health professionals both reflect and reproduce structural inequality between surgeons, anaesthetists and nurses within the team. In reality, where team work is characterized by social structures of inequality and clinical power – for example, surgeons and anaesthetists over nurses – critical reflection and dialogue, and thus the mobilization of alternative practices, are suppressed.

The discourse on work teams illustrates competing interpretations. On the one hand, the thinking and prescriptions in mainstream accounts tend to focus on the technical and the 'growth need' dimension of team-based work configurations, as well as the links between group processes and group performance. On the other hand, critical evaluations of team work focus on paradoxes and the effect of team ideology and behaviour on workers. Thus, team work arguably resembles Morgan's 'psychic prison' in the sense that peer pressure and self-surveillance are the norm, and this more accurately resembles reality than the optimistic notion of the learning-empowering, self-managed work team. In his book *Images of Organizations*,[88] Morgan explains that the notion of organizations as psychic prisons is a metaphor that connects the idea that organizations are a psychic phenomenon, in the sense that they are ultimately constructed and sustained by conscious and unconscious processes, with the belief that people can actually become imprisoned or confined by the ideas, thoughts and actions to which these processes give rise.

CHAPTER SUMMARY

- In this chapter, we have examined the background, nature and behavioural implications of work groups. We have suggested that the current wave of interest in work teams, often located within a cluster of other employment practices constituting what is called a 'high-performance workplace', is linked to lean forms of work organizations and the perceived shortcomings of large bureaucratic organizational structures.

- The chapter has emphasized that understanding group processes, such as groupthink, group leadership, informal group learning and intragroup conflict, is imperative for the successful management of the HPW system.

- Management tries to persuade workers of the need to work beyond their contract for the 'common' good and to engage in self-regulatory norms. The SMWT is said to be upskilling and empowering workers.

- However, we have also gone beyond management rhetoric, and presented arguments and evidence to suggest that self-managed teams shift the focus away from the hierarchy, directive and bureaucratic control processes, to a culture of self-control mechanisms.

- The discussion has emphasized that orthodox and critical accounts of team working provide very different views of this form of work organization and employment relations. Both perspectives, however, conceptualize team working as influencing individual behaviour and contributing to improved organizational performance. While both approaches make employee autonomy central to their analyses, each conceptualizes team membership as having a different influence. Additionally, autonomy is theorized as leading to different outcomes (such as growth need versus self-regulation) in each perspective.

KEY CONCEPTS

group dynamics
group processes
group structure
job characteristic model
peer pressure
psychic prison
work group
work team

VOCAB CHECKLIST FOR ESL STUDENTS

- Cohesiveness
- Empowerment, empower
- Formal work group
- Group context
- Group dynamics
- Group norms
- Group processes
- Group structure
- Groupthink
- Increment, incremental
- Informal group
- Job characteristics model
- Job design
- Job enlargement
- Job enrichment
- Job rotation
- Job satisfaction
- Paradox, paradoxical
- Role
- Role ambiguity
- Role conflict
- Role perceptions
- Self-managed work teams
- Systems theory
- Status
- Teams
- Work group

CHAPTER REVIEW QUESTIONS

1 How useful are group development models for understanding group or team behaviour?
2 What effect, if any, do you expect workforce diversity to have on group processes and outcomes?
3 Explain how the size of the work group might affect group dynamics and performance?
4 'Self-managed work teams are simply attempts by managers to control individuals at work by mobilizing group processes.' Do you agree or disagree? Discuss.
5 Students often complain about doing group projects. Why? Relate your answer to group processes and the critique of self-managed work teams.
6 What is meant by 'group think', and how important is it in deciding group performance?

CHAPTER RESEARCH QUESTIONS

1 Diversity is an organizational fact of life. In a group, we would like you to examine your own beliefs about diversity and how people stereotype others. Form a study

group. (a) Post each term from the following list on separate sheets of paper: Male, Roman Catholic, Asian, Generation Y, Disabled, American, Muslim, Female, Irish, Single mother, Over age 60, West Indian. (b) Circulate the sheets around the group, and write down one stereotype you have heard under each heading. Avoid repeating anything that is already written down. (c) After everyone has finished writing, each group member takes turns to read all the stereotypes under each category. (d) Group members should then discuss (i) their personal reaction, (ii) what they have learned about stereotyping others, and (iii) what managers can do to experience positive effects of diversity.

2 Obtain a copy of Bolton and Houlihan's book *Work Matters: Critical Reflections on Contemporary Work* (see Further Reading). After reading pages 162–79, explain how team working was introduced into a major supermarket chain. How much autonomy did the teams have? How did the leadership style differ between the teams? How was team productivity measured? How did team work help members cope with work-related stress? How might team diversity impact on the team dynamics?

3 Read Rolf van Dick et al.'s article, 'Group diversity and group identification: the moderating role of diversity beliefs' (see Further Reading). Does group diversity positively or negatively affect group decision making? What can managers do to improve the quality of group decision making?

FURTHER READING

Behfar, K., Peterson, R., Mannix, E. and Trochim, W. (2008) 'The critical role of conflict resolution in teams: a closer look at the links between conflict type, conflict management strategies, and team outcomes', *Journal of Applied Psychology*, **93**(1), pp. 170–88.

Belbin, R. M. (1993) *Team Roles at Work*, London: Butterworth/Heinemann.

Bolton, S. and Houlihan, M. (eds) (2009) *Work Matters: Critical Reflections on Contemporary Work*, Basingstoke: Palgrave.

Cole, M. S., Walter, F. and Bruch, H. (2008) 'Affective mechanisms linking dysfunctional behavior to performance in work teams: a moderated mediation study', *Journal of Applied Psychology*, **93**(5), pp. 945–58.

Cordery, J. (2002) 'Team working', pp. 326–50 in P. Warr (ed.), *Psychology of Work*, London: Penguin.

Danford, A., Richardson, M., Stewart, P., Tailby, S. and Upchurch, M. (2008) 'Partnership, high performance work systems and quality of working life', *New Technology, Work and Employment*, **23**(3), pp. 151–66.

Kasl, E., Marsick, V. and Dechant, K. (1997) 'Teams as learners', *Journal of Applied Behavioral Sciences*, **33**(2), pp. 227–46.

Kooij-de Bode, H. J. M., Hanneke J. M., van Knippenberg, D. and van Ginkel, W. P. (2008) 'Ethnic diversity and distributed information in group decision making: the importance of information elaboration', *Group Dynamics: Theory, Research and Practice*, **12**(4), pp. 307–20.

Proctor, S., Fulop, L., Linstead, S., Mueller, F. and Sewell, G. (2009) 'Managing teams', pp. 539–73 in S. Linstead, L. Fulop and S. Lilley (eds), *Management and Organization: A Critical Text* (2nd edn), Basingstoke: Palgrave.

Russell, N. and Gregory, R. (2005) 'Making the undoable doable: Milgram, the Holocaust, and modern government', *American Review of Public Administration*, **35**(4), pp. 327–49.

Sewell, G. (1998) 'The discipline of teams: the control of team-based industrial work through electronic and peer surveillance', *Administrative Science Quarterly*, **43**, pp. 406–69.

Taggar, S. and Robert Ellis, R. (2007) 'The role of leaders in shaping formal team norms', *Leadership Quarterly*, **18**, pp. 105–20.

van Dick, R., van Knippenburg, D., Hagele, S., Guillaume, Y. R. F. and Brodbeck, F. (2008) 'Group diversity and group identification: the moderating role of diversity beliefs', *Human Relations*, **61**(10), pp. 1463–92.

Case study 1

Building cars in Brazil

Setting

Founded in the earlier part of the century, the Cable Motor Company was a traditional, North American automobile manufacturer. They used Fordist management techniques and traditional assembly line production, and worked with a highly unionized workforce. By the mid-1980s, with their sales slumping, the company made the decision to purchase an obsolete automotive assembly plant in Brazil. The company quickly proceeded to upgrade the plant, resulting in a very large, modern, single-storey building of approximately 1.4 million square feet with four major manufacturing centres: stamping, body, paint and final assembly. The plan was to adopt the use of cooperative work teams, which had been used by Swedish car manufacturers such as Saab and Volvo, and to implement the Japanese lean production system originally created by Toyota and later adapted by Mazda.

The company spared no expense in planning for the workforce that would fit the plant's new approach to job design. There were extensive pre-employment screening and selection techniques used to recruit the 1200 people needed for the production run. Unlike the minimalist training normally provided under the Ford system, the company provided intensive classroom time and continuous on-the-job training for employees on the subject of self-managed work teams. Group decision making, integral to team success, was a strong focus.

The company found that the union representing the workers, the National Union of Cable Motor Company Workers, had little influence in the new Brazilian plant. This resulted in a much quicker implementation of the flexible production system. Production shifts of about 100 persons were scheduled with workers performing operations individually and in self-directed two-, three- or four-person teams. Any team member could pull a car off the line to check a quality issue. In such a case, a group walk-around decided if a car needed 'finessing'.

CEO John Miner was impressed with the initial look of the new production system. 'Minimal supervision and a self-directed workforce are what we strive to maintain and encourage,' he remarked. 'We will not get bogged down in traditional thinking, processes or paperwork. All workers are encouraged to be free-thinking and to get creative.'

The problem

The selection of the team leaders was conducted by the senior management group. Maria Lopez, a 30-year-old clerical worker, was moved from the administration office to head up one of the teams. Shortly after, production manager Clive Richards began to notice that Maria's team's production cycle times were increasing. He also noticed conflicts within her group. Clive decided to approach one of Maria's team members, Juan Fernandez, who had formerly worked in a team at another car company's assembly plant in Brazil. 'We can't work with Maria as our team leader,' Juan said. 'The team finds it hard because she is a woman. You have to remove her.'

While Clive struggled to decide what to do with Maria, other problems emerged. Employees were arriving to work late on a consistent basis. City buses, the main source of transportation for the plant workers, ran late if they ran at all. This was beginning to impact the continual on-the-job training as it required workers to arrive at work on time. Other employees were hesitant to do quality checks on their own work, saying that it would create the impression that the supervisors did not trust them.

Clive decided to meet with the CEO to let him know about the increasing issues so that action could be taken before the problems got worse. John was concerned when he heard what was happening at the new plant as he had just returned from a meeting where there were preliminary discussions on opening another in a different Brazilian location. 'I need you to do a presentation for the Board of Directors,' John said to Clive. 'We have to show what we've learned from this experience and how we can move forward.'

Tasks

Prepare a short presentation, incorporating the answers to the following questions:
1   How did Brazilian culture or work ideology contribute to the problems the company experienced with its use of teams?
2   In what alternative way could the team leader have been chosen which may have been more acceptable to the team members?
3   Should the conflicts in Maria's group only be viewed as a negative development?
Ask yourself:
4   Why do you think the use of teams could weaken a union's influence or power in the workplace?

Essential reading

Katz, H. C., Lee, W. and Lee, J. (2004) The New Structure of Labour Relations, New York: Cornell University Press.

Proctor, S., Fulop, L., Linstead, S., Mueller, F. and Sewell, G. (2009) 'Managing teams', pp. 539–73 in S. Linstead, L. Fulop and S. Lilley (eds), Management and Organization: A Critical Text (2nd edn), Basingstoke: Palgrave.

Note

Cable Motor Company is a fictitious company, but the background material for the case is derived from Muller, Rehder and Bannister (1998).[89] Some circumstances of the case organization have been altered. This case study was written by Lori Rilkoff, MSc, CHRP, Senior Human Resources Manager at the City of Kamloops, and lecturer in HRM at Thompson Rivers University, BC, Canada.

Case study 2

Teams at Land Rock Alliance Insurance

Visit www.palgrave.com/business/brattonob2e to view this case study

WEB-BASED ASSIGNMENT

Work groups and teams is one of the most important topics of organizational behaviour, and given that many students have experienced group working and will be called upon to work in groups in organizations, it is important to reflect on how groups influence human behaviour.

For this assignment, we would like you to gain more information on work teams by visiting www.workteams.org and www.berr.gov.uk. In addition, you are asked to explore examples of team working in European and North American companies by visiting the following websites: www.honda.com; www.sony.com; http://ptcpartners.com/Team/home.htm; www.berr.gov.uk.

What main principles can be identified as 'good' job design when applied to work teams? Looking at the companies that have introduced teams, what behaviours or 'norms' are expected of employees? How does the team-based model impact on other aspects of management such as human resource management? Discuss your findings with other students on your course.

OB IN FILM

The film *Twelve Angry Men* (1957) examines the behaviour of 12 members of a jury who have to decide on the innocence or guilt of a young man from a working-class background. At the beginning, 11 jurors are convinced of the youth's guilt and wish to declare him guilty without further discussion. One member of the jury (played by Henry Fonda) has reservations and persuades the other members to review the evidence. After reviewing the evidence, the jury acquits the defendant.

A modern version of this film can be seen in a 2005 episode of the television series *Judge John Deed*, in which Judge Deed (played by Martin Shaw) serves as a member of a jury and persuades the other members to review the evidence in a sexual assault case.

What group concepts do the film or the *Judge John Deed* episode illustrate? What types of power are possessed by the characters played by Henry Fonda and Martin Shaw? What pattern of influencing behaviour is followed by Henry Fonda and Martin Shaw?

REFERENCES

1. Johnson, D. W. and Johnson, F. P. (2000) *Joining Together: Group Theory and Group Skills* (7th edn), Boston: Allyn & Bacon.
2. Katzenbach, J. R. and Smith, D. (1994) *The Wisdom of Teams*, New York: Harper Business.
3. Kline, T. (1999) *Remaking Teams*, San Francisco: Jossey-Bass.
4. Orsburn, J. and Moran, L. (2000) *The New Self-directed Work Teams*, New York: McGraw-Hill.
5. Procter, S. and Mueller, F. (2000) *Teamworking*, Basingstoke: Palgrave Macmillan.
6. Bratton, J. (1992) *Japanization at Work*, Basingstoke: Macmillan.
7. Thompson, R and Ackroyd, S. (1995) 'All quiet on the workplace front: a critique of recent trends in British industrial sociology', *Sociology*, **29**(4), pp. 615–33.
8. Sewell, G. (1998) 'The discipline of teams: the control of team-based industrial work through electronic and peer surveillance', *Administrative Science Quarterly*, **43**, pp. 406–69.
9. Wells, D. (1993) 'Are strong unions compatible with the new model of human resource management?', *Relations Industrielles/Industrial Relations*, **48**(1), pp. 56–84.
10. Hertog, J. F. and Tolner, T. (1998) 'Groups and teams', pp. 62–71 in M. Poole and M. Watner (eds), *The Handbook of Human Resource Management*, London: International Thomson Business Press.
11. Buchanan, D. (2000) 'An eager and enduring embrace: the ongoing rediscovery of teamworking as a management idea', in S. Procter and F. Mueller (eds), *Teamworking*, London: Macmillan.
12. Yeatts, D. E. and Hyten, C. (1998) *High-performing Self-managed Work Teams*, Thousand Oaks, CA: Sage.
13. Bendix, R. (1956) *Work and Authority in Industry*, New York: Wiley.
14. Crawley, J. (1978) 'The lifestyles of the group', *Small Groups Newsletter*, **2**(1), pp. 26–39.
15. Gil, R., Rico, R., Alcover, C. M. and Barrasa, A. (2005) 'Change-oriented leadership, satisfaction and performance in work groups: effects of team climate and group potency', *Journal of Managerial Psychology*, **20**(3/4), pp. 312–29.
16. Simmel, G. (1908/1950) 'Subordination under a principle', pp. 250–67 in *The Sociology of Georg Simmel* (ed. and trans. K. Wolff), New York: Free Press.
17. Choi, J. N. (2007) 'Group composition and employee creative behaviour in a Korean electronics company: distinct effects of relational demography and group diversity', *Journal of Occupational and Organizational Psychology*, **80**, pp. 213–34.
18. Kooij-de Bode, H. J. M., van Knippenberg, D. and van Ginkel, W. P. (2008) 'Ethnic diversity and distributed information in group decision making: the importance of information elaboration', *Group Dynamics: Theory, Research and Practice*, **12**(4), pp. 307–20.
19. Slaughter, J. E. and Zicker, M. J. (2006) 'A new look at the role of insiders in the newcomer socialization process', *Group & Organization Management*, **31**(2), pp. 264–90.
20. Tuckman, B. and Jensen, M. (1977) 'Stages of small group development revisited', *Group and Organization Management*, **2**, pp. 419–27.
21. Gersick, C. J. (1988) 'Time and transition in workteams: towards a new model of group development', *Academy of Management Journal*, **31**, pp. 47–53.
22. Mayo, E. (1946) *The Human Problems of an Industrial Civilization*, New York: Macmillan.
23. Feldman, D. C. (1984) 'The development and enforcement of group norms', *Academy of Management Review*, **1**, pp. 47–53.
24. Taggar, S. and Ellis, R. (2007) 'The role of leaders in shaping formal team norms', *Leadership Quarterly*, **18**, pp. 105–20.
25. Zimbardo, P. (2008) BBC *Hardtalk* interview, April 22, 2008.
26. Romero, E. and Pescosolido, A. (2008) 'Humor and group effectiveness', *Human Relations*, **61**(3), pp. 395–418.
27. Wilson, F. M. (2003) *Organizational Behaviour and Gender*, Farnham: Ashgate.
28. Smith, J. W. and Calasanti, T. (2005) 'The influences of gender, race and ethnicity on workplace experiences of institutions and social isolation: an exploratory study of university faculty', *Sociological Spectrum*, **25**(3), pp. 307–34.
29. Hackman, J. and Oldham, G. (1980) *Work Redesign*, Reading, MA: Addison-Wesley.
30. Janis, I. L. (1972) *Victims of Groupthink*, Boston, MA: Houghton Mifflin.
31. Senge, P. (1990) *The Fifth Discipline*, New York: Doubleday.

32. O'Brien, D. and Buono, C. (1996) 'Building effective learning teams: lessons from the field', *SAM Advanced Management Journal*, **61**(3), pp. 4–11.

33. Jenkins, J. (2008) 'Pressurised partnership: a case of perishable compromise in contested terrain', *New Technology, Work and Employment*, **23**(3), pp. 167–80.

34. Thompson (1960). Cited in Robbins, S. P. (1990) *Organization Theory: Structure, Design, and Applications* (3rd edn), Englewood Cliffs, NJ: Prentice-Hall, p. 411.

35. Varela, O. E., Burke, M. J. and Landis, R. S. (2008) 'A model of emergence and dysfunctional effects of emotional conflicts in groups', *Group Dynamics: Theory, Research and Practice*, **12**(2), pp. 112–26.

36. Bolton, S. (2005) *Emotion Management in the Workplace*, Basingstoke: Palgrave.

37. Cole, M. S., Walter, F. and Bruch, H. (2008) 'Affective mechanisms linking dysfunctional behavior to performance in work teams: a moderated mediation study', *Journal of Applied Psychology*, **93**(5), pp. 945–58.

38. Dunlop, P.D. and Lee, K. (2004) 'Workplace deviance, organizational citizenship behavior, and business unit performance: the bad apples do spoil the whole barrel', *Journal of Organizational Behavior*, **25**, 67–80.

39. Behfar, K., Peterson, R., Mannix, E. and Trochim, W. (2008) 'The critical role of conflict resolution in teams: a closer look at the links between conflict type, conflict management strategies, and team outcomes', *Journal of Applied Psychology*, **93**(1), pp. 170–88.

40. Tajfel, H. (1978) 'Social categorization, social identity, and social comparison', pp. 61–76 in H. Tajfel (ed.), *Differentiation between Social Groups*, London: Academic Press.

41. Tajfel, H. (1981) 'Social stereotypes and social groups', in J. C. Turner and H. Giles (eds), *Intergroup Behaviour*, Oxford: Blackwell.

42. Turner, J. (1987) *Rediscovering the Social Group: A Self-categorization Theory*, New York: Basic Books.

43. Miller, N. and Brewer, M. B. (eds) (1984) *Groups in Contact: The Psychology of Desegregation*, New York: Academic Press.

44. Sherif, M., Harvey, O. J., White, B. J., Hood, W. R. and Sherif, C. W. (1961) *Intergroup Conflict and Cooperation*, Norman, OK: Oklahoma Book Exchange.

45. De Dreu, C. and Van de Vliert, E. (eds) (1997) *Using Conflict in Organizations*, London: Sage.

46. Hackman, H. R. (1986) 'The psychology of self-management in organizations', pp. 89–136 in M. S. Pallack and Perloff, R. O. (eds), *Psychology and Work: Productivity, Change and Employment*, Washington, DC: American Psychological Association.

47. Banker, R. D., Field, J. M., Schroeder, R. G. and Sinha, K. (1996) 'Impact of work teams on manufacturing performance: a longitudinal study', *Academy of Management Journal*, **39**(2), pp. 867–90.

48. Cohen, S. G. and Bailey, D. E. (1997) 'What makes team work: group effectiveness research from the shop floor to the executive suite', *Journal of Management*, **23**(3), pp. 239–90.

49. Steiner, I. D. (1972) *Group Processes and Productivity*, New York: Academic Press.

50. Horwitz, F. M., Chan feng Heng and Quazi, H. A. (2003) 'Finders, keepers? Attracting, motivating and retaining knowledge workers', *Human Resource Management Journal*, **13**(4), pp. 23–44.

51. Stewart, P. and Danford, A. (2008) 'Editorial: Union strategies and worker engagement with new forms of work and employment', *New Technology, Work and Employment*, **23**(3), pp. 146–50.

52. Asch, S. E. (1951) 'Effects of group pressure upon modification and distortion of judgements', in H. Guetzkow (ed.), *Groups, Leadership and Men*, New York: Carnegie Press.

53. Milgram, S. (1973) *Obedience and Authority*, London: Tavistock.

54. Russell, N. and Gregory, R. (2005) 'Making the undoable doable: Milgram, the Holocaust, and modern government', *American Review of Public Administration*, **35**(4), pp. 327–49.

55. Koring, P. (2004) 'Iraq war based on "flawed" reports', *Globe and Mail*, p. A11.

56. Winquist, J. and Franz, T. (2008) 'Does the stepladder technique improve group decision making? A series of failed replications', *Group Dynamics: Theory, Research and Practice*, **12**(4), pp. 255–67.

57. van Dick, R., van Knippenburg, D., Hagele, S., Guillaume, Y. R. F. and Brodbeck, F. (2008) 'Group diversity and group identification: the moderating role of diversity beliefs', *Human Relations*, **61**(10), pp. 1463–92.

58. Benders, J. and Van Hootegem, G. (1999) 'Teams and their context: moving team discussion beyond existing dichotomies', *Journal of Management Studies*, **36**(5), pp. 609–28.

59. Roethlisberger, F. J. and Dickson, W. J. (1939) *Management and the Worker*, Cambridge, MA: Harvard University Press.

60. Maslow, A. H. (1954) *Motivation and Personality*, New York: Harper.

61. McGregor, D. (1960) *The Human Side of Enterprise*, New York: McGraw-Hill.

62. Turner, A. N. and Lawrence, P. R. (1965) *Industrial Jobs and the Worker*, Boston: Harvard University, Graduate School of Business Administration.

63. Hoeve, A. and Nieuwenhuis, L. (2006) 'Learning routines in innovation processes', *Journal of Workplace Learning*, **18**(3), pp. 171–85.

64. Lowe, G. (2000) *The Quality of Work: A People-centred Agenda*, New York: Oxford University Press.

65. Klein, J. (1994) 'Maintaining expertise in multi-skilled teams', *Advances in Interdisciplinary Studies of Work Teams*, **1**, pp. 145–65.

66. 'Volvo's radical new assembly plant: "the death of the assembly line"?', *Business Week*, August 28, 1989.

67. Cressey, P. (1993) 'Kalmar and Uddevalla: the demise of Volvo as a European icon', *New Technology, Work and Employment*, **8**(2), pp. 88–96.

68. Elger, T. and Smith, C. (eds) (1994) *Global Japanization?*, London: Routledge.

69. Thompson, P. and Wallace, T. (1996) 'Redesigning production through teamworking', *International Journal of Operations and Production Management*, **16**(2), pp. 103–18.

70. Baldry, C, Bain, P. and Taylor, P. (1998) '"Bright satanic offices": intensification, control and team Taylorism', pp. 163–83 in P. Thompson and C. Warhurst (eds), *Workplaces of the Future*, Basingstoke: Macmillan.

71. Manz, C. C. and Sims, H. P. Jr. (1993). *Business Without Bosses*, New York: Wiley.

72. Danford, A., Richardson, M., Stewart, P., Tailby, S. and Upchurch, M. (2008) 'Partnership, high performance work systems and quality of working life', *New Technology, Work and Employment*, **23**(3), pp. 151–66.

73. Thompson, P. and McHugh, D. (2006) *Work Organizations: A Critical Introduction* (4th edn), Basingstoke: Palgrave.

74. Piore, M. and Sabel, C. (1984) *The Second Industrial Divide*, New York: Basic Books.

75. Turnbull, P. (1986) 'The Japanisation of British industrial relations at Lucas', *Industrial Relations Journal*, **17**(3), pp. 193–206.

76. Sayer, A. (1986) 'New developments in manufacturing: the just-in-time system', *Capital and Class*, **30**, pp. 43–72.

77. Tomaney, J. (1990) 'The reality of workplace flexibility', *Capital and Class*, **40**, pp. 29–60.

78. Clarke, L. (1997) 'Changing work systems, changing social relations? A Canadian General Motors Plant', *Relations Industrielle/Industrial Relations*, **52**(4), pp. 839–65.

79. Malloch, H. (1997) 'Strategic and HRM aspects of kaizen: a case study', *New Technology, Work and Employment*, **12**(2), pp. 108–22.

80. Willmott, H., (1995) 'The odd couple?: re-engineering business processes: managing human relations', *New/Technology, Work and Employment*, **10**(2), pp. 89–98.

81. Thompson, P. (1989) *The Nature of Work* (2nd edn), London: Macmillan.

82. Burawoy, M. (1979) *Manufacturing Consent*, Chicago: University of Chicago Press.

83. Burawoy, M. (2002) 'What happened to the working class?', pp. 69–76 in K. Leicht (ed.), *The Future of the Market Transition*, New York: JAI Press.

84. Shalla, V. (1997) 'Technology and the deskilling of work: the case of passenger agents at Air Canada', in A. Duffy, D. Glenday and N. Pupo (eds), *Good Jobs, Bad Jobs, No Jobs: The Transformation of Work in the 21st Century*, Toronto: Harcourt.

85. Wood, S. (1986) 'The cooperative labour strategy in the U.S. auto industry', *Economic and Industrial Democracy*, **7**(4), pp. 415–48.

86. Kasl, E., Marsick, V. and Dechant, K. (1997) 'Teams as learners', *Journal of Applied Behavioral Science*, **33**(2), pp. 227–46.

87. Finn, R. (2008) 'The language of teamwork: reproducing professional divisions in the operating theatre', *Human Relations* **61**(1), pp. 103–30.

88. Morgan, G. (1997) *Images of Organization* (2nd edn), Thousand Oaks, CA: Sage.

89. Muller, H. J., Rehder, R. R. and Bannister, G. (1998) 'The Mexican–Japanese–U.S. model for auto assembly in Northern Mexico', *Latin American Business Review*, **2**(1), pp. 47–67.

90. Proctor, S., Fulop, L., Linstead, S., Mueller, F. and Sewell, G. (2009) 'Managing teams', pp. 539–73 in S. Linstead, L. Fulop and S. Lilley (eds), *Management and Organization: A Critical Text* (2nd edn), Basingstoke: Palgrave.

91. Brown, S. P., Westbrook, R. A. and Challagalla, G. (2005) 'Good cope, bad cope: adaptive and maladaptive coping strategies following a critical negative work event', *Journal of Applied Psychology*, **90**, 792–8.

PERSONALITY

CHAPTER OUTLINE

- Introduction
- What is personality?
- Trait theories of personality
- The psychodynamic theory of personality
- Sociocultural theories of personality
- Identity and personality
- Applying personality theories in the workplace
- Summary and end-of-chapter features
- Chapter case study 1: Identifying leaders in Nigeria
- Chapter case study 2: Building Anna's self-esteem

CHAPTER OBJECTIVES

After completing this chapter, you should be able to:

- define personality and identity and understand their importance in the workplace
- distinguish between the trait and psychodynamic theories of personality
- understand how cultural and life-long social experience shapes personality
- critically assess how individual identity affects and is affected by the organization
- understand more of the main characteristics of your own personality and identity
- apply the key findings of personality research to the workplace

INTRODUCTION

At the morning coffee break, three nurses sat around a table in the hospital's cafeteria. Elizabeth spoke first. 'I'm really disappointed in Alan's behaviour. He became really excitable and loud again during the night shift when I asked him to assist in the emergency ward. He seems to be emotional and excitable whenever we have more than two or three critical cases in the ER. At the interview he came over as so confident and experienced.' And he had a wonderful CV,' Eleanor added.

'Interviews and good reference letters can't tell you about a person's personality and how they will perform under stress,' said charge nurse Judy Finnigan. 'He's not easy to get along with either, especially in the mornings. You ask a question and he jumps down your throat.'

'Yet, you know, he can be totally different outside the ER. He's sociable and pleasant when we go to the pub or when things are quiet on the ward,' replied Elizabeth.

How is Alan able to be such a different person in different situations? Are certain personality types better adapted for certain job types? Should managers try to recruit all employees with similar personalities? How does the personality characteristic influence motivation at work? Why do some people find it difficult to work in a team, while others excel as 'team players'? What personality types make for a 'good' team player?

Behaviour analysts have long been interested in relationships between personality traits and job performance, and whether personality homogeneity (people having similar personalities) facilitates a high-performance workplace. As we shall see in this chapter, many researchers have attempted to understand how both personality and identity are important factors shaping behaviour in the workplace.

In this chapter, we present psychological and sociological theories that have made significant contributions to our understanding of personality and identity, and some of the ways in which these theories are being applied in the workplace. There are at least 24 academics or groups of researchers who have contributed to theories of personality. Therefore our coverage in this chapter is highly selective, and we can hope to provide only a glimpse of the complexity and scope of the theories. We conclude the chapter with a discussion of the connections between personality and job performance, and personality and social integration, along with a critique of how personality tests are used in the workplace.

weblink

Go to www.queendom.com/tests.html and www.apa.org/science/testing.html for more information on personality testing instruments. In the UK, the British Psychological Society (www.bps.org.uk) assesses employment selection tests

WHAT IS PERSONALITY?

The notion of personality permeates popular culture and discussion in the workplace. In Western cultures, the mass media – print, radio, television, films and other communication technologies – endlessly discuss 'cool' or 'nice' personalities. And like Alan in our opening vignette, we sometimes meet people at work who seem to have a personality that does not 'fit' with the job requirements or work group. We all use the term 'personality' quite often, and most people feel they understand it intuitively. But what exactly is personality? Although there is no universally accepted definition, we define personality here as a relatively enduring pattern of thinking, feeling and acting that characterizes a person's response to her or his environment.

There are several aspects of this definition that need further explanation:

- The concept of personality refers to notions of individuality; people differ significantly in the ways in which they routinely think, feel and act.
- Personality refers to an enduring set of characteristics and tendencies of a person. An individual's personality encapsulates her or his way of responding to their world. Personality rests on the observation that people seem to behave somewhat consistently over time and across different life situations. Thus, we would not characterize a person as having a shy personality if that individual tended to be dominantly shy and retiring only some of the time, and on other occasions was frequently observed to be very sociable and outgoing.
- Similarly, we need to be aware that individual behaviour is influenced by social context. Individuals may be shy and retiring in a situation where they perceive the context to be unfavourable (such as meeting new people on the first day of employment), but outgoing when the situation is perceived as favourable. From this perceived consistency comes the notion of 'personality traits' that characterize

individuals' customary ways of responding to their environment. Research suggests that stability or consistency becomes greater as we enter adulthood, but even in adulthood, there remains a capacity for meaningful personality change.[1]

⊚ Finally, our definition of personality draws attention to the fact that, in studying personality, we are interested in factors within people that cause them to behave consistently as they do.

stop reflect
What do you think of these typical observations of people that give rise to the concept of personality? Do they accurately reflect how you form an opinion of a person's 'personality'?

The patterns of thinking, feeling and actions that are viewed as reflecting a person's personality typically have three characteristics. First, they are seen as elements of identity that distinguish that individual from other people. Second, the individual's behaviours seem to 'interconnect' in a meaningful fashion, suggesting an inner element that shapes and directs behaviour. Third, the behaviours are viewed as being caused primarily by 'internal' rather than contextual factors.

In studying personality, we need also to look at how social experience structures or shapes personality. People develop a personality by internalizing – or taking in – their social experiences or surroundings. Without social experience, personality cannot develop. Sociological research on the effects of social isolation on feral (meaning 'wild') children points to the crucial role of social experience in forming personality.[2–4] Sociologists suggest that, in the process of interacting with parents, siblings, relatives, teachers and others, people develop an individual identity. We shall examine identity later in this chapter, but we define it here as the core understandings human beings hold about who they are and what is meaningful to them. Figure 5.1 illustrates some perceived characteristics of behaviours that are seen as reflecting an individual's personality.

The trait, psychodynamic and sociocultural perspectives have guided the study of personality. These approaches provide very different conceptions of what personality is and how it functions. No doubt, you will find some of the theories more in accord than others with your own life views. Before we describe and evaluate each of the theories, we need to offer a few words of warning about personality in the workplace:

⊚ As we have already said, there is no 'one best' personality type. Some personality characteristics are useful in certain situations, and organizations need to appreciate the value of diversity. When all employees hold similar personality traits and have similar values, studies suggest that fewer rules are needed to get things done. For

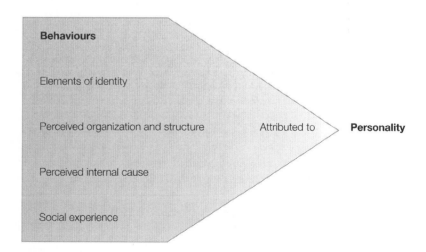

Figure 5.1 – Perceived characteristics of behaviours that are seen as reflecting an individual's personality

many managers, this may seem like a good thing, but in some circumstances this same homogeneity could hinder the organization's ability to adapt to change.[5]

- Although many organizations consider personality to be an important criterion for employment, personality tests are still considered to be a relatively poor instrument for selecting people for key positions, such as management roles.

- The excessive 'classification' of personality types may prevent others from appreciating a person's potential to contribute to an organization.

- If we draw attention to context and social experience, there is less likelihood of exaggerating the effect of personality on individual work-related behaviour. In highly structured situations – such as the armed forces – with clearly defined rules, roles and punishment contingencies, personality will have the least effect on work-related behaviour. In less structured situations – such as a volunteer community organization – personality will have the most effect on organizational behaviour.[6]

In what follows, we examine three approaches to the study of personality: the trait, psychodynamic and sociocultural approaches.

TRAIT THEORIES OF PERSONALITY

Almost two thousand years ago, the ancient Greeks used the humoral theory to explain individual differences in personality.[7] The body was thought to contain

Plate 1   Observable traits, such as friendliness, are those traits that are obvious to others.
Source: Getty Images

four humours or fluids: black bile, blood, phlegm and yellow bile. The personality of individuals was classified according to the disposition supposedly produced by the predominance of one of these humours in their bodies. Optimistic or sanguine people, who had a preponderance of blood (*sanguis*), were cheerful and passionate. Melancholic people, who had an excess of black bile, had a pessimistic temperament. Phlegmatic individuals, whose body systems contained an excessive proportion of phlegm, were calm and unexcitable. Choleric individuals, on the other hand, had an excess of yellow bile and were bad-tempered and irritable. Although subsequent research discredited the humoral theory, the notion that people can be classified into different personality types has persisted to this day.

If you were to describe the personality of a close friend or relative, you would probably make a number of descriptive statements, for example, 'He is a real extrovert. He likes to be the focus of attention, is abrasive in debate, but is also brilliant and charming. He works hard but he is generous with his time, and he is a truly caring person. He will always try to help if he can.' In other words, you would describe others by referring to the kind of people they are ('extrovert') and to their thoughts ('caring' and 'brilliant'), feelings ('attention'), and actions ('works hard'). Together, these statements describe personality traits, enduring personal characteristics that reveal themselves in a particular pattern of human behaviour in different situations.

The English dictionary contains approximately 18,000 words that could be used to describe personal traits, and obviously it would be impractical, even if it were possible, to describe people in terms of where they fell on some vast scale. Trait theorists therefore attempt to condense various descriptors into a manageable number of core personality traits that people display consistently over time, in order to understand and predict human behaviour.

Gordon Allport (1897–1967) pioneered research on personality traits. He believed that the set of words chosen to describe an individual reflect that person's central traits, personal characteristics that are apparent to others and that shape behaviour in a variety of environments. A central trait is equivalent to the descriptive terms used in a letter of reference (such as 'conscientious' or 'reliable'). Another aspect of what Allport called the 'building blocks' of personality is secondary traits, those which are more specific to certain situations and have less impact on behaviour. An example of a secondary trait is 'dislikes crowds'.[8]

factor analysis: a statistical technique used for a large number of variables to explain the pattern of relationships in the data

Psychologists have used the statistical tool of **factor analysis** to identify clusters of specific behaviours that are correlated with one another so highly that they can be viewed as reflecting basic personality traits. Different people fall into these different clusters. For example, you might find that most people who are shy and socially reserved stay away from parties and enjoy solitary activities such as reading. At the other end of the spectrum are people who are talkative and outward-going, like parties and dislike solitary activities such as reading. These behavioural patterns define a dimension that we might label introversion–extroversion. At one end of the dimension are highly introverted behaviours, and at the other end are highly extroverted behaviours. As we describe below, studies have found introversion–extroversion to be a major dimension of personality.

In 1965, Raymond Cattell, a British psychologist, built upon Allport's investigations to develop his theory of personality. Cattell used a process of factor analysis to identify clusters of traits that he believed represented a person's central traits. He analysed questionnaire responses from thousands of people, and also obtained ratings from people who knew the participants well, eventually identifying 16 basic behaviour clusters, or factors. These 16 traits he called 'source traits' because they were, in his view, the building blocks upon which personality is built. From his data, Cattell developed a personality test called the 16 Personality Factor Questionnaire (16PF) to measure individual differences on each of the dimensions, and provide personality profiles for individuals and for groups of people. Figure 5.2 compares the personality profiles of a hypothetical individual rated on Cattell's 16PF test.

Eysenck's three-factor model of personality

Hans J. Eysenck (1916–1997), another well-known British psychologist, also used factor analysis to devise his theory of personality. From his research, Eysenck concluded that normal personality can be understood in terms of three basic factors or dimensions: introversion–extroversion, stability–instability and psychoticism.[9] These factors are bipolar dimensions. Introversion is the opposite of extroversion, stability is the opposite of instability (sometimes called neuroticism), and psychoticism is the opposite of self-control.

Introversion refers to a reserved nature and the pursuit of solitary activities. Introverts tend to be shy, thoughtful, risk avoiders, and shun social engagements.

Extroversion refers to the opposites of these human characteristics. Extroverts tend to be sociable and spontaneous, thrive on change and be willing to take risks. *Psychoticism* refers to an aggressive, egocentric and antisocial nature. People high on psychoticism display such attributes as aggression, coldness and moodiness, are fraught with guilt and are unstable. People who score low on psychoticism do not show these attributes. Such people tend to be even-tempered and are characterized by emotional stability. Eysenck believed that the most important aspects of a person's personality can be captured by a two-dimensional model (Figure 5.3).

Figure 5.3 illustrates the effects of various combinations of the three dimensions of introversion–extroversion, stability–instability and psychoticism, and relates them to the four personality types described by the Greek physician Galen in the second century AD. We should note that the two basic dimensions intersect at right angles (meaning that they are statistically uncorrelated or independent). Therefore, knowing how extrovert an individual is reveals little about a person's level of emotional

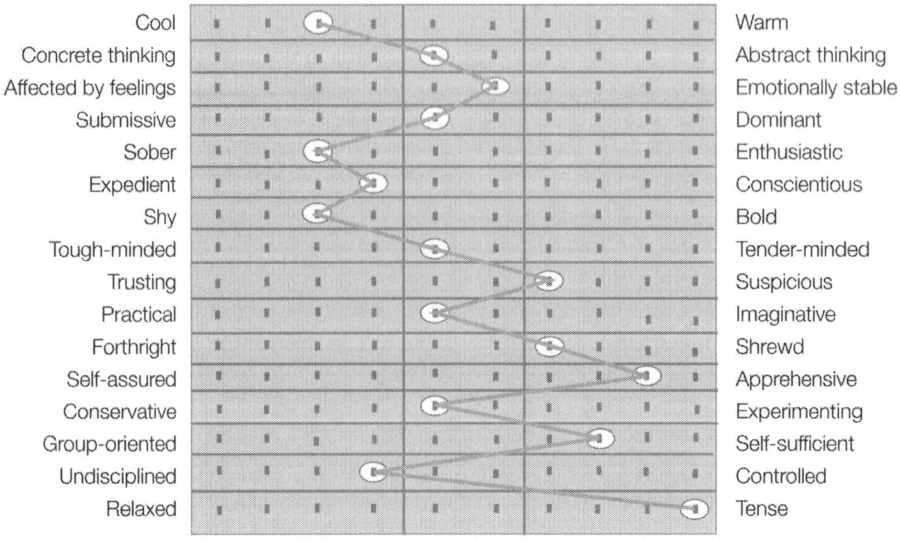

introversion: a personality dimension that characterizes people who are territorial and solitary

extroversion: a personality dimension that characterizes people who are outgoing, talkative, sociable and assertive

Figure 5.2 – Two hypothetical personality profiles using Cattell's 16PF test

stability – she or he could fall anywhere along the stability dimension. The secondary traits shown in the diagram reflect varying combinations of these two primary dimensions. Thus, we can see that the emotionally unstable (neurotic) extrovert is touchy, restless and aggressive. In contrast, the stable extrovert is a carefree, lively individual who tends to seek out leadership roles. The unstable introvert is moody, anxious and rigid, but the stable introvert tends to be calm, even-tempered and reliable.

Eysenck's research produced data to show that test scores measuring these two basic personality dimensions can predict people's key personality patterns, including specific behaviour tendencies or disorders. Leaders, for example, are likely to be in the 'sanguine' quadrant and tend to display outgoing, sociable behaviour. Criminals, on the other hand, are likely to be in the 'choleric' quadrant and tend to display aggressive and impulsive behaviour. Eysenck's trait theory of personality has received considerable support because the three dimensions have been replicated in factor analyses performed by many different researchers.[7]

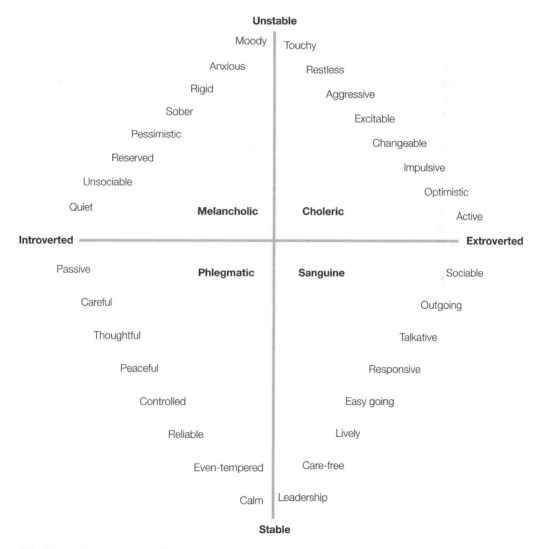

Figure 5.3 – Eysensk's major personality dimensions
Source: Eysenck (1973)[54]

The five-factor model of personality

As we have seen, trait theorists tend to divide into those who suggest that personality is best captured by measuring a large number of basic traits, such as Gordon Allport and Raymond Cattell, and those who suggest that the basic structure of personality can be captured by grouping 'high-order' dimensions, such as Hans Eysenck. The 'Big Five' model of personality trait structure proposes that personality is organized around only five core dimensions: openness, conscientiousness, extroversion, agreeableness and neuroticism.[10,11] These Big Five personality dimensions, represented by the handy acronym 'OCEAN' (or 'CANOE' if the words are reconfigured), are shown in Table 5.1.

Researchers using the Big Five model hold that when a person is placed at a specific point on each of these five core personality dimensions by means of a test or direct observations of behaviour, the essence of that person's personality is captured. These Big Five personality dimensions may be universal, since they were found to be consistent in a study of women and men in diverse Asian, European and North American cultures.[11–13]

stop reflect

Where would you place yourself on the personality scales? What is your reaction to the models? Are personality traits inherited or do they arise from social experience? What are the predictive advantages of the broad general traits and the narrow specific traits?

The research also shows evidence that some personality dimensions tend to be more stable than others over time. For example, introversion–extroversion tends to be quite stable from childhood into adulthood and across the adult years. When it comes to stability of behaviour across situations, personality again shows both a degree of stability and some capacity for change. For example, regarding the higher-order trait of 'conscientiousness', an employee might be highly conscientious in one situation (such as handing in class assignments on time to complete a college programme of studies) without being conscientious in another (such as coming to work on time).

nomothetic approach: an approach to explanation in which we seek to identify relationships between variables across many cases

Trait theorists have made an important contribution by focusing attention on the value of identifying, classifying and measuring stable and enduring personality characteristics. But this so-called **nomothetic approach** to understanding personality has severe limitations. It is argued elsewhere, for example, that researchers need to pay more attention to how traits interact with one another to affect various behaviours if we are to capture the true personality. There is a tendency for researchers to make predictions on the basis of a single measured personality trait without taking into account other personality factors that also might influence the action in question.[1]

THE PSYCHODYNAMIC THEORY OF PERSONALITY

Many social psychologists and organizational theorists believe that personality emerges from complex processes too dynamic to be captured by factor analysis. The

Table 5.1 – The Big Five model of personality trait structure and the associated lower-order traits

Dimensions	Lower-order traits
Openness	Artistically sensitive, intellectual interests, reflective, insightful, curious, imaginative
Conscientiousness	Efficient, reliable, responsible, scrupulous, ethical, persevering, organized, self-disciplined
Extroversion	Talkative, outgoing, candid, adventurous, sociable, assertive, gregarious, energetic
Agreeableness	Good-natured, forgiving, generous, non-critical, warm, gentle, cooperative, trusting, compassionate
Neuroticism	Anxious, self-pitying, nervous, tense, hostile, excitable, emotionally unstable, impulsive

Source: Adapted from Bernstein et al. (2000)[8]

Austrian physician Sigmund Freud (1856–1939) developed the influential psycho-analytic theory of personality, which claims that the dynamic interplay of inner psychological processes determines ways of thinking, feeling and acting. Freud's work introduced such terms as 'ego', 'fixation', 'libido', 'rationalization' and 'repression' into Western popular discourse, as well as having a profound effect on twentieth-century personality research. The significance of psychoanalytic theories of socialization pioneered by Freud has been recognized by sociologists.

When treating patients with the French neurologist Jean Charcot, Freud became convinced that conversion hysteria, a disorder in which physical symptoms such as paralysis and blindness appeared suddenly and with no apparent physical cause, was connected to painful memories, which were often sexual or aggressive in nature, and seemed to have been repressed by the patient. When his patients were able to re-experience these traumatic memories, their physical symptoms often markedly improved or disappeared.

weblink
Go to www.freud.org.uk, a site dedicated to Sigmund Freud and his work

Freud experimented with various techniques, including hypnosis and dream analysis, to unearth the buried contents of the unconscious mind. His research convinced him that personality develops out of each person's struggle to meet her or his basic needs in a world that often frustrates those efforts. Freud suggested that an individual's personality is determined by conscious, preconscious and unconscious brain activity, with the unconscious part of the mind exerting great influence on consciousness and behaviour. He proposed that most psychological events are located in what he termed the subconscious, a vast repository of traumatic events that a person apparently can no longer consciously recall without the use of hypnosis. The conscious mind, which consists of mental events of which people are presently aware, represented just the 'tip of the iceberg' (Figure 5.4).

The structure of personality: id, ego and superego

According to Freud, personality is made up three separate but interacting parts: the id, the ego and the superego. In Figure 5.4, the pointed arrows inside the 'Freudian iceberg' are meant to show the connections and the dynamic nature of the structure of personality. Freud saw the **id** (the Latin word for 'it') as the unconscious portion of the personality, where the libido, which is the primary source of life instincts, resides. The id is the only structure present at birth, and it functions in a totally irrational manner. The id operates on the pleasure principle, seeking the immediate gratifica-tion of impulses produced by two innate drives, sex and aggression.

id: Sigmund Freud's term for the component of personality that includes all of the individual's basic biological drives and needs that demand immediate gratification

ego: according to Sigmund Freud, the rational, reality-oriented component of personality that imposes restrictions on the innate pleasure-seeking drives of the id

superego: Sigmund Freud's term for the human conscience, consisting of the moral and ethical aspects of personality

For Freud, the id is:

> the dark, inaccessible part of our personality ... It is filled with energy reach-ing it from the instincts, but it has no organization, produces no collective will, but only a striving to bring about the satisfaction of the instinctual needs subject to the observance of the pleasure principle.[14]

The **ego** (Latin for 'I') is the thinking, organizing and protective self. It functions primarily at a conscious level, it controls and integrates behaviour, and it operates according to the reality principle. It negotiates a compromise between the pressures of the id and the demands of reality, deciding when and under what conditions the id can safely discharge its impulses and satisfy its needs. For example, the ego would seek sexual gratification within a consenting relationship rather than allow the pleas-ure principle to dictate an impulsive sexual assault.

The third component of personality is the **superego** (Latin meaning 'beyond' or 'above' the ego), which is subdivided into the conscience and the ego ideal, and tells

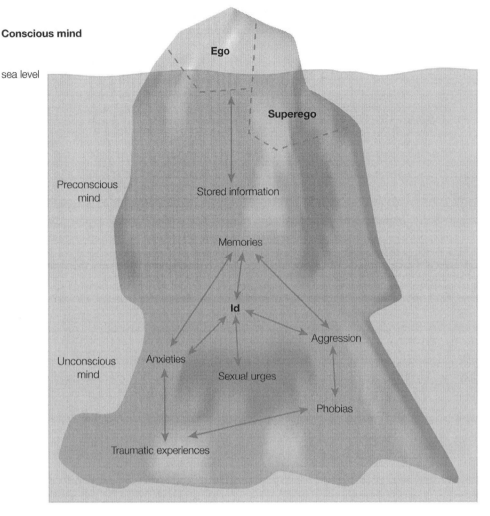

Conscious mind

sea level

Ego

Superego

Preconscious mind

Stored information

Memories

Id

Aggression

Unconscious mind

Anxieties

Sexual urges

Phobias

Traumatic experiences

Figure 5.4 – Freud's conception of the personality structure: 'the Freudian iceberg'

us what we should and should not do. The superego, the moral arm of the personality, determines which actions are permissible and punishes wrongdoing with feelings of guilt. Like the ego, the superego strives to control the instincts of the id, particularly the sexual and aggressive impulses that are condemned by Western society. Whereas the id screams 'I want!', the superego replies, 'Don't you dare! That would be wicked!' For the superego, moralistic principles take precedence over realist ones. Thus, the superego might cause a person to experience intense guilt over sexual deviance.

The ego must achieve a compromise between the demands of the id, the constraints of the superego and the demands of reality. This mediating role has earned the ego the title the 'executive of the personality'.[1]

Freud's theory of personality set the scene for a never-ending struggle between the id and the superego for control of the ego. When the ego confronts id drives that threaten to get out of control, anxiety results. Anxiety serves as a signal and motivates the ego to deal with the problem. Freud proposed a number of defence mechanisms to enable people to cope with these conflicts. Examples of defence mechanisms are described in Table 5.2. The principal defence mechanism is repression.

stop reflect
Have you ever found yourself using any of Freud's defence mechanisms? If so, what was the situation?

Plate 2 – Research into the genetic basis of personality suggests that traits such as extroversion may be inherited.
Source: Getty Images

Table 5.2 – Psychoanalytic defence mechanisms

Defence mechanism	Description	Example
Repression	An active defensive process through which anxiety-arousing impulses or memories are pushed into the unconscious mind	A sports celebrity who was sexually abused in childhood develops amnesia for the event
Denial	A person refuses to acknowledge anxiety-arousing aspects of the environment. The denial may involve either the emotions connected with the event or the event itself	A young man who is told he has terminal cancer refuses to consider the possibility that he will not recover
Displacement	An unacceptable or dangerous impulse is repressed, and then directed at a safer substitute target	A female employee who is harassed by her boss experiences no anger at work, but then goes home and abuses her husband and children
Rationalization	A person constructs a false but plausible explanation or excuse for an anxiety-arousing behaviour or event that has already occurred	An employee caught stealing justifies the act by pointing out that the company can afford the loss, and besides, other employees are stealing too

Source: Adapted from Passer et al. (2003)[1]

Freud believed that, in repression, the ego uses some of its energy to prevent anxiety-arousing thoughts, feelings and impulses from entering consciousness. Defence mechanisms operate unconsciously, so people are unusually unaware that they are using self-deception to ward off anxiety.

In Freud's theory, personality develops through seven psychosexual stages: oral, anal, phallic, Oedipus complex, Electra complex, latency and genital – which involve seeking pleasure from specific parts of the body called erogenous zones. A major shortcoming of psychoanalytic theory is that many of its concepts are ambiguous and difficult to define and measure operationally. A second major criticism is that Freud laid too much emphasis on the events of early childhood as determinants of adult personality.

weblink
Go to http://pandc.ca
for books and theorists
on personality and
consciousness

SOCIOCULTURAL THEORIES OF PERSONALITY

In this section, we present an introduction to the work of prominent social psychologists and sociologists who, in different ways, are interested in understanding personality from a sociocultural perspective. According to the trait and psychodynamic approaches, personality consists of traits that shape thoughts, feelings and actions. In contrast, those taking a sociocultural approach understand personality to be fundamentally rooted in life experience, communities of practice and relationships. This **idiographic approach** posits that personality is acquired through learning in an immediate social milieu – the social setting that is directly open to an individual's personal experience. In essence, its central tenet is that personality should not be located within typologies but be understood as a complex social entity, closely related to self-image and identity.

idiographic approach: an approach to explanation in which we seek to explain the relationships among variables within a particular case or event; it contrasts with nomothetic analysis

Sociocultural researchers examine how personality is connected with social experience and the society in which people live: the culture, socialization and social dynamics of social interaction and situations. To illustrate this broad sociocultural perspective, we consider significant *social-cognitive* and *phenomenological* approaches to personality.

The social-cognitive approach, sometimes called the social-learning approach, emphasizes the development of personality through people interacting with a social environment that provides learning experiences. The **phenomenological approach** to personality suggests that the way people perceive and interpret social experience forms their personalities and influences their thoughts, feelings and actions.

phenomenological approach: a philosophy concerned with how researchers make sense of the world around them, and whose adherents believe that the social researcher must 'get inside people's heads' to understand how they perceive and interpret the world

social-learning theory: a theory stating that much learning occurs by observing others and then modelling the behaviours that lead to favourable outcomes and avoiding the behaviours that lead to punishing consequences

The social-cognitive approach to personality

The most influential social-cognitive or **social-learning theories** are those of Julian Rotter and Albert Bandura.[15-17] These theorists have developed an approach that views personality as the sum total of the cognitive habits and behaviours that develop as people learn through experience in their social setting.

Julian Rotter (pronounced like 'motor') argued that a person's decision to engage in a behaviour in a given situation is determined by two factors:

- what the person expects to happen following the action
- the value the person places on the outcome, which is called the reinforcement value.

Expectancy is our perception of how likely it is that certain consequences will occur if we engage in a particular behaviour within a specific situation. 'Reinforcement

expectancy theory:
a motivation theory based on the idea that work effort is directed toward behaviours that people believe will lead to desired outcomes

locus of control: a personality trait referring to the extent to which people believe events are within their control

weblink
Go to http://sociologyindex.com for major ideas in the sociological study of socialization

self-efficacy: the beliefs people have about their ability to perform specific situational task(s) successfully

value' is basically how much we desire or dread the outcome that we expect the action to produce. For example, candidates for a particular position may spend a lot of money on new clothes to attend a job interview because past learning leads them to expect that doing so will help secure the job, and they place a high value on having the job.

Rotter also argued that people learn general ways of thinking about their environment, in particular about how life's rewards and punishments are controlled. Differences in this generalized expectancy concerning the degree of personal control that individuals have in their lives produced Rotter's influential concept of the internal–external **locus of control**. People with an internal locus of control believe that life outcomes are largely under personal control and depend on their own efforts. In contrast, people with an external locus of control believe that the environment is largely beyond their control, and that their fate has less to do with their own efforts than with the influence of external factors, such as luck.

Research suggests that the locus of control that people develop has important implications for personality in later life. For example, in the workplace, there is evidence that an internal locus of control is positively related to self-esteem and feelings of personal effectiveness, and the internally focused are less likely to experience depression or anxiety, and tend to cope with stress in a more active and problem-focused manner than do externally focused people.[18] One study has shown that because locus of control is fashioned by people's social experience, this aspect of personality can change.[19] In the workplace, for example, experiencing participative decision-making arrangements may cause a shift towards an internal locus of control in managers and non-managers alike.

According to Albert Bandura, neither personal traits nor the social context alone determines personality. Instead, he argues that the environment, the person and the person's behaviour interact in a pattern of two-way causal links to determine personality. In short, personality is determined by what Bandura calls *reciprocal determinism* (Figure 5.5).

One personal variable in this web of influence is particularly important in Bandura's view: **self-efficacy** refers to a person's beliefs about her or his ability to perform the actions needed to achieve desired outcomes. People whose self-efficacy is high have confidence in their ability to do what it takes to overcome obstacles and achieve their goals.

Self-efficacy not only determines whether a person will engage in a particular behaviour, but also determines the extent to which he or she will sustain that behaviour in the face of adversity. For example, if you believe that you are qualified for a job at the BBC, you are likely to apply for an interview. Even if you are turned down for the job, you are apt to apply for an interview at another TV company because you

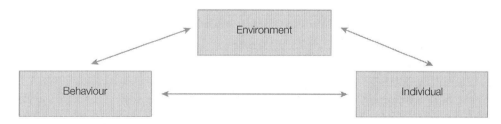

Figure 5.5 - Bandura's model of reciprocal determinism

are confident of your abilities. High self-efficacy can facilitate both the frequency and the quality of behaviour–environment interactions, and low self-efficacy can hamper both.[7]

stop reflect
Which environmental factors do you feel may be more important for shaping personality? What kinds of personality difference between males and females have you observed? Are these differences genuine or a product of your culture? How do you know?

For Bandura, self-efficacy beliefs are always specific to particular situations. Thus, we may have high self-efficacy in some situations and low self-efficacy in others. For example, those who have mastered sophisticated computer software skills do not feel more generally capable in all areas of their life, despite their enhanced computer abilities. Efficacy beliefs are strong predictors of future performance and accomplishment. In short, they become a kind of self-fulfilling prophecy.

The phenomenological approach to personality

The most influential phenomenological theories, also known as humanistic theories, of personality are those of Abraham Maslow (1908–1970) and Carl Rogers (1902–1987). These theorists emphasize the positive, fulfilling experiences of life, and argue that the way people perceive and interpret their social experiences forms their personality. Maslow believed that human motivation is based on a hierarchy of needs, and that understanding personality requires an understanding of this hierarchy of needs.[20] According to Maslow, personality is the expression of a basic human tendency towards growth and self-actualization. The innate drive for self-actualization, the realization of a person's true intellectual and emotional potential, is not specific to any particular culture. Maslow considered it as being a fundamental part of human nature: 'Man has a higher and transcendent nature, and this is part of his [sic] essence' (ref. 21, p. xvi).

Like Maslow, Carl Rogers saw personality as the expression of a basic human tendency towards growth and self-actualization.[22] However, unlike Maslow, he did not view personality development in terms of satisfying a hierarchy of needs. Rogers argued that personality development centres on a person's self-concept, the part of social experience that a person identifies as 'I' or 'me'. He believed that people who accurately experience the self – with all its preferences, approval, love, respect and affection – are en route to self-actualization.

The key to forming a psychologically positive personality is to develop a positive self-concept or image of oneself. How does a person do this? According to Rogers, people are happy if they feel that others are happy with them. Similarly, people are unhappy when others are dissatisfied or disappointed with them. People's feelings towards themselves depend significantly on what others think of them. From early childhood, we learn that there exist certain criteria or conditions that must be met before others give us positive regard. Rogers called these criteria 'conditions of worth'. In Rogers's view, rewards and punishment from others are important in personality development because they influence behaviour and shape self-perceptions. In short, personality is formed partly by the actualizing tendency and partly by others' evaluations.[8]

The social-self approach to personality

The traits (nomothetic) approach to understanding personality prevails in organizational behaviour literature, but the sociological concept of the *self* offers an alternative conception of the individual. For sociologists, the processes of socialization, the life-long social experience by which people learn culture and develop their human potential, has great relevance for understanding personality. A century ago in 1902, sociologist Charles Cooley (1864–1929) introduced the phrase the

looking-glass self:
Cooley's term for the way
in which a person's sense
of self is derived from the
perceptions of others

'looking-glass self' in his book *Human Nature and the Social Order* to mean a conception of self based largely on how we imagine we appear to others, and imagine judgements likely to be made about that appearance.[23]

Writing almost 30 years before the psychologist Carl Rogers, sociologist George Herbert Mead (1863–1931) expounded the concept of the looking-glass self, and developed a *process-relational theory* to explain how personality is formed through social activity and interaction with other people. Mead's writings have some similarities to those of Maslow and Rogers. Central to Mead's theory of personality is the concept of the 'self', that part of a person's personality composed of self-awareness and self image.[24] Mead believed that people form a personality by internalizing – or taking in – their locale. He rejected the notion that the self is inherited at birth and that personality is formed by biological inner impulses or drives, as argued by Sigmund Freud. According to Mead, the self develops only with social activity and social relationships, and if there is social isolation, as in the case of isolated children, the human body may develop but no self emerges.

After a self is formed, people usually, but not always, manifest it. For example, the novelist Daniel Defoe's character Robinson Crusoe developed a self while he was living in his own culture, and he continued to have a self when he was alone on what he thought was a deserted island. Thus, Crusoe continued to have the ability to take himself as an object.

The self is dialectically related to the human mind. The body, therefore, is not a self but becomes a self only when the mind has developed and engaged in reflexiveness. While Freud concentrated on the denial of the id's drives as the mechanism that generates the self's objective side, Mead drew attention to the source of the 'me' – how we become self-aware – by taking 'the role of the other'. People are interpretative creatures who must make sense of the world they live in. We learn to play different roles in this process. We are at different times children, students, friends, workers, parents and so on, and we do not behave in the same way in every situation. This process of role taking demonstrates that personality is a social product, and that 'group or collective action consists of aligning of individual actions, brought about by individuals' interpreting or taking into account each other's actions'.[25]

stop reflect
Make a list of the
personality traits you think
characterize you. Share
your list with others who
know you well, and ask
what they think. To what
extent, if at all, do you
think your own personality
originates from the
interaction between you
and your environment?
Can you give examples?

Language is an important aspect of socialization and the development of the self. As children learn to understand words and later to use them, they simultaneously learn to categorize their experience and evaluate their own behaviour and that of others. The first words many English or German children say is 'No' or 'Nein'. The use of language is one way individuals emphatically gauge different cultural meanings in disparate social situations and act accordingly. The self is reflexive, in that a person can become the object of her or his thought and actions. Language is central to the development of individual identity, the self. Moreover, 'the dynamics of the self and others are open to complex layers of interpretation and reflexive distancing' (ref. 24, p. 160).

Mead believed that the self has two parts: the 'I' (the unsocialized self) and the 'me' (the socialized self). The 'I' is the spontaneous, incalculable, impulsive, unsocialized and creative aspect of the self. Mead emphasized the 'I' because it is a key source of creativity in the social process, an individual's values are located in the 'I', it holds something that all individuals seek – self-realization – and finally, as society develops, people become increasingly dominated by the 'I' and less by the 'me'.

The 'me' is the social part of the self that is developed as the object of others' attitudes, beliefs and behaviour, including one's own reflections on one's self; it is 'the organized set of attitudes of others which one himself assumes' (ref. 23, p. 197). All

OB In focus Psychometric testing: ensuring the right fit

In spite of their best efforts, many organizations struggle with consistently finding and hiring successful job candidates. To make better selection decisions, many firms are turning to a less traditional tool: psychometric assessments. Psychometric assessments are scientifically designed to provide a standardized measure of a candidate's general intellectual ability, competencies and personality traits. While there are many different tests available, they can generally be classified into two broad types: ability and personality.

Ability is a measure of 'can do'. An ability assessment measures a person's current level of knowledge and her or his capability to acquire further knowledge and skills. It also reveals a candidate's capabilities and learning potential. Examples of assessments that fall in this area include measures of intelligence, verbal ability and mechanical aptitude. Ability assessments are among the best predictors of job performance.

Personality is a measure of 'will do'. A personality assessment measures typical behaviour, and discloses what candidates are likely to do on a daily basis. It is designed to measure a person's preference for behaving in certain ways. Personality measures also reveal whether the individual is easy to manage, works hard, offers innovative solutions and works well with others.

Psychometric tests are also used for assessing characteristics that cannot be developed through training but are acquired over long periods of time, such as personality traits or in-depth knowledge of a profession. The use of well-constructed assessments can improve organization fit and address counterproductive behaviours.

Shawn Bakker, a psychologist at Psychometrics Canada (www.psychometrics.com). Source: *Canadian HR Reporter,* March 27, 2006, p. 7.

peer group: a group of people who are linked by common interests, equal social position and (usually) similar age

social interaction has both parts: individuals initiate action (the 'I' phase of the self), and individuals continue their action based on how others respond to their behaviour (the 'me' phase of the self). Whereas the 'I' is associated with creativity, change and reconstruction of the self, the 'me' has a self-control aspect, in that it serves to stabilize the self. The combining of the 'I' and the 'me' leads to the formation of individual personality.[26] This reflexive process is invariably a social one, in which people form their sense of self in the context of family, peers and the mass media.[27] Thus, a person's personality will change across her or his life course as she or her participates in a community and interacts with different pervasive agents of socialization – family, school, **peer group** and mass media.

Mead's concept of the 'I' and the 'me' should not be confused with Freud's concept of the id and superego. As others have pointed out, Freud believed that the id and superego were firmly embedded in the biological organism, whereas Mead, on the other hand, rejected any biological element of the self. Furthermore, whereas the id and superego are locked in constant struggle, the 'I' and the 'me' work cooperatively.

interactionism: what people do when they are in one another's presence, for example in a work group or team

individualism: the extent to which a person values independence and personal uniqueness

Detractors argue that Mead's theory of personality is completely social, neglecting any biological element at all. Moreover, Mead's analysis of personality is rooted in the tradition of symbolic **interactionism**, a sociological perspective that focuses on the subjective meanings that people create through face-to-face communication in micro-level social settings. This was a perspective that resonated deeply in the North American **individualistic** culture and early US sociology.[28]

IDENTITY AND PERSONALITY

The term 'identity' is derived from the Latin root *idem,* implying sameness and continuity. Its precise meaning is contested, but here we define identity as a complex fusion of the interplay between the inner self and the outer communal culture and social interaction.[29] The identity approach to understanding personality is located within a process-relational view of the subject or individual. According to this perspective, individuals are conceived as having emerging identities that are developed by, and also develop, the institutions and processes of modernity.[30] As children develop, they identify social roles, first within their family and later in the community. They also develop an understanding of status differences, and the ways in which roles interact with class, gender, ethnicity and race to create complex patterns of social behaviour. This process of socialization is therefore affected by whether they are the son or daughter of a neurosurgeon or a hospital porter; whether they grow up in a two-parent or a single-parent household; whether they grow up in London or Londonderry; whether they speak English or Hindi; and whether they worship at a mosque or a synagogue. As a result of socialization, most people acquire a set of attitudes, values, skills and behaviours that enable them to form and sustain relationships with others, work cooperatively with co-workers, avoid deviant behaviour and form a sense of self and identity.

The difference between personality and identity can be understood by answering the question, 'Who am I?' You could respond to this question with a list of personality traits such as 'I am an introvert, thoughtful, and reliable person.' Alternatively, your response could be, 'I am a parent, I work part-time at the Body Shop, and I am a university student.' The second set of responses, unlike the first, makes no reference to personality traits, but portrays a sense of identity on the basis of how we are related to others (for example, partner, mother, employee or student), and as such is deeply contextualized within the multiple social relations within which we are embedded. Identity speaks to social relations, to a fluid process of 'becoming' rather than an end state of 'being'. Identity is not something we are born with: it is structured or shaped by, and also shapes, societal influences. For Peter Berger, identity is defined clearly to be 'socially bestowed, socially sustained and socially transformed' (ref. 31, p. 98; see also ref. 32).

Plate 3 –As children develop, they identify social roles, first within their family and later in the community. They also develop an understanding of status differences, and the ways in which roles interact with class, gender, ethnicity and race to create complex patterns of social behaviour.
Source: iStockphoto

personal identity: the
ongoing process of self-
development through
which we construct a
unique sense of ourselves
and our relationship to
the world around us

social identity: the
perception of a 'sameness'
or 'belongingness' to
a human collective
with common values,
goals or experiences

The concept of identity is complex and multifaceted. The main sources of identity include social class, gender, disability, sexual orientation and race and ethnicity. Anthony Giddens[33] identifies two types of identity: **personal identity** and **social identity**. Personal identity (or self-identity) refers to the ongoing process of self-development through which we construct a unique sense of ourselves and our relationship to the world around us. Identity is constructed through both social relations and discourses around, for example, gender (woman versus man), sexuality (straight versus gay) and race (black versus white). So, for example, ethnocultural factors may define identity. If I am Jewish, my religion may play a larger role in my identity than if I am agnostic, by virtue of the fact that Jewish people have been historically stigmatized. Identity draws upon the work of symbolic interactionists.[34]

If self-identity sets people apart as distinct individuals, social identity is the perception of 'sameness' or 'belongingness', the ways in which individuals are the same or members of some human collective – signs that denote who, in a basic sense, that person *is*.[33] Examples of social identities might include occupation, trade unionist, feminist, environmentalist, mother, Asian, disabled, Muslim and so forth. Social identities have a collective dimension and are predicated on a set of common values or goals or experiences. An individual can have multiple identities, some of which may be more dominant depending on a specific situation. What makes our identity dynamic, rather than static, is our capacity as self-conscious, self-reflexive human beings to constantly construct and reconstruct our identities.

Individuals spend a significant amount of time in work organizations and, unsurprisingly, derive a sense of identity from their occupation or from the organization or a work team within the organization. When a person says, 'I love my work; I am my work,' it connotes a sense of identity and its power to influence proactive behaviours. Each occupation, work group or organization will have a set of shared beliefs, values,

OB and globalization

Identity and instability in an uncertain economy

When first getting to know someone, it is common practice to ask them what they do for work. Being able to connect a person to a particular profession can help us to identify that person in relation to characteristics we associate with that line of work. For instance, we might imagine that someone working as a librarian might be shy or reserved, while a commodities broker might be assumed to be self-confident and assertive. Although such stereotypes often have little bearing on individuals' actual identities or personalities, we nonetheless persist in the notion that what someone does for work has something to say about who they are as a person. Likewise, many workers identify themselves in terms of the work they do and their social position in the workplace.

For workers in today's uncertain economy, the prospect of being made redundant generates stress not only about lost income, but also about the threat of an unmooring of their personal identities. Psychologists specializing in organizational behaviour note that, for many workers, their sense of self is inseparable from the work they do and the social environment of the workplace. The inability to engage in those familiar practices can leave them feeling ungrounded and even depressed. In a *Financial Times* article (Jacobs, 2008) dealing with redundancy and depression, a former banker explains how an organizational culture that promotes hard work, high achievement and an 'alpha male' approach can position workers for a long fall should they be made redundant:

> Some think the world revolves around them, in good times and bad. When things are good they feel like masters of the universe, but when the bubble bursts they take it very hard. It can be devastating.

In such situations, workers can stake their sense of self almost entirely on their work and, more specifically, on their place within the structure of the organization. Being unseated from their position within the organization can be equated to losing the reference point from which they are able to make sense of the world and their place in it. According to London therapist Christine Martin, 'Redundancy demands existential questions alongside the financial worries' (Jacobs, 2008).

Anthropologist Dorothy Holland and her colleagues (Holland et al., 1998) describe identity as a sense of self that is actively and continually constructed, tested and refigured through daily social practices. They explain that these social practices take place in particular cultural realms that provide resources and structures that individuals can draw on to formulate personal identities which reproduce (or resist) those cultural realms. The importance of improvisation, agency and creativity – within defined social worlds – is also central to identity formation.

Using Holland et al.'s approach to identity, we can consider workplace culture in the UK as a cultural realm that provides workers with a set of practices and social relations that they use to position themselves vis-à-vis their work tasks, relationships with colleagues and the world at large. Understanding the links between organizational culture, personal identity formation and economic stability (or instability) can help managers to provide appropriate support services to workers when redundancies are deemed necessary.

stop!   Do you think it is a positive or a negative thing for workers to have identities closely entwined with – even dependent upon – their work? Would such close links between identity and work benefit or hinder the workplace? How might they benefit or hinder other areas of workers' lives?

Sources and further research

Holland, D., Lachicotte, W. Jr., Skinner, D. and Cain, C. (1998) *Identity and Agency in Cultural Worlds*, Cambridge, MA: Harvard University Press.

Jacobs, E. (2008) 'Redundancy and a depression', *Financial Times*, August 19, 2008. Available at: www.ft.com; www.journalisted.com/article?id=763449.

Sheedy, B. (2005) 'All is not lost', *Management Today*, November/December 2005. Available at: www.aim.com.au/DisplayStory.asp?ID=571; www.doningtongroup.com/UserFiles/Media/0905-allisnotlost-SB-AIMmag.pdf.

Note: This feature was written by Gretchen Fox, PhD, Anthropologist, Timberline Natural Resource Group, Canada.

norms and demands particular to the group. Organizational goals and processes, such as sustainable products and practices, job design or rewards, can shape the relative value that individuals attach to joining and retaining their membership of groups or organizations. Equally, the termination of the employment relationship can lead to a loss of identity. The advocacy for a 'strong' organizational culture as a motivational strategy in an historical context of high-performance work systems underscores the importance of identity. Cultural control aims to have employees possess direct links to the values and goals of top managers in order to activate the emotion and create an identity that might elevate loyalty and commitment to the organization.

The power of social identity to define an occupation or organization's status relative to others can pose significant challenges to managers. For example, individuals may avoid or disassociate from a low-status organization considered to be managed without due regard to social responsibility, environmental sustainability and ethical practices. Some new theories of motivation, such as self-concept theory and whole-self theory, have linked the psychological treatment of work motivation to the notion of identity or self. Studies suggest that an individual's coherent sense of identity or loss of identity is far more important than most traditional treatments of work motivation acknowledge.[35,36]

APPLYING PERSONALITY THEORIES IN THE WORKPLACE

While managers tend to think of diversity in terms of such factors as gender, ethnic origin and disability, the variety of personalities in the workplace is also important. The nomothetic view of personality dominates management literature, partly because it enables management to render individuals 'knowable' and 'quantifiable' by identifying traits through personality testing.[37] Personality attributes determine how people interact with other workers, whether they can work on their own without supervision, whether they are conscientious or just do the minimum to 'get by', how they respond to change, whether they behave ethically or unethically, and much more.[38] For these reasons and others, organizations have developed an array of human resource management techniques to identify personality differences to help them to admit the 'right' people into the organization, and, once staff have been selected, this knowledge will help to identify those with the personality traits said to be required of an effective leader.

John Holland best articulated the view that organizations should consider aligning the requirements of the job and the characteristics of the workplace with personality characteristics.[39] In recent years, the awareness that organizations should focus on the degree of congruence between the individual and her or his work environment has expanded because of the need for workers to change and adapt to new work structures and employment relations. These include team working, individual-oriented performance-related compensation and a 'learning-oriented' organizational culture. Holland's personality–job fit model identifies six personality types – realistic, investigative, social, conventional, enterprising and artistic – each of which has a congruent occupational environment. Holland proposes that high congruence leads to satisfaction and the propensity to remain in that job or career. Table 5.3 defines these personality types and their personality attributes, and gives examples of congruent work environments.

Holland developed a model shaped like a hexagon that shows the relationships among occupational personality types, based on his Vocational Preference Inventory questionnaire, which contains 160 occupational titles. Respondents were asked to indicate which of the occupations they liked or disliked, and their answers were used to construct personality profiles. The closer two fields or orientations are in the hexagon, the more compatible they are. For example, the enterprising and social personality types are adjacent to each other in the hexagon model so, according to Holland's theory, individuals with both enterprising and social personalities have high compatibility (Figure 5.6).

There are three key points we should note about Holland's model:

- Intrinsic differences in personalities exist based on the restrictive Big Five personality model.
- Different types of occupation and work environment are better suited to certain personality types.
- Workers in workplaces and occupations congruent with their personality types should be more satisfied and more likely to remain with the organization than workers in incongruent occupations.

Research appears to strongly support the hexagonal model, but critics have pointed out that the model only incorporates the Big Five personality dimensions, and there are doubts whether the model can be generalized across cultures.[40–42]

With the resurgent interest in recruiting the 'right' people for the 'new' work regimes, and the 'discovery' of the Big Five personality model, research examining the relationships between personality traits and job performance, personality and social integration, and the efficacy of personality measuring instruments, has flourished. According to the new management parlance on knowledge work, workers are expected to create their own opportunities for innovation and positive change in the organization. Underlying the research on the relationship between personality traits and job

Table 5.3 – Holland's typology of personality and congruent work environments, and occupations

Personality type	Traits	Workplace characteristics	Congruent occupations
Realistic	Practical, shy, persistent, conforming, stable	Prefers physical activities that require skills and coordination	Mechanical engineer, farmer
Investigative	Analytical, creative, independent, reserved	Work involves thinking and analysing	Mathematician, biologist, systems analyst
Social	Sociable, friendly, outgoing, cooperative	Work involves helping and developing others	Social worker, teacher, counsellor, nurse
Conventional	Dependable, orderly, self-disciplined	Work is unambiguous, rule-regulated, orderly	Accountant, banker, administrator
Enterprising	Confident, ambitious, assertive, energetic	Prefers leading others, verbal activities, result-oriented setting	Lawyer, entrepreneur, salesperson, financial planner/ consultant
Artistic	Creative, disorderly, impulsive	Thrives on ambiguous and unstructured activities	Musician, architect, painter, designer

Source: Based on information from Holland (1985)[39] and Greenhaus (1987)[53]

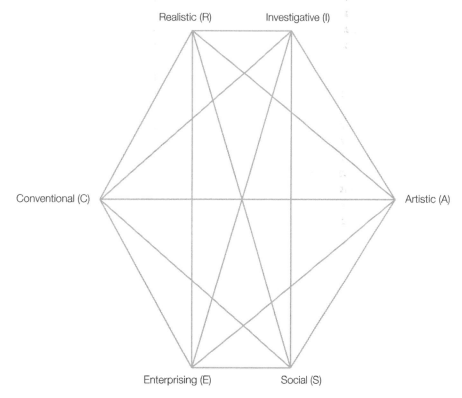

Figure 5.6 – Holland's individual–occupation hexagonal model
Source: Holland (1985). Reproduced in print by permission of Pearson Education, Inc. and digitally by permission of Psychological Assessment Resources, Inc.

performance is a presumption that a proactive personality – defined as a disposition to take action to influence one's environment – promotes job performance.[43] This is achieved by building a network of social relationships within an organization in order to gain access to information, wield influence and effect positive change – a process

social capital: the value of relationships between people, embedded in network links that facilitate trust and communication vital to overall organizational performance

referred to as **social capital**. In short, the social capital approach advocates a view that individual power within a work organization is predicated on developing a network of relationships, which in turn enhances job performance (Figure 5.7).

What do proactive employees do? By definition, employees with a proactive personality are inclined to construct their own environment. Proactive individuals are likely to seek ways to build a network of contacts in the organization that is conducive to their own self-interest. Proactive types, therefore, tend to seek allies and build alliances with other co-workers to support personal initiatives, and actively strive to become friends with people who occupy positions of influence and power. Thompson's quantitative study found a direct positive relationship between a proactive personality, network building and individual performance, suggesting that 'network building may occupy a critical stage in the process by which proactive personality engenders performance' (ref. 43, p. 1015).

Organizational behaviour theorists have long been interested in the connection between personality and innovative behaviours, and between personality and social integration. Henry Moon and his colleagues[44] identified personality and procedural fairness within a work organization as antecedents to proactive behaviour or 'taking charge'. Interestingly, the results show that the antecedents to proactive behaviour are based more on concerns about others than on self-interest. This suggests that getting employees to take charge within the firm may be more about 'we' than it is about 'me'.[44] An important aspect of the current wave of interest in self-managed work teams is the cultural dimension. In addition to changing methods of job performance, work teams demand changes in workers' attitude and behaviour.[45] Accordingly, organizational theorists are devoting increased attention to whether people with similar personalities make up more effective work teams.

The argument is that similar personalities might facilitate social integration among team members, increase the likelihood that co-workers will cooperate with each other, and foster trust between team leaders and members. Employment recruitment practices that create a homogeneous workforce of people with similar personalities and values may appear ideal in a team-based environment. As mentioned above, studies suggest that when employees hold similar personality characteristics, few rules, regulations and formal decision-making processes are needed to get work done. As a consequence, organizational leaders tend to choose people with personality traits similar to their own. The danger in top managers recruiting a workforce with similar personality traits is that homogeneity is a force potentially detrimental to change and long-term organizational survival.[5]

stop reflect
If you were recruiting people to join you on an important work project, would you try to hire people with a personality profile similar to your own? If so, why? Can you think of any advantages and disadvantages of this approach?

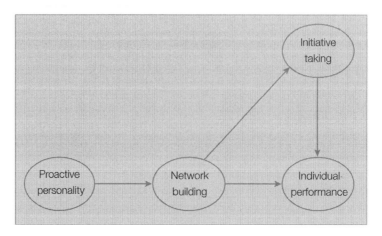

Figure 5.7 – A model of proactive personality and individual job performance

Work and Society: Why does she behave that way?

Many researchers who study work and personality stress the person–organization relationship. The assumption is that some personalities are a better 'fit' in particular organizational settings. Often, however, the question of person–organization fit is a complex one, and personality traits associated with highly skilled employees can sometimes be problematic.

One such personality trait is narcissism. A recent study suggests those with narcissistic personalities will have little to offer an organization:

> narcissists tend to lack empathy, engage in aggressive behavior and have self-serving motives ... narcissists should be especially unlikely to contribute positively to an organization's social and psychological climate by helping others, being courteous and a good sport, and going above and beyond the call of duty for the greater good.
>
> (Judge, et al., 2006, p. 765)

Narcissism would appear to be a personality trait that employers would want to avoid at all costs. However, it is important to realize that personality is only one of several factors that contribute to an individual's behaviour. Consider the following scenario. Sharon Smith had recently been hired by a mid-sized hospital as a specialist nurse practitioner – a new role situated midway between the physician and the traditional nurse. Those employed in more traditional nursing roles at the hospital resented the fact Sharon had taken over some of the more interesting and challenging aspects of their work. Sharon showed little sympathy for their concerns: 'Nurses need to understand that their education does not prepare them to perform these kinds of procedure safely.'

Sharon's interactions with physicians were also problematic. On one occasion, she clashed with Dr William Grant, a senior physician at the hospital. Dr Grant had questioned Sharon's recommendation that a particular patient could benefit from 'lifestyle changes'. Sharon responded without hesitation, 'There is no conclusive diagnosis for this patient, so why not proceed with the treatment the patient believes is best for him?' Later, in a conference with the ward manager, Sharon expressed her anger: 'Dr Grant has no right to question my judgement. In a situation like this, lifestyle changes are a perfectly reasonable course of action.'

Clearly, the idea of personality could prove useful in this context. Recognizing that Sharon exhibited many of the characteristics of a narcissistic personality might help managers make sense of a situation that seems to be getting out of control. However, it is possible to view Sharon's behaviour in a more positive light.

Perhaps Sharon's actions were the function of a conscientious rather than a narcissistic personality. Supporters of this more optimistic view might argue that Sharon was anxious to prove herself as an invaluable member of the healthcare team. But rather than working patiently to secure the trust and respect of her colleagues, she wanted immediate and unqualified validation. With the right 'coaching', however, Sharon could become aware of her personality traits, refine her social skills and make a genuine contribution to the hospital.

It is important to bear in mind that personalities are composed of a complex blend of 'traits' and, with appropriate mentoring, an individual may learn to manage various aspects of his or her personality. Issues of workplace design are also relevant here. When a new occupation is introduced into a well-established, hierarchical division of labour, conflicts are inevitable. Managers need to provide a clear rationale for change well in advance of the actual change. They must also create opportunities for dialogue among different members of the work team as the new occupation is integrated into established work roles and routines.

stop!   What do you think? Is Sharon 'programmed' by her personality to be an endless source of conflict at the hospital? Are there steps that could be taken help her become a productive member of a relatively harmonious work team?

What about the role of gender? Is the clash between Sharon and Dr Grant aggravated by the fact that healthcare workplaces have traditionally been dominated by men?

Sources and further information:

Austin, E. and Deary, I. (2002). 'Personality dispositions', pp. 187–211 in R. Sternberg (ed.), *Why Smart People Can Be So Stupid*, New Haven, CT: Yale University Press.

Judge, T., LePine, J. and Rich, B. (2006) 'Loving yourself abundantly: relationship of the narcissistic personality to self- and other perceptions of workplace deviance, leadership and task and contextual performance', *Journal of Applied Psychology*, 91(4), pp. 762–76.

For more information on the nurse practitioner, see the *Journal for Nurse Practitioners.*

Note: This feature was written by David MacLennan, Assistant Professor at Thompson Rivers University, BC, Canada.

Personality testing

The increased focus given to personality attributes, and how such attributes predict job performance and social integration, has led to increased research on selection methods in general, and personality testing in particular. Recent studies, for example, have explored the predictive validity of the Big Five personality model in relation to job performance through a meta-analysis of 36 studies that related validity measures to personality factors.[46] The empirically based research concluded that 'conscientiousness and emotional stability showed most validity for job performance, and that openness to experience was valid for training proficiency' (ref. 47, p. 239).

If you were a manager and had the task of writing within a week a complete personality description of an applicant you did not know for an important position in your organization, what would you do? Most likely you would seek information in a variety of ways. You might start by interviewing the applicant to elicit information about her strengths and weaknesses, interests and opinions. Based on the theories we have reviewed in this chapter, what questions would you ask? Would you ask questions related to the kinds of trait embodied in the Big Five model? Would you want to know about the person's early childhood experiences? Would you ask how she sees herself with others? Would you be interested in knowing how she responds to problems in various situations? You might ask her to complete a questionnaire that indicates her values, interests and preferences. You might also want to ask other people who know her well and obtain their views of what she is like. Finally, you might decide to ask her to perform job-related tasks and observe how she behaves in a variety of situations. As a manager or potential manager, your answers to these questions would tend to reflect your own view of what is important in describing personality.

The major methods used by organizations to assess personality and predict work behaviour are shown in Figure 5.8. These consist of the interview, inventories, behaviour assessment, personality tests and e-assessment.

The task of devising valid and useful personality measures is anything but simple, and it has taxed the ingenuity of psychologists for nearly a century.[1] To be useful from a managerial perspective, personality tests must conform to the standards of **reliability** and **validity**. Reliability refers to the extent to which a technique achieves consistency in what it is claiming to measure over repeated use. For example, a selection test that measures a stable personality trait should yield similar scores when administered to the same individuals at different times (test–retest reliability).

reliability: in sociological research, the extent to which a study or research instrument yields consistent results

validity: in sociological research, the extent to which a study or research instrument accurately measures what it is supposed to measure

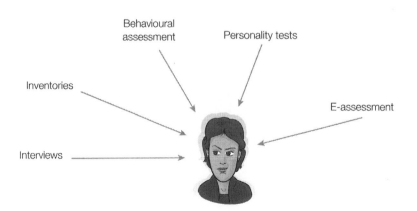

Figure 5.8 – Measurement approaches used to assess personality

In addition, different managers should score and interpret the test in the same way (interjudge reliability). Validity refers to the extent to which a test actually measures what it sets out to measure – in this case, the personality variable. A valid test allows us to predict a person's performance in work that is influenced by the personality variable being measured.

The interview is the oldest and most widely used method of personality assessment. For centuries, people have made judgements about others by talking with them and observing them. Structured selection interviews contain specific questions that are administered to every interviewee in order to obtain information about a candidate's thoughts, feelings and other internal states, as well as information about current and past relationships, experiences and behaviour.

Personality inventories, or scales, are used for assessing personality. These are usually self-completed questionnaires that include standard sets of questions, usually in a true/false or rating scale format, which are scored using an agreed-upon scoring key. Their advantages include the ability to collect data from many people at the same time, the fact that all people respond to the same items, and ease of scoring. Their major disadvantage is the possibility that some participants will 'fake' responses by choosing not to answer the items truthfully, in which case their scores will not be valid reflections of the trait being measured.[48]

Human resource practitioners can observe the behaviours they are interested in rather than ask participants about them. In behavioural assessment, psychologists devise an explicit coding system that contains the behavioural categories of interest. Trained human resource recruiters then observe candidates until there is a high level of consensus (interjudge reliability) about how to describe their behaviour.

On of the most widely used personality tests in North America is the **Myers–Briggs Type Indicator (MBTI).** The test contains 100 questions to participants about how they usually feel or act in certain situations. This personality test then labels participants as introverted or extroverted (I or E), intuitive or sensing (N or S), feeling or thinking (F or T) and perceiving or judging (P or J).

Online personality testing is also being used for personnel selection, a technique known as e-assessment. This form of assessment provides managers with the ability to conduct personality tests at any time and any place in the world, with the added advantage of the rapid processing of applicants.[47]

Whether the use of MBTI personality tests in fact accurately predicts future work performance is problematic.[49] It has been argued, for example, that broad traits such as Eysenck's 'Big Two' and the Big Five may be useful instruments for predicting behaviour across a whole range of work situations, much as a wide-beamed floodlight illuminates a large area. However, like a narrowly focused and intense spotlight, an analysis of specific traits such as Cattell's 16PF may be a better instrument in specific situations that call for the behaviours measured by the narrower traits. Personality testing provides organizations with insights into people's thoughts, feelings and behaviour. In other words, it makes aspects of personality quantifiable, and this allows the inner feelings of workers to be transmitted into measurements, about which management decisions can be made.

Some critical organizational theorists argue that psychometric testing measures what is effectively a stereotype of an 'ideal' worker or manager. It provides management with new ways of 'knowing' and managing managers and non-managers alike. It also represents a shift in management practices from the coercion of bodies through, for instance, time and motion and other Tayloristic techniques, to the attempted construction of self-regulated minds.[37,51,52] It is argued, for example, that

Myers–Briggs Type Indicator (MBTI): a personality test that measures personality traits

Critical insight

For many managers, personality tests such as the Myers–Briggs Type Indicator are useful instruments for measuring personality variables and helping to select suitable candidates to join the organization. Read pages 239–42 in Chapter 7, 'Recruitment and selection', in John Bratton and Jeff Gold's *Human Resource Management: Theory and Practice*,[50] for more information and discussion on psychometric testing. Also obtain a copy of Barbara Townley's *Reframing Human Resource Management: Power, Ethics and the Subject of Work*,[37] and read pages 83–98. What role, if any, does psychometric testing play in making workers known and manageable? Do you think Townley overstates her case? If so, why?

'The minutiae of the human soul – human interactions, feelings, and thoughts, the psychological relations of the individual to the group – [have] emerged as a new domain for management' (ref. 52, p. 72). Finally, personality assessment based on limited information can be damaging to the organization. For example, the over-emphasis on traits to identify 'ideal' personality types in which employees 'fit' into the workplace potentially reinforces the notion that workplace problems are embedded only in the personality characteristics of people, rather than being embedded in the organization at large and the inner tensions associated with managing the employment relationship.

CHAPTER SUMMARY

- Personality is the distinctive and relatively enduring pattern of thinking, feeling and acting that characterizes a person's response to her or his environment. In this chapter, we have examined a number of different approaches to personality. Each of these theories offers a view of how personality forms.

- Trait theorists try to identify and measure personality variables. They disagree concerning the number of traits needed to adequately describe personality. Raymond Cattell suggested a 16-factor model to capture personality dimensions, Eysenck offered a two-factor model, and McCrae and Costa suggested the Big Five factor model. Traits have not proved to be highly consistent across situations, and they also vary in consistency over time.

- We went on to examine Freud's psychoanalytic theory, which views personality as an energy system. He divided the personality into three structures: the id, the ego and the superego. According to Freud, the dynamics of personality involve a continuous struggle between the impulses of the id and the counterforces of the ego and superego.

- Sociocultural theorists emphasize the social context, the subjective experiences of the individual, and deal with perceptual and cognitive processes. We examined the theory of Albert Bandura, a leading social-cognitive theorist, who suggests that neither personal traits nor the social context alone determines personality. A key concept is reciprocal determinism, relating to two-way causal relations between personal characteristics, behaviour and the environment.

- Phenomenological theories, also known as humanistic theories, of personality were also examined. Influential humanist theorists such as Abraham Maslow and Carl Rogers emphasize the positive, fulfilling experiences of life, and argue that the way in which people perceive and interpret their social experiences forms their personality. Self-actualization is viewed as an innate positive force that leads people to realize their positive potential, if they are not thwarted by their social context.

⊚ In addition, the chapter examined Mead's theory of personality and his key concept of the self. He argues that people develop a personality by internalizing – or taking in – their immediate environment. He rejected the notion that the self is inherited and that personality is the product of biological inner impulses or drives, as argued by Sigmund Freud. According to Mead, the self develops only with social activity and social relationships.

⊚ The chapter has examined the role that an individual's identity (or identities) plays in determining behaviour in the workplace. Whereas personality is based on a cluster of traits, some of which are believed to be genetic and evident from birth, identity is perceived as socially constructed: it is developed by, and also develops, the institutions and processes of modernity. Identity is fluid and multiple, and emerges through our relationships with others.

⊚ Managers use a variety of instruments and techniques to assess personality. These include the interview, inventories, behaviour assessment, personality tests and e-assessment. We noted also that, to be useful to the organization, personality assessment instruments must conform to standards of reliability and validity.

KEY CONCEPTS

extroversion
factor analysis
Freudian iceberg
introversion
personality
personality traits
personality types
phenomenological approach
self-identity
social identity

VOCAB CHECKLIST FOR ESL STUDENTS

Ego
Expectancy theory
Extrovert, extroverted
Factor analysis
Id
Idiographic
Individual, individualism
Interactionism
Introvert, introverted
Locus of control
Looking-glass self
Nomothetic
Peer group
Phenomenology, phenomenological
Phlegmatic
Psychodynamic
Psychometric

Reliable, reliability
Sanguine
Self-efficacy
Social capital
Social learning theory
Superego
Valid, validity

CHAPTER REVIEW QUESTIONS

1 What is personality, and why is the concept difficult to define?
2 What is meant by the trait theory of personality? Choose one trait theory, and explain the strengths and weaknesses of this approach to personality assessment.
3 Drawing on your knowledge of Freud's psychoanalytic theory, explain why the ego is sometimes referred to as the 'executive of the personality'. What do you understand by 'defence mechanism', and what relevance has this concept to understanding behaviour in the workplace?
4. Assess critically the importance of understanding the terms 'social self' and 'socialization', and explain how attitudes and values are developed and changed.
5 How are the concepts of personality and identity different?

CHAPTER RESEARCH QUESTIONS

1 Form a diverse study group including, if possible, an international student(s). Discuss the following questions: In what ways has socialization bestowed, sustained and transformed your own sense of identity? What is the relationship between personality, self-identity and social identity? Discuss the power of agents of socialization. Use examples from your work experience or family, or from workplaces you have studied.
2 Read Anthony Giddens' opening chapter, 'The contours of high modernity' in *Modernity and Self-identity*.[30] After reading pages 10–15, how do you think Giddens links modernity to identity? Thinking about your own biography, how important, and why, are lifestyle choices in forming your self-identity?
3 Retrieve a copy of Cameron Anderson and others' (2008) article, 'Personality and organizational culture as determinants of influence' (see Further Reading, below), investigating personality as a determinant of influence in work organizations. How plausible is the evidence that individual effectiveness in initiating change and innovation depends largely on personality?

FURTHER READING

Anderson, C., Spataro, S. and Flynn, F. (2008) 'Personality and organizational culture as determinants of influence', *Journal of Applied Psychology*, **93**(3), pp. 702–10.

Arthur, W., Woehr, D. J. and Graziano, W. (2001) 'Personality testing in employment settings', *Personnel Review*, **30**(6), pp. 657–76.

Bandura, A. (1997) *Self-Efficacy: The Exercise of Control*. New York: Freeman.

Giberson, T. R., Resick, C. and Dickson, M. (2005) 'Embedding leader characteristics: an examination of homogeneity of personality and values in organizations', *Journal of Applied Psychology*, **90**(5), pp. 1002–10.

Institute of Personnel and Development (1997) *Key Facts: Psychological Testing*. London: IPD.

Moon, H., Kamdar, D., Mayer, D. and Takeuchi, R. (2008) 'Me or we? The role of personality and justice as other-centered antecedents to innovative citizenship behaviors within organizations', *Journal of Applied Psychology*, **93**(1), pp. 84–94.

Sternberg, R. (1999) 'Survival of the fit test', *People Management*, **4**(24), pp. 29–31.

Tucker, K. H. (2002) 'Freud, Simmel, and Mead: aesthetics, the unconscious, and the fluid self', pp. 193–227 in *Classical Social Theory*, Oxford: Blackwell.

Wiggins, J. S. (ed.) (1996) *The Five-Factor Model of Personality: Theoretical Perspectives*. New York: Guilford Press.

Chapter case study 1

Identifying leaders in Nigeria

Setting

Nigeria is Africa's most populous country, with over 140 million people. In 2004, the United Nations Development Index, which measures a country's life expectancy, literacy, educational attainment and gross domestic product (GDP) per capita, ranked Nigeria 151 out of 177 countries. Devastating poverty affects 57 per cent of its population, and of the 57.2 million people who make up the labour force, over 10 per cent are unemployed. It struggles to cope with an inadequate infrastructure and under-developed human capital.

Nigeria's economy also has a detrimental over-dependence on a capital-intensive oil sector. At the beginning of the twenty-first century, Nigeria's crude oil production was averaging around 2.2 million barrels per day and providing 20 per cent of GDP, 95 per cent of foreign exchange earnings, and about 65 per cent of government revenues. It is Africa's top oil producer.

In recent years, with a new civilian government taking over from the former military rulers, there have been attempts to diversify the economy. The government has strived to attract foreign investors, citing locally available raw materials and the large national market as opportunities for long-term investments and joint ventures. However, these efforts have been stalled by foreign investors' fears of continued corruption, weak regulations, poor surveillance and inefficiencies.

For those willing to deal with such market impediments, investment advisors recommend that companies thoroughly educate themselves on local conditions and business practices, and establish a local presence. Researchers point out the importance of blending African work principles, such as an emphasis on work group activities and assigning leadership positions based on age (which is associated with experience and wisdom), into the workplace. Instead of front-line supervisors being held responsible for hiring, Nigerian workers expect and respect the involvement of senior managers in the process. Despite this knowledge, contrary foreign management methods still dominate human resource management practices in the multinational companies based in Nigeria. This has resulted in confusion, frustration and malaise among the Nigerian workforce.

The problem

A leading gas company in Europe, German-owned Lebenskraft is one of 200 multinational companies settled in Nigeria. In its over 80-year history, Lebenskraft has developed from a German regional distributor to an international gas company. As Germany has relatively few natural resources, it must import large quantities of energy, and the company has found ample supplies through its operations in Nigeria, where it first became established nearly a decade ago.

Since its arrival in Nigeria, Lebenskraft's middle- and upper-level positions have been filled by candidates who have been educated and have lived in Germany. As a way of broadening its choice of candidates, Lebenskraft's senior management has decided to consider employees from the Nigerian operations to fill a recent management vacancy.

The company has always used personality testing when assessing individuals for promotional opportunities as part of an overall succession plan. The test they normally use, Review, was developed in Germany and has been previously applied within that country with great success. For this latest management recruitment, it has been suggested that a previously used tailored job benchmark, identifying the desired characteristics for leadership roles, should be used. The test would then be applied to compare the abilities, interests and personality traits of multiple Nigerian candidates to the benchmark to identify the best candidate for the current vacancy.

The company has created the customized benchmark using the characteristics of assessed top performers in their German operations as well as current management input. They hope that by using their Nigerian employees' assessment results, in conjunction with the benchmark, they will successfully fill the management vacancy and perhaps create an effective local succession plan. However, since the personality testing has never been used outside Germany, the company is hesitant to rely on its results. The human resources department in the Nigerian operations has been given the task of making recommendations on the selection process before the local management are asked to proceed.

Tasks

As a member of the human resources department, prepare a short report including answers to the following questions:
1   What advantages do you see in using the testing?
2   What cultural aspects of Nigeria should be considered by the Lebenskraft management team when considering the use of the test's benchmark and in developing the selection process?

Essential reading

Anakwe, U.P. (2002) 'Human resource management practices in Nigeria: challenges and insights', *International Journal of Human Resource Management*, 13(7), pp. 1042–59.

Cooper, D. and Robertson, I. (1995) 'Selection methods – psychometrics', Chapter 8 in *The Psychology of Personnel Selection*, London: Routledge.

Jackson, T. (2002) 'Reframing human resource management in Africa: a cross-cultural perspective', *International Journal of Human Resource Management*, 13(7), pp. 998–1018.

Note

This case study was written by Lori Rilkoff, MSc, CHRP, Senior Human Resources Manager at The City of Kamloops, and Lecturer in HRM at Thompson Rivers University BC, Canada

Chapter case study 1

Building Anna's self-esteem

Visit www.palgrave.com/business/brattonob2e to view this case study

WEB-BASED ASSIGNMENT

Form a group of three to five people, and visit the websites of any of the following organizations: Microsoft (www.microsoft.com/uk/graduates), Sainsbury's (www.sainsburys.co.uk), British Airways (www.britishairways.com), and Santander (www.santander.com). What personality attributes are these organizations seeking when they recruit new employees?

Go to www.queendom.com/tests.html and www.psychometricadvantage.co.uk (search for psychometrics) and examine the psychometric tests. Some of these you may take yourself without applying for a job. How accurate, in your view, is your personality profile as revealed by any of the psychometric tests? Do your close friends agree with the assessment? Which kind of psychometric tests do you suppose would be more effective in revealing the more important aspects of your personality? Why? How much weight should organizations give to psychometric test results in employment selection? Explain your reasoning. Write a report detailing your findings.

OB IN FILM

American Beauty (1999) follows the last few days in the life of Lester Burnham, an advertising space salesman with a mid-life crisis. The film is particularly good at showing the multiple factors influencing Lester's behaviour. Some of these reside in his personality and some in the environment. Interestingly, there are many instances when Lester's interaction with events surfaces his personality.

Drawing upon Bandura's model of reciprocal determinism, map Lester's descent into a mid-life crisis in terms of his personality, his environment and his behaviour. How does this analysis of Lester shape your understanding of personality and its role in shaping behaviour?

Note: This feature was written by Professor Jon Billsberry, Senior Research Fellow, Open University Business School, UK.

BONUS OB IN FILM FEATURE!

Visit www.palgrave.com/business/brattonob2e to see how *The Odd Couple* (1968) can be considered in relation to the subject of leadership.

REFERENCES

1. Passer, M., Smith, R., Atkinson, M., Mitchell, J. and Muir, D. (2003) *Psychology: Frontiers and Applications*, Toronto: McGraw-Hill Ryerson.
2. Curtiss, S. (1977) *Genie: A Psycholinguistic Study of a Modern-day 'Wild Child'*, New York: Academic Press.
3. Davis, K. (1940) 'Extreme social isolation of a child', *American Journal of Sociology*, **45**(4), pp. 554–65.
4. Rymer, R. (1994) *Genie*, New York: Harper Perennial.
5. Giberson, T. R., Resick, C. and Dickson, M. (2005) 'Embedding leader characteristics: an examination of homogeneity of personality and values in organizations', *Journal of Applied Psychology*, **90**(5), pp. 1002–10.
6. Adler, S. and Weiss, H. (1988) 'Recent developments in the study of personality and organizational behavior', in C. Cooper and I. Robertson (eds), *International Review of Industrial and Organizational Psychology*, New York: Wiley.
7. Carlson, N., Buskist, W., Enzle, M. and Heth, C. (2005) *Psychology* (3rd edn), Toronto: Pearson Education.
8. Bernstein, D. A., Clarke-Stewart, A., Penner, L. Roy, E. and Wickens, C. (2000) *Psychology* (5th edn), New York: Houghton Mifflin.
9. Eysenck, H. J. (1970) *The Structure of Human Personality* (3rd edn), London: Methuen.
10. Goldberg, L. R. (1990) 'An alternative "description of personality": the Big-Five factor structure', *Journal of Personality and Social Psychology*, **59**, pp. 1216–29.
11. McCrae, R. R. and Costa, P. T. (1995) 'Toward a new generation of personality theories: theoretical contexts for the five-factor model', pp. 51–87 in J. S. Wiggins (ed.), *The Five-Factor Model of Personality: Theoretical Perspectives*, New York: Guilford Press.
12. Dalton, M. and Wilson, M. (2000) 'The relationship of the five-factor model of personality to job performance for a group of Middle Eastern expatriate managers', *Journal of Cross-Culture Psychology*, March, pp. 250–8.
13. Paunonen, S. V. (1996) 'The structure of personality in six cultures', *Journal of Cross-Culture Psychology*, May, pp. 339–53.

14. Freud (1933). Quoted in Carlson, N., Buskist, W., Enzle, M. and Heth, C. (2005) *Psychology* (3rd edn), Toronto: Pearson Education, p. 462.

15. Rotter, J. B. (1966) 'Generalized expectations for internal versus external control of reinforcement', *Psychological Monographs*, **80**(1): 1–28.

16. Bandura, A. (1978) 'The self system in reciprocal determinism', *American Psychologist*, **33**, pp. 344–58.

17. Bandura, A. (1997) *Self-Efficacy: The Exercise of Control*, New York: Freeman.

18. Jennings (1990), quoted in Passer, M., Smith, R., Atkinson, M., Mitchell, J. and Muir, D. (2003) *Psychology: Frontiers and Applications*, Toronto: McGraw-Hill Ryerson, p. 565.

19. Frese, M. (1982) 'Occupational socialization and psychological development: an underemphasized research perspective in industrial psychology', *Journal of Occupational Psychology*, **55**, pp. 209–24.

20. Maslow, A. H. (1954) *Motivation and Personality*, New York: Harper.

21. Maslow, A. H. (1964) *Religions, Values, and Peak-Experiences*, New York: Viking.

22. Rogers, C. R. (1961) *On Becoming a Person*, Boston, MA: Houghton Mifflin.

23. Mead, G. H. (1934) *Mind, Self and Society*, Chicago: University of Chicago Press.

24. Ray, L. J. (1999) *Theorizing Classical Sociology*, Buckingham: Open University Press.

25. Blumer, H. (1969), quoted in Tucker, K. H. (2002) *Classical Social Theory*, Oxford: Blackwell, p. 218.

26. Pfuetze, P. (1954). *Self, Society and Existence: Human Nature and Dialogue in the Thoughts of George Herbert Mead and Martin Buber*, New York: Harper.

27. Tucker, K. H. (2002) *Classical Social Theory*, Oxford: Blackwell.

28. Brym, R., Lie, J., Nelson, A., Guppy, N. and McCormick, C. (2003) *Sociology: Your Compass for a New World*, Scarborough, ON: Thomson Wadsworth.

29. Mills, A. and Tancred, P. (eds) (1992) *Gendering Organizational Analysis*, Newbury Park, CA: Sage.

30. Giddens, A. (1991) *Modernity and Self-Identity*, Palo Alto, CA: Stanford University Press.

31. Berger, P. (1966) *Invitation to Sociology*, New York: Anchor Books.

32. Kellner, D. (1992) 'Popular culture and the construction of postmodern identities', pp. 141–77 in S. Lash and J. Friedman (eds), *Modernity and Identity*, Oxford: Blackwell.

33. Giddens, G. (2009) *Sociology* (6th edn), Cambridge: Polity Press.

34. Ravelli, B. and Webber, M. (2010) *Exploring Sociology*, Toronto: Pearson.

35. Fulop, L. and Linstead, S. (2009) 'Motivation and meaning', pp. 411–72 in S. Linstead, L. Fulop and S. Lilley, *Management and Organization: A Critical Text* (2nd edn), Basingstoke: Palgrave.

36. Herriot, P., Hirsh, W. and Reilly, P. (1998) *Trust and Transition: Managing Today's Employment Relationship*, Chichester: Wiley & Sons.

37. Townley, B. (1994) *Reframing Human Resource Management: Power, Ethics and the Subject of Work*, London: Sage.

38. Lee, S. and Klein, H. (2002) 'Relationships between conscientiousness, self-efficacy, self-description, and learning over time', *Journal of Applied Psychology*, **87**(6), pp. 1175–82.

39. Holland, J. L. (1985) *Making Vocational Choices: A Theory of Vocational Personalities and Work Environments* (2nd edn), Englewood Cliffs, NJ: Prentice Hall.

40. Brown, D. (1987) 'The status of Holland's theory of career choice', *Career Development Journal*, September, pp. 13–23.

41. Furnham, A. F. (1997) 'Vocational preference and P-O fit', in J. Arnold (ed.), 'The psychology of careers in organizations', *International Review of Industrial and Organizational Psychology*, **12**, pp. 1–37.

42. Young, R. A. and Chen, C. P. (1999) 'Annual review: practice and research in career counselling and development – 1998', *Career Development Quarterly*, December, p. 98.

43. Thompson, J. A. (2005) 'Proactive personality and job performance: a social perspective', *Journal of Applied Psychology*, **90**(5), pp. 1011–17.

44. Moon, H., Kamdar, D., Mayer, D. and Takeuchi, R. (2008), 'Me or we? The role of personality and justice as other-centered antecedents to innovative citizenship behaviors within organizations', *Journal of Applied Psychology*, **93**(1), pp. 84–94.

45. Procter, S. and Mueller, F. (2000) *Teamworking*, Basingstoke: Palgrave Macmillan.

46. Salgado, J. F. (1997) 'The five factor model of personality and job performance in the European Community', *Journal of Applied Psychology*, **82**, pp. 30–43.

47. Bratton, J. and Gold, J. (2003) *Human Resource Management: Theory and Practice* (3rd edn), Basingstoke: Palgrave.

48. Dalen, L. H., Stanton, N. A. and Roberts, A. D. (2001) 'Faking personality questionnaires in personal selection', *Journal of Management Development*, **20**(8), pp. 729–41.

49. Robertson, I. T., Baron, H., Gibbons, P., MacIver, R. and Nyfield, G. (2000) 'Conscientiousness and managerial performance', *Journal of Occupational and Organizational Psychology*, **73**(2), pp. 171–81.

50. Bratton, J. and Gold, J. (2007) *Human Resource Management: Theory and Practice* (4th edn), Basingstoke: Palgrave.

51. Hollway, W. (1991) *Work Psychology and Organizational Behaviour*, London: Sage.

52. Rose, N. (1990) *Governing the Soul: The Shaping of the Private Self*, London: Routledge.

53. Greenhaus, J. H. (1987) *Career Management*, Chicago: Dryden.

54. Eysenck, H. (1973) *The Inequality of Man*, London: Temple Smith.

Chapter

6

PERCEPTION

CHAPTER OUTLINE

- Introduction
- The basic features and process of perception
- The processing limitations underlying selective attention
- The influence of existing knowledge in perception
- Perceiving causes
- Perception and emotion
- Perception, emotion and employee relations
- Summary and end-of-chapter features
- Chapter case study: The blame game

CHAPTER OBJECTIVES

After completing this chapter, you should be able to:

- understand the basic nature of human perception and its far-reaching influence on the nature of decision making, behaviour and relationships in organizations
- identify and define the elements of the perception process, how they relate to each other, and why the sequence in which they occur will affect how individuals view people and situations
- understand how our emotions affect, and are affected by, our perception of people and situations
- explain the influence on perception of information-processing limitations and existing knowledge and expectations, including those arising from cultural background
- discuss how a knowledge of perception processes can generate insight into phenomena of particular significance in the workplace, such as human error, interpersonal conflict, stereotyping, performance expectations and intergroup relations

INTRODUCTION

If one manager's idea of creativity (or enthusiasm, or intelligence) is in his or her head and different from another's, how can employees know for sure that their potential and performance at work are being assessed fairly? If it happened to be another manager making the judgement, would that person have viewed things differently and given a particular employee that job, or that promotion, rather than turning her or him down? It is these types of concern about the accuracy and consequences of individuals' perceptions that drive the use of systematic assessment procedures in many organizations.

Systematic, formal procedures are used to make judgements in personnel selection and performance appraisals, and sometimes structured systems are used to assess the strategic options and risks that organizations face. In order to minimize the reliance on what is 'in the head' of one individual when important decisions are made, formal procedures usually aim to include multiple viewpoints rather than that of one person, and to use concrete definitions of the criteria by which a person or situation is to be assessed (for instance, 'creativity is defined as the number of brand new ideas generated'). But why is it necessary to employ complicated assessment procedures? Can we not just train each individual manager to be more objective so that managers will all make the same judgements when faced with the same decision?

perception: the process of selecting, organizing and interpreting information in order to make sense of the world around us

We show in this chapter how subjectivity in the way we perceive the world around us arises from the fundamental nature of human **perception** processes. It is not simply the result of lazy thinking, meanness or belligerence on the part of some individuals (although that is not to say that some people are not sometimes guilty of these things!). Subjectivity is the normal state of affairs in human judgement because of the particular way our senses gather information from the world, and the way our brains go about making sense of that information. So the task of ensuring a fair and good-quality assessment of people and situations in organizations is not about training individuals to see things as they 'really are'. Instead, the task is to understand how and why multiple realities will always exist in any given scenario, and to gain the benefits of them, or at least avoid the negative consequences of actions based on limited perspectives. In other words, the task is to understand perception.

The purpose of this chapter is to outline and discuss the psychological basis of perception: that is, what happens 'in the head' that leads us to perceive people and situations in particular ways. After introducing some examples of how individuals' perceptions can be consequential in organizational life, we explore the central features and processes of human perceptual systems that allow us to experience a seamless view of our world, through the use of cognitive efficiencies such as time- and energy-saving mental short cuts and the packaging of information for convenient retrieval.

In order to structure our discussion, the issues that arise from the workings of perception are grouped into two main themes: those relating to selective attention and those relating to the influence of existing knowledge. The central importance of context, and the background and characteristics of perceivers in determining what is perceived, will be emphasized throughout this discussion.

The final three sections of the chapter each focus on an aspect of perception that has particular significance in the workplace. First, we shall see how perceptions formed about the causes of behaviour and events experienced have an important influence on individuals' future behaviour and motivation to pursue particular courses of action. We then look at the role of emotions in perception. Finally, in the last section, focusing on perception, emotion and employee relations, the broader impact of individuals' perceptions on the social climate of organizations is highlighted.

The topic of perception lies at the heart of the study of human experience and behaviour, whether it occurs inside or outside work organizations, because it is through our perception that we decide what the reality of the world is. The truth is that perceptions, and therefore views of reality, are far more dependent on the perceiver than on what is actually 'out there'. The implication of this is that there is not one 'true' reality at any given moment waiting to be discovered, because what

each of us believes to be the basic reality of the world around us is 'mostly convenient, internally generated fiction' (ref. 1, p. 95). Based on our goals, experience and
personal qualities, we each create and then act upon our own unique perceptual
worlds. Crucially, this creative work is mostly automatic, so we tend to act confidently
upon our perceptions while remaining blissfully unaware that there might be alternative ways of seeing things.

The topic of perception is particularly important in organizational behaviour
because work organizations represent a real challenge to our perceptual abilities; to
use Weick's words, they are inherently 'puzzling terrain'.[2] So much of what occurs
in organizations is both constantly changing and ambiguous, especially because
workplaces are social settings, and interpreting other people's behaviour is rarely
straightforward. Changing market conditions and competitors, diverse people with
multiple roles and motivations, multiple communications in various media, organizational politics – all of these things contribute to the complexity of what people must
make sense out of when they go to work each day. Because 'the way things are' in an
organization is rarely indisputable, the particular perceptions formed by its members
become important influences on the nature of individuals' behaviour and relations
with each other, as well as on the nature and fate of the whole enterprise.

Take, for example, the role of employees' perceptions, particularly of fairness, in
the smooth running and performance of organizations, as illustrated by a spate of
so-called 'boss-napping' in France in the Spring of 2009. As the downturn in the global
economy took its toll on French businesses, French trade unions and workers reacted
angrily to news of job losses at a time when they perceived that company executives
were receiving large bonuses or generous early retirement packages. Employees at
3M, Scarpa adhesives and Sony expressed their anger by taking the law into their
own hands and holding senior company executives for ransom in their company
offices overnight in an effort to force the company to reconsider its position. Large
demonstrations were also held in the centre of Paris by employees of Total who were
angry about the announcement of significant job losses just days after the company
had announced the biggest annual profit in French corporate history (€13.9 billion).

These collective responses to perceived unfair treatment also serve to highlight the
social dimension of human perception. Our perceptions do not just form in isolation and then remain in our heads. The way we view ourselves, others and the world
around us will shape our behaviour, and our behaviour influences the perceptions and
behaviour of others. Although this interdependence underlies many of our actions,
the social dynamics of perception become more obvious in situations such as giving a
presentation, conducting a negotiation or joining a new work team.

A good example of the social (and emotional) dynamics of perception is a lecturer
giving a lecture to students. The lecturer may quickly lose confidence if he or she
perceives signs from the audience that things are not going well. Now lacking confidence and feeling anxious, he or she becomes self-conscious, begins to speak far too
quickly and forgets some of the key points. It is entirely possible that the lecturer has
misread the earlier signs from the watching students – they may have been whisper-
ing to each other because they were actually very interested in the talk. But ironically,
the lecturer's dive in confidence and collapse in performance may themselves have
created the negative audience perceptions he or she feared had occurred earlier. The
point is that our perceptions are formed in part on the basis of information or cues
picked up from the environment, to which we must then attach meaning. The way we
interpret the situation will then shape what we do next, which will affect our environment and the cues we pick up next, and so on and so on.

stop reflect
What other situations
can you think of when
individuals' perceptions
might have important
consequences in work
organizations?

These examples all illustrate the significance of understanding the links between individuals' perceptions and their behaviour in the work context. For one thing, different perceptions have different consequences for the performance and success of individuals and their organizations. But also, gaining an insight into how and why people form particular and differing perceptions in given circumstances means we have more chance of avoiding or preventing the escalation of conflict between people and groups of people. In order to discover why, like our poor anxious lecturer, we can be blind to our own perceptual processes, and why, like the employees at Total, we can find it extremely difficult to comprehend and accept the validity of alternative viewpoints, it is necessary to consider the basic workings of human perception. The rest of the chapter will explore the nature and consequences of perception in detail.

THE BASIC FEATURES AND PROCESS OF PERCEPTION

The basic features of perception

Before we explore the component processes involved in perception, it may be helpful to set the scene by highlighting some inherent features of the way we deal with information from the world. These features seem to provide good explanations for the phenomena highlighted in the introduction. Perception is selective, subjective, and largely automatic rather than conscious.

To function in the world, we need to gain information about the world around us. This information is gained through our six bodily senses of sight, hearing, touch, smell, taste and proprioception (the sense of the position and movement of our own body). Having sensed something, we then endeavour to make sense of what we are seeing, hearing, touching, tasting, smelling and/or feeling. This process is not always simply a matter of information processing of the kind carried out by a computer because we often experience an emotional reaction to the information we receive. This is most obvious when the primary information comes from our senses of smell or taste (certain odours and tastes provoking powerful feelings of disgust or nausea, for example), but, as our earlier example of 'boss-napping' illustrates, emotional feelings such as injustice and anger can be triggered by information gained from any of our senses. We will return to the role of emotion in perception later in this chapter.

We usually feel very certain about what we experience, and this certainty is actually helpful and adaptive because it allows us to go about our daily lives without having to think about every single thing we encounter. Our surroundings often make perfect sense to us without any conscious effort. We seem to need this feeling of order, but we actually have to work hard to create it, because the environment is not nicely ordered and organized. For one thing, there is just too much information available from the external environment for our senses to take it all in, and, to make things more difficult, this information comes in the form of raw data such as light and sound waves. So the basic ingredients of our perceptions are highly ambiguous sensory stimuli, and it takes a lot of 'brain work' to sift, organize and interpret them.

It is only possible for us to deal with the continuous bombardment of sights and sounds, smells and sensations because we employ **selective attention**. An obvious example is being able to focus on a companion's conversation in a busy cafe despite a myriad of sensory distractions such as others talking and laughing, background music, clattering plates, icy draughts or an uncomfortable chair. But the target of attention is determined by factors inside the person, as well as what stands out in the immediate context or setting. Individuals' preoccupations, emotional state and

selective attention: the ability of someone to focus on only some of the sensory stimuli that reach them motivation will cause them to focus attention on specific aspects of people or situations. A professional salesperson meeting a client will probably be monitoring his or her speech and body language specifically for buying signals such as precise questions about the product. A manager who suspects an employee of time wasting may start particularly to notice whenever he or she is away from his or her desk, or talking to colleagues.

So it is that two perceivers can genuinely capture different aspects of the very same situation through selective attention. We do not have unlimited capacity for taking in information, so focusing on some environmental cues necessarily means ignoring others. And because this process is automatic rather than conscious, we are usually not too aware that we have been selective. When it comes to perception, rather than acting as neutral receivers of signals, we select the part of the environment to which we attend by acting as 'motivated tacticians'.[3] The motivation at a particular time may be to prioritize speed, as when we scan information to 'get the gist of it'. We may perceive defensively, as when we 'block out' information that we do not want to receive, or we may be looking for specific types of information to support a particular theory, as when we think someone is lying to us. The point is that our intentions and emotions colour our perceptions, playing a large part in determining what we draw from the environment.

Beyond selective attention, another central feature of perception is that the interpretation or meaning we attach to the external information we receive is strongly influenced by our existing knowledge: our ideas, experiences and backgrounds, including our ethnic and cultural origins. In other words, what we experience is subjective because others are unlikely to base their perceptions on exactly the same

Plate 1 – It is estimated that 80 per cent of the information we perceive comes through our sense of sight. Even when someone is talking to us, we still rely heavily on a host of additional non-verbal, visual information when we attend to and interpret what is being said.
Source: iStockphoto

mix of motivations and prior knowledge. This principle applies to individuals who share cultural backgrounds, but culture-based assumptions will add an additional and powerful source of difference. So in the event that two individuals of different nationality, for instance, did manage to attend to exactly the same aspects of a shared situation, their cultural differences would mean that they would probably still not share the same thoughts about the meaning and relevance of the information.

It is estimated that 80 per cent of the information we perceive comes through our sense of sight. Even when someone is talking to us, we still rely heavily on a host of additional non-verbal, visual information when we attend to and interpret what is being said. The way we interpret much of this non-verbal communication is dependent on our cultural upbringing. Hand gestures offer a good example of this. Raising your hand and placing the tip of your index finger against the tip of your thumb so that the fingers form a circle is known as the 'ring gesture'. In English-speaking countries and in Indonesia, this gesture means 'everything is okay'. However, in France it can also mean zero or 'worthless', in Japan it can mean 'money', and in some Mediterranean countries it is used to infer that a man is homosexual. In Tunisia, the ring gesture means that the signaller feels extreme personal animosity towards you!

So existing knowledge, which includes culture-, gender- and age-related assumptions and expectations, as well as what we have learned and emotionally experienced in our lives, will influence how we interpret what we perceive. The key point is that existing factors specific to the perceiver will determine in good part the picture that he or she creates from the available information. So individuals' perceptions are likely to differ in the meaning attached to the information, as well as in the information picked up from the environment in the first place.

Critical insight

Get a copy of a paper by Dunkerley and Robinson, 'Similarities and differences in perceptions and evaluations of the communication styles of American and British managers',[4] and read about the different communication styles, perceptions and comments of the British and American managers in the study. What do you think we can do about the tendency to perceive our own cultural style as better than, rather than just different from, that of others?

The basic sequence and key factors in perception that we have discussed so far are shown in Figure 6.1. From the bombardment of sensory stimuli, the perceiver selects some of the information for attention and processing. Based on prior knowledge and current motivations, the perceiver then works out what the information means and responds accordingly. Once the person has responded in some way, her or his actions become part of the environment, and so influence the person's own and others' ongoing perceptions of what is happening.

In summary, human perception can be characterized as a process that is largely automatic, subjective and selective. Perception is not just something inside an individual; it has an emotional and a social dimension because perceptions affect our behaviour, which influences others. Although highly effective in helping us to easily and quickly make sense of the world around us, this amazing capability also has a downside. Our perceptions are most certainly providing only a limited perspective, because there will almost always be another point of view – and, dangerously, we are often 'blind' to this simple fact. By understanding how perception works, which means recognizing the inevitability of different world views, we become more able to understand and effectively manage our own and others' behaviour in organizations. The next section will examine the nature of perception processes in more depth.

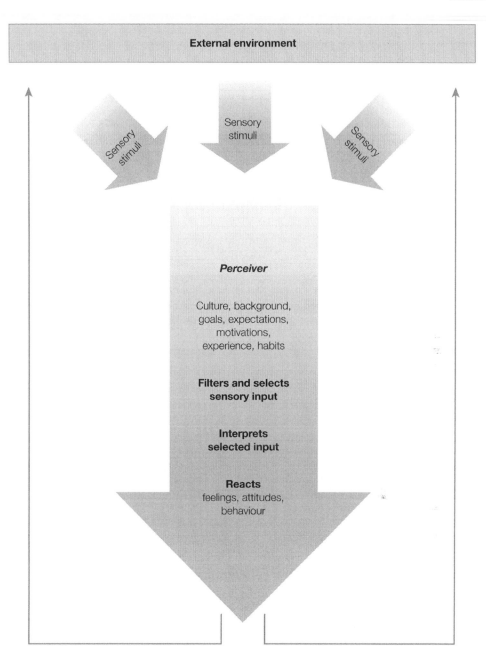

Figure 6.1 – The link between perception, behaviour and the environment

The process of perception

Perception is, then, a topic of significance in organizational behaviour because people's decision making and behaviour depend on how they interpret situations, and different interpretations are usually possible. But what exactly does the term 'perception' cover?

In truth, a definitive and comprehensive definition of human perception is not easy to find. The reason for this definitional difficulty is that perception is not really one topic or issue. Instead, the term 'perception' may be used in discussions about any one of a number of topics or issues, which can be placed at a number of different levels of analysis, from the physiological to the social. Research studies about human perception range from investigations of the inner workings of the human eye, to the impact of individuals' stereotypes on cross-cultural communication, to how others' perceptions affect people's choices about which careers to pursue. Nonetheless, it is still possible to identify a working definition to help us explore in more detail the psychological part of the perception process – the bit that happens inside our heads.

According to the cognitive psychologists Eysenck and Keane, 'At the very least, perception depends upon basic physiological systems associated with each sensory modality, together with central brain processes which integrate and interpret the output from these physiological systems' (ref. 5, p. 43). So our ability to 'perceive' depends upon three things:

1   *receiving*: being physically able to attend to and receive signals from the environment (for instance, having sight, hearing, touch, taste and smell, and being able to control which we employ at a given moment)
2   *organizing*: being able to mentally organize and combine those signals (which is what is happening when we see and hear speech in perfect synchronization, or see objects separate from their surroundings rather than as a mass of light patterns)
3   *interpreting*: being able to assign meaning or make sense of what we experience (for instance, attaching personal significance to particular combinations of sensory signals, like knowing when we are in a conversation and we need to talk back, or a person is threatening us, or a bus is approaching).

Figure 6.2 shows how these three elements are connected to each other.

To return to the features of perception already introduced, it is at the *receiving* stage that selective attention 'happens', and at the *interpreting* stage that subjectivity has its major influence. The *organizing* stage of perception is perhaps the most mysterious, in that our brains somehow work out those combinations of signals which are likely to go together, and those which are just not feasible. In this way, speech is attached to the face that is making the right movements even when there are other faces to choose from. This is how we know when we are looking at an image that is 'wrong' in some way, such as when the perspective is manipulated so the relative size of objects is unusual.

The sequence of perception: top-down or bottom-up?

Although it is helpful to separate the three elements of perception from one another so that we may better understand them, in reality they do not occur separately or in sequence; instead, they overlap and sometimes even occur in parallel. In addition, all three stages can be, and often are, influenced by our emotional reactions and dispositions. As we have discussed, our perceptions are actually constructed in a process that combines external information with our existing ideas about the world. Rarely do we start from scratch by piecing together the external 'clues' one by one. We have already attached some meaning to what we are in the process of perceiving while we are still receiving and organizing the external information. That is how we 'know' what someone is about to do or say, and why we are frequently surprised. The weight of evidence suggests that we almost always engage these three processes simultaneously.[5] Our relative reliance on external and existing information is not fixed, however, but will depend on the specific context.

When perception is led predominantly by gathering external sensory data and then working out what they mean, it is called 'bottom-up' or 'data-driven' information

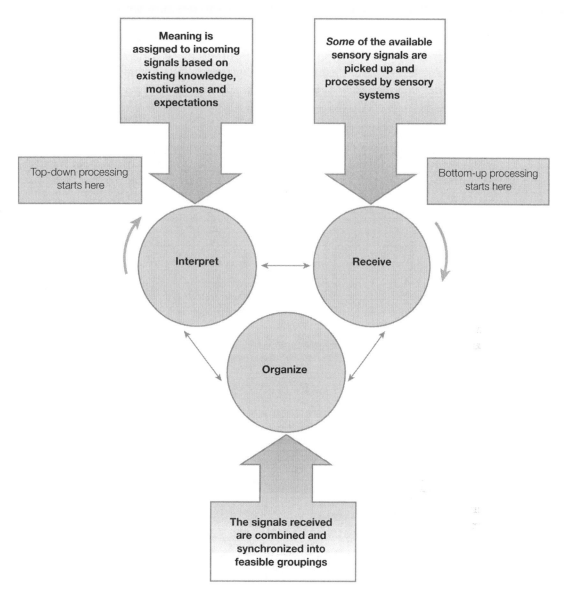

Figure 6.2 – The elements and process of perception

bottom-up processing:
perception led
predominantly by
gathering external
sensory data and
then working out
what they mean

processing. When we think there may be consequences in getting it wrong, we are likely to rely more heavily on **bottom-up processing**. For instance, the requirement in most assessment centres that assessors explain and justify the ratings they award to candidates is thought to exert a 'press of accountability'.[6] The need to justify their judgements publicly leads assessors to pay extra attention to all aspects of the candidates' behaviour.

Rather than always ensuring accuracy, 'thinking too much' can actually hinder our attempts at sound judgement and decision making. If we try too hard to take in as much information as possible, it can interfere with our ability to focus on the most important aspects of the situation. If that happens, irrelevant pieces of information end up being included in the decision-making process.

Some studies of the use of magnetic resonance imaging (MRI) technology in medical diagnosis bear this out. MRI scanners offer doctors incredibly detailed images of the interior of the body. However, research suggests that these images may contain so much misleading information that the accuracy of a doctor's diagnosis can be badly affected. In one study, the spinal regions of 98 people with no back pain or back-related problems whatsoever were scanned by an MRI machine. The pictures were then sent to doctors without any other information. After examining the pictures, the doctors reported that two-thirds of the scans revealed serious spinal problems, and many recommended immediate surgery.[7] The MRI pictures showed so much information that the doctors found it harder to know what they should be looking at. In fact, the serious problems they diagnosed were a normal part of the ageing process.

In contrast to the 'bottom-up' approach, perception being led predominantly by existing knowledge and expectations is called 'conceptually driven' or **top-down processing**. In this case, our working theory and expectations about what is happening will shape what we look for. We may fill in the scene from memory after perceiving a tiny number of cues that we think confirm our theory. Take a look at Figure 6.3. Can you see a black and white dog in this picture? If you can, you have just conformed to what psychologists called the 'law of closure', which states that if something is missing in an otherwise complete figure or object, we tend to try and complete it ('close the gaps') by adding additional information. In this case, our existing ideas of what a dog 'should' look like lead us to see a more complete picture of a dog than is actually there.

Researchers have found that we tend to rely on top-down processing in circumstances that are very familiar. For instance, Roth and Woods reported that novice operators in nuclear power plants relied heavily on feedback from monitoring the environment to guide their interventions – a bottom-up strategy.[8] Experienced

top-down processing: perception led predominantly by existing knowledge and expectations rather than by external sensory data

Figure 6.3 – The law of closure

operators, by contrast, relied much more on their existing knowledge of the operating systems, making much less frequent checks of environmental information.

However, there is a danger of relying too much on existing knowledge. The danger is that changes in the environment that really require a response from us may simply go unnoticed. This can happen because we are focused on the picture of the situation that already exists in our heads, so we fail to perceive the signals that the actual situation actually looks somewhat different from what we expected. When the cognitive task in question is making a judgement about someone or something, rather than maintaining a work system, we may never become aware of the failure to consider key bits of information. Sadly, there are no system alarms that go off when we judge people on their mistakes and forget about the things they did really well.

The dangers of 'thinking too little'[9] when making judgements have been well researched in the field of decision making. We have some **perceptual biases**, or automatic tendencies to attend to certain cues that do not necessarily support good judgements. The '**primacy effect**' is the term used to describe our tendency to pay too much attention to our first perceptions about someone. Although many people are aware of the power of first impressions, and try to avoid 'judging a book by its cover', it can be surprisingly difficult to change our initial perceptions. On the other hand, if we are not careful, we may be prone to the opposite bias,

perceptual bias: an automatic tendency to attend to certain cues that do not necessarily support good judgements

primacy effect: a perceptual error in which we quickly form an opinion of people based on the first information we receive about them

Plate 2 – Some people would be surprised to learn that this woman is a firefighter. The stereotype is of men doing such hazardous work.
Source: London Fire Brigade

recency effect: a
perceptual error in
which the most recent
information dominates
our perception of others

halo and horns effect:
a perceptual error
whereby our general
impression of a person,
usually based on one
prominent characteristic,
colours the perception
of other characteristics
of that person

stop reflect
Are you able to remember
situations when you have
used mostly a top-down
or mostly a bottom-up
perception strategy? Was
this a conscious decision
or did you become aware
of it afterwards?

overemphasizing the last things we perceived about someone, called the '**recency effect**'.

Another general tendency in person perception is making broad-based assumptions about a person's qualities on the basis of one or a small number of observations, the so-called '**halo and horns effect**'. For instance, if an employee makes a mistake on one job task that is considered to be very important, it may bias a manager's overall perceptions, so that he or she assumes that the person is incompetent in every aspect of the job. It is always useful to guard against such biases in dealing with others, but it becomes particularly significant in the context of selection and appraisal interviewing, or indeed any situation at work where we are evaluating a person in order to make a consequential decision. It is for this reason that good design is so crucial in assessment procedures.

The key point about our use of perception strategies is that there is a trade-off or balance to be struck between avoiding the risk of holding inaccurate perceptions that comes with top-down processing, while at the same time minimizing the mental effort of perceiving everything from the bottom up.

Perceptual tricks, manipulations and illusions

The goal of human perception seems to be to make sense of the environment as quickly as possible, even if a bit of accuracy is sometimes lost along the way. As a result, it is quite easy to trick our brains by 'setting off' these tendencies to seek meaning and certainty using various common tricks and illusions. These tricks make it possible for us to get some brief glimpses of some of the usually automatic, non-conscious, workings of our perceptual systems. Indeed, history suggests that we are endlessly amused by having our senses duped. Magicians capitalize on our selective attention when they use sleight of hand in card tricks and disappearing acts. Ventriloquists amuse us because we cannot stop our brains organizing, or associating the ventriloquist's voice with the dummy's mouth movements despite knowing the truth. There appears to be something pleasing for us about being perceptually confused, although – paradoxically – only as long as we know it is happening.

Some 'serious' artists such as Salvador Dali and M. C. Escher have also produced work that plays with a feature of visual perception that means we can visually reverse the figure and the background of an image. So, in a painting such as *The Great Paranoiac* by Dali, it is possible to see the image as being made up of many small scenes, or to 'phase out' the detail and see one large image of a man's head, which is actually made up of the smaller images. The simplest demonstration of figure-ground reversal is the Necker cube (Figure 6.4), which is named after Louis Albert Necker, who discovered in 1832 that the perspective of the cube spontaneously changes if it is looked at continuously. So the front face becomes the back one, or, if you prefer, the corner marked A 'moves' from being at the front to being at the back of the cube. This is a demonstration of what is called 'multistability' in perception.[10] When there are multiple possible interpretations of something, and they are equally good or feasible, we will sometimes choose one, sometimes another, but never two at the same time.

Using the same principles as illusionists, perception researchers manipulate sensory inputs in a controlled way in order to explore how the elements of the perception process work and how they relate to each other. A simple and now classic experimental image, the Mueller–Lyer illusion, is shown in Figure 6.5. The straight lines are actually the same length, but the placement of the arrowheads makes them appear to be different: the line on the left appears longer that the one on the right. Curiously, researchers have found that the Mueller–Lyer illusion tricks our eyes but

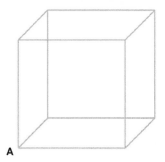

A

Figure 6.4 – The Necker cube

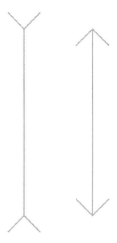

Figure 6.5 – The Mueller–Lyer illusion

not our hands. There was no illusory effect when the lines were made into three-dimensional figures and people were asked to reach out and grab them between their thumb and index finger.[11] In other words, the study participants positioned their fingers at the right distance apart to grab the figures in each case. The illusory effect also seems to depend to some extent on the cultural background of the perceiver. When the illusion is depicted in the form of the rectangular corners of walls, people from cultures where the built environment does not include these angular features are less likely to perceive the lines as being of different lengths.

In fact, the exact relationship between culture, particularly language, and thought or cognition is the subject of much research and debate among psychologists. Followers of the theory of **linguistic relativity** argue that the language we speak has such a fundamental influence on the way that we interpret the world that we actually think differently from those who speak a different language. There is a difference, for instance, between English and Nepalese speakers in the way that the relative position of two people or objects is described.[12] In English, the positions would be described egocentrically, in relation to one's own body (for example, 'He is on my left and she is on my right'). In Nepalese, however, an environmentally centred description would be given instead (such as 'He is on the west side and she is on the east side').

The question that researchers have been trying to answer is whether such linguistic differences are linked to basic differences in the way that people raised in different cultures select and interpret environmental information. The contrasting view to

linguistic relativity: the theory that the language we speak has such a fundamental influence on the way we interpret the world that we think differently from those who speak a different language

weblink
The Exploratorium, a museum of science, art and human perception based in San Francisco, has an excellent website where you can explore a number of classic visual illusions online. Go to: www.exploratorium.edu/exhibits

linguistic relativity is that language plays a much less fundamental role in perception and cognition. From this standpoint, it is our thoughts that come first, and we use the language available to us to express those thoughts. As is often the case in the social sciences, there seems to be good evidence to support both viewpoints. The 'compromise view' as explained by Bloom,[13] is that there are some universal perceptions and interpretations of the world that all people share, but that other distinctions in the meanings we attribute to what we experience are shaped by our native language.

The question of whether culture and language shape thought and perception clearly has important implications for our understanding of cross-cultural communication in organizations. Stated simply, the notion of linguistic relativity suggests that, for people attempting to live and work internationally, learning the language of the host country as an adult may not be enough to ensure that shared perceptions, understandings and ideas can be automatically developed with colleagues.

To focus on the context of organizational behaviour, not all of the perceptual tricks and illusions aimed at demonstrating the fundamental principles of perception, interesting as they are, can be applied directly to organizational life. One perceptual manipulation that has been used in a work context, however, is the old sales technique of the 'agreement staircase'. The technique involves making a series of requests to a customer to which he or she is highly likely to agree. The salesperson then immediately follows this with the main question – will the customer go ahead and buy? The idea is that the customer will instinctively say yes because he or she has fallen into the habit of doing so. Although, this technique sounds a bit naive, it can work if executed subtly because we do develop what are known as **perceptual sets**.

perceptual set: describes what happens when we get stuck in a particular mode of perceiving and responding to things based on what has gone before

A perceptual set describes what happens when we get stuck in a particular mode of perceiving and responding to things based on what has gone before. The same effect can occur if you read a list of French words followed by an English one, for instance.

Plate 3 – We know the fork is all in one piece, but our eyes deceive us.
Source: Nick Tutton

You will tend to pronounce the English word as if it were French – which can be stupidly amusing if it is a particularly unromantic word like 'cabbage'! These experiments and manipulations do raise an important point that needs to be included in our exploration of perception. They demonstrate the significant effect of context on how we interpret even apparently straightforward information that we receive from the environment. When that information becomes more complex, as in social encounters, that point becomes even more significant.

THE PROCESSING LIMITATIONS UNDERLYING SELECTIVE ATTENTION

We have already established that we attend to environmental information selectively. One central reason for selective attention is that there are actually physiological limits on how much information we can take in at once, as well as on how much mental work or processing we can do in a given time-frame. In other words, there are capacity constraints on two of the three elements of the perception process – receiving and organizing. Perception researchers have sought to understand how much of the different kinds of sensory information we can absorb, as well as what gets priority under different conditions.

An example of research in this area is the study of what is called 'dual-task interference', or when the attentional demands of one perceptual task limit our ability to do another at the same time. Put very simply, it is easier for us to do two tasks simultaneously if they involve different kinds of information input and require different kinds of response. Doing two computer screen monitoring tasks, each requiring a key stroke response, is more difficult than doing one visual and one auditory monitoring task simultaneously, for instance. As an example of the practical significance of this kind of knowledge, consider the controversy about the use of mobile cell phones while driving. This issue is of very real practical concern to the large number of people whose work involves driving, as well as to their employers.

One argument against their use is that mobile phones are a cause of road accidents because holding a phone and dialling numbers distracts motorists' attention from the road ahead and interferes with their ability to operate the vehicle's controls. In fact, two separate studies provide evidence that the interference with driving arises not from operating the phone, but rather from the amount of attention taken up by having a conversation. Whereas a passenger is aware of what is happening and will stop talking if the driver needs to act or concentrate, a person on the end of the phone cannot see what is happening in the car or on the road, so the conversation becomes more demanding for the driver. The findings reported in the studies included the statistic that drivers using mobile phones were four times more likely to be in an accident,[14] had slower reactions, and were two times more likely to miss traffic signals than those who were not on the phone.[15]

Other kinds of research study concerned with the limitations of information processing have identified two perceptual phenomena called 'change blindness' and 'inattentional blindness'. In these experiments, researchers test the focus of people's attention during various 'realistic' encounters by either changing the situation in some way, or introducing something unexpected and then finding out whether the manipulation was spotted. Change blindness refers to the fact that we simply do not seem to notice even large or obvious changes to things if they are not central to our concerns. In one experiment, somewhat reminiscent of a comedy sketch, members

weblink
Have a look at the gorilla video and other videos too, and find out about other studies in inattentional blindness and change blindness at the researchers' websites. For the gorilla video, go to http://viscog.beckman.illinois.edu/djs_lab/demos.html. See also www.nelliemuller.com/inattentional_blindness.htm

of the public who were giving directions to a researcher failed to spot that they were talking to a different person after two men carrying a door had walked in between them![16]

Another amusing experiment in the same vein, conducted by Simons and Chabris, involved a man in a gorilla suit.[17] Study participants were asked to watch a group of people passing a basketball between them and to count the number of passes that were made in a given time period. Amazingly, around 50 per cent of participants did not even see the man in the gorilla suit who walked among the ball players while they were counting the passes. This phenomenon has been termed 'inattentional blindness', because it seems we do not perceive even unusual or obvious things when we have focused our attention elsewhere. We appear to be very effective in automatically filtering out information that is not needed for the current task or goal. This propensity to reduce mental workload led to the characterization of human perceivers as 'cognitive misers',[18] using various short cuts to deal with limited processing capacity.

THE INFLUENCE OF EXISTING KNOWLEDGE IN PERCEPTION

So far we have emphasized the idea of perceivers as 'cognitive misers', seeking the quickest, most energy-efficient route to decisive perceptions with the use of a bit of external information and a lot of expectation and existing knowledge. Because existing knowledge is so influential, questions about what we store and how we store it are important in understanding perception. How we store knowledge matters as well as what knowledge we hold, because it affects how quickly and how often we are able to bring specific thoughts to mind in a particular circumstance. Our brains have the same basic architecture, so all individuals will go through the same perception process – receiving, organizing and interpreting information in some order. But similarities and differences in the content of the mental models held, and when they are used as a basis for perception, will help to determine the degree to which two or more people will form overlapping views of the same experience.

The reason that we are able to bring information to mind so quickly is because our knowledge is organized into packages of related content. This means that it is necessary to stimulate only one piece of information for all the related knowledge that is held with it to come to mind. These knowledge packages are ready-made 'mental models' or simplified representations of the world, which provide the frameworks and theories against which we then 'test' and place incoming data. Cognitive psychologists call these mental models 'schemas', or 'schemata', to be accurate. A **schema** can be described as:

> a set of interrelated cognitions (for example, thoughts, beliefs, attitudes) that allows us quickly to make sense of a person, situation, event, place and so forth on the basis of limited information. Certain cues activate a schema, which then fills in missing details. (ref. 19, p. 48)

Individuals have a large number of schemata, each of which will contain more or less information depending on how much exposure they have had to the phenomenon in question. Our schemata will include those for people (such as a close friend or your mother), for situations (such as a job interview or eating at a restaurant) and for roles (like managing director or student). Schemata about people, roles and places we have not experienced may contain very general, simplified information. For instance, we may hold snapshot, idealized images of exotic countries we have not yet visited,

schema: a set of interrelated mental processes that enable us to make sense of something on the basis of limited information and also associate those images with particular moods, feelings and personal goals. Even without having been there or read anything about it, a place like Zanzibar may, for someone from Northern Europe, conjure up images of golden beaches and sun-speckled blue seas that stimulate emotional feelings of warmth and relaxation, along with thoughts about winning the national lottery! By contrast, self-schemata, those which contain our thoughts and feelings about ourselves, will be both numerous and complex, and will include much more detailed information.

stop reflect
Can you map the mental associations that you make in relation to some familiar roles, situations and people, including yourself?

Schemata are based on our previous knowledge of and expectations about the world gained through the perceptual processes of receiving, organizing and interpreting information. Figure 6.6 shows how our schemata are activated and become progressively more accurate as they interact with the world. In the top-down processing mode, when perception begins with a clear theory or expectation, relevant schemata have already been activated and drive attention selectively towards external stimuli or cues that match or confirm the mental model in use. If I expect my boss to be angry, I will be selectively looking for signs of anger. So in the event that he or she smiles welcomingly at me, I might consider the possibility that I am seeing sarcasm in action, and look for other signs of anger rather than assume that my theory was wrong.

When people perceive in bottom-up mode, it is, as the diagram indicates, the cues that are noticed in the environment which drive the process. If I am going to see my boss and have no idea what mood he or she is in, I will start with the smile I see and build a theory based on all the signals I am getting. We tend to use distinctive and easily detected features such as a person's physical appearance as cues for choosing schemata.[19] The stimuli that grab our attention, those which are most salient, are received and organized, and these salient cues activate relevant schemata. The organization element of this process includes the basic categorization of the object, person or situation in question into a class or type before any meaning is attached. As an example, some person categories might be police woman, elderly foreign man or young trendy woman. This categorization process then determines which schema will be activated, and in turn how the perceiver will evaluate and respond to the encounter.

It is quite difficult to gain any mental control over the process of schema activation because it is so automatic. The associations between environmental cues, categories and schemata are not easily broken once formed. In fact, perhaps you have had personal experience of the research finding that trying to stop yourself having a

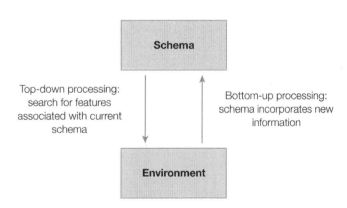

Figure 6.6 – The schema activation process

particular thought actually has the opposite effect. It appears that we suffer 'post-suppression rebound' when we try to block thoughts from our heads.[20] The effect has been found in experiments where people were asked, and failed, to suppress thoughts of white bears, sex and past romantic relationships among other things.

One explanation for this effect is that, in order to suppress thoughts, we first have to detect them and then replace them with an alternative. Whereas the 'ironic monitoring process' that scans our thoughts to check for 'forbidden' content is automatic, the replacement process is not automatic, and takes mental effort. So when we have a lot to think about and the amount of mental processing capacity available to us is diminished, the replacement process breaks down, but the monitoring process continues, making the unwanted thoughts more rather than less accessible to conscious awareness.

Like most aspects of perception, schema activation is not a neutral process. For each person, some schemata are more easily accessible than others as a result of previous experiences, one's emotional state and personality characteristics. These more accessible schemata will then be brought to mind and used more often, making them even more easily retrieved as time goes on. In this way, we develop habitual tendencies to perceive the world in particular ways. When certain schemata are frequently used by an individual, they are said to be 'chronically accessible schemata'. An expatriate for instance, accustomed to living and working within different nations, may be prone to make sense of social misunderstandings in terms of cultural differences rather than the personality of the other person involved. An extrovert may interpret a wide range of situations as opportunities for social contact, as anyone cornered on a long journey with one will testify!

The use and misuse of perceptual cues

Differences in schema accessibility and use also mean that some environmental cues will be routinely more salient for some people than others. This is because schemata drive the selectivity in our attention, and lead us to notice what we expect or hope to see. In the last section, we gave the example of physical appearance as a cue for activating schemata. However, there is evidence that some aspects of physical appearance can trigger the kind of perceptual biases we discussed earlier in the chapter. For example, research has shown that taller people are often perceived as more authoritative and more physically attractive than people of below average height. Indeed, in 2007 a survey found that 58 per cent of all CEOs of the Fortune 500 companies were over 462 cm (6 feet 2 inches) tall, whereas only 4 per cent of adult US males are this tall.[21] In addition, an analysis of 8590 people found a significant correlation between height and income.[22] It would seem that people receive higher evaluations and higher pay even when the job involved has nothing whatsoever to do with height. This is a good example of the 'halo effect' in action.

The fact that people routinely make judgements about people based on such cues has motivated many people to attempt to manage the way they are perceived by others. Indeed, the research just described suggests that, if you are of average height, your career prospects may be improved by the simple expedient of wearing shoes with higher heels. In fact, as individuals, we happen to be very good at influencing what others think of us, and seek to do so much of the time. **Impression management** (IM) is 'the process whereby people seek to control or influence the impressions that others form'.[23] We are motivated to manage the way we are perceived in order to make real the image of ourselves we prefer, and to exert some control over how others respond to us.

impression management: the process of trying to control or influence the impressions of oneself that other people form

Presenting the best possible picture of ourselves to others requires us to do two things: enhance our positive attributes, and minimize those which might be perceived negatively. Self-promotion techniques such as describing our actions or qualities in a selective and favourable way, as well as non-verbal behaviour such as eye contact and walking and dressing in a certain style, can serve to enhance the positive in a given situation. Techniques such as providing excuses and justifications for less desirable facts about us serve to meet the goal of minimizing negative aspects. Further IM behaviours are directed towards the other people involved, such as flattery and agreement, but these still serve to create a particular image of the actor.

Relating these techniques to what we know about perception processes, we can describe IM as the way in which individuals seek to actively direct others' selective attention towards the cues that will stimulate the desired interpretation. For example, by wearing a smart business suit and walking into an interview room assertively, we seek to stimulate a 'professional, confident applicant' schema in the mind of the interviewer. Actually, we are not always even aware we are managing our image, but when we know we are being evaluated, as in the case of a job interview, the process becomes more of a conscious effort.

The workplace presents many evaluative situations, both formal and informal, which makes IM an important concept in organizational behaviour. The significance of self-presentational techniques and their effects are perhaps most obvious in the formal setting of personnel selection and appraisal procedures. However, given that the point of paid work is to perform a specified role and set of tasks, workers' performance and behaviour will often be under a good deal of scrutiny from their peers, superiors and employees on an ongoing basis, which will motivate positive self-presentation.

One concern is that some people are just better at using IM techniques, so will be perceived more favourably than those with equal or greater talents who are less skilful or less motivated in their self-presentation. This is a key concern in relation to the accuracy and fairness of decisions about people at work and the resulting opportunities made available to them. In one study, women managers were less willing than male colleagues to use IM behaviours such as networking, self-promotion and ingratiation to get ahead in their organizations, preferring instead to rely on doing an excellent job.[24] The difficulty with the women's approach is that promotion decisions are affected by seniors' perceptions of potential and promotability, as well as actual performance. Because male managers tend to be more accepting of the need to 'play politics' to secure promotion, they are more willing to actively manage their image with their seniors, so may have an advantage over the women when it comes to promotion.

IM is not restricted to individual behaviour. Organizations also try to influence the way in which people perceive them. Corporate advertisements in the mass media are an obvious example of this, but researchers have discovered that many companies employ IM techniques in their design of annual reports to shareholders, particularly in the design of graphs of financial data. One of the most common used types of IM technique in financial graph design is called 'proportionality measurement distortion'. A basic principle of graph design is that the physical measurements of the graph should be in direct proportion to the numerical values displayed on the graph – for example, if sales have doubled in one year, the length of the bar representing current sales should be twice as long as the bar representing sales a year earlier. Unfortunately, not all company reports follow this principle, and empirical evidence reveals that annual reports of companies in the US, Canada, UK, France, Australia and Hong

Kong frequently contain graphs that distort financial information in this way.[25] Researchers have found that such measurement distortion tended to overemphasize the growth in sales and income and to underemphasize losses. In other words, the data were presented in such a way as to reinforce a favourable impression of the company's annual performance. Such an IM technique can be effective, as experimental studies reveal that people were significantly more likely to invest in companies with low growth rates when graphs of its performance were inaccurately drawn in this way than when the graphs were accurately drawn.[26]

The studies discussed above serve to highlight the controversial and ambiguous nature of IM behaviour. The line between simply highlighting one's best points and 'false advertising' is very difficult to determine, and each of us will have a different view about how far it is acceptable to 'manage' others' perceptions. Such controversy also surrounds IM behaviours that management stipulate as a contractual requirement of employee behaviour. In some organizations, the desire to create a favourable impression leads management to require some employees, especially those employees who regularly engage in face-to-face contact with customers, to carefully manage their emotional behaviours. Hochschild calls this behaviour *emotional management* – the

Work and Society: Smile to save the company

In the service sector, paid work involving direct contact with customers requires workers to provide more than just physical labour; it requires them also to manage their emotions in order to create a publicly observable facial display.

Faced with depleted profits, Air Canada (the country's largest carrier) vowed to restore competitive advantage by placing a renewed focus on customer service and by encouraging their cabin crew to display a smile. The aim was to follow the lead set by low-cost carrier WestJet, which had long prided itself on courteous staff. In an internal message to Air Canada staff, the company's CEO Montie Brewer wrote, 'While Air Canada has the lead in hard attributes, it's up to each and every one of us to work together to be sure that we're also out in front in the soft attributes such as a ready smile, eagerness to help customers and simply perform jobs well' (Brewer, 2006).

Arlie Hochschild (1983) has called this aspect of paid labour 'emotional labour'. Emotions are strong feelings that individuals express and experience, such as anger, love, joy and friendship. For front-line service workers, such as flight attendants, she argues that the emotion accompanying the service is part of the service itself. Moreover, this service must be delivered not only with a smile, but also, in an emergency, with reassurance. She quotes a flight attendant:

Even though I'm a very honest person, I have learned not to allow my face to mirror my alarm or my fright. I feel very protective of my passengers. Above all, I don't want them to be frightened. If we were going down, if we were going to make a ditching in the water, the chances of our survival are slim, even though we [the flight attendants] know exactly what to do. But I think I would probably – and I think I can say this for most of my fellow flight attendants – be able to keep them from being too worried about it. (p. 107)

For those employed as front-line service workers, the service cannot be separated from the mode of delivery. Hochschild's pioneering work emphasized that emotions are social and can be symbols that are widely recognized and form part of the way in which individuals manage and express themselves in social interaction. As social actors, workers' ability to manage emotions is based on their expectations of others and the expectations of others towards them. In understanding organizational behaviour, emotions become part of the social self and are one means that we use to interpret stimuli and develop an appropriate response.

stop!   Can you identify occupations where emotional labour might apply?
          How important is emotional labour in organizations?

Sources and further information

Ashforth, B. and Humphrey, R. (1993) 'Emotional labour and authenticity: views from service agents', pp. 184–203 in S. Fineman (ed.), *Emotion in Organizations* (2nd edn), London: Sage.

Brewer, M. *Globe and Mail*, November 11, 2008, p. B1.

Hochschild, A. (1983) *The Managed Heart: Commercialization of Human Feeling*, Berkeley, CA: University of California Press.

Morris, J. A. and Feldman, D. C. (1996) 'The dimensions, antecedents and consequences of emotional labour', *Academy of Management Review*, 21(4), pp. 986–1010.

management of employees who are paid to adjust their emotions to the needs of the customer and the requirement of the work situation.[27]

Hochschild conducted research to explore how attendants on board commercial passenger aircraft are trained to manage their 'real' emotions in order to present a pleasant, smiling demeanour to passengers regardless of how afraid, tired, irritated or angered they may actually feel. From the passengers' perspective, such a demeanour is perceived as pleasant and can enhance their enjoyment of the flight (and the likelihood of flying with that particular airline again). However, looking at it from the employees' perspective, Hochschild argued that such behaviour represents a distortion of their feelings of self-esteem and self-identity.

Critical insight

Get a copy of Dominique Moisi's book *The Geopolitics of Emotion* (2009) and read Chapter 1, 'Globalization, identity, and emotion'.[28] Moisi contends that it is possible to draft a global map of emotions because dominant emotions, like dominant colours in paintings, do exist. One task of governments, he argues, is to study the emotions of their respective peoples, to capitalize on them if they are positive, and to try to reverse or contain them if they are negative. What relevance, if any, is Moisi's thesis to understanding organizational behaviour? Do you think managers should attempt to diagnose the emotional state of the workforce? Why?

The stability of schemata

Schemata develop over time through learning and experience, and, once formed, can be remarkably resistant to significant change. Although we add complexity to our mental models as we experience new examples of a particular phenomenon, wholesale revision of a schema is less likely. This is because a schema acts as a lens through which relevant new information is interpreted. Data that are inconsistent with what we 'know' to be the case are just reinterpreted so that they do not challenge our existing views. As numerous recent reality television shows demonstrate, if you strongly believe yourself to be a very promising singing talent, even the most uncompromising feedback to the contrary can be easily discounted and fully explained by the nasty personality of the judge.

Some failures to take on board feedback and change mental models do, however, have more serious consequences than wounded pride. A serious fire in 1949 in the USA called the Mann Gulch disaster claimed many lives despite the fact that skilled firefighters were in attendance.[2] A central point to come from the analysis of the incident pointed to the failure of the fire crew to acknowledge quickly enough that this was not the type of fire they thought it was. As a result, the men did not respond appropriately to the situation they were actually in, because they reinterpreted discrepant information about what they were experiencing and continued to respond according to the routine for the wrong type of fire. Tragically, some of the men could have kept their lives if they had listened seriously to one of their colleagues, who was engaging in bottom-up processing and understood the need for different behaviour.

Most of what happens inside organizations is not a life-and-death matter, of course, but it does nonetheless affect people's livelihoods and well-being. The consequences of senior managers failing to adjust their schemata about the organization's competition and strategy quickly enough in response to new information has been a topic of interest to researchers. For instance, Hodgkinson[29] investigated UK estate agents' (realtors') perceptions of the competitive environment in the industry just before a recession hit the property market and again once the slump was established. The estate agents demonstrated 'cognitive inertia'. Their perceptions of the environment in which they were operating remained stable even though there was clear evidence of a downturn in the market. In other words, the estate agents were overly dependent on their schemata of the situation, failing to monitor and interpret environmental cues appropriately. As a consequence, their ability to respond effectively to the real threat to the organizations' viability posed by the downturn was seriously compromised.

Apart from demonstrating the stability of schemata, this study also illustrates that schemata are not always specific to an individual, but can be shared between groups of people. In this case, the estate agents' shared perceptions were a result of similar work roles and industry context. Broad similarities between people, such as gender, ethnicity, national culture and educational background, can also increase the chances that there will be some similarity in their perceptions about some things. A study found that two people randomly paired are likely to share only about 10 per cent of their chronic mental constructs, that is, their stable knowledge.[30] However, people who live or work together are not random pairings; they will share some common roles, backgrounds or experiences. **Stereotypes** are a class of schemata that appear to be shared between people, and are of particular consequence in organizational life because of their effects on perceptions of, and subsequent behaviour towards, individuals.

stereotyping: the process of assigning traits to people based on their membership of a social category

Stereotypes are a form of schema containing generalized ideas about the qualities and characteristics of individuals within particular groups,[19] for example people with financial worries make motivated salespeople, stock market traders are usually privately educated men in their 20s and 30s, Chinese men and women are the best mathematicians, and taller people are more authoritative. These are all examples of stereotypical beliefs about groups of people because they make an assumption that the characteristics in question will be true of all or most of the individuals in the category. Not all stereotypes are negative or unflattering, of course. But when assumptions about certain groups are automatically applied to individuals in the work context, unfair, potentially discriminatory and probably ineffective judgements and decisions can result.

A case in point is the issue of age discrimination by employers. In countries where this is prevalent, the exclusion of skilled and capable older workers from the work-force based on negative stereotypes of their potential to contribute is laying to waste a sizeable portion of that nation's available labour. As well as denying opportunities and income to the older workers, this exclusion of capable individuals based on non-performance-related characteristics is making it harder for organizations to recruit enough people, leading to reduced performance and profitability.

It is also known that people do not perform as well as they are able when they feel they are being stereotyped.[31] So even when given an opportunity, a worker who is a member of a minority group in an organization may not be able to contribute fully if he or she feels that the group membership is uppermost in others' minds. Gender-based stereotypes are of particular concern in organizations, because women still do not get the same rewards for paid work as their male counterparts, and some occupations appear to be 'gendered', or occupied predominantly by one or other sex.

The phrase 'think manager, think male' was coined by Virginia Schein[32,33] to describe the effect of sex-role stereotypes on the perceptions of what it takes to be a successful manager. Many studies have shown that both men and women, and people of different nationalities, describe successful managers as having characteristics that they also associate more with men than women, such as competitiveness, decisive-ness and ambition.[34] As well as affecting women's motivation and expectations, such perceptions may create a bias in the evaluation of potential and existing managers by decision makers if they are unaware of or unconcerned about the effect of gender-based stereotypes on their judgements.

As we have already discussed, it is actually very difficult to intervene in the automatic processes by which we associate people or situations with particular thoughts and feelings, even if we become aware of them. Trying to suppress stereotypical thoughts will probably result in 'thought rebound', bringing them even more to the forefront of our minds. We can, however, be vigilant about questioning and exploring our perceptions, reactions and decisions about people, in order to actively counter the inevitable biases and assumptions to which we would otherwise be prone.

It is hard to imagine a person who could not be stereotyped on some dimension, so we are all potentially at risk of being judged inaccurately at some point. Why then do we form stereotypes about people? We have already discussed the marvellous efficiency of schemata for making sense of the world quickly with minimum effort. Stereotypes allow us to size up people with the same efficiency, and apparently that includes ourselves. According to self-categorization theory, which is an extension of **social identity theory**,[35] stereotyping people occurs from the same process we use to categorize and understand the kind of person we are in relation to others. The basis of these influential theories is that part of our self-concept is defined in terms of the series of social groups to which we belong. Such groups include demographic ones based on age, gender and socioeconomic status, as well as those we have some choice about, including student, work, sports or more loosely defined groups such as 'clubbers' or classical music fans.

In order to decide whether an individual is a member of a particular group, we use as a basis what we consider to be the defining features or stereotypical attributes of members of that group. The effect of this process is to simplify the picture by maximizing the distinction between groups and minimizing any differences between individuals within groups. So we can then easily work out whether they, or we, have the key features necessary for membership. It has been suggested that one of two sources of motivation for this social comparison is to reduce uncertainty about the social world and how to behave in it, which, as we have discussed, is what our basic perceptual processes also appear to achieve.[36]

A second motivation for making these social distinctions concerns our need to maintain self-esteem, and this is crucial in relation to stereotyping. Although we categorize ourselves in the same way as others, this need to view ourselves positively means that we have an inherent tendency to evaluate the characteristics of the groups we belong to (**in-groups**) favourably, and those of other groups and their members (**out-groups**) negatively. So it is possible to see how perceptions of difference and negative stereotypes can form through basic social perception processes.

The ideas of self-categorization and social identity theories can be applied to try to understand some troublesome issues in contemporary organizations.[37] For instance, the evidence from reports of mergers and acquisitions is that 'people issues' are cited as one of the most difficult aspects of integrating two previously distinct firms.[38] From the perspective of social identity theory, the hostility and culture clashes that are a feature of firm integration can be explained by the tendency to favour our own groups and view others as both distinct or different, and less desirable. It is further suggested that events such as organizational restructuring may actually stimulate people to identify even more strongly with their in-groups as they seek to reduce the uncertainty that surrounds such events.[36] On the more positive side, the comparison groups we use are dynamic and flexible. So it may be possible to intervene in situations where there is unhelpful rivalry or hostility between work groups, by trying

stop reflect
Have you ever become aware you were being stereotyped? How did you feel about it? How did it affect your behaviour?

social identity theory: the theory concerned with how we categorize and understand the kind of person we are in relation to others

stop reflect
How would you define your social identity? Think about the types of people you identify positively with (your in-groups) and the types of people you are sure you are different from (your out-groups)

in-groups: groups to which someone perceives he or she belongs, which he or she accordingly evaluates favourably

out-groups: groups to which someone perceives he or she does not belong, which he or she accordingly evaluates unfavourably

to subtly change individuals' identity perceptions. Focusing all groups' attention on external competitors rather than each other is one example.

PERCEIVING CAUSES

As well as perceiving and judging people and situations, we are also naturally inclined to form perceptions about what has caused the behaviour and events we encounter. From the pursuit of religion to the public's fascination with getting 'into the mind' of serial killers, it is a human tendency to assume that there must be some meaning in all things, and some motive behind all people's actions. Hence, we develop ideas and expectations about causes and effects, and general ideas about how things happen and relate to each other, based on experience.

Broadly speaking, we distinguish between stable causes for things and transitory or changeable ones, and between two sources of explanation: those which are about the person (internal), and those which are about the situation (external). The explanations an individual chooses to use, '**causal attributions**' as they are called, are important because they can have a significant influence on his or her expectations and behaviour. This applies to expectations about ourselves, as well as about other people.

causal attribution: the explanations an individual chooses to use, either internal (about the person) or external (about the situation), and either stable or transitory

Consider the experience of being shortlisted but then not selected for a prestigious and challenging job. The reaction of many people is to spend some time thinking about why they were not considered to be the most suitable candidate. If the rejected applicant puts the result down to a lack of preparation on his or her part – an attribution to an internal but changeable cause – he or she might well consider applying for a similar job in the future, but make changes in his or her preparation for the interview. If on the other hand, the person perceives the main cause of the rejection to be a lack of the required level of intelligence – an internal, stable attribution – he or she will probably believe that such prestigious jobs are simply out of reach, and apply only for less challenging jobs in the future. Of course, the applicant might make an external attribution, deciding that the outcome was nothing to do with him or her at all, but was caused by the personal connections of the successful job seeker. In this case, the person's perceptions create no reason to reduce his or her ambitions based on this rejection, or indeed to make changes in approach.

This example demonstrates the way in which our perceptions about what causes things to happen can shape the options for any action that we consider, and our beliefs about what will result from that action. **Perceived self-efficacy** is the term used to describe the 'beliefs in one's capabilities to organize and execute the courses of action required to produce given attainments' (ref. 39, p. 3). Levels of self-efficacy for a specific activity or goal will determine what goals people actually attempt, how much effort they exert to achieve those goals, and how willing they are to persevere in the face of difficulty.

perceived self-efficacy: a person's belief in his or her capacity to achieve something

By definition, in order to develop high self-efficacy in an area, it is necessary to make at least some internal causal attributions for relevant outcomes, because efficacy requires us to believe in our ability to personally control what happens. The exception to this is the attribution of failures to stable, unchangeable personal qualities, which will naturally work to lower expectations of success. Of course, efficacy-lowering attributions are sometimes accurate, and in that sense they are useful. Failing to recognize appropriately when we do not have the skills or qualities required for a certain pursuit can be damaging in that it causes us to direct our effort in unproductive ways. It is when individuals' low expectations are not based on a realistic assessment of their capabilities that they constrain their ability to reach their potential.

There is solid evidence that efficacy beliefs are an important factor in determining many performance outcomes over and above actual ability.[39] An important example is in early study choices made at school, because these choices work to constrain the career options available to students later on. The sex-role stereotyping of subjects and occupations appears to affect girls' and boys' interests and expectations early on, through the subtle feedback and encouragement for different pursuits that children get from their social environments. From a young age, girls tend to have lower perceived self-efficacy for male-typed subjects such as maths and quantitative skills, regardless of their actual capabilities. For this reason, girls are less likely at school to choose and continue to study maths, which means they are not then well equipped to enter occupations for which continued exposure is required, such as science.

self-fulfilling prophecy: an expectation about a situation that of itself causes what is anticipated to actually happen

The case of girls and study choices shows how individuals' expectations can become **self-fulfilling prophecies.** That is, if we think that it is unlikely we can achieve a particular goal, we tend not to bother even trying, or to give up easily if we do try. This means we do not actually give ourselves the opportunity to succeed, so end up reinforcing our original expectation. Of course, this process can also work in a positive direction, where expectations of success can lead to engagement with, and increased effort to achieve, the goal in question. The implication of this information for organizational behaviour is that we cannot always assume that an individual's performance and attainment directly reflects her or his basic abilities. When setting goals, and when motivating and appraising performance, it may be helpful for individuals and their managers to examine causal beliefs and self-efficacy levels in order to identify potential barriers to achievement.

co-variation model: Kelley's model that uses information about the co-occurrence of a person, behaviour and potential causes to work out an explanation

Given its practical significance, there is a good deal of theory and research focused on the ways in which we might come to make one type of causal attribution over another, but the ideas of Kelley are particularly influential.[19] In his '**co-variation model**', Kelley suggested that we use information about the co-occurrence of the person, behaviour and potential causes to work out an explanation.[40] Specifically, three aspects of the occasion are considered:

- *Distinctiveness*: Does the person behave this way in other situations, or is the behaviour uncommon for them and specific to this situation?
- *Consistency*: Does the person always behave this way in this type of situation?
- *Consensus*: Does everyone behave this way in this type of situation, or is this person's behaviour different?

The pattern of answers to these three questions will rule out some potential causes and suggest others. Imagine that a colleague has just been very rude to you when passing on information. If this person is always rude to you (high consistency) but also rude to others (low distinctiveness), and everyone else in the organization is very friendly (low consensus), you will probably think that the person, and not you, is the cause of the problem. In the event that there is a lack of consistency in the person's behaviour in the situation – in this case, he or she is sometimes rude and sometimes friendly – we tend to discount the immediate possibilities and assume that there must be some other explanation.

One of the issues with Kelley's model is that it does not make too much sense unless we have experienced the person and situation more than once. If this is our only experience, we must use different criteria because we do not have the same information. In such cases, Kelley suggested that we use causal schemata as guiding frameworks for making attributions. There is supporting evidence for the co-variation model, but it is not actually clear whether we always or exclusively use this particular process to attribute causation. Nonetheless, the framework has proved a useful tool for understanding the implications of these perceptions.

As with the other aspects of perception discussed in this chapter, causal attribution is not a purely rational process free of selectivity and the workings of motivation. Just as we display biases towards perceiving some environmental cues over others, we are also subject to some general tendencies in the way we attribute causes to things. One bias that has been noted in our perception of causes is the **false consensus effect**, which is the tendency to over-estimate the degree to which other people will think and behave in the same way as we do. We also have a tendency to favour internal attributions for the behaviour of others but external ones to explain our own behaviour. So we are likely to assume that a colleague misses a deadline because she or he is unreliable or disorganized, whereas we miss our own deadlines because of unavoidable constraints. This is called the **fundamental attribution error.**

Actually, the error is not really fundamental in the sense of applying to all people. The extent to which people fall prey to this tendency appears to depend on their cultural background, because those from non-Western cultures are more likely to use external attributions.[41] It is also the case, mirroring the phenomenon of the chronic accessibility of certain schemata discussed earlier, that individuals appear to adopt particular 'explanatory styles', or have a predisposition to employ some types of explanation over others.

Two familiar explanatory styles are optimism and pessimism. Most of us have met someone who is unfailingly optimistic about life regardless of the circumstances, and someone for whom every silver lining has a cloud. Although we often treat such differences light-heartedly, they do have serious consequences. Optimism has been linked to achievement across life domains as well as physical health and psychological well-being, whereas pessimism has been linked with depression and lack of success.[42] It has been suggested that optimists are those who habitually favour external, unstable and specific (only affecting one part of their life) explanations for bad events.[43] By contrast, pessimists attribute bad results to internal, stable and global (affecting all aspects of their life) causes.

PERCEPTION AND EMOTION

Much has been written in recent years on the role that emotion plays in human perception and decision making. Like perception, emotions involve processes outside our conscious awareness, and research now shows that emotion plays a much bigger role in perception and thinking than was previously believed. Our schemata are not simply internal models of the world; they also contain emotional information and biases. Indeed, we have already seen in this chapter how feelings of anger, injustice, attractiveness, pessimism, wanting to belong, and desire to make a good impression on others can all influence how we interpret and interact with the world.

But it is not just our perception of other people that is coloured by our emotions. Take, for example, our perception of risk. Findings from neuroscientific research suggest that our emotions have a key part to play in the creation of a perceptual bias against risk taking.[44] Our emotional brain would appear to be 'pre-programmed' to maximize feelings of pleasure and minimize feelings of pain. In modern societies,

---

false consensus effect: the tendency to over-estimate the degree to which other people will think and behave in the same way as we do

fundamental attribution error: the tendency to favour internal attributions for the behaviour of others but external ones to explain our own behaviour

weblink
To find out more about learned optimism and other similar work, browse the website www.ppc.sas.upenn.edu. You will see that the researchers have made a number of questionnaires available for download, such as the Subjective Happiness Scale, which you could use for a research project of your own

these feelings are commonly associated with the gain and loss of something we value. We have an aversion towards loss because of the negative emotions this generates. Such loss aversion can seriously affect how we perceive and evaluate the riskiness of a particular situation. As a consequence, our desire to avoid feeling a sense of loss or regret can sometimes lead us to make very poor decisions. This may explain why investors put money into government bonds rather than corporate stocks even though the latter have historically out-performed the former by quite some margin[45] – bonds are perceived to be safer. It may also help us to understand why people sometimes continue on a particular course of action (for example, a large investment in a new organizational information system) even when that action is clearly failing: we don't want to regret wasting our 'sunk costs' even if the longer-term costs of continuing may end up being greater.

The neuroscientist Jonah Lehrer suggests that the emotional bias in our schemata to maximize pleasurable feelings lies at the heart of our irrational impulsive decision making.[46] He gives the example of the US subprime mortgage lending market (the collapse of which many economists blame for the onset of the 2009 global economic recession). The most common type of subprime mortgage is the 2/28 loan, which offers a very low fixed-interest rate for the first 2 years and a much higher variable rate for the next 28 years. This type of mortgage accounted for 20 per cent of all US mortgages before the housing market collapse in 2007. Clearly, for many people, the short-term benefits of these mortgages proved too tempting to resist. They were driven by the pleasurable feelings of getting a 'cheap deal' and overlooked the longer-term risk of rising interest rates. Our emotional brain is impulsive and not well equipped to look into the future. This is why decision making based on emotion and intuition is fraught with danger, and why so much research has been conducted on how to enhance the rationality of the decision-making process.

PERCEPTION, EMOTION AND EMPLOYEE RELATIONS

There is one final topic that needs to be included in this discussion about perception and organizational behaviour, namely the role that perception plays in shaping the tone of relations that exist in the workplace. Throughout the chapter, we have discussed how it is that two people can share an experience but form altogether different perceptions about what has happened and what it means. The reasons have included differences in attentional focus, expectations, emotional reactions and prior knowledge. We have also seen how unalterable factors such as gender and cultural background will influence these elements of perception processes, both by shaping the nature of individuals' learning and experiences, which impacts on expectations and knowledge, and through the social categorization and stereotyping processes by which we work out where we and others fit into the social world.

There is in the work domain another basic distinction between people that is of some importance in understanding behaviour in organizations: that between employers (and managers as the agents of employers), and employees or workers. The relations between these two groups are referred to as the employment relationship, and managing these relations is a central concern of human resource management. The relevance here is that the differences in roles, responsibilities, motivations and rewards associated with being either an employer or an employee mean that individuals in these two groups are likely to perceive and emotionally respond to what happens in the organization somewhat differently. This is significant because there

Plate 4 – Our emotional brain is impulsive and not well equipped to look into the future. This is why decision making based on emotion and intuition is fraught with danger. What is your view on the safety or otherwise of 'tombstoning' (see picture)? To what extent is that view based on emotions, and to what extent on rationality?

Source: iStockphoto

is evidence that the extent of the agreement between employers' and employees' perceptions about key aspects of work will have consequences for employees' work attitudes and performance.

Perceived unfair treatment can lead to industrial disputes, such as that highlighted earlier involving workers from Sony and Total in France. More broadly, such perceptions have been found to predict employees' feelings of job satisfaction and trust in managers, as well as their willingness to engage in discretionary behaviour such as staying to complete tasks beyond contracted hours and helping colleagues.[47] In fact, the notion of fairness or justice can be separated into two components: fairness of outcomes, or **distributive justice**, and fairness of procedures, or **procedural justice**. People tend to be concerned with the process by which decisions are made as well as the decision itself, and may in fact be willing to accept a personally disappointing outcome if the procedures used are perceived to have been equitable.

The importance of employees' perceptions about fairness or justice is not, however, restricted to how specific aspects of employment such as formal contract terms are viewed. The employment relationship is best seen as a series of agreements about a number of elements that are all of importance to the parties involved, such as working conditions, job security and commitment, management

distributive justice: justice based on the principle of fairness of outcomes

procedural justice: justice based on the principle of fairness of the procedures employed to achieve outcomes

OB and globalization

Emotional intelligence in the international oil and gas sector

International business relationships and partnerships are becoming more and more common in the natural resource sector. As the worldwide population grows and new industrialized economies, such as China, Brazil, India and Russia, emerge, there is increasing pressure on nations – and private companies within their borders – to secure access to the resources that literally fuel their economies.

One means of doing this is through the formation of international business partnerships to ensure that resources that exist only in certain locations can be extracted, transported and sold around the world. Such partnerships have become increasingly common in the oil and gas sector, and industry leaders must be savvy to the challenges of managing a global network of colleagues, clients and workers, many of whom have different, culturally based ideas about proper business relationships and effective organizational management.

In a recent industry publication, Weijermars et al. (2008) explain that the challenges of successful business relationships between Western European and Russian oil companies extend beyond the technical and political aspects of business and contract management. Whereas managerial culture in Russia has traditionally tended to be hierarchical and centralized, Western European business culture is more decentralized and reliant on networking. Building management tools to effectively address these different cultural expectations is integral to the success of the partnerships. According to Weijermars et al.:

> The hiring of a multicultural workforce from a range of countries, distinct company cultures and different age groups poses a challenge in itself through the increased risk of communication barriers or gaps … The common aim is to establish an emotionally balanced relationship between the two partners and to narrow the communication gap. This results in better alignment of cultural values, skill sets and common goals, which is important to overcome the residual Cold-War impediments of the past.

Such partnerships highlight the role of *emotional intelligence* as a management tool in international business. Emotional intelligence describes the ability to manage one's own emotions and, through verbal and non-verbal performance, to identify and manage the emotions of others (Goleman, 1995). Emotions, or emotional responses, are often linked to cultural experiences and worldviews, and in order for managers to effectively develop their emotional intelligence, they must recognize the cultural paradigms within which their partners' emotions are operating. This is the challenge facing the oil and gas sector today. In the increasingly global economy, strong emotional intelligence can be just as crucial to the success of business relationships as technical or fiscal intelligence.

stop!   Some professions, like airline attendant, healthcare worker and retail salesperson, are often said to demand high emotional intelligence. Think about your experiences with professionals in these fields. Describe some of the specific ways in which they might employ emotional intelligence in their work. How might this emotional labour benefit the workers as well as their customers, patients or clients?

Have you ever been in a situation where a friend or colleague from a different cultural background found it difficult to understand your emotional reaction to a situation, or vice versa? Describe how acquiring emotional intelligence about this person's culture might have helped you (or them) to understand and address the situation.

watch   Watch the BBC 2 television series *The Office* (2001–03), paying specific attention to how emotional intelligence is (or is not!) used by different characters, and to what effect.

Sources and further research

Goleman, D. (1995) *Emotional Intelligence: Why It Can Matter More Than IQ*, New York: Bantam Books.

Harwood, M. (2008) 'Relationships critical to overseas personnel protection'. Available at: www.securitymanagement.com/news/relationships-critical-overseas-personnel-protection (accessed September 2009).

Lorz, M. (2006) 'Leadership styles'. Available at: www.management-issues.co.uk/2006/8/8/opinion/leadership-styles.asp?section=opinion&id=3435&is_authenticated=0&reference=&specifier=&mode=print (accessed September 2009).

Weijermars, R., De Jong, V. and Van Der Kooi, K. (2008) 'Cultural challenges in oil and gas industry management', *World Oil*, 229(4), pp. 223–8.

Note: This feature was written by Gretchen Fox, PhD, Anthropologist, Timberline Natural Resource Group, Canada.

psychological contract: an individual's beliefs about the terms and conditions of a reciprocal exchange agreement between that person and another party

style, and pay and benefits. It is also an ongoing, dynamic interaction between the parties made up of a sequence of exchanges over time, each of which will influence the thoughts and perceptions of those involved. The **psychological contract**, has become important in organizational behaviour and human resource management.

It is a term used to capture individuals' general perceptions of the overall nature and balance of the employer–employee exchange.

A well-accepted definition of the psychological contract is provided by Rousseau, who describes it as 'individual beliefs, shaped by the organization, regarding the terms of an exchange agreement between individuals and the organization' (ref. 48, p. 14). In other words, it consists of employees' ideas about what they are expected to contribute to the organization and what they can expect to get back in return for their efforts. Two key points to note are that the psychological contract is unwritten and often unspoken, and that these are the perceptions formed by individual employees of the 'deal' promised by the employer. These expectations are formed during the recruitment process and when inside the organization, from what managers say and do, as well as the communications and culture of the company.

For all the reasons we have discussed for why people's perceptions may differ, one person's ideas about what the organization has promised and expects may not be fully or even partly shared by managers or indeed other employees. Much potential exists, then, for organizations to fall short of employees' expectations and vice versa, leading to feelings that agreed promises have been broken. The results from a number of studies suggest that violations of individuals' psychological contracts are linked to outcomes such as intentions to quit, reduced job performance and lower levels of commitment.[49]

Evidence from a study of supervisors and those they managed showed significant differences in relative perceptions of the extent to which aspects of the psychological contract related to pay, advancement opportunities and a good employment relationship were fulfilled.[50] Perhaps unsurprisingly, the supervisors felt that the employer's obligations had been fulfilled more fully than did their subordinates. This study also allows us to relate the issue of psychological contract violation to the process of causal attribution discussed earlier, and particularly the phenomenon of the fundamental attribution error. Where both parties agreed that some expectations were unmet, the employees were more likely to perceive the cause as intentional disregard by the employer, while the supervisors tended to see the cause as situational constraints, or events beyond the organization's control. Here then is another example of the very real and concrete organizational consequences of individuals' perceptions.

CHAPTER SUMMARY

- Perception is important in organizational behaviour because the fundamental nature of perceptual processes means that individuals usually interpret other people and situations differently and so routinely hold different views of reality, which in turn strongly influence their attitudes and actions. This means that avoiding conflict and ensuring that important workplace decisions are based on sound judgements is not a matter of training people how to see things as they 'really are', because multiple realities always exist. More can be gained from understanding how perception works, and shaping organizational activity so that the possibilities for negative outcomes (both emotional and behavioural) are minimized.

- 'Perception' refers to the process by which our senses gather information from the environment and our brains make sense of that information. The perception process is characterized as inherently selective, subjective and largely automatic rather than conscious. It can be broken down into three steps or elements – receiving, organizing and interpreting – representing the path by which we mentally transform sensory stimuli from the environment into meaningful information.

- The three elements of the perception process do not occur separately or in sequence, but overlap and sometimes occur in parallel. When perception proceeds from the sensory data received from the environment, it is called 'bottom-up' information processing. In contrast, when perception begins with existing knowledge that is used to interpret the incoming data, it is called 'top-down' processing. Whereas bottom-up processing requires a lot of mental effort, top-down processing carries the risk of assumptions and jumping to the wrong conclusions, so some balance is required between in the use of these two perception strategies.

- The processing limitations of our brains mean it is only because we employ selective attention that it is possible for us to experience the mass of sensory stimuli in the environment as orderly and meaningful. Our choice of what to attend to is driven by the environmental cues that are most salient, or by our own motivations, expectations, emotions and goals. This selectivity is highly resource efficient, but the downside is that we can miss crucial bits of information and form misleading perceptions of what we are experiencing. If we then act on those perceptions, we may suffer serious consequences.

- Existing knowledge has a powerful effect on how we perceive new experiences. We store knowledge in the form of mental models, or schemata: packages of related content (for instance, thoughts, emotions and attitudes) about people, situations and roles. Schemata do develop over time, but do not change much once formed because they act as lenses by which we view new information. New data that are inconsistent with what we 'know' are simply reinterpreted to fit. In perception, when one bit of information related to a schema is brought to mind, everything else in the package comes to mind also, so we can very quickly make sense of something on the basis of a small bit of information. But these stable, automatic linkages between thoughts can be unhelpful, as in the case of stereotypes. Although we can choose not to act upon stereotypes, it may not be possible to stop them coming to mind in the first place.

- Two specific classes of perception were identified that hold particular significance for organizations. The causes that people perceive (or attribute) for particular outcomes will significantly affect their future expectations and behaviour. If a person sees a failure to meet a goal as the result of stable, internal causes – such as intelligence – she or he is less likely to try again than if the cause of the failure is perceived to be more about his or her circumstances at the time. This knowledge is important for understanding individual performance and motivation. The second class of perception – employees' views of justice and fairness in the workplace – is significant because these impact on the employment relationship. If employees perceive that they are being treated unfairly by the organization, it will negatively influence their work attitudes and motivation. The difficulty is that employees and employers are very likely to perceive things differently by virtue of their respective roles and experiences, so it is a particular challenge for organizations to ensure that employees feel fairly treated.

KEY CONCEPTS

causal attribution
chronic accessibility
cognitive inertia
explanatory styles

false consensus effect
fundamental attribution error
mental models
perceived self-efficacy
perceptual biases
perceptual errors
perceptual sets
psychological contract
salient cues
schemata
selective attention
social identity theory
stereotypes

VOCAB CHECKLIST FOR ESL STUDENTS

- Bottom-up processing
- Causal attribution
- Co-variation model
- Distributive justice
- Emotional management
- False consensus effect
- Fundamental attribution error
- Halo and horns effect
- Impression management
- In-groups
- Linguistic relativity
- Out-groups
- Perceived self-efficacy
- Perception, perceiver, perceptive, perceive
- Perceptual bias
- Perceptual set
- Primacy effect
- Procedural justice
- Psychological contract
- Recency effect
- Schema, schemata, schematic
- Selective attention
- Self-fulfilling prophecy
- Social identity theory
- Stereotype, stereotyping
- Top-down processing

CHAPTER REVIEW QUESTIONS

1 Describe the basic features of human perception processes, and why these features explain the fact that people generally perceive the same situation differently.

2   Identify and explain two consequences of selective attention that can occur in the workplace.

3   Outline the pros and cons of the mental packaging of information into schemata.

4   What is causal attribution? Outline one scenario that might occur in an organization where a person's perceptions about the causes of things affect her or his motivation to achieve a goal.

5   In what ways can individuals' perceptions affect other people, groups of people and the social climate of an organization?

CHAPTER RESEARCH QUESTIONS

1   Get a copy of Jonah Lehrer's (2009) book, *The Decisive Moment*[45] and read the section entitled 'The danger of debt'. This section argues that the 2008/09 world economic downturn had as much to do with the way we perceive and emotionally respond to offers of credit cards and subprime loans as it had to do with broader political and economic forces.
    ⊙ How far do you agree with this argument?
    ⊙ Do you think the 'Save More Tomorrow' programme discussed at the end of the section could work? What might be the likely reactions of employers and employees if such a programme were to be introduced into an organization?

2   Get a copy of Stuart Sutherland's (2007) book *Irrationality*,[51] 'Distorting the evidence'. This chapter reveals how we often distort new evidence that disconfirms our current beliefs. What are the implications of this perceptual bias for a manager trying to explain to employees that long-established (and popular) working practices need to be fundamentally changed in order to achieve cost savings?

3   Get a copy of the paper 'The use of impression management tactics in structural interviews: a function of question type?' by Ellis et al. (2002),[52] and read about their study of the IM tactics used by job applicants in interviews using different types of question. Do you think organizations should try to prevent IM? Given that the way in which interviews are conducted seems to make a difference, do you consider it to be the responsibility of interviewers or of job applicants to check the accuracy of what applicants say?

FURTHER READING

Bandura, A. (1997) *Self-Efficacy: The Exercise of Control*, New York: Freeman.

Eysenck, M. W. and Keane, M. T. (2005) *Cognitive Psychology: A Student's Handbook* (5th edn), Hove: Lawrence Erlbaum.

Haslam, S. A. (2001) *Psychology in Organizations: The Social Identity Approach*, London: Sage.

Hogg, M. A. and Vaughan, G. M. (2004) *Social Psychology* (4th edn), Hemel Hempstead: Prentice Hall.

Lehrer, J. (2009) *The Decisive Moment: How the Brain Makes up its Mind*, Edinburgh: Canongate.

Rosenfeld, P., Giacalone, R. and Riordan, C. A. (2002) *Impression Management: Building and Enhancing Reputation at Work*, London: Thomson Learning.

Chapter case study

The blame game

Setting

This case is set in medium-sized factory specializing in the manufacture of metal boxes and cases. The factory workers employees are semi-skilled but receive a good wage. Employee relations are generally good.

Problem

It began as a normal day on the shop floor in the metal working factory of Chidi Manufacturing. By mid-morning, the manufacturing process was in full swing and Morenike, the factory manager, was able to take a short break to enjoy a well-earned cup of tea. However, just as she had sat down in her office, Daren (one of two line managers in the factory) came rather timidly into her office.

'I'm afraid we have a serious quality problem, boss,' he said apologetically. 'Edwin is turning out sub-standard work that is threatening to disrupt the whole production run'.

'Can't you sort this out, Daren?' Morenike replied. 'After all, this falls firmly within your remit as line manager.'

'That's true, but Edwin is adamant that he is not the cause of the problem, and he is getting quite angry about it,' Daren replied. 'I'd be grateful if you could help out.'

The two managers walked swiftly through the busy factory until they came to Workstation 42. Edwin stood by his machine, which appeared to be switched off despite the fact that the production run was in full flow all around him. A stockpile of work was building up by the side of his workstation.

'Okay, Edwin,' Morenike said quietly, 'would you like to tell me what is going on and why you're not working?'

'Good morning, boss' he replied. 'About an hour ago I realised that my workstation was beginning to produce material that was falling below quality standards. I told Daren and he just told me to "put things right" and maintain production speed. But it isn't my fault that the machine is faulty. I was working at Workstation 18 all last week, and there was never any problem with my work there. This Workstation 42 machine needs overhauling or something, and so there's no point in carrying on using it if it's not up to the job.'

'Oh, I see,' Daren interjected, 'you're saying that it is the machine's fault and not yours. How do you explain the fact that Workstation 42 was working perfectly well on the night shift and then started misbehaving only once you came to work? A bad worker always blames his tools.'

'I don't see how you know how well the machine was working last night. You weren't here and neither was I!', Edwin replied angrily.

'Gentlemen, let's keep our tempers here,' Morenike insisted. 'Edwin, your job is to operate Workstation 42, and if your line manager tells you to keep working then you darn well should. Please get back to work immediately or I'll be forced to enforce disciplinary procedures.'

Edwin shrugged his shoulders and muttered something under his breath. Nevertheless, he turned round and switched the machine back on. The two managers stayed for a few minutes to ensure that everything was working smoothly and then Morenike returned to her office. However, less than 10 minutes later, the line manager was back in her office complaining bitterly that Edwin had deliberately 'sabotaged' his workstation so that it now appeared incapable of functioning. 'Never mind disciplinary procedures. I want him sacked,' Daren declared. 'He's trying to undermine my authority and make me look as if I'm in the wrong and not him. I want your support on this matter.'

Tasks

1   Which theory or theories of perception best help us understand the causes of the conflict described in the case?
2   What should the factory manager do next?

Note

This case study was written by Martin Corbett, Associate Professor of Industrial Relations and Organisational Behaviour, Warwick Business School, UK.

WEB-BASED ASSIGNMENT

What attracts you to some organizations and not others?

Get a copy of the recruitment pages of a national newspaper or a professional publication, such as *People Management* or *The Economist*. From the advertisements, identify a selection of the recruiting organizations that differ from each other and provide details of their websites. Browse each of the sites, particularly looking at the pages aimed at potential job applicants. It would be ideal if you could do this with a colleague or friend so you can have a discussion about it.

Consider these questions:

- What are your perceptions of each organization as a potential employer? Are they your kind of place?
- Try to identify what perceptual cues from the advertisement and websites captured your attention, and the prior knowledge and expectations that led you to your conclusions. To what extent can you apply social categorization theory to explain your attraction or aversion to each organization?

OB IN FILM

Scottish cyclist Graham Obree is one of the greatest cyclists of all time. His fame does not stem from becoming world champion or breaking the 1-hour record twice, great though these feats are, but from the fact that he did so on a home-made bike made from washing machine parts. This aspect of his story was made all the more curious given the contrast with his closest rival, Chris Boardman, who rode a state-of-the art bicycle engineered by Lotus. In addition, Obree's story is all the more compelling because he has suffered from clinical depression and twice tried to commit suicide. The film revolves around the apparent contrast of psychological illness and sporting success.

In the hands of most directors, Obree's story would be a typical biopic capturing an interesting and complex life story. But the director of *The Flying Scotsman* (2006), Douglas Mackinnon, did quite something different with Obree's story. Not only did he create an engaging story, but he also critiques the whole way in which biopics are portrayed. He does this by playing a perceptual trick with the audience. After following convention and telling Obree's story, Mackinnon challenges the audience at the end when the camera looks straight into the cyclist's eyes. At this point, the viewer is forced to question whether or not they really understand what is going on inside the hero's head. As you watch the film, try to pick out how the director is influencing and manipulating your perception of Graham Obree.

Note: This feature was written by Professor Jon Billsberry, Senior Research Fellow, Open University Business School, UK.

BONUS OB IN FILM FEATURE!

Visit www.palgrave.com/business/brattonob2e to see how *A Beautiful Mind* (2001) can be considered in relation to the subject of perception.

REFERENCES

1. Ramachandran, V. S. and Rogers-Ramachandran, D. (2005) 'How blind are we?', *Scientific American Mind*, **16**(2), p. 96.

2. Weick, K. E. (2001) *Making Sense of the Organization*, Oxford: Blackwell.

3. Fiske, S. T. and Taylor, S. E. (1991) *Social Cognition* (2nd edn), New York: McGraw Hill.

4. Dunkerley, K. J. and Robinson, P. (2002) 'Similarities and differences in perceptions and evaluations of the communication styles of American and British managers', *Journal of Language and Social Psychology*, **21**, pp. 393–409.

5. Eysenck, M. W. and Keane, M. T. (2005) *Cognitive Psychology: A Student's Handbook* (5th edn), Hove: Lawrence Erlbaum.

6. Tetlock, P. (1983) 'Accountability and complexity of thought', *Journal of Personality and Social Psychology*, **45**, pp. 74–83.

7. Jensen, M. C., Brant-Zawadzki, M. N., Obuchowski, N., Modic, M. T., Malkasian, D. and Ross, J. S. (1994) 'Magnetic resonance imaging of the lumbar spine in people without back pain', *New England Journal of Medicine*, 331, pp. 69–73.

8. Roth, E. M. and Woods, O D. (1988) 'Aiding human performance. I: Cognitive analysis', *LeTravail Humain*, **51**, pp. 39–64.

9. Highhouse, S. (2001) 'Judgment and decision-making research: relevance to industrial and organizational psychology', in N. Anderson, D. Ones, H. K. Sinangil and C. Viswesveran (eds), *Handbook of Industrial Work and Organizational Psychology*, Volume 2: *Organizational Psychology*, London: Sage.

10. Attneave, F. (1971) 'Multistability in perception', in R. Held and W. Richards (eds), *Recent Progress in Perception*, San Francisco: W. H. Freeman.

11. Haart, E. G. O.-de, Carey, D. P. and Milne, A. B. (1999) 'More thoughts on perceiving and grasping the Mueller–Lyer illusion', *Neuropsychologica*, **37**, pp. 1437–44.

12. Mishra, R. C., Dasen, P. R. and Niraula, S. (2003) 'Ecology, language, and performance on spatial cognitive tasks', *International Journal of Psychology*, **38**, pp. 366–83.

13. Bloom, R. (2004) 'Children think before they speak', *Nature*, **430**, pp. 410–11.

14. Redelmeier, D. A. and Tibshirani, R. J. (1997) 'Association between cellular-telephone calls and motor vehicle collisions', *New England Journal of Medicine*, **336**, pp. 453–8.

15. Strayer, D. L. and Johnston, W. A. (2001) 'Driven to distraction: dual-task studies of simulated driving and conversing on a cellular telephone', *Psychological Science*, **12**(6), pp. 462–6.

16. Simons, D. J. and Levin, D. T. (1998) 'Failures to detect changes to people in a real-world interaction', *Psychonomic Bulletin and Review*, **5**, pp. 644–9.

17. Simons, D. J. and Chabris, C. F. (1999) 'Gorillas in our midst: sustained inattentional blindness for dynamic events', *Perception*, **28**, pp. 1059–74.

18. Nisbett, R. and Ross, L. (1980) *Human Inference: Strategies and Shortcomings of Social Judgement*, Englewood Cliffs, NJ: Prentice Hall.

19. Hogg, M. A. and Vaughan, G. M. (2004) *Social Psychology: An Introduction* (4th edn), Hemel Hempstead: Prentice Hall.

20. Macrae, C. N., Bodenhausen, G. V., Milne, A. B. and Jetten, J. (1994) 'Employee involvement management practices, work stress and depression in employees of a human services residential care facility', *Human Relations*, **54**(8), pp. 1065–92.

21. Gladwell, M. (2005) *Blink: The Power of Thinking Without Thinking*, Harmondsworth: Penguin.

22. Judge, T. A. and Cable, D. M. (2004) 'The effect of physical height on workplace success and income: preliminary test of a theoretical model', *Journal of Applied Psychology*, **89**, 428–41.

23. Rosenfeld, P., Giacalone, R. and Riordan, C. A. (2002) *Impression Management: Building and Enhancing Reputation at Work*, London: Thomson Learning.

24. Singh, V., Kumra, S. and Vinnicombe, S. (2002) 'Gender and impression management: playing the promotion game', *Journal of Business Ethics*, **37**, pp. 77–89.

25. Beattie, V. and Jones, M. J. (2000) 'Impression management: the case of inter-country financial graphs', *Journal of International Accounting, Auditing and Taxation*, **9**, 159–83.

26. Arunachalam, V., Pei, B. K. W. and Steinbart, P. J. (2002) 'Impression management with graphs: effects on choices', *Journal of Information Systems*, **16**, 183–202.

27. Hochschild, A. (1979) *The Managed Heart: Commercialization of Human Feeling*, Berkeley, CA: University of California Press.

28. Moisi, D. (2009) *The Geopolitics of Emotion: How Cultures of Fear, Humiliation, and Hope are Reshaping the World*, New York: Doubleday.

29. Hodgkinson, G. (1997) 'Cognitive inertia in a turbulent market: the case of UK residential estate agents', *Journal of Management Studies*, **34**, pp. 921–45.

30. Bargh, J. A., Lombardi, W. J. and Higgins, E. T. (1988) 'Automaticity of chronically accessible constructs in person × situation effects on person perception: it's just a matter of time', *Journal of Personality and Social Psychology*, **55**, pp. 599–605.

31. Steele, C. M., Spencer, S. J. and Aronson, J. (2003) 'Contending with group image: the psychology of stereotype threat and social identity threat,' pp. 102–15 in M. P. Zanna (ed.), *Advances in Experimental Social Psychology*, San Diego: Academic Press.

32. Schein, V. E. (1973) 'The relationship between sex role stereotypes and requisite management characteristics', *Journal of Applied Psychology*, **57**, pp. 95–100.

33. Schein, V. E. (1975) 'The relationship between sex role stereotypes and requisite management characteristics among female managers', *Journal of Applied Psychology*, **60**, pp. 340–4.

34. Schein, E.A. (1996) 'Culture: the missing concept in organization studies', *Administrative Science Quarterly*, **41**, pp. 229–40.

35. Tajfel, H. and Turner, J. C. (1979) 'An integrative theory of intergroup conflict', in W. G. Austin and S. Worchel (eds), *The Social Psychology of Intergroup Relations*, Monterey, CA: Brooks/Cole.

36. Hogg, M. and Terry, D. J. (2000) 'Social identity and self-categorization processes in organizational contexts', *Academy of Management Review*, **25**, pp. 121–40.

37. Haslam, S. A. (2001) *Psychology in Organizations: The Social Identity Approach*, London: Sage.

38. Chartered Institute of Personnel and Development (2000) *People Implications of Mergers and Acquisitions, Joint Ventures and Divestments: Survey Report*, London: CIPD.

39. Bandura, A. (1997) *Self-efficacy: The Exercise of Control*, New York: Freeman.

40. Kelley, H. H. (1973) 'The process of causal attribution', *American Psychologist*, **28**, pp. 107–28.

41. Morris, M. W. and Peng, K. P. (1994) 'Culture and cause: American and Chinese attributions for social and physical events', *Journal of Personality and Social Psychology*, **67**, pp. 949–71.

42. Peterson, C. (2000) 'The future of optimism', *American Psychologist*, **55**, pp. 44–55.

43. Seligman, M. E. P. (1991) *Learned Optimism*, New York: Knopf.

44. Montague, R. (2007) 'Neuroeconomics: a view from neuroscience', *Functional Neurology*, **22**, 760–67.

45. Zweig, J. (2008) *Your Money and Your Brain*, New York: Simon Schuster.

46. Lehrer, J. (2009) *The Decisive Moment: How the Brain Makes up its Mind*, Edinburgh: Canongate.

47. Gilliland, S. W. and Chan, D. (2001) 'Justice in organizations: theory, methods and applications', in N. Anderson, D. Ones, H. K. Sinangil and C. Viswesveran (eds), *Handbook of Industrial, Work & Organizational Psychology*, Volume 2: *Organizational Psychology*, London: Sage.

48. Rousseau, D. M. (1995) *Psychological Contracts in Organisations: Understanding Written and Unwritten Agreements*, Thousand Oaks, CA: Sage.

49. Taylor, M. S. and Tekleab, A. G. (2004) 'Taking stock of psychological contract research: assessing progress, addressing troublesome issues, and setting research priorities', in J. A.-M. Coyle-Shapiro, L. M. Shore, M. S. Taylor and L. E. Tetrick (eds), *The Employment Relationship: Examining Psychological and Contextual Perspectives*, Oxford: Oxford University Press.

50. Lester, S. W., Turnley, W. H., Bloodgood, J. M. and Bolino, M. (2002) 'Not seeing eye to eye: differences in supervisor and subordinate perceptions of and attributions for psychological contract breach', *Journal of Organizational Behavior*, **23**, pp. 39–56.

51. Sutherland, S. (2007) *Irrationality*. London: Pinter & Martin.

52. Ellis, A. P. J., West, B. J., Ryan, A. M. and DeShon, R. P. (2002) 'The use of impression management tactics in structured interviews: a function of question type?', *Journal of Applied Psychology*, **87**, pp. 1200–8.

THE ROLE OF HRM

OUTLINE

OBJECTIVES

After studying this chapter, you should be able to:

1 Explain the development of human resource management (HRM)
2 Define HRM and its relation to organizational management
3 Explain the central features of the contract in the employment relationship
4 Summarise the scope of HRM and the key HRM functions
5 Explain the theoretical issues surrounding the HRM debate
6 Appreciate the different approaches to studying HRM

INTRODUCTION

This book is concerned with managing people, both individually and collectively, in the workplace. Emerging from the worst cyclical economic recession since 1945, human resource management (HRM) has assumed new prominence as concerns about global competitiveness, the demographics of ageing and climate change persist. It is argued that these global drivers of change require managers to adjust the way in which they manage in order to achieve innovation, sustainable growth and an effective use of employees. For some, HRM is associated with a set of distinctive 'best' practices that aim to recruit, develop, reward and manage people in ways that create what are called 'high-performing work systems'. For others, the HRM stereotype is simply a repackaging of 'good' personnel management practices – the 'old wine in new bottles' critique – or more fundamentally exposes enduring conflicts and paradoxes associated with labour management. As managers strive to reduce costs, most follow conventional wisdom – downsizing, restructuring and outsourcing work to ever cheaper labour markets – rather than looking to HRM in order to create competitive advantage or provide superior public services. Critical management theorists point to the need to address the conflict between the dual imperatives of competitiveness and control, and the cooperation and commitment of employees. Within the academic study of HRM, this conflict is often framed in terms of 'the rhetoric versus the reality' of HRM.

This chapter examines the complex debate surrounding the nature and significance of contemporary HRM. After defining HRM, we will examine the nature of the employment relationship and HRM functions. We will also explore some influential theoretical models that attempt to define HRM analytically. We will begin, however, by briefly examining the development of HRM.

Reflective question

Based upon your reading or work experience, how important is HRM to individual performance at work or to organizational success?

THE DEVELOPMENT OF HRM

Despite the fact that 'human resource management' outwardly appears to be a relatively neutral management term, the language used to talk about it is imbued with ideologies that reflect radical changes in society over time. As understood in the approach we are taking here, innovations in management must be analysed within a framework of existing social relationships and interdependencies in society. The notion that HRM is *embedded* in society helps to capture and express the importance of culture, national politics, practising law and indigenous business-related institutions, for example employment tribunals, in explaining how work and people are managed. Thus, developments in HRM respond to and are shaped by changes in markets, social movements and public policies that are the products of the economic and political changes in society.

Keynesianism: collectivism and personnel management

The roots of people management can be traced back to the Industrial Revolution in England in the late eighteenth century. However, we begin our discussion on this history with the economic and political conditions prevailing after the Second World War. The years 1950–74 were the 'golden age' of the Keynesian economic doctrine, as evidenced by the post-war Labour government's commitment 'to combine a free democracy with a planned economy' (Coates, 1975, p. 46). It was a period when both Conservative and Labour governments, anxious to foster industrial peace through conciliation, mediation and arbitration (Crouch, 1982), passed employment laws to improve employment conditions and extend workers' rights, which also encouraged the growth of personnel specialists. The Donovan Commission (1968) investigated

HRM in practice: A new role for HR professionals

There has been increased awareness and understanding of the impact that business activity has upon social and political systems as a result of high-profile corporate scandals, such as the alleged phone hacking at News International and the politicians implicated. Awareness has also been raised by global development initiatives such as the Business Leaders Initiative on Human Rights (a business-led organization aiming to find practical ways of implementing the Universal Declaration of Human Rights in a business context). As a result, organizations are increasingly being pushed to develop their business practices in order to operate within socially acceptable parameters. The 'triple bottom line' (Elkington, 1998) of *profit*, *people* and *planet* provides a convenient manifesto for the 'social contract' now expected from business. There is little doubt that there is tension between social obligations and the demands of shareholders. But who is awarded the daunting task of integrating the economic, social and environmental objectives into an organization's strategy, thus dealing with the complex task of balancing ethics and income? The need to define, balance and carry out these objectives has been intensified as the effects of the economic downturn are felt around the globe. A recent People Management article highlights this growing expectation that businesses will accept such responsibility:

> *The fallout from the world financial crisis continues unabated. For the first time since the Great Depression of the 1930s, some of the most sacred tenets of Western capitalism are being questioned in mainstream debate. Chief among these is our most basic assumption that growth is the primary goal of economic activity. There seems to be a widespread acceptance of the need for corporations to be more responsible as global tenants, to pay more attention to the broader consequences of economic activity and to adopt more sustainable practices ... While the recklessness of the financial services industry seems to have been pivotal, our research suggests that the crisis was the culmination of a far wider malaise affecting how organisations operate, what leaders do, and how they are developed ... Businesses are increasingly seen as participants in a wider ecology with responsibility for minimising their environmental impact and improving their contribution to social welfare. (Casserley and Critchley, 2010, p. 21)*

Much is made of the wide-ranging responsibilities of the human resources (HR) function. Alongside the strategic influence of their new role as a business partner in many organizations, and the ongoing need for them to provide operational support, HR professionals are facing renewed and unrelenting pressure to act as moral and ethical compasses for organizations. This is rooted in the welfare role of the personnel function prior to the advent of HRM. The HR function has been awarded great responsibility as a guardian of the ethos and values that must be embedded in an organizational culture if HR specialists are to be successful. The changing expectations of organizational stakeholders can be attributed to notable cases of corporate mismanagement and stakeholders' growing awareness that their reputation could be damaged. This has led to a competitive need to justify not only what organizations do with their profits, but also how those profits are generated in the first place. Cross-border business and an emphasis on employee welfare and social, legal and philanthropic responsibilities have all forced organizations to nominate 'natural' leaders to be responsible for internal and external ethical responsibility.

Stop!   Should corporations behave in an ethical manner because it is morally right or because there is a 'business case' for management ethics? Should HR professionals act as the 'moral compass' for organizations?

Sources and further information

For further information, see the Business Leaders Initiative on Human Rights website www.blihr.org. See also Casserley and Critchley (2010), Francis and Keegan (2005) and Watson (2007).

Note

This feature was written by Lesley McLean (née Craig) at Edinburgh Napier University.

Source: Mat Coleman

UK industrial relations and recommended, among other things, that management should develop joint (trade union–management) procedures for the speedy settlement of grievances. The idea that there were both common and conflicting goals between the 'actors' – employers and trade unions – and the state's deep involvement in managing and regulating employment relations provided the *pluralist* framework for managing the employment relationship.

HRM web links

Go to the website of the HR professional associations (for example, Australia www.hrhq.com; Britain www.cipd.co.uk; Canada www.hrpa.org; and USA www.shrm.org). Then click on the 'Mission statement' or 'History'. Evaluate the information you find in relation to the history of personnel management. What are the origins of the association?

Neo-liberalism: individualism and HRM

In the 1980s and 90s, there was a radical change in both the context and the content of how people were managed. Western economies saw the renaissance of 'market disciplines', and there was a strong belief that, in terms of economic well-being, too much government intervention was the problem. The new political orthodoxy focused on extending market power and limiting the role of the government, mainly to facilitate this laissez-faire agenda (Kuttner, 2000). The rise of the political ideology of Thatcherism in Britain represented a radical break from the consensual, corporatist style of government, which provided the political backcloth to this shift in managerial ideas and practices. Whereas it was alleged that traditional personnel management based its legitimacy and influence on its ability to deal with the uncertainties stemming from full employment and trade union growth, HRM celebrated the *unitary* philosophy and framework. Strongly influenced by the up-and-coming neo-liberal economic consensus, HRM subscribed to the idea that there was a harmony of goals and interests between the organization's internal members. The new approach was therefore to marginalize or exclude 'external' influences such as the state or trade unions.

The landmark publication *New Perspectives on Human Resource Management* (1989), edited by John Storey, generated the 'first wave' of debate on the nature and ideological significance of the normative HRM model. Debate focused on 'hard' and 'soft' versions of the HRM model. The 'hard' version emphasizes the term 'resource' and adopts a 'rational' approach to managing employees, that is, viewing employees as any other economic factor – as a cost that must be controlled. The 'soft' HRM model emphasizes the term 'human' and thus advocates investment in training and development, as well as the adoption of 'commitment' strategies to ensure that highly skilled and loyal employees give the organization a competitive advantage. For some academics, the normative HRM model represented a distinctive approach to managing the human 'input' that fitted the new economic order (Bamberger and Meshoulam, 2000); in addition, being much more concerned with business strategy and HR strategy linkages, it signalled the beginnings of a new theoretical sophistication in the area of personnel management (Boxall, 1992). For those who disagreed, however, the HRM stereotype was characterized as a cultural construct concerned with making sure that employees 'fitted' corporate values (Townley, 1994), even attempting to 'govern the soul' (Rose, 1999). In this way, the HRM model, among both its advocates and its detractors, became one of the most controversial topics in managerial debate (Storey, 1989). The displacement of personnel management by HRM can be seen as the outcome of neo-liberalism ideology, much as the 'social contract' of the 1970s was an outcome of Keynesian economic planning and the 'Old' Labour government–union partnership.

MANAGEMENT AND HRM

HRM, in theory and in practice, encompasses a diverse body of scholarship and managerial activities concerned with managing work and people. An early definition of HRM by Michael Beer and his colleagues focuses on all managerial activity affecting the employment relationship: 'Human resource management (HRM) involves all management decisions and actions that affect the nature of the relationship between the organization and employees – its human resources' (1984, p. 1). Acknowledging HRM as only one 'recipe' from a range of alternatives, Storey (1995a, 2001) contends that HRM plays a pivotal role in sophisticated organizations, emphasizing the importance of the strategic dimension and employee 'commitment' in generating HR activities. In his view:

> Human resource management is a distinctive approach to employment management which seeks to achieve competitive advantage through the strategic deployment of a highly committed and capable workforce using an array of cultural, structural and personnel techniques. (Storey, 2007, p. 7)

Conceptualizing HRM as a high-commitment management strategy limits the discipline to the study of a relatively small number of distinct organizations as most firms continue to provide low wages and a minimal number of training opportunities (Bacon and Blyton, 2003). In contrast, Boxall et al. (2008, p. 1) define HRM as 'the management of work and people towards desired ends'. These authors advance the notion of 'analytical HRM' to emphasize that the primary task of HRM scholars is to build theory and gather empirical data in order to identify and explain 'the way management *actually behaves* in organizing work and managing people' (Boxall et al., 2008, p. 4, emphasis added).

This approach to HRM has three interrelated analytical themes. The first is a concern with the '*what*' and '*why*' of HRM, with understanding management behaviour in different contexts and with explaining motives. The second is a concern with the '*how*' of HRM, that is, the processes by which it is carried out. The third is concerned with questions of '*for whom and how well*', that is, with assessing the *outcomes* of HRM. The third characteristic in particular implies a critical purpose and helps us to rediscover one of the prime objectives of the social sciences – that of asking tough questions about power and inequality. It also reminds all of those who are interested in studying the field that HRM is 'embedded in a global economical, political and sociocultural context' (Janssens and Steyaert, 2009, p. 146).

Almost 50 years ago, sociologist Peter Berger wrote that the first wisdom of sociological inquiry is that 'things are not what they seem' (1963, p. 23). A deceptively simple statement, Berger's idea suggests that most people live in a social world that they do not understand. The goal of sociology is to shed light on social reality using what the late C. Wright Mills called the 'sociological imagination' – the ability to see the relationships between individual life experiences and the larger society, because the two are related (1959/2000, pp. 3–4). Sociologists argue that the sociological imagination helps people to place seemingly personal troubles, such as losing a job to outsourcing or local environmental degradation, into a larger national or global context. For Watson (2010), a critical approach to studying HRM provides inspiration and an invitation to apply Mills' 'sociological imagination' to matters of HRM 'outcomes' that have 'wider social consequences'. In the context of the post-2008 crisis and the search for the 'new economic philosophy', Delbridge and Keenoy (2010) provide a persuasive argument for critical HRM (CHRM), an intellectual activity, grounded in social science inquiry, that contextualizes HR practices within the prevailing capitalist society, challenges the maxims of what Alfred Schutz has called the 'world-taken-for-granted' and is more inclusive of marginal voices.

We need a definition of the subject matter that conceptualizes HRM in terms of employment or people management, one that distinguishes it from a set of 'neutral' functional practices, and one that conceives it as embedded in a capitalist society and its associated ideologies and global structures. The following attempts to capture the essence of what contemporary HRM is about:

> Human resource management (HRM) is a strategic approach to managing employment relations which emphasizes that leveraging people's capabilities and commitment is critical to achieving sustainable competitive advantage or superior public services. This is accomplished through a distinctive set of integrated employment policies, programmes and practices, embedded in an organizational and societal context.

Following on from this definition, CHRM underscores the importance of *people* – only the 'human factor' or labour can provide talent to generate value. With this in mind, it goes without saying that any adequate analytical conception of HRM should draw attention to the notion of *indeterminacy*, which derives from the employment relationship: employees have a *potential* capacity to provide the added value desired by the employer. It also follows from this that human knowledge and skills are a *strategic resource* that needs investment and skilful management. Moreover, the emergent environmental management literature provides a role for HRM in improving an organization's performance in terms of overall *sustainability*. Also implicit within our definition is the need for radical organizational and social change. Another distinguishing feature of HRM relates to the notion of *integration*. A cluster of employment policies programmes and practices needs to be coherent and integrated with the organization's corporate strategy. Finally, the 2008 global financial implosion and the 2011 nuclear crisis in Japan remind us that the economy and society are part of the same set of processes, and that work and management practices are deeply embedded in the wider sociocultural context in which they operate. The conception of CHRM put forward here resonates with analytical frameworks holding that HR practices can only be understood in the context of economic-societal factors that shape or direct those practices. The approach adopted can be summed up in the succinct phrase 'context matters'.

This book is oriented towards helping people manage people – both individually and collectively – more effectively, equitably and with dignity. It is plausible to argue that if the workforce is so critical for sustainability performance, HRM is too important to be left solely to HR specialists but should be the responsibility of *all* managers. Furthermore, human dignity *in* and *at* work is, or *ought* to be, at the heart of contemporary HRM (Bolton, 2007). The dignity dimension provides support for a reconceptualized HRM model of empowered, engaged and developed employees, the 'missing "human" in HRM' critique (Bolton and Houlihan, 2007). Recently, critics have voiced concerns regarding the 'moribund and limited' nature of mainstream HRM (Delbridge and Keenoy, 2010, p. 800). The demands for dignity in the workplace are a key dimension of CHRM that provides strong support for extending the analysis of HRM outcomes beyond employee performance and commitment to include the 'dignity' aspects of the employment relationship and equality. To grasp the nature and significance of HRM, it is necessary to understand the management process and the role of HRM within it. But before we do this, we should explain why managing people or the 'human' input is so different from managing other resources.

The meaning of 'human resource'

First and foremost, labour is not a commodity. It is people in work organizations who set overall strategies and goals, design work systems, produce goods and services, monitor quality, allocate financial resources and market the products and services. Human beings, therefore, become human capital by virtue of the roles they assume in the work organization. Employment roles are defined and described in a manner designed to maximize particular employees' contributions to achieving organizational objectives. Schultz (1981) defined human capital in this way:

> Consider all human abilities to be either innate or acquired. Every person is born with a particular set of genes, which determines his [sic] innate ability. Attributes of acquired population quality, which are valuable and can be augmented by appropriate investment, will be treated as human capital. (Schultz, 1981, p. 21; quoted in Fitz-enz, 2000, p. xii)

In management terms, 'human capital' refers to the traits that people bring to the workplace – intelligence, aptitude, commitment, tacit knowledge and skills, and an ability to learn. But the contribution of this human resource to the organization is typically variable and unpredictable. This indeterminacy of an employee's contribution to her or his work organization makes the human resource the 'most vexatious of assets to manage' (Fitz-enz, 2000, p. xii) and is helpful in understanding Hyman's (1987) assertion that the need to gain both *control over* and *commitment from* workers is the *leitmotiv* of HRM.

Managing people in a democratic market society extends beyond the issue of control. If the employer's operational goals and the employee's personal goals are to be achieved, there must necessarily be *cooperation* between the two parties. This reciprocal cooperation is, however, often accompanied by different forms of *resistance* and

These chefs provide an example of human capital in the context of a restaurant.
Source: ©istockphoto.com/Huchen Lu

conflict. The nature of employment relations reminds us that people differ from other resources because their commitment and cooperation always has to be won: they have the capacity to resist management's actions and join trade unions to defend or further their interests and rights. At the same time, employment entails an economic relationship and one of control and cooperation. This duality means that the employment relationship is highly *dynamic* in the sense that it is forged by the coexistence of control, cooperation and conflict in varying degrees (Brown, 1988; Edwards, 1986; Watson, 2004). Thus, HRM is inevitably characterized by structured cooperation and conflict.

The meaning of 'management'

The word *manage* came into English usage directly from the Italian *maneggiare*, meaning 'to handle and train horses'. In the sixteenth century, the meaning was extended to include a general sense of taking charge or directing (Williams, 1976).

The answer to the question 'Who is a manager?' depends on the manager's social position in the organization's hierarchy. A manager is an organizational member who is 'institutionally empowered to determine and/or regulate certain aspects of the actions of others' (Willmott, 1984, p. 350). Collectively, managers are traditionally differentiated horizontally by their function activities (for example, production manager or HR manager) and vertically by the level at which they are located in their organizational hierarchy (for example, counter manager or branch manager).

Management has been variously conceptualized as 'the central process whereby work organizations achieve the semblance of congruence and direction' (Mintzberg, 1973), as 'art, science, magic and politics' (Watson, 1986) and as a process designed to coordinate and control productive activities (see, for example, Thompson and McHugh, 2009). In his seminal work, Fayol (1949) envisioned management as a science. For Fayol, management is primarily concerned with internal planning, organizing, directing and controlling – known as the 'PODC' tradition. The creation of a formal organizational structure and work configuration is, therefore, the *raison d'être* for management. This classical stereotype presents an idealized image of management as a rationally designed system for realizing goals, but there are competing theoretical perspectives, as we will explain later in this chapter.

THE NATURE OF THE EMPLOYMENT RELATIONSHIP

The nature of the social relationship between employees and their employer is an issue of central analytical importance to HRM. The employment relationship describes an asymmetry of reciprocal relations between employees (non-managers and managers) and their work organization. Through the asymmetry of the employment contract, inequalities of power structure both the economic exchange (wage or salary) and the nature and quality of the work performed (whether it is routine or creative). In contemporary capitalism, employment relationships vary: at one end of the scale, they can be a short-term, primarily but not exclusively economic exchange for a relatively well-defined set of duties and low commitment; at the other, they can be complex long-term relationships defined by a broad range of economic inducements and relative security of employment, given in return for a broad set of duties and a high commitment from the employee.

The employment relationship may be regulated in three ways: unilaterally by the employer; bilaterally, by the employer and the trade unions, through a process of collective bargaining; and trilaterally, by employers, trade unions and statutes, through the intervention of the government or state (Kelly, 2005). What, then, is the essence of the employment relationship? Research into the employment relationship has drawn attention to economic, legal, social and psychological aspects of relations in the workplace.

At its most basic, the employment relationship embraces an *economic relationship*: the 'exchange of pay for work' (Brown, 1988). When people enter the workplace, they enter into a pay–effort bargain, which places an obligation on both the employer and the employee: in exchange for a wage or salary, paid by the employer, the employee is obligated to perform an amount of physical or intellectual labour. The pay–effort bargain is relevant for understanding how far the employment relationship is structurally conflictual or consensual. In the capitalist labour market, people sell their labour and seek to maximize their pay. To the employer, pay is a cost that, all things being equal, reduces profit and therefore needs to be minimized. Thus, as Brown (1988, p. 57) states, 'Conflict is structured into employment relations' as the benefit to one group is a cost to the other.

The 'effort' or 'work' side of the contract also generates tensions and conflict because it is inherently imprecise and indeterminate. The contract permits the employer to buy a potential level of physical or intellectual labour. The function of management is therefore to transform this potential into actual value-added labour. HR practices are designed to narrow the divide between employees' potential and actual performance or, in Townley's (1994, p. 14) words:

> Personnel practices measure both the physical and subjective dimensions of labour, and offer a technology which aims to render individuals and their behaviour predictable and calculable ... to bridge the gap between promise and performance, between labour power and labour, and organizes labour into a productive force or power.

The second component of the employment relationship is that it involves a *legal relationship*: a network of contractual and statutory rights and obligations affecting both parties to the contract. Contractual rights are based upon case law (judicial precedent), and the basic rules of contract, in so far as they relate to the contract of employment, are fundamental to the legal relationship between the employer and the employee. It is outside the scope of this chapter to provide a discussion of the rules of contract. But, to use Kahn-Freund's famous phrase, the contract of employment, freely negotiated between an individual and her or his employer, can be considered to be the cornerstone of English employment law (Honeyball, 2010).

Statutory rights refer to an array of legislation that affects the employer–employee relationship and employer–union relationship: the 'right not to be unfairly dismissed' or the 'right to bargain', for example. Statutory employment rights provide a basic minimum or 'floor' of rights for all employees. A complex network of UK and European Union statutory rights regulates the obligations of employers and employees even though these are not (for the most part) formally inserted into the employment contract itself. If they are violated, legal rights can be enforced by some compulsory mechanisms provided by the state, for example a tribunal or the courts. Table 7.1 provides an overview of how UK employment legislation has helped to shape the legal regulation of employment relations. In broad terms, the employment laws of the 1979–97 Conservative government sought to regulate the activities of trade unions. Cumulatively, the changes marked 'a radical shift from the consensus underlying "public policy" on industrial relations during most of the past century' (Hyman, 1987, p. 93). The changes in the law tilted the balance of power in an industrial dispute towards the employer (Brown et al., 1997).

The influence of European Union (EU) law increased steadily during the same period. Although it is not a comprehensive body of employment legislation, EU employment law does draw on the Western European tradition, in which the rights of employees are laid down in constitutional texts and legal codes. Under the 1997 'New Labour' government, a plethora of legislative reform in employment law facilitated trade union organization and collective bargaining and extended protection to individual employees. For example, the 2006 Work and Families Act gave additional protections in relation to pregnancy – the right to maternity leave, time off for antenatal care and the right to maternity pay (Lockton, 2010).

Table 7.1 – Selective UK Employment Statutes and Statutory Instruments, 1961–2007

Year	Act
1961	Factories Act (Safety)
1963/72	Contract of Employment Act
1965	Industrial Training Act
1968	Race Relations Act
1970	Equal Pay Act
1971	Industrial Relations Act
1973	Employment and Training Act
1974	Health and Safety at Work etc. Act
1974/76	Trade Union and Labour Relations Act
1975/86	Sex Discrimination Act
1975	Employment Protection Act
1978	Employment Protection (Consolidation) Act
1980	Employment Act
1982	Employment Act
1984	Trade Union Act
1986	Wages Act
1988	Employment Act
1989	Employment Act
1990	Employment Act
1992	Trade Union and Labour Relations (Consolidation) Act
1993	Trade Union Reform and Employment Rights Act
1996	Employment Rights Act
1996	Employment Tribunals Act

Table 7.1   Continued

Year	Act
1998	Employment Rights (Disputes Resolution) Act
1998	National Minimum Wage Act
1999	Employment Relations Act
2002	Employment Act
2003	National Minimum Wage (Enforcement) Act
2003	Employment Equality (Sexual Orientation) Regulations
2003	Employment Equality (Religion or Belief) Regulations
2004	Gender Recognition Act
2004	Employment Relations Act
2005	Disability Discrimination Act
2006	Employment Equality (Age) Regulations
2006	Work and Families Act
2006	Equality Act
2007	Corporate Manslaughter and Corporate Homicide Act

Reflective question

Based on your own work experience or that of a friend or relative, can you identify three statutory employment rights?

The third distinguishing component of the employment relationship is that it involves a *social relationship*. Employees are not isolated individuals but members of social groups, who observe social norms and mores that influence their actions in the workplace. This observation of human behaviour in the workplace – which has been documented since the 1930s – is highly relevant given the increased prevalence of work teams. Furthermore, unless the employee happens to be an international football celebrity, the employment relationship embodies an uneven balance of power between the parties. The notion in English law of a 'freely' negotiated individual agreement is misleading. In reality, without collective (trade union) or statutory intervention, the most powerful party, the employer, imposes the agreement by 'the brute facts of power' (Wedderburn, 1986, p. 106).

Inequalities of power in turn structure the nature of work. Most employees experience an extreme division of labour with minimal discretion over how they perform their tasks or opportunity to participate in decision-making processes. Thus, the social dimension is concerned with social relations, social structure and power – *people with power over other people* – rather than with the legal technicalities between the parties. As such, employment relations are deeply textured and profoundly sociological (Bratton et al., 2009). Looking at the development of the mainstream HRM canon over the last 25 years, it can be seen how little these inherent inequalities figure, despite the fact that they can be readily observed in the contemporary workplace.

In recent years, mainstream HRM scholarship has focused on another component of the employment relationship: the *psychological contract*. This is conceptualized as a dynamic two-way exchange of perceived promises and obligations between employees and their employer. The concept has become a 'fashionable' framework within which to study aspects of the employment relationship (Guest and Conway, 2002; Rousseau and Ho, 2000). The 'psychological contract' is a metaphor that captures a wide variety of largely unwritten expectations and understandings of the two parties about their mutual obligations. Rousseau (1995, p. 9) defines this as 'individual beliefs, shaped by the organization, regarding terms of an exchange agreement between individuals and their organization'. Guest and Conway (2002, p. 22) define it as 'the perceptions of both parties to the employment relationship – organization and individual – of the reciprocal promises and obligations implied in that relationship'. At the heart of the concept of the psychological contract are levers for individual commitment, motivation and task performance beyond the 'expected outcomes' (Figure 7.1).

The psychological contract has a number of important features that employers need to appreciate. First, ineffective practices may communicate different beliefs about the reciprocal promises and obligations that are present (Guest and Conway, 2002). Thus, individuals will have different perceptions of their psychological contract, even when the legal contract is identical. Managers will therefore be faced with a multitude of perceived psychological contracts (PPCs) within the same organization (Bendal et al., 1998). Second, the PPC reaffirms the notion that the employment relationship is thought to be one of exchange – the promissory exchange of offers and the mutual obligation of the employer and employee to fulfil these offers. Third, PPCs are shaped in particular contexts, which includes HR practices. Rousseau argues that HR practices 'send strong messages to individuals regarding what the organization expects of them and what they can expect in return' (Rousseau, 1995, pp. 182–3). In the current post-crisis era, 'downsizing' has become a ubiquitous fact of organizational life (Datta et al., 2010; Mellahi and Wilkinson, 2010). Research suggests that those organizations downsizing can reduce the likelihood of psychological contract violation by ensuring that HR practices contribute to employees' perceptions of 'procedural fairness' (Arshad and Sparrow, 2010).

On any reading, the essence of the PPC thesis is the idea that a workforce is a collection of free, independent people, as though individual beliefs are fixed features of an employee's day-to-day behaviour. However, this addresses concerns of individual

Figure 7.1 – The employment and psychological contract between employees and employers

motivation and commitment within a *unitary* ideological framework. In doing this, in total contrast to critical paradigms, it neglects a well-established body of research grounded in sociology showing that people's beliefs and expectations about employment form *outside* the workplace. The work experiences of parents, for instance, shape the attitudes and career aspirations of their teenage children. The idea that family members and peer groups can influence expectations about career opportunities and the everyday reality of work is called 'orientation to work' (Goldthorpe et al., 1968; Hyman and Brough, 1975).

Reflective question

What do you think of the concept of the psychological contract? Why does there appear to be more interest now in managing it? How important is it to manage the psychological contract for (1) non-managerial employees, and (2) managerial employees?

SCOPE AND FUNCTIONS OF HRM

HRM is a body of knowledge and an assortment of practices to do with the organization of work and the management of employment relations. The mainstream literature identifies three major subdomains of knowledge: micro, strategic and international (Boxall et al., 2008).

The largest subdomain refers to *micro HRM* (MHRM), which is concerned with managing individual employees and small work groups. It covers areas such as HR planning, job design, recruitment and selection, performance management, training and development, and rewards. These HR subfunctions cover a myriad of evidence-based practices, training techniques and payment systems, for instance, many of them informed by psychology-oriented studies of work (see, for example, Warr, 2008). The second domain is *strategic HRM* (SHRM), which concerns itself with the processes of linking HR strategies with business strategies and measures the effects on organizational performance. The third domain is *international HRM* (IHRM), which focuses on the management of people in companies operating in more than one country.

Drawing on the work of Squires (2001), these three major subdomains help us address three basic questions:

- What do HRM professionals do?
- What affects what they do?
- How do they do what they do?

To help us answer the first question, the work of Harzing (2000), Millward et al. (2000) and Ulrich (1997) identifies the key *MHRM* subfunctions of HR policies, programmes and practices that have been designed in response to organizational goals and contingencies, and have been managed to achieve those goals. Each function contains alternatives from which managers can choose. How the HR function is organized and how much power it has relative to that of other management functions is affected by both external and internal factors unique to the establishment. A regulation-oriented national business system, with strong trade unions, employment laws on equity and affirmative action, and occupational health and safety regulations, elevates the status of the HR manager and strengthens the corporate HR function. In contrast, a market-oriented corporate culture, with employee pay based on going market rates, minimum investment in employee training and shorter employment contracts, is associated with outsourcing and decentralization of the HR function, which weakens the corporate HR function (Jacoby, 2005).

The size of the organization also appears to negatively affect the extent to which HR services are provided internally by HR specialists from the central HR unit. Klass et al.'s (2005) study, for example, found that an increasing number of small and medium-sized organizations – defined as those with 500 or fewer employees – have established a business relationship with a professional employer organization that assumes responsibility for delivering their HR services and interventions, a process usually referred to as 'outsourcing'. Klass et al. argue that the choice is not between an internal HR department and outsourcing the HR services, but is one in which limited resources mean that it is a case of either obtaining HR expertise and services externally or foregoing such services. In addition, an increasing number of European organizations have transferred responsibility for their HR functions from the central HR department to line management. This process of 'decentralization' has occurred as HR has assumed a more strategic role (Andolšek and Štebe, 2005; CIPD, 2006a).

SHRM underscores the need for the HR strategy to be integrated with other management functions, and highlights the responsibility of line management to foster the high commitment and motivation associated with high-performing work systems. SHRM is also concerned with managing sustainability, including, for example, establishing a low-carbon work system and organization, communicating this vision, setting clear expectations for creating a sustainable workplace, and developing the capability to reorganize people and reallocate other resources to achieve the vision. As part of the integrative process, all managers are expected to better comprehend the strategic nature of 'best' or better HR practices, to execute them more skilfully, and at the same time to intervene to affect the 'mental models', attitudes and behaviours needed, for instance, to build a high-performing sustainable culture (Pfeffer, 2005). Furthermore, national systems of employment regulation shape SHRM: 'the stronger the institutional framework ... the less [sic] options a company may have to impose its own approach to regulating its HRM' (Andolšek and Štebe, 2005, p. 327).

HRM web links

Go to the website of the 2004 Workplace Employment Relations Survey (www.dti.gov.uk/employment/research-evaluation/grants/wers/index.html) for data on the job responsibilities of HR specialists. Has there been any change in the functions performed by HR specialists over the past decade? Are HR specialists involved in all the key areas of activity described in the text?

The peculiarities of national employment systems and national culture shape the employment relationship, and these forces and processes create different tendencies in HR practice operating across national boundaries. As such, they relate to the second question we posed earlier – what affects what managers and HR professional do? The HR activities that managers perform vary from one workplace to another depending upon the contingencies affecting the organization. These contingencies can be divided into three broad categories: external context, strategy and organization. The external category reinforces the notion that organizations and society are part of the same set of processes – that organizations are *embedded* within a particular market society that encompasses the economic and cultural aspects. The external variables frame the context for formulating competitive strategies. The internal organizational contingencies include size, work, structure and technology. Global as well as local factors can affect what managers do. For those managers in companies that cross national boundaries, *micro* HR policies and practices relating to global and local recruitment and selection, training and development, rewards and the management of expatriates will be affected by a particular country's institutional structure and cultural setting. These micro HR functions, when integrated with different *macro* contexts and overall strategy considerations, define the subdomain of *IHRM*.

It is important, therefore, to recognize that HR policies and practices are contingent upon external and internal contexts and are fundamentally interrelated. For example, a company responding to competitive pressures may change its manufacturing strategy by introducing 'self-managed' teams. This will in turn cause changes in recruitment and selection (for example, hiring people perceived to be 'team players'), and training and reward priorities (for example, designing crossfunctional training and designing a reward system that encourages the sharing of information and learning). HR practices, therefore, aim to achieve two objectives: to produce a synergy that improves employee performance and to enhance organizational effectiveness.

The third of our three basic questions – how do managers and HR professionals do what they do? – requires us to discuss the means or skills by which managers accomplish their HRM goals. Managers and HR specialists use technical, cognitive and interpersonal – such as mentoring and coaching – processes and skills to accomplish their managerial work (Agashae and Bratton, 2001; Senge, 1990; Squires, 2001; Yukl, 2005). Power is important because it is part of the influence process, as are legal procedures. In addition, communication practices and skills convey the formal and psychological contract to employees (Guest and Conway, 2002). Managing people is complex, and individual managers vary in terms of their capacity or inclination to use established processes and skills. These processes and skills therefore concern human relationships and go some way to explaining different management styles and the distinction between a manager and a leader (Bratton et al., 2004a). The micro, strategic and international domains, the contingencies influencing domestic and international HR policies and practices, and managerial skills are combined and diagrammatically shown in a three-dimensional model in Figure 7.2.

The model implies not only that HRM is a multidimensional activity, but also that its analysis has to be multidirectional (Squires, 2001). We might, for that reason, examine the effect of new technology (a contingency) on HR functions, such as

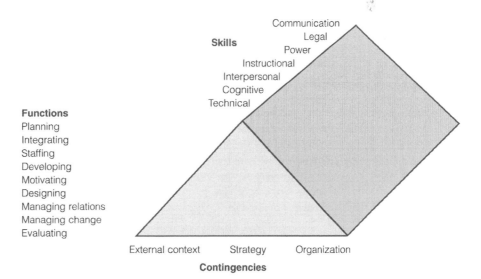

Figure 7.2 – HRM functions, contingencies and skills
Source: Adapted from Squires (2001)

training and development, and how HR functions are translated into action, such as learning processes. The model is useful in other ways too: it serves as a pedagogical device that allows its users to discover and connect a specific aspect of HRM within a consistent, general framework. It also helps to develop an 'analytical conception' of HRM by building theory and generating data based on managers' *actual* social actions in managing work and people across workplaces, sectors and different market societies (Boxall et al., 2008) – the classic rhetoric–reality gap notably highlighted by Legge (1995, 2005). It also offers HR specialists a sense of professional 'identity' by detailing professional functions, processes and skills. Finally, it helps HR specialists to look beyond their immediate tasks and to be aware of the 'totality of management' (Squires, 2001, p. 482).

HRM web links

Go to the website of the HR professional associations (for example Australia www.hrhq.com; Britain www.cipd.co.uk; Canada www.hrpa.org; or the USA www.shrm.org). Click on the 'Accreditation and/or certification' button. Using the information you find, compare the practices that HR professionals are formally accredited to practise with those practices listed in Figure 7.2. Does the information on the website give a comprehensive picture of 'What HRM specialists do'?

THEORETICAL PERSPECTIVES ON HRM

Practice without theory is blind.

(Hyman, 1989, p. xiv)

So far, we have focused on the meaning of management and on a range of HRM practices used in the contemporary workplace. We have explained that HRM varies across organizations and market societies depending upon a range of external and internal contingencies. In addition, we have identified the skills by which managers accomplish their HRM goals. We will now turn to an important part of the mainstream HRM discourse – the search for the defining features and goals of HRM – by exploring the theoretical perspectives in this area.

Over the past two decades, HRM scholars have debated the meaning of the term 'human resource management' and attempted to define its fundamental traits by producing polar or multiconceptual models. A number of polar models contrast the fundamental traits of HRM with those of traditional personnel management, while others provide statements on employer goals and HR outcomes. These models help to focus debate around such questions as 'What is the difference between HRM and personnel management?' and 'What outcomes are employers seeking when they implement a HRM approach? Here, we identify six major HRM models that seek to demonstrate in analytical terms the distinctiveness and goals of HRM (Beer et al., 1984; Fombrun et al., 1984; Guest, 1987; Hendry and Pettigrew, 1990; Storey, 1992). These models fulfil at least four important intellectual functions for those studying HRM:

- They provide an analytical framework for studying HRM (for example, HR practices, situational factors, stakeholders, strategic choice levels and HR and performance outcomes).
- They legitimize HRM. For those advocating 'Invest in People', the models help to demonstrate to sceptics the legitimacy and effectiveness of HRM. A key issue here is the distinctiveness of HRM practices: 'it is not the presence of selection or training but a *distinctive approach* to selection or training that matters. It is the use of high performance or high commitment HRM practices' (Guest, 1997, p. 273, emphasis added).

HRM in practice: Twenty-first-century senior HR leaders have a changing role

Early debate on HRM centred on the question 'How does HRM differ from personnel management?' For some, HRM represents a new approach to managing people because, in theory at least, it was envisioned to be integrated into strategic planning. HRM models also make reference to performance outcomes, predicting that a coherent 'bundle' of HR practices will enhance employee commitment and improve performance. To meet the challenges of the twenty-first century, it is argued, organizations therefore need a new senior manager, the chief human resources officer (CHRO). As one writer put it:

> The modern CHRO is required increasingly to act as both strategist and steward. Jeff Schwartz, of Deloitte Consulting, said: 'The requirements and perception of HR are changing dramatically as this function's leadership is now expected to play a central role in building and shaping – not just staffing – the enterprise strategy.' 'The role of the CHRO as an enterprise business leader is still evolving – but this transformation has never been more timely or relevant.' 'This is an environment that HR leaders have longed for – where their executive peers would view HR as a business partner, rather than as a back-office administrator.'[1]

In contrast, detractors argue that HRM is more a matter of repackaging 'progressive' personnel management. They emphasize that relatively few organizations have integrated HRM planning into strategic business planning, a central element in the HRM model. They also point to the incontrovertible evidence of a shift towards 'individually oriented' cultures that is symbolized by the growth of contingency pay, as well as the fact that a large proportion of UK firms are still preoccupied with traditional cost-focus strategies. The empirical evidence therefore suggests a lack of fit between knowledge of the normative HRM model and actual management practice.

Stop! Debates on HRM offer an interesting perspective on the issues of state intervention in a market society. Among academics, HRM is highly contentious, and its antecedents, its defining characteristics and its outcomes are much disputed. What is your view? Is HRM different from personnel management?

Sources and further information

[1]Deloitte Consulting's Strategist and Steward report, available at www.deloitte.com/us, and search for 'Strategist and Steward'. For a discussion on employee commitment and HRM, see Guest (1998); for evidence of the growth of 'individualism', see Kersley et al. (2005); and for further insight into the HRM debate, see Legge (2005).

Note

This feature was written by John Bratton.

Source: ©istockphoto.com/Daniel Laflor

- They provide a characterization of HRM that establishes the variables and relationships to be researched.
- They serve as a heuristic device – something to help us discover and understand the world of work – for explaining the nature and significance of key HR practices and HR outcomes.

The Fombrun, Tichy and Devanna model of HRM

The early HRM model developed by Fombrun et al. (1984) emphasizes the fundamental interrelatedness and coherence of HRM activities. The HRM 'cycle' in their model consists of four key constituent components: selection, appraisal, development and rewards. In terms of the overarching goals of HRM, these four HR activities are linked to the firm's performance. The weaknesses of Fombrun et al.'s model are its apparently prescriptive nature and its focus on four HR practices. It also ignores different stakeholder interests, situational factors and the notion of management's strategic choice. The strength of the model, however, is that it expresses the coherence of internal HR policies and the importance of 'matching' internal HR policies and practices to the organization's external business strategy. The notion of the 'HRM cycle' is useful as a heuristic framework for explaining the nature and significance of key HR practices that make up the complex field of HRM.

The Harvard model of HRM

As was widely acknowledged in the early HRM literature, the 'Harvard model' offered by Beer et al. (1984) provided one of the first comprehensive statements on the nature of HRM and the issue of management goals and specific HR outcomes. The Harvard framework (Figure 7.3) consists of six basic components:

1 Situational factors
2 Stakeholder interests
3 HRM policy choices
4 HR outcomes
5 Long-term consequences
6 A feedback loop through which the outputs flow directly into the organization and to the stakeholders.

In the Harvard model of HRM, the *situational factors* influence management's choice of HR strategy. This normative model incorporates workforce characteristics, management philosophy, labour market regulations, societal values and patterns of unionization, and suggests a meshing of 'product market' and 'sociocultural logics' (Evans and Lorange, 1989). Analytically, both HRM scholars and practitioners will be more comfortable if contextual variables are included in the model because this reflects the reality of what they know: 'the employment relationship entails a blending of business and societal expectations' (Boxall, 1992, p. 72).

The *stakeholder interests* recognize the importance of 'trade-offs', either explicitly or implicitly, between the interests of business owners and those of employees and their organizations, the trade unions. Although the model is still vulnerable to the charge of 'unitarism', it is a much more pluralist frame of reference than is found in later models.

HRM policy choices emphasize that management's decisions and actions in HR management can be fully appreciated only if it is recognized that they result from an interaction between constraints and choices. The model depicts management as a real actor, capable of making at least some degree of unique contribution within

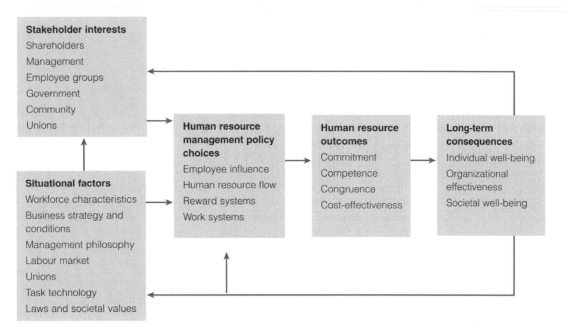

Figure 7.3 – The Harvard model of HRM
Source: Beer, M. et al. (1984), Managing Human Assets, The Free Press

the environmental and organizational parameters present and of influencing those parameters itself over time (Beer et al., 1984).

In terms of understanding the importance of management's goals, the *HR outcomes* of high employee commitment and competence are linked to longer term effects on organizational effectiveness and societal well-being. The underlying assumptions built into the framework are that employees have talents that are rarely fully utilized in the contemporary workplace, and that they show a desire to experience growth through work. Thus, HRM is indivisible from a 'humanistic message' about human growth and dignity at work. In other words, the Harvard framework takes the view that employment relations should be managed on the basis of the assumptions inherent in McGregor's (1960) classic approach to people-related issues, commonly called 'Theory Y', or, to use contemporary parlance, in conditions of human dignity at work.

The *long-term consequences* distinguish between three levels: individual, organizational and societal. At the level of the individual employee, the long-term HR outputs comprise the psychological rewards that workers receive in exchange for their effort. At the organizational level, increased effectiveness ensures the survival of the firm. In turn, at the societal level, as a result of fully utilizing people at work, some of society's goals (for example, employment and growth) are attained. The strength of the Harvard model lies in its classification of inputs and outcomes at both the organizational and the societal level, creating the basis for a critique of comparative HRM (Boxall, 1992). A weakness, however, is the absence of a coherent theoretical basis for measuring the relationship between HR inputs, outcomes and performance (Guest, 1997).

The sixth component of the Harvard model is a *feedback loop*. As we have discussed, situational factors influence HRM policy and choices. Conversely, however, long-term outputs can influence the situational factors, stakeholder interests and HR policies, and the feedback loop in Figure 7.3 reflects this two-way relationship.

As was observed by Boxall (1992), the Harvard model clearly provides a useful analytical basis for the study of HRM. It also contains elements that are analytical (that is, situational factors, stakeholders and strategic choice levels) and prescriptive (that is, notions of commitment, competence, and so on).

The Guest model of HRM

In David Guest's (1989, 1997) framework, different approaches to labour management are examined in the context of goals, employee behaviour, performance and long-term financial outcomes. According to this HRM model, managers are advised to consider the effects of a core set of integrated HR practices on individual and organizational performance.

For Guest, HRM differs significantly from personnel management, and he attempts to identify the major assumptions or stereotypes underpinning each approach to employment management. Personnel management seeks 'compliance', whereas HRM seeks 'commitment' from employees. In personnel management, the psychological contract is expressed in terms of a 'fair day's work for a fair day's pay', whereas in HRM it is 'reciprocal commitment'. In the area of employee relations, personnel management is said to be pluralist, collective and 'low trust', whereas HRM is unitarist, individual and 'high trust'. The points of differences between personnel management and HRM are also reflected in the design of organizations. Thus, organizations adopting the personnel management model exhibit 'mechanistic', top-down and centralized design features, whereas firms adopting HRM are allegedly 'organic', bottom-up and decentralized. Finally, the policy goals of personnel management and HRM are different. In the former, they are administrative efficiency, standard performance and minimization of cost. In contrast, the policy goals of HRM are an adaptive workforce, an improvement in performance and maximum utilization of human potential.

According to these stereotypes, HRM is distinctively different from personnel management because: (1) it integrates HR into strategic management; (2) it seeks employees' commitment to organizational goals; (3) the HR perspective is unitary with a focus on the individual; (4) it works better in organizations that have an 'organic' structure; and (5) employer goals prioritize the full utilization of human assets.

Implicit in the contrasting stereotypes is an assumption that the dominant HRM model is 'better' (allowing enhanced commitment and flexibility) within the current more flexible labour markets and in decentralized, flexible, empowering and organic organizational structures. However, as Guest correctly states, 'variations in context ... might limit its effectiveness' (1987, p. 508). The central hypothesis of Guest's (1997) framework is that managers should adopt a distinct set or 'bundle' of HR practices in a coherent fashion; the outcome will be superior individual and organizational performance.

Guest's model has six components:

1 An HR strategy
2 A set of HR policies
3 A set of HR outcomes
4 Behavioural outcomes
5 Performance outcomes
6 Financial outcomes.

The model acknowledges the close links between HR strategy and the general business strategies of differentiation, focus and cost. The 'core' hypothesis, however, is that HR practices should be designed to lead to a set of HR outcomes of 'high employee commitment', 'high quality' and 'flexibility'. Like Beer et al., Guest sees high employee commitment as a critical HR outcome, concerned with the employer's goals of binding employees to the organization and obtaining the behavioural outcomes of increased effort, cooperation and organizational citizenship. 'Quality' refers to all aspects of employee behaviour that relate directly to the quality of goods and services. Flexibility is concerned with how receptive employees are to innovation and change. The model focuses on the link between HR practices and performance. Only when all three HR outcomes – commitment, quality and flexibility – are achieved can superior performance outcomes be expected. As Guest (1989, 1997) emphasizes, these HRM goals are a 'package': 'Only when a coherent strategy, directed towards these four policy goals, fully integrated into business strategy and fully sponsored by line management at all levels is applied will the high productivity and related outcomes sought by industry be achieved' (1990, p. 378).

Guest (1987, 1989, 1997) recognizes a number of conceptual issues associated with the dominant HRM model. The first is that the values underpinning the model are predominantly individualist-oriented: 'There is no recognition of any broader concept of pluralism within society giving rise to solidaristic collective orientation' (Guest, 1987, p. 519). The second concerns the status of some of the concepts, such as that of commitment, which is suggested to be 'a rather messy, ill-defined concept' (Guest, 1987, pp. 513–14). A third issue is the explicit link between HRM and performance. This raises the problem of deciding which types of performance indicators to use in order to establish the links between HR practices and performance. It has been argued elsewhere that Guest's model may simply be a polar 'ideal type' towards which organizations can move, thus proposing unrealistic conditions for the practice of HRM (Keenoy, 1990, p. 367). It may also make the error of criticizing managers for not conforming to an image constructed by academics (Boxall, 1992). Furthermore, it presents the HRM model as being inconsistent with collective approaches to managing the employment relationship (Legge, 1989).

In contrast, the strength of the Guest model is that it clearly maps out the field of HRM and classifies its inputs and outcomes. The model is useful for examining the key employer goals usually associated with the normative models of HRM: strategic integration, commitment, flexibility and quality. The constituents of the model hypothesizing a relationship between specific HR practices and performance can be empirically tested by research. Guest's constructed set of theoretical propositions can also provide a framework for a critical dialogue on the precise nature, tensions and contradictions of HRM.

The Warwick model of HRM

The Warwick model emanated from the Centre for Corporate Strategy and Change at the University of Warwick, UK, and with two particular researchers: Hendry and Pettigrew (1990). The Warwick framework extends the Harvard model by drawing on its analytical aspects. The model takes account of business strategy and HR practices, the external and internal context in which these activities take place and the processes by which such changes take place, including interactions between changes in both context and content. The strength of the model is that it identifies and classifies important environmental influences on HRM. It maps the connections between the outer (wider environment) and the inner (organizational) contexts, and explores how HRM adapts to changes in context. The implication is that those organizations achieving an alignment between the external and internal contexts will experience superior performance. A weakness of the model is that the process whereby internal HR practices are linked to business output or performance is not developed. The five elements of the model are as follows:

1 Outer context – socioeconomic, technical, political-legal, competitive
2 Inner context – culture, structure, leadership, task-technology, business outputs
3 Business strategy content – objectives, product market, strategy and tactics
4 HRM context – role, definition, organization, HR outputs
5 HRM content – HR flows, work systems, reward systems, employee relations.

The Storey model of HRM

The Storey framework attempts to demonstrate the differences between what John Storey terms the 'personnel and industrials' and the HRM paradigm by creating an 'ideal type'. He devised the model by reconstructing the 'implicit models' conveyed by some managers during research interviews. We should note that the usage of an 'ideal type' is a popular heuristic tool in the social sciences. It is a 'mental image' and cannot actually be found in any real workplace. Its originator Max Weber wrote in *The Methodology of the Social Sciences*, that 'In its conceptual purity, this mental construct [*Gedankenbild*] cannot be found empirically anywhere in reality' (Bratton et al., 2009, p. 216). An ideal type is not a description of reality; neither is it an average of something, or a normative exemplar to be achieved. It is a *Utopia*. Its purpose is to act as a comparison with empirical reality in order to establish the differences or similarities between the two positions, and to understand and explain causal relationships.

Storey posits that the HRM model emerged in the UK as a 'historically situated phenomenon' and is 'an amalgam of description, prescription, and logical deduction' (Storey, 2001, p. 6). The four main elements in his HRM framework (Table 7.2) are:

- Beliefs and assumptions
- Strategic aspects
- Role of line managers
- Key levers.

According to the stereotypes depicted in Table 7.2, the HRM 'recipe' of ideas and practices prescribes certain priorities. In this framework, the most fundamental *belief and assumption* is the notion that, ultimately, among all the factors of production, it is labour that really distinguishes successful firms from mediocre ones. It follows logically from this that employees ought to be nurtured as a valued asset and not simply regarded as a cost. Moreover, another underlying belief is that the employer's goal should not merely be to seek employees' compliance with rules, but to 'strive' for 'commitment and engagement' that goes 'beyond the contract' (Storey, 2001). The *strategic qualities* contained in Storey's framework show that HRM is a matter of critical importance to corporate planning. In Storey's words, 'decisions about human resources policies should ... take their cue from an explicit alignment of the competitive environment, business strategy and HRM strategy' (p. 10).

The third component, *line management*, argues that general managers, and not HRM specialists, are vital to the effective delivery of HRM practices (Purcell et al., 2009). Research evidence from 15 UK 'core' organizations suggests that line managers have emerged in almost all cases as the crucial players in HR issues (Storey, 1992).

The *key levers* element in the model focuses on the methods used to implement HRM. In researcher–manager interviews on HRM, Storey found considerable unevenness in the adoption of these key levers, such as performance-related pay, harmonization of conditions and investment to produce a work-related learning company. What

Table 7.2 – The Storey model of HRM

Personnel and industrial relations (IR) and human resource management (HRM): the differences		
Dimension	**Personnel and IR**	**HRM**
Beliefs and assumptions		
Contract	Careful delineation of written contracts	Aim to go 'beyond contract'
Rules	Importance of devising clear rules/mutuality	'Can do' outlook; impatience with 'rules'
Guide to management action	Procedures/consistency/control	'Business need'/flexibility/commitment
Behaviour referent	Norms/custom and practice	Values/mission
Managerial task vis-à-vis labour	Monitoring	Nurturing
Nature of relations	Pluralist	Unitarist
Conflict	Institutionalised	De-emphasised
Standardisation	High (for example 'parity' an issue)	Low (for example 'parity' not seen as relevant)
Strategic aspects		
Key relations	Labour–management	Business–customer
Initiatives	Piecemeal	Integrated
Corporate plan	Marginal to	Central to
Speed of decision	Slow	Fast
Line management		
Management role	Transactional	Transformational leadership
Key managers	Personnel/IR specialists	General/business/line managers
Prized management skills	Negotiation	Facilitation
Key levers		
Foci of attention for interventions	Personnel procedures	Wide-ranging cultural, structural and personnel strategies
Selection	Separate, marginal task	Integrated, key task
Pay	Job evaluation; multiple fixed grades	Performance-related; few if any grades
Conditions	Separately negotiated	Harmonisation
Labour–management	Collective bargaining contracts	Towards individual contracts
Thrust of relations with stewards	Regularised through facilities and training	Marginalised (with exception of some bargaining for change models)
Communication	Restricted flow/indirect	Increased flow/direct
Job design	Division of labour	Teamwork
Conflict handling	Reach temporary truces	Manage climate and culture
Training and development	Controlled access to courses	Learning companies

Source: Storey (1992)

HRM and globalization: The HRM model in advancing economies?

Contemporary globalization is the defining political economic paradigm of our time. In terms of HR strategy, HRM policies and practices have to be aligned to the global activities of transnational enterprises, and must be able to attract and retain employees operating internationally but within different national employment structures. The word 'globalization' became ubiquitous in the 1990s. It was, and still is, a thoroughly contested concept depending on whether scholars view it as primarily an economic, a political or a social phenomenon.

In the economic sphere, globalization is understood as a worldwide process of integration of production and consumption resulting from the reduction of transport and communication costs – a global system of economic interdependences. Arguments that build only on these technical conceptions emphasize the positive aspects of globalization, and draw attention to the outsourcing of manufacturing jobs to China and India from high-wage Western economies. The economic argument is captured by this extract from a Foresight2020 research report:

> On a per-capita basis, China and India will remain far poorer than Western markets and the region faces a host of downside risks,' Laza Kekic, director of forecasting services at the Economist Intelligence Unit, says. 'Asia will narrow the gap in wealth, power and influence, but will not close it.' The report assumes that world economic growth depends on the pace of globalization. Labour-intensive production will continue to shift to lower-cost countries but the report concludes that fears of the death of Western manufacturing are premature. Workers in the low-cost economies will benefit but Chinese average wages, for example, will rise only to about 15% of the developed-country average in 2020 compared with today's 5%.

Writers who conceptualize globalization in terms of politics and power argue that 'big business' has relegated national governments to being the 'gatekeepers' of free unfettered markets. Because there is little competition from alternative ideologies, twenty-first century capitalism 'is more mobile, more ruthless and more certain about what it needs to make it tick' (Giddens and Hutton, 2000, p. 9). Modern capitalism has been called a 'febrile capitalism' that is serving the needs of Wall Street and the financial and stock markets.

Stop!   Critics charge that national governments have lost power over their own economies as a handful of large corporations are being permitted to control natural resources and social life. In other words, civil society is perceived principally through the 'prism of economics'. Take a moment to assess critically the various standpoints in the globalization debate. What economic and political forces encourage outsourcing? What are the implications of outsourcing for HRM?

Sources and further information

See Giddens and Hutton (2000), Hoogvelt (2001), Chomsky (1999), and Gereffi and Christian (2009). To download Foresight2020 free of charge, visit www.eiu.com/foresight2020.

Note

This feature was written by John Bratton.

Source: ©istockphoto.com/Jessica Liu

is persuasive about the HRM narrative, observes Storey (2007), is evidence of a shift away from personnel procedures and rules as a basis of good practice, to the management of organizational culture as proof of avant-garde practice.

Ulrich's strategic partner model of HRM

To overcome the traditional marginalization of the personnel function and to strengthen the status of the profession, the UK Chartered Institute for Personnel and Development (CIPD) has long sought to demonstrate the added value of HR activities in business terms. Such a position requires a transition from the functional HR orientation, with the HR department primarily involved in administering policies, towards a partnership orientation, with the HR professional engaged in *strategic* decisions that impact on organizational design and organizational performance. In the last decade, the HRM model most favoured to support such a move has been provided by David Ulrich's (1997) 'business partner' model. Ulrich presents a framework showing four key roles that HR professionals must accomplish in order to add the greatest value to the organization (Figure 7.4). The two axes represent focus and activities. HR professionals must focus on both the strategic and the operational, in the both the long and the short term. Activities range from managing processes to managing people. Therefore these two axes delineate four principal roles:

- *Strategic partner* – future/strategic focus combined with processes
- *Change agent* – future/strategic focus combined with people
- *Administrative expert* – operational focus combined with process
- *Employee champion* – operational focus combined with people.

A later variant of the model integrates the change agent role into the strategic partner role, and gives greater emphasis to HR professionals playing a leadership role (Ulrich and Brockbank, 2005). As such, the first two roles require a strategic orientation; for example, as a strategic partner, HR professionals work with other managers to formulate and execute strategy, and as a change agent, they facilitate transformation and significant change. During the 2000s, the Ulrich business partner model was widely espoused in the mainstream HRM literature, partly because of the perceived increase in status and prestige of HRM, because the strategic partner and change agent roles proved highly attractive to many ambitious HR practitioners, and because of its rhetorical simplicity (Brown et al., 2004). Furthermore, the administrative role provides for processes to 're-engineer' the organization towards great efficiency, while

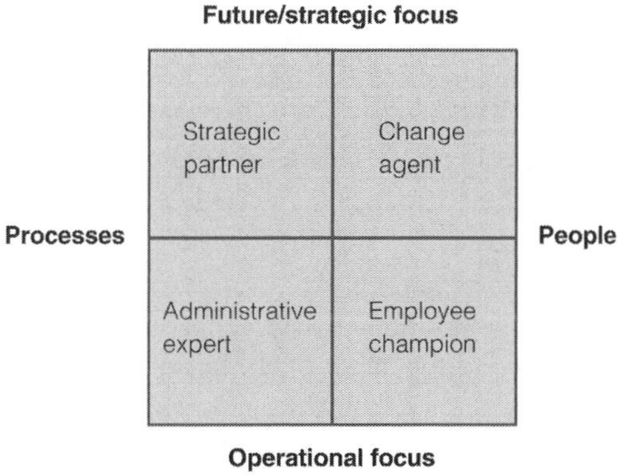

Figure 7.4 – Ulrich's human resources business partner model

the employee champion relates to listening to employees and providing resources for employees. Research shows, however, that, of the small sample surveyed, few HR practitioners considered their primary roles to be those of the 'less trendy' employee champion and administrative expert (Guest and King, 2004; Hope-Hailey et al., 2005).

Although it has been influential, the way in which this model has been implemented would suggest a degree of pragmatism, probably to reduce cost, with the four roles being combined into three, but with implications for how HR departments are structured (Reilly et al., 2007). For example, administrative roles would be structured into a shared services centre, with the task of providing cost-effective processes to run transactional services such as payroll, absence monitoring and simple advice for employees. Centres of excellence provide specialist knowledge and development to produce innovations in more complex areas such as talent, engagement and leadership and management development. Strategic business partners take on the work with managers and leaders, influencing and helping the formation of strategy, perhaps as members of a management team.

Perhaps inevitably, the role of the strategic business partner attracts most attention, while the employee champion role, which concerns the well-being of staff, tends to be left to line managers and is therefore likely to be neglected (Francis and Keegan, 2006). With the recession following the 2008 financial crisis, there has been concern with sustaining organizational performance through leadership, shared purpose, engagement, assessment and evaluation, agility and capacity-building (CIPD, 2011). It is, however, suggested that none of these can be achieved without a good process of learning and development for HR practitioners. Despite the popularity of the business partners' model, a survey of managers revealed that only 47 per cent polled believed that Ulrich's model was successful in their organization, and 25 per cent said the model was ineffective (Pitcher, 2008).

HRM web links

For more information on Ulrich's HRM model, go to: http://hrmadvice.com/hrmadvice/hr-role/ulrichs-hr-roles-model.html.

Reflective question

Reviewing the six models, what beliefs and assumptions are implied in them? What similarities and/or differences can you see? How well does each model define the characteristics of HRM? Is there a contradiction between the roles of 'change agent' and 'employee champion' as outlined in Ulrich's model? Is it realistic to expect HR professionals to be 'employee champions'?

STUDYING HRM

It has become commonplace to point out that HRM is not a discipline in its own right, but a field of study drawing upon concepts and theories from core social science disciplines including anthropology, psychology, sociology, law and political science. This provides relatively elastic boundaries within which to analyse how the employment relationship is structured and managed. In addition, these elastic boundaries generate multiple ways of making sense of the same organizational phenomenon or the differing standpoints found in the HRM canon. How we understand work and HRM is very much influenced by key social discourses, a discourse being a number of ideas that together form a powerful body of thought that influences how people think and act. Management in the twenty-first century is being influenced by multiple social discourses that include globalization, environmental destruction, social injustice and fundamental neo-liberal economic failure. We should also note that management research and education is going through a process of post-crisis reflexivity (Currie et al., 2010).

In understanding the recent debate that management education and pedagogy should be more reflexive and critical, it is crucial to develop a knowledge base of competing ideological perspectives or paradigms. For our purposes here, we will define paradigms as established frameworks of interrelated values, beliefs and assumptions that social science scholars use to organize their reasoning and research. Each paradigm in the social sciences makes certain bold assertions about the nature of social reality and, in turn, provides legitimacy and justification for people's actions (Babbie and Benaquisto, 2010). When people ask, 'What paradigm are you using?' they might just as well be asking, 'What is your own bias on this aspect of social life?', as each paradigm has a particular bias based on a particular version of knowing about social reality (Hughes, 1990). Paradigms are a 'lens' through which we view the world of work. Thus, when we refer to a particular paradigm to study the HRM phenomenon, we are speaking of an interconnected set of beliefs, values and intentions that legitimize HR theory and practice. For the purpose of developing a critical, analytical conception of HRM, we will in this section compare and contrast three major paradigms – *structural-functionalism*, *conflict* and *feminism* – that have emerged to make sense of work, organizations and HRM.

The intellectual roots of the *structural-functional paradigm* can be traced to the work of the French philosopher Auguste Comte (1798–1857) and French sociologist Emile Durkheim (1858–1917). Comte believed that society could be studied and understood logically and rationally, and he used the term *positivism* to describe this research approach. Durkheim studied social order and argued that the increased division of labour in modern societies created what he called 'organic solidarity', which maintained social harmony: 'The division of labour becomes the chief source of social solidarity, it becomes, at the same time, the foundation of moral order' (Durkheim, 1933/1997, p. 333).

The popularity of the structural-functionalist approach is commonly attributed to the US sociologist Talcott Parsons (Mann, 2011). For Parsons, organizations can function in a stable and orderly manner only on the basis of shared values. In his words: 'The problem of order, and thus the nature of the integration of stable systems of social interaction ... thus focuses on the integration of the motivation of actors with the normative cultural standards which integrate the action system' (1951, p. 36). Although there are variations and tensions, the structural-functional paradigm takes the view that a social entity, such as a whole market society or an organization, can be studied as an organism. Like organisms, a social system is composed of interdependent parts, each of which contributes to the functioning of the whole. A whole society or an organization is held together by a consensus on values, or a value system. The view of an organization as a social system thus looks for the 'functions' served by its various departments and members and the common values shared by its members.

It is frequently assumed that managerial functions and processes take place in organizations that are rationally designed to accomplish strategic goals, that organizations are harmonious bodies tending towards a state of equilibrium and order, and that the basic task of managers is to manage resources for formal organizational ends. Thus, the structural-functionalism paradigm, sometimes also known as 'social systems theory', becomes inseparable from the notion of efficiency. The focus of much of the research and literature on management using this 'lens' is about finding the 'winning formula' so that more managers can become 'effective' (Thompson and McHugh, 2009). Common to all variations of structural-functionalism, which is often seen as the dominant or mainstream perspective, is a failure to connect management processes to the 'master' public discourse on market-based societies and globalization.

The intellectual roots of the *conflict paradigm* are most obviously found in the works of the German philosopher Karl Marx (1818–1883). The German sociologist Max Weber (1864–1920) also devoted much research to work and organizations within advanced capitalist societies. In his early manuscripts of 1844, Marx analysed the fundamental contradiction of capitalism that arose from structured tensions between capital (employers) and labour (employees). Specifically, he made the assumption that these two social classes have competing interests. For Marx, the relationship between capitalists and workers was one of contradiction. Each is dependent upon the other, and the two must cooperate to varying degrees. Yet there is a fundamental conflict of interest between capital and labour: the capitalist seeks to minimize labour costs; the workers seek the opposite. As a result, economic forces compel employers and employees to cooperate, but also there are forces that simultaneously cause conflict between the two groups.

Equally importantly, workers experience alienation or 'estrangement' through the act of labour. Marx describes alienation explicitly as an absence of meaning or self-worth. Alienated workers are people 'robbed' of the unique characteristic or the 'essence' of human beings – their ability to be creative through productive work. Marx's analysis of alienation continues to inform contemporary studies of work and the prerequisites for dignity *in* and *at* work (see, for example, Bolton, 2007).

Similar to Marx, Weber's analyses of advanced capitalist societies centre on work and organizations, especially large bureaucracies. Two themes within Weber's work are especially relevant to understanding contemporary theories of work and management. One is the notion of *paradox* in market societies. In *The Protestant Ethic* (1904–05/2002), Weber pessimistically warns of creeping rationalization and of the tendency of people to experience a debilitating '*iron cage*'. The process of rationalization is, according to Weber, unremittingly paradoxical (Bratton et al. 2009). He, and subsequent writers in the Weberian tradition, focused on the notion of '*paradox of consequences*' – two or more positions that each sound reasonable yet conflict or contradict each other. For example, an organization invests in new technology and achieves higher levels of efficiency, and ultimately rising profits. However, the performance benefits of the technology are accompanied by behaviours that reduce long-term efficiency as work becomes increasingly devoid of meaning or dignity for the employees. Thus, a paradox of consequence results when managers, in pursuit of a specific organizational goal or goals, call for or carry out actions that are in opposition to the very goals the organization is attempting to accomplish.

A second theme that lies at the centre of Weber's sociology is his analysis of *power* and domination by social elites (Bratton et al., 2009, p. 235). In *Economy and Society* (1922/1968), Weber stresses that power is an aspect of virtually all social relationships. However, Weber was primarily interested in legitimate forms of domination or power, or what he called 'legitimate authority', which allocates the right to command and the duty to obey. He argued that every form of social elite attempts to establish and cultivate belief in its own legitimate authority. For example, *legal-rational* domination, which Weber defined as 'a belief in the legality of enacted rules and the right of those elevated to authority under such rules to issue commands' (Weber, 1922/1968,

p. 215), is exercised through bureaucracy, itself a product of the systematic rationalization of work and society. Weber viewed bureaucratic domination with some apprehension. The more perfectly bureaucracy is developed, 'the more it is 'dehumanized' (p. 975) as it 'reduces every worker to a cog in this [bureaucratic] machine and, seeing himself in this light, he will merely ask how to transform himself from a little into a somewhat bigger cog' (p. iix).

Critical scholars draw heavily on the works of Marx, and to a lesser extent Weber, to explain management activities in terms of basic 'logics' underlying capitalist production and society: goods and services are produced for a profit; technology and bureaucratic principles provide new opportunities for increasing both the quantity and the quality of work; and the agents acting for the capitalists – the managers – decide how and where goods and services are to be produced within the context of powerful economic imperatives that do not allow for substantial differences in management style or approach. Thus, managerial control is a *structural* imperative of capitalist employment relations, causing what Edwards' (1986) calls '*structural antagonism*'. Labour process analysis is part of the conflict school of thought. It represents a body of theory and research that examines 'core' themes of technology, skills, control and worker resistance, as well as, more recently, new 'postmodern territories' with a focus on subjectivity, identity and power (Thompson and Smith, 2010). The conflict paradigm, when applied to work organizations, sets out to discover the ways in which power, control, conflict and legitimacy impact on contemporary employment relations. It emphasizes that HRM can only be understood as part of a management process embedded within the wider sociocultural and political economy order of a capitalist society, which determines the nature of work and employment practices. The various critical approaches to HRM attempt to demystify and contextualize the situation of HRM by focusing on the interplay of economic, social and political forces, power and systematic inequality, and structured antagonism and conflict (see Delbridge and Keenoy, 2010; Thompson and Harley, 2008; Watson, 2010).

The third social science paradigm examined here, the *feminist paradigm*, traces its intellectual roots to eighteenth-century feminist writings, such as Mary Wollstonecraft's *A Vindication of the Rights of Woman* (1792/2004) and, in the 1960s, to Betty Friedan's *Feminine Mystique* (1963). Whereas Marx chiefly addressed the exploitation of the working class, the early feminist writers provided a 'sophisticated understanding into gender-based, persistent, and pervasive injustices that women continue to experience in all areas of life' (Bratton et al., 2009, p. 11). Researchers looking at the market society from a feminist perspective have drawn attention to aspects of organizational life that are overlooked by other paradigms. In part, feminist scholarship has focused on gender differences and how they relate to the rest of society. Over the decades, gender has become a concept to be wrestled with, but here we use the word to refer to a set of ideas that focuses on the processes of gender roles, inequalities in society and in the workplace, problems of power, and women's subordination and oppression.

Theoretically, one of the most important consequences of gender analysis is its power to question the research findings and analysis that segregate studies of HRM from those of gender divisions in the labour market (Dex, 1988), patriarchal power (Witz, 1986), issues of workplace inequality (Phillips and Phillips, 1993) and 'dual-role' and work–life issues (Knights and Willmott, 1986; Platt, 1997; Warhurst et al., 2008). More importantly, however, including the dimension of gender in the study of contemporary HRM has the potential to move the debate forward by examining the people who are deemed to be the 'recipients' of HRM theory and practice (Mabey et al., 1998a). For example, Dickens (1998) has noted that the equality assumption in the HRM model, which emphasizes the value of diversity, is part of the rhetoric rather than the reality. Reinforcing this observation, a large-scale Canadian study showed that women face a gender bias when it comes to career advancement. In addition, women from visible minorities face a 'double bias' favouring white men at all levels, from entry-level to middle managers right up to chief executive officers (Yap and Konrad, 2009). The feminist paradigm takes it as self-evident that gender inequality in the workplace can only be understood by developing a wider gender-sensitive understanding of society and employment practices.

Reflective question

It is important to explore your own values and views and therefore your own perspective on HRM. What do you think of these social science paradigms? How do they help us to explain the actions and outcomes of behaviour in organizations? Which perspective seem to you to be more realistic, and why? How do these paradigms help us to understand the uncertainties and conflicts evident in contemporary workplaces?

CRITIQUE AND PARADOX IN HRM

Since Storey's (1989) landmark publication, the HRM canon has been subject to 'external' and 'internal' criticism (Delbridge and Keenoy, 2010). The external critique has come from academics within the broad field of critical management studies and labour process theory. These critics include Alvesson and Willmott (2003), Godard (1991), Thompson and McHugh (2009) and Watson (2004). They expose structured antagonisms and contradictions, and contend that HR practices can only be understood in the context of the wider cultural and political economy factors that shape or direct those practices. Critical management theorists also argue that mainstream HRM researchers have routinely neglected or marginalized those most directly impacted by HR practices – the employees. Generally, there has been an intellectual failure to engage in the process of 'denaturalization' – of questioning 'taken-for-granted' beliefs and assumptions and 'unmasking' the questionable results of HRM research. Finally, critics hold that most HRM researchers have largely failed to subject employment practices to a critical scrutiny of 'unintended consequences', 'contradictions' or the 'collateral damage' resulting from their application (Delbridge and Keenoy, 2010, p. 803).

The principal 'internal' critics of HRM include Karen Legge (2005), who provides a sustained critique with respect to the divide between what she describes as the 'rhetoric' and the 'reality' of HRM. Similarly, Barbara Townley (1994) offers a sustained Foucauldian analysis and critique of HRM, and Winstanley and Woodall (2000) present a sustained ethical critique of HRM. More generally, Keenoy and Anthony (1992) have sought to explore the ambiguity associated with the term 'human resource management' itself. This relates to the question of where the emphasis of strategic management policy is placed: is it on the word *'human'* or on *'resource'* in management? This ambiguity generated the notion of 'soft' and 'hard' HRM and, more recently, provoked a collection titled *Searching for the 'H' in HRM* in the 'moral' market society (Bolton and Houlihan, 2007).

Analytically, critical commentaries of the HRM phenomenon echo the belief that the contemporary workplace mirrors the capitalist society at large: a social entity that may be characterized by creativity, innovation, wealth, but also one that exhibits constant change, strategic variation, human degradation, inequality, social power, differential interests, contradiction and paradox. Charles Dickens (1859/1952), in *A Tale of Two Cities*, nicely captures the existence of paradox in modernity: 'It was the best of times, it was the worst of times, it was the age of wisdom, it was the age of foolishness ...'. This duality of creativity and wealth alongside degradation and inequality in the workplace is neatly captured by a well-known drawing found in first-year psychology textbooks, an image that can be seen at the same time as a beautiful young woman and an old crone.

Drawing upon Weber's work, the 'internal' critics of HRM have used the paradox of consequence to encourage their audiences to view the reality of HRM differently. For example, new job and work designs were promoted to revitalize organizations in order to enlist workers' knowledge and commitment, but what have emerged are downsizing and work intensification. A similar contradiction emerges in new reward systems with the introduction of variable pay arrangements, but what can emerge is a 'bonus culture' that undermines other espoused employer goals such as loyalty and commitment, or, as the 2008 banking crisis attests, risk-aversion. Legge's incisive critique identifies the basic paradox that the dominant HRM model simultaneously seeks both control over and the commitment of employees, the tensions in the 'soft' and 'hard' schools of HRM, and the rhetoric that asserts 'we are all managers now'. Paradoxically, the inclusion of the HR director in the strategic management team, the process of 'decentralization' or the act of 'giving away HR management' to line managers, as well as the outsourcing of HR activities, might ultimately lead to the demise of the HR professional, thereby undermining the ongoing quest of HRM specialists for centrality and credibility (Legge, 2005).

Critical accounts of HRM also suggest a paradox of consequence arising from new networked organizational designs (Rubery et al., 2002). The short-lived nature of multiemployer networks, differentiated by employer, business contracts and employment contracts, encourages subcultures that may counter any efforts to create a 'high-commitment' culture and/or violate the psychological contract. As Legge explains, in discussing interfirm relationships: 'When flexibility is the justification and watchword ... pragmatism ... is likely to moderate, if not supplant, a truly strategic approach to HR' (2007, p. 54). Furthermore, when employers are urged to adjust to Britain's ageing workforce (Brindle, 2010), investment in work-based learning is at odds with the reality of 'HRM's organizationally sponsored ageism' (Lyon and Glover, 1998, p. 31).

In our view, studying HRM remains relevant. The global and environmental drivers of change that are reshaping Western economies and societies will cast a long shadow over contemporary organizations as managers struggle to control work and employment activities. Analytical HRM is, therefore, highly relevant given that its *raison d'être* is, using a variety of approaches or styles, to leverage people's knowledge and capabilities and manage employment relationships. In particular, given the need for organizations to develop sustainably oriented strategies, a reflexive, critical analysis of HRM is increasingly important to understanding organizational life.

Furthermore, with regard to concerns about an absence of reflexive critique in business schools, Delbridge and Keenoy's (2010) contribution elaborating what constitutes CHRM is both important and timely. In writing this text, we have found concepts from the social science paradigms to be highly relevant, albeit through the lens of our own cultural bias. As in previous editions of *Human Resource Management: Theory and Practice*, we are concerned with developing a context-sensitive understanding of work and practices of HRM. Throughout the book, we emphasize that paradox and antagonism is structured into the employment relationship. Many mainstream HRM writers have not been realistic about the nature of capitalism (Thompson and Harley, 2008). From our perspective, it goes without saying that different work systems and HR strategies and practices can only be understood in the context of the wider cultural-political economy, technological, environmental and market factors that direct or influence work regimes.

We are aiming to provide a more critical, nuanced account of the realities of the workplace in market societies, one that encourages a deeper understanding and sensitivity with respect to employment and HR-related issues. We hope that *Human Resource Management: Theory and Practice* captures the range of change evident in today's workplaces, and will moreover lead to the kind of sensibilities that encourage the reader to question, to be critical and to seek multicausality when analysing contemporary HRM.

Case Study

Canterbury Hospital

Setting

In the twenty-first century, New Zealand is tackling environmental issues similar to those of many countries: the more sustainable use of water, managing marine resources, reducing waste and improving energy efficiency. The country is particularly concerned about the decline of its unique plants, animals and ecosystems. The country is striving to build a positive image of New Zealand through exporting environmentally sensitive products and maintaining a reputation of being sustainable at home and abroad. The government has therefore recognized that there is a need to increase reporting on sustainable practices among New Zealand businesses in order to raise the profile of New Zealand globally on this important issue.

For the last few years, the Ministry for the Environment has promoted several grant-funding programmes to support environmental initiatives. In an attempt to control administration costs and improve the evaluation of the programme's outcomes, a decision was recently made to combine the funds supporting environmental initiatives at the community level. It is hoped that merging these funds will mean that the programme will be more streamlined and that there will be more flexibility to meet government priorities.

The combined funding programme, called the Community Environment Fund (CEF), aims to support community groups, businesses and local government in taking environmental actions. To be eligible for funding, applicants have to demonstrate that their projects will support one or more of the following objectives:

○ Raise awareness of environmental damage
○ Support and strengthen partnerships between community, industry, Maori populations and local government on practical environmental initiatives

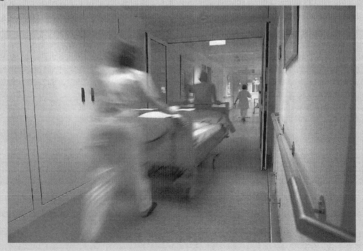

Source: ©istockphoto.com/Dr. Heinz Linke

The CEF funding process

Eligible to apply →

Project selection →

Funding approval →

Check eligibility online

Apply for funding
Stage I

Develop project plan
Stage II

Sign funding deed

Start project

Source: www.mfe.govt.nz/withyou/funding/community-environment-fund/; Ministry for the Environment (New Zealand) (2011)

○ Involve the community in practically focused action for the environment
○ Empower the community to take action that improves the quality of the environment
○ Increase community-based advice, educational opportunities and public information about environmental legislation.

Eligible environmental projects will be considered for a minimum of $10,000 and up to a maximum of $300,000 of funding per financial year.

The problem

Canterbury Hospital, located near the city of Christchurch, provides a wide range of complex medical, surgery and mental health services, and is not only one of New Zealand's largest healthcare centres, but also its oldest. The hospital has a poor reputation in terms of its HRM and struggles with adversarial union relations. Workers are given low autonomy in their jobs, and the organizational structure contains several layers of management. Decision-making is primarily centralized.

The hospital's administration recently became aware of the funding provided by the government's new environmental initiative. Subsequently, in a public meeting, Chief Executive Officer Heather Nicol announced the creation of an Environmental/Sustainability Innovation Committee, made up of staff members chosen by management from the various hospital departments: 'Environmental stewardship is a key component of our hospital's strategic and operational planning, and through this new committee we will be contributing to our organization's and the country's goals to become more sustainable.' The committee, she said, would recommend and develop projects that would meet the funding criteria outlined by the government.

This new and revolutionary approach by the hospital administration took most of the staff by surprise. Although many were eager to learn about the environmental issues and contribute their ideas through this experience, others were suspicious of management's motives in involving staff members when they had never been asked to participate in such a public initiative before. Shortly before the initial meeting of the selected group, the HR department received an angry call from the union executive questioning why they had not been asked to sit on the committee and asking what criteria had been used to select the employees who were to participate. The union demanded a meeting with management to discuss how workloads and jobs would be impacted by the employees' involvement.

Assignment

Working either alone or in a study group, prepare a report drawing on this chapter and other recommended material addressing the following:

1 Using one of the five major HRM models, identify which aspects of the case illustrate traditional personnel management and HRM approaches.
2 What contribution can a set of 'best' HR practices make to this organization?
3 Reflecting upon the national business system, discuss how the effectiveness of HR practices depends on the context of an organization.

Note

Your report may be written to fit your own national business and legal context.

Essential reading

Dunphy, D. C., Griffiths, A. and Benn, S. (2003) *Organizational Change for Corporate Sustainability: Understanding Organizational Change*. London: Routledge.
Enhert, I. (2009) Sustainability and human resource management: reasoning and applications on corporate websites. *European Journal of International Management,* **3**(4): 419–38.

Jones, G. (ed.) (2011) *Current Research in Sustainability.* Prahan: Tilde University Press.

Tyler, M. and Wilkinson, A. (2007) The tyranny of corporate slenderness: 'corporate anorexia' as a metaphor for our age. *Work, Employment and Society,* **21**(3): 537–49.

For more on New Zealand's Community Environment Fund, go to: www.mfe.govt.nz/withyou/funding/community-environment-fund.

Note

This feature was written by Lori Rilkoff, HR Manager at City of Kamloops, BC, Canada.
  Visit the companion website at www.palgrave.com/business/bratton5 for guidelines on writing reports.

SUMMARY

- In this introductory chapter, we have emphasized the importance of managing people, individually and collectively, over other 'factor inputs'. We have examined the history of HRM and emphasized that, since its introduction, it has been highly controversial. The HRM phenomenon has been portrayed as the historical outcome of rising neo-liberalism ideology, closely associated with the political era of Thatcherism.

- We have conceptualized HRM as a strategic approach, one that seeks to leverage people's capabilities and commitment with the goal of enhancing performance and dignity *in* and *at* work. These HRM goals are accomplished by a set of integrated employment policies, programmes and practices within an organizational and societal context. We suggest that the HRM approach as conceptualized here constitutes CHRM, extending the analysis of HRM outcomes beyond performance to include equality, dignity and social justice.

- To show the multiple meanings of the term 'human resource management', we have examined five theoretical models. We have discussed whether HRM now represents a new orthodoxy; certainly, the language is different.

- We have explained that tensions are omnipresent. These include tensions between profitability and cost-effectiveness and employee security; between employer control and employee commitment; and between managerial autonomy and employee dignity. Throughout this book, we illustrate and explain some of these tensions and inevitable paradoxes to encourage a deeper understanding of HR-related issues.

- Finally, workplace scholars use a variety of theoretical frames of reference or paradigms – here the focus has been on structural-functionalism, conflict and feminist paradigms – to organize how they understand and conduct research into HRM.

VOCAB CHECKLIST FOR ESL STUDENTS

- analyse (v), analysis (n), analytical (adj)
- arbitrate (v), arbitrator (n), arbitration (n)
- bureaucrat (n), bureaucracy (n), bureaucratic (adj)
- capitalize (v), capital (n), capitalist (n), capitalism (n)
- conflict (n), conflict perspective (n)
- contract (v), contract (n), contractor (n), contractual (adj)
- controversy (n), controversial (adj)
- criticize (v), critic (n), critical (adj)
- downsize (v), downsizing (n)
- economize (v), economics (n), economy (n), economist (n), economical (adj)

- employ (v), employee (n), employer (n), employment (n)
- equity (n), equitable (adj), equal (adj)
- globalize (v), globe (n), globalization (n), global (adj)
- idea (n), ideology (n), ideological (adj)
- interdepend (v), interdependencies (n), interdependent (adj)
- international human resource management (IHRM) (n)
- liberalize (v), liberalism (n), liberal (n) (adj)
- manage (v), manager (n), management (n), managerial (adj)
- mediate (v), mediator (n), mediation (n)
- micro human resource management (MHRM) (n)
- norm (n), normative (adj), normal (adj)
- oblige (v), obligation (n), obligatory (adj)
- outsource (v), outsourcing (n)
- paradigm (n)
- paradox (n), paradoxical (adj), paradoxically (adv)
- recruit (v), recruit (n), recruitment (n)
- restructure (v), restructuring (n)
- rhetoric (n), rhetorical (adj)
- sociology (n), sociologist (n), sociological (adj)
- stakeholder (n)
- stereotype (v), stereotype (n), stereotypical (adj)
- strategic human resource management (SHRM) (n)
- strategize (v), strategy (n), strategist (n), strategic (adj)
- sustain (v), sustainability (n), sustainable (adj)
- theorize (v), theory (n), theorist (n), theoretical (adj)
- unionize (v), union (n), unionization (n)

NOTE

some words are denoted as nouns (n) when in fact the word is a gerund; for example, 'restructuring' is in the gerund form; however, gerunds function grammatically as nouns, so the general term of noun (n) is used.

Visit www.palgrave.com/business/bratton5 for a link to free definitions of these terms in the Macmillan Dictionary, as well as additional learning resources for ESL students.

REVIEW QUESTIONS

1 What is 'human resource management' and what role does it play in work organizations?
2 To what extent does the emergence of HRM reflect the rise and ideology of neo-liberalism?
3 To what extent is HRM different from conventional personnel management – or is it simply 'old wine in new bottles'?

FURTHER READING TO IMPROVE YOUR MARK

1. Reading these articles and chapters can help you gain a better understanding and potentially a higher grade for your HRM assignment.

2. The changing role of HRM is explored in R. Caldwell (2001) Champions, adapters, consultants and synergists: the new change agents in HRM. *Human Resource Management Journal*, **11**(3): 39–52.

3. Critical studies are also found in the following:

4. Delbridge, R. and Keenoy, T. (2010) Beyond managerialism? *International Journal of Human Resource Management*, **21**(6): 799–817.

5. Dickens, L. (1998) What HRM means for gender equality. *Human Resource Management Journal*, **8**(1): 23–45.

6. Kochan, T. (2008) Social legitimacy of the HRM profession: a US perspective. In P. Boxall, J. Purcell and P. Wright (eds) *The Oxford Handbook of Human Resource Management* (pp. 599–619). Oxford: OUP.

7. Legge, K. (2005) *Human Resource Management: Rhetorics and Realities*. London: Palgrave Macmillan.

8. Storey J. (ed.) (2007) Human resource management today: an assessment. In J. Storey (ed.) *Human Resource Management: A Critical Text* (pp. 3–20). London: Thompson Learning.

9. Thompson, P. and Harley, B. (2008) HRM and the worker: labour process perspectives. In P. Boxall, J. Purcell and P. Wright (eds) *The Oxford Handbook of Human Resource Management* (pp. 147–65). Oxford: OUP.

10. Watson, T. (2010) Critical social science, pragmatism and the realities of HRM. *International Journal of Human Resource Management Studies*, **21**(6): 915–31.

Visit www.palgrave.com/business/bratton5 for lots of extra resources to help you get to grips with this chapter, including study tips, HRM skills development guides, summary lecture notes, and more.

RECRUITMENT AND SELECTION

OUTLINE

OBJECTIVES

After studying this chapter, you should be able to:

1 Understand the importance of recruitment and selection in the formation of the employment relationship
2 Understand the key features of recruitment and selection policies
3 Explain the nature of attraction in recruitment
4 Explain the effectiveness of various selection methods

INTRODUCTION

'You're hired!' And with these words, on an annual basis, Lord Alan Sugar selects his latest recruit. Each year, a range of budding apprentices present themselves to Lord Sugar and his panel as part of the BBC's flagship recruitment and selection programme. Although it is clearly a balance between human resources (HR) practice and entertainment, and is presented as the job interview from hell, *The Apprentice* also covers some of the key features of recruitment and selection, effective or otherwise. First, a position is made available, to which apparently several thousand people are attracted. Whereas it is not entirely clear what is in the job description or personnel specification, suffice it to say that there is a six-figure salary. Then, through a series of 'auditions' as well as interviews, around 70 applicants are selected for a second round, followed by psychological tests, from which the short list of 16 are presented to Lord Sugar. In the following weeks, through a series of tasks, aided by the assessment of trusted colleagues, choices are made about the applicants – usually resulting in the immortal line 'You're Fired!' – until an appointment is made in the final week of the programme.

It is often the case that those who make it to the final are strikingly different in terms of their education, experience and personality characteristics. These are, however, less relevant than the chance for Lord Sugar and his panel to base their assessments on what they see so that they can predict how a potential employee might behave in the future and fit into the organization. Of course, whether the winner's job with the organization meets their expectations as part of an evolving employment relationship and a positive psychological contract based on a mutual and reciprocal understanding is something that is left to our imagination.

Reflective question

What are your expectations for employment? What attracts you to employment opportunities in the current economic climate?

RECRUITMENT AND SELECTION POLICIES

Recruitment and selection have always been critical processes for organizations. We discussed ethics in recruitment and selection practices and how such practices can change or reinforce a particular culture. After a period during which recruitment difficulties had been reported in many organizations, and employer branding in terms of recruitment and selection was needed to stand out as a 'good employer' (Chartered Institute of Personnel and Development [CIPD], 2005b), the recession in the late 2000s led to a significant reduction in the number of vacancies. According to CIPD's (2010c) survey of over 480 organizations, fewer organizations were experiencing recruitment problems, and some had even cut or reduced their graduate schemes, although for many these remained the same (at 42 per cent). In circumstances where many applicants chase fewer jobs, just like in *The Apprentice*, employers clearly have more power, and therefore many approaches to recruitment and selection emphasize this power. Traditional approaches to recruitment and selection attempt to attract a wide choice of candidates for vacancies before screening out those who do not match the criteria set in the job descriptions and personnel specifications. Figure 8.1 shows an overall view of the stages of recruitment and selection, and the connection of these processes to workforce planning.

There are wide variations in recruitment and selection policies and practices, reflecting an organization's strategy and its philosophy of people management. In large multinational organizations, for example, there is a distinction between policies to attract those destined for international careers and policies suited to local conditions (Sparrow, 2007). Where indicated by the workforce plan, an organization will seek ways of attracting a pool of applicants and then differentiating between them, avoiding the costs of hiring the 'wrong' ones (Newell, 2005, p. 115). In recent years, there has been interest in the idea of an employer brand (Knox and Freeman, 2006), based on the image the organization wishes to project to potential applicants in order to attract them. Many larger organizations use their websites for this purpose or employ recruitment agencies to help them (CIPD, 2010c).

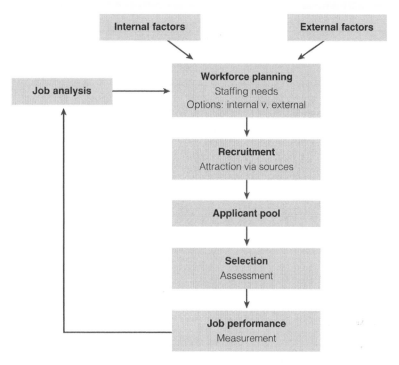

Figure 8.1 – The stages of recruitment and selection

Visit www.palgrave.com/business/bratton5 to read an HRM in practice feature on how Adidas attracts new staff.

The employer brand will also be reflected in the psychological and behavioural characteristics expected of employees, which are expressed through competency frameworks (Roberts, 1997); we will explore these below. Such frameworks have allowed organizations to adopt a range of sophisticated recruitment and selection techniques in order to identify and admit the 'right' people. In this way, as 'organizationally defined critical qualities' (Iles and Salaman, 1995, p. 204), a competency framework augments an organization's power. For example, one tool of assessment we will consider is personality testing, and a survey by Piotrowski and Armstrong (2006) found that popular qualities for testing included integrity and potential for violence. Such information can be used to make judgements about who to admit. Crucially, however, such models need to work within the constraints of a legal context and policies for diversity management (Daniels and Macdonald, 2005).

HRM in practice: Employer branding and the employment 'deal'

Employer branding is now recognized as an important part of the HR 'toolkit', stimulated by a growing awareness of the application of marketing principles in attracting better applicants and leveraging employee engagement and retention. This places the spotlight on the employer's 'brand promise', which has been defined as the employee value proposition (EVP) or employment 'deal', initially promoted by recruitment consultancies since the 1990s as part of the 'war for talent'. This centres around promoting a positive image of the organization as a good place to work, as illustrated by Google's portrayal of the 'Top 10 Reasons' to work for the company, such as having fun, fulfilling work and a supportive workplace (Google, 2012).

Consultancy-driven recipes for 'employer of choice' strategies have become very popular, and employers are increasingly seeking more sophisticated means of linking their HR strategy and the corporate brand, beyond the aim of attracting job applicants. The challenge is to find a way of building employees' 'buy-in' to a new brand articulation in ways that enhances their engagement and performance, especially during periods of redundancy and cost-cutting. More active employee involvement is key, as shown by the Co-operative Group's attempts to reinvent its company brand during a time of declining performance. In the words of the Director for HR (MacLeod and Clarke, 2009, p. 45):

> The engagement strategy was a catalyst for re-building trust and confidence between individuals, their line managers and the organisation. We asked people how they felt about working here, why they felt that way and what should be done to change things.

Research into making and keeping an employer brand promise has been informed by exchange concepts, notably the idea of the psychological contract. This is commonly described in terms of a reciprocal relationship of inducements from employers in exchange for contributions from their employees – for example, meaningful work pay and benefits in return for the employees' initiative and discretionary effort.

Detractors have, however, pointed to the somewhat passive role accorded to employees in the current modelling of human resource management (HRM) and EVP, treating them essentially as *consumers* 'buying into' their employer's vision and brand, rather than as active *producers* of HR practices or employer brand. This is promoted by an over-reliance on statistical instruments concerned with the mechanistic cause-and-effect relationships between organizational 'drivers' and employees' performance. More research work needs to be done on how employers might reformulate the design process of EVPs in order to facilitate more authentic employee involvement and participation that are of mutual benefit to the stakeholders involved.

Stop!   Academic debates about the emergent concepts of EVP and engagement have pointed to unrealistic *unitarist thinking* about the employment relationship, which assumes that what is good for the organization is always good for employees and vice versa. What is your view?

Sources and further information

See MacLeod and Clarke's (2009) report to the government, *Engaging for Success*, and for further insight into employee engagement, see Balain and Sparrow (2009). An examination of how linkages between social exchange, EVP and engagement can be applied in practice is contained in Francis and Reddington (2012).

Note

This feature was written by Professor Helen Francis and Dr Martin Reddington at Edinburgh Napier University.

Visit the companion website at www.palgrave.com/business/bratton5 for bonus HRM in practice features on how Adidas attracts new staff, and on the Co-op's internship scheme.

Reflective question

How would an employer prove to you that it was seeking to develop its employer brand based on a positive psychological contract? Go to BP Global Careers at www.bpfutures.com. How has BP's image and brand been affected by the Gulf Oil Disaster?

RECRUITMENT AND ATTRACTION

Recruitment is the process of attracting the interest of a pool of capable people who will apply for jobs within an organization. In this definition, we can highlight three crucial issues. First, there is a need to attract people's interest in applying for employment. This implies that people have a choice about which organizations they wish to work for, even though during times of recession such choices might be limited. Second, people may be capable of fulfilling a role in employment, but the extent to which this will be realized is not totally predictable. Third, how capability is understood is increasingly determined by an organization's approach to talent management. There are some choices to be made, especially in terms of whether there should be an exclusive or an inclusive focus (Lewis and Heckman, 2006).

Under different labour market conditions, power in the recruitment process will swing between the buyers or sellers of labour – the employers and employees, respectively. It is therefore important to understand that the dimension of power will always be present in recruitment and selection, even in organizations that purport to have a high-commitment HR strategy. Thus, in conditions of recession, employers are likely to reduce recruitment budgets and costs, giving more attention to developing the talent that has already been employed (CIPD, 2010c).

Tania Hummel   Group Human Resources Director, Macmillan Publishers www.macmillan.com

Macmillan Publishers Ltd is one of the largest international publishing groups in the world, with 7000 staff operating in more than 80 countries. Macmillan publishes a variety of academic and scholarly, fiction and non-fiction books and online content, as well as STM (science, technical and medical) and social science journals, educational course materials and dictionaries, and higher education textbooks. Divisions of the company include NPG (Nature Publishing Group), Macmillan Education, Pan Macmillan, Picador and Palgrave Macmillan.

Tania Hummel joined Macmillan in 2006 as Personnel Manager for the London divisions, having spent many years in publishing, most notably with Rough Guides and Lonely Planet publications. She has an MSc in HRM, with a special interest in management development.

Visit www.palgrave.com/business/bratton5 to watch Tania talking about recruitment, diversity and the challenges faced by HR in the publishing industry, and then think about the following questions:

1 How does Tania describe the differences between personnel management and HRM?
2 What does she see as the role of HR in the business?
3 What issues are facing recruitment today? How do companies ensure diversity in the workplace?

HRM as I see it

Budgetary factors will also affect how recruitment channels are used, with more use of online recruitment, as we will consider below. Generally, there needs to be an intelligent use of recruitment channels in all circumstances. For example, the ageing profile of the workforce requires an adjustment of recruitment polices (Lyon and Glover, 1998). Henkens et al. (2005) found that the use of the Internet and agencies for recruitment reflected a bias towards younger applicants, whereas older workers were more dependent on formal channels of recruitment such as newspapers and journals.

In addition, since the early 1990s, there have been more graduates entering the labour market, but the number of 'graduate' jobs has not kept pace, with a consequent reduction in the power of many new graduates to find employment on advantageous terms (Brannie, 2008). This means that many graduates will take longer to find employment that matches their skills and aspirations. It might also affect the perceptions of value to be gained from studying for a degree against the price of a degree. Among today's graduates are those referred to as Generation Y (those born between 1977 and 1994), who are said to be confident and thrive on challenging but flexible work, expecting quick feedback and reward while maintaining a balanced lifestyle (Broadbridge et al., 2009).

HRM web links

Go to www.ashridge.org.uk/Website/Content.nsf/wFARCRED/Generation+Y?opendocument to find out about Ashridge's Generation Y research project.

Reflective question

Do you consider yourself as part of Generation Y? What are your expectations for working, and what do you expect in recruitment?

Fitting the person to the environment, organization and job

Effective recruitment depends on the extent to which the overall management philosophy supports and reinforces an approach to HRM that focuses on the utilization and development of new employees once they have joined an organization. Although HR policies will be designed to achieve particular organizational targets and goals, those policies will also provide an opportunity for individual needs to emerge and be satisfied. This view assumes that a fit between a person and the environment can be found so that their commitment and performance will be enhanced (Kristof, 1996). Some commentators doubt that such mutuality could ever occur on an equal basis, and believe that organizational needs, as determined by senior management, will always take precedence; however, individual needs may, through HRM activities, influence how the organization's needs are perceived. Recruitment and then selection processes will therefore aim to attract and admit those whom management view as the 'right' people for such an approach. In one sense, an organization already knows who the right people are for its vacancies since they are the very people who are already employed and are present in the company's talent pool. Such internal recruitment might be based on performance assessment and the decisions of senior managers, whose choices could be made on the basis of candidates' similarity to themselves (see Mäkelä et al., 2010).

Taking a strategic view of recruitment requirements starts with the strategic plan. Research by Tyson (1995) found that although there were many differences between organizations, HRM could help to shape the direction of change, influence culture and 'help bring about the mindset' that would decide which strategic issues were considered. HR considerations, including the results of a review of the quantity and quality of people, should thus be integrated into the plan. The goals, objectives and targets that then emerge set the parameters for performance in an organization and for how work is organized into roles and jobs. A key role for HR is

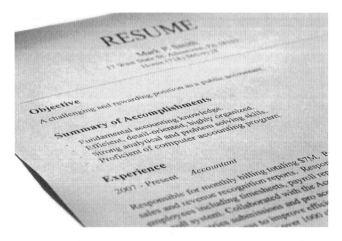

Recruitment is a process of attracting the right people to apply for the job.
Source: ©istockphoto.com/Anatoly Vartanov

to align performance within roles with the organization's strategy, so recruiting the right people for a role depends on how that role is defined in terms relating to the performance needed to achieve the strategy (Holbeche, 1999). Once a recruitment strategy has been formed, an organization might outsource its implementation, especially where there are a large number of staff to be recruited (Tulip, 2004), although recent moves to focus on the talent already employed might reduce this tendency (Ordanini and Silvestri, 2008).

Traditionally, creating a specification containing the requirements for a particular role has required the use of *job analysis techniques*; these may include a range of interviews, questionnaires and observation processes that provide information about work carried out, the environment in which it occurs and, vitally, the knowledge, skills and attitudes needed to perform the job well. In recent years, information derived from the analysis of work performance has been utilized to create a taxonomy or framework of either criterion-related behaviours or standards of performance referred to as *competencies*. Although most frameworks are developed within organizations and are based on the meanings of behaviour that exist within an organization, there are also frameworks that can be applied more generally or to specific groups in different organizations. According to the CIPD (2010d, p. 1), competencies are 'the behaviours that employees must have, or must acquire, to input into a situation in order to achieve high levels of performance'. (This definition, focusing on behaviour patterns, differs from the idea of competence used with Vocational Qualifications, which are related to performing activities within an occupation to a prescribed standard. You can read more about the development of Vocational Qualifications at www.qcda.gov.uk/qualifications/60.aspx.) Competency frameworks are concerned with behaviour that is relevant to the job and the effective or competent performance of that job, although factors such as equipment and the behaviour can also have an impact.

Competency frameworks are widely thought to help an organization to align its objectives with the various HR activities of recruitment and selection, appraisal, training and reward (Holbeche, 1999). In addition, competencies enhance a common understanding of effective behaviour at work and provide a basis for more consistency in assessment practices (Whiddett and Hollyforde, 2003).

HRM web links

SHL is one of the main suppliers of job assessment software that can be used to develop competencies. Details of its Universal Competency Framework can be found at www.shl.com/WhatWeDo/Competency/Pages/UniversalCompetency-Framework.aspx. SHL also provides a useful book on job analysis techniques, which you can download at www.shl.com/assets/resources/Best-Practice-Job-Analysis.pdf.

Table 8.1 shows how one large financial services organization in the UK sets out its competencies. Each competency is defined and described by a range of indicators that enables assessment and measurement. The competency of 'creating customer service' is, for example, indicated by:

- Anticipating emerging customer needs and planning accordingly
- Identifying the customers who will be of value to the company
- Recommending changes to current ways of working that will improve customer service
- Arranging the collection of customer satisfaction data and acting on them.

The analysis and definition of competencies should allow the identification and isolation of dimensions of behaviour that are distinct and are associated with

Table 8.1 – Competencies in a financial services organization

Personal focus	Self-control Self-development Personal organization Positive approach
Customer focus	Creating customer service Delivering customer service Continuous improvement
Future focus	Delivering the vision Change and creativity
Business focus	Delivering results Providing solutions Systemic thinking Attention to detail
People focus	Developing people Working with others Influencing Leading

competent or effective performance. Competencies can therefore be used to provide, at least from an organization's point of view, the behaviours needed at work to achieve the business strategy. On this assumption, the assessment of competencies is one means of selecting employees, as will be discussed below. Competencies will enable organizations to form a model of the kinds of employee they wish to attract through recruitment.

HRM web links

Competency frameworks are now widely established in all kinds of organization. Check how the British Medical Association advocates the use of its framework at www.bma.org.uk/about_bma/bma_jobs/HRCompetencies.jsp?page=1. Note how this framework is used in recruitment.

Whatever the model constructed, an organization's commitment to its HR processes will form part of its evolving value system and make it even more attractive to those seeking employment. Many organizations seek to express their values by statements of visions and missions. For example, the following can be found at www.morrisons.co.uk/Corporate/Corporate-responsibility-2011/Responsible-retailing/Our-values.

> Our values are at the heart of everything we do, defining what we expect of each other and what our customers can expect of us as we aim to deliver our vision of becoming the 'Food Specialist for Everyone'.
>
> CAN DO
>
> Can do is about making things happen. It's about getting the job done and delivering results. It's about being positive and rising to a challenge.
>
> ONE TEAM
>
> One team is about working together to reach a common goal. It's about keeping our promises, building trust and respect, and valuing each other's contribution.

BRINGING THE BEST OUT OF OUR PEOPLE

Bringing the best out of our people is about developing ourselves and those around us. It's about constantly learning so we can improve the way we work and the experience we give our customers.

GREAT SELLING AND SERVICE

Great selling and service is about delivering a great experience for our customers. It's about sharing our knowledge and know-how and always striving to do better.

GREAT SHOPKEEPING

Great shopkeeping is about setting high standards and taking care of every detail. It's about having pride in our work and making quality our top priority.

FRESH THINKING

Fresh thinking is about finding new and better ways of working. It's about greater awareness, asking questions and coming up with bright ideas that give us the edge.

Such statements form part of the image, or 'brand' in talent management terms, that is projected by the company. Projected images, values and information on espoused goals will be made sense of by people in external labour markets, including both those employed and those unemployed. This interaction will determine how attracted potential recruits feel to an organization.

Reflective question

Think about an organization you would like to work for. What images, values and information related to that organization come into your mind? What is the brand of that organization?

The image projected by an organization and the response from potential employees provide the basis for a compatible person–organization (P–O) fit, a variant of the person–environment fit referred to earlier (in addition to P–O fit, person–vocation fit, person–job fit, person–preferences for culture fit, and person–team fit; see Barber, 1998; Wheeler et al., 2005.) Schneider (1987), using a theory of interactional psychology, proposed an attraction–selection–attrition framework to explain the workings of this process and the differences between organizations that are caused by

Source: Courtesy of Morrisons PLC

the attraction of people to the organization's goals, their interaction with those goals and the fact that 'if they don't fit, they leave' (Schneider, 1987, p. 437). The proposed framework is shown in Figure 8.2. Schneider argued that people are attracted to an organization on the basis of their own interests and personality. Thus, people of a similar type will be attracted to the same place. Furthermore, the attraction of similar types will begin to determine the place. Following selection, people who do not fit, because of either an error or a misunderstanding of the reality of an organization, will leave, resulting in attrition from that organization.

At the heart of the framework lie organizational goals, originally stated by the founder and/or articulated by top managers, and out of these emerge the structures and processes that will form the basis of decisions related to attraction. This framework was supported by research conducted by Judge and Cable (1997), who found that applicants seek P–O fit, attempting to match their values with the reputation surrounding an organization's culture. Understanding the operation of P–O fit can prevent unnecessary and expensive attrition. One area that suffers from high staff turnover is call-centre work. McCulloch and Turban (2007) considered P–O fit related to selection in 14 call centres in the USA and Canada among over 200 staff who stayed and those who left, showing that taking P–O fit into account during selection can play a key role in preventing high attrition.

Furthermore, P–O fit can be enhanced by an attention to socialization processes once new employees have been selected (Cable and Parsons, 2001), and in recent years, there has been growing interest in retaining talent through *onboarding* programmes (Dai and de Meuse, 2007). For example, Google's onboarding programme for software engineers includes face-to-face, online and on-the-job training, mentoring, membership of a support community and practice-based learning, all deemed to be successful in creating a congruence between Google's values and the values of those seeking sustained employment in the company (Johnson and Senges, 2010).

In addition to P–O fit, there is also interest in the extent to which there is a match between an individual's skills, knowledge and abilities and the requirements of a job,

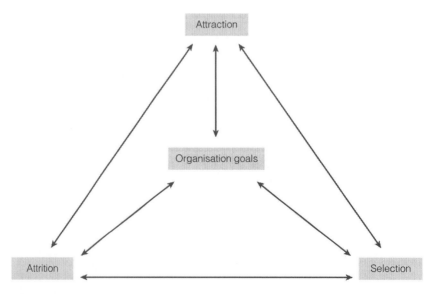

Figure 8.2 – An attraction–selection–attrition framework
Source: Schneider (1987), p . 440. Reproduced with the permission of John Wiley & Sons, Inc.

referred to as the 'person–job' (P–J) fit. Research by Carless (2005) found that both P–O and P–J fit were positively linked to attraction – the perception that an organization was a desirable place to work. However, P–J fit becomes more important in relation to a candidate's intention to accept a job offer, suggesting that once applicants move toward job acceptance, they become more concerned with how they will use their abilities than with working in an organization that matches their values. There is also the issue of person–team fit (Hollenbeck, 2000), which considers how people can be matched to variations in organizational structure. For example, in a decentralized structure in which the focus is on self-managing teams, different characteristics might be required compared with more centralized or departmental structures.

This analysis of attraction, based on images and congruence of values, and then use of abilities, has been complicated by recent concerns about attracting a more diverse workforce. Recent changes in legislation have also set limits on the expression of values. For example, images used in advertisements for recruits need to take into consideration possible discrimination against older applicants.

Recruitment channels

The main means of attracting applicants can be summarised as follows:

- Walk-ins
- Employee referrals
- Advertising
- Websites
- Recruitment agencies
- Professional associations
- Educational associations.

Advertising and other recruitment literature comprise a common means by which the organization's values, ethos and desired image are made manifest, often in the form of glossy brochures. The utilitarian approach that focused on specifying job details, terms and conditions has been superseded by advertising that attempts to communicate a message about the company image, possibly over a long period of time through 'low-involvement' advertisements that seek to create awareness of an organization rather than generate recruits (Collins and Han, 2004). A good example might be the series of adverts for BT broadband, which clearly advertises a product but maintains ongoing awareness of BT as a brand and an organization. There has been a marked shift towards recruitment advertisements that are creative and reflect the skills normally used in product marketing. Recruitment advertising is now fully established within mainstream advertising.

HRM web links

Go to www.makeupyourownmind.co.uk/quality-scouts-home.html to find out about McDonald's Quality Scouts. What are the various methods used to attract applicants?

Over the last decade, there has been a rapid growth in online recruitment, e-recruitment having become another facet of the rapid progression of e-HRM. As a result, organizations are advised to consider the design of their websites and the terms that applicants might use to carry out job and vacancy searches (Jansen and Jansen, 2005). It has also been shown that the usability of a company's website affects an applicant's perception of a job (Cappelli, 2001), and that content features such as testimonials by current employees, pictures, policies and awards can affect perceptions of the organization's culture (Brady et al., 2009). Some companies use websites combined with 'smart phone' apps in recruitment.

According to the CIPD (2010c), 63 per cent of organizations regard their own website as their most effective method of attracting applications. The survey also found that 33 per cent make use of commercial job boards such as Monster (www.monster.co.uk) and StepStone (www.stepstone.com), although evidence from other surveys suggests that such sites can also attract unsuitable applicants (Parry and Tyson, 2008). Further research also found different attitudes towards commercial job boards in comparison to company websites, including the potential of reaching a wider pool of applicants and the convenience of the method (Parry and Wilson, 2009).

In many cases, especially at a time when there are more applicants than vacancies, online applications via websites can be a way of saving costs in recruitment and also allowing a faster response and turnaround. Although cost saving is clearly a major benefit, some companies see online recruitment more strategically. For example, when Whitbread faced the problem of recruiting managers for its 400-site Brewsters and Brewers Fayre restaurant business, it developed its own recruitment website. The site was searched over 100,000 times in the first 4 months, with 1300 applications. This enabled the company to build a database and maintain contact with potential candidates. Another benefit to the company was its ability to establish consistency in its brand to potential employees (Smethurst, 2004).

As online recruitment has developed, it has been accompanied by the use of tools for filtering applicants and tools for starting the selection process (Parry and Tyson, 2008), probably much valued by employers during a recession when the ratio of applications to positions available will be high. Pollitt (2008) reports the approach of the mobile phone company 3, who work with a commercial e-recruitment operator that provides five online 'gateways' for both external and internal recruitment. Applicants can view video clips of employees talking about working for 3, as well as upload their details and create e-mail alerts for jobs that become available. They can also monitor the progress of any application made and receive messages on their mobile phone.

HRM web links

Check the services provided by ActiveRecruiter at www.taleo.com/solutions/recruiting and Real Match at www.realmatch.com.

Reflective question

Go to either the British Airways website at www.britishairwaysjobs.com/baweb1, or that of investment company Merrill Lynch at www.totalmerrill.com/publish/mkt/campaigns/careers/index.aspx. How do you think these websites filter out those who do and do not wish to work for British Airways or Merrill Lynch? Did you take the interactive challenges? Does online recruitment increase the power of employers in the graduate labour market?

In the late 2000s, social networking sites such as Facebook and LinkedIn, and social media such as Twitter, have grown in popularity, and all of these allow information about vacancies in organizations to be shared. While informal 'word of mouth' information about jobs has long been recognized for its accuracy and effectiveness in employee referrals (Iles and Salaman, 1995), employees can quickly, through Web 2.0 social networking, refer their friends or contacts towards vacancies – although how useful this will be to an organization will depend on the value of those people's social networks (Casella and Hanaki, 2008). It is, of course, also possible for organizations to explore the public pages of network sites to assess the extent and value of a person's links or to find other applicants within a network. Research in Belgium suggests there is some interest among recruiters in the use of social networking sites, especially LinkedIn, but also the possibility that such interest will lead to biased decisions on selection based on profile pictures and personality as indicated by the person's presence on a site (Caers and Castelyns, 2010).

Internships or placements

One method of attracting applicants is through internships or placements, which are often used by students for work-based research as part of their programmes (Hynie et al., 2011), but also provide an opportunity for students to gain experience and increase their marketability. If students then take up positions within the organization, the organization gains through the motivation of students to work and in terms of savings on training and induction. Research suggests that experience gained from internships increases employment prospects and starting salaries. Where internees perform well, employers place more value on such programmes (Gault et al., 2010). Because internships and placement offer employers an advanced opportunity to assess potential applicants, a selection process is increasingly used, involving some of the methods we will consider below.

HRM web links

Explore internship opportunities and the selection process at www.graduatesyorkshire.co.uk/internships.

Visit www.palgrave.com/business/bratton5 to read an HRM in practice feature on the Co-op's internship scheme.

Job descriptions

A further manifestation of the image projected by an organization to which recruits will be attracted is a description of the actual work that potential employees will be required to do. The traditional way of providing such information is in the form of a *job description*, usually derived from a job analysis and a description of the tasks and responsibilities that make up the job. Against each job description, there is normally a specification of the standards of performance. A typical format for a job description is given in Figure 8.3.

In addition to a job description, there is, in the form of a *personnel or person specification*, some attempt to profile the 'ideal' person to fill the job. It is accepted that the ideal person for the job may not actually exist, and that the specification will be used only as a framework within which a number of candidates can be assessed. In the past, a format for a personnel specification has been the seven-point plan, based on the work of Rodger (1970) and shown in Figure 8.4. An alternative to the seven-point plan was Munro-Fraser's fivefold grading system (1971), as in Figure 8.5. In both forms of personnel specification, it was usual to indicate the importance of different requirements. Thus, certain requirements might be expressed as essential and others as desirable.

Both job descriptions and personnel specifications have been key elements in the traditional repertoire of HR managers. Over the years, various attempts

JOB DESCRIPTION

Job title

Department

Responsible to ...

Relationships

Purpose of job/overall objectives

Specific duties and responsibilities

Physical and economic conditions

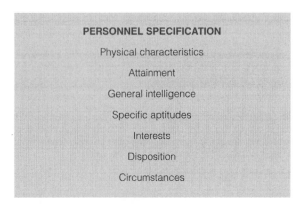

Figure 8.3 – Job description format

PERSONNEL SPECIFICATION

Physical characteristics

Attainment

General intelligence

Specific aptitudes

Interests

Disposition

Circumstances

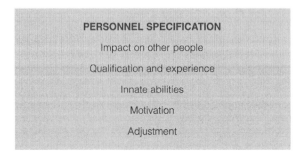

Figure 8.4 – Rodger's seven-point plan

PERSONNEL SPECIFICATION

Impact on other people

Qualification and experience

Innate abilities

Motivation

Adjustment

Figure 8.5 – Munro-Fraser's fivefold grading system

have been made to develop and fine-tune techniques and practices. One such development has been the shift of emphasis in job descriptions away from specifying tasks and responsibilities towards the results to be achieved (Plachy, 1987). There has, however, been a growing awareness of the limitations and problems of such approaches. Watson (1994) noted that job analysis, used to produce job descriptions and person specifications, relied too much on the analyst's subjective judgement in identifying the key aspects of a job and deriving the qualities that related to successful performance. In addition, the use of frameworks such as the seven-point plan may provide a 'cloak for improper discrimination' (Watson, 1994, p. 189). Current legislation on discrimination needs to be carefully considered in job descriptions and person specifications. For example, criteria set for physical characteristics might discriminate against applicants with a disability who in fact have the ability to do the job.

HRM web links

In the UK, ACAS provides examples of job descriptions and personnel specifications at www.acas.org.uk/index.aspx?articleid=1393.

The move towards flexibility and changing work practices has seen the appearance of new forms of work description. It is argued that traditional job descriptions are too narrow and may restrict opportunities for development and growth within jobs (Pennell, 2010). Some organizations have replaced or complemented job descriptions with performance contracts. These contain details of what a job-holder agrees to accomplish over a period of time, summarising the purpose of a job, how that purpose will be met over the time specified and how the achievement of objectives will be assessed. This approach allows job requirements to be adjusted by agreement between the job-holder and his or her manager. It also allows a clear link to other HR processes. Performance contracts signal to new recruits the expectation that their jobs will change and that they cannot rely on a job description as the definitive account of their work. Adler (Adler, N. J., 2002) refers to this reorientation as performance-based recruitment and selection.

As we have already discussed, competencies are used to create a specification of the characteristics of those sought for particular positions (Industrial Relations Services, 2003a; Roberts, 1997). It has been argued (Feltham, 1992) that the use of competencies allows organizations to free themselves from traditional stereotypes in order to attract applicants from a variety of sources. Stereotypes of the ideal person may be contained within personnel specifications, and organizations may, despite warnings, be reinforcing the stereotype in their recruitment practices. Competencies appear to be more objective, have a variety of uses in attracting applicants and allow an organization to use more reliable and valid selection techniques.

The test of success of a recruitment process is whether it attracts a sufficient number of applicants of the desired quality within the budget set (Connerley et al., 2003). Traditionally, applications are made by a combination of letter, a completed application form and/or a CV. Increasingly, such forms can be submitted by email or completed online (Parry and Wilson, 2009). Recruiters might reasonably expect a number of applicants per position available, referred to as the recruitment ratio, thus allowing a choice to be made. Too many applicants may reduce the cost per applicant but add further costs in terms of the time taken to screen the applications. Too few applicants may be an indication of a tight labour market but may also be an indication that the values, ethos and image projected by the organization onto the market, including information on the work, as provided by job descriptions and specifications, are poor attractors. Recruiters need to monitor the effect of such factors on the recruitment process. If there are insufficient applicants from particular ethnic groups, too few men or women or disabled applicants, the recruitment process may indirectly discriminate and/or fail to meet legal requirements.

SELECTION

As we have seen, it is usual for an organization that wishes to recruit new employees to define criteria against which it can measure and assess applicants. Increasingly, such criteria are set in the form of competencies composed of behavioural characteristics and attitudes. Rather than trust to luck, organizations are using more sophisticated selection techniques. Organizations have become increasingly aware of making good selection decisions, since selection involves a number of costs:

- The cost of the selection process itself, including the use of various selection instruments
- The future costs of inducting and training new staff
- The cost of labour turnover if the selected staff are not retained.

The CIPD's research (2010c) on selection methods used in UK organizations showed that competency-based interviewing was the most common approach (78 per cent), followed by interviewing following the contents of the CV/application form (that is, biographical; 64 per cent), structured panel interviews (61 per cent) and telephone interviews (47 per cent). Other methods being used were references before interviews, group exercises and tests for specific skills, general abilities, literacy/numeracy, attitudes and personality; in addition, 42 per cent also used an assessment centre.

The configuration of selection techniques chosen will depend on a number of factors. As argued by Wilk and Cappelli (2003, p. 117), it is not simply a case of 'more is better'. Selection methods will depend on the characteristics of the work and the level of pay and training. It is also crucial to remember that decisions are being made by both employers and potential employees, even during a recession, and that the establishment of mutually agreed expectations during selection forms part of the psychological contract, which will strongly influence an employee's attitudes and feelings towards the organization (Herriot et al., 1997). According to Hausknecht et al. (2004), there are good reasons why organizations need to consider the reaction of applicants to selection methods:

- If selection is viewed as invasive, the attraction of the organization may be diminished.
- Candidates who have a negative experience can dissuade others.
- A negative selection experience can impact on job acceptance.
- Selection methods are covered by legislation and regulations relating to discrimination.
- Mistreatment during selection will put off future applications and may also stop applicants from buying the organization's products or using their services.

Reflective question

How would you react to a negative experience in a selection process?

An important factor is the perception of fair treatment, and this applies to both the methods used and the process as a whole, referred to as procedural justice or fairness (Gilliland, 1993). Bauer et al. (2001) have sought to measure the reactions of applications for jobs using a procedural justice scale relating to selection. Items in the scale include the job-relatedness of tests, the 'opportunity to perform', which is the chance to demonstrate knowledge, skills and abilities, the provision

HRM in practice: Trapped in the 'marzipan layer'

The *Sex and Power 2011* report by the Equality and Human Rights Commission found that the rate of progress towards gender equality in senior management had remained extremely slow, and that the process had even reversed in some sectors. Despite women starting on their career ladder often better qualified than men, after some years women either drop out of management or remain trapped in 'the marzipan layer' below senior management, leaving the higher ranks to be dominated by men (as quoted in *Guardian*, August 17, 2011).

This phenomenon, often referred to as the 'glass ceiling', has been attributed to both continuing direct discrimination (which remains unlawful) and more subtle indirect discrimination such as an expectation to work long hours that clashes with family responsibilities (a clash still less likely to be experienced by men).

A good example of the way these pressures permeate a whole organizational culture is shown by Jacqueline Watts' examination of women civil engineers in the extremely male world of the construction industry (Watts, 2009). When newcomers who are different (in their gender or ethnicity) join an existing group, one response is what is called 'boundary heightening', in which the majority deliberately emphasize their group characteristics. Thus, when a woman enters predominantly male territory such as a building site, the amount of sexual innuendo and jokes or displayed pornography may actually increase. Similarly, in the setting of the boardroom, the pre-business conversation may be devoted to male sports interests, effectively excluding the sole woman present.

Watts' women engineers all remarked on the expectation that they would work long hours (the general feeling that 'hard working means long working') and on the predominantly male management style; this was seen by the women respondents as authoritarian and top-down compared with their own preferred style of more inclusive, participative management. When on site and faced with the boundary-heightening behaviour described above, the women engineers felt compelled to defeminize their clothing and appearance (no make-up or heels) 'otherwise you'd never survive'. All, however, found the heightened visibility, sexual harassment and intimidation to be emotionally draining, and this had led one participant to leave the profession.

The chances of resisting these pressures were seen as slim to non-existent: to emphasize work–life balance in the face of the 'heroic narrative' of staying late would cast them as slackers and open them up to criticism. The women felt they had no option but to collude with the male style of management in choosing, for example, not to voice any concerns they might have over staff workloads in case they were seen as less committed.

Watts concludes that:

Women managers experience challenges not faced by male counterparts because of the dominant masculinist ethos of corporate management culture that privileges men, ranks some men above others and places women on the periphery of the managerial class.

Stop!   The continued exclusion of women from senior decision-making roles is clearly a huge waste of talent and expertise. How would you remedy this, given that the equality legislation has had relatively little effect on the cultural pressures indicated above?

Sources and further information

See Watts (2009) for more information of her study of women in engineering.

Note

This feature was written by Chris Baldry at the University of Stirling.

Source: ©istockphoto.com/Peter Close

of feedback and treatment with warmth and respect. The scale could be used by organizations to evaluate the fairness of their selection procedures and the correction of problems. Positive reactions to selection can result in greater efforts to perform, which can in turn help organizations to identify the best candidates (Hausknecht et al., 2004).

Underlying the process of selection and the choice of techniques are two key principles:

- *Individual differences* – Attracting a wide choice of applicants will be of little use unless there is a way of measuring how people differ. People can vary in many ways, for example intelligence, attitudes, social skills, psychological and physical characteristics, experience and so on.
- *Prediction* – Recognition of the way in which people differ must be extended to a prediction of performance in the workplace.

Selection techniques will, to a varying degree, reflect these principles of measuring differences and predicting performance. Organizations may increasingly use a variety of techniques, and statistical theory is used to give credibility to those techniques which attempt to measure people's attitudes, attributes, abilities and overall personality. Some commentators would suggest that this credibility is 'pseudoscientific' and that many limitations remain with selection techniques. Iles and Salaman (1995), for example, claim that this 'psychometric' model appears to value:

- *Individualism* – in which individual characteristics are claimed to predict future performance
- *Managerialism* – in which top managers define the criteria for performance
- *Utility* – in which the costs and benefits, in monetary terms, of using different selection techniques are assessed.

Reflective question

What do you think are the implications associated with individualist, managerialist and utilitarian values in the selection process?

We are once again reminded that power is an important consideration when making decisions about employing people. Selection instruments often seem to be neutral and objective, but the criteria built into such instruments that allow the selection and rejection of applicants make up a knowledge base that provides the organization and its agents with power.

Reliability and validity issues

Two statistical concepts – reliability and validity – are of particular importance in selection. *Reliability* refers to the extent to which a selection technique achieves consistency in what it is measuring over repeated use. If, for example, you were being interviewed by two managers for a job in two separate interviews, you would hope that the interview technique would provide data such that the interviewers agreed with each other about you as an individual. Alternatively, if a number of candidates were given the same selection test, you would want to have some confidence that the test would provide consistent results concerning the individual differences between candidates. The statistical analysis of selection techniques normally provides a reliability coefficient, and the higher the coefficient (that is, the closer it is to 1.0), the more dependable the technique.

Validity refers to the extent to which a selection technique actually measures what it sets out to measure. There are different forms of validity, but the most important in selection is criterion validity, which measures the results of a technique against set criteria; this may be the present success of existing employees (concurrent validity) or the future performance of new ones (predictive validity).

Validation is in practice a complex process, and studies involving a large number of candidates would be required in order to allow a correlation coefficient to be calculated – in testing with criteria, this is referred to as a *validity coefficient*. If the coefficient is less than 1.0, an imperfect relationship between the test and the criterion is indicated. Even if the coefficient indicates such a relationship, a selection technique may, however, still be worth using: that is, you would be better to use the instrument than not use it. In addition, different selection techniques can be assessed in relation to each other according to their validity coefficient results. One difficulty is that it usually takes a long time to conduct validity studies, and by the time such studies were completed, it would be highly likely that the work from which some of the criteria were derived would have changed. Validity is also related to the particular environment in which performance is carried out. Such problems have not, however, stopped many organizations using tests and other selection techniques that have been validated by the test designers in a range of organizations or situations. (Go to www.socialresearchmethods.net/kb/measure.php for more details on validity and reliability.)

CVs and biodata

For many positions, applicants will be asked to provide a CV (a curriculum vitae, called a résumé in the USA and Canada), which enables them to set out their experience, skills and achievements. Importantly, it also provides an early chance for the organization to screen the applicants before moving to the next stage of selection. There has been interest in how selectors make decisions on the basis of information contained in CVs, and whether such decisions are informed by the criteria set out in the job descriptions and specifications, or are subject to personal bias. For example, would an applicant who attended a particular university be more likely to be selected on the basis of their CV? Proença and de Oliveira (2009) examined the assessment of CVs in selection and the reasoning used by selectors. They found some interesting contradictions between the use of objective knowledge and criteria, as set out in the formal documentation, and more implicit knowledge and emotion.

In addition to CVs, there is growing interest in information about a person's past experiences and behaviours in particular situations. This can be gathered by questionnaires including several multiple-choice questions and/or scenarios seeking data that can be verified as factual. Such information is referred to as *biodata*. Items can then be scored to predict against aspects of future behaviour such as job performance and absenteeism, results that have been shown to have relatively high validity (see Becton et al., 2009).

Selection interviewing

Of all the techniques used in selection, the interview is the oldest and most widely used, along with application forms and letters of reference, referred to by Cook (1994, p. 15) as 'the classic trio'. In recent years, with the advent of secure technology, interviews can also take place by video. Various attempts have been made to classify selection interviews, and it may be useful to point out some of the categories that have been developed:

- *Information elicited* – interviews have a specific focus and require information at different levels:
  - An interview may focus on facts. The style of the interview will be direct, based on a question and answer session.
  - An interview may focus on subjective information once the factual information has been obtained.
  - There may also be a focus on underlying attitudes, requiring intensive probing techniques and usually involving qualified psychologists.
- *Structure* – interviews may vary from the completely structured, based on planned questions and responses, to the unstructured, allowing complete spontaneity for the applicant and little control for the interviewer. A compromise between the two extremes is most likely, the interviewer maintaining control by the use of guided questions but allowing free expression on relevant topics.
- *Order and involvement* – the need to obtain different kinds of information may mean the involvement of more than one interviewer. Applicants may be interviewed serially or by a panel.

The selection interview has been the subject of much review and research over the past 60 years. During much of that time, overall results on the validity and reliability of interviews have been disappointing. In 1949, Wagner carried out the first comprehensive review of research associated with the employment interview. Wagner noted that, in the 174 sets of ratings that were reported, the reliability ranged from a correlation coefficient (r) of 0.23 to one of 0.97, with a median value of $r = 0.57$. Validity, from the 222 results obtained, ranged from $r = 0.09$ to $r = 0.94$, with a median of $r = 0.27$ (Wagner, 1949). Wagner considered such results to be unsatisfactory. This pattern of low-validity results continued in other research for the next four decades. In their review, for example, Ulrich and Trumbo (1965) agreed that the interview seemed to be deficient in terms of reliability and validity, and they were forced to conclude that judgements about overall suitability for employment should be made by other techniques.

There have been two lines of research to examine the reasons behind such poor results for the selection interview. The first focuses on how interviewers process information that leads to a decision on acceptance or rejection. The second focuses on the skills of effective interviewing. Table 8.2 outlines a summary of this research.

By 1982, Arvey and Campion (1982) were able to report less pessimism about reliability and validity when interviews were conducted by boards (panels) and based on job analysis and job information. In particular, reference was made to the success of *situational interviews* (Latham et al., 1980). In these, interview questions are derived from systematic job analysis based on a critical incident technique (see Flanagan, 1954). Questions focus on descriptions of what an applicant would do in a series of situations. Responses are judged against benchmark answers that identify poor, average or excellent employees.

In addition to situational interviews, Harris (1989) reported on other developments in interview format that relied on job analysis. These included *behaviour description interviews*, which assess past behaviour in various situations, and *comprehensive structured interviews*, which contain different types of question, for example situational, job knowledge, job simulation and work requirements. Such developments have resulted in an enhanced effectiveness of the selection interview and improved scores for reliability and validity. To achieve the benefits of such improvements,

HRM and globalization: Unpacking the meaning of credentials

In a fascinating new study of higher education in the USA, sociologist Ann Mullen writes 'we need to look not just at *who* goes to college, but at who goes *where* to college' (Mullen, 2010, p. 5). The main thrust of her argument is that even though more and more students are attending college and earning credentials, post-secondary education in the USA remains highly stratified. Even when students graduate with the same credential (the baccalaureate or bachelor's degree), its value and prestige will depend on the institution that awarded it.

Mullen's analysis alerts us to a challenge in employee recruitment. What do credentials stand for? At first glance, they appear to solve the problem of globalizing markets for educated labour. Employers seem justified in believing that knowledge and skill would be similar between similar credentials earned in different countries. But if the meaning of the same credential varies within a developed country such as the USA, as Mullen suggests, one must obviously proceed cautiously when attempting to evaluate the meaning of credentials earned in different countries.

As a starting point, it is helpful briefly to consider different theories of credentialism. Steven Brint provides an overview starting with a definition: 'By credentialism, I mean the monopolization of access to rewarding jobs and economic opportunities by the holders of educational degrees and certificates' (Brint, 2006, p. 166). He then proceeds to review various criticisms of credentialism. Many of these criticisms focus on the question of whether credentials are 'information-rich': does the possession of a credential tell us whether a person has the knowledge and skill that will enable them to perform the tasks and duties of a particular job? If the answer is 'yes', they are indeed information-rich.

But perhaps credentials are not information-rich in the way suggested above. Perhaps they just tell us that a person is trainable (or educable): the person has qualities of attentiveness and perseverance that will enable them to learn on the job. Or perhaps credentials are merely signals of a person's social background: an employer may believe that a particular university produces upper-class applicants who are a better 'fit' for the organization. Here, credentials are not information-rich, at least not in the sense that they tell employers specific things about job-related knowledge and skill.

The question of whether credentials are information-rich becomes even more challenging when we are referring to situations in which HR professionals from one country are responsible for hiring credentialled workers from another country. This situation, which is becoming more common all the time, forces us to think critically about what credentials mean and what they tell us about the person who has earned them. To answer this question satisfactorily, we must know something about the education system in the country where the credential was earned, and this knowledge is often not readily available.

Stop!   The credentials demanded for access to particular occupations sometimes seem unjustified. Provide one example of a situation where demands for higher entry-level credentials are justified, and one example of where they are not. If such increased demands are not justified, why are they made?

You have been accused of discrimination for your criticisms of the credentials earned in a developing country. As an HR professional, how would you respond? What institutions have been created to evaluate the meaning and value of credentials?

Sources and further information

See Brint (2006) and Mullen (2010) for more information on credentials.

Note

This feature was written by David MacLennan at Thompson Rivers University.

Source: ©istockphoto.com/ericsphotography

Table 8.2 – Reasons for poor results from selection interviewing

Processing of information	
Pre-interview	Use of application forms to reject the applicant on grounds of sex, academic standing or physical attractiveness
First impressions	Decisions made quickly lead to a search during the rest of the interview for information to support those decisions. Negative information will be heavily weighted if the decision is rejection, but a positive early decision may lead to warm interviewer behaviour
Stereotypes	Interviewers may hold stereotyped images of a 'good' worker against which applicants are judged. Such images may be personal to each interviewer and are potentially based on prejudice
Contrast	Interviewers are influenced by the order in which applicants are interviewed. An average applicant who follows below-average applicants may be rated as above average. Interviewers may compare applicants against each other rather than against objective criteria
Attraction	Interviewers may be biased towards applicants they 'like'. This attraction may develop where interviewers hold opinions and attitudes similar to those of the applicant
Skills of interviewing	
Structure	Variations in interview structure affect reliability, low scores being gained for unstructured interviews
Questions	Interviewers may use multiple, leading, embarrassing and provocative questions
Listening	Interviewers may talk more than listen, especially if they view the applicant favourably. Interviewers may not be 'trained' to listen effectively
Retention and interpretation	Interviewers may have a poor recall of information unless guides are used and notes made. Interviewers may have difficulty in interpreting the information

organizations need to pay more attention to providing formal training on structured selection interviewing. This is, however, not always easy to achieve since untrained interviewers may believe they are doing a good job in predicting future performance (Chapman and Zweig, 2005).

The use of questions about past behaviour combined with competencies in selection interviews has enhanced effectiveness even further. Pulakos and Schmitt (1995) compared the validity results during the selection process for experience-based (or behavioural) questions and situational questions. The former are past-oriented questions and are based on the view that the best predictor of future performance is past performance in similar situations. Applicants are asked job-relevant questions about what they did in other situations. This contrasts with situational questions, in which applicants are asked what they would do in response to particular events in particular situations. Responses to both types of question can be scored on behaviour scales, but experience-based questions have shown better results with respect to predictions of job performance, that is, predictive validity.

These results can then be used by organizations with competency frameworks. An ICT company has, for example, a competency relating to 'managing meetings'. Interviewers could base their questions around an applicant's past behaviour in managing meetings by asking the applicant to explain what she or he did in managing a specific meeting. Follow-up questions can be used to reveal further features of the applicant's performance, which can then be assessed against the competency indicators. Research by Campion et al. (1997, p. 655) found that these were 'better questions' that enhanced the effectiveness of the interview.

Barclay (1999) found a rapid increase in the use of structured techniques as part of a more comprehensive approach to selection. In particular, it was found that behavioural interviewing was being used systematically, especially in combination with a competency framework. Further research by Barclay (2001) found that behavioural interviewing was referred to in a variety of ways in organizations, for example competency-based interviewing, criterion-based interviewing, skills-based interviewing, life questioning and behavioural event interviewing. It was claimed that, however it was referred to, behavioural interviewing had improved the selection process and decisions made, a finding supported by Huffcutt et al. (2001) in their study of the use of interviews for positions of high complexity.

However, these approaches to interviewing have not been without criticism. First, since behavioural or competency-based questions are based on past behaviour, there is an assumption that behaviour is consistent over time, allowing prediction into the future. This assumption can be challenged on the basis that people do learn from their mistakes and can learn new ways of behaving. Furthermore, it might be suggested that people also tend to behave according to contingent factors such as time, place and especially the presence of others. A second assumption is that the questions allow a fair comparison between different candidates. They might, however, disadvantage those candidates with more limited experience or a poor recall of their experience, even though they might possess attributes or ideas that are not revealed in an interview (Martin and Pope, 2008). Even though a structured approach provides a degree of control over the interview, it still might possible for applicants to prepare their answers in advance or distort their responses to create a desirable impression (Levashina and Campion, 2006).

It is interesting at this point to note that much of the progress in interviews as a selection technique has occurred where organizations have sought to identify behaviour and attitudes that match their models of employees to be selected. This has required an investment in more sophisticated techniques of analysis. It is agreed that traditional job analysis techniques allow the production of job models in terms of tasks and responsibilities; however, organizations faced with change and seeking to employ workers whose potential can be utilized and developed will increasingly turn to techniques of analysis producing inventories of the characteristics and behaviours, such as competencies, that are associated with effective performance in the present and the future.

One consequence of more structured approaches to interviewing, including the training of interviewers, is the impact on applicants' reactions. A review by Posthuma et al. (2002) reported growing research interest in such reactions, generally showing that applicants prefer interviews compared with other selection instruments – the interview had greater *face validity* – which concerns whether applicants judge selection techniques to be related to the job (Smither et al., 1993).

One interesting dilemma, however, emerges for organizations – should the interview focus on establishing a good relationship with an applicant to elicit a positive reaction from the candidate about the selection process, or should the interview be concerned with using good structure and sophisticated questions that have higher predictive validity? In their research, Chapman and Zweig (2005, p. 697) found that this tension exists, with some interviewers preferring less structure in favour of building a rapport that 'potentially contaminates an otherwise standardized procedure'. Organizations need to recognize that the interview is a source of anxiety for applicants, inevitably affecting their performance. The danger is that an anxiety-affected interview performance may mask an applicant's ability to perform the job (McCarthy and Goffin, 2004). In addition, applicants' self-evaluation can impact on their perception of fairness and reactions to interviews in selection. Applicants who evaluate themselves positively are more likely to view the interview as fair (Nikolaou and Judge, 2007).

HRM web links

Selection interviews can be quite daunting for candidates. For particular guidance on competency-based interviews, try www.allaboutmedicalsales.com/competency.html.

PSYCHOMETRIC TESTING

Selection based on competencies and attitudes has been one result of the increased attention given to identifying psychological factors through testing, and to how such factors predict job performance. Testing, it would seem, offers organizations a cost-effective process in their search for the right people to match the company's personality. For example, during the expansion of the coffee house chain Costa, 1800 new 'team' members were sought. The company worked with a testing house to develop a team-member personality questionnaire based on the company's values that measured particular qualities, such as a person's achievement orientation (Dawson, 2005).

We can make the following distinctions between different kinds of test:

- *Ability tests* – these focus on mental abilities such as verbal reasoning and numerical power, but also include physical skills testing such as keyboard speeds. In such tests, there may be right/wrong answers or measurements that allow applicants for a position to be placed in ranked order.
- *Inventories* – these are usually self-report questionnaires about personality, indicating traits, intelligence, values, interests, attitudes and preferences. There are no right/wrong answers but instead a range of choices between possible answers.

Taken together, tests of personality and ability are referred to as *psychometric tests* and have a good record of reliability and validity. Most people have some fears related to any test, and this has caused confusion over the meaning, use and value of psychometric tests. The 1990s saw a rapid growth in the number of organizations using such tests, which was the result of more people, especially HR practitioners, being trained to administer them (McHenry, 1997). The CIPD survey (2010c) indicated that 44 per cent of organizations used personality/attitude/psychometric questionnaires, 43 per cent used literacy and/or numeracy tests, and 27 per cent used general ability tests.

Both forms of test provide a set of norms, developed from the scores of a representative group of people (the 'norm' group) of a larger population, for example UK adult men or women in a sales role. Figures are then expressed in percentiles, which allows for standardization. Thus, a raw score of 120 on a personality test or a section of a test might be placed in the 60th percentile, indicating that the applicant's result is higher than that of 60 per cent of the norm group but less than the score obtained by 40 per cent of the group. If the test had good predictive validity, this would be a valuable indicator allowing a comparison to be made between different applicants. Inventories would also include some allowance for 'distortions' and 'fake' responses (Dalen et al., 2001) as personality tests are generally thought to be less reliable than ability tests. An important issue here is the extent to which a test might discriminate against particular groups of people, which can lead to legal challenges (Jackson, 1996).

Reflective question

A personality questionnaire contains the item 'I think I would make a good leader.' This was answered 'true' by twice as many men as women, implying that men are twice as likely to become good leaders. What do you think of such an item and its implication?

Ability tests may be of a general kind, for example those relating to general mental ability or abilities such as verbal fluency and numerical ability. In addition, there are also tests for specific abilities, often referred to as aptitude tests, for example for manual dexterity and spatial ability. Furthermore, there are tests for specific jobs, such as computer aptitude and sales aptitude (Toplis et al., 2005).

For many years, there has been a great deal of interest in the extent to which general mental ability and cognitive abilities can be shown to be valid in terms of predicting performance and can be generalized across a range of occupations (see Schmidt, 2002). For example, Bertua et al. (2005) sought to examine whether general mental ability and cognitive ability tests were valid predictors of job performance and training success in UK organizations. They did this by completing a meta-analysis of 56 papers and books covering 283 samples of testing. The analysis showed that the tests were valid predictors of performance and training success across a range of occupations, including senior managers. This was also the case for changes in the composition of job roles. The authors claimed that the results provided 'unequivocal evidence for the continued and expanded use of general mental ability tests for employee selection in UK organizations' (Bertua et al., 2005, p. 403).

HRM web links

The Watson–Glaser test measures high-level verbal reasoning abilities and is often used in selecting managers and professionals. Go to www.talentlens.co.uk/select/watson-glaser-critical-thinking-appraisal.aspx#description for more details.

On the personality front, there has over the past 25 years been growing interest in what has been referred to as the five-factor model as an explanation of the factors that determine a person's personality (Wiggins, 1996). The five-factor model – sometimes called the 'big five' model of personality – proposes that differences between people can be measured in terms of degrees of:

- *Emotional stability (neuroticism)* – adjustment versus anxiety, level of emotional stability, dependence versus independence
- *Extroversion* – sociable versus misanthropic, outgoing versus introverted, confident versus timid
- *Openness to experience* – reflection of an enquiring intellect, flexibility versus conformity, rebelliousness versus subduedness
- *Agreeableness* – friendliness versus indifference to others, a docile versus a hostile nature, compliance versus hostile non-compliance
- *Conscientiousness* – the most ambiguous factor, seen as educational achievement, or as will or volition.

Salgado (1997) sought to explore the predictive validity of the five-factor model in relation to job performance through a meta-analysis of 36 studies that related validity measures to personality factors. It was found that conscientiousness and emotional stability showed most validity for job performance, and that openness to experience was valid for training proficiency.

There are, however, doubts about an over-reliance on personality tests with respect to their use in predicting future performance, especially in relation to complex tasks such as management. Within the five-factor model, for example, conscientiousness has been highlighted as a predictor of overall job performance. However, a study by Robertson et al. (2000) attempted to test the link between conscientiousness and the performance of 453 managers in five different companies. The results showed no overall statistical relationship, although there was a link with particular performance factors such as being organized and being quality-driven. It was also found that there might be an inverse relationship between conscientiousness and promotability. This result supports the view that suitability for complex work cannot be assessed on the basis of a narrow measurement of a psychological profile.

This situation also applies to the assessment of intelligence. Ceci and Williams (2000) suggest that the measurement of intelligence, although used in various ways by HR departments, does have drawbacks if such measurement is based on the assumption of intelligence as a fixed property of individuals. They argue that intelligent behaviour such as complex thinking is strongly connected to the setting, composed of the task, the location and the other people involved.

Limitations on the value of intelligence, as measured by intelligence quotient tests, as a predictor have led to a growing interest in the assessment of another kind of intelligence based on feelings, sensing others' feelings and the ability to perform at one's best in relationship with others. This is referred to as *emotional intelligence* (Dulewicz and Higgs, 2000), and there is mounting evidence that employers are attempting to utilize this view of intelligence in their competency frameworks (Miller et al., 2001). Emotional intelligence has been popularized by the work of Daniel Goleman (2006), who divides emotional intelligence into five emotional competencies:

- The ability to identify and name one's emotional states and to understand the link between emotions, thought and action
- The capacity to manage one's emotional states – to control emotions or to shift undesirable emotional states to more adequate ones
- The ability to enter into emotional states (at will) associated with a drive to achieve and be successful
- The capacity to read, be sensitive to and influence other people's emotions
- The ability to enter and sustain satisfactory interpersonal relationships.

Partly as consequence of the interest in emotional intelligence, efforts have been made to develop a test with valid and reliable psychometric properties. For example, Akerjordet and Severinsson (2009) describe the design of an Emotional Intelligence Scale and an Emotional Reactions and Thoughts Scale for use in maternity care. Interestingly, they suggested that self-reporting might pose difficulties.

HRM web links

Find out more about emotional intelligence tests at www.haygroup.com/ww/services/index.aspx?id=1566. You can try a test online at www.ivillage.co.uk/test-your-emotional-intelligence-eq/74101.

Self-reporting in the completion of tests is a key issue considered by Morgeson et al. (2007a), who provide a fascinating review of personality testing based on the author's considerable experience and expertise in the field. They conclude that, in view of the self-reporting process that most tests employ, faking should not only be expected, but could also actually be seen as an ability that could be useful in certain situations. They highlight the generally low validity figures for such tests, suggesting that measures which are more job-related carry greater face validity because the results can be explained more easily. They also suggest a need for an alternative to self-report measures.

An interesting finding about tests is that academics' debates on validity are not especially significant for practitioners, who tend to choose tests because they are well-known (Furnham, 2008). This means that the most popular tests are the:

- Myers–Briggs Type Indicator (www.myersbriggs.org/my-mbti-personality-type/mbti-basics)
- 16PF Questionnaire (www.ipat.com/about/16pf/Pages/default.aspx)
- Belbin Team Role (www.belbin.com/rte.asp?id=8)
- Occupational Personality Questionnaire (www.shl.com/assets/resources/OPQ-UK.pdf).

Online testing

Online testing is also being used for selection and other HR purposes, this being referred to as e-assessment. One feature of testing is to provide a filter for organizations in order to reduce the number of unsuitable candidates (Czerny, 2004), although such a process may also screen out good applicants. A CIPD (2010c) survey found that 32 per cent of organizations were using preapplication elimination/progression questions, and most of this would have occurred online. The banking organization Lloyds TSB, for example, has an online application form based on its competency framework; this acts as the first stage in filtering applicants. For the second stage, there is a 20-minute numerical reasoning test, also completed online (Pollitt, 2005). The results of this test are then scored electronically, and this feeds into the bank's recruitment management system.

It is claimed that online testing provides organizations with the ability to test at any time and any place in the world, with the added benefit of being able to process the applicants quickly (Lievens and Harris, 2003). Furthermore, as tests are taken, the

Online testing, or e-assessment, is a popular form of candidate selection, especially in the early stages of recruitment, when it can be used to filter out applicants.
Source: ©istockphoto.com/webphotographeer

results can be accumulated and used to improve the validity of the tests. There might even be a correlation between performance in online tests and successful learning at work. One difficulty, however, is that there is a loss of control over the administration of a test; thus, you can take a test at any time and in any place in the world – but also with anyone else to help. Toplis et al. (2005, p. 52) pose the question, 'How do you know who is responding to the test at the end of the line?' There is, however, interest in comparing Internet testing with traditional paper and pencil testing. One issue, for example, is whether a person has an understanding of computers, which can affect the perceptions of a test (Weichman and Ryan, 2003).

Potosky and Bobko (2004) compared the responses of 65 students to Internet and paper and pencil versions of untimed and timed tests. They also assessed the students' understanding of computers in advance of the process and their reactions at the end. One interesting finding was the issue of timing; that is, it was reported that time on the Internet (virtual time) was different from actual time. This affected the time to find and read the instructions or the time to download a test online. The appearance of a test is also affected online, with fewer items being seen compared with a full paper test. This may also affect the order in which items are responded to since it is easier to move around a paper test compared with its online counterpart. The results showed interesting differences in test performance between the Internet and paper and pencil versions on the timed test. For the untimed test, there was little difference.

Another issue is the perception of efficiency and user-friendliness of the website in taking tests online. For example, sites that are difficult to navigate will affect applicants' overall satisfaction , especially in the earlier stages of selection (Sylva and Mol, 2009).

Reflective question

How do you feel about taking a test online?

Whatever developments occur in the use of e-assessment in recruitments, all tests need to conform to the requirements of discrimination laws. In the UK, tests should be endorsed by the British Psychological Society, which will check for any sexual and ethnic bias within the test. In addition to this endorsement, the impact of tests needs to be followed up and monitored to ensure that a test does not result in discrimination in practice against one sex or particular ethnic groups.

HRM web links

You can find many tests to take yourself – without applying for a job. Go to www.myskillsprofile.com/index. php?partnerid=2221. From there, for example, you can take an online emotional intelligence test at www.myskillsprofile. com/instructions/eiq16.

Assessment centres

In their examination of organizational selection practices, Wilk and Cappelli (2003) found that as the complexity and demands of work increased, there was a need for a variety of selection methods. The CIPD (2010c) found that 42 per cent of organizations used assessment centres during selections. Given the weakness of single measures, organizations can combine techniques and apply them together at an event referred to as an assessment centre. Such events may last for 1–3 days, during which a group of applicants for a post will undergo a variety of selection techniques. For example, in the case of Lloyds TSB referred to above (Pollitt, 2005), the last stage of the selection process is attendance at an assessment centre, lasting 24 hours (from 5 pm until 5 pm the following day). Candidates attend in groups of 12 or 24 and are observed by assessors as they complete an interview, a case study presentation, group exercises and a role play. They also complete a numerical reasoning test to verify the online test.

We can make a distinction here between development centres, which yield information to help identify development needs, and assessment centres, which are designed to yield information to help make decisions concerning suitability for a job. Assessment centres can also be used to select participants for training programmes, especially for leadership and management development, and to promote internal applicants to more senior positions (Thornton and Gibbons, 2009).

It is argued that it is the combination of techniques, providing a fuller picture of an applicant's strengths and weaknesses, that makes assessment centres so valuable. Woodruffe (2000) outlines four generalizations about assessment centres:

- Participants are observed by assessors who are trained in the use of measurement dimensions such as competencies.
- Assessment is by a combination of methods and includes simulations of the key elements of work.
- Information is brought together from all the methods, usually under competency headings.
- Participants can be assessed in groups.

Although there may be no such thing as a 'typical' assessment centre (Spychalski et al., 1997), the general methods used are group discussions, role plays and simulations, interviews and tests. The following activities were, for example, used in the assessment centre to select customer service assistants for European Passengers Services Ltd (Mannion and Whittaker, 1996, p. 14):

- Structured interview
- Perception exercise
- Communication exercise
- Personality inventory
- Customer service questionnaire
- Tests for clear thinking and numerical estimation.

The objectives for using these methods were to generate information about:

- The ability to work under pressure
- Characteristic behaviour when interacting with others
- Preferred work styles
- The ability to think quickly
- The ability to make quick and accurate numerical estimates
- Experience and aptitude for a customer service role.

The European Passengers Services assessment centre process was judged to be a success, underpinned by the objectives and standardized decision-making of the assessors. Candidates attending an assessment centre will be observed by assessors who should be trained to judge candidates' performance against criteria contained within the dimensions of the competency framework used.

There has been interest in assessment centres that measure dimensions of personality and/or behaviour, referred to as dimension-based assessment centres (Lance,

2008), based on the judgement of assessors while candidates complete the exercises. A common problem is that assessor ratings may be affected because there are too many people to assess at the same time during an exercise (Melchers et al., 2010), and this problem may become more difficult to solve when organizations attempt to save costs by reducing the number of assessors. One possibility is to focus more on interviews with higher validity possibilities that measure dimensions similar to those of an assessment centre, thus screening out applicants who score less well at the interview and reducing the number to measure at the assessment centre (Dayan et al., 2008). Another possibility is to use measurement dimensions that are more focused and specific to particular tasks, in contrast to measurements that are used across all exercises. This approach is a feature of task-based ACs, where attention is given to specific dimensions of behaviour for each task, which are observable in the outcomes of participating in that task (Jackson et al., 2010).

Reflective question

Have any of your colleagues applying for graduate training programmes been put through an assessment centre? What was their reaction to this process?

If your colleagues were to relay negative reactions to you about their experience of selection techniques with one organization, this might affect your image of it. Again, the question of face validity is important – whether the applicants feel that the selection techniques are connected to the job. For example, in response to the problem that an assessment centre lacked realism and variety, the accountancy firm Ernst and Young ran its centre in real offices, having candidates answer emails and telephone calls. This apparently made the organization's expectations clearer (Trapp, 2005). Kolk et al. (2003) found no difference to the process in terms of validity when they made an assessment centre more transparent to candidates by revealing, prior to their attendance, the dimensions of assessment that would be observed and used to make judgements.

Pre-employment activities

During recruitment and selection, even in times of recession, both parties in the relationship are making decisions. It is therefore important for an organization to recognize that high-quality applicants, attracted by the organization's image, could be lost at an early stage unless they are supplied with realistic organization and work information. Applicants have expectations about how the organization will treat them, and recruitment and selection represent an opportunity to clarify these.

Realistic job previews (RJPs) provide a means of achieving this by offering 'accurate, favourable, and unfavourable job-related information to job candidates' (Templer et al., 2006, p. 158). RJPs can take the form of case studies of employees and their work, the chance to 'shadow' someone at work, job sampling and videos, the aim being to enable applicants' expectations to become more realistic. One possibility therefore is that expectations about work and an organization can be lowered, allowing applicants to deselect themselves; however, for those who continue into employment, organizational commitment, job satisfaction, performance and job survival are likely to increase (Phillips, 1998; Premack and Wanous, 1985).

A key feature of RJPs is their promotion of accurate pre-employment expectations that serve to 'vaccinate' employees for when they are faced with job demands once employed. RJPs also serve to communicate an organization's honesty about such demands (Hom et al., 1999). For example, if the work is located overseas, there is a need for information about living in another country, referred to as a realistic living conditions preview (Templer et al., 2006). Research in Canada by Richardson et al. (2008) highlighted the importance of realistic living conditions previews in revealing non-work factors such as the well-being of the partners and children of those employees who live abroad.

What is clear is that recruitment and selection provide an arena for engagement between organizations and potential employees in which both parties develop an 'image' of each other. If managers fail to understand the mutuality of this process, they endanger the attractiveness of the organization and thereby threaten the organization's ability to recruit good applicants (Hausknecht et al., 2004). In combination with RJPs, organizations such as Siemens and DaimlerChrysler provide applicants with a link to current employees who act as mentors (Spitzmüller et al., 2008), and this can play a role in increasing attraction.

Case Study

WATSON AND HAMILTON LAWYERS

Setting

In England and Wales, the provision of legal services has been slowly moving in the direction of increased competition between law firms, prompted by changes in the regulatory framework that seeks to remove restrictive barriers so that clients can benefit. Many law firms, especially those which operate in commercial law, have already sought to enhance their position in the market by embracing marketing expertise and placing more focus on the achievement of outcomes that satisfy client requirements.

Watson and Hamilton Lawyers (WHL) is a medium-sized firm of UK commercial lawyers, based in the Midlands. Within the firm, there are around 50 directors who have an equity stake in the firm, with a further 60 staff who are professionally qualified as lawyers, 50 staff who are qualified as legal executives and around 40 support staff including HR and marketing. WHL's strategy is to pursue a path of expansion and growth based on offering high-quality legal services to clients.

A key finding has been the recognition that around 80 per cent of fee income is generated from 20 per cent of clients, who are seen as crucial to the delivery of the firm's strategy in two ways: first, such clients need to be retained and, second, they also need to be the focus of the development of business relationships. Therefore, in a difficult market, the senior directors of the firm saw the retention of key clients and the development of opportunities for future business with clients as paramount. Following research, a number of crucial behaviours and actions that needed to be enacted were identified (see the table). Once such behaviours had been identified, it was recognized that they could be used in a variety of ways at WHL, such as:

○ In selecting new staff
○ In assessing the potential of lawyers for future development, including self-assessment and development

It is vital for WHL that its employees develop and maintain good business relationships with their clients.
Source: ©istockphoto.com/Alexander Raths

Retaining clients	Developing opportunities for future business
1.1 Establishing contact	2.1 Working in partnership
1.2 Attending to needs and requirements	2.2 Delivering a quality service
1.3 Making the relationship work	2.3 Nurturing
1.4 Building value	2.4 Seeing the opportunities
1.5 Adding value	2.5 Exploiting those opportunities

- For senior staff coaching and developing more junior staff
- In setting targets and goals for development
- In reviewing progress against targets
- As a common language for the firm to talk about performance.

The problem

Soon after the development of these behaviours, it became obvious that recruitment and selection procedures would need to change. The firm had a poor history relating to these areas, particularly in relation to professional staff, who were essential for fee-earning. Applicants were most commonly attracted through informal contacts, and decisions for employment were made on 'feel'. While the strategy and senior directors provided the parameters for decisions on recruitment and selection, managers were then 'given free rein', and most recent staff had been recruited on the basis of 'word of mouth' information obtained informally using 'field knowledge'.

Job descriptions (and personnel specifications) were not always produced, and evidence suggested that there was little involvement on the part of HR. There was no information on selection methods, questions used, criteria for assessing responses or judgements made on suitability. There was a 'perception of secrecy', with a strong possibility that decisions were biased towards the status quo and towards reinforcing the culture within a department.

There was apparent confusion over responsibility for determining vacancies for fee-earning staff and over how potential applicants were identified, especially with respect to the use of 'field knowledge'. Given the importance of behaviours relating to retaining clients and developing opportunities for future business, those involved in selection seemed to have little understanding of such requirements for fee-earners, nor were they using selection methods to make such assessments.

Assignment

Working in a group or on your own, prepare a report that argues for changes to the recruitment and selection policy incorporating the crucial behaviours of retaining clients and developing opportunities for future business. Explain how the 'perception of secrecy' can be tackled through a more effective assessment process based on these behaviours.

Note

This feature was written by Jeff Gold.

Visit the companion website at www.palgrave.com/business/bratton5 for guidelines on writing reports.

SUMMARY

- This chapter has examined the nature of recruitment and selection in organizations.
- The attraction and subsequent retention of employees is crucial to an employment relationship, which is based on a mutual and reciprocal understanding of

expectations. Employers have, however, significant power in recruitment and selection. The overall approach taken will reflect an organization's strategy and its philosophy towards people management.

- Recruitment and selection practices are bound by the law of the land, especially with respect to discrimination in terms of sex, race, disability, age and sexual orientation. In the UK, the Equality Act 2010 provides a simplification of discrimination legislation. Unless exempted by the provisions of occupational requirement, discrimination is against the law directly, indirectly or by harassment or victimization. The antidiscrimination legislation set forward over the past 35 years provides the foundation for a growing interest in diversity at work.

- It is essential that organizations see that, whatever the state of the labour market and their power within it, contact with potential recruits is made through the projection of an 'image' that will impact on and reinforce the expectations of potential recruits.

- Competency frameworks have been developed to link HR practices to the key requirements of an organization's strategy. Competencies can be used to form a model or 'image' of the kinds of employee that an organization is seeking to attract and recruit. The response to the image provides the basis for a compatible P–O fit. Images or the 'brand' will feature in recruitment literature and, increasingly, on the Internet via e-recruitment.

- There has been a growth in online recruitment as a form of e-recruitment, with recent surveys showing that 63 per cent of organizations regard their own website as the most effective method of attracting applications. Features on websites such as testimonials by current employees, pictures, policies and awards can affect perceptions of an organization's culture. Social networking sites now allow a sharing of information about vacancies and applicants.

- Key documents in recruitment and selection are job descriptions and personnel specifications, although there is a growing awareness of the limitations of traditional approaches to their construction. Some organizations have switched to performance contracts, which can be adjusted over time. In addition, personnel specifications may be stated as competencies, which appear more objective.

- Selection techniques seek to measure differences between applicants and provide a prediction of future performance at work. Techniques are chosen on the basis of their consistency in measurement over time – reliability – and the extent to which they measure what they are supposed to measure – validity. Applicants' experience of selection methods, especially perceptions of fair treatment, strongly influences feelings their towards the organization.

- There are a range of selection techniques, the most common of which is the interview, and this has been the subject of much research. Recent years have indicated that a structured approach and the use of behavioural interviewing based on competencies increase the effectiveness of interviews in selection. The use of competencies in selection is a reflection of the current interest in assessing personality and abilities by the use of psychometric tests. Techniques of selection may be combined in assessment centres to provide a fuller picture of an applicant's strengths and weaknesses.

- Online testing allows organizations to process applicants more quickly. This may, however, filter out good applicants as well as unsuitable ones.

- Applicants have expectations about how the organization will treat them, and the recruitment and selection process represents an opportunity to clarify these. The use of RJPs can increase commitment and job satisfaction by clarifying expectations and communicating an organization's honesty.

VOCAB CHECKLIST FOR ESL STUDENTS

- aptitude (n)
- assessment centre (n)
- attrition (n)
- coefficient (n)
- competencies (n), competent (adj)
- competing framework (n)
- curriculum vitae (CV) (n)
- discriminate (v), discrimination (n), discriminatory (adj)
- face validity (n)
- flagship (n)
- opportunity to perform (n)
- person–job (P–J) fit (n)
- personnel specification (n)
- person–organization (P–O) fit (n)
- pessimism (n), pessimist (n), pessimistic (adj)
- procedural justice (n)
- pseudoscientific (adj)
- realistic job preview (RJP) (n)
- realistic living conditions preview (n)
- recruitment ratio (n)
- reliability (n), reliable (adj)
- validity (n), validation (n), valid (adj)

Visit www.palgrave.com/business/bratton5 for a link to free definitions of these terms in the Macmillan Dictionary, as well as additional learning resources for ESL students.

REVIEW QUESTIONS

1 Who holds the power in recruitment and selection?
2 How can recruitment and selection support an organization's diversity strategy?
3 How can the predictive validity of the employment interview be improved?
4 Should job descriptions be abandoned in recruitment and selection?
5 'Appeal to their guts instead of just their brains.' How far do you agree with this view of graduate recruitment?
6 Are assessment centres a fair and valid way of selecting employees?

FURTHER READING TO IMPROVE YOUR MARK

Reading these articles and chapters can help you gain a better understanding and potentially a higher grade for your HRM assignment.

1. Selection techniques and methods have always been subject to criticism at a variety of levels, including measurement criteria, validity and reliability, decision-making and applicant reactions. For a broad-ranging review of the research in this area, see P. Sackett and F. Lievens (2008) Personnel selection. *Annual Review of Psychology,* **59**: 419–50.

2. A key issue in selection is the perception of fairness of the methods used. A very interesting cross-national comparison of procedural justice can be found in N. Anderson and C. Witvliet (2008) Fairness reactions to personnel selection methods: an international

comparison between the Netherlands, the United States, France, Spain, Portugal, and Singapore. *International Journal of Selection and Assessment*, **16**(1): 1–13.

3. Diversity issues are increasingly important in recruitment and selection. M. Van den Brink, M. Brouns and D. Waslander, D. (2006), in their article Does excellence have a gender? *Employee Relations*, **28**(6): 523–39, consider the recruitment of professors in The Netherlands, finding gender differences in terms of selection and recruitment procedures.

4. There is an interesting debate about the value of personality tests in selection. An argument in favour of tests is presented by D. S. Ones, S. Dilchert, C. Viswesvaran and T. A. Judge (2007) In support of personality assessment in organizational settings. *Personnel Psychology*, **60**: 995–1027. A response is provided by F. P. Morgeson, M. A. Campion, R. L. Dipboye, J. R. Hollenbeck, K. Murphy and N. Schmitt (2007b) Are we getting fooled again? Coming to terms with limitations in the use of personality tests for personnel selection. *Personnel Psychology*, **60**: 1029–49.

Visit www.palgrave.com/business/bratton5 for lots of extra resources to help you get to grips with this chapter, including study tips, HRM skills development guides, summary lecture notes, and more.

PERFORMANCE MANAGEMENT AND APPRAISAL

OUTLINE

- Introduction
- Performance measurement and human resource management
- The purpose and processes of performance management
- Performance, judgements and feedback
- HRM in practice: Performance target culture: 'I have been near breaking point …'
- Appraisal interviews
- Performance and development
- HRM and globalization: Mindset: how views of ability influence the quality of performance appraisals
- Case study: Robertson Engineering
- Summary, Vocab checklist for ESL students, Review questions and Further reading to improve your mark

OBJECTIVES

After studying this chapter, you should be able to:

1. Explain the purpose and uses of performance management, assessment and appraisal
2. Provide a model of performance management
3. Assess various approaches to understanding performance at work
4. Understand contrasting approaches to assessment and appraisal
5. Explain the use of performance management and appraisal in employee development
6. Understand the use of different performance-rating techniques

INTRODUCTION

Ever since you arrived at university or college, you knew that there would at some point be an assessment of your work performance. Whether in the form of examinations, assignments, group activities and so on, you have had the chance to demonstrate your capabilities and develop your potential. The results of the assessment are used in an appraisal of what you will do next. So, as in a workplace, your life as a student has to be connected to a performance management system (PMS) in which assessment and appraisal are crucial activities.

Of course, any information you receive about your performance rating as a student will depend on your response to feedback, which in turn will depend on the judgements you make about your own performance, or self-appraisal. Consider for a moment your reactions to the feedback you received on your last assignment. Did you regard the judgement as a valid measurement of your performance? Perhaps you might see more value in receiving feedback from people other than your tutors. You can make use of multisource feedback (MSF) from other students in group work, employers in job placements or even your parents so you get a 360-degree appraisal of your performance. And obviously it is not just students whose performance is assessed. In recent years, through the National Student Survey (see www.heacademy. ac.uk/ourwork/supportingresearch/nss), students have been able to provide feedback on the performance of their university or college as a form of upward appraisal.

Because performance management and appraisal are often seen as key features of an organization's drive towards achieving competitive advantage and high performance, such information can be used in goal-setting as part of a performance and development plan (PDP). In this chapter, we will explore the working of PMSs, especially appraisal and assessment, and seek to explain some of the contentious features that have, in the past, failed to find respect among employers and employees alike. The chapter will, however, also explore how performance management has the potential to reverse the negative images of its past so that it can become the source of continuous dialogue between an organization's members.

Reflective Question

How well does the PMS operate in your university or college?

PERFORMANCE MEASUREMENT AND HUMAN RESOURCE MANAGEMENT

Performance management refers to the set of interconnected practices designed to ensure that a person's overall capabilities and potential are appraised, so that relevant goals can be set for work and development, and so that, through assessment, data on work behaviour and performance can be collected and reviewed. This has in many organizations resulted in the development of an integrated PMS, often based on a competency framework (Strebler et al., 1997) .

At the centre of the PMS is work performance, in which the key ideas are that the principal dimensions of a person's work can be defined precisely in performance terms, allowing measurement over agreed periods of time that also takes account of particular constraints within the performance situation (Furnham, 2004). Measurement yields data that become information, allowing rational, objective and efficient decision-making that can be used in performance appraisals, objective-setting, assessment of development needs, regular feedback to individuals and regular review meetings (Chartered Institute of Personnel and Development [CIPD], 2009b). Through the use of assessment metrics that connect to business objectives, appraisal and performance management provide the possibility of matching human resources (HR) practices with organizational strategy. Performance management forms the nub of the strategic link between HR inputs and practices and organizational performance (Ferguson and Reio, 2010); it is also a vital feature of the development of high-performance work systems (Macky and Boxall, 2007) and the intent of sustained organizational performance (CIPD, 2009b).

Significant attention has been paid to setting organizational goals and directions so that business performance can be improved, and, importantly, to how such improvements can be measured. Based on the well-known dictum that 'if you can't measure it, you can't manage it', finding ways of measuring performance has become a major preoccupation in many organizations in both the public and the private sectors. All organizations have some means of measuring performance, and whichever methods of measurement are chosen, they are considered to play a key role in the efficient and effective management of the organization (Kennerley and Neely, 2002). Both now and in the future, performance data and indicators that can be quickly produced by information and communication technology are likely to affect decision-making in all sectors (Hatry, 2010), with a direct impact on how performance is managed and goals are set (Kagaari et al., 2010).

It is argued that measurement of performance is an indication of an organization's culture and the strategic thinking of its managers (Pun and White, 2005). Indeed, measurement is a crucial determinant of culture and what managers consider in their thinking. If, for example, turnover and costs are the key measures, these will form the indicators used in setting objectives for others and deciding how achievement is judged. Traditionally, of course, performance measurement has been based on accountancy models, with embedded assumptions relating to turnover, costs and especially profit – the bottom line. This provides an underpinning rationale for a 'control approach' to an organization's activities, including performance management and appraisal. It is argued that the control approach is an outcome of the drive towards rationality and efficiency found in our organizations, and in recent years perhaps simply of the drive towards survival, especially in small and medium-sized enterprises (SMEs). Such beliefs may certainly become part of a set of taken-for-granted assumptions that dominate life in organizations and may also be difficult to challenge. This is certainly the case for the HR profession, who have sought to provide a clear link between their activities and organizational outcomes, usually expressed in financial terms (Prowse and Prowse, 2010).

Organizational leaders, managers and employees are often unaware of the ways in which such beliefs are embedded in their actions. For example, much of the language of organizations, and many of the processes developed, can be related back to such a mechanical assumption of organizing. Mintzberg (1989, p. 339) argued that the form of structure called 'machine bureaucracy' has dominated thinking on how organizations should be constructed, and that terms such as 'getting organized', 'being rational' and 'achieving efficiency' represent evidence of this domination. As Mintzberg (1990, p. 340) wrote: 'I believe that to most people, what I am calling machine bureaucracy is not just a way to organize, it is the way to organize; it is not one form or structure, it is structure.'

Reflective Question

Does a mechanical assumption of organizing underpin how people talk about work? What effect does such talk have in terms of how judgements and decisions are made?

There have been growing efforts to prove the special value of *people* in organizations by measuring and expressing human resource management (HRM) in financial terms (Toulson and Dewe, 2004). This is a partial acceptance of the control approach that is implied in traditional accountancy models. There has, however, been interest in developing alternatives to a financial measure. An example of this is return on investment, which aims to identify value-drivers in organizations (Scott, 1998), such as customer satisfaction and loyalty, and intellectual capital – although the intangibility of these can make some value-drivers more difficult to develop. There are, however, measurement models that take a wider view, perhaps more strategic and long term, which encompass a range of values rather than just financial, and can stimulate continuous improvement (Pun and White, 2005). For example, the total quality management (TQM) movement, which emerged in the 1980s and is still prevalent in many organizations, provides tools and measurements to bring about lasting change. The idea of continuous improvement in TQM is referred to as *kaizen*, and there is a close connection to another system of continuous improvement and measure called Six Sigma – find out more at www.isixsigma.com.

The European Foundation for Quality Management (EFQM) 'excellence model' provides a way of understanding how the whole organization works based on nine elements of 'excellence', including people. Each element can be judged on a range of criteria, and improvements can then be planned accordingly. For example, one of the criteria for people is that 'people are involved and empowered'. Another holistic measurement framework is Kaplan and Norton's (2000) 'balanced scorecard', in which a variety of perspectives are considered under the headings of customer, financial, internal business, and innovation and learning. Measures can be set for each, and these can then be aligned with strategy. Managers and employees can subsequently develop their own measures in response.

Over the last 15 years, there have been significant efforts to reconfigure the value-drivers in the public sector through more measurement against targets. In the late 1990s, there was a shift towards a more a customer-oriented approach to performance measurement (Mwita, 2000), referred to as 'new managerialism'. A Best Value framework was introduced in England in 1997, followed by five dimensions of performance indicator:

- *Strategic objectives* – why the service exists and what it seeks to achieve
- *Cost/efficiency* – the resources committed to a service and the efficiency with which they are turned into outputs
- *Service delivery outcomes* – how well the service is being operated in order to achieve the strategic objectives
- *Quality* – the quality of the services delivered, explicitly reflecting users' experiences of the services
- *Fair access* – ease and equality of access to services.

The overall aim of Best Value was to encourage a reorientation of service delivery towards citizens and customers, and to produce a quality-driven organization (Sheffield and Coleshill, 2001). By 2008, the Best Value performance indicators had been replaced by nearly 200 National Indicators used to monitor and measure local government performance, but by 2010 these had been abolished as they were seen by the new UK government to be too much micromanagement. In parallel, Scotland, Wales and Northern Ireland had their own policies for local authority performance management – for Scotland, go to www.scotland.gov.uk/Topics/Government/PublicServiceReform/14838/564; for Wales go to www.wlga.gov.uk/english/wales-programme-for-improvement; and for Northern Ireland, go to www.doeni.gov.uk/index/local_government.htm. However, local authorities and the public sector as a whole then faced large cuts in budgets from 2010 while still being required to meet some standards on front-line services.

A 'not-for-profit' social enterprise is a business that measures performance against social objectives, and reinvests profits or 'surpluses' into projects that help the community or environment.
Source: © Lisa F. Young/Fotolia.com

Although the public sector is facing significant flux, some attention is being given to community and voluntary groups, of which there are many thousands throughout the UK. Even though such groups are also likely to face funding difficulties, there is interest in how volunteerism as performance can help to meet some of society's needs. One part of what is called the 'third sector' of businesses measures performance against social objectives, in which profits or 'surpluses' are reinvested in projects that help the community or environment. Such social enterprises have been seen as a source of creativity and responsible work that raise the standards of ethical and socially responsible business (Cabinet Office, 2007).

SMEs, usually understood as any business with between 10 and 249 staff (along with businesses with fewer than 10 staff, which are referred to as microenterprises), make up over 95 per cent of all organizations. For many years, there has been concern about their performance and their potential for growth (see Gold and Thorpe, 2010). Research suggests that most SMEs have little time for an analysis of performance, and that measurement is mostly responsive to problems as they emerge. This, for the most, means a basic profit and loss measurement to ensure survival (Garengo et al., 2005). It has been suggested that, by close attention to helping managers of SMEs deal with their immediate problems and concerns, more complex measures of performance can be introduced (Gold and Thorpe, 2008).

HRM web links

There are a variety of approaches and frameworks for setting performance measures. Try www.som.cranfield.ac.uk/som/cbp, the home page of the Centre for Business Performance, which researches the design and implementation of performance measurement and management systems. You can find out more about the balanced scorecard at www.balancedscorecard.org. There is more about the EFQM excellence model at www.bqf.org.uk/performance-improvement/about-efqm-excellence-model.

THE PURPOSE AND PROCESSES OF PERFORMANCE MANAGEMENT

There is considerable pressure on organizations to show that they are organized and systematic in their approach to the management of employee performance, and that there is a clear link between such performance and the organization's goals. The recent interest in talent management policies highlights the importance of ensuring that employees are able to use their talents effectively in the performance of work (Baron, 2009). In addition, effective performance management can result in increased employee engagement (Mone et al., 2011).

Activities such as appraisal and assessment have traditionally been completed in isolation and have not always been able to demonstrate their value to organizational performance. Therefore, during the 1990s, there was a growing interest in performance management to ensure that HRM could be seen as being vital to an organization's concerns, leading to performance improvement and competitive advantage (Armstrong and Baron, 2004). The adoption of a PMS represents an attempt by an organization to show a strategic integration of its HRM processes, which can together be linked to the goals and direction of an organization. However, this move relies very much on the role of managers and the quality of their relationships with employees (Sparrow, 2008), and it therefore represents something of a conundrum for HR managers. That is, the activities of a PMS, designed and assembled by HR, require the serious attention and commitment of other managers for their effective operation, and this cannot always be assured (Rao, 2007).

It is a strategic focus on business objectives that gives performance management its distinctive position in HRM (Baron, 2009), providing the link between the organization's values, performance and competitiveness (Boudreau and Ramstad, 2009). However, the degree to which strategic aims and a PMS are integrated is open for discussion, creating a gap between the rhetoric and the reality of claims for the contribution of performance management to organizational effectiveness (Stanton and Nankervis, 2011).

For example, according to a survey by the CIPD (2009b) of over 500 companies in the UK, there was a high level of agreement regarding the importance of performance management and the inclusion of regular review meetings (90 per cent), objective-setting (82.5 per cent), regular feedback to individuals (83 per cent), performance appraisals (82.8 per cent) and assessment of development needs (75.1 per cent). However, in reality such activities were not always completed – for example, only 62.7 per cent completed regular review meetings to assess their progress against targets and only 75.3 per cent set objectives or targets. Performance appraisal was more likely, at 81.3 per cent. The survey found a trend towards greater integration by incorporating talent management, developing potential, planning careers and providing coaching or mentoring as part of a PMS, although we can see the working of the conundrum that we referred to above in the responses on the impact and benefit of a PMS. For example, only 20 per cent replied that performance management had had a positive impact on individual performance, and only 19 per cent replied that line managers benefitted most from performance management. Just 37 per cent thought that performance management would help line managers to develop the capability to manage people better.

Reflective Question

Why do you think there is so much variation in the impact and benefits of PMSs in organizations?

A key feature of a PMS is its attempt to provide a link between all levels of an organization through goals, critical success factors and performance measures. An organization's goals will thus be derived from business strategy and translated into sector goals, departmental goals, manager goals and employee and/or team goals respectively.

Visit www.palgrave.com.business/bratton5 to read an HRM in practice feature on coaching for performance at Morrisons.

As Locke and Latham (2009, p. 22) have argued, 'Purposeful activity is the essence of living action', and people who commit to goals are likely to exert more effort and sustain it over time. At each stage, there will be an attempt to provide measurable performance indicators of the achievement of goals. Furthermore, in response to the dynamic conditions of globalization and technical change, there is a need to review and reset goals and targets through the year (Rose, 2000). A PMS will also provide a means of supporting performance through diagnosing development needs, providing ongoing feedback and review and coaching where required. In a PMS, the attitudes of line managers are crucial because they are the key actors in implementing the various HR processes in the cycle. The integrated nature of a PMS is outlined in the performance management cycle shown in Figure 9.1.

A PMS might incorporate, especially for managers, development centres, which are the same as assessment centres in that assessment tests and exercises are used to provide a report on individual strengths and limitations. Development centres do, however, differ in their emphasis on diagnosing development needs, leading to suggested development activities and a PDP (Ballantyne and Povah, 2004). Although a range of activities may be used, a development centre usually involves psychometrics

Figure 9.1 – A performance management cycle

and feedback from a qualified occupational psychologist, MSF and a self-diagnosis against the organization's competency framework. A PDP also includes an attempt to link the overall business aim with key areas of responsibility, the competencies that are expected to be demonstrated in performing a role, and goal-setting with measurable objectives.

Although development centres are concerned with development needs, their similarity to assessment centres may make it difficult to escape the tension between judgement and development that is a feature of all processes concerned with assessing and appraising people at work. Carrick and Williams (1999) suggest that development centres may, for some participants, result in the diagnosis of many development needs and have a demotivating influence. Because this may be the expected outcome for some potential participants, this may influence their decision to participate, and their overall performance if they do. As Woodruffe (2000, p. 32) warned, 'Assessment centres masquerading as development centres are wolves in sheep's clothing.'

Overall, there is a need for considerably more research into the value of development centres. However, some research carried out by Halman and Fletcher (2000) highlights examples of the tensions inherent in development centres and performance management more generally. This relates to assessment and performance. In their research, 111 customer services staff attended a development centre. Prior to attending, each person self-assessed his or her performance and was then rated by assessors as part of the development centre. The research revealed a variety of responses to self-ratings depending on whether participants under-rated, over-rated or even accurately rated their performance. For example, those who over-rated their performance tended to make little adjustment in response to any feedback provided, possibly due to their view that they did not need to improve their performance. We will consider the issues of ratings, judgement and feedback in performance management in more detail below.

Reflective Question

How do you respond to critical feedback when you believe you have performed well?

HRM web links

SHL is of one of the UK's biggest providers of development centre methods – see www.shl.com/images/uploads/cs_CocaCola.pdf for a case study of the development centre provided for Coca Cola.

Once a PDP has been established, according to the performance management cycle, work is carried out to meet the objectives set. There should also be ongoing coaching from the immediate manager and support for any training and development needs identified. Over the last 10 years, coaching has become a key activity managers can use to support change and development in organizations. Such is the belief in the value of coaching that many organizations seek to develop a 'coaching culture' (Garvey et al., 2009).

Objectives and performance are reviewed, perhaps every quarter- or half-year, in order to monitor progress and make any adjustments. During the course of the year, feedback might be obtained from different sources, this being used to improve performance as well as being fed into the end-of-year review, at which an overall assessment and appraisal might also be carried out.

PERFORMANCE, JUDGEMENTS AND FEEDBACK

A PMS can be used for a variety of purposes, which can be broadly categorized as follows:

- To make administrative decisions concerning pay, promotions and careers, and work responsibilities – the *control purpose*
- To improve performance through discussing development needs, identifying training opportunities and planning action – the *development* purpose.

Both categories require judgements to be made. In the first category, a manager may be required to make a decision about the value of an employee both in the present and in the future, and this may cause some discomfort. For example, several decades ago, McGregor (1957, p. 89) reported that a key reason why appraisal failed was that managers disliked 'playing God', which involved making judgements about the worth of their employees. Levinson (1970) thought that managers experienced the appraisal of others as a hostile and aggressive act against employees that resulted in feelings of guilt related to any criticism given. Such views highlight the tension between appraisal as a process to control employees and appraisal as a supportive development process. It is a tension that has never been resolved and lies at the heart of most debates on the effectiveness of appraisal in particular and, as we will explain below, performance management more generally.

The ability to make judgements about employees' performance that can lead to decisions about their contribution, value, worth, capability and potential has to be considered as a vital dimension of a manager's relationship with those employees. Decisions will be interpreted by an employee as feedback, defined as 'actions taken by (an) external agent(s) to provide information regarding some aspect(s) of one's task performance' (Kluger and DeNisi, 1996, p. 254). Gilliland (1993) have pointed to the importance of feedback that is timely as well as informative for a perception of fairness. What is particularly interesting is the way in which individuals respond to feedback or how people perceive the accuracy of the feedback received, referred to by Anseel and Lievens (2009) as 'feedback acceptance', which is based on the extent to which feedback confirms how people see themselves.

There is no simple formula for how feedback can be used to motivate people, even though managers may be quite convinced, in their own minds, that there is. However, we do know that feedback has a definite influence in terms of demotivation (Coens and Jenkins, 2002). Figure 9.2 shows the range of responses from employees to feedback on their performance at work.

Reflective Question

What motivates you to work? Make a list of these factors, and then make another list of what demotivates you. It is likely that the latter will be longer, covering a wide range of factors.

As suggested, the response to feedback can result in two possibilities: validation if there is agreement with the judgement made, or a defensive posture when there is disagreement. The latter is especially likely when feedback is negative or critical, and the impact on subsequent performance can also be negative.

DeNisi and Kluger (2000) conducted a review of research considering the relationship between feedback and performance. They found that, in one-third of cases, feedback had a negative effect on performance. As DeNisi and Kluger highlighted, when feedback does have the potential to help someone focus on what is to be done

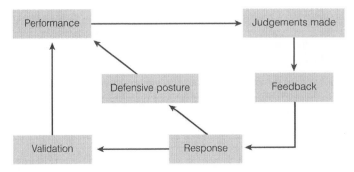

Figure 9.2 – Responses to feedback on performance at work

in performing a task or learning details, performance usually improves. The main danger, however, occurs with feedback that can have a potentially strong impact on an employee's view of 'self', for example self-belief and self-esteem. The response to feedback, especially critical feedback, is likely to be affective or emotional, which can be detrimental to performance.

Because of the dangers of negative feedback, Kluger and Nir (2009) have suggested a positive approach, especially in appraisal interviews, called *feedforward*. A win-win approach is adopted that avoids a retreat into defensive emotions by focusing on stories of experience from work that can look forward to provide support so that performance can improve.

HRM web links

Kluger has set up a site devoted to feedforward at http://www.feedforward.co.il. The idea of feedforward is drawn from the technique of appreciative inquiry – see www.appreciative-inquiry.co.uk/?idno=4 for more details.

As well as feedback provided to employees on their performance, some might prefer to take a more proactive stance, seeking feedback themselves. Such behaviour may be undertaken in pursuit of a goal, as well as to provide protection for a person's image or ego (Anderson et al., 2003). Contextual factors such as the attitudes of managers and leaders can influence a person's approach to seeking feedback, and given the importance of feedback on each person's sense of self, there is growing interest in creating more open feedback environments (Anseel et al., 2007).

Particular problems for fostering a diversity agenda can arise from the basis on which many judgements are made in the various processes that form a PMS. PMSs are used for many purposes, including helping in decision-making regarding people's careers, the development they will undertake, the payment they will receive and their future direction in the organization. Well-documented patterns in organizations suggest that some groups suffer disadvantages in these areas.

For example, in the UK, around 40 per cent of the workforce, but only around 30 per cent of managers, are women, with far fewer women becoming senior managers or directors of organizations (Sealy et al., 2008). This is the so-called 'glass ceiling' for women, suggesting that there are limits on their progress in organizations. There is a similar problem for black, Asian and minority ethnic managers; figures here suggest that 10 per cent of the population, but only 6.8 per cent of managers, are classified within this grouping (Race for Opportunity, 2008). There are many reasons for this, largely relating to biased and stereotyped judgements about performance. As in

HRM in practice: Performance target culture: 'I have been near breaking point ...'

In February 2007, a 38-year-old employee at Renault's Technocentre came home from work while his wife and small son were on holiday and took his own life. His wife later told the French newspapers that her normally calm and poised husband had been pushed to exhaustion by his work to the extent that he was 'beyond sleep': 'he suffered from enormous pressure, bringing files home and waking in the middle of the night to work'. His was the third suicide at the centre in four months (*Guardian* Work Supplement, March 10, 2007).

Management has always felt the need to monitor employee performance, often setting desirable performance targets or offering target-based incentives such as bonus payments. However, when those targets become *minimum* performance standards rather than goals to be aimed for, the consequences of failing to reach them can be experienced by employees as coercive.

What is significant here is that the Renault suicides were not those of car assembly employees (where the stress and health consequences of intensified track-working have been well documented for several decades), but those of highly qualified engineers and technicians, working in a £700 million research and design plant set in 150 acres of countryside and with its own restaurants, bank and other facilities. The primary cause of the spate of suicides, according to the French unions, was Renault's application of quantitative production targets to the creative process.

It would seem that there has been a general increase in the spread of quantitative performance targets, first pioneered by F. W. Taylor over a century ago in the context of manufacturing, to areas of white-collar and professional work formerly characterized by a high degree of autonomy. Andrew Danford and his colleagues have examined the introduction of the so-called 'lean' management techniques used to achieve these quantitative targets into the UK Revenue and Customs Service (HMRC) (Carter et al., 2011). Lean essentially means 'doing more with less' – less time, less labour power and less materials.

Source: ©istockphoto.com/courtyardpix

When, however, these management techniques begin to diffuse into areas of white-collar work, problems can arise. In their study of HMRC, the researchers found that previous performance standards had shared normative understandings of how much case work could be completed in a given time period, and most staff enjoyed sufficient autonomy and job discretion to manage their own workloads within such broad parameters. The new 'lean' model meant the imposition of targets based on 'results' rather than on the quality of service delivery. Targets were generated by the introduction of 'time and motion studies', which involved lean advisers and line managers armed with clipboards and stopwatches, generating sets of optimum work cycle times. Line managers announced daily and hourly targets at team meetings and then conducted patrols, on the hour, to monitor individual performance against them.

Moreover, staff also had to meet quality targets. If one piece of work out of a large batch was found to be in error, the complete batch would be failed and the officer concerned could be publicly rebuked. When surveyed, just 1 per cent of respondents indicated they had felt 'very pressurized' prior to 'lean' management, whereas 63 per cent felt this way after 'lean' management had been introduced. One employee commented:

The job now is very stressful and I have been near breaking point several times since working under Lean. I never ever felt like this before. I used to love my job; now I feel at times like an empty shell.

Stop!   How useful are targets in boosting or maintaining output or service delivery? Is there any support for the view that although the negative consequences for employees are regrettable, they are necessary in order for an organization to stay competitive?

Sources and further information

See Carter et al. (2011) for more information on the HMRC case, and Bain et al. (2002) for a study of call centres.

> **Note**
>
> This feature was written by Chris Baldry at the University of Stirling.
> Visit the companion website at www.palgrave.com/business/bratton5 for bonus HRM in practice features on 720-degree feedback at Cadbury and coaching for performance at Morrisons.

selection decisions, distortions occur in how people and their performance are rated (Grote, 1996), such as when managers make judgements based on stereotypes and generalizations, demonstrate similarity bias (rating people who are similar to them more highly) and relying on first impressions or comparisons with others to make judgements.

One explanation for the occurrence of these distortions in judgement during PMS is provided by social role theory (Eagly, 1987). This suggests that social structures influence the roles that people can adopt and the behaviours expected. For example, if it is expected that women will become mothers, this will affect how the different genders are viewed in a PMS. As women leave work to care for children, this reinforces the consistent expectation of the social role of women (Diekma and Eagly, 2000), and even when women return to work, it is expected that there will be conflicts between family and work (Benschop and Doorewaard, 1998). As a consequence, women's performance at work may be less highly rated than men's. However, the recent trend of men taking time away from work for family has also been linked to a poor performance rating; that is, both men and women suffer the family care stereotype (Butler and Skattebo, 2004).

Reflective Question

Have you ever felt your work performance to be judged unfairly against a social stereotype?

APPRAISAL INTERVIEWS

We define 'appraisal' here as a process that provides an analysis of a person's overall capabilities and potential, allowing informed decisions to be made for particular purposes. It is a process that is central to the purpose of stimulating performance (Aguinis, 2009) and an important part of the process is assessment, whereby data on an individual's past and current work behaviour and performance are collected and reviewed. The process of appraisal is usually completed by means of an interview, once or twice a year, between an employee and his or her line manager.

As well as stimulating performance improvement, there are a variety of other declared purposes and desired benefits for appraisal, including:

- Improving motivation and morale
- Clarifying expectations and reducing ambiguity related to performance
- Determining rewards
- Identifying training and development opportunities
- Improving communication
- Selecting people for promotion
- Managing careers
- Counselling
- Discipline
- Planning remedial actions
- Setting goals and targets.

This potential list of purposes for appraisal has led to the view that appraisal is something of a 'panacea' in organizations (Taylor, 1998), although expectations and hopes are more often than not confounded. A recent development has been the link made in many organizations between appraisals as performance reviews and bonus payments.

Reflective Question

Why do you think it is difficult to meet the hopes for and expectations of appraisal systems at work?

When we consider the history of appraisal, it soon becomes apparent that, of all the activities comprising HRM, appraisal is arguably the most contentious and least popular among those who are involved. Managers do not seem to like doing it, and employees see no point in it (Heathfield, 2007). HR managers, as guardians of an organization's appraisal policy and procedures, often have to stand by and watch their work fall into disrepute. Although most organizations seek to complete appraisals in one form or another, often under the heading of Performance Development and Review, with normative guidelines and training available, there is evidence of a gap between such direction and what actually happens. For example, guidelines might emphasize a ratio of time to talk that is tilted towards the employee or appraisee, but research suggests that this ratio is in reality rarely achieved. Crucially, negativity is often the main feature of appraisal conversations, which makes the interaction difficult for the participants (Asmuß, 2008).

Remarkably, despite the poor record of appraisal within organizations, it is an accepted part of management orthodoxy that there should be some means by which performance can be measured, monitored and controlled (Barlow, 1989). Indeed, a failure to show that management is in control would be regarded as highly ineffective by those with an interest in the affairs of an organization. As a result, appraisal systems have for some time served to prove that the performance of employees is under control, or at least to give the appearance of its being so. As Barlow (1989, p. 500) has stated, 'Institutionally elaborated systems of management appraisal and development are significant rhetorics in the apparatus of bureaucratic control.' It is not surprising therefore that most appraisal schemes are underpinned by a 'performance control approach' (Randell, 1994, p. 235), which we present as Figure 9.3, with a focus on setting targets or key performance indicators linking individuals to an organization's strategic direction. As one manager in CIPD's (2009b, p. 14) survey stated:

> Ultimately there is no point doing performance management if it does not deliver the business objectives. It should enable you to take action at the individual level if people are pulling in the right direction ... everyone whatever level they are knows where their personal [key performance indicators] fit.

The idea of control may perhaps lie at the heart of the problem of appraisal in organizations, and this stems from the key points we raised above about judgements and feedback. There is always a danger in any situation when a manager has to provide feedback to employees that the outcome will be demotivated employees. The seminal study that highlighted this was carried out by Meyer et al. (1965) at the General Electric Company. Although this work was carried out in the mid-1960s, it is remarkable how the lessons have been forgotten and how the mistakes uncovered then have been repeated many times over in many organizations since.

Meyer et al.'s study looked at the appraisal process at a large plant where appraisal was judged to be good. There were 92 appraisees in the study who were appraised

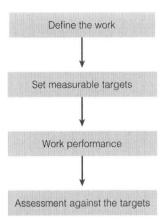

Figure 9.3 – Performance control in appraisal
Source: Adapted from Randell (1994)

- Criticism often has a negative effect on motivation and performance
- Praise has little effect – one way or another
- Performance improves with specific goals
- Employees' participation in goal-setting helps to produce favourable results
- Interviews designed primarily to improve performance should not at the same time weigh salary or promotion in the balance
- Coaching by managers should be day to day rather than just once a year

Figure 9.4 – Summary of findings from Meyer et al.'s (1965) study

by their managers on two occasions over 2 weeks. The first interview discussed performance and salary, the second performance improvement. The reactions of the appraisees were gathered by interviews, questionnaires and observation. It was discovered that although interviews allowed for general praise, criticism was more specific and prompted defensive reactions. Defensiveness on the part of appraisees involved a denial of shortcomings and blaming others. On average, 13 criticisms were recorded per interview, and the more criticism received, the more defensive the reaction of the appraisee. The study revealed that the defensive behaviour was partly caused by most appraisees rating themselves as above average before the interviews – 90 out of 92 appraisees in fact rated themselves as average or above. It was also found that, subsequent to the interviews, criticism had a negative effect on the employees' performance. A summary of some of the conclusions from this study is set out in Figure 9.4.

Since this study, there has in many respects been a long search to find a way of appraising employees that reduces the negative; however, we should not be surprised therefore to find an attachment by many managers to the idea of control in appraisal (Townley, 1994), and a perception by employees that they are being controlled by appraisal systems. Barlow (1989) took the argument further, pointing out that appraisal serves to make rational, simple and static a relationship between managers

Some critics have argued that appraisal attempts to simplify a relationship between managers and employees that is ambiguous, complex and dynamic.
Source: ©istockphoto.com/Anna Bryukhanova

and employees that is ambiguous, complex and dynamic. Ambiguity, complexity and dynamism cannot be eliminated in reality, and therein lies the falseness of the experience of appraisal. For many employees, appraisal is just not seen as relevant. The following reflects the opinion of one manager about appraisal, gathered in a field study in a sector of the petrochemicals industry (Barlow, 1989, p. 505):

> If we were asked for a good man, we certainly wouldn't go hunting through appraisal forms. We'd do it by personal knowledge and I suppose, to some extent, by rule of thumb. Appraisal forms are no use. It's what's left out rather than what's put in that's important.

When an organization seeks to implement strategic changes to improve performance based on principles of learning, communication and employee involvement, there is an apparent contradiction when appraisal is part of performance management, as this is oriented towards control. For example, Soltani et al. (2005) studied a number of organizations that were seeking to utilize principles of TQM. It was found that although there was a recognition that appraisal should match the requirements of TQM, there was little evidence of this occurring. Indeed, appraisal was often characterized as ineffective, based on high subjectivity that ignored individual objectives, and managers unqualified in providing feedback. These factors tended to work against the changes sought through TQM.

Generally, appraisal as an informal and continuous process will make the formal appraisal less isolated and less prone to negativity. It must, however, be acknowledged that, given the importance of appraisal in making judgements and decisions that can have a significant bearing on a person's future, appraisal is bound to be perceived as a political process (Poon, 2004). Employees who believe that their appraisal is based on subjectivity or bias and subjects them to unfair punishments are likely to experience appraisal as being of low quality, resulting in less satisfaction at work, lower commitment and greater intention to leave (Brown et al., 2010) (although in times of high unemployment, they may remain under sufferance). There are concerns about how bias and prejudice, albeit implicit, might influence ratings during appraisal (Wilson and Jones, 2008). In addition, older employees may miss out on appraisal and on any opportunities arising (Grund and Sliwka, 2009).

It is important that appraisal is perceived to be fair and ethical (Ilgen et al., 1979; Sillup and Klimberg, 2010), particularly with respect to what is called 'procedural justice', which concerns perceptions of *how* appraisal is conducted and completed rather than the outcomes of appraisal (Cawley et al., 1998). Research completed in China by Chen et al. (2011), for example, found that perceptions of procedural justice moderated employees' responses to appraisals. They found that if procedural justice was high, this increased employees' acceptance of performance goals, even if the appraisal was negative.

There is still, however, a tendency to associate feedback with criticism even though most people do their work well most of the time (Swinburne, 2001). One suggestion is that employees may not have realistic expectations about appraisal and perhaps need training on how to use feedback and take action (Cook and Crossman, 2004). Another approach is to work with the feedforward principles referred to above. Bouskila-Yam and Kluger (2011) report on the development of a strength-based performance appraisal and a goal-setting process that focuses on the patterns of strengths of an employee and how these can be expanded in the future. Weaknesses are not ignored but are minimized, so that a ratio of three positives to one negative is maintained to ensure positive energy and emotions (Fredrickson and Losada, 2005).

It is also possible to widen the sources of feedback. In recent years, for example, there has been a growth in the popularity of MSF (Smither et al., 2008), during which individuals receive feedback from different people, including peers, subordinate staff, customers and themselves. Where feedback is received from 'all round' a job, this is referred to as 360-degree appraisal or feedback, or – with variations – 180-degree, 270-degree or 540-degree feedback (McCarthy and Garavan, 2001; see also below). The growth in such approaches is based on the view that feedback from different sources allows for more balance and objectivity than the does single view of a line manager. We will examine MSF and 360-degree appraisal in more detail later in this chapter.

A further development is the move to online appraisal, probably a feature of integrated human resources information system processes or talent management packages. The apparent value of such approaches is the way in which information about employees in particular positions is stored against their skills and competencies (see www.peopleadmin.com/position-management for an example). HR managers can also monitor the completion of appraisals and consider the pattern of ratings. Payne et al. (2009) compared employee reactions between those who completed online appraisals and those who used a more traditional paper and pencil approach. The results indicated greater participation in the process, in terms of completing self-ratings, by the online appraisees, but there was also a perception that the online process was of lower quality, perhaps because of the limited feedback, which lacked detail.

HRM web links

Because of the difficult nature of appraisal, a plethora of resources and training programmes is available. For basic advice on appraisal interviewing, check the Advisory, Conciliation and Arbitration Service (ACAS) at www.acas.org.uk/media/pdf/o/q/B07_1.pdf. ACAS also publishes a booklet on appraisal-related pay at www.acas.org.uk/index.aspx?articleid=625.

PERFORMANCE AND DEVELOPMENT

It is highly unlikely that the pressure for rationality, efficiency and control in organizations will disappear as it is a powerful force that underlies any organized activity. However, for a PMS to be seen as a driver of organizational performance, it also has to include an alignment with the organization's talent management policies based on people first developing skills and then also being challenged to develop themselves (Baron, 2009). This view, of course, provides a contrast to the control orientation of a PMS and questions the underlying principles that are required to develop a culture supporting and reinforcing the ideas and practices of high-performance HRM based on employee engagement, commitment and trust. This can be a painful process. It may, for example, be difficult to resist the requirements of financial controllers seeking to control costs during a recession. It is therefore no surprise that surveys continue to show ambivalent support for performance management as a helpful process for skill development and careers (CIPD, 2009b).

In a seminal paper, Walton (1985) wrote about disillusionment with the apparatus of control that assumed low employee commitment and mere obedience, reporting on a number of organizations that had attempted to move towards a workforce strategy based on high employee commitment. Performance management and appraisal can serve as the fulcrum of such a movement, although considerable difficulties can arise (Wilson and Western, 2000). The contrast between control approaches and commitment could not be greater for managers: the former involves a concentration on techniques, the latter a shift towards attitudes, values and beliefs. The skill for HRM practitioners is to acknowledge the importance of the former while arguing for a greater place for the latter.

Reflective Question

What particular skills are needed by HRM practitioners to argue for two potentially conflicting points of view, such as the need for control and the need for commitment?

A developmental PMS that attempts to harness potential would, for many organizations, mean a more inclusive approach to talent management (Iles and Preece, 2010). It has been accepted that discussions of potential and prospects for development have been confined to leaders and managers, thereby sending a strong message to the rest of the organization that only managers are worthy of such attention – with the implicit assumption that non-managers cannot develop.

More recently, attention has expanded to those doing key jobs in strategically key positions, referred to by Huselid et al. (2005) as the 'A' positions, but this still represents an exclusive approach to talent. Changes in employment conditions through the 1990s have meant that more employees are included in PMS and appraisals. This has also been brought about by changes in organizational structure in the 2000s that have sought to move decision-making to the point of interaction with customers and clients, and see such interactions as the source of creativity. This provides line managers with significant responsibility to ensure that effective communication and feedback are given to employees (Industrial Relations Services, 2003b).

In putting more emphasis on the development of potential, the suspicion that has surrounded control approaches may be reinforced, which should not be surprising as there has been pressure to shift the orientation for some time. As long ago as 1983, Harper suggested dropping the word 'appraisal' because it put employees on the defensive. He recommended instead a shift towards future-oriented review and development that actively involved employees in continuously developing ways of improving performance in line with needs, similar to Kluger and Nir's (2009) feedforward interview process referred to earlier. Moving in such a direction requires a more flexible approach on the part of line managers. It also results in inevitable tensions because such objectives might be concerned with immediate performance set against

HRM and Globalization: Mindset: How views of ability influence the quality of performance appraisals

What are the roots of outstanding performance, and how can performance be improved? These basic questions lie at the heart of performance management and appraisal. How we answer these questions depends on how we view the relationship between skill, knowledge and ability.

The work of psychologist Carol Dweck provides provocative new insights into this topic. Dweck (2008) argues that thinking about ability and performance tends to fall into one of two categories or mindsets. The fixed mindset sees ability as something you either possess or fail to possess. The growth mindset sees ability as something that changes over time. Those who endorse this latter view believe that, with good 'coaching' and plenty of practice, individuals can improve their performance on any given task.

Obviously a manager's mindset will influence his or her approach to performance management and appraisal. The performance appraisals of managers who hold incremental (or growth) views of ability will produce better results than the performance appraisals of managers who hold entity (or fixed) views of ability. One could argue that the dominant trend is towards growth views of ability. Indeed, performance appraisals should be getting better all the time!

Although this claim about a dominant trend may be plausible, it is easy to imagine exceptions to the general rule. In situations where managers cling to stereotypes about particular groups or individuals, we would expect to encounter versions of the fixed view of ability. This would be the case even in developed nations where women seek access to non-traditional occupations. But fixed views of ability may be especially prevalent in developing nations where traditional gender roles persist to a greater degree and women have yet to attain legal protection against workplace discrimination.

Consider the case of videographers working for a British company undertaking PR and advertising for multinationals that operate in India and China. Women represent a rapidly growing segment of the workforce in these two nations, and the HR team is seeking to increase the number of female videographers they employ. However, women who work with more experienced videographers (mostly men) typically receive low evaluations. The goal of increasing the number of female videographers seems out of reach. Questioned about the feedback and instruction they were receiving, the women made the following comments: 'Mostly he just criticizes me, pointing out the various things I am doing wrong. He never takes the time to show me what I might do to improve my performance. Often his tone of voice seems to suggest: "This is a waste of time; women are not suited for this kind of work."'

Stop!   What is going on here? How could the experienced male videographers be encouraged to accept a growth mindset? Would a change in mindset lead to better quality performance appraisals? Explain why.

Sources and further information

For more information on Carol Dweck and her ideas, see Dweck (2008) and also check out the website www.mindsetonline.com.

Note

This feature was written by David MacLennan at Thompson Rivers University.

Source: ©istockphoto.com/Paul Vasarhelyi

Figure 9.5 – Performance as a transformation process

current tasks and standards, but employees and even their managers might also be concerned with a variety of work and personal changes such as a change of standards, task, job role or even career.

Once employees have been encouraged to pay attention to their progress at work, the organization must be able to respond to their medium- and long-term aspirations. The manager's role will be to resolve the inevitable tension that will result between individual goals and the manager's interpretation of organizational goals. But how can data about employees be gathered for such purposes? Of necessity, there has to be a shift in attention towards the performance of work. This will provide a link to the value of a PMS as a means of recognizing employees via feedback on what they have done, and engaging them in a dialogue about improving performance (Armstrong and Baron, 2004) that considers the importance of trust and perceptions of justice (Farndale et al., 2011). In such a context, it becomes possible to identify how learning and development can help employees to meet their needs and aspirations.

The performance of a work task can be presented as a relationship between means and outcomes (Ouchi, 1979). The means take the form of the attributes, skills, knowledge and attitudes (competencies) of individual employees that are applied to a task in a specific context. The outcomes take the form of results achieved, which may be measurable either quantitatively or qualitatively against an explicit or implicit standard or target. Between means and outcomes lies the behaviour of the individual in a transformation process, as shown in Figure 9.5.

Although all phases of this process can form the focus of performance management, particular attention to behaviour in the transformation process will reveal how an individual has applied knowledge, skills and attitudes to practice when carrying out a task; this will include taking account of all aspects of the context, including time and place, machinery and equipment, other employees and other circumstances. For example, the presence of a manager might have an impact on an employee's performance. There is significant interest in this part of the transformation process, because it is in practice that new knowledge can be created (Newell et al., 2002). Research has partly focused on the importance of knowledge that people learn informally in practice, which is acquired intuitively and implicitly, often without intention (Sternberg and Horvath, 1999). Such knowledge is often referred to as 'tacit knowledge', a rather ambiguous term but one that is seen as key in knowledge creation as it emerges from practice (Nonaka et al., 2000a), and as a key feature of workplace learning (see Gold et al., 2010c).

We must also remember that practice occurs in a context, that contextual factors can have a significant bearing on overall performance, and that these need to be considered in the various PMS processes of managing, measuring, assessing and rewarding performance (CIPD, 2009b). Thus, attention paid to how an employee performs will provide rich data on that employee's current effectiveness and potential for further development. If, for example, we assume that an employee has been trained to complete a basic task, attention to practice in the transformation process will provide data on a number of issues. The first time she completes the task, an assessment of her behaviour will reveal nervousness until completion, when the results achieved can be compared against a standard. This nervousness can be corrected by adjustments to the employee's skills and practice until she has gained confidence. Further study reveals that, once confidence has been gained, the employee will perform with some sense of rhythm and flow that achieves a perfect result.

Given static conditions and standards, this is as far as the employee can go in this task. She can continue to perform with confidence, but after some time this becomes too easy. This feeling prompts her to ask for some adjustment, possibly at first to the work targets and then to an extension of tasks within the job. The important point is that ease within the transformation process, assessed by the employee and others, leads to developmental adjustments. Continued attention to the process may eventually result in a further range of adjustments, such as increased responsibility through job enlargement and job enrichment, and a reconsideration of the employee's future direction within the organization. On the way, the organization may benefit from rising her efficiency and effectiveness, including better standards.

Through attention to the behaviour of an employee in the transformation process, data can thus be provided for a whole gamut of developmental decisions over time, starting with adjustments to reach minimum standards and then addressing career changes and progression. Individual employees are able to set targets, objectives and goals for each stage through appraisal.

The focus on practice as the starting point for PMS processes is brought into greater prominence when we consider that many people now perform tasks that are knowledge-intensive within what is recognized as a knowledge economy and a knowledge society (Rohrbach, 2007). Highly skilled jobs require significant and ongoing learning, or life-long learning. Furthermore, such work often requires a response to unusual or changing situations, where on-the-spot decisions are needed with little time for considered deliberation. This is not untypical of professional work or work requiring high levels of expertise (Beckett, 2000).

A number of techniques have been developed that allow for a consideration of practice against the various stages of the transformation process. The ability to employ various techniques in performance management will depend on a number of contingencies. Ouchi (1979) has provided a framework specifying these and allowing for a choice to be made; Figure 9.6 has been adapted from his work. This framework can be used to reconcile the dilemma that organizations may face in performance management and appraisal, that is, the dilemma between the desire to maintain control and the desire to foster a developmental emphasis. Forms of control depend on the feasibility of measuring desired performance – 'the ability to measure either output or behaviour which is relevant to the desired performance is critical to the 'rational' application of ... bureaucratic forms of control' (Ouchi, 1979, p. 843).

In Ouchi's framework, if an organization either has high ability to measure outputs or behaviour, or has perfect knowledge of the transformation process involved in production, it could opt for a bureaucratic control approach and base appraisal on behaviour, output measurements or both. Thus, in cell 1, typical of traditional manufacturing and service organizations where work process steps can be clearly stated, both behaviour and output techniques can be used. Appraisal interviews or online measures can include ratings against dimensions drawn from a competency framework, with a focus on behaviour or outputs that can be assessed.

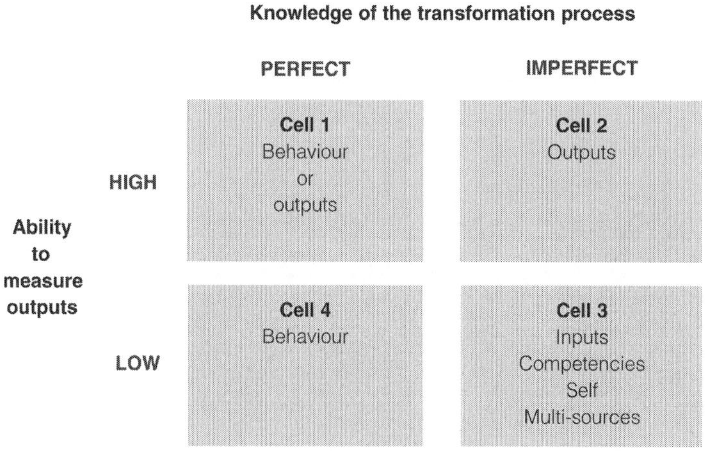

Knowledge of the transformation process

	PERFECT	IMPERFECT
HIGH	**Cell 1** Behaviour or outputs	**Cell 2** Outputs
LOW	**Cell 4** Behaviour	**Cell 3** Inputs Competencies Self Multi-sources

Ability to measure outputs

Figure 9.6 – Contingencies in performance management
Source: Adapted from Ouchi (1979)

In cell 2, only outputs can be successfully measured, perhaps because work processes cannot be directly observed; this may occur with field sales workers, for example. The key issue here seems to be how such outputs are judged and the criteria utilized. Research by Pettijohn et al. (2001), for example, which sought to understand salespersons' perspectives of appraisal, found that although appraisal was a common practice within sales management, there was some dissatisfaction with the criteria used. In particular, salespersons preferred to be appraised with respect to customer satisfaction and the product knowledge that lay within their control. The failure to include such criteria had implications for morale, turnover and overall performance. Even if outputs provide more objective measurement criteria, it is still possible for subjective criteria to affect how sales staff are evaluated. Vilela et al. (2007) showed how factors such as physical attractiveness and being in favour with a supervisor can affect the judgement of a salesperson's performance.

Approaches are now moving from cell 1 to cell 2 in areas such as police work (Shane, 2010), where performance appraisal has traditionally been based on a model of compliance and control that fits a bureaucratic framework. Instead, it is argued that there could be a stronger focus on what the police achieve, as indicated by empirical measures.

In cell 4, employees' behaviour can be observed, but outputs are more difficult to discern; this may be the result of groups of employees producing group outputs or measurable outputs over a long period of time, for example in research work. Particular difficulties occur when appraisal, which is inherently an individual process, is applied to a group or team – you may already have had experience of group work and the problems that occur when a group mark is given for assessed work. In the workplace, there may be variations of effort and variations in the skill required. There is also variability in the life of teams, some teams coming together for a single project, others working together over several tasks. In addition, a team may increasingly have to operate over different locations.

All this suggests that the performance management of teams requires a considera-tion of relevant circumstances rather than a 'one-size-fits-all' prescription (Scott and Einstein, 2001), including the situations faced and the beliefs and motives of team members (Chang et al., 2008). Van Vijfeijken et al. (2002) suggest that effective group performance management requires a combination of goal-setting and rewards based on group performance. This needs to consider the degree of interdependence between tasks completed by group members, the complexity of tasks and the interdependence of goals, which considers how one person's goal is affected by or affects the attainment of goals by others.

HRM web links

Team appraisal is often a difficult process. You can view a short online video on team appraisal at www.staffs.ac.uk/about_us/university_departments/personnel/policies/team_good_example.jsp.

In all the above cases, the logic of control may be extended to some form of performance- or merit-related pay system. In cell 3, however, there is an imperfect knowledge of transformation and a low ability to measure outputs directly, making bureaucratic control more difficult. Ouchi refers to this cell as a 'clan' based on a ritualized, ceremonial or 'cultural' form of control arising from shared attitudes, values and beliefs. Cell 3 would include the work of professionals and knowledge workers, as well as most managers and, increasingly, forms of work organization in which higher levels of discretion and autonomy are granted to individual employees. It also includes teams within a network, where expertise must be used selectively and leadership shared between team members (Friedrich et al., 2009). Behaviour, although difficult to observe formally, can be observed by those present at the point of production.

A university can, for example, bureaucratically control who becomes a lecturer through its selection processes; hence it is possible to assess 'inputs' through qualifications and other attributes. Once the lecturer is in place, however, his or her performance is much more difficult to assess and appraise. Some universities have used competency frameworks. For example, one institution is seeking to base performance management on an 'assessment of the outcomes and competence requirements established during the Performance and Development Review'. The difficulty here is the attempt to measure outcomes when the work is non-standardized. Furthermore, the use of competencies has been widely criticized as a reduction and fragmentation of complex work, but one giving power to those who seek to control such work (Gold et al., 2010b).

Consider further the work of professionals in the public sector, in which performance management and appraisal have been seen as a shift towards managerialist language and techniques. In response to deregulation and competition, often sponsored by central government as part of the trend referred to as new managerialism or new public management (Pollitt, 2000), there have been various attempts to curtail the power of professionals within the public sector and remove or usurp their monopoly (Exworthy and Halford, 1999). Research so far suggests the emergence of new relationships and a reordering of professions and management: head teachers, for example, require leadership skills that include the assessment of their staff. In the UK, the National College for School Leadership has been established with the aim of ensuring 'that school leaders have the skills, recognition, capacity and ambition to transform the school education system into the best in the world' (for further details, see www.nationalcollege.org.uk).

In the UK's National Health Service (NHS), with over 1 million employees, many of whom are professionally qualified, appraisal was developed in the 1980s and has been seen as one of the tools necessary to bring about a change in culture. Research by Redman et al. (2000) found that, after several years of experience, appraisal was generally valued, with particular strengths being the setting of objectives, personal development planning and, where they occurred, having quarterly 'mini' reviews. There was, however, also evidence of 'patchy application' (p. 59). Although there remains little systematic evidence of PMS in the NHS, such evidence as does exist points to the importance of feedback and participation in setting goals (Patterson et al., 2010).

Generally, the performance management of people whose work is knowledge-based is difficult to observe and requires a longer timeframe for measurement. Reilly (2005) suggests that one cannot impose performance management in such circumstances. Furthermore, such workers tend not to want hierarchical career progression, and many will resist moves into managerial posts. Career-planning tools can help them to determine their own career paths.

Approaches to rating performance

We can see that there are a number of opportunities for performance rating to occur. The different approaches to rating can be classified as inputs, results and outcomes, and behaviour.

Rating *inputs* is a broad and potentially vague category that has traditionally been concerned with listing traits or personality attributes. Typical attributes are dependability, loyalty, decisiveness, resourcefulness and stability. Because such attributes may be difficult to define, there will be little agreement on their presence in employees between the different groups using lists of measures. The use of personality attributes in performance management and appraisal can lack reliability, giving rise to charges of bias, subjectivity and unfairness. This is normally the case when managers attempt to measure their employees in appraisal interviews. As indicated above, many organizations now prefer to use reliable and valid psychometric instruments as a way of helping employees to diagnose strengths and weaknesses for a development plan.

Ratings based on the *results and outcomes* of work performance provide the most objective technique for collecting data for appraisal. When available, measurements can be taken at different points in time and comparisons made with objectives. Typical measurements might relate to production, sales, the number of satisfied customers or customer complaints. The CIPD (2009b) survey clearly indicates the popularity of such an approach, with 85 per cent of respondents claiming the use of objective-setting and review as part of their PMS. Ratings might utilize the language of standards as set out in vocational qualifications. Such standards attempt to describe what competent people in a particular occupation are expected to be able to do. The outcomes achieved can be assessed against performance criteria for each standard. It is not surprising that most measurements are quantifiable, although many organizations will attempt to modify quantification with qualitative measurements or comments.

The attractiveness of results and outcomes as objective sources of data makes them a feature of many PMSs, but do such approaches reflect performance control or development approaches? Factors for consideration will relate to how objectives, targets and goals are set, how managers and employees interact in work towards their achievement, and the whether employees use the measurements as feedback in order to develop further. As Pettijohn et al. (2001) found, it is important that the criteria used to judge performance are controllable by those being judged: a failure here affects morale and overall performance.

During the 1960s, for example, there was a growth in schemes of management by objectives, which were designed to control the performance of managers and stimulate them in terms of their development. If this could be achieved, it was believed, the needs of managers and the organization could be integrated. Such schemes soon came under attack, however, and many fell into disrepute. Levinson (1970, p. 134) attacked the practice of management by objectives as self-defeating because it was based on 'reward–punishment psychology', which put pressure on individuals without there being any real choice of objectives. Modern approaches to objective-setting will face similar charges unless managers pay as much attention to the process by which objectives are set as to the content and quantification of objectives, and the environment in which employees work towards their achievement.

Attention to the *behaviour* of employees as practised in the transformation process will reveal how an individual has applied aptitudes, attitudes and competencies to the performance of work and will provide rich data on current effectiveness and the potential for further development. This attention can occur on a continuous basis, taking into account both subjective and objective data. Such an approach forms the foundation of a PMS concerned with the direction of performance and support for employees' continuing development. Once these processes have been established, employees may be more willing to accept more codified approaches to rating their behaviour. Frameworks of competencies associated with effective performance can, for example, provide the integrating link within a PMS between identifying key performance factors and setting objectives that can then be reviewed and rated; there is, however, evidence that the competencies identified are not always included in an appraisal process (Abraham et al., 2001).

Two kinds of ratings scale can be developed:

- *Behaviour-anchored rating scales* (BARSs) provide descriptions of important job behaviour 'anchored' alongside a rating scale. The scales are developed by generating descriptions of effective and ineffective performance from people who know the job; these are then used to develop clusters of performance and scales (Rarick and Baxter, 1986). Each scale describes a dimension of performance that can be used in appraisal. For example, in a scale developed for the behaviour of 'planning', the performance scale can vary between 'Excellent' and 'Unacceptable', and in between would lie a range of possible behaviours with varying degrees of effectiveness.
- *Behavioural observation scales* (BOSs) involve the people doing the rating assessing the frequency of specific job-related behaviours that are observable. Figure 9.7, for example, shows BOSs that have been derived from a financial services company.

Both BARSs and BOSs are based on specific performance and on the descriptions of employees involved in a particular job. Research by Tziner et al. (2000) provided a comparison between BARSs and BOSs with respect to the satisfaction of those being rated with their appraisal and with the setting of goals to improve performance. It was found that goals developed using BOSs were more specific than those set using a BARS since they were based on what a 'rater' actually observed rather than on evaluation. Furthermore, since BOSs require a rating of several behaviours rather than the identification of a single 'anchor', as in BARSs, this reduces bias and allows more specific feedback, with the formation of clearer goals. What is particularly interesting is the potential for such instruments to enhance self-appraisal and allow a dialogue between employees and others based on more objective criteria.

Self-appraisal

Referring back to our earlier analysis, we saw that have been significant problems associated with performance appraisal. These stemmed mainly from the way in which

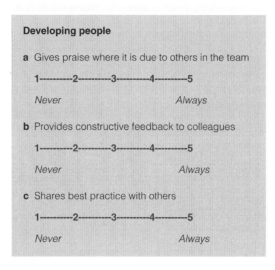

Figure 9.7 – BOSs in a financial services company

systems were put in place as a way of superiors evaluating employees for a variety of purposes, for example improving performance, pay and promotion. What cannot be escaped, however, is that all employees have an opinion on how well they are performing, the rewards they desire and deserve, and the training they require. That is, whatever techniques of appraisal are employed, self-appraisal and self-rating will always be there too. When the emphasis of PMS is on evaluation and control, it is only to be expected that differences will exist between an individual's self-appraisal and the appraisal of his or her superior. Campbell and Lee (1988) put forward a number of discrepancies between self-appraisal and supervisory appraisal:

- *Informational* – there is disagreement over the work to be done, how it is done and the standards to be used in judging the results.
- *Cognitive* – behaviour and performance are complex, and appraisers attempt to simplify this complexity. Different perceptions will result in disagreement between appraisers and appraisees.
- *Affective* – the evaluative nature of performance control appraisal is threatening to appraisees and triggers defence mechanisms, leading to bias and distortions in interpreting information. Appraisers also may find appraisal threatening.

All this suggests that self-appraisal in an environment of evaluation and control is not effective, which is not surprising. Campbell and Lee (1988, p. 307), however, suggested that 'such pessimistic conclusions did not rule out the possibility that self-appraisals can be used as important developmental and motivational tools for individuals'. We have already shown that employees are able to observe their own performance and obtain data for appraising strengths and weaknesses, and for identifying future goals, from the processes of working. Self-appraisal as a minimum condition allows the emergence of data for use in a discussion about performance, especially where the work is complex or knowledge-intensive (Ryan and Tipu, 2009). The extent to which employees are able to appraise themselves objectively becomes a question of how willing they are to seek and accept feedback from their work behaviour and the environment they are in. Employees can learn to appraise themselves and will treat this as part of their own development if they can see its value for themselves rather than viewing it as a manipulative management tool.

HRM web links

Multisource feedback

Self-appraisal for development will not occur unless it is set in an environment that facilitates and encourages such a process. If a positive experience is gained from self-appraisal, employees may then be willing to share their thoughts on the process with others. Many organizations have sought to increase the amount of feedback received and the number of sources of feedback. Kettley (1997) claimed that the popularity of MSF had arisen from a number of factors:

- It is a way of empowering employees and promoting teamwork by allowing employees to appraise their managers.
- It increases the reliability of appraisals and balance in 'flatter' (that is, less hierarchical) organizations.
- It reinforces good management behaviour by allowing people to see themselves as others see them.

The various sources of feedback might include:

- The immediate manager
- Staff (upward appraisal)
- Peers (peer appraisal)
- The manager and/or other staff (180-degree appraisal)
- The manager, staff and peers (360-degree appraisal)
- The manager, staff, peers, customer, suppliers and others (540-degree or 720-degree feedback).

Visit www.palgrave.com.business/bratton5 to read an HRM in practice feature on 720-degree feedback at Cadbury.

As the number and range of MSF schemes have grown, so too has interest in their impact. The crucial factor is the extent to which self-rating is supported by the ratings of others. What do you think the outcome would be if a manager had a positive perception of his or her performance but was rated less well by others, for example staff and internal customers? Yammarino and Atwater (1997) have provided an examination of possible HRM outcomes based on the range of agreements between 'self' and 'other' ratings. For example, where self-ratings are higher than the ratings of others, this is likely to lead to negative outcomes, whereas self-ratings that are lower than the ratings of others will result in a mixture of positive and negative outcomes.

MSF is growing in popularity, although the CIPD's (2009b) survey found that only around 25 per cent of organizations used 360-degree feedback. There is evidence of both its benefits and its difficulties. For example, *upward appraisal* for managers leads to performance improvement where managers start from a low or moderate rating and the feedback process is sustained over time; there is less impact, however, on managers who already have a high performance rating (Reilly et al., 1995). Managers prefer feedback from people they can specify, although staff, understandably perhaps, prefer anonymity (Antonioni, 1994). Most importantly, upward appraisal provides a powerful message to managers that performance will be assessed and improvement is expected. Managers can prepare themselves by becoming aware of the behaviours being assessed.

However, managers can also treat ratings with ambivalence or worse. For example, Atwater et al. (2000) found that managers who faced feedback from staff during a period of organizational change demonstrated a low impact where the change had been cynically introduced. Research by Van Dierendonck et al. (2007) in the NHS suggested that upward appraisal had only a small positive effect but, more importantly, that there was a gap between the self-ratings of managers and those of their staff. This led to some reduction of ratings by managers but no change of behaviour. Perhaps one of the most valued features of upward appraisal is the opportunity for staff to express their views in a constructive manner, which adds to their sense of being included (Howe et al., 2011).

Peer appraisal appears to be especially suitable for professional and knowledge-based workers such as doctors, teachers and researchers. The responses can be unpredictable, but research suggests that some will undertake further learning as a consequence (Colthart et al., 2008), and that peer-led discussions about learning and development are more acceptable than other alternatives (Main et al., 2009). There are, however, some possible tensions, since peers in managerial roles are usually connected with each other through their work or more informal relationships, and may be unwilling to offer formal feedback or make comparisons between their peers. Within teams, peer feedback can lead to resistance and avoidance of blame if the team is not performing well (Peiperl, 2001).

Reflective Question

Do you review the performance of your group after any work completed? Do you provide feedback to each other?

Moving round from upward and peer appraisal, *360-degree appraisal* completes the circle of MSF. Such a move does, however, require confidence and trust in the way it works because the outcome can become demoralizing and negative for the target group of appraisees, usually managers and leaders. 360-degree appraisal usually requires ratings from a sample of relationships, probably no fewer than eight. The feedback is collected by questionnaire, increasingly completed online, which can speed up the process (Mason et al., 2009) and can be seen as a more objective approach.

As with all approaches to appraisal, there can be both positive and negative reactions. Where appraisees are open-minded and willing to use the views of others to assess their self-perceptions, the process can be positive (Taylor and Bright, 2011). Individuals can, however, be hurt by too much negative feedback, and there might be confusion over whether the process is for development or for judgement relating to pay or promotion (Handy et al., 1996). Recent research into leadership development in a university in Australia (Drew, 2009) suggests that responses range from 'no surprising feedback' (that is, just reinforcement and affirmation) to 'new insights' that lead to plans for change.

The value of the 360-degree appraisal will also depend on how the process is positioned in an organization, on how a climate of support is established and facilitated for its implementation, and on amelioration of the negative effects. In particular, organizations need to consider employees' willingness to give and receive feedback and to use the various rating techniques. Training programmes are crucial before the implementation of MSF schemes. It would also seem that such schemes have more value as development and performance improvement processes rather than as a judgement mechanism involved in pay and promotion (McCarthy and Garavan, 2001).

Smither et al. (2005) sought to explore the impact of MSF on performance over time by examining 24 studies. However, they found only small improvements in performance, suggesting that other factors were also important. Their research suggested that the following factors were important in determining how much performance improvement might result from MSF:

- The characteristics of the feedback
- Initial reactions to the feedback
- Personality
- The feedback orientation of those receiving feedback
- The perceived need for change
- Beliefs about change
- Goal-setting
- Taking action.

Each of these factors could have an impact ranging from the nature of the feedback, for example positive or negative, to beliefs about the ability to take action. There are no clear paths to performance improvement from MSF feedback. Instead, the process will benefit some employees and not others. In particular, an organization needs to assess the impact of any MSF feedback scheme, and provide support by developing a coaching culture (DeNisi and Kluger, 2000), especially as a common problem reported by managers is a lack of interest on the part of others (including the employees' immediate line managers) (Garavan and McCarthy, 2007). In addition, as we indicated earlier, perceptions of procedural justice are important in appraisal, and this is significant for the acceptance of MSF, as is the decline of cynical attitudes of managers towards MSF (McCarthy and Garavan, 2007). Smither et al. (2008) showed how wider features of context can affect the impact of MSF over time. They found that, 9 months after completing MSF, 145 managers tended to recall strengths rather than weaknesses, and there was little evidence of performance improvement. MSF needs to be supported by reviews, coaching and perhaps learning projects, especially since the process is often used with development programmes for leaders and managers.

HRM web links

Go to www.psytech.com/Documents/Guidelinesfor360Feedback.pdf for a free booklet on 360-degree feedback. https://www.leadingpeople.co.uk/leadership360-1.asp provides an example of an online approach to 360-degree feedback for leadership development. Notice how the findings are reviewed through one-to-one coaching that leads to an action plan.

Given the potential for tension between performance management and appraisal that is oriented towards judgements, in contrast to process oriented towards development, there needs to be some way of providing reconciliation. The development of competency frameworks, along with other measurement devices, has improved the reliability and validity of feedback on employees' attitudes, aptitudes and performance. This still does not, however, remove the underlying emphasis on control. Indeed, some would claim that the use of the various techniques within a PMS serves to enhance the 'manageability' of employees (Townley, 1994). PMSs also place a great deal of faith in the support of the management team as the assessors and facilitators of other people's development. There is no guarantee of either, and our understanding of what really happens in performance management and in organizations generally is still limited.

Importantly, so much of the literature concerning performance management and appraisal works from the neo-human relations assumption that all employees have an interest in achieving the objectives set or in responding to measurements when they have participated in the process (Newton and Findlay, 1996). Employees do, of course, have an interest in what they do at work, but they also have many other interests with only a tangential connection to workplace performance, possibly including many activities that work against management requirements for performance, such as gossiping and having fun, but also more serious forms of behaviours such as theft of the organization's property (Ackroyd and Thompson, 1999).

Case Study: Robertson Engineering

Setting

Robertson Engineering is a family-owned business that designs and manufactures equipment for mining. Based in the North-East of England, the company grew by serving local coal mines, but since the 1980s it has sought new customers. Having survived the demise of the UK market, the business has been successful in securing contracts for Chinese and Australian mining companies. There are currently 45 staff, but this is likely to grow over the next few years.

The company's MD is Bill Robertson. He is a third-generation owner of the business, and recognizes that more attention needs to be given to performance management. In particular, there needs to be a more systematic process so that talent can be identified to enable growth. Although he believes that things are happening informally, the MD is aware is that he needs to demonstrate, using objective data, that he has control of the business. This means that people's performance has been agreed against targets that are tied to business objectives.

The problem

Until recently, any assessment of performance had been undertaken rather informally. This is traditional in small businesses, and most of the staff were used to a 'friendly chat' with their line manager. There are four line managers, and they had all been appointed from within the business and therefore had close relationships with the people they managed. Owing to the size of the business, Bill ran 'a tight ship', with only the line managers between him and the rest of the staff, so performance management was very much left to the managers.

When action or changes were needed, such as promotions or replacements of staff, Bill relied on information from the managers to make a quick decision. It had always been the case that people were promoted from within, and that training needs could be identified 'as and when' needed. This did not please everyone, and Bill knew that some of the staff were not always happy with the way managers made judgements about work performance, or with their support (or lack of support) for training. Most of the time, however, any clear differences and variations in performance could be 'smoothed over', and the annual company profit share tended to satisfy the bulk of the workforce.

There had been little attention given to setting goals, and hardly any attempt had been made to record and monitor targets. Because production tended towards fairly lengthy time scales, it was felt that as long as people knew when delivery was required, and that everyone had a 'rough' idea when their input was needed, goals could be 'loose'. As long as delivery was achieved on schedule, profit would be secured.

But some changes were needed, and Bill saw an increasing connection between the performance management of staff and the expansion of the business, although he did not want to lose the informality that had come from being a smaller business. He certainly did not want to create a bureaucratic process of unnecessary form-filling. He was also aware that many staff were very sensitive to feedback, and this could become difficult if judgements about performance were written down formally.

But there was an attraction in understanding more about staff performance, albeit through the eyes of line managers, and he wanted individuals to have their own development plans. Being an engineer, he could also see the logic of a talent pipeline and, as most staff were likely to stay with the company, some connection to career development. Indeed, he could see how performance management might provide him with the perfect process to move the business forward.

Until recently, Robertson Engineering had used an informal appraisal system with its employees.
Source: ©istockphoto.com/Pali Rao

Assignment

Working as a group or on your own, prepare a report for Bill that outlines the way forward. You will need to consider:

○ An appropriate approach to performance management in this organization
○ The purpose of the exercise, and what skills would be needed by the managers
○ The issue of staff sensitivity to feedback
○ Whether training would be needed, and what methods would be used.

Note: This feature was written by Jeff Gold.
Visit the companion website at www.palgrave.com/business/bratton5 for guidelines on writing reports.

SUMMARY

⊚ The key idea of a PMS is that the principal dimensions of a person's work can be precisely defined in performance terms, allowing measurement over agreed periods of time, and also takes account of particular constraints within the situation of performance. Performance management forms the nub of the strategic link between HR inputs and practices and organizational performance.

⊚ Through its link to measurement, performance management provides evidence that management is rationally, efficiently and effectively controlling an organization. There are, however, measurement models that take a wider view, perhaps more strategic and long term, which encompass a range of values (not just financial) and can stimulate continuous improvement.

⊚ Research evidence shows the importance of performance management, with a wide range of activities featured. Different criteria are used to judge performance and to help diagnose development needs, providing a link to the organization's goals. A performance management cycle integrates various HR processes, including development centres, objective-setting and personal development planning, feedback and reviews. There is, however, often a gap between the rhetoric and the reality of claims for its contribution to organizational effectiveness.

- Performance management has a 'control' purpose to aid decisions about pay, promotion and work responsibility, and a 'development' purpose in improving performance, identifying training opportunities and planning action.
- A PMS might incorporate development centres, which are the same as assessment centres in that assessment tests and exercises are used to provide a report on individual strengths and limitations. However, they differ in their emphasis on diagnosing development needs, leading to suggested development activities and a PDP.
- Managers have a vital role to play in providing feedback, both formally as part of a PMS and informally as part of everyday work. The acceptance of feedback as valid will depend on its frequency as part of an ongoing relationship and on how well managers understand the perceptions of their staff.
- The performance control approach to appraisal is still seen as evidence of rationality and efficiency at work. Such beliefs often become taken-for-granted assumptions and difficult to challenge. Employees who believe that their appraisal is based on subjectivity or bias and subjects them to unfair punishments are likely to experience appraisal as being of low quality.
- A more developmental approach to performance management and appraisal has to include an alignment with talent management policies based on people developing their skills and being challenged to develop themselves.
- Performance can be rated in different ways. Inputs, in the form of personality attributes or traits, may lack reliability and may be seen as subjective and unfair. Results and work outcomes allow quantifiable measurement and are therefore seen as being more objective. Rating behaviour within performance allows the use of such techniques as BARSs and BOSs.
- Performance might be reviewed and appraised using a variety of MSF processes, including self-appraisal and feedback from managers, peers, subordinates and others as part of a 360-degree appraisal process.

VOCAB CHECKLIST FOR ESL STUDENTS

- 360-degree appraisal (n)
- appraise (v), appraisal (n)
- behavioural observation scale (BOS) (n)
- behaviour-anchored rating scale (BARS) (n)
- cognition (n), cognitive (adj)
- feedback (n)
- feedforward (n)
- high-performance work system (n)
- key performance indicator (n)
- mentor (v), mentor (n), mentoring (n)
- multisource feedback (MSF) (n)
- panacea (n)
- peer appraisal (n)
- performance and development plan (PDP) (n)
- performance development and review (n)
- performance management system (PMS) (n)
- psychometrics (n), psychometric (adj)
- self-appraisal (n)

- tacit knowledge (n)
- total quality management (TQM) (n)
- upward appraisal (n)

Visit www.palgrave.com/business/bratton5 for a link to free definitions of these terms in the Macmillan Dictionary, as well as additional learning resources for ESL students.

REVIEW QUESTIONS

1 What should be the purpose of performance management and appraisal?
2 What is the role of 'objectives' in performance management? Can performance be 'managed by objectives'?
3 Does a PMS enhance strategic integration within HRM?
4 Can knowledge workers and/or professionals be performance-managed?
5 Do you think that students should have more say in appraising and assessing themselves and each other?
6 Do you think that appraisal and assessment techniques enhance the 'manageability' of employees?

FURTHER READING TO IMPROVE YOUR MARK

Reading these articles and chapters can help you gain a better understanding and potentially a higher grade for your HRM assignment.

1. It is argued that most research on PMS is intended to serve a managerialist agenda leading to prescribed behaviours. S. McKenna, J. Richardson and L. Manroop (2011) Alternative paradigms and the study and practice of performance management and evaluation. *Human Resource Management Review*, **21**(2): 148–57 call for more innovation in research using a variety of approaches or paradigms.

2. A. Neely (2007) *Business Performance Measurement*. Cambridge: Cambridge University Press sets performance management in a wider context and considers connections to measurement frameworks and methodologies.

3. B. Townley (1993) Performance appraisal and the emergence of management. *Journal of Management Studies*, **30**(2): 221–38 provides an analysis of appraisals based on the work of Michel Foucault.

4. For a well-considered view of appraisal and feedback, based on research, try Clive Fletcher's (2004) *Appraisal and Feedback: Making Performance Review Work* (3rd edn). London: Chartered Institute of Personnel and Development.

5. The importance of fairness and justice has been highlighted, and more research on this issue can be found in P. W. Thurston and L. McNall (2010) Justice perceptions of performance appraisal practices. *Journal of Managerial Psychology*, **25**(3): 201–28.

6. The importance of ethics in performance management has been considered by Diana Winstanley and Kate Stuart-Smith (1996) Policing performance: the ethics of performance management. *Personnel Review*, **25**(6): 66–84.

Visit www.palgrave.com/business/bratton5 for lots of extra resources to help you get to grips with this chapter, including study tips, HRM skills development guides, summary lecture notes, and more.

10

ETHICS AND THE CORPORATION (CSR)

CHAPTER OBJECTIVES

- To understand, and to be able to criticize, the case for human resource management (HRM) as a new way of managing people at work.
- To recognize some of the inherent tensions and contradictions implicit in HRM.
- To be able to differentiate between (i) business orientated; and (ii) academic, critical literature on HRM.
- To understand some of the different models of HRM, and to be aware of their ethical implications.

Case study

Introductory case study

The sweet factory and the ethics school

Kondo (1990) gives a vivid account of everyday life on the shop floor of a small family-owned sweet factory in Tokyo ... she is sent to an ethics school with two other employees ... Here is a brief description of the activities before breakfast each day. The day started at 5 am with a call to rise. Waking up late was regarded as unnatural, indulgent, selfish, slovenly. Cleaning came next and was a standard ingredient of spiritual education. Each cleaning task was to be performed with a glad heart. The counsellors would lead the group in chants of 'Fight!' as they hosed down the toilets, emptied the tins of sanitary napkins, and scrubbed the floors. After cleaning, they jogged to the statue of the founder and after a rousing shout of good morning, they were lectured on an inspirational theme. A tape recorder played the national anthem as the flags were raised. They then had shouting practice where they were required to scream greetings at the top of their voices or shout 'I am the sun of 'x' company. I will make 'x' company number one in Japan.' Every word was rewarded by shouts of encouragement from the others and rounds of applause. The idea was to inculcate receptiveness and a willingness to greet and appreciate others and eliminate resistance toward responding positively towards authority. They ran for at least 2.4km as a rehearsal for the 7.5 km marathon scheduled for the end of the programme. Shouting and chanting was required during running. Speed was not the issue, it was more important to finish and not give up. Neglect of the body was seen as lack of appreciation of the gift of life. Ritual ablution ceremonies with cold water, in order to give thanks to water, followed. The morning classes were for reciting in unison phrases like 'Hardship is the gateway to happiness' and 'Other people are our mirrors'. Students would be given instructions on how to bow at the proper angle, have a pleasant facial expression, and use the appropriate language level.

(*Source*: Wilson, 1999)

Question

Is this what you would think of as a 'school'? If not, what other kind of organization(s) does it seem like to you?

10.1 INTRODUCTION: DIFFERENT WAYS OF INTERPRETING THE ETHICS SCHOOL CASE

There are a number of ways of looking at this extract from Fiona Wilson's introduction to organizational behaviour. It can be understood in a fairly neutral way as describing a company's training programme to instil a customer ethic, and to encourage bonding among employees. Each of the exercises and the associated rituals could also be described as a way of forming corporate identity, or of 'managing culture'. To more sceptical eyes it may seem as though this is a form of brainwashing. The ethics school (and those running the organization) could be described as breaching the boundaries of individual liberty, or as contravening basic human rights – for example, the right to dignity at work. From the perspective of a Western European liberal democracy, some of the rituals do seem somewhat strange (what do they have to do with making sweets?) and even a little chilling. To require sessions of orchestrated screaming at work seems frightfully un-British, for example. In the ethics school it can seem even more unsettling and oppressive to the individual that these sessions are scheduled shortly after hearing the national anthem, since this can appear to be another way of legitimizing domination and subordination. On the other hand, in any country in the developed or developing world, there will be family-owned businesses run by petty tyrants that are vehicles of worse oppression. Perhaps one could argue that, unlike the case of the petty tyrant who is head of the family firm, there is some rationality at work in this ethics school. It could also be argued that what takes place in this ethics school differs by only a matter of degree (if at all) from what happens on some of the more exotic training courses inflicted on Western executives. In 2006, for example, a training consultancy – Si Group – ran a fire-walking exercise in South London designed to build confidence among Deloitte's staff. One senior accountant burnt her feet so badly she had to take two weeks off work, and Si Group was fined £3,000 and had to pay over £4,500 in costs (Thomas, 2006).

From all these different perspectives (training programme/a way to manage culture/a form of brainwashing/an abuse of human rights/cultural relativism/no worse than other apparently bizarre practices), the case of the ethics school prompts us to consider the duties owed by organizations to their employees. It also prompts us to reflect on the way in which those employees are managed. The type of behaviour expected in Kondo's ethics school may seem completely inappropriate if we compare it with the typical practices of a contemporary Western factory. However, such behaviour is not far removed from what might be expected in other communities or organizations. Consider, for example, the devotion required in a monastery, or the strict discipline and obedience to a regime expected in different ways by a school, a prison or a hospital (Foucault, 1979). As well as acknowledging some cultural relativism, we might allow for some trans-organizational relativism. We might also acknowledge that even in cultures that are (stereotypically) less deferential and more individualist than Japan, collective screaming is acceptable or even normal in some settings: among the temporary communities at a football match or rock concert, say.

Kondo's case study reveals that our notions of what is appropriate or acceptable when it comes to organizational behaviour, and managing people in organizations, can be dramatically different in different cultures, in different communities and in different types of organization. In the workplace, we may also have more flexible standards of appropriateness regarding certain activities. Consider, for example, a training course, where we might allow that learning something new involves moving beyond established boundaries. We could also be more flexible in acknowledging that at certain stages of one's career within an organization, periods of greater and lesser intensity are both natural and appropriate. Consider the cases of an induction period for graduate trainees, and a mid-career assessment centre to determine who is fit for promotion, for example. In both of these cases the organization may reasonably be expected to test or train employees in a more intensive way than in the course of their daily work. One could even make an ethical case for this difference – it could be argued that it would be unfair to promote someone who was not able to cope with the demands of a more senior position (assuming, of course, that the assessment centre was a valid and reliable way of evaluating these demands).

The case of the ethics school also prompts us to think about what similarities there are in the management of people across different organizations and cultures. For example, if we find the idea of orchestrated screaming and flag saluting offensive, or un-British (or un-French or whatever) why might we think it acceptable for Western firms to expect their employees to undergo the rites of passage and cult-like rituals associated with some training programmes – whether it's paint-balling to build teamwork, or fire-walking to develop inner strength and confidence? Aren't these experiences rather similar, and if so, why should we be offended by one and not the other? It seems as though a more thoughtful reading of the case of the ethics school is encouraging a drift towards relativism: the denial of any absolute standards of rightful conduct. This is unsettling because it suggests that, when it comes to the management of people, what seems to be acceptable rather than unacceptable, or ethical rather than unethical, is at least partly subjective. We do not judge health and safety conditions in contemporary factories against the standards of the nineteenth century, for example. On the one hand this may seem obvious, but even if we think such standards would be totally unacceptable, as consumers, global capitalism means that we may continue to buy products manufactured in factories overseas where conditions are as bad as or worse than they once were in the developed world (Gibson, 2007: 68–73; Scholte, 2005). There are many ways in which we can blur the lines between what is acceptable and unacceptable, strange and familiar, ethical and the unethical. This should encourage us to take a critical perspective of even well-received ideas about how people are managed. There is always scope to question and consider alternative approaches since the management of people is inescapably enmeshed with ethical implications (Legge, 1998a). In terms of the themes of the opening chapter of our book, in our search for the science of the good we need to scrutinize the received 'truths' that dominate present-day thinking about how people are managed. The management of people is also the management of values and of meaning. As the Nietzsche quote in our opening chapter suggests, it is an arena where, 'a prejudice, a notion, an "inspiration", generally a desire of the heart sifted and made abstract, is defended ... with reasons sought after the event'. We might even go further and suggest that, in the context of this chapter, those claiming to have the answers to how to manage people, 'are one and all advocates who do not want to be regarded as such, and for the most part no better than cunning pleaders for their prejudices, which they baptize "truths"' (Nietzsche, 1886/1973, 1(5)).

10.2   A NEW WAY OF MANAGING PEOPLE?

Later in this chapter we look at the phenomenon of human resource management (HRM). HRM came to the fore in the 1980s and subsequent discussion of it can be separated into two strands of literature: a business orientated or managerial literature on what HRM is or should be, and how to do it (Dessler, 2000; Fowler, 1987); and an academic, largely critical literature that attempts to address or highlight failings in the HRM model(s) and expose the gap between the rhetoric of HRM and what happens in practice (Keenoy, 1999; Legge, 1995; Storey, 1995). The classical conception of the relationship between employer and employee was based on the notion of a free contract between the two parties, essentially for their mutual benefit (Hoffman and Moore, 1990: 269). Employers were expected to pay fair wages, and, in return, employees were to give their loyalty and obedience, and above all, a satisfactory performance (Hoffman and Moore, 1990). In modern organizations, however, the management of people is more complex and involves several stakeholders: the government, unions, shareholders, employees and management, to mention just a few. HRM management practices are affected strongly by the economic, political, technological, legal and social contexts within which they operate. These contexts pull the HRM function in different directions. While some writers argue for more protection of employees' interests and rights, others call for the protection of shareholders' interests at the expense of employees' rights and fair treatment. These debates take place amid a more turbulent economic environment.

HRM came to the fore as an ostensibly 'new' way of managing people to improve business performance (Beer *et al.*, 1984, 1985; Fombrun *et al.*, 1984; Hendry and Pettigrew, 1986; Walton, 1985). Before examining the business-orientated and academic approaches to HRM, it is important to set out the argument for a new way of managing people that in its own way has become a contemporary 'truth' about behaviour in organizations. The argument for a new way of managing people can be expressed as follows: the twentieth century and the opening years of the twenty-first have been characterized by rapid technological change and corresponding changes in the ease of transport, both of which have 'shrunk' the world. The early twentieth century witnessed mass production designed to deliver 'one size fits all' goods for a uniform, mass market. Henry Ford's Model T car was famously suited to the customer – who could have 'any colour they wanted as long as it was black' – in other words, no choice at all.

The advent of global consumerism challenged standardized production and, in turn, traditional ways of managing people. Since the 1960s, the influence of information technology has increased, with the advent and subsequent omnipresence of the computer and silicon chip. More recently, phenomena such as the internet, and global capitalism have led to the restructuring of society, the redefinition or abolition of national boundaries, and the emergence of new organizational forms (Scholte, 2005). Each *day*, $3 trillion dollars of currency is electronically traded on the international money markets. This is a sum greater than the wealth of any one state, and the amount traded has doubled in just over a decade (Progressive Policy Institute, 2007). The complexity (speed and anonymity) and scale of these transactions have led to various forms of insecurity across the globe. This is reflected in the corporate climate of today's multinationals, and through them to smaller companies everywhere. We now live in a business environment where prediction and control are ultimately unrealizable, because of the inter-relatedness, and instability, of the global financial system. This global instability has consequences for an organization's environment, and consequently how it has to manage its people. In times of uncertainty, the security of 'jobs for life', which some organizations historically have been able to afford employees, has gone for ever (Maund, 2001). Consequently, organizations have to look at new ways of encouraging employee loyalty and commitment. External uncertainties (such as those caused by complexity in the business environment), have translated into internal uncertainties (the problems of managing people within the organization).

One way to represent the effect of environmental complexity is using Ashby's Law of Requisite Variety. This was originally developed in the field of cybernetics but it has also been applied more specifically to look at behaviour in organizations (Morgan, 1995). Put simply, an organism (such as an organization) must be as complex as its environment to survive: the global environment is now more complex, and standardized production is not capable of meeting the needs of a diverse market which – in terms of the Ford Model T example – want black and every other colour as well. If we accept that it is appropriate to apply Ashby's Law in this context, it can give us a very powerful way of understanding the rise of new (post-bureaucratic, or sometimes post-Fordist) organizational forms, and of demonstrating the consequent challenges to effective people management. Seen in this light, HRM can be portrayed as the necessary 'silver bullet' (Legge, 1998b) to slay uncertainty and promote performance.

The case for a new mode of management is typically set out in the context of new technologies, changes in modes of consumption, the rise of post-Fordist and post-bureaucratic ways of working and global capitalism (globalization). However, even if we accept this is a fair description of the context, these changes have ethical implications that are very old and familiar. For example, let us suppose that we buy into the idea that traditional bureaucracies and hierarchies are no more and that we are all living in a knowledge economy (incidentally, not everyone does believe this, and it is certainly not the case that it is true for everyone, everywhere, as we suggest below). A critical (Marxist) perspective in this context would suggest that HRM (which is at the forefront of these new ways of managing people) is a fundamentally *managerialist* approach. That is, advocates of HRM are interested first and foremost in advancing the interests of managers and ultimately of a powerful elite, rather than those of workers or the masses. In these terms, HRM is basically a way of introducing changes to the way people are controlled – a necessity, given the changes brought about by global capitalism. This change is orchestrated in such a way that it serves the interests of those in power. Strategic HRM scholars such as Tsui (1987) have argued for the thesis of 'strategic fit' between HRM policies and practices, and overall corporate strategy. In a business environment characterized by relentless competition and a quest to achieve and sustain competitive advantage, the strategic role of the HRM function is to help the organization achieve its strategic goals regardless of whether HRM policies and practices are ethical or not. The key measuring criteria on this view is: do all practices help the company achieve a better than average return on investment? This prompts ethical questions relating to justice, rights and fairness.

A contrast to this Marxist analysis still prompts ethical considerations for HRM. Assuming that the scenario of the knowledge economy makes sense, this can also be used as the basis for recognizing the increasing importance and worth of the person in an organization. If 'knowledge workers' become increasingly prevalent and important, then organizational worth will reside in the workforce rather than in other factors of production (land, machinery, other fixed assets, financial capital and so on). Newer organizational forms will be increasingly dependent on their knowledge workers, largely through the way that they use information. Organizations and their employees will need to learn to remain competitive (Argyris and Schön, 1978; Pedler *et al.*, l, 1991). Thinking about this in the context of one of the founders of ethics, in Aristotelian terms this is potentially a positive development. Learning is a uniquely human characteristic: reasoning is the difference that makes us human, and from that follows our ability to learn and our ability to behave (un)virtuously. It is what makes us individuals. In a post-bureaucratic era there would seem to be more focus on people as people, and individuals in organizations would seem to have greater power because of their valuable expertise.

There are some problems with this argument, however. First, it neglects the fact that bureaucratic structures and many elements of standardization continue to be highly cost-effective. Consequently, many of today's 'knowledge workers' may be difficult to distinguish from workers on a traditional (Fordist) mass-production assembly line. Consider the relatively recent phenomenon of the call centre, for example. Though call centre operatives may be providing a service (working in the knowledge economy), in effect they are often highly regulated and have to complete a certain number of calls in a given time. They may also have to stick rigidly to a standard script, and be monitored by having each call recorded (see Figure 10.1).

A second problem with a more positive take on the case for a new way of managing people is that the type of learning that is important to organizations is not really the kind of contemplative reasoning that Aristotle recognized as being uniquely human. Learning within organizations is typically learning for instrumental purposes – that is, for the benefit of the organization. It is very rare to find organizations sponsoring any forms of learning other than those that are believed to have a direct impact on the bottom line. Third, while in the developed world a greater proportion of people work in tertiary or quaternary sectors (that is, service industries and the knowledge economy), across the globe as a whole many people still work in agriculture and manufacturing (the primary and secondary sectors of industry). The danger of the high-flying rhetoric of a knowledge economy is that it ignores the fact that people somewhere still have to make things, and that often to compete in a global market this means that the cost of labour is ruthlessly driven down. The luxury that supports the knowledge economy has its roots in the systematic oppression of the majority of the world's workforce.

Reflective exercise

Should the business environment dictate how we manage people in organizations? What if the business context suggests some workers have to give up basic rights? Consider the 'business case' for slavery: 'if other people are using slave labour then their costs are low; we have to use it too otherwise we won't be able to compete'. What is wrong with this argument?

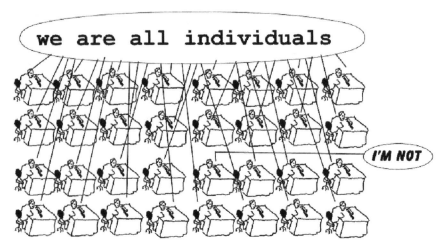

Figure 10.1 – Spot the knowledge worker (apologies to Monty Python)

It is important to look at the case for a new way of managing people, because if we can find problems and contradictions in that case, then we are left with the same kind of uncertainty we feel when deciding whether Kondo's ethics school is appropriate or not. Unless there is a compelling argument for one best way, then it seems as though deciding on how we should manage people at work is always something that can be contested. Resisting the claim to 'truths' about the best way to manage people is an ethical endeavour, just as challenging taken-for-granted assumptions about the good is an ethical endeavour. As well as finding problems with the argument for a new way of managing people, there is a rich and detailed literature that identifies some of the problems and contradictions with the specifics of HRM itself. Before discussing briefly this academic and critical perspective on HRM, it is appropriate to start by looking at the descriptive, business-orientated or managerial literature on HRM. In that way, we shall have a clear idea about what we're talking about before moving on to criticizing it and examining the ethical implications.

The significance of a critical perspective on HRM is that this brings ethical issues into the foreground. It raises questions such as, what is the fair and right way to manage people, what sorts of expectations are legitimate from an employer, and what obligations can reasonably be expected of an employee. Though there is not enough space to do this critical tradition justice in this chapter, it is perhaps fair to say that its main theme is that HRM constitutes a new architecture of control, where traditional imbalances in power between the employer and employee are simply reconstituted or reinforced (rather than being abolished, or HRM being seen in any way as democratizing). This perspective allows us to be sceptical about claims that HRM is in some way necessarily liberating – as is implied, for example, in the title of Walton's (1985) influential paper 'from control to commitment in the workplace'. It also allows us to be sceptical about claims that HRM is genuinely new (and by association, in some way an improvement over the old). A Marxist analysis of work suggests that society is ordered in such a way that workers will be exploited increasingly under capitalism. The effect of capitalism in a global economy – what Scholte (2005) has called 'hypercapitalism' – means that workers are increasingly being turned into mere objects to be manipulated (Freire, 2003; Hanlon, 2007). In one sense, then, the label for this activity of 'human resource' management is remarkably transparent about such exploitation. The same could be said about its precursor, found in the title of the seminal text, 'managing human assets' (Beer *et al.*, 1984). There remain basic tensions between the liberating rhetoric associated with HRM and the ruthless pull of the bottom line. Advocates of HRM may well preach about high commitment management and an environment where people are the most important asset, but this is not reflected in terms of investment in those assets. Tom Peters, writing in the US context, stated that, 'investment in training is a national disgrace' (1989: 324). Michael Hammer, the architect of business process re-engineering, referred to this as the 'biggest lie told by most organizations' (Lancaster, 1995: 1). These tensions suggest that the unitarism (defined on p. 172) underpinning HRM is illusory, and that there can be very real differences between the interests of middle managers and their workers, and the interests of the board of directors.

10.3   WHAT IS HRM?

When discussing the academic and critical perspective on HRM, it is also important to acknowledge what the advocates of different versions of HRM have described.

Though these advocates are many and varied, and there is no single real model of HRM, there are some similarities across various texts and authors. Because there is no one way of actually 'doing' HRM, it is difficult to talk about HRM as though it is a coherent phenomenon (Morrell, 2002a). This makes it difficult when thinking about the ethical implications of HRM, because there is no single place to stand in relation to HRM. A wide variety of management initiatives can fall under the banner of HRM, and some of these may even contradict one another. For example, some approaches to HRM place an emphasis on managing culture, communication and leadership striving for high employee commitment, while other approaches may entail widespread use of numerical flexibility and de-layering or downsizing – this distinction is sometimes referred to as the gap between 'soft' and 'hard' HRM, respectively (Morrell, 2002b). Additionally, it can be unclear how closely the actual effects of HRM initiatives relate to descriptions of these initiatives; in other words whether the realities of HRM in practice can match the various rhetorics of its advocates (Legge, 1995). In addition to these definitional and contextual complexities, we need to be aware that there are various interest groups, each with a stake or vested interest in 'HRM'. One way of making sense of this confusion is to look for conceptual frameworks (or models) which outline a particular version or interpretation of HRM (Morrell, 2002a). We can then take an ethical stance in relation to each conceptual framework.

The Harvard model, developed by Beer and his colleagues at Harvard University in the 1980s (Beer *et al.*, 1984), is perhaps the best-known model of HRM. It acknowledges the role of context-specific factors in the choice of HRM policies. These comprise situational factors (such as workforce characteristics, business strategy, the labour market), and stakeholder interests (such as shareholders, management, unions, employees, government). These influence the way in which HRM policy choices (for example, systems of pay) lead to HR outcomes (for example, commitment) and how they influence consequences over the long term (for example, organizational effectiveness, individual and societal well-being). An advantage of this model is the degree to which it emphasizes that HR initiatives need to fit the particular industry context, thus allowing for flexibility in terms of the choice of an HR strategy. This sets it apart from other, less flexible, models, which may have a more 'unitarist' conception of HRM, ignoring the role of different interest groups (briefly, unitarism is the belief that all the members of an organization share the same goals). From an ethical perspective, one advantage of the Harvard model is that it acknowledges that there may be differences in the interests of various groups. There is also a degree of flexibility built into the model, which suggests that it may discourage a dogmatic or ideological perspective on the employment relationship because, as circumstances change, the Harvard model suggests that our way of managing people should change too. This can also be a disadvantage, however, because it may encourage a more pragmatic approach to the employment relationship and there is certainly less emphasis on principle with a model that allows environmental factors to dictate how the workforce is managed.

Drawing in part on the Harvard model, David Guest (1987, 2000) has outlined a framework for assessing the effectiveness of organizations, based on the testing of propositions such as 'strategic integration', 'quality', 'flexibility' and 'commitment'. While the extent to which these propositions are open to testing remains a matter of debate, there is no doubt that his extension of the Harvard model is potentially useful in so far as it gives an example of how fairly abstract notions of 'commitment' and 'organizational effectiveness' might be operationalized (made concrete and testable), and be seen to interrelate. Guest's model of HRM places organizational commitment at its core, and to this extent it is also useful in terms of drawing a clear distinction between HRM and traditional systems of personnel management/industrial relations, which are said to centre more on compliance (Guest, 1989). None the less, it should be recognized that the belief that high commitment is key to organizational effectiveness remains an assumption that has received limited direct empirical support. More worryingly, despite considerable research interest over time (Boxall and Purcell, 2000; Guest et al., 2003; Hope et al., 2005; MacDuffie, 1995; Patterson et al., 1997; Truss, 2001) the link between HRM and organizational performance remains contested. This is not least because, as noted above, there is no single thing that can be said to be HRM (Boselie et al., 2005; Hyde et al., 2006). Setting aside this rather sweeping challenge, Guest's account has a number of ethical implications. Starting with a less obvious inference, he has provided a way in which some of the claims of advocates of HRM may be tested by trying to make notions such as flexibility testable. This is important because it offers a way of challenging some of the rhetoric that surrounds HRM. Another, more obvious, ethical implication is that it forces us to examine the role of commitment in the employment relationship. On the one hand, it seems desirable that employers try to secure a commitment from their employees to the enterprise. This suggests that there is at least some consideration given to employee well-being – it is difficult to be committed to something without feeling positive towards it. On the other hand, though, the emphasis on commitment suggests a degree of encroachment by the organization into employees' personal feelings. Should it not be enough that people do their job well without expecting that they also be 'committed' to it?

John Storey (1992, 1995) proposed a 25-item checklist to differentiate the newer model of HRM from the older versions of personnel management/industrial relations (PM/IR). This offers a comprehensive way of thinking about the difference between HRM (as an ideal type) and PM/IR as a system of management. For each of twenty-five 'dimensions' of management, Storey's checklist sketches the difference between HRM and PM/IR. So, for example, in the dimension of 'conflict handling', for PM/IR we have 'reach temporary truces', whereas for HRM we have 'manage climate and culture'. Again, for the dimension of 'contract', for PM/IR we have 'careful delineation of written contracts', whereas for HRM we have 'aim to go "beyond contract" '. This offers another way of thinking about whether HRM is something new. It also suggests that some of the more important differences between these models are captured by Guest's emphasis on commitment. One argument for moving from a compliance mode to a commitment mode is that more and more work nowadays is carried out in the context of a knowledge economy. Since this work involves processes that cannot be observed directly (because they relate to intellectual capital) it is not enough to secure compliance; one must have commitment too. If we consider the example of someone building a wall, it is easy to see how many bricks they have laid in an hour, and by extension how much they could reasonably be expected to do in a week. In contrast, if somebody is designing a piece of software or providing a service to people, that cannot be observed directly or checked on intermittently with any degree of reliability. There has to be a new form of control or surveillance (Ouchi, 1979). Hence, returning to Storey's checklist, there may be a need to manage climate and culture, and to ask people to go beyond contract, since we cannot specify in precise detail just how people should be served.

Karen Legge nicely identified some ethical implications of such a model (comparing and contrasting the old with the new). She pointed out that, whereas models of HRM were aspirational and setting out an ideal, the models of the old PM/IR way of managing the employment relationship were often caricatures. It is important to note this difference because this contrast was often used to support the change to a new way of managing (controlling) people. If this new way was simply rhetoric then this has profound implications. It can be argued generally that, however comprehensive a model may be, it is bound to be an oversimplification of what happens 'in real life', and as such, using a model may distract us from thinking about the inherent complexities involved in managing people. More specifically, the extent to which HRM models or theories are 'normative' (that is, accounts of how things should be) or 'descriptive' (that is, accounts of how things actually are) is problematic. One criticism levelled at comparisons between HRM as seen as a new and better way of managing people, and other traditional models such as PM is that they blur this distinction. Models of PM describe or caricature what is actually going on (are descriptive), whereas models of HRM are idealized or 'normative'. Writers such as Legge have argued there is little or no difference between the normative ambitions of PM and HRM. This is a fundamental challenge to the coherence of the argument for HRM because it suggests that HRM is not a new way of managing people at all.

10.4   ETHICAL IMPLICATIONS OF HRM

Karen Legge (1998a) noted that 'Thirty years ago, the answer to the question "Is HRM Ethical?" certainly in the mind of the lay person – would probably have been: "Of course personnel management is ethical. It's there to help people, isn't it?" 'Personnel professionals, at least publicly, might have gone along with this and pointed to the supposed origins of people management in benevolent paternalism and social welfare. But if asked the same question today, would there be a more hesitant response? First, there would be some difficulty in presenting 'one consistent image' (Legge, 1996: 34). Several writers have examined the reasons for the rise of ethical concerns over contemporary HRM practices in considerable depth (Legge, 1996, 1998a, 2000; and Winstanley *et al.*, 1996). One compelling reason would be that current HRM models, policies and practices partially reflect the macroeconomic and political environments of the 1980s and 1990s. These were characterized by global competition and cut-throat competition. They focused management concerns on survival and on achieving sustainable competitive advantage by obtaining higher-than-average returns on investment. Obviously, these exigencies would, in most cases, make managers unsympathetic to ethical HRM practices unless they were proven to help the company achieve its strategic advantage or at least not to damage it. In addition, in the UK, successive Conservative governments, and even the New Labour government, have given management a relatively free hand to improve the economy's competitiveness by doing what they see fit. Legge (1998a: 150) noted that:

> There was no 'other alternative', if a cure [for the British disease] was to be effected, then a strong dose of monetarism and market competition was in order, never mind if the side effects ... threatened to kill the patent. Such medicine was seen as the *right* way to combat the evils of low productivity, high inflation and poor competitiveness.

As a result, the HRM function since the 1980s has embodied managerialist values focusing its aim primarily on helping the organization to achieve and sustain its competitive advantage at all costs. Keenoy (1990) describes the HRM function in the 1980s as a 'wolf in sheep's clothing'.

Because of the nature of the HRM function, HR managers must frequently make and implement decisions with ethical implications. This explains why HR managers may have reason to make the HR department the organizational locus of responsibility for ethical behaviour at work. During the process of making and executing HRM policies and practices, however, HR managers are often torn between strong conflicting pressures associated with the field (Hosmer, 1987), surveillance and at the same time upholding the right to privacy, making provision for whistle-blowing; and policing disloyalty, to mention just a few. HR managers face other dilemmas on a regular basis involving favouritism in employment – old boys' network, inconsistencies in pay (Heery, 2000), sex and race discrimination, and breaches of confidentiality, for example. Downsizing and outsourcing often lead to problems in maintaining employee motivation and a sense of well-being in the face of growing job insecurity. There is no easy way to deal with these dilemmas. Winstanley and Woodall (2000: 278) note that 'HRM managers must inevitably confront ethical dilemmas, and that some of these may be neither apparent nor easily resolved'. This explains the extensively debated widening cleavage between rhetoric and reality in HRM (see Table 10.1). In such a contradictory context, today's HRM managers and professionals are increasingly advised not to see their attitudes as dichotomous choices, but in some way to embrace 'paradox' as the simultaneous expression of diverse attitudes. HR managers are urged to strike a balance between these competing, and sometimes contradictory, values based on their reflection, personal experience and professional ethical codes of conduct. In her analysis of the ethics of HRM policy and practices, Legge (1998a) argues that, because people are used as a means to an end – achieving sustainable competitive advantage, HRM decision-making is firmly grounded in utilitarianism. She added that even the 'soft' model of HRM, which genuinely seeks to treat people in a humane way and would pass 'muster in terms of the deontologists', applied to all

Table 10.1 – Sisson's model of rhetoric and reality in HRM

Rhetoric	Reality
Customer first	Market forces supreme
Total quality management	Doing more with less
Lean production	Mean production
Flexibility	Management 'can do' what it wants
	Core and periphery. Reducing the organization's commitment.
	Devolution/delayering. Reducing the number of middle managers
Downsizing/right-sizing	Redundancy
New working patterns	Part-time instead of full-time jobs
	Empowerment. Making someone else take the risk and responsibility
Training and development	Manipulation
Employability	No employment security
Recognizing contribution	Undermining the trade union of the individual and collective bargaining
Teamworking	Reducing the individual's discretion

Source: Legge, 1998a.

employees, has several embedded contradictions. Indeed: 'The contradictions embedded in HRM are illustrative of the Kantian dilemma that second-order moral rules can clash and that resolutions can often only be achieved by back-door admission of utilitarianism' (Legge, 1998a: 162).

A survey conducted by the Society for Human Resource Management/Ethics Resource Center (SHRM/ERC) (accessed from the website on 2 December 2009) in the USA showed that 47 per cent of the HRM professionals surveyed reported that they 'feel pressured by other employees or managers to compromise their organization's standards of ethical business conduct in order to achieve business objectives'. The list below shows that 'aggressive financial business objectives' are the main 'moralizing' factors – half of the HRM professionals surveyed felt pressure to compromise their ethical business conduct. Note that the first five key factors listed below are related to the survival and well-being of the organization, and not to individuals. Only 16 per cent felt pressure to save jobs. HRM professionals reported that they do not compromise their ethics for personal gain (4 per cent). They identified the following pressures:

Meeting overly aggressive financial business objectives	50%
Meeting schedule pressures	38%
Helping the organization survive	30%
Rationalizing that others do it	22%
Resisting competitive threats	18%
Saving jobs	16%
Advancing the career interests of my boss	15%
Feeling peer pressure	12%
Advancing my own career or financial interests	4%

Source: SHRM/ERC (DATE?) Ethics Survey Snapshot (http://www. shrm.org).

10.5   HRM AND ETHICAL CODES OF CONDUCT

Many firms give the HR managers a key leadership role in establishing and maintaining their ethical code of conduct (Driscoll and Hoffman, 1998). This is often carried out through seeking – and providing – sources of ethical information and advice, as well as developing and executing ethical programmes (ibid.). As a result, certain aspects of HRM practices have become more formalized through the establishment of both a professional code of ethics within the HRM field, and the internal codes of conduct within many Western corporations. To outsiders, codes of conduct are the most visible sign of a company's ethical policy. In the UK, the ranks of companies gaining the IIP (Investors in People) status have swelled rapidly; the certification process includes a commitment to ethical HRM practices. Similarly, in the USA, the certification process is often linked to espoused goals of creating an ethical organization culture (Payne and Wayland, 1999: 300). Again, a survey of 1,500 American employees showed that the percentage of respondents reporting that their organization had in place a set of written ethical standards increased from 60 per cent in 1994 to 79 per cent in 1999 (SHRM, 2001). The survey also revealed that training on ethics increased from a third in 1994 to 55 per cent in 1999. Another survey of US employees, sponsored by the Society of Financial Service Professionals, reported that almost 90 per cent of respondents claimed that their companies have a written code of ethics and standards of conduct. According to the President of the ERC, Michael Daigneault, 'workplace ethics involves more than just applying the laws and regulations, ethical behaviour refers to standards of conduct such as honesty, fairness, responsibility and trust'. Evidence from the above survey suggests that written ethical codes of conduct have a positive impact on employees' behaviour only when top and line managers live by them and set good ethical examples. Otherwise, they build cynicism and scepticism, and companies would be better off not having them. This is because the ethical conduct of the organization requires the support of the top management.

None the less, Payne and Wayland (1999: 304) noted that HRM is 'still largely relegated to a role of serving strategic and control interests, defined mostly by owners, institutional investors and managers in work organizations, rather than conceived of as a force in helping shape alternative organizational potential'. Consequently, HRM practice 'inhibits the consciousness' of HRM managers towards 'potentially expanding ethical obligations' towards employees. They noted that while HRM managers may accept much of what is found in the ethical codes of professional organizations such as the Chartered Institute of Personnel and Development (CIPD) and SHRM, in practice, they lack the power and the ethical will to confront a powerful management paradigm geared towards competitive advantage at any cost. In brief, while the growing desire to make the HRM function more ethical by binding it to a moral code of ethics is understandable, it cannot, we believe, become an ethical function merely by producing a code of ethics.

10.6   HRM AS PRACTICE

The main activities of HRM can be understood in terms of the CIPD framework that has been used by leading authors spanning the business-orientated and academic divide (Marchington and Wilkinson, 1996, 2002). Using this framework, HRM can be understood in terms of four main activities: employee resourcing (Taylor, 2005) (recruitment and retention, or getting the right people in the right place at the right time): employee reward (Armstrong, 2002) (pay, recognition and motivation); employee relations (Gennard and Judge, 2005) (managing the employment contract and relationship); and training and development (Harrison, 2005) (often expressed in terms of individual and organizational learning – though, as mentioned earlier, this learning is ultimately for the organization's benefit).

Ethical challenges for HRM in practice include such themes as discrimination, psychological testing, anti-union activity, work design, employment security, employee discipline, confidentiality, and employee privacy (Gandtz and Hayes, quoted in Payne and Wayland, 1999). Danley *et al.*'s survey of over 1,000 US HRM professionals reported that the 'most serious ethical situations' US HRM professionals face are: favouritism in hiring, training, promotion, pay and discipline due to friendship with top management; sexual harassment; inconsistent discipline practices; not maintaining confidentiality; sex discrimination in promotion; compensation and recruitment; non-performance factors used in appraisal; and arrangement with vendors or consulting agencies leading to personal gain (quoted in Payne and Wayland, 1999: 300).

10.6.1   Ethics in selection

10.61.1   *Interviews*

Firms use employment interviews widely in the selection process. Different types of interviews are used: structured, semi-structured, focused, and unstructured. For many years, academics and practitioners have attempted to develop scientific interviewing techniques to help predict a candidate's behaviour, attitudes and efficiency, and thus select the most appropriate person for the job. It is argued that these techniques will reduce bias and allow interviewees to reach a fair, efficient and objective decision. However, fairness is a vague term and hard to measure, especially when interviewing candidates from different ethnic groups and/or from cross-cultural backgrounds – members of different ethnic groups or different cultures behave differently during interviews and say things differently. In its narrowest sense, however, fairness refers to choosing a person according to job-related criteria. Choosing, or not choosing, a person because of his or her race, colour, look, gender, nationality and age is generally considered to be unfair (see Arvey and Sackett, 1993).

Pearn and Seer (quoted in Spence, 2000: 46) suggest the following measures to help avoid such discrimination and unfair recruitment practices:

- Interviews should be properly conducted along professional lines.
- Interviewers should be properly trained.
- Interviews should be as consistent as possible.
- Interviews should only be used to assess abilities which cannot be more directly and accurately assessed by other means.

Spence (2000: 55) lists three steps towards 'best ethical practice' in employment interviewing. Interviewers should:

Step 1. Acknowledge individual interviewer influence on interviewing and identify actual practices.

Step 2. Understand the reasons for those practices.

Step 3. Clarify and communicate with all participants in interviewing the preferred ethical stance of the firm.

10.6.1.2   *Psychometric testing*

Psychometric tests are often used in the selection process and considered as an 'important component' of the selection event (Baker and Cooper, 2000: 61). Baker and Cooper (2000) note that 'the ethics of occupational testing is one area of human resource management where there has already been established ethical debate'. Manese's (1986) book *Fair and Effective Employment Testing* highlights several ethical issues facing (and 'best practices' for) occupational testing in the North American context. Since this book was first published, the literature has grown rapidly. Perhaps this reflects the widespread usage of psychometric testing by Western firms as well, and the manner in which it is deployed. Saville and Holdsworth (1993) note that around 70 per cent of large firms use personality and cognitive measures in their selection processes. In some countries such Sweden, however, there is strong concern about tests and invasion of individual privacy (Baker and Cooper, 2000: 61). Advocates of psychometric testing claim that, if used properly and in a professional manner, it will help the firm to predict the performance and behaviour of employees better than interviews and other subjective techniques (Cooper and Robertson,

1995). According to Baker and Cooper, 2000: 60–1), psychometric tests, when used properly, can:

> provide common and neutral language to discuss and understand differences between people;
>
> provide powerful results in a short time span;
>
> offer an idea of strengths and development areas and give a good starting point for open discussion;
>
> provide focus for changing behaviour;
>
> offer people the way to understand themselves better; and
>
> generate objective, benchmarked, and impartial results.
>
> (Beardwell and Holden, 1997).

However, several articles written by professionals and academics alike have raised concern over the use of psychometric tests in the selection process. These concerns range from employers not following the suggested guidelines of 'good practice' (Baker and Cooper, 1985; Commission for Racial Equality (CRE), quoted in Baker and Cooper, 2000), to the manner in which tests are carried out, and 'fairness, cross-cultural issues and biases of race and gender, test selling practice ... types of tests such as integrity and honesty tests, facets of testing practices and testing practices and disabled candidates' (Baker and Cooper, 2000: 63). Iles and Robertson (1997) highlight the negative impact of testing on individuals undertaking genetic, integrity, honesty and computer-based tests, because of intrusiveness and their impact on the individual concerned.

Baker and Cooper (2000: 66) note that the changing emphasis in HRM on strategic fit and achieving sustainable competitive advantage has opened a range of new ethical concerns. The testing process seeks not only to predict attitudes and behaviours, but also to tell whether the person would fit within the overall corporate strategic vision and structure. Iles and Robertson (1997) argue that, because of the strategic integration of the HRM function and the quest for 'strategic fit', tests have shifted from the traditional job/role and person fit to 'cultural values person fit'. For example, the results of the tests are widely used to help identify 'core' and 'periphery' workers.

Jackson (1997) reports cases where companies used testing not in a job selection process, but to justify who should go when downsizing takes place. Baker and Cooper (2000: 66) argue that using tests in this way 'is inappropriate because they are measuring constructs that were arguably not genuine occupational or job requirements. An example would be when existing data input clerks re-applying for similar jobs are rejected on the grounds of not displaying enough "creativity"'.

Baker and Cooper (2000: 68–9) examined testing from a range of different ethical frames of reference and reported the following from different frames:

- Utilitarianism: Mistakes and negative impacts on candidates are regrettable, but are acceptable as long as tests have utility for the system as a whole.
- A deontological approach: Stresses the regulatory process, and best practices and procedures to avoid harming candidates. A variation of this would be a perspective firmly grounded in Kantian 'universalism': emphasis is placed on testing processes and criteria so that tests meet the ethical principle of 'doing unto others as you would have done unto you'.
- Rights-based perspective: stresses egalitarianism, equity, fairness and equity of opportunity.

10.7   HRM AS STRATEGY

As well as considering the ethical implications of particular activities, HRM is distinctive (or at least advocates of this new way of managing people claim that it is distinctive) because there is also a commitment to greater alignment with business strategy. So, one claim within the new model of HRM is that these activities are brought under one umbrella and organized in such a way that they are mutually supporting (sometimes referred to as 'horizontally integrated'). An example might be that, if we want to encourage people to take risks (which might be part of our training and development or learning strategy) then we move away from reward systems that encourage conservatism (a fixed annual wage) to ones that reward entrepreneurship (additional bonuses for demonstrating innovation). As well as being horizontally integrated, these activities should be aligned with the main organizational business strategy (so they are also 'vertically integrated') (Marchington and Wilkinson, 2002: 9). An example might be that if as our main business strategy we want our organization to grow, then we concentrate on retaining existing staff and recruiting sensibly (the resourcing 'bit'), but in doing this we also look at what makes us a potentially attractive employer – for example, our terms and conditions (the relations 'bit') and pay package (the reward 'bit') as well as the opportunities the organization provides for growth and learning (the training and development 'bit').

The claim to be more in line with business strategy and more coherent is often contrasted with the more piecemeal approach of the old-fashioned model of personnel management or industrial relations (though how fair that comparison is, is open to debate, as we have shown). Leading academic authors such as David Guest (1987, 1997) have identified how managing for greater commitment is also a distinctive claim or aspect of HRM. For each of the associated activities (resourcing, reward, relations, training and development) advice can be found for those with responsibilities for HRM in terms of selecting the right staff, excellence in compensation (pay) management, managing culture and motivating staff, driving through organizational learning and so on. Though these kinds of topics have been popular among managers as long as there has been a management industry (Kaufman, 2007), a distinctive claim within the managerialist literature on HRM is that this newer model of managing people brings together these different activities under one function: the 'human resource' manager. There is a surface rationality to this since, if we accept that people are just one of a number of resources the organization brings to bear, than having somebody manage the 'human resource' makes as much sense as having an IT director (to manage the IT resource), a facilities manager (to manage buildings and associated resources), or an accountant (to manage capital): hence the title of Beer *et al.*'s (1984) seminal work, *Managing Human Assets*.

10.8   CONCLUSIONS: HUMAN BEINGS – ENDS IN THEMSELVES OR RESOURCES – MEANS TO AN END?

From an ethical perspective there is an immediate and basic problem with treating people in this way. Immanuel Kant, one of the most influential ethical philosophers, argued that in order to behave ethically we had to ensure that we never treated people as a means to an end. He based his moral philosophy on the idea that people were always ends in themselves. Though this may at times seem unrealistic in a business environment – where the end is to make money, or at least to stay in business – there are troubling consequences if we believe that people are only one of a number of resources or assets *a la* Beer *et al.* (1984). Some of the tensions inherent in colliding the two words 'human' and 'resource' are played out in critical perspectives on HRM (Legge, 1989; Noon, 1992). Some authors have even argued that the phenomenon of HRM is so beset with contradictions and internal incoherence that it is impossible to treat it as a distinct entity and instead that it should be seen as mere rhetoric or only understood through metaphor (Keenoy, 1999; Keenoy and Anthony, 1992).

Even looking at HRM in a fairly abstract way (and setting aside for the moment the difficulty of defining HRM), one can see there are ethical implications for this newer way of managing people. If the organization's needs change, then one implication of the HRM model is that this, above all else, should determine how we manage people across the board. So, rather than respecting people as ends in themselves, they are seen as a means to an end, another resource to be managed. One could say that this is true of any organization – there may come a point at which individual rights are sacrificed in order to preserve the goals and viability of the organization. However, the difference between HRM and the stereotype of the old-fashioned way of managing people is that management of the human resource becomes much more closely linked to business strategy. Simply put, the personnel department with its adherence to rules and procedures (the means) makes way for HRM with its eye firmly on the bottom line (the ends). Similarly, the focus on securing commitment has ethical implications (Legge, 1998a). Positively, it could imply people will enjoy work more if they are involved in it and invest in work outcomes. More troublingly, managing for high commitment could be seen as corporate brainwashing – the management of meaning. This is another, more subtle, architecture of control (Townley, 1993, 2004). More insidious than the (personnel management) insistence on adherence to agreement and contracts, HRM implies people go beyond contract because they are expected to be committed to organizational ideals and strategies (Legge, 2001). This could be a more subtle, and potentially therefore more dangerous, means of manipulation than the brazen devices of Kondo's ethics school.

10.9   A NEW WAY OF MANAGING PEOPLE?

Some of the tensions identified in this chapter are apparent when we consider the way in which large companies extravagantly reward those at the top of their organization. In considering the case below it seems that even in a supposedly new business environment, the traditional divide between an elite class of capitalists (the 'fat cats') and a mass of workers holds true.

Case study

Closing case study

Pay for 'fat cats': why severance and golden parachutes are hot topics ...

Bob Nardelli's lavishly paid ouster as CEO from Home Depot has provided the latest material for headlines trumpeting controversial exit CEO packages – further stirring indignation among investors, the public, and some key politicians. Nardelli's departure on Jan. 2, 2007, triggered a payout of $210 million. But the embattled ex-CEO is far from alone in seeing his exit package flare up into controversy.

In what some may see as fitting symbolism, two of the most notorious examples of excessive compensation were anchored in Wall Street and Disneyland. The first involved Dick Grasso's $187.5 million compensation package after being forced from the top job at the New York Stock Exchange; and the second, the $140 million severance pay that Michael Ovitz received after 14 months as president at Disney. Both packages sparked lawsuits. Grasso is demanding a jury trial and has appealed a trial judge's ruling ordering him to return millions to the Big Board. In the Disney case, the Delaware court found that the directors had not violated their fiduciary duty – but also noted that the board's actions of 1996 fell short of today's expectations and best practices.

Excessive severance gives rise to shareholder complaints over 'pay for failure.' Strictly speaking, though, the 'severance' portion is often a relatively small part of the overall exit payout. Nardelli's, for example, includes $20 million in cash severance – a hefty sum in absolute terms, but less than 10 percent of the overall exit package. More glaring was the payment of $32 million in retirement benefits – for just six years of service at Home Depot. The balance of the exit payout included millions of dollars for bonuses, unvested deferred stock awards, unvested options, earned and vested deferred shares, and 'other entitlements' under his employment contract. As the company noted, the entire payout of $210 million consists of 'the amounts [Nardelli] is entitled to receive under his pre-existing employment contract entered into in 2000.' And that's the point. If payouts are egregious [stand out for their reprehensible nature], it is because of the decisions that the board made earlier – seven years earlier, in this case, when Home Depot directors recruited Nardelli, a runner-up in the three-way battle to succeed Jack Welch at General Electric Co. But it is the exit package that aggregates all the disparate elements of an executive's pay, bringing to light any and all past errors of judgment. It is a sharp and unrelenting glare, beaming in on a single, all-inclusive number: a $210 million payout for a CEO here, a package of $180 million there.

Severance agreements kick in when an executive leaves the company, but the company itself experiences no change in control. Golden parachute arrangements, on the other hand, unfold after a change in control of the company, such as a merger or acquisition, which in turn leads to the loss of an executive's position or a substantial change in its terms … Excessive golden parachutes also draw fire from investors. Sometimes the executive gets her golden parachute even if she stays on in the same capacity in the new company – or when the deal is scuttled and the merger never takes place. Other times, the size of the payment itself generates controversy. Often there seems no earthly reason for such stratospheric payments. Other times, however, dispassionate analysis might argue that the payment, while large, was indeed deserved. Take, for example, the $164 million payment for severance and benefits that James Kilts, the head of Gillette Co., received when the company was acquired by Procter & Gamble Co. for $57 billion in 2005. Warren Buffett insisted that Kilts 'earned every penny.' As with severance payouts, golden parachutes draw attention because they reduce complex terms to a single, glaring number. Parachute payments inevitably raise a critical question for investors: did the executives have incentives to chase or make deals that are in their personal interests, but against the long-term interests of the company and its shareholders?

…Given the controversies over excessive exit packages, it's worth stepping back and asking what their purpose is. Proponents of severance agreements see advantages on both the front and back ends. A severance agreement can help in recruiting, because it mitigates the financial and reputational risks to the incoming CEO – especially if the new company is experiencing difficulties. And on the back end, when the executive's employment is terminated, the employment agreement will make the terms clear. That relieves both the departing executive and the board from having to negotiate severance terms on an ad hoc basis. Some observers also see a corporate governance advantage to an agreement that removes the need for board discretion on severance when the executive is forced out. Last but not least, severance agreements mitigate the risk that an ousted executive will file suit for wrongful termination.

But employment and severance agreements also have their detractors. Critics note, for example, that the employment terms should not outlast the dicey situation that gave rise to the severance agreement in the first place: have the risks to the company and its CEO subsided after time has passed – time in which the executive has been well paid? And not everyone agrees that severance and change-in-control agreements are needed in the first place. Rank-and-file employees have no such agreements, so why should executives? In the words of Kenneth D. Lewis, chairman and chief executive of Bank of America, 'I don't understand why a C.E.O. should have a safety net when others don't.' Jeffrey Immelt, chairman and chief executive of General Electric Co., also spoke out recently against multi-year employment agreements. In a November 2006 interview with the *Financial Times*, he 'argued that chief executives should not have multi-year contracts, which could lead to large pay-offs if they were dismissed … '

… some prominent companies and chief executives are working with no employment contracts. GE's Immelt is one. So, too, are the new chief executives of Exxon Mobil Corp., PepsiCo Inc., Pfizer Inc., and Wm. Wrigley Jr. Co., as well as the heads of Citigroup Inc. and Procter & Gamble Co. Other companies with no employment agreements for executives include Intel Corp. (which states that it has no executive employment agreements, severance payment arrangements or change-in-control arrangements), Cisco Systems (which also has no employment or severance agreements), Health Management Associates and home improvement company Masco Corp.

And the following chief executives voluntarily have given up their employment agreements:

○ Bank of America's Lewis voluntarily canceled his agreement in December 2003. Bank of America has no employment, severance, or change in control agreements, according to its 2006 proxy statement.
○ Wachovia Corp. CEO G. Kennedy Thompson voluntarily terminated his employment agreement in December 2005. Other executives at the bank, however, do have employment agreements.
○ ConocoPhillips CEO James J. Mulva voluntarily gave up his employment agreement Oct. 1, 2004. All listed executive officers serve without an employment agreement.

Even with no employment agreements, differences between companies emerge in other severance and post-employment benefits. While neither HMA nor Masco offers employment agreements, their equity compensation plans include change-in-control provisions for cash payments and accelerated vesting, respectively. Senior executives at Exxon Mobil have no employment contracts, severance programs, or benefits triggered or subject to acceleration upon a change in control. The company, does, however, offer a defined benefit plan based on a percentage of final average salary and bonus. When CEO Lee Raymond retired in January 2006, he received a lump sum retirement benefit of $98.4 million.

(*Source:* Taken verbatim from 'Exit Pay Best Practices in Practice', with the permission of Stephen Deane of the RiskMetrics Group, previously, Institutional Shareholder Services)

Comment on Case

In terms of the fourfold CIPD structure we introduced earlier (resourcing, relations, reward, training and development), this case study can be seen to be located in the 'reward' domain. However, it does have implications for the other practices too. Severance deals are part of the incentives that attract top talent, so in that sense this topic also relates to resourcing. The ability to attract and retain exceptional chief executives and directors is also pertinent when we consider how HRM strategies should be integrated with business strategy, particularly if we consider how shareholders' opinions will be affected by large payouts. In a less obvious but perhaps equally important sense, there are implications in terms of how such stellar sums influence employee relations. In one sense, having extremely high pay for the chief executives of large multinational corporations is consistent with the notion in HRM that we have individualized contracts – the argument for this would be that chief executives need to be rewarded differently because they are exceptionally talented. For the wider workforce, however, if exceptional payouts to outgoing chief executives go hand-in-hand with organizational failures (which in turn have a negative effect on staff conditions, or even cause redundancies), employees may well feel that their relationship with their organization is compromised and consequently become de-motivated. This would compromise the claim of the HR department to be able to manage culture effectively, a well as damaging what is sometimes referred to as the psychological contract between employers and their organizations (this refers to a bundle of beliefs that each employee has relating to how they feel they should be treated by their organization; for example, with fairness, dignity, respect and so on) (Guest and Conway, 2001). A report in the HR magazine *Personnel Today* (Overell, 2004) in referring to the, 'great fat cat pay heist' neatly summarised this issue under the heading 'differentials disincentivise' and argued that 'Executive pay should never be isolated from pay in general [that is, pay among the wider workforce] because differentials are fundamental to the calculus of just reward.' From an ethical perspective, the topic of differential pay relates to basic notions of justice and fairness. If we think of it in terms of an Aristotelian framework of virtues and vices, some of these severance packages simply appear greedy. In contrast, the actions of those who voluntarily give up such packages could be described as (at least comparatively) virtuous.

Questions

What is the case for paying executives a great deal of money?
What are the ethical implications of this for management of the 'human resource'?

REFERENCES

1. Argyris, C., and Schön, D. 1978. *Organizational Learning: A Theory of Action Perspective.* Reading, Mass.: Addison Wesley.

2. Armstrong, M. 2002. *Employee Reward*, 3rd edn. London: CIPD.

3. Arvey, R. D. and Sackett, P. R. 1993. 'Fairness in Selection: Current Developments and Perspectives', in N. Schmitt and W. Borman (eds), *Personnel Selection*. San Francisco: Jossey-Bass.

4. Baker, B. and Cooper, J. 1995. 'Fair or Foul: A Survey of Occupational Test Practices in the UK', *Personnel Review*, 24: 67–82.

5. Baker, B. and Cooper, J. 2000. 'Occupational Testing and Psychometric Instruments: An Ethical Perspective', in D. Winstanley and J. Woodall (eds), *Ethical Issues in Contemporary Human Resources Management*. Basingstoke: Palgrave.

6. Beardwell, I. and Holden, L. 1997. *Human Resource Management: A Contemporary Perspective*, 4th edn. London: Pitman.

7. Beardwell, I. and Holden, L. 2001. *Human Resource Management: A Contemporary Approach.*

London: Prentice Hall.

8. Beer, M., Spector, B., Lawrence, P. R., Mills, D. Q. and Walton, R. E. 1984. *Managing Human Assets*. New York: Free Press.

9. Beer, M., Spector, B., Lawrence, P. R., Mills, D. Q. and Walton, R. E. 1985. *Human Resource Management: A General Manager's Perspective*. Glencoe, Ill.: Free Press.

10. Blyton, P. and Turnbull, P. 1992. *Reassessing Human Resource Management*. London: Sage.

11. Boselie, P., Dietz, G. and Bon, C. 2005. 'Commonalities and Contradictions in HRM and Performance Research', *Human Resource Management Journal*, 15,3: 67–94.

12. Boxall, P. and Purcell, J. 2000. 'Strategic Human Resource Management: Where Have We Come From and Where Should We Be Going?', *International Journal of Management Reviews*, 2,2: 183–203.

13. Cooper, D. and Robertson, I. 1995. *The Psychology of Personnel Selection*. London: Routledge.

14. Dessler, G. 2000. *Human Resource Management*, 8th edn. London: Prentice Hall.

15. Driscoll, D. and Hoffman, M. 1998. 'HR Plays a Central Role in Ethics Programs', *Workforce*, April.

16. Fombrun, C. J., Tichy, M. M. and Devanna, M. A. 1984. *Strategic Human Resource Management*. New York: John Wiley.

17. Foucault, M. 1979. *Discipline and Punish*. Harmondsworth: Penguin.

18. Fowler, A. 1987. 'Comment: When Chief Executives Discover HRM', *Personnel Management*, 19,1: 1–3.

19. Freire, P. 2003. *Pedagogy of the Oppressed*. New York: Continuum International Publishing Group.

20. Gennard, J. and Judge, G. 2005. *Employee Relations*, 4th edn. London: CIPD.

21. Gibson, K. 2007. *Ethics and Business: An Introduction*. Cambridge: Cambridge University Press.

22. Guest, D. 1987. 'Human Resource Management and Industrial Relations', *Journal of Management Studies*, 24,5: 503–21.

23. Guest, D. 1989. 'Personnel and HRM: Can You Tell the Difference?', *Personnel Management*, 21: 48–51.

24. Guest, D. 1997. 'Human Resource Management and Performance: A Review and Research Agenda', *International Journal of Human Resource Management*, 8: 263–76.

25. Guest, D.E. 2000. 'HR and IR', in J. Storey (ed.), *Human Resource Management: A Critical Text*. London: IT.

26. Guest, D. and Conway, N. 2001. *The Psychological Contract: Public and Private Sector Perspectives*. London: CIPD.

27. Guest, D. E., Michie, J., Conway, N. and Sheehan, M. 2003. 'Human Resource Management and Corporate Performance in the UK', *British Journal of Industrial Relations*, 41,2: 291–314.

28. Guest, D., Michie, J., Sheehan, M., Conway, N. and Metochi, M. 2000. *Human Resource Management and Performance: First Findings from the Future of Work Study*, Chartered Institute of Personnel Development Issue Series. London: CIPD.

29. Hanlon, G. 2007. 'HRM Is Redundant? Professions, Immaterial Labour and the Future of Work', Proceedings of the 5th Critical Management Studies Conference, Electronic Journal of Radical Organization Theory. Available at: http://www.mngt.waikato.ac.nz/ejrot/; accessed 22 August 2007.

30. Harrison, R. 2005. *Learning and Development*. London: CIPD.

31. Heery, E. 2000. 'The New Pay: Risk and Representation at Work', in D. Winstanley and J. Woodall (eds), *Ethical Issues in Contemporary Human Resource Management*. Basingstoke: Palgrave.

32. Hendry, C. and Pettigrew, A. 1986. 'The Practice of Strategic Human Resource Management', *Personnel Review*, 15,5: 3–8.

33. Hoffman, W., and Moore, J. 1990. *Business Ethics: Readings and Cases in Corporate Morality*. New York: McGraw-Hill.

34. Hope, H. V., Farndale, E. and Truss, C. 2005. 'The HR Department's Role in Organizational Performance', *Human Resource Management Journal*, 15,3: 49–66.

35. Hosmer, L. 1987. 'Ethical Analysis and Human Resource Management', *Human Resource Management*, 26: 313–30.

36. Hyde, P., Boaden, R. B., Cortvriend, P., Harris, C., Marchington, M., Pass, S., Sparrow, P. R. and Sibbald, B. 2006. *Improving Health through Human Resource Management: Mapping the Territory*. London: CIPD.

37. Iles, P. and Robertson, I. 1997. 'Impact of Selection Procedures', in N. Anderson and P. Herriot (eds), *International Handbook of Assessment and Selection*. Chichester: John Wiley.

38. Institutional Shareholder Services. 2007. 'Exit Pay Best Practices in Practice', Rockville, Md., USA, March.

39. Jackson, K. 1997. 'Globalizing Corporate Ethics Programmes', *Journal of Business Ethics*, 16,12/13: 1272–35.

40. Kaufman, B. A. 2007. 'The Development of HRM in Historical and International Perspective', in P. Boxall, J. Purcell and P. Wright (eds) *The Oxford Handbook of Human Resource Management*, Oxford: Oxford University Press, pp. 19–47.

41. Keenoy, T. 1990. 'HRM: A Case of the Wolf in Sheep's Clothing', *Personnel Review*, 19, 2: 363–384.

42. Keenoy, T. 1999. 'HRM as Hologram: A Polemic', *Journal of Management Studies*, 36,1: 1–23.

43. Keenoy, T. and Anthony, P. 1992. 'HRM: Metaphor, Meaning and Morality', in . Blyton and P. Turnbull (eds), *Reassessing Human Resource Management*. London: Sage.

44. Kondo, D. K. 1990. *Crafting Selves: Power, Gender, and Discourses in a Japanese Workplace*. Chicago: University of Chicago Press.

45. Lancaster, H. 1995. 'Re-engineering Authors Reconsider Re-engineering', *The Wall Street Journal*, 7 January: B1.

46. Legge, K. 1989. 'Human Resource Management: A Critical Analysis', in J. Storey (ed.), *New Perspectives on Human Resource Management*. London: Routledge.

47. Legge, K. 1995. *Human Resource Management: Rhetorics and Realities*. London: Macmillan.

48. Legge, K. 1996. 'Morality Bound', *People Management*, 2,25: 34–7.

49. Legge K. 1998a. 'Is HRM Ethical? Can HRM Be Ethical?', in M. Parker (ed.), *Ethics and Organizations*. London: Sage.

50. Legge, K. 1998b. 'The Morality of HRM', in C. Mabey, D. Skinner and T. Clark (eds), *Experiencing Human Resource Management*. London: Sage.

51. Legge, K. 2000. 'The Ethical Context of HRM: The Ethical Organization in the Boundaryless World', in D. Winstanley and J. Woodall (eds), *Ethical Issues in Contemporary Human Resource Management*. Basingstoke: Palgrave.

52. Legge, K. 2001. 'Silver Bullet or Spent Round? Assessing the Meaning of the "High Commitment Management"/Performance Relationship', in J. Storey (ed.), *Human Resource Management: A Critical Text*. London: Thomson.

53. MacDuffie, J. P. 1995. 'Human Resource Bundles and Manufacturing Performance: Organizational Logic and Flexible Production Systems in the World Auto Industry', *Industrial and Labor Relations Review*, 48,2: 197–221.

54. Manese, W. R. 1986. *Fair and Effective Employment Testing*. London: Quorum Books.

55. Maund, L. 2001. *An Introduction to Human Resource Management: Theory and Practice*. Basingstoke: Palgrave.

56. Marchington, M. and Wilkinson, A. 1996. *People Management*. London: CIPD.

57. Marchington, M. and Wilkinson, A. 2002. *People Management and Development: Human Resource Management at Work*. London: CIPD.

58. Morgan, G. 1995. *Images of Organization*. London: Sage.

59. Morrell, K. 2002a. 'Models of HRM', in T. Redman and A. Wilkinson (eds), *The Informed Student Guide to Human Resource Management*. London: Thomson.

60. Morrell, K. 2002b. ' "Hard" and "Soft" HRM', in T. Redman and A. Wilkinson (eds), *The Informed Student Guide to Human Resource Management*. London: Thomson.

61. Nietzsche, F. (1886) 1973. *Beyond Good and Evil*, trans. R. Hollingdale. Harmondsworth: Penguin.

62. Noon, M. 1992. 'HRM: A Map, Model or Theory?', in P. Blyton and P. Turnbull (eds), *Reassessing Human Resource Management*. London: Sage.

63. Ouchi, W. G. 1979. 'A Conceptual Framework for the Design of Organizational Control Mechanisms', *Management Science*, 25,9: 833–48.

64. Overell, S. 2004. 'Time to Thin Down Fat Cat Pay', *Personnel Today*, 17 February. Available at: http://www.personneltoday.com; accessed 20 August 2007.

65. Patterson, M. G., West, M. A., Lawthom, R. and Nickell, S. 1997. *Impact of People Management Practices on Performance*. London: IPD.

66. Payne, S. and Wayland, R. 1999. 'Ethical Obligations and Diverse Values Assumptions in HRM', *International Journal of Manpower*, 20,5: 297–308.

67. Pedler, M., Burgoyne, J. and Boydell, T. 1991. *The Learning Company. A Strategy for Sustainable Development*. London: McGraw-Hill.

68. Peters, T. 1989. *Thriving on Chaos*. London: Pan.

69. Progressive Policy Institute. 2007. 'Currency Trading Totals $3 Trillion a Day', *Trade Fact of the Week*, 14 March. Appropriate website accessed 8 October 2007.

70. Saville, P. and Holdsworth, R. 1993. *Equal Opportunity Guidelines for Best Practice in Occupational Testing*. Esher: Saville and Holdsworth.

71. Scholte, J. A. 2005. *Globalization: A Critical Introduction*. Basingstoke: Palgrave Macmillan.

72. SHRM. 2001. 'Business Paying More Attention to Ethics: Management Support Essential'. Available at: http://www.shrm.org/...les/default.asp? page=bna0614c.htm. Spence, L. 2000. 'What Ethics in the Employment Interview?', in D. Winstanley and J. Woodall (eds), *Ethical Issues in Contemporary Human Resource Management*. Basingstoke: Palgrave.

73. Storey, J. 1992. *Development in the Management of Human Resources: An Analytical Review*. Oxford: Basil Blackwell.

74. Storey, J. 1995. *Human Resource Management: A Critical Text*. London: Routledge.

75. Taylor, S. 2005. *People Resourcing*, 3rd edn. London: CIPD.

76. Thomas, D. 2006. 'Firewalking Firm Fined after Accountant Has to Hotfoot It to Hospital', *Personnel Today*, 3 February. Available at: http://www. personneltoday.com. accessed 20 August 2007.

77. Townley, B. 1993. 'Foucault, Power/Knowledge and Its Relevance for HRM', *Academy of Management Review*, 18,3: 518–45.

78. Townley, B. 2004. 'Managerial Technologies, Ethics and Managing', *Journal of Management Studies*, 41,3: 425–45.

79. Truss, C. 2001. 'Complexities and Controversies in Linking HRM and Organizational Outcomes', *Journal of Management Studies*, 38,8: 1121–49.

80. Tsui, A. S. 1987. 'Defining the Activities and Effectiveness of the Human Resource Department: A Multiple Constituency Approach', *Human Resource Management*, 11: 601–18.

81. Walton, R. E. 1985. 'From Control to Commitment in the Workplace', *Harvard Business Review*, 63: 77–84.

82. Wilson, F. 1999. *Organizational Behaviour: A Critical Introduction*, Oxford: Oxford University Press.

83. Winstanley, D. and Woodall, J. (eds). 2000. *Ethical Issues in Contemporary Human Resources Management*. Basingstoke: Palgrave Macmillan.

84. Winstanley, D., Woodall, J. and Heery, E. 1996. 'Business Ethics and Human Resource Management – Themes and Issues', *Personnel Review*, 25,6: 5–12.

Chapter

11

ORGANIZATIONAL STRUCTURE AND DESIGN

CHAPTER OUTLINE

◎ Introduction
◎ Organizational structure and design
◎ Dimensions of structure
◎ Typologies of organizational structure
◎ Determinants of organizational structure: making strategic choices
◎ Organizational restructuring: a conceptual framework
◎ Traditional designs of organizational structure: bureaucracy
◎ Emerging organizational designs: post-bureaucracy?
◎ Gender, sexuality and organizational design
◎ Summary and end-of-chapter features
◎ Chapter case study 1: Strategy and design in Australia's tourist industry
◎ Chapter case study 2: ABC's just-in-time supply chain

CHAPTER OBJECTIVES

After studying this chapter, you should be able to:

◎ identify and define the foundation concepts of organizational structure and design
◎ understand the meaning and significance of complexity, formalization and centralization
◎ explain the relationships between strategy, size, technology and capitalist development, and the different forms of organizational design
◎ describe the difference between classical and modern thinking about organizational design
◎ describe some of the emerging contemporary forms of organizational design and identify the potential impact on workplace behaviour
◎ explain and illustrate the basis of criticism of managerial thinking about organizational design with reference to power, gender and sexuality

INTRODUCTION

In his influential book *Beyond Reengineering*,[1] Michael Hammer cited the Ford Motor Company as an exemplar of how a few American corporations had restructured and transformed 'beyond recognition' their old ways of doing things in order to meet the challenges of global competition. In February 2009, Ford chairman and CEO Bill Ford and other CEOs from General Motors and Chrysler were publicly explaining to the US Senate banking committee why they needed US\$17 billion of emergency financial infusion to prevent bankruptcy. And in March 2009, US President Barack Obama rejected General Motors' and Chrysler's restructuring plans that had been submitted in February, while demanding the resignation of General Motors' CEO, Rick Wagoner, as part of the government's offer to help General Motors to accelerate and deepen their restructuring plans (see OB in focus, below).

In the same period, corporate bail-outs and the restructuring of European companies such as Fiat SpA, Renault SA, Volvo and Opel were reported. These restructuring initiatives were not unique to the manufacturing sector. Accelerated by dysfunctional financial markets and deteriorating global trade, venerable financial firms such as American International Group, Fannie Mae, Freddie Mac, Citigroup, Bank of America, Northern Rock, Bradford and Bingley, Royal Bank of Scotland and HBOS have been bailed out, restructured or nationalized.

Organizational restructuring entails a significant decrease in the resources that it allocates to process activities or product markets in which it has previously engaged, or a reallocation of resources to new geographical locations.[2] A plethora of studies have analysed such a 'downsizing' as part of a process of 'outsourcing' many functions originally assigned to permanent employees. Restructuring has been wrapped in the mantra of flexibility, lean and mean and competitiveness.[3-12] These studies emphasize that 'corporate anorexia' can fundamentally change how work is performed as well as reshape employment relations. Thus, the study of organizational structure and design is essential for a deeper understanding of workplace behaviour. What exactly are senior managers 'restructuring'? What determines organizational design? What is the right relationship between the centre of a company and its periphery? How does the psychological contract between the worker and the employer change after restructuring? And how does organizational design and redesign modify behaviour?

The answer to these questions is the focus of this chapter. We begin by explaining the meaning and nature of organizational structure and design. To help with our analysis of different organizational forms, we offer a conceptual framework of the various types of organizational reconfiguring. We then move on to examine some traditional **formal organizational** designs: functional, product/service, divisional and matrix. New organizational designs that have allegedly supplanted the traditional forms are also examined. We conclude this chapter with a discussion on the links between gender, sexuality and organizational design.

formal organization: a highly structured group formed for the purpose of completing certain tasks or achieving specific goals

stop reflect
Think about an organization where you have worked or studied. Can you identify a set of characteristics that help to describe its structure?

OB In focus: Corporate restructuring and the car industry

Since the start of the recession, downsizing has become the management trend around the world, and corporate restructuring has become key to survival. In just one week in November 2008, Britain's BT, Canada's Nortel and German-owned DHL were just three of many firms announcing massive job cuts. In addition to having to trim down the number of employees, businesses are having to rethink the organization of their headquarters. Many are struggling with the problem of maintaining the right relationship between the centre and the periphery. In the 1970s, large multinationals created large headquarters. In the 1990s, the fashion changed to modest, simple centres. In the twenty-first century, headquarters were beginning to expand again – but the recession will probably force organizations to revert to minimalism.

The car industry has been hit especially hard by the recent economic downturn. Three of the largest US car manufacturers – General Motors (GM), Chrysler and Ford – have been forced to make significant changes to how they operate, while the government has had to step in to help out. All three organizations were in the midst of implementing vast restructuring and cost-cutting strategies when they were knocked back again by tightening credit and rising oil prices. The revelation that GM was in danger of running out of cash concentrated executive minds. Although not quite as desperate, Ford was in a similar position, while Cerberus Capital Management (which owned 80 per cent of Chrysler) sought to offload the car maker to another firm. So the struggling car manufacturers were left with just two options: either the US government would have to come to the rescue, or the biggest car companies in America would have to seek bankruptcy protection.

Chrysler did in the end file for bankruptcy (despite evidence that customers would be likely to abandon the products of a car manufacturer that took this step). The US government bailed out GM, and President Obama expressed his hope that the company would emerge 'leaner and meaner' as a result of its financial woes. In some ways, it seems that the Obama administration's automotive task force holds the fate of the US car industry and its future structure in its hands.

Sources: Anonymous (2008) 'Centres of attention', *The Economist*, November 13; Anonymous (2008) 'Follow the money', *The Economist*, October 18, p. 72; Anonymous (2008) 'On the edge', *The Economist*, November 15, 2008, p. 75; Keenan, G. (2009) 'Losses force GM to question its future', *Globe and Mail*, February 27, p. B1; http://news.bbc.co.uk/1/hi/business/8065760.stm.

ORGANIZATIONAL STRUCTURE AND DESIGN

Organizations are created to produce goods or services and to pursue dominant goals that individuals acting alone cannot achieve. According to Peter Drucker, the purpose of the work organization 'is to get the work done'.[13] However, organizational structure is not easy to define because it is not a physical reality, but rather a conceptual one. Let us begin to explain the concept in this way. To accomplish its strategic goals, an organization typically has to do two things: divide the work to be done among its members, and then coordinate the work. **Organizational structure** refers to the formal division of work and the formal configuration of relationships that coordinate and control organizational activities. The **organizational design** is the planning and implementation of a structural configuration of roles and modes of operation. Arguably, theories of organizational structure are a product of modernity, because they are largely based on Weber's notions of rationality and bureaucratic specialization.

Thus, work is divided horizontally into distinct tasks that need to be done, either into jobs, subunits or departments. This horizontal division of labour is associated

organizational structure: the formal reporting relationships, groups, departments and systems of the organization

organizational design: the process of creating and modifying organizational structures

Plate 1 – In a small restaurant, the horizontal divisions might be divided into three main work activities: preparing the food, service and running the bar. A vertical division of labour would describe the coordinating and directing work of the head chef, the restaurant supervisor and the head bar tender, all of whom report to the restaurant manager.
Source: iStockphoto

with specialization on the part of the workforce. The vertical division of labour is concerned with apportioning authority for planning, decision making, monitoring and controlling: who will tell whom what to do? For example, in a small restaurant, the horizontal divisions might be divided into three main work activities: preparing the food, service and running the bar. A vertical division of labour would describe the coordinating and directing work of the head chef, the restaurant supervisor and the head bar tender, all of whom report to the restaurant manager.

This small business has a simple structure. However, the structure could become more complex as more people were hired and as coordination and control became more difficult. As business expanded and management became more complicated, the manager might not have enough time to deal with the accounts and hiring and training of new staff. To solve these problems, the restaurant manager might hire an accountant and a human resource manager, which would increase the vertical division of labour. The growth of an organization might therefore lead to a greater degree of specialization of its workforce.

Alternatively, the restaurant manager might create work teams and allow the team members to coordinate their work activities and hire and train their members. This limited 'empowerment' of the workers would then free up time for the head chef, the restaurant supervisor and the head bar tender to handle the accounts for their departments.

specialization: the allocation of work tasks to categories of employee or groups. Also known as division of labour

Specialization occurs when people focus their effort on a particular skill, task, customer or territorial area. Our simple example of the restaurant illustrates two important points: managers have choices over how to divide labour, and different organizational configurations impact on people's work experience. (For instance, if teams were introduced, additional tasks would have to be learnt and the pace of work might intensify.)

organization chart: a diagram showing the grouping of activities and people within a formal organization to achieve the goals of the organization efficiently

An **organization chart** graphically shows the various parts as boxes, and the coordination and control by lines that connect the boxes. This system is used in Figure 11.1 to demonstrate the simple structure of the restaurant just described, and is used in the sample organization charts that follow. Organizational design refers to the process of creating a structure that best fits a strategy, technology and environment. For example, Ford Motor Company has created a structure on a product basis, with separate divisions for specific models. So why do managers redesign structures? Management designs new structures in order to reduce costs, to respond to changing customer buying patterns or business boundaries, to reset priorities, to shift people and align capabilities, to shift perceptions of service among users, or to 'shake things up'.[14]

Why is organizational structure important? From a managerial perspective, structure may make the task of managing employees more complex, bringing into play the questions of efficiency and consistency that are likely to arise more often when different groups report directly to departmental managers, rather than to a single owner or manager in an organization employing relatively few people. Structure therefore defines lines of responsibility and authority. In terms of organizational performance, a 'good' structure is not a panacea, but it is very important, argues management guru Peter Drucker: 'Good organizational structure does not by itself produce good performance ... But a poor organization structure makes good performance impossible, no matter how good the individual managers may be' (ref. 15, p. 4). The structure of an organization also affects the ability of workers to learn, to be creative, to innovate and to participate in decision making.[16,17]

From a worker's perspective, different structural configurations affect not only productivity and economic results, defined by the marketplace, but also job

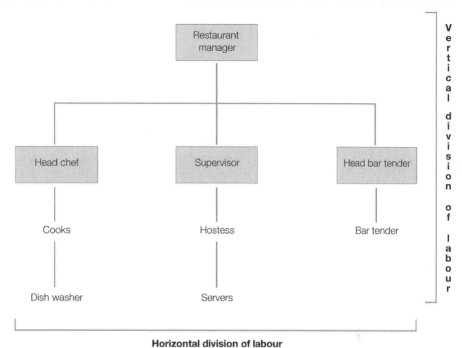

Figure 11.1 – An example of a simple organizational structure

satisfaction, commitment, motivation and perceptions about expectations and obligations. Redesigning organizational structure will therefore affect the intangible 'psychological contract' of each individual worker.

The concept of the psychological contract has an important implication for those redesigning organizational structures. Each individual employee will have different perceptions of his or her psychological contract, even when the structure within which he or she works is identical. Therefore, there will be no universal notion of mutual expectations and obligations.[18] Changes in the organization's structure also affect employee relations and organizational governance. All this serves to remind us that organizational success and failure depend on the behaviour of people, who work within the formal structure and who mould and imprint their personality into their work activities.

So far, we have given what could be described as the orthodox or mainstream position, in which organizational structure is rationally designed by managers to meet dominant organizational goals in as efficient a way as possible within the constraints they perceive. However, a critical approach to studying organizational behaviour examines the **informal aspects of structure**, which consist in part of unofficial working arrangements, social **networking** cabals and the internal **politicking** of people. Conceptually, it is argued that these two aspects of organizational structure – the formal and the informal – are dialectically related, in that they are influenced by each other, and activities in one encourage activities in the other.[19,20] For example, a team-based organizational structure designed by senior management to increase flexibility may invite unofficial strategies among line managers who choose to resist being relocated. An organizational structure reflects internal power relationships.[21,22]

informal structure: a term used to describe the aspect of organizational life in which participants' day-to-day activities and interactions ignore, bypass or do not correspond with the official rules and procedures of the bureaucracy

networking: cultivating social relationships with others to accomplish one's goals

organizational politics: behaviours that others perceive as self-serving tactics for personal gain at the expense of other people and possibly the organization

DIMENSIONS OF STRUCTURE

stop reflect
Think about an organization where you or someone you know well has worked. Can you identify a management practice that was designed to encourage one behaviour but also resulted in another behaviour that impacted on the activity?

A variety of dimensions can be used to conceptualize organizational structure. There is a disagreement among theorists over what makes up the term 'structure', but a relatively recent way of thinking about organizations and structure is as 'discursive metaphors'. Advocates of this approach suggest that organizations are 'texts', created through discourses, which have symbolic meaning for managers and workers. These meanings are open to multiple readings even when particular meanings become sufficiently privileged and concrete. Here, we take a more orthodox approach to examine how researchers have analysed structure, before discussing how it affects organizational behaviour.[23] While we acknowledge the elastic definitions and various labels attached to organizational phenomena, here we examine three aspects: complexity, formalization and centralization.

Complexity

complexity: the intricate departmental and interpersonal relationships that exist within a work organization

weblink
Go to www.shell.com for an example of team-based organizational design

Complexity is the degree of differentiation in the organization. Complexity measures the degree of division of tasks, levels of hierarchy and geographical locations of work units in the organization. The more tasks are divided among individuals, the more the organization is *horizontally complex*. The most visible evidence in the organization of horizontal complexity is specialization and departmentalization.

Specialization refers to the particular grouping of activities performed by an employee. Division of labour – for example, accounting activities – creates groups of specialists (in this case, accountants). The way these specialists are grouped is referred to as departmentalization. As the vertical chain of command lengthens, more formal authority layers are inserted between top management and front-line workers. In such circumstances, the organization becomes more *vertically complex*. Therefore, vertical complexity refers to the depth of the organization's hierarchy: the number of levels between senior management and the workers. Organizations with the same number of workers need not have the same degree of vertical complexity. Organizations can be 'flat', with few layers of hierarchy, or 'tall', with many levels of management between the top CEO and front-line employees (Figure 11.2).

During the last decade, organizations have moved towards flatter configurations by eliminating whole levels of middle managers and generally 'doing more with less'. This form of restructuring, commonly called 'downsizing', increases the span of control for the managers who remain. The **span of control** defines the number of subordinates that a single manager or administrator can supervise effectively. If this span is narrow, managers have few subordinates reporting to them. If it is wide, managers

span of control: the number of people directly reporting to the next level in the organizational hierarchy

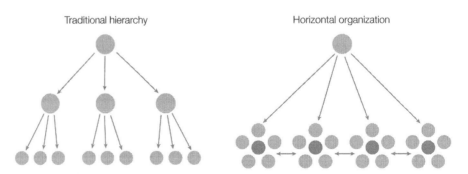

Figure 11.2 – A tall organization structure versus a flat (team-based) structure

are responsible for many subordinates. The larger the span, the less potential there is for control by direct supervision. When work tasks are routine, the control of subordinates through technology and output performance substitutes for direct supervision. At lower operational levels, it is not unusual to have spans of control of up to 20 individuals. In the managerial ranks, work is less routine, and spans of control tend to be smaller. Thus, the complexity of the task often dictates the span of control.

Vertical complexity can also affect managerial behaviour by impacting on other factors such as communication networks and manager–worker dynamics. For example, a wide span of control makes it more difficult for a manager to hold face-to-face meetings.

An organization can perform the same work activities in geographically separate locations, a fact emphasized by globalization. The existence of multiple workplaces increases complexity. *Spatial complexity* refers to the degree to which the organization's operations and core workforce are geographically dispersed. As spatial complexity increases, managers face coordination, control and communication challenges relating to their subordinates.[24]

Formalization

formalization: the degree to which organizations standardize behaviour through rules, procedures, formal training and related mechanisms

Formalization is the second core dimension of organizational structure, and describes the degree of standardization of work and jobs in the organization. It refers to the extent to which work is defined and controlled by rules. The more rules there are about what is to be done, when it is to be done and how it should be done, the more an organization is formalized. Where formalization is low, employees are given freedom to exercise discretion in their work. The degree of formalization can vary widely within and among organizations.

The extent of formalization typically varies with the nature of the work performed and the size of the organization.[25] The most complex and creative paid work is amenable to low degrees of formalization. Formalization also tends to be inversely related to the hierarchical level in the organization. Individuals lower in the organization are engaged in activities that are relatively simple and repetitive, and therefore these people are most likely to work in a highly formalized environment. Although formalization regulates workers' behaviour, it can also impose constraints on managers and subordinates. In a unionized workplace, for instance, contract rules negotiated by union and management can constrain managers' ability to mobilize the skills, creativity, commitment and values of their subordinates.[26]

CENTRALIZATION

centralization: the degree to which formal decision authority is held by a small group of people, typically those at the top of the organizational hierarchy

Centralization, the third core dimension of organizational structure, refers to the degree to which decision making is concentrated at a single point in the organization. In essence, it addresses the question, who makes the decisions in the organization? A decentralized organization is one in which senior managers solicit input from members when making key decisions. The more input members provide or the more autonomy they are given to make decisions, the more decentralized the organization.

The degree of centralization affects workers' ability to make decisions, levels of motivation and the manager–subordinate interface. An ongoing challenge for managers is to balance the degree of centralization necessary to achieve control on the one hand, and to gain commitment through participation and work-related learning on the other.

TYPOLOGIES OF ORGANIZATIONAL STRUCTURE

mechanistic organiza-
tion: an organizational
structure with a narrow
span of control and high
degrees of formalization
and centralization
organic organization: an
organizational structure
with a wide span of
control, little formalization
and decentralized decision
making

The three core dimensions of formal organizational structure – complexity, formalization and centralization – can be combined into a number of different types or models. Two popular descriptive models have received much attention: the mechanistic model and the organic model.[27]

The **mechanistic organization** has been characterized as a machine. It has high complexity, high formalization and high centralization. A mechanistic organization resembles a bureaucracy. It is characterized by highly specialized tasks that tend to be rigidly defined, a hierarchical authority and control structure, and communications that primarily take the form of edicts and decisions issued by managers to subordinates. Communication typically flows vertically from the top down.

Organic organizations are the antithesis of mechanistic organizations. They are characterized by being low in complexity, formality and centralization. An organic organization is said to be flexible and informally coordinated, and managers use participative decision-making behaviours. Communication is both horizontal (across different departments) and vertical (down and up the hierarchy), depending on where the information resides.

stop reflect
Can you identify organizations that have organic features and organizations that display mechanistic features?

DETERMINANTS OF ORGANIZATIONAL STRUCTURE: MAKING STRATEGIC CHOICES

The underlying rationale for mechanistic and organic organizations is, according to conventional organizational theory, explained by the choice of competitive strategy. The mechanistic organization strives for **competitive advantage** by maximizing efficiency and productivity, whereas an organic organization's competitive strategy is based on maximum adaptability and flexibility. Thus, structural characteristics concern contextual factors within the organization and affect the management process. So far, although we have examined a number of core organizational design concepts, we have not provided much insight into why organizational structures vary so much, or into the forces behind corporate restructuring. The purpose of this section is to discuss theories of organizational design in terms of their relevance for understanding current restructuring endeavours.

competitive advantage: the ability of a work organization to add more value for its customers and shareholders than its rivals, and thus gain a position of advantage in the marketplace

Early management theorists put forward universalistic organizational structure theories: that is, the 'one size fits all' principle applied to organizations. Over the last 30 years, organizational analysts have modified the classical approach by suggesting that organizational structure is contingent (or depends) on a variety of variables or contextual factors. The contingency approach to organizational design takes the view that there is no 'one best' universal structure, and emphasizes the need for flexibility. The significant contingency variables are strategy, size, technology and environment.

weblink
Visit http://www.12manage. com/methods_ contingency_theory.html and http://changingminds. org/disciplines/ leadership/theories/ contingency_theory.htm for more information on contingency theory

Strategy and structure

Strategy can be viewed as a pattern of activity over time to achieve performance goals. The classical position that 'structure follows strategy' assumes that managers choose the structure they have: 'A new strategy required a new or at least refashioned structure' (ref. 28, p. 15). This hypothesis is represented in Figure 11.3.

For example, if top management chooses to compete through product and service innovation and high quality – a differentiation strategy – then managers need to

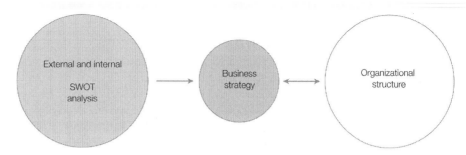

Figure 11.3 – The strategy-structure thesis

adopt an organic or horizontal organizational structure. A cost leadership strategy, on the other hand, requires products or services to be standardized with minimum costs. A mechanistic, functional structure with more formalization and centralization is most appropriate with this strategy, so that managers can closely control quality and costs.

A counter-thesis sees strategy as related less directly to organizational design. In this view, 'strategy follows structure'.[29] The design of the organization is the context in which top managers form the business strategy. Thus, the existing organizational configuration affects top managers' perceptions of internal strengths, weaknesses, threats and opportunities (SWOT) outside the organization, and helps shape a strategy.

Empirical research offers support for both views of strategy affecting the design of an organization; this is illustrated in Figure 11.3 by a two-headed arrow between structure and strategy. This recognizes that the link between strategy and structure is affected by other contingency factors, such as size, technology and environment.

In her book *No Logo*, globalization critic Naomi Klein provides a more controversial account of the link between corporate strategy – a focus on 'branding' and the relocation of manufacturing capacity from the core capitalist economy to the periphery, where wage levels are low – and multifaceted structures spanning national frontiers:

> The astronomical growth in the wealth and cultural influence of multinational corporations over the last fifteen years can arguably be traced back to a single, seemingly innocuous idea developed by management theorists in the mid-1980s, that successful corporations must primarily produce brands, as opposed to products ... The very process of producing – running one's own factories, being responsible for the tens of thousands of full-time, permanent employees – began to look less like the route to success and more like a clunky liability.

> At around this time a new kind of corporation began to rival the traditional all-American manufacturers for market share; these were the Nikes and Microsoft, and later the Tommy Hilfigers and Intels ... What these companies produced primarily were not things, they said, but images of their brands. Their real work lay not in manufacturing but in marketing. This formula, needless to say, has proved enormously profitable, and its success has companies competing in a race towards weightlessness: whoever owns the least, has the fewest employees on the payroll and produces the most powerful images, as opposed to products, wins the race. (ref. 30, p. 4)

Of course, as globalization theorists have observed, the notion of 'weightlessness' is only feasible because of the developments in transportation, namely containerization and the Internet.

weblink
Visit www.corpwatch.org, a US-based organization that monitors and critiques global capitalism through education and social action

Size and structure

Most studies define organizational size as the total number of employees, and researchers suggest that larger organizations have different structures from smaller organizations. As organizations increase in size, they tend to develop more written rules and procedures, and division of labour becomes more specialized. A number of theorists have argued that size is an important factor affecting organizational design.[31–33] It seems credible that there is a positive relationship between size and the degree of formalization, specialization and centralization.

Critics of the size imperative have countered that neither formalization nor complexity can be inferred from organizational size. An equally valid alternative interpretation of early empirical data is that size is the result, not the cause, of structure.[34] The key point here is that there are obvious structural differences between large and small organizations, but a statistically significant relationship between size and structural dimensions does not imply causation. For example, technology influences structure, which in turn determines size.

Technology and structure

Technological change is quintessentially a defining feature of the 'knowledge economy', and is also another important contingency variable explaining organizational structure. Researchers have adopted either a restrictive or an expansive definition of technology, and the early research on technology suggests a positive relationship between type of technology and organizational structure.[35,36]

The 'technology–structure' thesis has sought to analyse technology as an independent explanatory variable. The British academic Joan Woodward, for example, classified production technology into three main categories for analysis: unit production (as in a tailor's shop), mass production (as in an automotive plant), and continuous process production (like that of a pulp mill). Perrow classified four types of technology: routine, engineering, craft and non-routine. Routine technologies have few exceptions and easy-to-analyse problems (for example, pulp and paper mills or chemical plants belong to this category). Engineering technologies have a large number of exceptions, but can be managed in a systematic manner (as with the construction of bridges). Craft technologies deal with relatively difficult problems with a limited set of exceptions (such as in hand-crafted furniture making). Non-routine technologies are characterized by many exceptions and difficult-to-analyse problems (as with research and development).

The research found evidence of different types of technology being associated with different organizational designs. Non-routine technology, for instance, is positively associated with high complexity. So as the work becomes more customized, the span of control narrows. Studies also suggest that routine technology is positively related to formalization. Routine technologies allow leaders to implement rules and regulations because the work is well understood by their followers. It has been proposed that routine technology might lead to centralized decision making and control systems if formalization is low. Within this theoretical framework, it is suggested that technology mediates mechanical and integrated forms of management control, which are incorporated into the technology itself. Thus, employee performance is subject to control by technology rather than by direct human supervision.

Joan Woodward died in 1971, but her thesis that technology is a crucial contingency influenced the American sociologist Howard Aldrich. For Aldrich in 2002, as for Woodward, the technology in use in the organization had high priority in accounting for the degree of organizational structure.[37] Both structure and technology are multi-dimensional concepts, and it is not realistic to relate technology to structure in any simple manner. In addition, all the technological paradigms have their strengths and weaknesses. Conceptualizing technology by degrees of 'routineness' leads to a generalizable conclusion that technology will shape structure in terms of size, complexity and formalization. The strategic choice discourse also suggests that it is managerial behaviour at critical points in the process of organizational change – possibly in negotiation with trade unions – that is critical in reshaping managerial processes and outcomes, including organizational structure.

Environment and structure

environment: refers to the broad economic, political, legal and social forces that are present in the minds of the organization's members and may influence their decision making and constrain their strategic choices, such as the national business system

stop reflect
Can you think of any developments in the UK or Europe that have changed organizational design?

The **environment** is everything outside the organization's boundary. The case for the environmental imperative argues that organizations are embedded in society, and therefore a multitude of economic, political, social and legal factors will affect organizational design decisions. The attack on the World Trade Center on September 11, 2001 and the global economic recession that began in 2008–09 are two catastrophes outside organizations that resulted in major restructuring within many airlines and banks.

An early study by Burns and Stalker in 1966 proposed an environment–structure thesis.[27] In essence, their study of UK firms distinguished five different kinds of environment, ranging from 'stable' to 'least predictable', and two divergent patterns of managerial behaviour and organizational structure – the organic and the mechanistic configurations. They suggested that both types of structural regime represented a 'rational' form of organization that could be created and sustained according to the external conditions facing the organization. For instance, uncertainty in the environment might cause top managers to restructure in order to be more responsive to the changing marketplace.

An organization's environment can also range from *munificent* to *hostile*. Organizations located in a hostile environment face more competition, an adversarial union–management relationship and resource scarcity.

These four distinct dimensions of environments shape structure. The more dynamic the environment, the more 'organic' the structure, and the more complex the environment, the more 'decentralized' the structure.[38] The explosive growth of e-commerce, for example, has created a dynamic complex environment for much of the retail book and clothing industry, and is therefore spawning highly flexible network structures. Despite the criticisms of contingency theory, it has provided insights into understanding complex situational variables that help to shape organizational structure.

Globalization and organizational restructuring

globalization: when an organization extends its activities to other parts of the world, actively participates in other markets, and competes against organizations located in other countries

Our aim in this chapter is to offer a multidimensional understanding of organizational structure and restructuring. Existing organizational behaviour texts tend to be more narrowly focused, and give limited, if any, coverage to the causation and consequences of global capitalism.

As a field of study, the term **globalization** is controversial, as are its alleged effects. Clearly, a detailed study of globalization is beyond the scope of this chapter, but to ground the arguments on organizational structure we need to at least acknowledge the interplay of continuity, restructuring and the diversity of experiences of globalization.

Work and Society: Fordism for Doctors?

For those who study occupational change, the professions represent an interesting case. 'Professional' occupations span a broad range of areas – from established occupations such as doctor or lawyer, to so-called 'semi-professional' occupations such as teacher or social worker. What makes the professions unique is that they appear to have resisted many of the trends that have changed the face of work in the twentieth century. Although specialized, the professional worker is not alienated. He or she enjoys considerable discretion over how work is done, the settings in which it is done, and the ways in which it is evaluated. Traditionally, professional workers have maintained control over their work processes, despite efforts by managers and consumers to challenge that control.

The world of professional work has undergone significant change in the last two decades. Professional authority has been contested, and there have been efforts to subordinate professional authority to managerial authority. Some of the more dramatic instances of this kind of challenge have occurred in Britain's National Health Service (NHS). Referring to specific moments in this process of reform, David Hunter (1994), a Professor at the Nuffield Institute for Health, offers the following analysis:

> Much of the impetus beyond the 1989 reform proposals ... can be seen as an attempt to secure a shift in the balance of power between doctors and managers in favour of the latter. They seek to achieve such a shift in the context of advocating improved efficiency in the use of resources and in the provision of services. Much of the management problem in the NHS has centered on the notion of undermanagement in respect of the medical side of the service. Getting a grip on the freedom enjoyed by clinicians and holding them to account for expenditure they incur is seen as the last unmanaged frontier in the NHS. (p. 6)

As Hunter suggests, the rationale behind this attempt to limit the professional power of doctors was efficiency. But what is the larger historical context of this managerial initiative? Richard Sennett argues that the rationale for reform of this kind can be traced back to Henry Ford's views on how work should be organized. In Sennett's view, 'Fordism' entails a particular perspective on the division of labour: 'each worker does one task, measured as precisely as possible by time-and-motion studies; output is measured in terms of targets that are ... entirely quantitative' (Sennett, 2008, p. 47). Sennett goes on to suggest how Fordism has shaped reforms in the NHS: 'Fordism monitors the time doctors and nurses spend with each patient; a medical treatment system based on dealing with auto parts, it tends to treat cancerous livers or broken backs rather than patients in the round' (p. 47).

How effective has this approach been to managing the clinical world of healthcare? Hunter maintains that while the power of doctors was constrained in some ways, doctors continued to exert considerable influence over how health and disease should be understood, and consequently on how the work of producing health and preventing illness should be organized. Moreover, as Sennett notes, 'doctors create paper fictions' to circumvent the practice guidelines imposed by managers in the NHS: 'Doctors in the NHS often assign a patient a disease in order to justify the time spent exploring a puzzling body' (p. 49).

The challenge of how to organize and manage professional work remains a central issue in the field of organizational design. We have yet to answer the question of what might constitute the optimal balance between professional and managerial power. Perhaps the best way to approach this question is to attempt to envision a situation where shared power enhances productivity and quality in the provision of healthcare.

stop! Taking the doctor as an example, where would you position the threshold beyond which too much managerial power might erode productivity and decrease the quality of patient care? Provide some concrete examples to illustrate how a sharing of power between professionals (including allied professionals, such as nurses) and managers will enhance the overall effectiveness of the NHS and national health systems more generally.

Can you identify the major source of managerial authority in a system like that of the USA where private corporations play a key role in the delivery of healthcare?

Consider how these issues may apply to other professions, such as law and teaching.

Sources and further information

Freidson, E. (1998) *Professionalism Reborn*, Chicago: University of Chicago Press.

Hunter, D. (1994) 'From tribalism to corporatism: the managerial challenge to medical dominance', pp. 1–22 in J. Gabe, D. Kelleher and G. Williams (eds), *Challenging Medicine*, London: Routledge.

Sennett, R. (2008) *The Craftsman, New Haven, CT: Yale University Press.*

Note

This feature was written by David MacLennan, Assistant Professor at Thompson Rivers University, BC, Canada.

For some, globalization involves the spread of transplanetary connections between people.[39] For others, globalization primarily revolves around two main phenomena. First is the emergence of a capitalist global economy based on a sophisticated system of production, finance, transportation and communication driven by transnational corporations (TNCs). Second is the notion of global culture, which focuses on the spread of particular patterns of consumption and the ideology of consumerism at the global level.[40]

The more radical globalization literature helps us to locate the main driver of organizational design and restructuring in the dialectical development of global capitalism. This argument is based on the theory that organizational restructuring occurs because of systematic contradictions.[41] This approach, which has occupied an immense space in Marxist literature, searches for inherent tendencies in the global capitalist system that create tension and bring about their own conflicts, until such a system can no longer maintain itself without far-reaching structural adjustments. Thus, every phase of capitalist expansion is characterized by the particular model through which business organizations 'make their profits'. In Marxist literature, this is referred to as 'accumulation'.

To apply accumulation theory to the various restructuring initiatives shown in Figure 11.5, below, profit maximization was achieved in the first half of the twentieth century through the use of bureaucracies modelled on Fordist-style production and employment relations. The whole point about bureaucratic Fordism as a profitable undertaking is that it achieves economies of scale: the system produces standardized products at relatively low unit costs.

However, the downside to Taylorism and Fordism is that the success of the operation depends on an expanding market for the same standard product, and mass production cannot readily adjust to changing consumer tastes. The offer to consumers of 'Any colour of car provided it's black' is less compelling when the market is saturated with black cars and competitors are offering a choice of colours. It is perhaps not surprising that, in order to maintain profitability, an early response of employers to the catalogue of problems associated with bureaucratic Fordism was to decentralize and transplant assembly-line systems from core capitalist countries (such as Germany) to the periphery (for example, to Mexico), where wage levels were very low. The systematic contradiction of Fordism and corporate imperatives created divisionalized structures, including strategic business units, as manufacturing was relocated to the newly industrialized economies (NIEs) of South-East Asia, Brazil and Mexico.

weblink

Visit https://www.cia.gov/library/publications/the-world-factbook for more information on the relative size, by revenue, of TNCs

In recent years, market changes compelled further restructuring and 'downsizing' towards 'horizontal' or 'lean' organizations. As two US management theorists write, 'American companies were weighted down with cumbersome organizational charts and many layers of management' (ref. 42, p. xiii). Critical accounts of organizational restructuring also describe the associated changes in social relations: non-standard or precarious employment, and a new 'international division of labour' in which a small number of NIEs participate in the global dispersal of manufacturing by TNCs.

Feminist scholars have highlighted the exploitative and patriarchal nature of the new international division of labour. The critics of global capitalism argue that, as the dominance of the capitalist global system spreads and deepens, it simultaneously sows the seeds of organizational restructuring by providing resources, forms of organizational capacity and the ideological rationale.[40]

Figure 11.4 offers a synthesis of current thinking. It suggests that organizational structure is influenced by business strategy, size, technology, environment and the

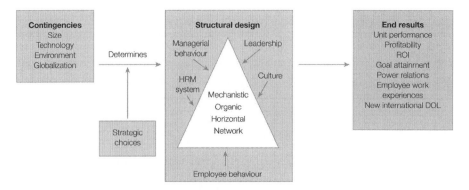

Figure 11.4 – Determinants of organizational structure and end-results. DOL, division of labour: ROI, return on investment

economics of global capitalism. It is also influenced by internal situational variables, such as culture, managerial and worker behaviour, and the strategic choices available to dominant organizational decision makers. The end results include increased profits for corporations and a new international division of labour.

ORGANIZATIONAL RESTRUCTURING: A CONCEPTUAL FRAMEWORK

Much discussion on organizational structure in standard organizational behaviour textbooks tends to be historically blind, economically shallow, culturally illiterate and politically naive. Although organizational structure and redesign are widely assumed to influence behaviour in the workplace, most treatment of the subject gives scant attention to the complex interplay of organizational structure, management strategies and changes in global capitalist development. To help the analysis of the interplay of different dimensions that appear to have been critical in recent organizational restructuring, we have drawn upon the work of Mabey and his colleagues[43] and constructed a conceptual framework using four interconnected dimensions. Each of these is shown in Figure 11.5.

On the bottom horizontal axis is the dimension of capitalist global development over the last century, from national economies to a global scale. On the right vertical axis is the dimension of competitive strategy, covering the spectrum from low cost to differentiation. On the left vertical axis is the dimension of formalization, showing the contrast between high/directive and low/autonomous, and on the horizontal axis at the top of the figure is the dimension relating to decision making, which contrasts centralized and decentralized modes.

At the risk of oversimplification, some alternative structural designs are shown for illustrative purposes. In the first half of the twentieth century, at the lower left of Figure 11.5, the bureaucratic form is located to suggest a low-cost, mass-production competitive strategy, a high degree of formalization and direction, and a centralized decision-making mode. Ascending and moving to the right in the figure, from about the 1960s, we see the development of divisionalized configurations, to the development of strategic business units and then networks and virtual organizations.

In addition to the changes in conventional structural boundaries, organizations have recently undertaken other types of restructuring involving new commercial

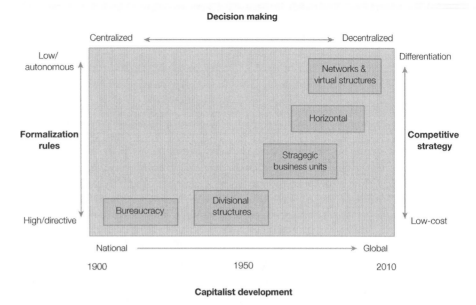

Figure 11.5 – Types of organizational restructuring
Source: Adapted from Mabey, Salaman and Storey (1998),[43] p. 235

relationships. Manufacturing companies have outsourced the production of some parts – note the influence of just-in-time systems – and services (such as payroll, training and benefits handling), and in the public sector so-called non-core activities (such as laundry, catering and cleaning) have been privatized.

This framework is useful in illustrating the different organizational forms and design options facing top managers, when considered in relation to the core dimensions of formal organizational structure and in relation to each other. The argument of this book is that if we are to understand contemporary workplaces and explain what is happening in them, we need to locate restructuring initiatives in a multidimensional framework that includes capitalist global development. While we believe that the actions of TNCs and the international division of labour are intimately interconnected with organizational design and restructuring, the inclusion in the framework of capitalist global development does not suggest any inevitable linear progression.[39,43] We must remember that millions of people still work in 'sweatshops' and bureaucratic organizations in core economies and NIEs, and these traditional modes of organizing work exist alongside 'new' horizontal and process-based forms and 'frame-breaking' network-based organizations.

The next two sections review the traditional and contemporary types of organizational structure shown in Figure 11.5.

TRADITIONAL DESIGNS OF ORGANIZATIONAL STRUCTURE: BUREAUCRACY

In Henry Mintzberg's *Structure in Fives: Designing Effective Organizations*,[44] he suggests that any work organization has five core parts, which vary in size and importance (Figure 11.6). Three line roles include senior management (the strategic apex), middle management (the middle line), and the production (operating, technical) core. The production core consists of those who do the work of the organization, making its products or servicing its customers. Two staff roles include technical support (technological structure) and clerical support (support staff). The model suggests that, given these five different parts, organizations can adopt a wide variety of structural configurations, depending on which part is in control.

At its simplest, work organizations must perform four essential functions to survive and grow in a capitalist economy:

1 A product or a service must be developed that has value.
2 The product must be manufactured or the service rendered by employees who rely on paid work as their only or major source of income.
3 The product or service must be marketed and made available to those who are to use it.
4 Financial resources are needed in order to develop, create and distribute the product or service provided.

These 'task' functions are the basic activities of the organization, and are undertaken within each of Mintzberg's five basic elements: developing (support), manufacturing the product or providing the service (technostructure and operating core), marketing the product and service (support), and financing the organization (strategic apex and support).

The process of developing, manufacturing the product or providing the service, and marketing it in a capitalist economy also results in a number of organizational imperatives (an imperative being something that dictates something) that centre on issues of control. For those who sit at the strategic apex and for middle-line managers, producing for a market creates pressures to control costs and control uncertainties. Organizations that compete in the marketplace typically face two types of competitive pressure: pressure for cost reductions and pressure to be responsive to changing customer tastes.

Responding to pressures for cost reductions means that managers must try to minimize unit costs by, for example, producing a standardized product and achieving economies of scale. On the other hand, responding to pressures to be responsive to customers requires that managers differentiate the firm's product offering in an effort to accommodate differences in consumers' tastes and preferences. These two types of competitive pressure are even more intense in the global marketplace.[45]

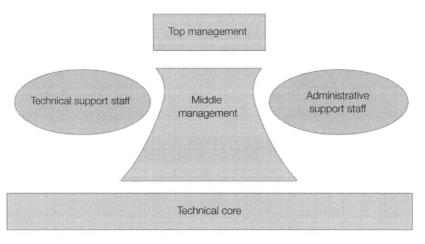

Figure 11.6 Five basic elements of an organizational structure

Plate 2 – Government organizations are typically bureaucratic. They have numerous rules and procedures that white-collar workers must follow, and concentrate decision making with high-ranking bureaucrats. This photo shows part of the parliament building in Wellington, New Zealand.
Source: iStockphoto

Additionally, the indeterminacy of employees' job performance creates pressures to render individual behaviour predictable and manageable. The control imperatives inherent in capitalist production and employee relations create a need for other managerial behaviour that is supportive of the operating functions of the organization, including human resource management (HRM), industrial relations and public relations. Together, the pressures arising from 'task' functions and 'control' functions shape formal organizational structure as a hierarchy, where decision making is top-down, with subunits or departments, and with managers hired to control employee behaviour.

In the industrial technology era, the organizational dynamics just described caused managers to adopt one of four common structural configurations. They could structure the organization by:

- function
- product/service
- division
- function and product, a matrix.

No formulas exist to guide the choices for organizational structure. Each structure has advantages and disadvantages. The guiding principle is that although there is no one right organizational structure, the right structure for top managers is the one that offers the most advantages and the fewest limitations, or, to put it another way, the one that 'makes their profits'.

Several newer contemporary forms of organizational design have evolved over the last two decades, and are well established in the organizational discourse. These new designs focus on processes or work teams, or the electronic connection of widely dispersed locations and people to form an extended 'virtual' organization. Understanding the strengths and limitations of each structural design helps us to understand what informs design choices, as well as the interplay between different structural configurations and organizational behaviour.

A **functional configuration** is one in which managers and subordinates are grouped around certain important and continuing functions. For example, in an engineering company, all design engineers and planners might be grouped together in one department, and all marketing specialists grouped together in another department (Figure 11.7). In a functionally designed organization, the functional department managers hold most of the authority and power. Key advantages of functional organizations include the development of technical expertise and economies of scale: it is the classic bureaucratic structure. Disadvantages can include the encouragement of narrow perspectives in functional groups, alienation and demotivation, and poor coordination of interdepartmental activities.

A product or service design arrangement is one in which managers and subordinates are grouped together by the product or service they deliver to the customer. For example, at Volvo Motors there is a car division, a truck division and so on (as schematized in Figure 11.8). Another example is a hospital where a medical team and support workers are grouped together in different departments or units dealing with particular treatments, such as maternity, orthopaedic surgery and emergencies.

The advantages of product or service structures include increased coordination of functional departments, improvements in decision making, and the location of accountability for production and profit. Disadvantages of product or service structures can include a loss of economies of scale, the duplication of scarce resources and the discouragement of cooperation between divisions.

> **functional configuration:** an organizational structure that organizes employees around specific knowledge or other resources

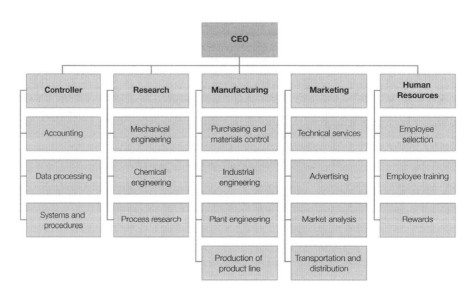

Figure 11.7 – Engineering company with a functional design

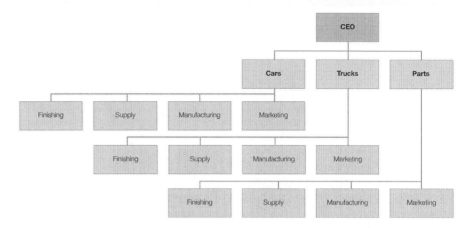

Figure 11.8 – An auto company with a product design

A **divisional structural** arrangement uses decentralization as its basic approach. The decentralized divisions can group employees together in one of three ways: by the products or services on which they work, by the sets of customers they serve, or by the geographical locations in which they operate. In the 1980s, these divisional structures developed into **strategic business units**, often with 20 levels of management between the corporate CEO and front-line employees in the business units.

The Body Shop uses a divisional structure based on its major operating regions around the world. The company's products are sold in different markets in different parts of the globe. This is based on the premise that marketing The Body Shop's products in Canada is different from marketing skin and hair products in the UK or the Asian region.

Figure 11.9 shows one possible conception of a multidivisional corporation with strategic business units, built around core products and core competencies. Organizations often evolve from a functional design to a divisional arrangement. As the external environment changes and becomes more complex and uncertain, management might find that it must diversify its operations to remain competitive.[24,45,46] Divisional organizational design emphasizes autonomy in divisional managers' decision making.

There are several advantages associated with a divisional configuration. It improves decision making by allowing many decisions to be delegated to divisional managers, who are generally more knowledgeable about the local markets. Divisional managers are more accountable for their decisions. In many divisional organizations, units are 'profit centres', and divisional managers are evaluated on the overall performance of their unit.

The disadvantages of a divisional structure come partly from its decentralized activities. Economies of scale are lost because many task functions of the organization, such as marketing, and control functions, such as accounting and HRM, are duplicated in each division. Specialists in one division may not be able or willing to share information with similar specialists in other divisions. Thus, the autonomy given to each division to pursue its own performance goals becomes an obstacle to achieving overall corporate goals. As a consequence, warn Hamel and Prahalad in *Competing for the Future*, 'corporate' strategy is little more than 'an amalgamation of individual business unit plans' and managerial strategic behaviour tends to be parochial, focusing only on existing business units (ref. 24, p. 309). From a worker's

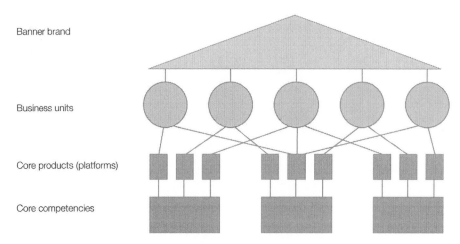

Banner brand

Business units

Core products (platforms)

Core competencies

Figure 11.9 – Divisional organizational structure based on strategic business units
Source: Hamel and Prahalad (1994),[24] p. 279

perspective, the outcome can be catastrophic: relocating to another geographical location means job loss as the firm's products or services are relocated to typically low-wage economies or outsourced and, in the case of public corporations, privatized.

In the **matrix structure**, both functional specialities and product or service orientation are maintained, and there are functional managers and product managers. Functional managers are responsible for the selection, training and development of technically competent workers in their functional area. Product managers, on the other hand, are responsible for coordinating the activities of workers from different functional areas who are working on the same product or service to customers. In a matrix design, employees report to two managers rather than to one (Figure 11.10).

matrix structure: a type of departmentalization that overlays a divisionalized structure (typically a project team) with a functional structure

EMERGING ORGANIZATIONAL DESIGNS: POST-BUREAUCRACY?

Since the 1980s, faced with accelerated changes in global capitalism, the limitations of bureaucracy and new technologies, such as the Internet, new post-bureaucratic forms of organization have emerged in the management literature: the flexible firm,[47] the cellular configuration,[48,49] the adhocracy configuration,[38] the postmodern organization,[50] the individualized corporation,[51] the re-engineered corporation,[52] and the virtual[53] and the networked[54] organization. All the post-bureaucratic forms of organization are conceived as substituting a hierarchical model of structure and implementing a more flexible work regime that gives workers limited empowerment.[55] A centre-piece of employment relations in the post-bureaucratic organization is a 'new pay' paradigm linking individual or group performance to rewards.[56,57] Three leading-edge post-bureaucratic configurations, which we examine here, are shown in Figure 11.5, above: horizontal, virtual and network.

The **horizontal or 'lean' structure** is the division of work into teams or 'cells' that are responsible for completing a whole process. A team-based organization uses decentralization to move decisions to the work teams, and gives limited autonomy to those teams to decide about product and service design, process design, quality and

horizontal or 'lean' structure: an integrated system of manufacturing, originally developed by Toyota in Japan. The emphasis is on flexibility and team work

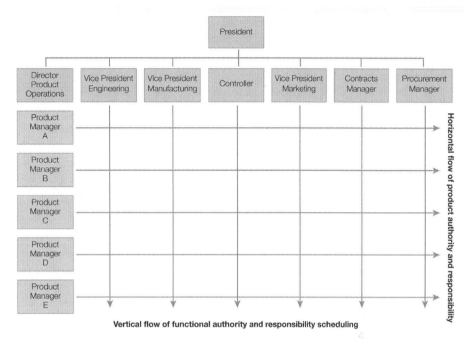

Figure 11.10 – An engineering company with a matrix design

customer service. Typically, work-based regimes are accompanied by other management techniques such as just-in-time and total quality management.

Business process re-engineering

One design methodology with a process emphasis in a horizontal structure is **business process re-engineering** (BPR). According to the re-engineering guru James Champy, BPR is 'about changing our managerial work, the way we think about, organize, inspire, deploy, enable, measure, and reward the value-adding operational work. It is about changing management itself' (ref. 26, p. 3).

Structurally, the typical pyramid-shaped industrial model is stood on its head, management structures are leaner or 'delayered', and decision making is pushed down to the 'front line' to meet the contemporary demands for quality, flexibility, low cost and entrepreneurial autonomy. Some writers have described these anti-hierarchical characteristics in organizational design as a shift from 'modernist' to 'postmodernist' organizational forms and employee relations practices.[52]

The re-engineered organization allegedly has a number of common characteristics (Table 11.1). Central to these organizational forms is the 'reconceptualization' of core employees, from being considered to be a variable cost to being represented as a valuable asset; capable of serving the customer without the need for a directive style of organizational leadership.[58] With the ascendancy of 'customer democracy', employees are encouraged not only to exercise initiative, but also to display **emotional labour** in creating value for customers. According to BPR proponent Hammer, 'Loyalty and hard work are by themselves quaint relics ... organizations must now urge employees to put loyalty to the customer ... because that is the only way the company will survive' (ref. 1, pp. 158–9). Unlike earlier movements in organizational design, re-engineering is market driven – the 'dictatorship of the customariat' – and, by focusing on the social interaction between the buyer and seller of services, rather

business process re-engineering: a radical change of business processes by applying information technology to integrate operations, and maximizing their value-added content

emotional labour: the effort, planning and control needed to express organizationally desired emotions during interpersonal transactions

Table 11.1 – The re-engineered and virtual organization

Characteristic	Bureaucratic model	Re-engineered model
Market	Domestic	Global
Competitive advantage	Cost	Speed and quality
Resources	Capital	Information
Quality	What is affordable	No compromise
Focal point	Profit	Customer
Structural design	Hierarchical	Flattened
Control	Centralized	Decentralized
Leadership	Autocratic	Shared
Labour	Homogeneous	Culturally diverse
Organization of work	Specialized and individual	Flexible and in teams
Communications	Vertical	Horizontal

weblink

Visit www.wbs.ac.uk/
faculty/research, the
website at the University of
Warwick, for information
on publications on BPR.
Alternatively, visit www.
accenture.com and search
for 'business process
engineering'

than the relationship between employer and employee, BPR emphasizes emotional labour as a key aspect of competitiveness.

Re-engineering has been criticized largely by academics.[58–63] It is argued, for example, that the 'leaner' organization actually gives more power to a few: 'Removing some of the middle layers of organizations is not the same as altering the basic power structure ... By cutting out intermediary levels [of management] ... the power resources of those at the top can be increased' (ref. 60, p. 192).

Virtual organizations

'virtual' organization: an
organization composed of
people who are connected
by video-teleconferences,
the Internet and
computer-aided design
systems, and who may
rarely, if ever, meet face
to face

core competency: the
underlying core characteristics of an organization's
workforce that result in
effective performance
and give a competitive
advantage to the firm

network structure: a set of
strategic alliances that an
organization creates with
suppliers, distributors and
manufacturers

In the age of the Internet, it is not unsurprising that the **'virtual' organization** has captured the attention of organizational analysts. The virtual organization is a temporary or permanent arrangement of otherwise independent companies or individuals, with a lead firm, to produce a product or service by sharing costs and core competencies. This ever-changing constellation of organizations is connected not through formal rules, but rather through virtual networks. A **core competency** is a knowledge and expertise base that resides in the organization.[24] The Internet, the World Wide Web and information technology connect members of the network wherever they are in the world. Typically, data are electronically transferred around the virtual network and separate competency sets work on the data either sequentially or in parallel.[64] Several factors have driven organizations to adopt network-based modes of organizing: an increased requirement for flexibility and global learning, reducing market uncertainty, managing joint production, a high-tech base and the perceived need to manage cultural diversity.[65]

Corporate global network connections have forerunners in the eighteenth and nineteenth centuries, but they have figured as a pervasive, major aspect of organizational life in the twenty-first century.[39] A **networked organization** is a constellation of several independent organizations or communities of people, usually linked on a large project basis, such as aerospace alliances between specialist engineering

to produce and market a product. Members of the network work together on a long-term basis to find new ways to improve efficiency and increase the quality of their products

firms. The firms or groups in the network have a more formal and long-term commercial relationship than in the virtual organization.[66] Hierarchy is sacrificed in order to speed decision making, and vertical integration is supplanted by horizontal integration across group boundaries. Each group in the network focuses on a set of competencies. This structure enables each community of people to be flexible and responsive to changes.[64]

Networks, argues Castells, have had a transformational effect on structures.[67] Examples of network structures exist at Amazon.com, Cisco Systems, Dell Computers and Mozilla Corporation. Perhaps the best-known company using a network structure is Amazon.com, a virtual bookstore with no inventory, online ordering and electronic links to its customers. Cisco Systems, another exemplar, produces 80 per cent of the world's Internet hardware using a global network of employees and suppliers using web-based technology. In a recent book, Clay Shirky argues that Internet technologies make it increasingly easy to create constellations of networked project groups (see the Critical Insight 'Business without Organizations', below).[68]

A virtual or network structure has neither a corporate head office nor an organizational chart. Mitchell Baker, the CEO of Mozilla Corporation, developer of the Firefox web browser, for example, describes her role not as head of the organization but as 'the coordinator and motivator of a group effort'.[69] Bartlett and Ghoshal describe an integrated global network structure with, for example, a firm in France receiving flows of components from across the globe.[70] The concept of an integrated networked structure emphasizes the shift from inflexible to permeable structures and processes, accompanied by significant flows of components, resources, information and people. Unilever is an example of a networked company that has pursued a transnational strategy, with 17 different and largely decentralized detergent plants in Europe alone.

The network structure offers employers access to wider markets, lower production costs, and the potential to respond quickly to new product and service developments and markets. The weakness of the network arrangement is that associates have little direct control over the functions done by other members of the network. The number of independent members in the network creates a high-dependency relationship between each company within the network. This requires new behaviours and a high trust in network members. Managers and knowledge workers need to radically modify their behaviours as strategic planning, for example, is no longer an independent activity, but a process needing coordination, information sharing and global learning.[70]

Although the networked organization may have been the favoured paradigm of the 1990s, the global economic recession of 2008/09 has caused firms to reassess the efficacy of the networked model. As *The Economist* reported, management wisdom had for two decades been to make companies as lean as possible, expanding just-in-time supplier networks around the globe and outsourcing all but core competencies, lubricated by cheap credit. In September 2008, the abrupt closure of the overnight commercial paper market to lubricate the system meant that most companies need to accumulate cash to meet such basic obligations as paying their employees. Thus, 'ultra-lean supply chains no longer look like a brilliant idea when you have to find cash to keep a supplier afloat that cannot get even basic trade credit' (ref. 71, p. 17). A case perhaps of 'just-in-time' being substituted for a 'just-in-case' network.

More sceptical analysts have found the 'dark side' of networks. A characteristic signature of networks is the exploitation of the less powerful by the more powerful members. Buttressing this assertion is evidence that employees experience 'uncertainty, ambiguity and frustration' in their attempts to enact their professional roles within this organizational form.[72] Countering the academic hype around 'post-bureaucratic' organizations is a recent study by Pulignano and Stewart. Analysing primarily qualitative data from global automotive companies, they persuasively argue that new employment arrangements have, paradoxically, revitalized Weber's typology of bureaucracy. According to the researchers, new employee performance-related incentives have generated behavioural rules that reinforce bureaucratic control at Fiat, VW and Renault: 'Thus, intriguingly, the use of bureaucratic control emerges as the main element of labour control in this type of workplace' (ref. 56, p. 104). Arguably, the binary bureaucratic/post-bureaucratic view of organizational design is a somewhat misleading analytical paradigm. In reality, new organizational structures are likely to be hybrids, new forms coexisting alongside some old enduring elements of bureaucracy.[73]

Critical insight

Business without organizations

The Internet and social networking sites are bringing people together like never before. Websites such as Facebook and Bebo make it extraordinarily easy to meet like-minded people, join groups and exchange ideas. What impact might this be having on business? Clay Shirky, author of the recent book *Here Comes Everybody: The Power of Organizing Without Organizations*,[68] argues that these new technologies could revolutionize the way in which businesses operate. But how? The story of rival web browsers Microsoft Internet Explorer and Mozilla Firefox provides an excellent example.

In the early 1990s, Internet Explorer appeared to have an unassailable lead in the web browser market, with an estimated market share of around 95 per cent in 2002. Microsoft's supremacy seemed assured when rival company AOL abandoned its own Netscape browser, leaving Internet Explorer with a near-monopoly. What happened next is a lesson in the growing power of informal networks and their increasing ability to take on big business. Former Netscape employees grouped together under the title The Mozilla Foundation and, using a small investment from AOL, began work on a new web browser. But The Mozilla Foundation was (and still is) no ordinary company: it is a non-profit-making organization, made up of not only staff, but also a network of volunteers and contributors – essentially, a community of Mozilla enthusiasts whose efforts are organized and coordinated electronically using the open-source model. In the words of Mozilla's CEO, Mitchell Baker, 'we build software, but we also build communities of people who build software and share a particular vision for what the future of the Internet should look like'.

This open-source model has enabled Mozilla to draw on a vast array of talent and creativity without having to become a huge, unwieldy corporation – and in this way, it gains competitive advantage over more traditional business set-ups. Any given individual might only contribute one idea to the development of the browser – their output could be very limited, but their input to the project could be crucial. Mozilla can harness the skills of such individuals without having to employ them full time – meaning that it can avoid becoming a vast, bureaucratic and hierarchical organization.

The success of Mozilla's model speaks for itself: Firefox's market share has increased to around 20 per cent since its foundation, and it now has over 100 million users worldwide – an incredible achievement and a very speedy growth rate, particularly given that it was pitting itself against the fearsome might of an established Microsoft product.

Consider the following question: Do you think that traditional corporations are the *solution* to our problems or *are* the problem? How can Facebook and Twitter transform organizational structure and design?

Source: Based on an article by Ken Hunt (2009), 'The chaos theory of organization', *Report on Business*, March, pp. 16–18. Further research: Shirky, C. (2008) *Here Comes Everybody: The Power of Organizing Without Organizations*, New York: Penguin.[68]

Implications for organizational behaviour

The downsizing and restructuring to create 'lean and mean' high-performance workplaces hit employees across the globe with cataclysmic force in the global economic recession that emerged in 2008–09. By definition, downsizing and restructuring include both high and poor performers. Employees are therefore usually correct in predicting job losses, extensive changes in the way they perform their work, work intensification, skill changes and changes in employee relations.

It is well documented that relocating operations to an NIE or outsourcing and privatizing a service in a public sector organization can have major employment implications. Downsizing has a chilling effect on the psychological climate, much as high levels of unemployment depress wage rates. Well-documented empirical research shows that, for the survivors of corporate restructuring, there can be detrimental effects on work motivation and commitment building, as well as fundamentally redefining the contours of employment relations.[43] The trauma of downsizing has predictable negative effects on the psychological well-being of individuals. 'Survivors typically are less loyal and less willing to provide service to customers and support for fellow employees,' opines Denise Rousseau (ref. 74, p. 212). The effects of the global recession and downsizing on the psychological climate also include negative perceptions about corporate leaders and decreased trust in management on the part of the survivors and the public generally.[75]

GENDER, SEXUALITY AND ORGANIZATIONAL DESIGN

Alongside management debates on organizational structures, there is a body of critical literature that focuses on relationships between gender, sexuality and organizational design. The term 'sexuality' refers to sexual characters and sexual behaviour in the workplace. Sexuality pervades organizations through pornographic pin-ups, innuendo, gossip and sexist joking. While it serves to affirm men's sense of shared masculinity, sexuality can, in a male-dominated workplace, serve to make women feel uncomfortable. Leaving the organization is often seen as the only alternative.[76,77]

Studies of the gendering of organizations emphasize that gender and sexuality make an overwhelming difference to organizational reality.[78-82] The studies draw attention to the double problem of women entering work organizations: discrimination and gender harassment. The first part of the problem is entering occupations and professions that have traditionally been occupied by men (for example, manual trades and white-collar professions).[83] The notion that 'gendered occupations', that is, ones that associate job requirements with the perceived qualities of a particular sex, has generated debate in organizational studies over the extent to which organizations and their hierarchical structures can be considered as gendered. The second part of the problem is that, once in the organization, many women face gender harassment, making it difficult for women to move into positions of authority. This is often referred to as a 'glass ceiling' – invisible, informal barriers to promotion to higher positions of authority in the organizational hierarchy.

Legislation making direct gender discrimination and harassment unlawful means that it is more common for male and even some female subordinates to hinder in indirect ways the promotion of women. Indirect gender harassment may be an identifiable element of an organization's culture, a feature of the workplace. Gender analysis questions research findings and analysis that segregate studies of organizational behaviour from those of gender divisions in the labour market, patriarchal power, issues of workplace inequality and 'dual-role' work–family issues.[84] More importantly, however, including the 'gender and sexuality paradigm' in the study of the organizational structure and restructuring has pushed the boundaries of organizational

OB and globalization Gender equality in times of economic transition: women workers in Russia

The late twentieth century brought significant changes to world of work in Eastern Europe and the former Soviet Union. The fall of Communist state governments was accompanied by a massive restructuring of national and local economies, and of the social lives of the workers who populated these institutions. While old-order policies and practices were pushed aside in favour of open markets, social and cultural attitudes about gender endured, often extending into the offices and boardrooms of organizations navigating this massive capitalist shift.

By the late 1990s, the new Russian economy was starting to look up, buoyed by successes in high-tech and natural resource sectors. Russian women, in particular, made strides in the new economy, creating successful businesses catering to the burgeoning Russian consumer culture. Two decades after this transition, scholars and journalists are turning a critical eye to how gendered experiences of work in post-Soviet Russia continue to be affected by enduring cultural attitudes about women in Russian society.

According to Russian Vogue magazine editor Alyona Doletskaya, although career opportunities for women in Russia have changed significantly over the past few decades, women workers continue to overpopulate sectors such as fashion, service and public relations (Weir, 2005). Furthermore, women's salaries are substantially lower than those of their male counterparts. Weir writes, 'A recent survey of living standards … suggested that of the poorest 15 percent of Russians, 68 percent are women. Many of the poor are well-educated women who find their skills unrewarded in the new economic order.'

The contemporary experiences of Russian women in the workforce can be linked to the Soviet era, when women were often relegated to undesirable, low-wage work, a pattern that reflected state support for, and reproduction of, wider cultural attitudes about gender roles. Today, although the transition to a free market economy has resulted in access to new types of work for Russian women workers, enduring cultural attitudes about gender roles continue to affect women's abilities to participate fully in the new Russian economy. This period of economic, political and social transition in Russia provides us with an opportunity to consider how cultural attitudes about gender can span major systemic changes, influencing local people's experience of such transitions. It also raises questions about how, over time, the new economic and political orders in Russia will affect local constructions of gender.

stop!   Using gender as an example, consider the often-entwined relationships between cultural beliefs and economic and governance systems. How do local attitudes about gender influence government and economic policy and practice? How do governments and economies influence local constructions of gender?

What kinds of societal attitude and practice related to gender extend into workplaces where you live? Who should be responsible for regulating gender roles and gender equity in the workplace?

How should 'gender equality' be defined? Are there different organizational approaches to achieving equity?

In times of political and economic upheaval, support for social conservatism can surge. How might this claim be used to explain – or dispute – the experiences of Russian women workers described above?

Sources and further information

Ashwin, S. (2005) *Adapting to Russia's New Labour Market: Gender and Employment Strategy*, New York: Routledge.

Brainerd, E. (1998) 'Winners and losers in Russia's economic transition', *American Economic Review*, 88(5), pp. 94–115.

McGregor, C. (2003) 'Getting beyond the glass ceiling', *Moscow Times*, February 10. Available at: www.clumba.com/news.asp?ob_no=2927 (accessed October 2, 2009).

Weir, F. (2005) 'For Moscow's businesswomen, a powerful new role', *Christian Science Monitor*. Available at: www.csmonitor.com/2005/0308/p07s01-woeu.html; www.usatoday.com/news/world/2005-03-07-russsia-women_x.htm (accessed October 2, 2009).

Note: This feature was written by Gretchen Fox, PhD, Anthropologist, Timberline Natural Resource Group, Canada.

behaviour by examining the people who are deemed to be the 'recipients' of organizational design.

As sociologist Judy Wajcman observes in her insightful study, the individual and the modern bureaucracy are not gender-neutral. Indeed, more controversially perhaps, she presents a powerful argument for gender-inclusive organizational theories if we accept her main premise that 'gender is woven into the very fabric of bureaucratic hierarchy and authority relations' (ref. 84, p. 47).

CHAPTER SUMMARY

- We have attempted to cover a wide range of complex issues in this chapter. Organizational structure refers to the formal division of work or labour, and the formal pattern of relationships that coordinate and control organizational activities, whereas organizational design refers to the process of creating a structure that best fits a strategy, technology and environment.

- The three core dimensions of formal organizational structure – complexity, formalization and centralization – can be combined into different types or models. Three descriptive models were examined: mechanistic, bureaucratic and organic. The mechanistic organization has been likened to a machine. It is characterized by highly specialized tasks that tend to be rigidly defined, a hierarchical authority and control structure, and communications that primarily take the form of edicts and decisions issued by managers to subordinates. Communication typically flows vertically from the top down. Thus, it has high complexity, high formalization and high centralization. A mechanistic organization resembles a bureaucracy. A bureaucratic organization is a rational and systematic division of work. Within it, rules and techniques of control are precisely defined. A bureaucratic design allows for large-scale accomplishments. The disadvantages associated with bureaucracy include suppression of initiative through overcontrol.

- Organic organizations are the antithesis of mechanistic organizations. They are characterized by being low in complexity, formality and centralization. A post-bureaucratic organizational structure, such as team-based structures and those produced by BPR, is organic and highly adaptable. However, the binary bureaucratic/post-bureaucratic view of organizational design may be a somewhat misleading analytical device.

- The contingency view of formal organizational design focuses on strategy, size, technology and environment. A change in business strategy may require changing the manufacturing process and the organizational design, for example moving from a functional to a team-based organizational structure. Large organizations will tend to be more centralized and have more rules and techniques of control. Organizations with complex non-routine technologies will tend to have more complex organizational arrangements. Organizations with routine technologies will tend to use written rules and procedures to control people's behaviour, and decision making will be more centralized than in establishments using non-routine technologies.

- An organization's external environment can range from 'stable' to' dynamic' and from 'hostile' to 'munificent'. Distinct external environments help to explain divergent patterns of managerial behaviour and organizational structure. For example, organic configurations are better suited to dynamic and hostile environments so that organizational members can adapt more quickly to changes.

- The external context has a significant impact on managerial and employee behaviour. The external domain influences the formal structure and functioning of a work organization, and in turn the organization's leaders influence the wider society. The linkage between external contexts and the search for competitive advantage through employee performance and managerial activities is complex. We have therefore emphasized that organizational behaviour studies must be able to deal with the new complexities and nuances. Caught up in the drama of severe economic recession, there is a need for a multidimensional approach to the study of organizational behaviour.

⊚ The analysis offered here provides a guide to how formal organizational structure helps to shape the behaviour of managers and employees. The contingency elements identified – strategy, size, technology, environment, culture and HRM systems – are not separate, but are integrated and linked in complex ways. It is within this integrated framework that interpretations of competing resources, conversations and interests take place, and influence people's behaviour in many ways.

KEY CONCEPTS

bureaucracy
horizontal
mechanistic
network structure
organic
technological change
virtual organization

VOCAB CHECKLIST FOR ESL STUDENTS

- ⊚ Artefacts
- ⊚ Business process re-engineering
- ⊚ Capitalist, capitalism, capitalize
- ⊚ Centralization, centralize, central
- ⊚ Competitive advantage
- ⊚ Complexity, complex
- ⊚ Core competency
- ⊚ Divisional structure
- ⊚ Emotional labour
- ⊚ Environment, environmental
- ⊚ Formal organization
- ⊚ Formalization
- ⊚ Functional configuration
- ⊚ Globalization, globalist, globalize, global
- ⊚ Horizontal structure
- ⊚ Information structure
- ⊚ Lean structure
- ⊚ Matrix structure
- ⊚ Mechanism organization
- ⊚ Networking, network
- ⊚ Network structure
- ⊚ Organic organization
- ⊚ Organization chart
- ⊚ Organizational design
- ⊚ Organizational politics
- ⊚ Organizational structure
- ⊚ Span of control
- ⊚ Specialization, special, specialize

- Strategic business unit
- Virtual organization

CHAPTER REVIEW QUESTIONS

1 Compare and contrast a 'mechanistic' and a 're-engineered' organization. What is it like to be a manager making decisions in these two types of organization? What employees' behaviours are likely to be rewarded? What type of competitive strategy is each best suited to?
2 Why is there no 'one best way' to design an organization's structure?
3 What is the link between organizational structure and technology?
4 Why do organizations in fast-change and unstable environments have different structures from those in stable environments?
5 Review the 'new' forms of organizational design described in this chapter. Discuss the designs that you and other students finding appealing and challenging. Explain your reasons.
6 Does Internet web-based technology have the potential to demolish bureaucracy?

CHAPTER RESEARCH QUESTIONS

1 Read the Critical Insight 'Business without Organizations', above. Form a study group. Thinking about how you use Facebook and Twitter, sketch out how new social networking sites (a) provide an opportunity to change the form of organizational structure and design, (b) can create new services or products, and (c) can enhance the delivery of your orgnizational behaviour course and other courses in your university programme.
2 Obtain a copy of *The Oxford Handbook of Work and Organization* (see Further Reading). 'Post-bureaucracy?', discuss why the authors believe that emerging post-bureaucratic forms operate more as a means of *legitimating* change and innovation than as a concrete indicator of changing forms of work organization.
3 Read the article by Jonathan Morris et al. (2008), listed in Further Reading. What empirical evidence do the researchers provide of a shift towards new governance post-bureaucratic forms of work organization?

FURTHER READING

Acker, J. (2008) 'Helpful men and feminist support: more than double strangeness', *Gender, Work and Organizations*, **15**(3), pp. 288–93.

Alvesson, M. and Thompson, P. (2006) 'Post-bureaucracy?', pp. 485–507 in S. Ackroyd, R. Batt, P. Thompson and P. Tolbert, (eds), *The Oxford Handbook of Work and Organization*, York New: Oxford University Press.

Armstrong-Stassen, M. and Schlosser, F. (2008) 'Taking a positive approach to organizational downsizing', *Canadian Journal of Administrative Science*, **25**, pp. 93–106.

Bakan, J. (2004) *The Corporation*, London: Penguin.

Currie, G., Finn, R. and Martin, G. (2008) 'Accounting for the "dark side" of new organizational forms: the case of healthcare professionals', *Human Relations*, **61**(4), pp. 539–64.

Du Gay, P. (2000) *In Praise of Bureaucracy*. London: Sage.

Fulop, L., Hayward, H., and Lilley, S. (2009) 'Managing structure', pp. 195–237 in S. Linstead, L. Fulop and S. Lilley (eds), *Management and Organization: A Critical Text* (2nd edn), Basingstoke: Palgrave.

Grey, C. (2005) *A Very Short, Fairly Interesting and Reasonably Cheap Book about Studying Organizations*, London: Sage.

Hammer, M. (1997) *Beyond Reengineering*, New York: Harper Business.

Lazonick, W. (2006) 'Corporate restructuring', pp. 577–601 in S. Ackroyd, R. Batt, P. Thompson and P. S. Tolbert (eds), *The Oxford Handbook of Work and Organization*, Oxford: Oxford University Press.

Morris, J., Hassard, J. and McCann, L. (2008) 'The resilience of institutionalized capitalism: managing managers under "shareholder capitalism" and "managerial capitalism"', *Human Relations*, **61**(5), pp. 687–710.

Pulignano, V. and Stewart, P. (2006) 'Bureaucracy transcended? New patterns of employment regulation and labour control in the international automotive industry', *New Technology, Work and Employment*, **21**(2), pp. 90–106.

Tyler, M. and Wilkinson, A. (2007) 'The tyranny of corporate slenderness: "corporate anorexia" as a metaphor for our age', *Work, Employment and Society*, **21**(3), pp. 537–49.

Case Study   Strategy and design in Australia's tourism industry

Setting

Tourism is a strong contributor to Australia's economy, with over a half million people employed in the sector, and tourism spending reaching over $85 billion a year. The country promotes its beautiful landscapes, Aboriginal art and culture, coastal lifestyles and the outback as main attractions for visitors.

Australia's top five international tourism markets are New Zealand, the UK, Japan, the USA and China. Visitor numbers from the emerging markets of China and India have grown strongly, while the numbers of Japanese and Korean tourists have declined in the last few years. China is now Australia's fifth largest international tourism market, bringing it into second place with New Zealand, and this is set to grow over the next decade.

However, Australia's share of global tourism continues to drop, with a decrease of 14 per cent between 1995 and 2008. Since its peak in 2001, it has also declined as a proportion of Australia's gross domestic product. The Australian tourism industry continues to struggle from the effects of a series of crises, starting with a pilot strike in 1989 and the worldwide economic outfalls of the Iraq War and the SARS outbreak in more recent years. Skilled staff shortages are also contributing to the industry's troubles, with an estimated 42,000 employees needed by 2015.

The problem

Established in the early 1990s, Outback Inc. is an adventure-based tour company located in Sydney, Australia. The company offers a variety of services, including guided tours, accommodation and meals, to those wishing to visit remote and regional areas of Australia. Outback's comprehensive packages of services appeal to travellers from all over the world, particularly visitors from Japan, who typically make up over 80 per cent of their client base. However, despite increased marketing efforts aimed at the general Asian market, the company has seen a decrease in bookings from its traditionally reliable Japanese sector. Outback has yet to attract new clients from China or other Asian countries experiencing more favourable economic conditions.

Although Outback grew from a small, family-owned business in the early 1990s to a moderately sized company with sales of several million dollars a year, it still retains its original functional organizational structure. Outback's managers, typically members of the company's founding family, head up the various departments, which are structured around traditional functions such as marketing, finance and human resources. Although the company does have its own website, management has been hesitant to move away from using standard travel agencies for their client booking purposes.

As with most organizations in the hospitality field, the Outback management uses a traditional leadership style, with decisions made at the top levels of management and communicated downwards. The majority of Outback's employees are young, highly motivated and eager for learning opportunities, but the company struggles to retain them, facing a turnover rate higher than even what is expected in an industry with a notorious turnover culture.

Management recently made the decision to hire a consultant whom they hoped could make some recommendations to help attract new clients and stop the flow of employees walking out of the door.

Tasks

As a consultant hired by the Outback management, prepare a short presentation addressing the following questions:

1 Would you recommend a change in the company's functional structural arrangement? If yes, which of the other three common structural configurations (product/service, division, matrix) would you recommend? Why?
2 How does your recommended structure fit with a strategy that could help with Outback's goal to attract new clients?
3 Would you characterize Outback as a mechanistic organization? How might this contribute to a high turnover of its staff?

Essential reading

Navickas, V. (2007) 'The reasons and consequences of changes in organizational structures of tourism companies', *Economics and Management*, pp. 809–13.

Ogaard, T., Marnburg, E. and Larsen, S. (2008) 'Perceptions of organizational structure in the hospitality industry: consequences for commitment, job satisfaction and perceived performance', *Tourism Management*, **29**(4), pp. 661–71.

Tribe, J. (1997) *Corporate Strategy for Tourism*, London: International Thomson Business Press.

For more information on Australia's tourism industry and the challenges it faces, go to www.tourism.australia.com/home.asp

Note

This is a fictional case study. It was written by Lori Rilkoff, MSc, CHRP, Senior Human Resources Manager at the City of Kamloops, and lecturer in HRM at Thompson Rivers University, BC, Canada.

Case Study   ABC's just-in-time supply chain

Visit www.palgrave.com/business/brattonob2e to view this case study.

WEB-BASED ASSIGNMENT

This chapter discusses the different types of organizational design, and the interconnectedness between structure and restructuring, and organizational behaviour. Organizations can adopt a large number of structures to match their strategy, size, technology and profit-making imperative. Restructuring affects job design and individual workers' perception of the employer and work motivation.

This web-based assignment requires you to explore the web to find a site that displays an organizational chart, or that discusses a method of managing its structure. For example, enter the website of Dell Computers (www.dell.com), Canadian TV and media company Globalmedia (www.globalmedia.ca) or car manufacturer Saturn (www.saturn.com) for an example of a 'flatter' organizational structure.

Consider these questions:

⊙ What kind of organizational structure does the company have (for example, in terms of decision making, is it centralized or decentralized)?
⊙ In what ways is the organizational structure appropriate for the company?

OB IN FILMS

The documentary film *The Corporation* (2003) offers an excellent collection of case studies, anecdotes and true confessions from corporate elites, which reveal structural contradictions and behind-the-scenes tensions. The documentary also features many critical perspectives, including interviews with Noam Chomsky, Michael Moore, Maude Barlow and Naomi Klein.

What examples are given to substantiate the claim that corporations, if left unregulated, behave much like individuals with 'a psychopathic personality', creating destruction? What examples of corporate crime does the film illustrate?

REFERENCES

1. Hammer, M. (1997) *Beyond Reengineering*, New York: Harper Business.
2. Lazonick, W. (2006) 'Corporate restructuring', pp. 577–601 in S. Ackroyd, R. Batt, P. Thompson and P. S. Tolbert (eds), *The Oxford Handbook of Work & Organization*, Oxford: Oxford University Press.
3. Baumol, J. W., Blinder, S. A. and Wolff, N. E. (2003) *Downsizing in America*, New York: Russell Sage Foundation Press.
4. Delbridge, R. (1998) *Life on the Line in Contemporary Manufacturing*, Oxford: Oxford University Press.
5. Gowing, M. K., Kraft, J. D. and Campbell Quick, J. (eds) (1997) *New Organizational Reality: Downsizing, Restructuring, and Revitalization*, Washington, DC: American Psychological Association.
6. Hales, C. (2002) 'Bureacracy-lite and continuities in management work', *British Journal of Management*, **13**(1), pp. 51–66.
7. Innes, P. and Littler, C. (2004) 'A decade of downsizing: understanding the contours of change in Australia, 1990–99', *Asia Pacific Journal of Human Resources*, **42**(2), pp. 229–42.
8. Legge, K. (2000) 'Personal management in the lean organization', pp. 43–69 in S. Bach and K. Sisson (eds), *Personal Management*, Oxford: Blackwell.
9. Littler, C. and Innes, P. (2004) 'The paradox of managerial downsizing', *Organizational Studies*, **25**(7), pp. 1159–84.
10. Moody, K. (1997) *Workers in a Lean World*, London: Verso.
11. Womack, J., Jones, D. and Roos, D. (1990) *The Machine that Changed the World*, London: HarperCollins.
12. Tyler, M. and Wilkinson, A. (2007) 'The tyranny of corporate slenderness: "corporate anorexia" as a metaphor for our age', *Work, Employment and Society*, **21**(3), pp. 537–49.
13. Drucker, P. F. (1997) 'Toward the new organization', pp. 1–5 in F. Hesselbein, M. Goldsmith and R. Beckhard (eds), *The Organization of the Future*, San Francisco: Jossey-Bass.
14. Gadiesh, O. and Olivet, S. (1997) 'Designing for implementability', pp. 53–78 in F. Hesselbein, M. Goldsmith and R. Beckhard (eds), *The Organization of the Future*, San Francisco: Jossey-Bass.
15. Drucker, P. (1954/1993) *The Practice of Management*, New York: HarperCollins.
16. Galbraith, J. R. (1996) 'Designing the innovative organization', pp. 156–81 in K. Starkey (ed.), *How Organizations Learn*, London: International Thomson Business Press.
17. Bratton, J. (1999) 'Gaps in the workplace learning paradigm: labour flexibility and job design', in Conference Proceeding of Researching Work and Learning, First International Conference, University of Leeds, UK.
18. Herriot, P. (1998) 'The role of human resource management in building a new proposition', pp. 106–16 in P. Sparrow and M. Marchington (eds), *Human Resource Management: A New Agenda*, London: Financial Times Management.

19. Watson, T. (1995) *Sociology of Work and Industry* (3rd edn), London: Routledge.

20. Thompson, P. and McHugh, D. (2006) *Work Organizations: A Critical Introduction* (4th edn), Basingstoke: Palgrave.

21. Clegg, S. and Dunkerley, D. (1980) *Organization, Class and Control*, London: Routledge & Kegan Paul.

22. Hardy, C. and Clegg, S. R. (1999) 'Some dare call it power', pp. 368–87 in S. R. Clegg and C. Hardy (eds), *Studying Organization*, London: Sage.

23. Clegg, S., Hardy, C. and Nord, W. (eds) (1999) *Managing Organizations: Current Issues,* Thousand Oaks, CA: Sage.

24. Hamel, G. and Prahalad, C. K. (1994) *Competing for the Future*, Boston, MA: Harvard Business School Press.

25. Daft, R. (2001) *Organization Theory and Design* (7th edn), Cincinnati, OH: South-Western.

26. Champy, J. (1996) *Reengineering Management*, New York: HarperCollins.

27. Burns, T. and Stalker, G. M. (1966) *The Management of Innovation* (2nd edn), London: Tavistock.

28. Chandler, A. (1962) *Strategy and Structure*, Cambridge, MA: MIT Press.

29. Keats, B. W. and Hitt, M. (1988) 'A causal model of linkages among environmental dimensions, macro organizational characteristics, and performance', *Academy of Management Journal*, September, pp. 570–98.

30. Klein, N. (2000) *No Logo*, London: Flamingo.

31. Blau, P. M. and Schoenherr, R. A. (1971) *The Structure of Organizations*, New York: Basic Books.

32. Pugh, D., Hickson, C, Hining, R. and Turner, C. (1969) 'The context of organization structures', *Administrative Science Quarterly*, **14**, pp. 91–114.

33. Child, J. (1972) 'Organizational structure, environment and performance: the role of strategic choice', *Sociology*, **6**(1), pp. 331–50.

34. Aldrich, H. (1972) 'Technology and organizational structure: a re-examination of the findings of the Aston Group', *Administrative Science Quarterly*, **17**(1), pp. 26–43.

35. Woodward, J. (1965) *Industrial Organizations: Theory and Practice*, London: Oxford University Press.

36. Thompson, J. D. (1967) *Organizations in Action*, New York: McGraw-Hill.

37. Aldrich, H. E. (2002) 'Technology and organizational structure: a reexamination of the findings of the findings of the Aston Group', pp. 344–66 in S. R. Clegg (ed.), *Central Currents in Organization Studies,* London: Sage

38. Mintzberg, H. (1993) *Structure in Fives: Designing Effective Organizations* (7th edn), Englewood Cliffs, NJ: Prentice Hall.

39. Scholte, J. A. (2005) *Globalization: A Critical Introduction*, Basingstoke: Palgrave Macmillan.

40. Sklair, L. (2002) *Globalization: Capitalism and its Alternatives*, Oxford: Oxford University Press.

41. Hoogvelt, A. (2001) *Globalization and the Postcolonial World* (2nd edn), Basingstoke: Palgrave.

42. Orsburn, J. and Moran, L. (2000) *The New Self-Directed Work Teams*, New York: McGraw-Hill.

43. Mabey, C., Salaman, G. and Storey, J. (1998) *Human Resource Management: A Strategic Introduction* (2nd edn), Oxford: Blackwell.

44. Mintzberg, H. (1983) *Structure in Fives: Designing Effective Organizations*, Englewood Cliffs, NJ: Prentice Hall.

45. Hill, C. and Jones, G. (2004) *Strategic Management Theory*, New York: Houghton Mifflin.

46. Jacoby, S. M. (2005) *The Embedded Corporation: Corporate Governance and Employment Relations in Japan and the United States*, Princeton, NJ: Princeton University Press.

47. Atkinson, J. (1984) 'Manpower strategies for flexible organizations', *Personnel Management*, August, pp. 14–25.

48. Bratton, J. A. (1992) *The Japanization of Work*, London: Macmillan.

49. Miles R. E., Snow, C. C., Matthews, J. A. and Coleman, H. J. (1997) 'Organizing in the knowledge area: anticipating the cellular form', *Academy of Management Executive*, **11**(4), pp. 7–20.

50. Hassard, J. and Parker, M. (1993) *Postmodernism and Organizations*, London: Sage.

51. Ghoshal, S. and Bartlett, C. A. (1997) *The Individualized Corporation: A Fundamentally New Approach to Management: Great Companies Are Defined by Purpose, Process, and People*. New York: Harper Business.

52. Hammer, M. and Champy, J. (1993) *Reengineering the Corporation: A Manifesto for Business Revolution*, New York: Harper Business.

53. Goldman, S. L., Nagel, R. N. and Preiss, K. (1995) *Agile Competition and Virtual Organizations: Strategies for Enriching the Customer*, New York: Van Nostrand Reinhold.

54. Powell, W. W. (2003) 'Neither market nor hierarchy: network forms of organization', pp. 315–30 in M. J. Handel (ed.), *The Sociology of Organizations*, Thousand Oaks, CA: Sage.

55. Clarke, T. and Clegg, S. R. (1998) *Changing Paradigms: The Transformation of Management for the 21st Century*, London: Collins.

56. Pulignano, V. and Stewart, P. (2006) 'Bureaucracy transcended? New patterns of employment regulation and labour control in the international automotive industry', *New Technology, Work and Employment*, **21**(2), pp. 90–106.

57. Corby, S., Palmer, S. and Lindop, E. (2009) *Rethinking Reward*, Basingstoke: Palgrave.

58. Willmott, H., (1995) 'The odd couple?: re-engineering business processes: managing human relations', *New/Technology, Work and Employment*, **10**(2), pp. 89–98.

59. Reed, M. I. (1993) 'Organizations and modernity: continuity and discontinuity in organization theory', pp. 163–82 in J. Hassard and M. Parker (eds), *Postmodernism and Organizations*, London: Sage.

60. Thompson, P. (1993) 'Fatal distraction: postmodernism and organizational theory', in. J. Hassard and M. Parker (eds), *Postmodernism and Organizations*, London: Sage.

61. Craig, J. and Yetton, P. (1993) 'Business process redesigns critique of *Process Innovation* by Thomas Davenport as a case study in the literature', *Australian Journal of Management*, **17**(2), pp. 285–306.

62. Oliver, J. (1993) 'Shocking to the core', *Management Today*, August, pp. 18–21.

63. Grint, K. and Willcocks, L. (1995) 'Business process re-engineering in theory and practice: business paradise regained?', *New Technology, Work and Employment*, **10**(2), pp. 99–108.

64. Davidow, W. H. and Malone, M. A. (1992) *The Virtual Corporation: Structuring and Revitalizing the Corporation for the 21st Century*, New York: HarperCollins.

65. Ferlie, E. and Pettigrew, A. (1998) 'Managing through networks', pp. 200–22 in C. Mabey, G. Salaman and J. Storey (eds), *Strategic Human Resource Management: A Reader*, London: Sage.

66. Rocket, J. F. and Short, J. E. (1991) 'The networked organization and the management of interdependence', in M. S. Scott Morton (ed.), *The Corporation of the 1990s: Information Technology and Organizational Transformation*, Oxford: Oxford University Press.

67. Castells, M. (2000) *The Information Age: Economy, Society and Culture*, Volume 1: *The Rise of Network Society* (2nd edn), London: Blackwell.

68. Shirky, C. (2008) *Here Comes Everybody: The Power of Organizing Without Organizations*, New York: Penguin.

69. Baker, M. Quoted in Hunt, K. (2009) 'The chaos theory of organization', *Report on Business*, March, p. 18.

70. Bartlett C. A. and Ghoshal, S. (1989) *Managing Across Borders: The Transnational Solution*, London: Random House.

71. Anonymous (2008) 'All you need is cash', *Economist,* November 22, p. 17.

72. Currie, G., Finn, R. and Martin, G. (2008) 'Accounting for the "dark side" of new organizational forms: the case of healthcare professionals', *Human Relations*, **61**(4), pp. 539–64.

73. Dunford, R., Palmer, I., Benveniste, J. and Crawford, J. (2007) 'Coexistence of "old" and "new" organizational practices: transitory phenomenon or enduring feature?', *Asia Pacific Journal of Human Resources*, **45**(1), pp. 24–43.

74. Rousseau, D. M. (1995) *Psychological Contracts in Organizations*, Thousand Oaks, CA: Sage.

Clarke, J. and Koonce, R. (1995) 'Engaging organizational survivors', *Training and Development*, **49**(8), pp. 22–30.

Mills, A. and Tancred, P. (eds) (1992) *Gendering Organizational Analysis*, Newbury Park, CA: Sage.

Hearn, J., Sheppard, D., Tancred-Sheriff, R. and Burrell, G. (eds) (1989) *The Sexuality of Organization*, London: Sage.

Dex, S. (1988) 'Gender and the labour market', pp. 281–309 in D. Gallie (ed.), *Employment in Britain*, Oxford: Blackwell.

Witz, A. (1986) 'Patriarchy and the labour market: occupational control strategies and the medical division of labour', in D. Knights and H. Willmott (eds), *Gender and the Labour Process*, Aldershot: Gower.

Knights, D. and Willmott, H. (eds) (1986) *Gender and the Labour Process*, Aldershot: Gower.

Phillips, R. and Phillips, E. (1993) *Women and Work: Inequality in the Canadian Labour Market*, Toronto: Lorimer.

Wilson, F. M. (2003) *Organizational Behaviour and Gender*, Farnham: Ashgate.

Ledwith, S. and Colgan, F. (eds.) (1996) *Women in Organizations: Challenging Gender Politics*, London: Palgrave Macmillan.

Wajcman, J. (1998) *Managing Like a Man: Women and Men in Corporate Management*, Cambridge, MA: Polity Press/Penn State University Press.

ORGANIZATIONAL CULTURE

CHAPTER OUTLINE

- Introduction
- National culture and culture dimensions
- Understanding organizational culture
- Perspectives on organizational culture
- Managing cultures
- Summary and end-of-chapter features
- Chapter case study: Changing the University of Daventry's culture

CHAPTER OBJECTIVES

After studying this chapter, you should be able to:

- explain the relationship between national culture and organizational culture
- define organizational culture and be aware of its importance for understanding behaviour in the workplace and organizational performance
- explain the three levels of organizational culture and notions of dominant culture, cultural diversity, subcultures and countercultures
- explain mainstream and critical theoretical perspectives on organizational culture
- describe how managers seek to manage cultures and how leaders strive to change the culture of their organization

INTRODUCTION

In Malcolm Bradbury's *The History Man*, Professor Marvin, sitting at the head of the table, starts the department of sociology's monthly meeting at 2 pm by calling 'Can we come to order gentlemen?' The story goes on: 'Immediately the silence breaks; many arms go up, all around the table; there is a jabber of voices. "May I point out, Mr. Chairperson, that of the persons in this room you are addressing as 'gentlemen', seven are women?" says a female character. "May I suggest the formulation 'Can we come to order persons?' or perhaps 'Can we come to order colleagues?'" "Doesn't the phrase itself suggest we're somehow normally in a state of *dis*order?,"' states another. The meeting goes on, and it is 2.30 before Professor Marvin manages to begin item 1 of the 34-item agenda.

This amusing incident providing an insight into the ways of doing things in one particular work domain is an example of **organizational culture**, as is

organizational culture: the basic pattern of shared assumptions, values and beliefs governing the way employees in an organization think about and act on problems and opportunities

predatory sexual harassment, or espousing the value of research-informed teaching, or a belief that university students are not 'customers'. Redesigning complex organizations to create new hierarchical arrangements and new subunits, as well as installing new technology, sets the context within which people interact and work. However, the ways in which organizational members *experience* these formal structures of organizational charts and technology is shaped by the social and psychological scaffolding that governs what we believe, what we value and what we see as legitimate.[1] These informal structures at work can be thought of as organizational 'culture'.

Organizational culture has become a pivotal concept in studies on organizational behaviour over the last two decades. Implicitly, its importance in the mainstream literature is an acknowledgement of the imperfections of formal arrangements and practices, and, as such, culture has been cast in the role of transforming the workplace to unlock the 'holy grail' of individual and collective employee commitment, and to achieve extraordinary performance. Cultural change has historical roots in *paternalistic management practices*, which are partly based on the premodern assumption that employers have a moral responsibility to look after the welfare of their workers. Always a minority phenomenon, well-known examples of paternalistic cultures are companies such as Cadbury, Pilkington, Rowntree and Marks & Spencer in the UK, and IBM in the USA.[2]

As a contemporary strategy for managing people, the concept of organizational culture became prominent in North American literature in the 1980s, in response to a particular interpretation of the perceived competitive advantages of Japanese 'ways of doing'. Japanese management scholarship led to a recognition that national and organizational culture mattered.[3,4] In a globalized post-industrial world, it became common parlance that competitive advantage stemmed from mobilizing the creativity of workers and from managing cultural factors in the workplace.

This chapter begins by a brief discussion of national culture before examining the concept of organizational culture: what it is, how it manifests itself within the workplace, and its importance for understanding organizational behaviour, development and performance. We look at the three levels of organizational culture and notions of dominant culture, cultural diversity, subcultures and countercultures. We examine mainstream and critical theoretical perspectives on organizational culture, and finally consider whether managers can change the culture of their organization.

NATIONAL CULTURE AND CULTURE DIMENSIONS

culture: the knowledge, language, values, customs and material objects that are passed from person to person and from one generation to the next in a human group or society

The word 'culture' originates from the Latin *cultura*, meaning cult or worship. Cult members believe in specific ways of doing things, and thus develop a culture, which safeguards those beliefs. Partly because of its historical development, but mainly because of its use in several distinct intellectual disciplines, Raymond Williams believes culture to be one of several most complicated words in the English language.[5] The complexity of its modern usage can be appreciated when, in everyday speech, we refer to painting, music, ballet or the opera as 'high culture', and such activities as football, rock music and Hollywood film-going as 'popular culture' or 'mass culture'. When anthropologists and sociologists use the term, it includes all such social activities, but far more than is implied in everyday conversation.

Culture refers to the ways of life of a human society, or of groups within a society. The concept is perhaps easier to grasp by a description than a definition. For example, suppose a young female student from Iran has joined your university class. It is immediately evident that her culture is different from yours: you can see it in her clothing. Although she will be at least bilingual, you can hear it in her language, and in class discussions you may hear her express different beliefs and values about the world. All these traits are indicative of culture. Anthropologists have produced scholarship rich in a description of culture as comprising three levels: inner patterns of thought and perception; deep-level verbalization (for example, the syntax in language), of which a native speaker is seldom aware; and visible patterns of behaviour, which are also culturally determined.

Cultural variations among human beings are linked to different types of society. You might think of culture as a societal tapestry of woven threads that makes each society unique, or as a national characteristic – English as opposed to Indian or Chinese, for example. Culture has been defined as 'the collective programming of the mind'.[6] Alternatively, it can refer to the complex collection of shared values, patterned ways of thinking, feeling and behaving shared by a people, including their embodiment in physical objects or **artefacts** socially transmitted from one generation to the next.[7]

The culture of a human society is a manifestation of the complex interaction of symbols, values and behaviours learned and exhibited by its members, as shown in Figure 12.1.

Individuals and groups in a human society express culture and its normative qualities through symbols; these are ideas that convey meaning, such as language and mathematical signs. Symbols allow people to classify experiences, to learn and to generalize from them. These symbols in turn determine the values they hold about the world around them. Values can be both unconsciously and consciously held. These values in turn shape the form of human behaviour considered most appropriate and effective in different social situations. **Mores** (the Latin word for 'customs', pronounced MOR-ays) are norms that specify social requirements. For example, if a woman walks down the street in Tehran without a head-cover, she is violating the mores of that society. People are usually punished when they violate norms. The strongest norms are taboos. When a person violates a **taboo**, for example incest, it causes revulsion in most communities, and punishment is severe.

artefacts: the observable symbols and signs of an organization's culture

weblink

Visit www.tnellen. com/ted/tc/schein. html for an article on culture and leadership; and www.hcgnet.com/ ArticlesAndResearch.asp and www.new-paradigm. co.uk/describing_culture. htm for a description of organizational culture

mores: norms that are widely observed and have great moral significance

taboos: mores so strong their violation is considered to be extremely offensive, unmentionable and even criminal

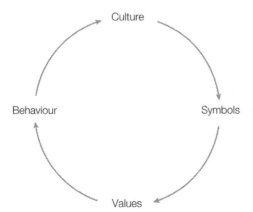

Figure 12.1 – The influence of culture on human behaviour and behaviour on culture
Source: From ADLER. *International Dimensions of Organizational Behavior*, 5E. © 2008 South-Western, a part of Cengage Learning, Inc. Reproduced by permission. www.cengage.com/permissions[11]

Plate 1 –In many Muslim countries, if a woman walks down the street without a head-cover, she is violating that society's mores.
Source: iStockphoto

socialization: the life-long process of social interaction through which individuals acquire a self-identity and the physical, mental and social skills needed for survival in society

The process by which each generation, or other new members of society, learn the way of life of their society is called **socialization**. Shared values and behaviour, although socially embedded, often change over time and generations. During the last 200 years, the period of modernity, both Western and Eastern societies have witnessed tremendous social changes caused by industrialization and the secularization of thought, which has changed values, beliefs and patterns of behaviour. Thus, the continually changing patterns of individual and collective behaviour eventually influence the society's culture, and the cycle begins again. Anthropologists suggest that a national culture has five defining features: it is learned, cumulative, transmitted, shared and a product of human interaction.[8] These five defining aspects of national culture are important in understanding the complexity of culture and how people maintain their social uniqueness over time.

Many scholars have written about the variation in cultural traits between Western and Eastern societies. Perhaps the best known in the field of management is Hofstede's research,[9] which measured national culture, in terms of values, in 64 countries. His data, based on one global corporation, IBM, initially identified four independent dimensions of national cultural differences:

1 *power distance* – the extent to which the less powerful accept that power is distributed unequally (see Chapter 16)
2 *individualism* versus *collectivism* – the degree to which members of society are integrated into communities
3 *masculinity* versus *femininity* – the general acceptance of sex-biased values and the sexual division of labour
4 *uncertainty avoidance* – which refers to society's tolerance for ambiguity and uncertainty; this ultimately deals with the search for truth.

Cross-cultural management literature examines the implications of different national cultures for managing people at work. For example, in Maslow's hierarchy, self-actualization is seen as the supreme human need. Drawing on Hofstede's

weblink
Visit Geert Hofstede's website at www.geert-hofstede.com, which includes summaries of his work, and http://geert-hofstede.international-business-center.com, which includes critiques of Hofstede's work

OB and globalization

Saving face – an important component in US–China business relationships

In many Asian cultures, 'saving face' is an integral component of personal and business relationships. In this context, 'face' describes the identity or image that a person projects to the world, and is closely linked to concepts of honour and respect. Saving face can be understood as an ongoing social negotiation in which a person works to maintain their honour and dignity – and the honour and dignity of their family, friends and colleagues – by avoiding behaviours that are viewed as bringing humiliation, weakness or disloyalty. The workplace behaviours and expectations of Asian workers can differ significantly from those of workers from Western countries.

As a result of the increased globalization of business interactions, some Western companies have begun teaching their workers how to ensure that their Asian colleagues' cultural sensitivities are respected. In one example from the USA, Bruzzese (2008) describes how understanding the concept of saving face can present management challenges to American managers working overseas in China. 'Many U.S. managers are learning a hard lesson when they are on assignment in China,' she writes. 'The practices they used in America to be successful may very likely bring them failure in China.' In particular, Bruzzese asserts, the indirect communication style that often characterizes saving face can puzzle Western managers seeking feedback from their workers:

> The challenge for managers is figuring out if someone is having problems and then finding a way to get the worker to talk about [it] … Further, cultural constraints can inhibit the manager's ability to give performance feedback.

Saving face is an important concept to understand in the cross-cultural workplace, where organizational behaviours viewed as standard practice in a European or North American workplace may be seen as dishonourable or embarrassing to workers from other cultures. Scholars like Miroshnik (2002) assert that efforts to save face are a characteristic feature of collectivist societies, like China, where emphasis is placed on maintaining harmony, recognizing structured hierarchies and supporting group interests. In contrast, Europe and North America have been described as individualist societies, where valued behaviours and beliefs include assertiveness, direct communication and self-interest (Hofstede, 2001).

Values associated with collectivist and individualist societies often extend to organizational structure and behaviour, and conflicts can arise when workers from one culture inadvertently transgress the values and expectations of workers from another. Understanding how concepts like saving face feature in cross-cultural business relationships can help organizations and workers to identify and work successfully with their colleagues from other cultures.

stop! Are workers from Asian cultures the only ones concerned about saving face in the workplace? What are the values that workers from your culture try to project and maintain at work? Can you identify some practices that reflect their efforts to save face?

Sources and further information

Bruzzese, A. (2008) 'On the job: U.S. managers must learn new rules in China', *Gannett News Service*, July 30. Available at: www.mycentraljersey.com/apps/pbcs.dll/article?AID=/20080730/BUSINESS/807300321/1022/RSS07; www.tucsoncitizen.com/ss/related/91243.

Gries, P. H. and Peng, K. (2002) 'Culture clash? Apologies East and West', *Journal of Contemporary China*, 11(30), pp. 173–8.

Hofstede, G. (2001) *Culture's Consequence: Comparing Values, Behaviours, Institutions and Organizations Across Nations* (2nd edn), Thousand Oaks, CA: Sage.

Miroshnik, V. (2002) 'Culture and international management: a review', *Journal of Management Development*, 21(7): 521–44.

Ting-Toomey, S. (1994) *The Challenges of Facework: Cross-cultural and Interpersonal Issues*, Albany: SUNY Press.

Note

This feature was written by Gretchen Fox, PhD, Anthropologist, Timberline Natural Resource Group, Canada.

cultural analysis, however, this assumption presupposes an *individualist* culture in which the ties between individuals are loose and everyone is expected to look after themselves and their immediate family. In the West, assertiveness has been much advocated as a way for women to communicate, but communication scholars point out that the effectiveness of this means of communicating is culture related.

The work of Geert Hofstede and his core assumption that countries have a singular national culture has attracted considerable criticism. The empirical basis for his assertion that a national population shares a singular culture is based on a statistical averaging of the quantitative data – the survey responses from IBM's employees. An average of personal values claiming to measure the values of a national culture is about as meaningful as an average of personal income. As has been well established elsewhere, in the same way that there is a wide variance in personal income in any population, so there is wide dispersion in the personal values of that population.[10]

stop reflect
The problem of identifying a national culture is soon apparent when we examine values. Taking Britain or Australia, for example, just what are core 'British values' or core 'Australian values'? How do we complete the phrases 'as British as ...?' or 'as Australian as ...?'

Among the developed countries in the global economy, few are likely to exhibit a single cultural orientation, but they are more likely to have a plural orientation with hyphenated identities such as African-American, Chinese-Canadian, Anglo-Indian and so on. The empirical evidence at the centre of Hofstede's claims is problematic, and the term 'national culture' is misleading. Nonetheless, deep cultural undercurrents structure human behaviour in subtle but highly regular ways, and managers and other employees carry their cultural heritage and ethnicity to the workplace.[11] Research on the relationships of national cultures, based mainly on values, to organizational cultures are, however, 'loose ones'.[6] Sociological research demonstrates that cultural diversity is a global fact of human life. In the face of such plurality, will this diversity be reflected at work?

UNDERSTANDING ORGANIZATIONAL CULTURE

The notion of organizational culture is a complex concept because it lends itself to very different uses. In the literature, the terms 'corporate culture', 'organizational culture' and 'organizational climate' are common. The distinction between corporate culture and organizational culture is that the former is devised and transmitted down to subordinates by management executives as part of a strategy of mobilizing employee commitment, and emphasizes actors as 'culture-takers'. Organizational culture, on the other hand, is a product of members' creativity and emphasizes actors as 'culture-makers'.[12]

Schneider[1] notes that *'organizational climate'* is the 'elder child' in cultural scholarship, and the terms *culture* and *climate* are used interchangeably by some culture researchers. Others refer to the disagreements over whether the two concepts are distinguishable constructs as 'paradigm wars'.[13] Organizational culture and organizational climate are two complementary constructs, but reveal overlapping nuances in the social and psychological life of complex organizations. The former tends to take a sociological approach, using qualitative methodology derived from anthropology, to examine symbolic and cultural forms of organizations. Climate researchers, however, attempt to measure individuals' perceptions of autonomy, leadership, growth or whatever (see Critical Insight, p. 351), and the meaning they assign to them, using quantitative methods derived from the nomothetic traditions in organizational psychology. The distinction between culture research and climate research lies in the different methodological traditions, what they consider to be significantly meaningful and their agendas. The sociologist Martin Parker argues that the psychological treatment of culture largely reflects 'a neo-human relations agenda' (ref. 14, p. 132).

Writers have offered various definitions of organizational culture (Table 12.1), and a synthesis of these definitions captures most of the essential elements of

Table 12.1 – Some definitions of organizational culture

Social or normative glue that holds an organization together … The values or social ideals and the beliefs that organization members come to share. These values or patterns of beliefs are manifested by symbolic devices, such as myths, stories, legends and specialized language. (Smircich, 1983, p. 344)[20]
Talking about organizational culture seems to mean talking about the importance for people of symbolism – of rituals, myths, stories and legends – and about the interpretation of events, ideas, and experiences that are influenced and shaped by the groups within which they live. (Frost et al., 1985, p. 17)[101]
The shared beliefs and values guiding the thinking and behavioral styles of members. (Cooke and Rousseau, 1988, p. 245)[102]
Culture is 'how things are done around here'. It is what is typical of the organization, the habits, prevailing attitudes and grown-up pattern of accepted and expected behaviour. (Drennan, 1992, p. 3)[103]
For me values are less central and less useful than meanings and symbolism in cultural analysis … Culture is not primarily 'inside' people's heads, but somewhere 'between' the heads of a group of people where symbols and meanings are publicly expressed, for example in work group interactions, in board meetings but also in material objects. Culture then is central in governing the understanding of behaviour, social events, institutions and processes. Culture is the setting in which these phenomena become comprehensible and meaningful. (Alvesson, 2002, pp. 3–4)[36]

organizational culture. It is about the importance of the shared values, beliefs and language that shape and perpetuate this network of values of organizational reality, so that employees behave predictably to achieve the organization's goals.

To help us understand organizational culture, we need to examine its parts, even though any organizational culture is greater than the sum of its parts. Drawing on the work of Edgar Schein,[15] Figure 12.2 shows three fundamental levels of organizational culture: *artefacts*, *values* and *basic assumptions*. These can be imagined as the skins of an onion, artefacts representing the less abstract and basic assumptions the deepest manifestations of organizational culture, with values lying in between. Here, we use an alternative image, the iceberg. The uppermost subtriangle might be viewed as the 'tip of an iceberg' representing observable parts of organizational culture, which are embedded in shared values, basic assumptions and beliefs that are invisible to the human eye. Each level of culture influences another level.

The first level shown in Figure 12.2 comprises visible culture, the *artefacts* and material objects such as buildings, technology, art and uniforms that the organization 'uses' to express its culture. For example, when a company only uses e-mail for internal communication, the cultural message is that IT is a highly valued resource. Displaying art on office walls signals to members and visitors that creating a stimulating cultural context in which employees can explore ideas and aesthetics is highly valued.[16] Other examples are the wearing of a professorial gown in universities and the doctor's white coat in the National Health Service.

The visible culture also includes *language*. How managers describe other employees is an example of using symbols to convey meaning to each other. For example, Walmart refers to its employees as 'associates', and at Disneyland they are known as 'cast members'. Social *behaviour* is another aspect of observable organizational culture and includes rituals and ceremonies. **Rituals** are collective routines that 'dramatize' the organization's culture. For example, the office party can be viewed as a ritual for *integrating* new members into the organization. **Ceremonies** are planned and represent more formal social artefacts than rituals, for example the 'call to the bar' ceremony for graduating lawyers.

The second level of organizational culture comprises shared work-related *values*, which are not visible, but which we recognize influence patterns of observable

stop reflect
Looking at Table 12.1, does your university have a culture? How does this differ within and between different faculties, schools or departments within the university?

rituals: the programmed routines of daily organizational life that dramatize the organization's culture

ceremonies: planned events that represent more formal social artefacts than rituals

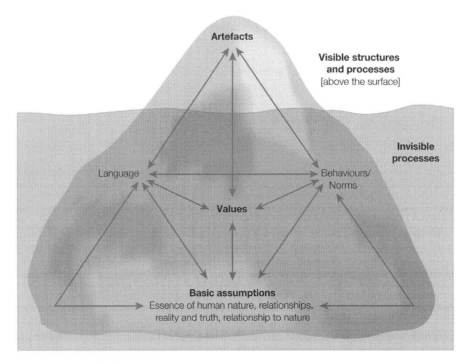

Figure 12.2 –The three levels of organizational culture

Plate 2 –Rituals are collective routines that 'dramatize' the organization's culture. For example, the office party can be viewed as a ritual for integrating new members to the organization. Ceremonies are planned and represent more formal social artefacts than rituals, for example the 'call to the bar' ceremony for graduating lawyers.
Source: Catherine Travers

weblink

Visit http://en.wikipedia.
org/wiki/Organizational_
culture
for more information on
Edgar Schein

behaviour at work. For example, in healthcare, standard medical practice is influenced by a belief in evidence or a commitment to patient-centred care. In many universities, practice is influenced by the espoused value of 'We are a teaching-centred institution.' Employment-related espoused values possess six characteristics:

1 They involve moral or ethical statements of 'rightness'.
2 They pertain to desirable modes of behaviour at a given point in time.
3 They directly influence employee behaviour and experiences, and act as significant moderators.
4 They are typically associated with strategic goals and address questions like 'What are we doing?' and 'Why are we doing this?'
5 They guide the selection and evaluation of members.
6 They may vary in respect to male/female, demographic and cultural differences,[17] for example that women in the armed forces should not engage in combat roles.

The term 'shared' in cultural analysis implies that organizational members are a whole. Each member has been exposed to a set of dominant values, although not every member may internalize and endorse them.

The third level of organizational culture relates to *basic assumptions*, which are invisible, unconscious, taken for granted, difficult to access and highly resistant to change. These are the implicit and unspoken assumptions that underpin everyday choices and shape how members perceive, think and emotionally react to social events. For example, in healthcare, assumptions about the relative roles of doctors and nurses, about patients' rights or about the sources of ill-health underpin everyday decisions and actions.[18] The basic assumptions/beliefs about human nature, human relationships, relationship to nature and how the world works form the base from which employees, who as social beings enter the workplace with life histories and experiences, build their values of how the world *should* be. Assumptions and values then shape organizational behaviour and the artefacts with which members surround themselves.

stop reflect

Think about your own
university or college. As
a student, do you expect
a student-centred focus?
Are teaching and support
staff helpful? Do teaching
staff primarily focus
on their teaching or on
research interests? Try
to assess your answer at
three levels: observable
artefacts, shared values
and basic assumptions of
the culture

PERSPECTIVES ON ORGANIZATIONAL CULTURE

Social scientists adopt different perspectives on the study of workplace behaviour. The genealogy of the different perspectives on organizational culture is rooted in classical sociological theory. The work of Durkheim and Weber is representative of the canonical literature on understanding behaviour in organizations as a social and cultural phenomenon. Here, for example, Weber stresses that individuals behave 'not out of obedience, but either because the environment approves of the conduct and disapproves of its opposite, or merely as a result of unreflective habituation to a regularity of life that has *engraved itself as a custom*' (ref. 19, p. 312, emphasis added). From the 1950s, influential management writers, such as Peter Drucker, have stressed the importance of *integrity* of character and *values* in the practice of management.

Contemporary culture analysis can essentially be divided into what by now should be two familiar schools of thought: managerialist and critical. The managerialist-oriented perspective on the topic is functionalist in that theorists in this school stress the value of culture from the premise that it can play a role in building organizational consensus, building harmony and improving performance. Organizational culture is viewed as a *variable* – an attribute that an organization possesses or 'has', and as such can be produced by senior managers.[20] The critical-oriented school, on the other hand, focuses on describing and critically explaining cultural processes, how culture emerges through day-to-day social interaction, power relations, shaping communities of practice, emotion and norms of workplace behaviour. Viewed through a sociologist's lens, culture is something that a work organization '*is*' and emphasizes the symbolic, consciousness and subjective aspects of the workplace, the role of culture in strengthening management control over employees, and the interrelationships between organizational cultures *inside* and social inequalities *outside* the workplace.

The managerialist perspective on organizational culture

functional theory a sociological perspective emphasizing that human action is governed by relatively stable structures

The **functionalist** perspective is based on the assumption that the organization is a stable, orderly system that serves specific functions. Organizational culture, in terms of attitudes, beliefs, values and norms, is generated and managed according to organizational goals and needs. Cultural analysis from a functionalist perspective is based on the theoretical insights of Emile Durkheim, whose sociological studies focus on the integrative and social stabilizing ability of culture.

Neo-management theorists primarily understand organizational culture as a unifying phenomenon, in which cultural processes can create organizational stability and consensus, focusing on how culture can be managed and disseminated downwards by senior management. Thus, mainstream theorists are said, in Martin's words, to follow an '*integration*' perspective. In this sense, management-inspired cultural processes and interventions attempt to mitigate the many forms of the ever-present conflict that arise from managing the labour process. This approach focuses on building a culture that binds members together around the same core values, beliefs and norms, which are considered prerequisites for achieving strategic goals. For integration or functionalism theorists, culture is conceptualized as 'organization-wide agreement with values espoused by top management'.[21] The notion of 'cultural engineering' – creating the 'right' kind of culture to align with strategic goals – is seen as a 'lever' for fostering commitment and loyalty in the workforce.

Searching for excellence and innovation

A cluster of functionalist writers put forward ideas about causality by attempting to demonstrate positive linkages between the 'right' corporate culture and performance.[3,22,23] Within this genre, Peters and Waterman's influential pop-management book, *In Search of Excellence*, is probably the best well-known example of the 'has' school. These gurus view culture as an elixir that binds together specific human qualities and skills that lead to organizational excellence and success. They write:

> What our framework has really done is to remind the world of professional managers that 'soft is hard.' It has enabled us to say, in effect, 'All that stuff you have been dismissing for so long as the intractable, irrational, intuitive, informal organization *can* be managed ... you [are] foolish to ignore it.' (ref. 22, p. 11)

What constitutes the 'right culture' for excellence is a matter of debate. A popular approach in functionalism is *contingency* theory. Based on the belief that senior managers need to consider a range of different external and internal variables when deciding what kind of culture best fits their particular organization, Deal and Kennedy[23] and Handy[24] identify a fourfold typology of culture, in which the choice of each culture depends on an assessment of organizational situations. Contingencies that have been identified as important include level of risk, size and design of the organization, ownership and governance, market preference, technology, national culture and need for innovation.

Table 12.2 – Typologies of organizational culture

Deal and Kennedy's ideal types	Handy's ideal types
Process culture This type is concerned with ensuring that members follow uniform procedures, and is associated with low-risk hierarchical organizations; for example, hospitals	*Role culture* This type is mechanistic and highly formalized, abounds with rules, and is dominated by authority and the hierarchical structure; for example, utility services
Work hard/play hard culture This type is team- and customer-focused and stresses 'fun' at work; for example, Google	*Person culture* This type centres around 'star' performers who are loosely attached to the organization; for example, barristers, surgeons and architects
Bet-your-company culture This type characterizes high-investment, long-term, highly technical members; for example, the NASA space agency	*Power culture* This type exhibits a single power source, with centralized policy and decision making; for example, a family-owned and operated company
Macho culture This type is characterized by fast decision making and high risk; for example, traders in merchant banks	*Task culture* This type is organic, informal and product and project based, the opposite of role culture; for example, firms of management consultants

For functionalist theorists, leaders can create 'strong' corporate cultures. Leadership studies consider change as a situation-driven contingency that moderates the effectiveness of certain leadership styles. It is suggested that transformational leadership is especially effective in shaping and guiding organizations towards innovation-oriented cultures. Thus, in Rosabeth Moss Kanter's *The Change Masters*, she notes that employees 'find their stability and security not in specific organizational arrangements but in the *culture* and direction of the organization. It requires that they feel *integrated with the whole* rather than identified with the particular territory of the moment, since that is changeable' (emphasis added).[25] In turn, the 'right' culture is counterposed to bureaucratic cultures. In Hammer and Champy's *Reengineering the Corporation*, the authors contend that 'the reigning values and beliefs in an organization must support the performance of its design process' (ref. 26, p. 81). Similarly, in Champy's *Reengineering Management*, it is posited that 'values are our moral navigational devices', and for real change to occur, leaders need 'cultural warriors' at every level of the organization to communicate new values to their peers (ref. 27, p. 79).

Whereas modern management gurus like Ouchi, Peters and Waterman, Deal and Kennedy, and Hammer and Champy focus on values that foster 'strong cultures', Handy and Kanter are more sensitive to the complexities and problematic aspects of culture (Table 12.2).

Subcultures and counter-cultures

As is the case with anthropological studies of national cultures, contingency literature draws attention to cultural heterogeneity. Martin[28] refers to such studies as the '*differentiated*' perspective. A large complex organization, for example British Airways, might have one dominant culture expressing senior management's core values, but they also have sets of *subcultures* typically defined by professional occupations, spatial separation and departmental designations. These work groups might share a distinctive set of values, beliefs and norms that differ in some significant way from that of the organization's dominant values and philosophy. The concept of cultural heterogeneity has been applied to distinctions ranging from professional identities associated with engineers, artists, healthcare practitioners, researchers and ethnic- and religion-based groups, to small reservoirs of employees presumed to be marginalized from the larger organization as a result of distinctive work paradigms or the particular demands of the occupation. A subculture emerges to bind members working intensely together, as a means of coping with common frustrations concerning the demands of emotional labour, or as a way to preserve their distinctive identity.[29]

stop reflect
Does a complex organization like the UK National Health Service have subcultures? What are the management implications if core subcultures exist?

In the context of healthcare organizations, a recent study revealed that 'complex multiple cultural values are often hierarchical and are commonly interpreted in ways that ascribe differentiated, fragmented and collective meaning' (ref. 30, p. 61). For example, healthcare professionals may collectively interpret the espoused value of providing the 'best possible care' for patients. But the delivered 'care' will be performed differently by the various professional groups, each with distinctive interpretations of what 'best care' means. For doctors, it may mean eradicating the cause of illness, whereas for occupational therapists it may mean helping patients to achieve greater mobility and improved quality of life.[31] In contrast, a macho and highly aggressive subculture might exist among male manual workers doing repetitive, mundane work or among abattoir workers slaughtering animals.[32,33] The analyses of subcultures reveal a wide variation in values, norms and assumptions both within and across subcultures, which might cause conflict – but this is a normal part of organizational life.

Sociologically informed analysis of culture acknowledges the existence of *counter-cultures* in organizations. As others have observed, these create their own form of organizational reality through a subculture that actively opposes the dominant values and norms.[34,35] For example, a change in status of an education institution, from a college to a university, may produce counter-cultures. A particular teaching faculty may strongly reject university values on research and a 'publish-or-perish' culture. In the private sector, mergers and acquisitions may produce counter-cultures. There may be a 'clash of corporate cultures' when the values, beliefs and norms held by the members of an acquired organization are inconsistent with those of the acquiring organization. The debate surrounding the existence of subcultures and counter-cultures emphasizes the complexities and interwoven character of organizational culture, and avoids an overly static and monolithic picture of everyday organizational life.

Critical perspectives on organizational culture

Although all critical theorists share a similar view on the role of culture – that values and norms are deeply embedded but can change over time – they typically see organizational culture through somewhat different lenses as they are guided by different theoretical perspectives in their research. What do these critical perspectives tell us about organizational culture? In contrast to the mainstream functionalist perspective that understands culture as something that an organization '*has*', critical perspectives proceed, as we saw earlier in the chapter, from the root-metaphor idea that the organization '*is*' a culture. Therefore, critical-oriented perspectives promote a view of organizations as manifestations of human consciousness, as a source of power and as a socializing and controlling force, and are studied in terms of their networks of symbols and shared meanings. Moreover, advocates of the 'is' view of culture are likely 'to play down the pragmatic results that can help management increase effectiveness in favour of more general understanding and reflection as the major emphasis of cultural studies' (ref. 36, p. 25). Here, we look at three critical-oriented perspectives: the symbolic-interactionist, the conflict and the feminist. These perspectives will serve as alternative lenses through which to see organizational culture.

The symbolic-interactionist perspective

symbolic interactionism: the sociological approach that views society as the sum of the interactions of individuals and groups

The **symbolic-interactionist** approach, using a micro-level analysis, understands organizational culture as the sum of all its members' interactions. In this school of thought, culture plays the role of a vehicle for shared meaning (hence 'symbolic'), and is produced by workers and managers in face-to-face encounters (hence 'interactionist') as they go about their everyday workplace activities. Culture is constructed by organizational actors and reproduced by the networks of symbols and meanings that workers and managers share, and that make shared social behaviour possible. The analysis of organizational culture can therefore be through studying observable artefacts, language, action and the beliefs and values of organizational members.

In the realm of shared *artefacts*, displayed mission statements, framed photographs of individuals and ceremonies, technology, paintings and sculptures are all manifestations of culture. Space is an element of culture. For example, if senior management has allocated privileged parking within the organization's boundary while others park outside in the street, the cultural message is that hierarchy and status are highly valued by the organization. Symbolic interactionists explore how *language* and emotion are used to communicate effectively in order to make social action possible. Shared stories, myths and legends serve to construct a common ground for understanding social behaviour. For example, an account of a dramatic event in the past history of the company serves to create shared meaning of how workers are expected to handle problems in the present. Also scrutinized is shared social *action*. Rites commonly found in the workplace are those of acceptance (for example, an invitation to the office party), of recognition (for example, the employee of the month award), of conflict (for example, a disciplinary hearing) and of severance (for example, dismissal to emphasize unacceptable behaviour).

Plate 3 –If senior management has allocated privileged parking within the organization's boundary while others park outside in the street, the cultural message is that hierarchy and status are highly valued by the organization.
Source: iStockphoto

Symbolic interactionists also examine shared *beliefs* and *values*. Beliefs are the dominant assumptions of the organization concerning the society and how it works, while values contain an 'ought to' implicit in them. In organizational talk, the assertion of 'values' is omnipresent, either of legislative provisions not always heeded (for example, antidiscrimination laws) or of espoused values not adequately funded. Groups in the organization will clothe their proposals around 'values' rhetoric to elevate these demands over more pedestrian ones, for example diverting resources from one department to another – from production to employee training – because a core 'value' is continuous work-related learning. This approach to cultural analysis highlights how members produce and reproduce the culture of an organization through day-to-day social interaction. However, symbolic interactionism tends to underemphasize how larger social structures cause disagreement on meanings.

The conflict perspective

conflict perspective the sociological approach that views groups in society as engaged in a continuous power struggle for the control of scarce resources

Conflict perspectives are based on the assumption that conflict is a basic feature of organizational life as members seek to control scarce resources.[37] Unlike the integration perspective, critical theorists insist on treating conflict as a central concept in exploring how values, beliefs and norms develop to sustain the power and control of senior management. The conflict perspective sets out to develop an understanding of organizational culture by situating it in the context of capitalist relations of domination and control.

As early conflict theorist Karl Marx emphasized, ideas are the cultural constructs of a society's most powerful social elite. The creation of ideas, of conceptions of consciousness, is directly interwoven with work-related activity and the material interaction of people, the language of real organizational life. As Marx states, 'The production of ideas, conceptions, of consciousness is, to begin with, immediately involved in the material activity and the material interaction of men [sic], the language of real life.'[38] Many conflict theorists agree with Marx's assertion that social elites use

ideology: a term with multiple uses, but in particular referring to perceptions of reality as distorted by class interests, and the ideas, legal arrangements and culture that arise from class relations (a term taken from Marx)

ideology, a non-material element of culture, to shape the thoughts and actions of members of other social classes – the common idea, for example, that an unfettered market can best decide society's economic priorities because 'Governments cannot pick winners' or 'What's good for Ford is good for America.' Public discourse often supports these views, since no other alternatives are debated or offered.

Conflict views on culture emphasize perpetual tension, conflict and resistance between different groups in the organization. This emphasis on a structured antagonism between 'capital' and 'labour', and concomitantly on managerial control, focuses on motive – the 'who' of power and the 'how' of employee commitment. It tends to dismiss conceptualizing organizational culture as the 'organization's personality' or as an overarching catch-all to describe 'the way we do things around here'. Instead, the focus is on how corporate culture attempts to generate *real*, as opposed to hollow, employee commitment and self-control by mobilizing values, beliefs and emotions. The study by Ray is an example of cultural control as an employment strategy:

> The top management team aims to have individuals possess direct ties to the values and goals of the dominant elites in order to activate the emotion and sentiment which might lead to devotion, loyalty and commitment to the company. (ref. 39. p. 294)

For Ray, control by corporate culture did not rely on direct supervision, but primarily on an acceptance of values and peer enforcement. It was the 'last frontier', in that a 'strong' corporate culture had enabled top management to generate employee emotion and commitment, at the same time internalizing control by fusing individual with corporate identity. Shared social activities outside the organization's space and time, such as weekend 'retreats' or social events for employees' families, expand cultural controls by integrating both manual staff and managerial employees, and developing a sense of community or 'family' through what Thompson and McHugh describe as a form of 'compulsory sociability' (ref. 40, p. 203).

Around this thesis has developed a body of literature which argues that cultural control overlaps and exists alongside, rather than replaces, more traditional forms of management control strategies, such as bureaucracy, new technology and human resource management (HRM) practices. Weberian internal bureaucratic control focuses on rules, internal labour market structures and reporting hierarchies. Computer-based technology can be used for the surveillance of employees by recording attendance, output or productivity and time logged after hours as measure of commitment. The HRM function plays a central role in the development of strong corporate cultures and in managing emotion by integrating a complex array of recruitment, training, reward and discipline practices, as well as policies to deal with trade unions, if necessary, that are designed to direct work processes, to secure commitment and to control the workforce. In this sense, faced with a complex set of internal and external forces, systems of cultural hegemony do not replace but *complement* other employment strategies adopted over time that are aimed at increasing the loyalty and control of employees, and ultimately their efficiency.

The picture represented by conflict theorists is more likely to be one that represents contradictory, fluid and unstable cultures. Drawing on the postmodernist discourse that characterizes modern life as ephemeral, fragmentary and contingent,[41] Joanne Martin describes this approach to understanding culture as the 'fragmentary' perspective.[28] Organizational culture is characterized by so much ephemerality, ambiguity and change, and so exposes the truth claims of monolithic and united corporate cultures, that, she argues, culture is 'a loosely structured and incompletely shared system that emerges dynamically as cultural members experience each other, events, and the organization's contextual features' (ref. 28, p. 152). The value of this fragmentary approach to organizational culture is in its exposure of the naivety of thinking that there is no ambiguity in what cultural members believe and do. For example, it exposes claims to the espoused truth that 'We are an equal opportunity employer' while masking gender or race inequality arising from the cultural values and beliefs of a male-dominant or white-dominant workplace.[42–44]

There are other contributions to debates on organizational culture that warn of a neo-Orwellian nightmare of creeping omnipresent cultural control. Whereas Weberian sociology laments about rationalization processes creating the 'iron cage' of the modern bureaucracy, insidious corporate culture apparently seeks the 'governance of the employee's soul'. Powerful cultural processes, it is argued, seek to replace the 'iron cage' of bureaucratic controls with a 'velvet cage' of managed emotion, self-surveillance and self-subordination.[45–48] Others rightly acknowledge that although corporate culture is a key ideological element in the labour process, its effectiveness as the ultimate means of moulding employees' acceptance of managerial initiative should not be exaggerated. Empirical studies show the limits of culture, and reveal that employees are not passive recipients of corporate social engineering. As one British Airways manager acknowledged: 'We know it's hype – they know it's hype. It's okay ... But do I believe in it? – well that's a totally different question' (ref. 49, p. 205). Employees may comply with the demands for adherence to corporate language, and

stop reflect

Go back to Figure 1.2. What external and internal factors drive development in managerial employment strategies? To what extent will the financial and economic crisis facing the global economy cause managers to change the mix of strategies, including cultural control, with which they experiment?

participate in organizational rites and obey cultural values as espoused through the mission statements, but '*without* internalizing the values and therefore generating the "real" commitment' (ref. 50, p. 205). However, this does not imply that interventions to change organizational culture have no effect, which we examine below.

The feminist perspective

As with all perspectives, a focus on conflict and control has the effect of silencing other ways of seeing. Thus, there is a body of literature that is rooted in a critical analysis of capitalism, but which draws attention to aspects of organizational life that other perspectives we have examined do not reveal. The **feminist perspective** argues that gender is a central aspect of organizational analysis. A gender perspective in organizational culture analysis is important for at least three essential reasons:

1 Membership of the organization through recruitment, selection and appraisal practices often conforms to and extends sex-biased societal values that discriminate against women.

2 Cultural values associated with notions of masculinity and femininity are often reflected in organizational processes, for example processes that privilege the rationality and 'objectivity' associated with masculine attributes while suppressing emotion, associated with family and 'natural' feminine attributes.

3 Some organizations (e.g. schools, media and popular culture) directly play a part in the socializing processes in which people acquire gender identities.[51,52] For example, the social association between masculinity and physical danger contributes to the gendered nature of 'the way things are done' in an organization, justifying 'masculine occupations'.

The deep-rooted assumptions about the nature of human nature have affected the manner in which society and organizations have been studied. In Western thought, the social arrangements have, since the European Enlightenment at least, been generally understood as the result of the 'rule of the mind and the rational element over the passionate'. Aristotle, for example, thought that 'the female was an incomplete version of the male' (ref. 53, p. 3). The view that male hegemony in human society is a 'natural' phenomenon, and gave rise to a resultant 'natural' superiority of men over women, continued in nineteenth-century Western classical sociological theory and twentieth-century organizational analysis.[54]

The argument is that, with notable exceptions, mainstream organizational analysis has generally reflected dominant social beliefs about gender roles, that men inhabit the 'public' domain of action, decision making, power and authority, and women the 'private' domestic world. Thus, feminist scholars have contended that the standard treatment of organizational culture neglects how gender, a patriarchal system and sexuality in organizations influence the dynamics of organizational culture. The term 'sexuality' refers to sexual characters and sexual behaviour in the workplace. Sexual harassment can be an entrenched feature of organizations through pornographic pin-ups, taunting and innuendo, and predatory conduct. And organizational culture is a crucial determinant of sexual harassment.[55,56]

Workplaces exhibit both heterogeneity and harassment. After overcoming the challenge of the 'glass ceiling', female managers who progress into positions of authority have problems exercising that authority. Moreover, female managers and supervisors are significantly more likely to be sexually harassed in the workplace than are female subordinates because male co-workers target woman managers as a way to equalize power in the workplace.[57] One female manager, for

feminist perspective the sociological approach that focuses on the significance of gender in understanding and explaining the inequalities that exist between men and women in the household, in the paid labour force, and in the realms of politics, law and culture

Plate 4 – Sexual harassment can be an entrenched feature of organizations through pornographic pin-ups, taunting and innuendo and predatory conduct. And organizational culture is a crucial determinant of sexual harassment. While sexuality serves to affirm men's sense of shared masculinity, it can serve to make women feel uncomfortable and leaving the organization is often seen as the only alternative.
Source: iStockphoto

example, recalled her subordinates joking: 'If we had somebody with balls in this position, we'd be getting things done.' As McLaughlin and her colleagues argue, 'By objectifying women, it strips them of any power or prestige that they hold in the workplace.'[57] While sexuality serves to affirm men's sense of shared masculinity, it can serve to make women feel uncomfortable, and leaving the organization is often seen as the only alternative.[58] Sexual harassment is less about sexual desire or innuendo than about control and male domination. Studies of the gendering of organizations emphasize that gender, sexuality and sexual harassment make an overwhelming difference to the reality of organizational life for women.[59,60] Gender analysis questions research findings and analysis that segregates studies of organizational culture from those of gender divisions in the labour market, patriarchal systems, the processes of male institutionalized power, workplace inequality and 'dual-role' work–family issues.

Observing Indian culture in 2009, journalist Stephanie Nolen illustrates the interrelation of a patriarchal system, sexuality and gendered work organizations. She describes the culture shock for a Western woman moving to work in India like this:

> I am reminded more incessantly of the sexism here. It started when I signed our lease, and had to provide either my father's name or my husband's. I've had to adjust to the fact that every repair person, shopkeeper and many potential staff members utterly ignore anything I say to them, waiting for the voice of authority, my male partner, to tell them what they really ought to do. (ref. 60, p. A13)

National culture with its societal value system and norms of behaviour and organizational culture are deeply intertwined in a **dialectical** relationship: each is fashioned and refashioned by the other. In an important way, by including the gender–sexuality paradigm in the study of the organizational culture, feminist writers have pushed the

dialectic: refers to the movement of history through the transcendence of internal contradictions that in turn produce new contradictions, themselves requiring solutions

Work and Society: 'Farmers' wives' working at Wal-Mart

Why is the idea of culture so important to the understanding of organizational behaviour? One reason is because it encourages us to move beyond narrowly individualistic accounts of what happens in organizations. To recognize the importance of culture in organizations is to recognize that there is a 'supra-individual' level of reality – shared values, for example – that influences what people in organizations do.

It makes sense to think about the ways in which cultural values influence behaviour, but we should never lose sight of the fact that people vary in the ways they respond to cultural values and the extent to which they care about those values. Sociologist Margaret Archer develops this point in a series of monographs on the complex interactions between structural factors like culture and another set of factors she groups under the heading 'agency' (the human capacity to act in, and on, the world). Given the powers and preferences that individuals bring to any given situation, they have the capacity to respond in various ways to different cultural values and different forms of cultural conditioning. We must take these variations into account when we develop cultural explanations of organizational behaviour.

Take the case of Wal-Mart, widely recognized as one of the most successful companies in the world. Critics have argued that Wal-Mart's success has come at the expense of some of its employees. A review of several major studies of Wal-Mart describes the 'harshness' of Wal-Mart's working conditions (compared with similar companies, such as Costco) and suggests that some Wal-Mart employees 'have ... been subjected to relentless harassment' (Head, 2004, p. 4). Women are particularly likely to experience harassment at Wal-Mart, and the reviewer, Simon Head, refers to evidence from 'the Dukes case, a class-action lawsuit brought in 2001 by six female employees and named for one of the six, Betty Dukes' (p. 4).

Head goes on to offer the following cultural explanation of the problematic features of the Wal-Mart approach to management:

Sex discrimination at Wal-Mart has a long history. Bethany Moreton, a doctoral candidate in history at Yale, has stressed the importance of Wal-Mart's origins in the rural, small-town culture of the Ozarks, where Wal-Mart's corporate headquarters at Bentonville, Arkansas, is still located. In the early years some of the women who worked at Wal-Mart were the wives of local Ozark farmers, and the women's earnings were a meagre supplement to their husbands'. The women in the Dukes case say that some of their store managers still often think of them as resembling those farmers' wives. Ramona Scott, a Dukes case petitioner who worked for Wal-Mart in the 1990s, was told by her store manager that "men are here to make a career and women aren't. Retail is for housewives who just need to earn extra money" (pp. 4–5)

This review of research on Wal-Mart contains a factual claim: the reviewer notes that some studies have discovered instances of harassment and discrimination at Wal-Mart. The review also makes reference to an explanatory claim: some researchers who study Wal-Mart have used a cultural explanation to account for documented cases of harassment and discrimination. In this context, the cultural explanation – the specific reference to rural, small-town culture – may seem persuasive.

However, bearing in mind Archer's more nuanced approach to culture, it is worth questioning whether all, or even most, managers at Wal-Mart see female employees as farmers' wives and therefore as deserving of the second-class status such a characterization supposedly entails. Perhaps this is typical only of male managers in certain geographical regions and would not be found, for instance, among female managers in Alaska.

Consider another possibility: perhaps many managers do not see women this way but are 'forced' to treat their employees harshly for other reasons. For example, earlier in the review, Simon Head notes that Wal-Mart typically fails to provide managers with the budgets they need 'to staff their stores at adequate levels' (Head, 2004, p. 3). Perhaps harsh treatment of employees is more the result of pragmatic managers seeking to keep their jobs than it is the result of the managers' internalization of rural, small-town values.

To conclude, the idea of culture provides a valuable perspective on organizational behaviour, but we must be careful not to portray people as 'cultural dopes' whose behaviour is wholly determined by the cultural values to which they have been exposed.

stop! Develop a cultural explanation of organizational behaviour, but be sure that your explanation recognizes the agentic powers of the people whose behaviour you are explaining.

Sources and further information

Archer, M. (2000) *Being Human: The Problem of Agency*, Cambridge: Cambridge University Press.

Head, S. (2004) 'Inside the Leviathan', *New York Review of Books*, 51(20), pp. 1–8.

Note: This feature was written by David MacLennan, Assistant Professor at Thompson Rivers University, BC, Canada.

Table 12.3 – The major perspectives on organizational culture

Perspective	Analysis level	Primary concern	Nature of organizations
Functionalist	Macro level	Maximizing efficiency/loyalty	A system comprising interrelated parts/groups that work together with no inherent conflict. Power is not important. Culture is something that an organization 'has'
Symbolic-interactionist	Micro level	How culture is learned/equity	Organizational culture is constructed and reproduced by symbols and shared meanings in interaction with members. Culture is a metaphor for the organization. It is something that an organization 'is'
Conflict	Macro level	Elimination of power imbalances	Organization is characterized by economic/power inequality/conflict over scarce resources. Culture is fragmented in complex and conflicting ways. It is something that an organization 'is'
Feminist	Macro level *and* micro level	Elimination of sexual inequality	Organization is characterized by pervasive sexuality/power inequality/sexual discrimination. Culture is fragmented, something that an organization 'is'

stop reflect
Looking at Table 12.3, what are the key differences between the 'has' perspective and the 'is' perspective on organizational culture? Which of these perspectives do you consider most useful for understanding the nature of organizations and shared behaviour, and why?

boundaries of organizational behaviour by examining the people who are deemed to be the 'recipients' of organizational culture. As sociologist Judy Wajcman observes in her insightful study, the individual, work groups and the modern organization are not gender neutral. Indeed, more controversially perhaps, she presents a powerful argument for gender-inclusive cultural theories if we accept her main premise that 'gender is woven into the very fabric of bureaucratic hierarchy and authority relations' (ref. 62, p. 47). The feminist perspective shares with the differentiation approach concerns with inequality and redressing discriminatory workplace practices.

Each of the four major ways of thinking about organizational culture we have examined involves different assumptions. As a result, each perspective leads us to ask different research questions and to view the realities of organizational life differently. Table 12.3 reviews the four perspectives in terms of three characteristics: (1) their primary level of analysis; (2) the primary concern of the theorists associated with each; and (3) how each understands the nature of organizations. These major perspectives can be used as a theoretical compass for navigating through the myriad competing views found in the organizational culture literature.

MANAGING CULTURES

Much management 'integrationist' theory identifies a robust corporate culture as an important factor in promoting work motivation. Proponents advocate that senior managers abandon bureaucratic 'command and control' regimes for a 'strong' corporate culture to win the commitment of their workers, much like a magnet will realign a chaotic collection of iron filings into a discernible pattern. A strong culture can help to activate latent employment-related values, which workers possess but have laid dormant or discouraged. In this narrative, corporate culture functions as the ultimate form of management control: self-control consistent with management expectations. Thus, developing a 'strong' culture in which members develop a fierce loyalty to the company is seen as central to modern management for its potential to close the 'gap' in the employment relationship and thereby release worker's creative capacity.[63-65]

It is considered central to 'soft' HRM practices to manage the *psychological contract*, to change the employment relationship from a binary, hierarchical, low-trust and low-commitment relation to a participatory, high-trust and high-commitment one,[66] and to capture, manage and control emotion in the organization.[29] Drawing on concepts from the sociologist Erving Goffman from the 1950s and 60s, work that analogizes the interactions between individuals to what goes on in drama, a robust corporate culture provides normative and behaviour 'scripts' for employees when management seeks to capture and manage emotional labour and introduce new initiatives, such as high-performance work systems and team-total quality control.[67,68]

Ways of managing culture

Cultural theorists and managers alike have tried to identify effective ways to change manifestations of organizational culture: visible *artefacts*, including language and shared behaviour, and work *values*, which are invisible but can be espoused. This section reviews strategies of planned culture change in three ways:

1 reframing social networks of symbols and meanings through artefacts, language, rituals and ceremonies
2 initiating new HRM practices to change behaviour and norms
3 leadership processes that aim to create the motivation to change behaviour, with particular emphasis on their symbolic content.

All three strategies implicitly adhere to Kurt Lewin's three-stage model of planned change, which involves 'unfreezing' present inappropriate behaviours, 'changing' to new behaviour patterns and positive reinforcement to 'refreeze' the desired changes.[69]

Reframing of social networks and meanings

The reframing of social networks of symbols and meanings to strengthen commitment to the organization and work-related values is manifested through changes in physical artefacts ranging from displaying a framed copy of the organization's new mission statement, and redesigning departments to create 'open-plan' office spaces or work teams with greater autonomy and new work uniforms, to establishing an R&D centre to emphasize the importance of research and innovation. Many organizations have reframed shared symbols and meanings by changing the language to promote the values of customers and quality. Stories and story telling are pervasive in culture management. Stories often contain, explicitly and implicitly, arguments for and against work-related values; they help members to locate work experiences and to develop new insights, which in turn promote sense making or sense giving and new ways of behaving.[70-72] Notable examples of language and narrative strategies to achieve cultural change are British Airways 'Putting People First' and Hewlett Packard's 'HP Way'. Others include the 'corporate' university, where students are increasingly conceptualized as 'clients' and professors as 'service providers' who must 'brand' their institutions and sell their 'products' to 'clients', as do car and beer manufacturers.[73]

Rituals aim to change behaviour. For example, the 3M Corporation has its own version of a Nobel Prize for innovative employees. The general gist of this change strategy is that, properly introduced, the reframing of cultural artefacts is seen to be potentially very effective in disconfirming the appropriateness of employees' present behaviours, providing employees with new behavioural models and affirming new ways of doing things.

HRM practices to change culture

The values that employees bring into the workplace may be identified through the selection process, and it is also posited that a particular culture can be created by a galaxy of HRM practices that select, retrain, reward or replace employees. Human resources selection techniques are an important means of 'knowing' and managing a culture change.[74] Personality- and competency-based tests are the psychological calculation of suitability that enables managers to find the 'best person' for the new culture. Changing and managing culture involves formal and informal work-related learning. This includes a process of socialization, through which employees learn the symbols and meanings and the shared practices: 'The fact that organizational cultures are composed of practices rather than values makes them somewhat manageable: they can be *managed* by changing the practices' (ref. 75, p. 240, emphasis added).

The performance appraisal system is a systematic HRM mechanism used to classify and rank employees hierarchically according to how well they integrated the newly defined set of beliefs, values and actions into their normal ways of doing things. The new espoused work values are incorporated into appraisal systems to allow employees to be compared with each other, to render them 'known' and to reinforce the desired change. The reinforcement effect is further secured when appraisals are linked to performance-related rewards. For example, given the general **commodification** of education, new contracts in university education reinforce a 'research culture' when promotion and pay are tied to research productivity rather than teaching. Such HRM initiatives help with 'cultural doping' so that employees exhibit new behaviours and attitudes.[76] Thus, a metaphorical 'glue' bonds employees and encourages each to internalize the organization's culture because it fulfils their need for social affiliation and identity.

commodification: in Marxist theory, the production of goods and services (commodities) for exchange in the marketplace, as opposed to the direct consumption of commodities

Leading cultural change

The role of leadership in generating employees' support for cultural change is rooted in the leadership literature (see, for example, Bass and Riggio[77]). There are sociologically informed writers who recognize that cultures can be changed to match strategic goals. In contrast to the crudely prescriptive functional approach, Morgan, for example, cautiously argues that:

> Managers can influence the evolution of culture by being aware of the symbolic consequences of their actions and by attempting to foster desired values. But they can never control culture in the sense that many management writers advocate … An understanding of organizations as cultures … [does] not always provide the easy recipe for solving managerial problems that many managers and management writers hope for. (ref. 78, p. 152)

The guiding maxim for implementing successful strategies for cultural change is that of meeting 'complexity with complexity'.[79]

One approach that subsumes Kurt Lewin's change model and recognizes complexity is John Kotter's either-step sequential model, which focuses on what specific behaviours leaders should engage in when leading change (Table 12.4).[80] Steps 1–4 represent Lewin's 'unfreezing' stage, steps 5, 6 and 7 represent the 'changing' stage, and step 8 represents the 'refreezing' process. Kotter's model attempts to change culture through a empiricist-rational strategy, that is, with the view that individuals will make rational choices if provided with 'correct' information. In an economic and political crisis, Canadian writer Naomi Klein reminds us that 'unfreezing' and organizational change may occur through 'shock therapy' as well as adroit management.[66,81] The practitioner approach offered by Kotter does not address whether the change-appropriate behaviours are less or more likely to be exhibited by certain types of organizational leader.[82]

Is managing culture desirable?

Assuming that senior managers are able to transform organizational cultures, is this necessarily desirable? If the central premise of the 'has' theory is that ideas within a social work group are homogeneous, unified and uncontested, a strong culture can be a double-edged sword. It can give members an organizational identity, facilitate collective commitment, provide social stability and influence behaviour without the need for bureaucratic controls. If fundamental changes are needed, however, a strong corporate culture can actually be an impediment to creative thinking, to informal learning, creativity and innovation, and to change, and may thus undermine organizational excellence and success. The learning–creativity paradigm as a decisive source of competitive advantage is based upon spontaneity, irrational and idiosyncratic rather than conventional ideas and solutions, risk taking and rule breaking; it celebrates the creative potential of deviant thinking and action.[83]

Table 12.4 – A strategy for cultural change

Step	Description of action
1. Establish a sense of urgency	Examine competitive realities. Identify and discuss realities, crises or opportunities relating to why cultural change is needed
2. Create the guiding coalition	Create a cross-functional group of people with enough power to lead the cultural change
3. Develop a vision and strategy	Create a vision and strategic plan to help direct the change process
4. Communicate the change vision	Develop and implement a communication strategy that consistently communicates the new behaviour expected of employees
5. Empower broad-based action	Eliminate obstacles to change, and use target individuals and groups to transform the organization. Encourage risk taking and creative thinking and problem solving
6. Generate short-term wins	Plan for and create visible short-term improvements or 'wins'. Recognize and reward people who contribute to the wins
7. Consolidate and produce more change	Consolidate gains. The guiding coalition uses credibility from short-term wins to create more change. Reinvigorate the change process with new change agents and new projects
8. Anchor new approaches in the culture	Create better customer- and productivity-oriented behaviours. Ensure a reconnection between new behaviours and processes and organizational success. Develop methods to ensure leadership development and succession

Source: Kotter (1996),[80] p. 21.

The much-vaunted 'learning organizations' in contemporary managerial lexicon meet the learning goals only if learners engage in critical reflection and open dialogue activities that may be considered deviant in organizations attempting to create cultural homogeneity.[84,85] The current managerial and political infatuation with Richard Florida's concept of 'creative economy' must be squared with the complexities of managing 'inherent tensions' between learning-creativity and control.[86,87] Furthermore, a strong corporate culture can undermine effective decision making because it encourages the phenomenon of group conformity or **groupthink** . Thus, although prescriptive literature presents organizational culture as a variable that can be manipulated at will to produce ideal types of coherence and integration to 'fit' new corporate aims, reservations exist on the appropriateness of such a strategy.

groupthink: the tendency of highly cohesive groups to value consensus at the price of decision quality

Evaluating cultural change strategies

Much cultural analysis is framed within an effort–performance relationship in which a 'strong' culture increases commitment, great loyalty to the organization and better all-round performance. Despite published accounts of 'culture change' initiatives, demonstrating an empirical relationship between a strong culture and organizational performance is problematic. To say that culture and performance are correlated requires the measurement of particular attributes of one variable against particular attributes of the other. In addition, correlation in itself does not constitute a causal relationship between the two variables, although this is one criterion of causality. The methodology for ensuring high internal validity would ideally permit a calculation of how different cultures – 'weak' versus 'strong' – affect organizational performance while controlling the other factors that might influence those performance outcomes. The data must demonstrate the extent to which a stable group of employees have internalized the new value demands, and the extent of the successful socialization of new members into these values, compared with a particular set of performance variables over a period of time.

reliability: in sociological research, the extent to which a study or research instrument yields consistent results

validity: in sociological research, the extent to which a study or research instrument accurately measures what it is supposed to measure

These measurement challenges underscore the importance of the statistical concepts of **reliability** and **validity**, which raises questions concerning the appropriateness of 'culture change' and performance measures. For example, there is the challenge of isolating external variables. Exchange rates can, for instance, significantly affect the financial bottom line, which makes it difficult to measure accurately the impact of a culture change. To be confident about the culture–performance link, we need credible evidence and a theory about how much of the variance can be explained by the culture factor. Otherwise, as two researchers have admitted, 'We cannot be sure of the extent to which the companies we studied were actually successful in creating that commitment or whether that commitment contributed to their success. All we can say is that the managers in question reported that their efforts ... produced a significant improvement' (ref. 88, p. ix).

The arguments around lack of rigor in research methodology have been well rehearsed;[89–93] see also Bratton and Gold[94] for an overview of measuring the effect of human factors on organizational performance. A small sample size, the exclusion of unfavourable data and citing corporate leaders as incontrovertible evidence of a culture–performance linkage is evidence of allegedly deficient research. When CEOs project an image of the organization by espousing values to the outside world (for example, the researcher), the image and the values may be inconsistent with what they truly value – referred to as enacted values – and what internal stakeholders experience. In this respect, given the dynamics between employee insiders and

Plate 5 – Exchange rates can significantly affect the financial bottom line, which makes it difficult to measure accurately the impact of a culture change.
Source: iStockphoto

community outsiders, incongruence between the corporate culture (or image) projected outwards and what is fed back into the organization is likely to breed cynicism, because the openly espoused values do not match the values and norms of the organization.[95] Additionally, it must be kept in mind that individuals within the same workplace will not necessarily internalize the culture of their workplace in the same way, and predictions of a 'strong culture' creating commitment and motivating one employee does not necessarily work with all employees. The evidence for a positive culture–performance link is tenuous. Indeed, it is so deficient that some have argued that it should not be dignified with serious attention.[47]

The most sceptical detractors argue that organizational culture *as a whole* cannot be 'created, discovered or destroyed by the whims of management' (ref. 96, p. 209). Organizational culture is embedded in potent informal shared interactions and norms. Hugh Willmott[47] – a deflater of the 'balloons of academic beliefs' – argues that resistance to strong cultures, or what he calls 'corporate culturalism', is found among powerful professional groups with considerable autonomy over how they perform their work. For example, Schein found that a strategy for cultural change that focused on the 'bottom line' and expected engineers to 'sell their services to clients' caused many to resist and threaten resignation.[97] Resistance to strategies for cultural change has also occurred in universities, healthcare and the BBC in the UK. This concept of 'misbehaviour' emphasizes that acts of resistance to new cultural demands can be less overt, less familiar and barely observable to the 'outsider'. And in what Sharon Bolton[29] describes as 'small spaces of resistance', employees' misbehaviour is changing from the familiar acts of soldiering and absenteeism towards more subtle acts of resistance that are far more difficult for managers to manage.

Not surprisingly therefore, the critical school tend to be highly sceptical about claims of managing cultures, regarding such claims as naive and unethical. Moreover, a strong corporate culture does little to alter the nature of the employment relationship, at least not in any meaningful way. The preoccupation with culture may obscure enduring structural antagonism and conflict. It does nothing to obviate the need for top management to try to reduce labour costs, to intensify the pressure of work and, sometimes, to render employees redundant.[37]

The binary conflict of interest between capital and labour that exists within a 'negotiated order' of mutual cooperation and combinations of values and norms suggests that the significance of organizational culture cannot be grasped unless it is related to structures of power within a context of market exigencies. In other words, culture can never be wholly managed, argue detractors, because it emerges from complex processes involving how employees construct their sense of identity in ways that are beyond management's control. The scope for misbehaviour and indifference to values and the efficacy of culture change strategies is captured by Erving Goffman thus:

> We find that participants decline in some way to accept the official view of what they should be putting into and getting out of the organization ... Where enthusiasm is expected, there will be apathy, where loyalty, there will be disaffection; where attendance, absenteeism; where robustness, some kind of illness; where deeds are to be done, varieties of inactivity ... Wherever worlds are laid on, under-lives develop. (ref. 98, p. 267)

survey: a research method in which a number of respondents are asked identical questions through a systematic questionnaire or interview

These arguments stress that participants' work values are shaped by outside variables such as class, gender, race and profession or trade. At the very best, culture change interventions are only successful at the observable behavioural level rather than the subconscious level.[99]

Finally, adding to the complexity of managing culture is the omnipresent Internet. It has, for example, been argued that the Internet adds both new operational capacities and a 'space dimension' that affects organizational culture in new ways.[100]

Critical insight   Can quantitative measurements capture organizational culture?

Organizational culture is an important area of the organizational behaviour field, but academics disagree on the best way to measure it. Ashkanasy et al. undertook research in 2000 to investigate the question of how best to carry out research into organizational culture. They found that the best research method really depends on *where* organizational culture is considered to be 'based'. If it is founded in values, the best way to carry out research is to use a technique that is able to access these deep-rooted, qualitative aspects – such as observations and interviews. On the other hand, if organizational culture is seen as being 'rooted in perceived practices rather than values', more standardized, quantitative techniques, such as questionnaires, may have an important part to play. Such quantitative techniques have a number of benefits, as Ashkanasy et al. state: 'We note that self-report **surveys** allow respondents to record their own perceptions of reality, and quantitative techniques allow for replication, cross-sectional comparative studies and provide data that can be analyzed through multivariate statistical techniques.'

But how should these questionnaires be designed? Ashkanasy et al.'s work found a lack of consensus on this question – in part, perhaps, because many researchers lack valid and reliable research tools to investigate organizational culture. In an effort to investigate this problem and perhaps provide a solution, Ashkanasy et al. devised the 'OCP' survey, which produced an 'organizational culture profile' based on questions relating to 'leadership, structure, innovation, job performance, planning, communication, environment, humanistic workplace, development of the individual and socialization on entry'. Initially, they surveyed 151 individuals using their OCP approach, but their results 'provided only mixed support for the reliability and validity of the OCP'. However, the results of a second OCP survey, using a larger sample, were more encouraging.

Ashkenasy et al.'s work investigating research methods for quantitative culture led them to conclude that 'multidimensional measures of organizational culture offer greater interpretive power and have a continuing role in advancing our knowledge of organizational culture.' They also provide the following advice to budding organizational culture researchers:

- Carry out research in order to establish a more theoretical basis for the measures being used in the questionnaire.
- Ensure that the dimensions being measured are clearly distinguishable.
- Use a wide spectrum of respondents.
- Gather qualitative data on the nature of the sample and subcultures.

○ Apply controls for environmental stability, in order to establish that the culture measures are valid.
○ Use longitudinal studies to establish causal relationships between the cultural dimensions and outcome the variables.

Do you agree? Do you think that surveys and questionnaires can capture the richness of organizational culture or deviant subcultures?

Source: Based on N. M. Ashkanasy, L. E. Broadfoot and S. Falkus (2000) 'Questionnaire measures of organizational culture,' pp. 131-45 in N. M. Ashkanasy, C. P. M. Wilderom and M. F. Peterson (eds), *Handbook of Organizational Culture and Climate*, Thousand Oaks, CA: Sage.

CHAPTER SUMMARY

○ In this chapter, we have explored the nature of organizational culture – a unique configuration of shared artefacts, common language and meanings and values that influence ways of doing things in the workplace. The culture of an organization influences what employees should think, believe or value in this social discourse.

○ The belief that organizational culture can be produced and managed has become closely associated with organizational redesign and management theories around HRM, the management of emotional labour and transformation leadership.

○ Three fundamental levels of organizational culture comprise visible artefacts (buildings, technology, language and norms), underpinned by values, which are invisible, and basic assumptions, which are also invisible, unconscious and resistant to change.

○ We explained that culture analysis can be divided into two schools of thought: managerialist and critical. The managerialist perspective is functionalist in that it stresses that culture can play a role in building consensus and harmony, and how culture can improve performance. It views organizational culture as a *variable*: it is something that an organization '*has*' and, as such, can be produced and managed.

○ The prescriptive literature tends to present too uniform a view of organizational culture. Alternative approaches point out the existence of *subcultures* and *counter-culture*. These concepts are important if we believe that organizations consist of individuals and work groups with multiple sets of values and beliefs.

○ The critical perspective focuses on a sociological concern to describe and critically explain cultural processes, how culture emerges through social interaction, power relations, social inequalities, influencing communities of practice, emotion and norms of individual and group behaviour. Viewed through a sociologist's lens, culture is something that a work organization '*is*'.

○ The critical literature emphasizes the symbolic and subjective aspects of the workplace, the role of culture in strengthening management control, and the relationships between social inequalities and patriarchal systems *outside*, and work socialization and behaviour *inside*, the workplace.

○ We have discussed how national culture and organizational culture are deeply intertwined, each influencing the other and with latter embedded in society. Gender refers to culturally specific patterns of human behaviour and is culturally learned or determined. Unarguably therefore, gender is a central facet of organizational analysis. Yet standard accounts of organizational culture have tended to neglect how gender, patriarchy and sexuality in society and in workplaces influence the dynamics of organizational culture.

○ This chapter described a model for culture change. We emphasized that managers must be aware of the complexities of cultures. Finally, we discussed the problem of a strong corporate culture undermining decision making because it may encourage conformity or groupthink.

KEY CONCEPTS

artefacts
corporate culture
counter-cultures
misbehaviour
national culture
organizational climate
organizational culture
rituals
stories
subcultures
values

VOCAB CHECKLIST FOR ESL STUDENTS

- Artefacts
- Assumptions, assume
- Commodification, commodity
- Culture, cultural
- Development, develop, developed, developing
- Differentiated, differentiate
- Dominance, dominate, dominant
- Fragment, fragmentary
- Functionalist
- Groupthink
- Ideology, ideological
- Integration, integrate
- Invisible structures
- Macho
- Mores
- Nation, nationalize, national
- Organizational climate
- Organizational culture
- Paternal, paternalistic
- Reliability, rely, reliable
- Ritual, ritualistic, ritualize
- Socialization, socialize, social
- Soldiering
- Subculture
- Taboo
- Validity, validate, valid
- Values, value, valuable
- Visible structures

CHAPTER REVIEW QUESTIONS

1 What is meant by organizational culture, and how does it relate to national culture?

2 What are the three levels of culture, and how do they operate?

3 Review the 'mainstream' and 'critical' perspectives on organizational culture described in this chapter. Discuss the perspectives that you and other students find appealing and plausible. Explain your reasons.

4 What mainstream interventions have been used for changing or reinforcing organizational culture? What are the strengths and weaknesses of each?

5 What impact do cultural values and expectations about gender have upon the design and operation of organizations, and how, in turn, does this impact on gender?

6 To what extent, if at all, do notions of masculinity and femininity reinforce or challenge traditional notions of organizational culture?

CHAPTER RESEARCH QUESTIONS

1 One way to understand organizational culture is to observe your own university or college and reflect on students' comments in class. What visible artefacts, ceremonies and practices of the teaching faculty indicate, for example, a 'strong' focus on research or on teaching students? Talk to other students and ask them what the distinctive facets of their national culture are. Give examples of their value statements that may be considered reflective of a national culture.

2 Obtain a copy of Peter Warr's article 'Work values: some demographic and cultural correlates'.[17] What does the World Values Survey tell us about work values in countries with a different cultural heritage? What are the implications of the findings for international managers?

3 Mats Alvesson's *Understanding Organizational Culture*[36] emphasizes the importance of avoiding 'quick fixes' when it comes to organizational culture. What are Alvesson's 'seven sins' in organizational culture thinking? How do these 'seven sins' compare with more traditional management texts on the subject?

FURTHER READING

Aaltio, I. and Mills, A. J. (2002) *Gender, Identity and the Culture of Organizations*, Routledge: London.

Alvesson, M. (2002) *Understanding Organizational Culture*, London: Sage.

D'Amato, A. and Zijlstra, D. (2008) 'Psychological climate and individual factors as antecedents of work outcomes', *European Journal of Work and Organizational Psychology*, **17**, pp. 33–54.

de Cieri, H. (2008) 'Transnational firms and cultural diversity', pp. 509–29 in P. Boxall, J. Purcell and P. Wright (eds), *The Oxford Handbook of Human Resource Management*, Oxford: OUP.

Dennison, D. R. (1996) 'What is the difference between organizational culture and organizational climate? A native's point of view on a decade of paradigm wars', *Academy of Management Review*, **21**, pp. 619–54.

Linstead , S. (2009) 'Managing culture', pp. 149–94 in S. Linstead, L. Fulop and S. Lilley (eds), *Management and Organization: A Critical Text* (2nd edn), Basingstoke: Palgrave.

McSweeney, B. (2002) 'Hofstede's model of national cultural differences and their consequences: a triumph of faith – a failure of analysis', *Human Relations*, **55**(1), pp. 89–118.

Martin, J. (2002) *Organizational Culture: Mapping the Terrain*, Thousand Oaks, CA: Sage.

Martin, J., Knopoff, K. and Beckman, C. (1998) 'An alternative to bureaucratic impersonality and emotional labour: bounded emotionality at the Body Shop', *Administrative Science Quarterly*, **43**(3), pp. 429–69.

Morgan, P. I. and Ogbonna, E. (2008) 'Subcultural dynamics in transformation: a multi-perspective study in health care professionals', *Human Relations*, **61**(1), pp. 39–65.

Ogbonna, E. and Harris, L. (2006) 'Organizational culture in an age of the Internet: an exploratory case study', *New Technology, Work and Employment*, **21**(2), pp. 162–75.

Parker, M. (2000) *Organizational Culture and Identity*, London: Sage.

Schneider, B. (2000) 'The psychological life of organizations,' pp. xvii–xxi in N. M. Ashkanasy, C. P. M. Wilderom and M. F. Peterson (eds), *Handbook of Organizational Culture and Climate*, Thousand Oaks, CA: Sage.

Case Study   Changing the University of Daventry's culture

Setting

The UK higher education sector generally is facing uncertainty about a continuing national demand for higher education as the level of unemployment, caused by the global economic recession, is increasing. Other challenges facing higher education are changes to student fee regimes, changing political agendas and public funding, as well as the unpredictable demand from international students. The increase in student fees has sharpened students' focus on the value they receive from their universities. Combined with an increase in the number of new universities entering the sector, and at least a short-term reduction in student applications, this will increase the pressure on universities to make their programmes and services more attractive to students while maintaining their academic standards. Globalization has created a booming market in higher education, and, aided by new technologies and the dissolution of national market borders, international partnerships have developed to create 'super' universities with overwhelming competitive advantages over individual locally or regionally focused institutions.

Background

Located in central England, the University of Daventry, created from the amalgamation of Daventry College and Daventry Institute of the Arts, gained university status in 2009. Student numbers have grown steadily in the past few years, and it recruited to meet its target level or the first time in 2007/08. The headcount is 8500 full- and part-time students. The University's core activity is helping students succeed. The vast majority of students attend the University to improve their career prospects or to change career. Daventry offers programmes across a comprehensive range of disciplines. Historically, it has been strong in business studies, but more recently technology, health studies and the creative programmes have experienced significant growth. Daventry has always attracted a high proportion of mature students, and its geographical location, discipline mix and entrance policies have made it attractive and accessible to a diverse student population drawn from larger cities such as Coventry, Leicester, Bedford and Peterborough. Mature students account for 50 per cent of full-time undergraduates, and international students account for 9 per cent of the student population.

The University of Daventry must reduce its dependence on undergraduate students funded by the Higher Education Funding Council for England, and create a more diverse portfolio of income streams without putting its core activity at risk. The University's strategic plan is to deliver high-quality, innovative, flexible programmes both on and off the campus. It also aims to work closely with employers, schools, colleges and agencies in the region to offer excellence in research, scholarship and knowledge transfer, which will shape and support cultural and economic development in support of a sustainable agenda.

The University of Daventry has a number of identifiable strengths: a significant proportion of teaching staff with professional qualifications and experience in addition to their teaching qualifications; an increasing number of programmes with professional accreditation with recognition by over 30 professional bodies; and a high student satisfaction rate and reputation for excellent student support. The University also recognizes some weaknesses, including a low proportion of teaching staff engaged in research, a poor track record in attracting students with high qualifications upon entry, and a low number of departments with strong working partnerships with relevant professional employers. In setting a course to achieve its new strategic vision, the University has established five strategic goals: (1) helping all career-motivated students to achieve their career aspirations; (2) consistently delivering academic excellence; (3) building the University's track record in applied research and innovation; (4) developing the capacity to generate income; and (5) contributing to the cultural and economic prosperity of the region.

Ad Hoc Joint Committee Meeting: developing research capacity

The Ad Hoc Joint Committee established by the University's Board of Governors, which consisted of representatives from the teaching staff, deans, students' union and human resources, and was chaired by the President, Heather Gannon, was mandated to develop an action plan to build the University's track record in research (goal 3). At the first meeting, James Duncan, the Human Resource Manager for University of Daventry, presented data on external research funding and research-based activities gleaned from the websites of six medium-sized universities. In closing his presentation, he remarked that although Daventry's teaching staff were highly committed to teaching, few engaged in research, and this was unlikely to change any time soon because 'There is no incentive to do so,' he said.

Bill Warren from the Department of Management forcefully countered, 'Teaching staff don't have time to do research', going on to say that 'The strength of the University lies in the quality of our teaching, not research.' Dr Michael Peters, from the Department of Applied Sciences, then responded to this by saying, 'High-quality teaching and research go together. If the University is to attract and retain students with high qualifications on entry, they must have the opportunity to become involved in research with their professors. When our teaching staff and their undergraduate students learn with each other and from each other, the result is powerful.'

A perceptive contribution came from the mature undergraduate student representative, Alex Boxall: 'Students are worried that if teachers are promoted on the books they write, they will be less interested in teaching.' Dr Margaret Cinel, Dean of Social Sciences and recently recruited from a large 'research-intensive' university, added that, compared with her previous institution, few of the teaching staff discussed research: 'This is a teaching institution, and if we are to achieve the strategic goals, we have to change the culture,' she said.

The President, Heather Gannon, summed up the contributions from around the table. Finally, following extended discussion, it was agreed that Dr Margaret Cinel, Dr Michael McLennan, Bill Warren, Alex Boxall and Mr James Duncan would draft a discussion paper for the next meeting on what could be done to change the culture at the University of Daventry.

Tasks

Workings in a small group, and role playing the five members of the subcommittee, prepare a report for the Ad Hoc Joint Committee drawing on the material from this chapter and addressing the following:

1   What change interventions can senior administrators introduce in order to create a culture at the University of Daventry that is more aligned with the new strategic vision?
2   What role, if any, should members of the Ad Hoc Joint Committee play in the culture change programme?

Additional Information

Arthurs, H. (2007) 'Publish-or-perish culture at universities harm the public good', *Ottawa Citizen*, November 3. Available at: http://osgoode.yorke.ca/media2.nsf/

Levin, J. S. (2003) 'Organizational paradigm shift and university colleges in British Columbia', *Higher Education*, 46, pp. 447–67.

Note

This case was written by John Bratton. Although the case draws upon material from UK and Canadian universities, the names of Daventry University and the individuals in the case study are fictitious.

WEB-BASED ASSIGNMENT

This chapter discusses the significance of culture in work organizations and the interconnectedness between national culture, and organizational culture and behaviour in organizations and businesses. The mainstream or managerialist perspective tends to focus on changing organizational culture to match business strategy and improve efficiency and profitability. This perspective focuses on achieving an organizational culture in which all members subscribe to one set of values and beliefs, normally decided by senior management. Critical perspectives tend to focus on how multiple viewpoints, values and beliefs are controlled or ignored by senior managers. This web-based assignment requires you to explore the Internet to find a website that provides insight into different cultures in organizations. For example, visit the websites of:

- Cosmetics retailer The Body Shop, at www.thebodyshop.com
- US entertainment corporate giant Disney, at http://disney.go.com
- Swedish homeware chain IKEA, at www.ikea-group.ikea.com
- South American agricultural and food giant Bunge, at www.bunge.com/about.html.

1 What kind of organizational culture do these organizations have (for example, what are their espoused values)?

2 What would critical theorists make of the cultures at these companies (or any others you have found)?

OB IN FILM

In recent years, there has been a growing backlash against corporate leaders accused and convicted of falsifying financial documents, misleading investors and engaging in fraudulent accounting practices. In 2002, American President George W. Bush's rhetoric promised harsh punishment for senior executives who 'cooked the books' and violated the public trust, the premise being that removing a minority of corporate malefactors could solve corporate white-collar crime. The American film *Wall Street* (1987), directed by Oliver Stone, offers an insight into the culture of financial corporations premised on greed. What examples of organizational culture does the film illustrate? What examples are given to substantiate the claim that a culture of anomie and avarice, not simply a few unscrupulous individuals or 'bad apples', contributed to the historic 2008/09 market crisis?

REFERENCES

1. Schneider, B. (2000) 'The psychological life of organizations,' pp. xvii–xxi in N. M. Ashanasy, C. P. M. Wilderom and M. F. Peterson (eds), *Handbook of Organizational Culture and Climate*, Thousand Oaks, CA: Sage.
2. Ackers, P. J. and Black, J. (1991) 'Paternalist capitalism: an organization in transition', in M. Cross and G. Payne (eds), *Work and the Enterprise Culture*, London: Falmer.
3. Ouchi, W. G. (1981) *Theory Z*, Reading, MA: Addison-Wesley.
4. Wicken, P. (1987) *The Road to Nissan*, London: Macmillan.
5. Williams, R. (1983) *Key Words*, New York: Oxford University Press.
6. Hofstede, G. (1997) Cultures *and Organizations: Software of the Mind* (2nd edn), New York: McGraw-Hill.
7. Giddens, A. (2009) *Sociology*, Cambridge: Polity Press.
8. Ravelli, B. (2000) 'Culture', pp. 39–61 in M. Kanwar and D. Swenson (eds), *Canadian Sociology* (3rd edn), Dubuque, IA: Kendall-Hunt.
9. Hofstede, G. (1991) *Cultures and Organizations: Software of the Mind*, Maidenhead: McGraw-Hill.
10. McSweeney, B. (2002) 'Hofstede's model of national cultural differences and their consequences: a triumph of faith – a failure of analysis', *Human Relations*, **55**(1), pp. 89–118.
11. Adler, N. J. and Gundersen, A. (2008) *International Dimensions of Organizational Behavior* (5th edn), Mason, OH: Cengage Learning [formerly Thomson-South-Western].
12. Linstead, S. and Grafton-Small, R. (1992) 'On reading organizational culture', *Organization Studies*, **13**(3), pp. 331–55.
13. Payne, R. L. (2000) 'Climate and culture: how close can they get?', pp. 163–76 in N. M. Ashkanasy, C. P. M. Wilderom and M. F. Peterson (eds), *Handbook of Organizational Culture and Climate*, Thousand Oaks, CA: Sage.

14. Parker, M. (2000) 'The sociology of organizations and the organization of sociology: some reflections on the making of a division of labour', *Sociological Review*, **48**(1), pp. 124–46.
15. Schein, E. H. (1985) *Organizational Leadership and Culture*, San Francisco: Jossey-Bass.
16. Harding, K. (2003) 'Working with art', *Globe and Mail*, August 20, p. C1.
17. Warr, P. (2008) 'Work values: some demographic and cultural correlates', *Journal of Occupational and Organizational Psychology*, **81**, pp. 751–75.
18. Davies, H. T. O. (2002) 'Understanding organizational culture in reforming the National Health Service', *Journal of the Royal Society of Medicine*, **95**(3), pp. 140–2.
19. Weber, M. (1922/1968) *Economy and Society*, Los Angeles: University of California Press.
20. Smircich, L. (1983) 'Concepts of culture and organizational analysis', *Adminstrative Science Quarterly*, **28**, pp. 33–58.
21. Martin, J and Frost, P. (1996) 'The organizational cultural war games: a struggle for intellectual dominance', pp. 599–621 in S. R. Clegg, C. Hardy and W. Nord (eds), *Handbook of Organization Studies*, London: Sage.
22. Peters, T. and Waterman, R. (1982) *In Search of Excellence*, New York: Harper & Row.
23. Deal, T. E. and Kennedy, A. A. (1982) *Organization Cultures: The Rites and Rituals of Organizational Life*, Reading, MA: Addison-Wesley.
24. Handy, C. (1993) *Understanding Organizations*, London: Penguin.
25. Kanter, R. M. (1982) *The Change Masters*, New York: Simon & Schuster.
26. Hammer, M. and Champy, J. (1994) *Reengineering the Corporation*, New York: HarperBusiness.
27. Champy, J. (1996) *Reengineering Management*, New York: HarperCollins.
28. Martin, J. (1992) *Culture in Organizations: Three Perspectives*, New York: Oxford University Press.
29. Bolton, S. C. (2005) *Emotion Management in the Workplace*, Basingstoke: Palgrave.
30. Morgan, P. I. and Ogbonna, E. (2008) 'Subcultural dynamics in transformation: a multi-perspective study in health care professionals', *Human Relations*, **61**(1), pp. 39–65.
31. Fitzgerald, J. A. and Teal, A. (2004) 'Health reform and occupational subcultures: the changing roles of professional identities', *Contemporary Nurse*, **16**(1/2), pp. 9–19.
32. Collinson, D. L. (1988) '"Engineering humour": masculinity, joking and conflict in shop-floor relations', *Organization Studies*, **9**(2), pp. 181–99.
33. Ackroyd, S. and Crowdy, P. (1990) 'Can culture be managed? Working with raw material: the case of the English slaughtermen', *Personnel Review*, **19**(5), pp. 3–13.
34. Martin, J. and Siehl, C. (1983) 'Organization culture and counterculture', *Organizational Dynamics*, **12**, pp. 52–64.
35. Jones, R., Lasky, B., Russell-Gale, H. and LeFevre, M. (2004) 'Leadership and the development of dominant and countercultures: a narcissistic perspective', *Leadership and Organization Development Journal*, **25**(1/2), pp. 214–33.
36. Alvesson, A. (2002) *Understanding Organizational Culture*, Los Angeles: Sage.
37. Edwards, P. K. (1990) 'Understanding conflict in the labour process: the logic and autonomy of struggle', pp. 125–52 in D. Knights and H. Willmott (eds), *Labour Process Theory*, Basingstoke: Macmillan.
38. Marx, K. (with Friedrich Engels) (1845/6/1978) 'The German ideology', p. 154 in R. Tucker (ed.), *The Marx–Engels Reader* (2nd edn), New York: Norton.
39. Ray, C. A. (1986) 'Corporate culture: the last frontier of control?', *Journal of Management Studies*, **23**(3), pp. 287–97.
40. Thompson, P. and McHugh, D. (2002) *Work Organizations* (3rd edn), Basingstoke: Palgrave.
41. Harvey, D. (1990) *The Condition of Postmodernity*, Oxford: Oxford University Press.
42. Calás, M. B. and McGuire, J. B. (1990) 'Organizations as networks of power and symbolism', pp. 95–113 in B. Barry (ed.), *Organizational Symbolism*, Berlin: de Gruyter.
43. Martin, J. (2000) 'Hidden gender assumptions in mainstream organizational theory and research', *Journal of Management Inquiry*, **9**(2), pp. 207–16.
44. Mills, A. (1995) 'Managing subjectivity, silencing diversity: organizational imagery in the airline industry: the case of British Airways', *Organization*, **2**(2), pp. 243–69.

45. Deetz, S. (1998) 'Discursive formations, strategized subordination and self-surveillance', pp. 151–72 in A. Kinlay and K. Starkey (eds), *Foucault, Management and Organization Theory*, London: Sage.

46. du Gay, P. and Salaman, G. (1992) 'The cult(ure) of the customer', *Journal of Management Studies*, **29**(5), pp. 615–33.

47. Willmott, H. (1993) 'Strength in ignorance, slavery is freedom: managing culture in modern organizations', *Journal of Management Studies*, **30**(4), pp. 515–52.

48. Sewell, G. and Wilkinson, B. (1992) 'Empowerment or emasculation? Shopfloor surveillance in a total quality organization, in P. Blyton and P. Turnbull (eds), *Reassessing HRM*, London: Sage.

49. Höpfl, H. (1992) 'The challenge of change: the theory and practice of organizational transformation', presented to the Employment Research Unit Annual Conference, Cardiff Business School, September. Quoted in P. Thompson and D, McHugh (2009), *Work and Organizations*, Basingstoke: Palgrave-Macmillan, p. 205.

50. Thompson, P. and McHugh, D. (2009) *Work and Organizations*, Basingstoke: Palgrave Macmillan.

51. Mills, A. (1988) 'Organization, gender and culture', *Organization Studies*, **9**(3), pp. 351–69.

52. Helm Mills, J. C. and Mills, A. (2000) 'Rules, sensemaking, formative contexts, and discourse in the gendering of organizational culture', pp. 55–70 in N. M. Ashkanasy, C. P. M. Wilderom and M. F. Peterson (eds), *Handbook of Organizational Culture and Climate*, Thousand Oaks, CA: Sage.

53. Sydie, R. A. (1994) *Natural Women, Cultured Men*, Vancouver: UBC Press.

54. Bratton, J. , Denham, D. and Deutschmann, L. (2009) *Capitalism and Classical Sociological Theory*, Toronto: UTP.

55. Watts, J. H. (2007) 'Porn, pride and pessimism: experiences of women working in professional construction roles', *Work, Employment and Society*, **21**(2), pp. 299–316.

56. Chamberlain, L. J., Crowley, M., Tope, D. and Hodson, R. (2008) 'Sexual harassment in organizational context', *Work and Occupations*, **35**(3), pp. 262–95.

57. McLaughlin, H., Uggen, C. and Blackstone, A (2009) 'A longitudinal analysis of gender, power and sexual harassment in young adulthood', presented at the American Sociological Association's 104th annual meeting, August 8. Quoted in *Globe and Mail*, August 11, 2009, p. L1, L3.

58. Brewis, J. and Linstead, S. (2000) *Sex, Work and Sex Work: Eroticizing Organization*, London: Routledge.

59. Mills, A. and Tancred, P. (eds) (1992) *Gendering Organizational Analysis*, Newbury Park, CA: Sage.

60. Hearn, J., Sheppard, D., Tancred-Sheriff, P. and Burrell, G. (eds) (1989) *The Sexuality of Organization*, London: Sage.

61. Nolen, S. (2009) 'From Johannesburg to New Delhi', *Globe and Mail*, January 10, p. A13.

62. Wajcman, J. (1998) *Managing Like a Man: Women and Men in Corporate Management*, Cambridge: Polity Press/Penn State University Press.

63. Burns, J. M. (1987) *Leadership*, New York: Harper & Row.

64. Kirkpatrick, S. A. and Locke, E. A. (1996) 'Direct and indirect effects of three core charismatic leadership components on performance and attitudes', *Journal of Applied Psychology*, **81**(1), pp. 36–51.

65. Soder, R. (2001) *The Language of Leadership*, San Francisco: Jossey-Bass.

66. Legge, K. (2005) *Human Resource Management: Rhetorics and Realities*, Basingstoke: Palgrave.

67. du Gay, P. (1996) *Consumption and Identity*, London: Sage.

68. Thompson, P. and Findley, T. (1994) 'Changing the people: social engineering in the contemporary workplace', in A. Sayer and L. Ray (eds), *Culture and Economy after the Cultural Turn*, London: Sage.

69. Lewin, K. (1951) *Field Theory in Social Sciences: Selected Theoretical Papers*, London: Tavistock.

70. Boyce, M. E. (1997) 'Organizational story and storytelling: a critical review', *Journal of Organizational Change*, **9**(5), pp. 5–26.

71. Gold, J., Holman, D. and Thorpe, R. (2002) 'The role of argument analysis and story telling in facilitating critical thinking', *Management Learning*, **33**(3), pp. 371–88.

72. Taylor, S. S., Fisher, D. and Dufresne, R. (2002) 'The aesthetics of management storytelling', *Management Learning*, **33**(3), pp. 313–30.

73. Gingras, Y. (2009) 'Marketing can corrupt universities', *University Affairs*, February, p. 39.

74. Townley, B. (1994) *Reframing Human Resource Management*, London: Sage.

75. Hofstede, G. (1998) 'Organization culture', pp. 237–55 in M. Poole and M. Warner (eds), *The Handbook of Human Resource Management*, London: International Thomson Business Press.

76. Alvesson, M. and Willmott, H. (1996) *Making Sense of Management: A Critical Introduction*, London: Sage.

77. Bass, B. M. and Riggio, R. E. (2006) *Transformational Leadership*, Mahwah, NJ: Erlbaum.

78. Morgan, G. (1997) *Images of Organizations* (2nd edn), Thousand Oaks, CA: Sage.

79. Bate, P. (1995) *Strategies for Cultural Change*, Oxford: Butterworth-Heinemann.

80. Kotter, J. (1996) *Leading Change*, Boston: Harvard University Press.

81. Klein, N. (2007) *The Shock Doctrine: The Rise of Disaster Capitalism*, Toronto: Alfred Knopf.

82. Herold, D. M., Fedor, D. B., Caldwell, S. and Liu, Y. (2008) ' The effects of transformational and change leadership on employees' commitment to a change: a multilevel study', *Journal of Applied Psychology*, **93**(2), pp. 346–57.

83. Bratton, J. A. and Garrett-Petts, W. F. (2008) 'Art in the workplace: innovation and culture-based economic development in small cities', pp. 85–98 in D. W. Livingstone, K. Mirchandani and P. H. Sawchuk (eds), *The Future of Lifelong Learning and Work*, Rotterdam: Sense.

84. Fenwick, T. (1998) 'Questioning the concept of the learning organization,' pp. 140–52 in S. Scott, B. Spencer and A. Thomas (eds), *Learning for Life*, Toronto: Thompson Educational.

85. Coopey, J. (1996) 'Crucial gaps in the "learning organization": power, politics and ideology', pp. 348–67 in K. Starkey (ed.), *How Organizations Learn*, London: International Thomson Business Press.

86. Thompson, P., Jones, M. and Warhurst, C. (2007) 'From conception to consumption: creativity and the missing managerial link', *Journal of Organizational Behavior*, **28**, 625–40.

87. DeFillippi, R., Grabher, G. and Jones, C. (2007) 'Introduction to paradoxes of creativity: managerial and organizational challenges in the cultural economy', *Journal of Organizational Behavior*, **28**, 511–21.

88. Martin, P. and Nichols, D. (1987) *Creating a Committed Workforce*, London: Institute of Personnel Management.

89. Antony, P. A. (1994) *Managing Culture*, Milton Keynes: Oxford University Press.

90. Guest, D. E. (1992) 'Right enough to be dangerously wrong: an analysis of the in search of excellence phenomenon', in G. Salaman (ed.), *Human Resource Management*, London: Sage.

91. Ogbonna, E. and Wilkinson, B. (1990) 'Corporate strategy and corporate culture: the view from the checkout', *Personnel Review*, **19**(4), pp. 9–15.

92. Silverman, J. (1987) 'The ideology of excellence: management and neo-conservativatism', *Studies in Political Economy*, **24**, pp. 105–29.

93. Smith, P. and Peterson, M. (1988) *Leadership, Organizations and Culture*, London: Sage.

94. Bratton, J. and Gold, J. (2007) *Human Resource Management: Theory and Practice* (4th edn), Basingstoke: Palgrave.

95. Herrbach, O. and Mignonac, K. (2004) 'How organizational image affects employee attitudes', *Human Resource Management Journal*, **14**(4), pp. 76–88.

96. Lynn Meek, V. (1992) 'Organizational culture: origins and weaknesses', pp. 192–212 in G. Salaman (ed.), *Human Resources Strategies*, London: Sage.

97. Schein, E. H. (2004) *Organizational Culture and Leadership* (3rd edn), San Francisco, CA: Jossey Bass.

98. Goffman, E. (1961) *Asylums*, London: Penguin. Quoted in S. Bolton (2005), *Emotion Management in the Workplace*, Basingstoke: Palgrave, p.267.

99. Ogbonna, E. (1992) 'Organization culture and human resource management: dilemmas and contradictions', pp. 74–96 in P. Blyton and P. Turnbull (eds), *Reassessing Human Resource Management*, London: Sage.

100. Ogbonna, E. and Harris, L. (2006) 'Organizational culture in an age of the Internet: an exploratory case study', *New Technology, Work and Employment*, **21**(2), pp. 162–75.

101. Frost, P. J. , Moore, L., Louis, M., Lundberg, C. and Martin, J. (1985) *Organizational Culture*, Newbury Park, CA: Sage.

102. Cooke, R. A. and Rousseau, D. M. (1988) 'Behavioural norms and expectations: a quantitative approach to the assessment of organizational culture', *Group and Organization Studies*, **13**, pp. 245–73.

103. Drennan, D. (1992) *Transforming Company Culture*, London: McGraw-Hill.

Chapter
13

POWER AND POLITICS

CHAPTER OUTLINE

- Introduction
- Power: a matter of definitions
- Power: evidence from the workplace
- Summary and end-of-chapter features
- Chapter case study 1: Aiming for a paperless world
- Chapter case study 2: Las Vegas general strike

CHAPTER OBJECTIVES

After completing this chapter, you should be able to:

- recognize and explain key debates concerning the concept of power in the context of the organizational behaviour field
- understand and explain the following key concepts: systems of power, authority, influence and hegemony
- compare and contrast major macro-theoretical approaches to the concept of power in the writings of Mann, Foucault, Lukes, Weber and Gramsci
- discuss possible implications of theories and research for workplace practice

INTRODUCTION

In the field of physics, 'power' is defined as a quantity expressing the rate at which energy is transformed into work. In fact, thermodynamic laws see energy as flowing in one direction only. In addition, power is active. The concept that slows it down, 'resistance', is passive. We begin with these points for a reason. Simply put, some of these basic principles appear remarkably persistent in many common-sense views about the notion of 'power' in its more general forms, what it is and how it works.

This chapter takes up the issue of power and behaviour in work organizations. It provides an introduction to a range of thinking and research in order to help provide tools with which to expand your understanding. As some recent researchers have commented, 'Changes in power almost invariably lead to changes in behavior' (ref. 1, p. 135). (See also Ailon[2] for further commentary on the gaps in organizational theorists' thinking about power, and Crane et al.[3] for a discussion of this matter in relation to business studies, with a specific focus on the work of Michel Foucault.)

Throughout, however, we explicitly reject the common-sense view of power. We argue that power is not simply something the powerful have and the powerless lack. Power, to borrow from the late French philosopher Michel Foucault, is not possessed – it is exercised. In addition, power does not simply limit what people do (that is, as Foucault also says, it does not simply 'say no'), but rather it is productive too (it also says 'yes' to certain behaviours). Across the work of the many intellectuals we discuss in this chapter, some look at macro-phenomena such as politics, society and history, and some look at micro-phenomena such as everyday practice. Still others focus on the many elements in between and the connections between the two. What is clear is that the most astute understandings of power see it as being, at its heart, relational or interactive in nature.

Although it is most often a charge levelled at the work of others, it has been fairly common in recent organizational behaviour writing to note that power as a concept is underdeveloped in this literature. In fact, it has been noted in the editorial introduction to a special journal issue devoted to the concept of power that very little has been written by behavioural analysts on the topic.[4] There are some important indications that this trend may, however, be changing. Nevertheless, it runs like a thread throughout the chapter that, building on what has just been established, power is not an individual phenomenon. Despite the fact that the figure of the 'powerful person' appears in all our lives, there is in fact no individual who creates, constitutes or sustains 'power' as such.

Imagine, for example, the power of a police officer, a judge, a professor or a CEO. What are all the 'things' – the history, the traditions, the institutions, the distribution of resources, the socially granted authority and so on – that are necessarily in place to create this seemingly individual embodiment of 'power'? Take away the vastly networked, social, material, historical, cultural and ideological dimensions of the phenomenon, and what we find is that the person's 'power' virtually disappears. Imagine the power of a plumber (for example, when you have a flooded bathroom) or a secretary (for example, when their manager needs some important documents in an emergency). Here too, the power that these individuals may appear to embody, upon closer examination, rests on the particular situation as much as on any individual possession of power per se.

The point here is that while individuals may embody a variety of traits that seem to constitute and legitimize their 'power', we must not confuse individual traits with power as such, because where changes occur across the many dimensions of power – the cultural, the organizational, the political or the situational – the meaning of these traits can be radically transformed. Indeed, it is important to also remember that the exercise of power is often more contested, more conflictual, than is sometimes evident at first glance.

In this sense, we begin, as we usually must, with the matter of definitions and related but distinct terms. Indeed, a sizeable proportion of this chapter must grapple directly with these matters of definition.

POWER: A MATTER OF DEFINITIONS

A reasonable starting point for many discussions of **power** is some version of the sociologist Robert Dahl's much-quoted phrase, 'A has power over B to the extent

stop reflect
Before proceeding with your reading of the chapter, take a moment to think about your definition of the term 'power'.
Do you hold any of the 'common-sense' views on power discussed above? As you make your way through your reading, be sure to keep in mind that a good definition of power should offer you the capacity to see the areas through which it might be questioned, challenged or altered where warranted

power: a term defined in multiple ways, involving cultural values, authority, influence and coercion as well as control over the distribution of symbolic and material resources. At its broadest, power is defined as a social system that imparts patterned meaning

Plate 1 – Imagine the power of a plumber (for example, when your boiler is broken and you have no heating or hot water in winter), a firefighter (for example, when your house is on fire), or a secretary (for example, when their manager needs some important documents in an emergency). The power that these individuals may appear to embody, upon closer examination, rests on the particular situation as much as on any individual possession of power per se.
Source: iStockphoto

that he can get B to do something that B would not otherwise do' (ref. 5, p. 202–3). Closely related to this is a definition by French and Raven that likewise focuses on the potential ability of one individual to influence another within a certain social system.[6] In fact, French and Raven went on to develop five bases of power, the most important of which, first suggested by Warren,[7] are those related to systemic reward and coercion.

Our goal in this chapter is to incorporate such statements into a more comprehensive understanding of power, and then test the current analyses of power in work organizations in relation to this new understanding. In doing this, we might add to Dahl's basic definition to relate it directly to the paid workplace: power is the ability to say no to certain behaviours, yes to others, and to shape how something should be done. And, building further on this as Alion does, we can add that it is equally vital to know as much as possible about what 'B would otherwise do'.[2] Alion's article offers a summary of the six ways in which 'what B would otherwise do' are typically understood by organizational researchers, arguing that there is an important difference between what are referred to as 'political' versus 'Foucauldian' approaches to power in organizations

This, of course, is inseparable from many of the other issues addressed in the text, including equity and diversity, the organization of labour processes, the selection of technologies, the technical and social divisions of labour, and the accountability and reporting structures and pacing that shape, or rather influence, 'power' in organizations.

It is vital that we recognize that, to complicate matters further, the concept of 'power' is often confused with the relatively distinct questions of 'influence' and 'authority'. We see this, in fact, in the definitions of both Dahl and French and Raven. The goal of our definition here is to recognize that **authority** is closely related to, but analytically distinct from, the concept of power. Authority, as it is defined in the social science literature, also tends to have a complex relational dimension, but can be said to involve power granted by some form of active or passive consent – whether the consent is linked to specific individuals, groups or institutions – which bestows on it some level of legitimacy. (A fascinating treatment of this notion of coercion, consent and legitimacy can be read in the analysis of the American system of slavery as documented by Genovese.[8]) Some theorists use these words in ways that overlap a good deal. For example, the German sociologist Max Weber's work deals with issues of power but mostly elaborates on types of authority.

The issue of **legitimacy** opens up a range of important questions, which we discuss more directly below. Legitimacy depends on one's perspective in communities, organizations, institutions and the world (as a worldview). What is legitimate for some may not be legitimate for others, and this can and does change over time, and according to situations.

Even here, in these conceptually humble beginnings, we see that our rejection of individual models of power in favour of relational ones holds firm. In order to move further beyond conventional discussions of power, we can look beyond organization-based literature to some of the most general, macro approaches.

Traditionally, the field of social theory has understood the concept of power in broad macro terms. Indeed, there is a noticeable preoccupation with how the state, the Church, electoral politics, the military, and sometimes corporations and economic systems, may or may not be involved in systems of power. One of the key writers of this type is Michael Mann. His *Sources of Social Power* is considered a key text in these theoretical discussions, and builds from a detailed study of ancient Rome and world religions.[9] The 'sources of social power' are determined to be ideological, military, political and economic. Indeed, Mann goes on to say that the object of this type of social power approach should be the development of an analysis of 'multiple overlapping and intersecting socio-spatial networks of power' (ref. 9, p. 1).

Power, in this approach, is diffuse and what we might call 'infrastructural'. It can be understood, according to Mann, by taking into account a specific set of universal relations or dynamics: universalism–particularism, equality–hierarchy, cosmopolitanism–uniformity, decentralization–centralization and civilization–militarism. Each is concerned with the dynamic between control and diffuse freedoms and, when applied to his four sources of social power, produces a way of thinking about power that has been influential in social theory as well as history.

Mann's type of approach more or less rejects the explanation of power as simply a form of 'institutionalization' (which we discuss in relation to Weber below), but another key example that is influential in the mainstream social theory tradition is the work of Anthony Giddens.[10] His work on the 'central problems of social theory' seeks to provide an overarching approach while avoiding what he sees as the pitfalls of many broad social theories of power (from schools of social theory such as Marxism, phenomenology and structural-functionalism). His theory of **structuration** is intended to demonstrate the complex interrelations of human freedom (or agency) and determination (or structure), and emphasizes that, in the modern world, there

authority: the power granted by some form of either active or passive consent that bestows legitimacy

legitimacy: a term describing agreement with the rights and responsibilities associated with a position, social values, system and so on

structuration: a concept focusing on balancing the dichotomies of agency, or human freedom, and social organization, or structures where individual choices are seen as partially constrained, but they remain choices nonetheless

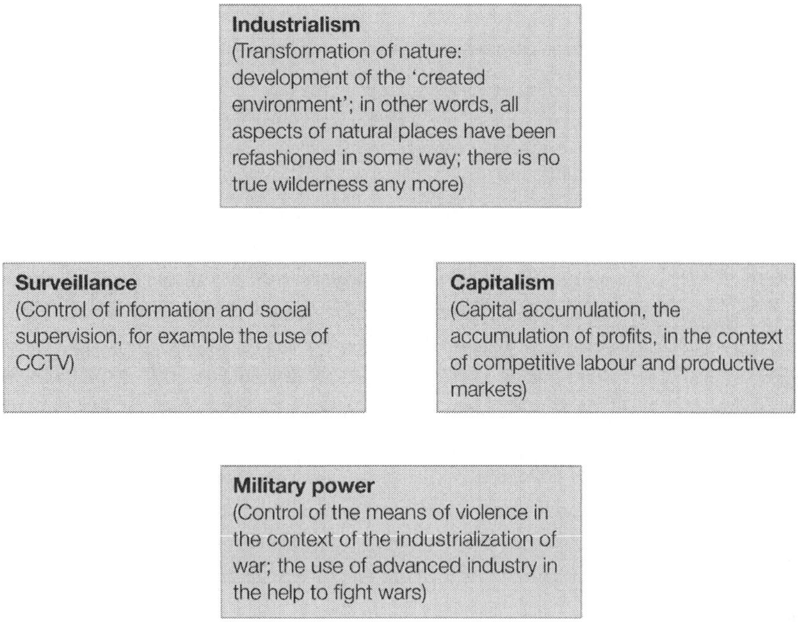

Industrialism
(Transformation of nature: development of the 'created environment'; in other words, all aspects of natural places have been refashioned in some way; there is no true wilderness any more)

Surveillance
(Control of information and social supervision, for example the use of CCTV)

Capitalism
(Capital accumulation, the accumulation of profits, in the context of competitive labour and productive markets)

Military power
(Control of the means of violence in the context of the industrialization of war; the use of advanced industry in the help to fight wars)

Figure 13.1 – Giddens' model of power

has been a fundamental shift based on the enormous growth in the resources (what he refers to as 'containers') of power. Central to Giddens' thesis are societal surveillance, capitalist enterprise, industrial production and centralized control over the 'means of violence' by the state (Figure 13.1).[10]

It is important to the theory of structuration that these sources of power are not 'out there', but are rather the result of specific forms of human interaction mixed with 'authority' and a distribution of 'resources', which together shape and control time and space. This is important, in part, because of its lack of what we would call 'closure'. That is, power is always an open, historical question: things can and do change.

Although we do not review it here, it is worth noting the meta-theory of German social theorist Jürgen Habermas. He describes **ideology** as structure of communication (in his theory of communicative action) that has been systematically distorted by power in such a way as to mostly exclude the realm of daily human activity (what Habermas calls the 'lifeworld') when its activity does not align with dominant institutions and their unique interests and needs. Such domination comes to penetrate individuals' lifeworld, personal identity and inner mental experience – on the same level of analysis dealt with by Giddens' approach to human interaction – leading to their further domination by social systems.

Finally, we should note that, for Giddens, all individuals 'have power', but this power is influenced and constrained by the distribution of different types of resource. In this model, there are 'allocative resources', which refer to control over physical things such as money or property, and there are also 'authoritative resources', which involve control over people's practices. For example, a business owner has the allocative resources of her capital, as well as authoritative resources granted by our legal institutions to set her workplace up in the way she feels most appropriate.

This can lead us to a deeper discussion of the relations between power and authority. Having influenced researchers including Mann, Giddens and Habermas, Max Weber's

ideology: a term with multiple uses, but in particular referring to perceptions of reality as distorted by class interests, and the ideas, legal arrangements and culture that arise from class relations (a term taken from Marx) work on the basic types of authority is closely linked to, although not the same as, the theories of power we have outlined. That is, Weber's theory of authority can be much more closely related to individuals, despite the fact that, ultimately, his approach too is a relational one. Authority necessarily involves others who grant this authority or legitimacy through complex systems of power.

Weber outlines three types of authority:

- *Charismatic authority* refers to leaders who are able to exercise power based on their personal traits.
- *Traditional authority* is dependent on a historical trajectory of past authority.
- *Rational authority*. Weber is most widely known for his analysis of this in his writing on bureaucracy. Here, authority rests on a specific system of laws or rules that establish a hierarchy in, for example, a public or private sector work organization.

Weber's perspective on authority is echoed in the work of Wrong, who lays out a basic model of the relations between influence and power (Figure 13.2).[11]

Another key body of writing on the concept of power is Steven Lukes' *Power: A Radical View*.[12] Lukes' theory is partially summarised in Figure 13.3. Lukes understands power and authority with the notion of 'bringing about consequences' not unlike, for instance, the way a teacher might seek to encourage students to complete their reading assignments prior to lectures. Part of this type of analysis is the recognition that obtaining compliance can require a multifaceted effort. It can be secured by the use of force or by people choosing to surrender to (or be led by) others. In fact, each is usually involved, as we shall see in our discussion of Gramsci later on. When people choose to accept the will of others as legitimate, we can, according to Lukes, describe the relationship as one of authority. Some of the studies of behaviour in organizations that we discuss in the following section of this chapter appear to draw on this type of approach.

conflict of interest: a condition in which the needs of one party (such as an individual or group) run counter to the needs of another

Equally important to Lukes' explanation are the conditions of a **conflict of interest**. The identification of structural and idiosyncratic conflicts of interest is a key challenge for organizational behaviour literature. Where, for example, is

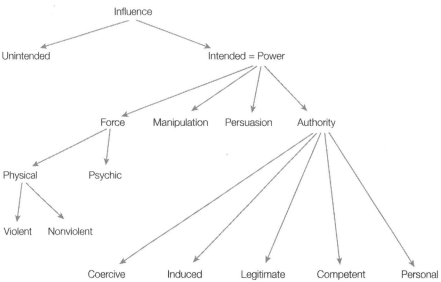

Figure 13.2 – Wrong on influence and power
Source: Wrong (1979),[11] p. 24

Work and Society: Worker autonomy as a contentious issue: the many dimensions of power

In their major study of work in contemporary society, Tilly and Tilly (1998) identify a broad range of issues that may prove contentious for workers. This list includes employer coercion, compensation (wages), outsourcing, discrimination, qualifications, union rights and worker autonomy. How such contentious issues are resolved depends on the exercise of power.

But what do we mean by power in this context? Steven Lukes (2007, p. 59) offers the following definition:

In social and political contexts, we typically attribute power to agents when we hold them responsible for bringing about significant outcomes.

Power, Lukes continues, always involves 'a mechanism – a causal process that links the powerful with the outcomes they can bring about' (p. 59). He adds that 'power, in its most general sense, involves the capacity to advance one's interests and affect the interests of others, whether negatively or positively' (p. 60).

Much of this is quite straightforward. It would be possible to use Lukes' definition of power to analyse how any one of the contentious issues outlined above was resolved. For example, we could identify the agents who exercise power and investigate the mechanisms they employ to advance their interests with respect to any of these contentious issues.

However, the study of power becomes more complicated when two other aspects of power are considered. The first complication in the study of power concerns what some would call the structural dimensions of power. Examples of the structural dimensions of power are large-scale inequalities in resource allocation and the formal rules (for example, laws and regulations) present in the environments where power is exercised. A second complicating issue in the study of power concerns what some would call its symbolic dimension. The symbolic dimension of power is evident when the values and thought processes of the less powerful support the exercise of power by the powerful.

Lukes' approach to power will become clearer if we focus on one of the Tillys' contentious issues. The issue of autonomy includes both task complexity and worker discretion. Autonomy is widely recognized as a key aspect of job satisfaction. It has also been associated with creativity, quality and productivity at work. In what sense is autonomy a political issue?

Using Lukes' analysis as a guide, we could respond by asking 'Who has an interest in expanding or restricting worker autonomy, and what mechanisms do they employ to advance their interests?' When we look at general trends in the world of work, it would appear that there has been a tendency for employers to consider worker autonomy as somehow not in the interests of the employer. How else would one explain various initiatives to deskill workers throughout the industrialized world?

But Lukes' analysis of power would lead us to proceed carefully in exploring the question of interests. Lukes insists that it is a mistake to think that 'the power of the powerful [always] affects others' interests adversely' (p. 60). According to Lukes, 'power can be empowering, even transformative, increasing others' resources, capabilities and effectiveness' (p. 60). So the work of identifying different interest groups in the workplace does not provide us with an automatic answer to how power will be exercised in the area of worker autonomy. In some instances, powerful groups may believe that it is in their interest to increase the capabilities of the less powerful and therefore to encourage worker autonomy.

What about the structural and symbolic dimensions of power? With regard to the structural dimension, it is worth noting that there are significant cross-national variations in how powerful groups view the issue of worker autonomy. In some countries, governments have stepped in and made the defence of worker autonomy a focus of regulation and state action (Gallie, 2007). With regard to the symbolic dimensions of power, Lukes would ask us to consider the circumstances in which worker autonomy emerges as a contentious issue. Perhaps the culture of some work environments makes it almost unthinkable to raise the question of worker autonomy.

stop! Take a moment to reflect on some of the issues raised by Lukes' approach to power. Can you think of examples of situations where employer groups have sought to encourage worker autonomy?
Why have some governments made worker autonomy a focus of regulation and state action? In what work environments would the issue of worker autonomy fail to make the agenda of contentious issues?

Sources and further information

Gallie, D. (2007) 'Production regimes, employment regimes, and the quality of work', pp. 1–34 in D. Gallie (ed.), *Employment Regimes and the Quality of Work*, Oxford: Oxford University Press.

Lukes, S. (2007) 'Power', *Contexts*, 6(3), pp. 59–61.

Tilly, C. and Tilly, C. (1998) *Work Under Capitalism*, Boulder, CO: Westview Press.

Note: This feature was written by David MacLennan, Assistant Professor at Thompson Rivers University, BC, Canada.

conflict just a matter of fine-tuning existing organizational structures and simply rooted in the contingencies and unpredictability of everyday life, and where might conflict be so deeply rooted in a structure that to challenge it is to simultaneously challenge the very nature of the organization itself? As Figure 13.3 shows, where

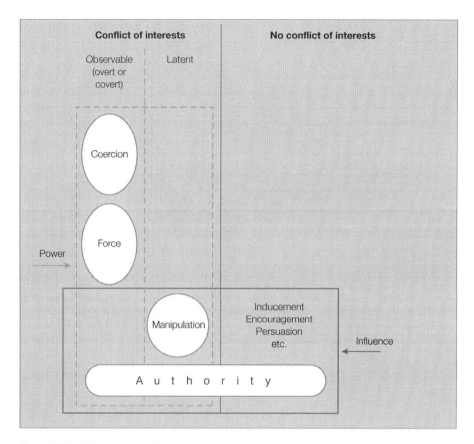

Figure 13.3 – Steven Luke's vision of power

Stop Reflect
Take a moment to
think back to your own
employment experiences
(or those of friends or
family members, if you
have none of your own
as yet). How can you
distinguish between
Weber's concept of
'authority' and the broader
systems of power as
discussed in Lukes or
Giddens? How has the
social infrastructure of
power systems supported
the 'authority' of those
in charge?

such structural conflicts of interest do not exist, Lukes uses the word 'influence'. Where structural conflicts of interest exist, he uses the word 'power'. Both planned decision making (overt and covert varieties) and latent (or unintended) uses of power play a role in Lukes' model, while issues of authority, not unlike those outlined by Weber, operate in both non-conflict and conflict of interest contexts.

ADDITIONAL DEFINITIONS OF POWER TO CONSIDER

Up to this point, we have looked at what can be called traditional social theory approaches to power. They help us think outside common-sense views. There are, however, still other perspectives to consider. One of these is found in the work of Michel Foucault, another key thinker in the field of social theory. His work in, among many other texts, *Discipline and Punish* and *Power/Knowledge*,[13,14] although oriented by a stated interest in the 'micro-politics' of power and preoccupied with individual identity or 'subjectivity', is in the end a very broad macro theory as well. In this way, Foucault, like Giddens, is interested in breaking down the distinction between individuals and society, or 'agency' and 'structure'. Unlike Lukes, however, Foucault's definitions of power make it even clearer that there is a double edge to power. It prevents some behaviours while at the same time positively encouraging others, both at the broadest political and historical levels and at the deepest level of individual identity:

> it seems to me now that the notion of repression is quite inadequate for capturing what is precisely the productive aspect of power. In defining the effects of power as repression, one adopts a purely juridical conception of such power, one identifies power with a law which says no, power is taken above all as carrying the force of a prohibition. Now I believe that this is a wholly negative, narrow, skeletal conception of power, one which has been curiously widespread. If power were never anything but repressive, if it never did anything but to say no, do you really think one would be brought to obey it? What makes power hold good, what makes it accepted, is simply the fact that it doesn't only weigh on us as a force that says 'no', but that it traverses and produces things, it induces pleasure, forms knowledge, produces discourse. It needs to be considered as a productive network which runs through the whole social body, much more than a negative instance whose function is repression. (ref. 14, p. 119)

For Foucault, power is all-pervasive. Indeed, power constitutes what we know as a society, including, of course, how we think about work organizations. Power is everywhere: 'there are no "margins" for those who break with the system' (ref. 14, p. 141). Thus, in Foucault's analysis, power is discussed in terms of the many ways through which it is exercised – 'economies of power', 'regimes of power', 'networks of power', 'technologies of power'.[3]

An important distinction that some researchers make here, however, concerns the difference between Foucauldian approaches to power and what are often referred to as political theories of organizational power:

> Foucaultians claimed that the two are characterized by an all-encompassing inseparability. Political theorists claimed that *politics* are everywhere: people always seek ways to fulfill their parochial interests, always want to impose upon others that which they would otherwise do despite legitimate power structures and at times in contrast to them. Foucaultians claimed that *power* is everywhere: what people see as their interests as well as the strategies they devise for achieving these interests are determined by existing power structures or discursive practices and to a considerable extent serve to reinforce them. (ref. 2, p. 783)

For a key example of the political approach to power in organizations, see Astley and Sachdeva.[15]

Thus, although there are important overlaps between the Foucauldian and political approaches to power, an important distinction should be recognized. An important tool for this recognition is hegemony. **Hegemony** is an important term in critical political theory that involves the complexity and mixture of consensus and conflict, and hence power relations in a broad sense. It derives from the Greek, where it originally referred to a leader or ruler (*egemon*), but was taken up in the English language in the nineteenth century, and has come to describe a very nuanced form of sociopolitical predominance. It describes control that is both direct and indirect, and rests on the notion of a whole way of seeing the world, a 'normal reality' or 'common sense'.

Specifically, the term 'hegemony' can express two types of power relations. The first describes a group's *domination* over other groups, and the second describes a group's *leadership*. The concept represents a whole body of practices as well as expectations, assignment of energies, and ordinary understandings of the world in

hegemony: a conception of power that includes both conflict as well as consent and leadership by generating a particular worldview or 'common sense' on relevant and appropriate action terms of meanings and values. In essence, the concept expresses the relationships of leadership and domination that produce a general sense of coordinated reality for most people. However, it is a concept that lends itself to a wider discussion than Foucault's thesis encourages. Power is seen as all-pervasive in the sense that there can also be something called 'counter-hegemony'. Counter-hegemony is composed of and expresses competing ways of seeing the world and behaving, although this behaviour can at times be clandestine and underdeveloped.

The term 'hegemony' is now most closely associated with the writings of an early twentieth-century Italian Marxist, Antonio Gramsci. Gramsci used a historical analysis of specific periods of French and Italian society in order to refer to a system of alliances within a 'hegemonic bloc' of interests. A bloc necessarily contains significant competing interests, but it is unified on some core principles. This bloc was dependent on what Gramsci referred to as the 'powerful system of fortresses and earthworks' of civil society, including the multitude of social, economic, cultural organizational, group and corresponding ideologies among which there is significant room for compromise (although only on non-hegemonic terrain).[16] As the English cultural studies theorist Raymond Williams notes, however, much influential work on counter-hegemonic practices has ignored contemporary scenes of consensus and conflict, including work organization. This is not without its problems.[17]

Critical   Insight

Based on your own current or past employment experiences, try to apply Gramsci's notion of a 'hegemonic bloc' by tracing the key groups that hold sway in an organization. Look at how they differ and what principles they share a commitment to. Finally, consider any 'counter-hegemonic' groups in the organization. How unified are they? How is their degree of unity related to how they challenge the hegemonic bloc?

An important contribution to our general understanding of power, and in turn of power as it relates to work organizations and behaviour, comes from the notion of emergent forms of practice that lie in some form of opposition to a dominant or hegemonic bloc in the sense that Gramsci and Williams described. First, the notion provides a basic framework for understanding the character of alternative (resistant) practices in opposition to a complex of dominant presumptions. An entire subschool of industrial sociology/organizational studies literature has specifically addressed the issue of resistance.[18] Building from this notion, we can see that organizational behaviour emerging from non-dominant (that is, workers' rather than managers') standpoints need not strictly reproduce a particular hegemonic order. It can at times run tangentially to it, and possibly even in direct opposition to it. In both cases, it represents an active, living process in which alternatives struggle against incorporation.

In less abstract terms, we are talking about people's behaviour that is rooted in processes that align with the basic assumptions and structures of the organization, have little to do with these dominant assumptions, or in some cases actively resist the major premises upon which the organization is based. This type of resistance can be ongoing and persistent, or more likely it is to be seen in certain conflictual situations such as during collective bargaining, or within a specific department of an organization that is having difficulties for one reason or another. To put this in the language of social class, we are talking about organizational behaviour that can be easily incorporated into capitalism, is somehow outside this logic, or opposes capitalism in some way either persistently or idiosyncratically (and everything in between).

These macro theories of power in studies of society set the context. We can now turn to a consideration of theories of power in local, everyday interaction or behaviour. Analyses of micro-interaction form another distinct set of theories on power. For example, we can ask what Nietzsche's '**will to power**' (a term that defines social interaction as an ongoing contest between people constantly striving to exercise power over others) might mean in terms of behaviour in organizations. Is the 'will to power' a generalized (overt or covert) phenomenon, as Nietzsche's work suggests, or are there other central motivations in people's lives?

The work of another famous micro-sociologist, Erving Goffman, is also relevant in this context. His analysis of 'contests' as a major frame of social interaction offers a fascinating exploration of how people think and negotiate order in their daily interactions. Another concept that has similarities, although it is not the same as Goffman's notion of 'contests', comes from the school of sociology called **game theory**. This is a subset of the rational choice tradition,[19] and is popular among economists and economic sociologists for its apparent pragmatism.

This school of thought, which focuses on the notion of contests or games, invites us to understand individual actors as acting in a way in which they believe will provide the best outcome for them, given their objectives, resources and circumstances as they see them. Its focus is on voluntary actions and inter-actor exchange, and it encompasses both conflictual contests and cooperative games. In relation to game theory and the rational choice tradition, it begins from the rather traditional economic assumption that individuals act to maximize their utility (that is, to do as well as is possible in the circumstances).

We can also consider micro-interactions through the work of discourse analyst Robin Tolmach Lakoff, which is discussed by Krippendorff.[20] How might 'power' be evident in this simple, everyday exchange?:

> Man: Wanna go to the movies?
> Woman: Oh, I don't know. Do you?

Krippendorf correctly points out that this is one example of a very common, gendered 'language game' that allows us to explore a host of possibilities. The male makes a proposal. The female has several options in response, including ignoring, accepting, counter-proposing and clarifying (and in fact a vast array of others).

Her different options (including the response she gives above) allow us to consider the system of power in operation at the micro level. For example, a counter-proposal might signal some sort of equal power relation; a stern rejection might signal an unequal power relation; a deferral (as in her response above) might signal another form of unequal power relation; and of course any and all of the possibilities might be part of a clever, expanded set of negotiations that defy simplistic categorization.

Ailon's work can, in turn, be used to understand the option potentially open to this woman in terms of Dahl's traditional definition of power, which we used to begin this chapter.[2] In this exchange, of course, the word 'power' is never used. The point here is that we can quite easily, even in this smallest of examples, draw into our analysis the concept of power. We can also see how it can include a whole infrastructure of, for example, gender relations.

Finally, returning to the work of Erving Goffman for a moment, micro-power can also be understood as part of people's 'presentation of self in everyday life'.[21] It is echoed in the work of a range of others such as Finkelstein,[22] who writes extensively on how people's physical appearance or self-presentation involves a whole range of broader 'macro-forces' or systems of power.[23]

will to power: the notion that people are inherently driven to develop and expand power and control in their environments

game theory: a social theory premised on the notion that people do what is best for themselves given their resources and circumstances, as in some form of a competitive game

Stop Reflect
The example of going to the movies can readily be extended to a work context. How might you go about a micro-analysis of the following exchange?
Woman: Tell me how to fix this Xerox machine.
Man: Oh, don't you worry about this, honey. Leave it to me.
Now take a next step and continue the exchange, taking account of the distinct backdrops of power and/or gender relations

Plate 3 – The micro-management of appearances has been understood for some time to be a vital component of how 'power' operates. The distinctive wig and black robe give barristers an air of distance and authority.
Source: Cheryl Dainty and Ben Harding

Stop Reflect

Can the management of appearances hold the balance between success and failure in organizations? What instances of this have you seen in your own experiences? How are appearances given meanings in relation to broader 'systems of power' within and beyond a specific work organization? Explore company dress codes as best you can over the Internet. Although some dress code demands are related to health and safety, others are not. How does power in organizations work in terms of a dress code? What ideological values are represented in such codes? A recent book by Ruth Rubenstein discusses *Dress Codes:*

In a particularly striking section of her book, Finkelstein gives an example of a Jewish prisoner in a Nazi concentration camp. His memoirs show him taking incredible pains to keep himself 'respectable' in appearance. As the prisoner notes, his captors' general beliefs about his 'respectability' could in fact hold the balance between life and death: 'He needed no more than his spruce suit and his emaciated and shaven face in the midst of the flock of his sordid and slovenly colleagues to stand out and thereby receive benefits from his captors' (ref. 22, p. 136). This is an extreme example, but the point is that the micro-management of appearances has been understood for some time to be a vital component of how 'power' operates. It provides a mechanism of sorting, in Finkelstein's terms of 'social passport and credential', for how people can participate in the systems of power they are presented with.

POWER: EVIDENCE FROM THE WORKPLACE

Through the 1990s and into the new millennium, the number of strikes by employees in industrialized countries around the world has tended to decline.[25] What are we to make of this? Should we conclude that the power struggles in organizations have been reduced, giving way to greater consensus? Not according to some researchers.[26,27] Collinson's work is worth looking at in detail for its discussion of power in organizations. It represents an important type of research that has linked past discussions from industrial sociology and labour process theory (a stream in the field of sociology of work) to more contemporary concerns about individuals, identity and meaning under what are sometimes referred to as 'postmodern' conditions of globalization and the (apparently) 'new' knowledge or information economy.

Meaning and Messages in American Culture.[24] What further details does it give you about the relationship between appearance and power?

Collinson argues that despite the decline of formal workplace disputes, the power struggle continues to rage on in diffuse and pervasive forms. Power is exemplified not simply by either domination *or* resistance in organizations, but rather domination *and* resistance. In this context, power is to be found in situations of apparent consent and domination as well as where there is resistance. Collinson maintains that labour process theory has made a distinctive contribution to the analysis of work by highlighting the 'irreducible interrelationship between employee resistance and managerial control ... Emphasizing the extensive power asymmetries in contemporary organizations' (ref. 26, p. 25). He goes on to claim that the founding preoccupations of traditional labour process theory with scientific management and Taylorism are still relevant, as is the classic critique offered in the work of Harry Braverman.[28]

Collinson's specific contribution, however, emerges from his assessment that knowledge and information are key aspects of power. He draws on the work of Foucault, on writers who make use of Mann's work on power[29] and on the 'game metaphor',[30] but goes on to say that, despite the seemingly uneven distribution of access to organizational knowledge and information, other forms of knowledge are available to workers (that is, technical and production-based knowledge). These alternative resources can be mobilized through a wide variety of strategies, and this variety in turn accounts for the very uneven and variegated results of power struggles in organizations.

The first of the two main strategies he outlines is 'resistance by distance', in which workers restrict information from management. This is referred to as a type of 'escape attempt', and a denial of involvement or interest in work processes. The second strategy, 'resistance through persistence', involves efforts to extract information from management. In a sense, this involves voluntarily increasing involvement and interest in work processes. Of course, management in this framework tries to use the opposite strategies of extracting and restricting information respectively, and this results in a complex spiral of control resistance, greater efforts at control and so on, or rather a series of strategies and counter-strategies.

Finally, Collinson emphasizes the role played by both management and workers' personal identities, or we might say social background, which significantly shapes which strategy is used. He qualifies his conclusions, which depend heavily on the exact context, but in general concludes that 'resistance through persistence' turns out to be a more effective strategy. However, as he notes, neither strategy constitutes a deep challenge to the structure of power (that is, management rights) in organizations.

The key point for this chapter is that, although power is often revealed in overt forms of conflict and resistance (such as strikes, sabotage or simply a lack of cooperation), both subtle and alternative forms of resistance can also be identified. You should be able to understand that better in the light of the various conceptual frameworks we explored earlier in the chapter.

Even the existence of consensus can be used to support the claim that work organizations are in many ways constituted by power relations. Drawing on Collinson as well as Kondo,[31] we can note that effective resistance requires elements of conformity to a rival power source. Collinson sees this as discursive and knowledge based, but we would suggest that this concept can easily be extended to include well-functioning communities of workers: bargaining units, neighbourhoods, social movements or occupational groupings. This brings us back in a sense to Giddens' claim that 'everyone has power', but that it is expressed in different ways depending on the (allocative and authoritative) resources. There is the power of enforcing democracies, forcing people to learn, and ultimately the power to remake existing power relations into something better.

Although there is not exactly a flood of interest in power issues in most of the recent empirical research outlined in the main organizational behaviour journals, these nevertheless reveal a significant consideration of issues of power. Studies in this area deal with a variety of topics, such as practical governance and managerial practices in work organizations. Often, although not exclusively, there is a particular interest in organizational change initiatives. Below we explore some key findings of the most recent studies that touch on important issues in the field. The aim is to balance our earlier conceptual discussion with some more concrete findings.

In a provocative study of relations between supervisors and their subordinates, Elangovan and Xie[32] explore the results and perceptions of supervisory 'power.' Even this brief introductory line reveals that they conceive power in a way that is partially, not absolutely, at odds with the relational perspective we have developed here. The focus is on employees and supervisors, which is obviously a relational issue, but Elangovan and Xie tend to see power largely as something a supervisor has, rather than as a dimension of the social system (on the macro or micro level). A relational perspective, on the other hand, would highlight how power is systemic, put into effect or reproduced by all individuals subjected to the system, and not, for example, simply traceable to the characteristics of a particular supervisor. Nevertheless, they offer some important findings on how power is *experienced* by the individuals subject to it.

Among the important issues in workplaces today are motivation, on the one hand, and stress and people's individual and collective responses to it, on the other. These authors find that people's backgrounds play an important role in their behaviour. For example, they focus on the issue of 'self-esteem'. This is seen as a product of nurture as opposed to nature: that is, it is inextricably linked to people's lives inside the workplace, as well as to their lives outside work, and indeed developmentally before they ever began to work. Broader theories of power also see these expansive connections as important. Elangovan and Xie conclude that those with low self-esteem show signs of higher motivation and lower stress as their perceptions of supervisory power increase. Importantly, those with high self-esteem actually show lower motivation and increased stress when they give a higher score to the perceived power of their supervisor.

This has important implications for the types of worker that the typical work organization appears to favour. Elangovan and Xie go on to explore the concept of 'locus of control', which we discussed earlier, looking at workers with internal or external orientations. Those with an internal orientation were seen to respond to different types of power, authority and influence (the authors tending to see these as equivalent). Their motivation levels drop in relation to the perceived rewards and the levels of coercive power that they associate with supervisors. Those with a predominantly external locus of control had lower stress levels when they gave higher assessments of expert power to their supervisors.

Broadly similar dynamics to those analysed by Elangovan and Xie are seen in two other important recent studies. Overbeck and Park,[33] and Raghubir and Valenzuela,[34] explore the relationship between positional power and the strategic use of 'social in/attention' in different work team contexts. Like Elangovan and Xie, these researchers make some important observations, particularly about how managerial decision making takes place, but the way in which they frame 'power' in organizational behaviour as involving an individual/positional use of resources tends to downplay the broader systemic nature of power as something that is exercised.

Plate 3 – Surveillance and control is more often something that the powerful do to the less powerful. Might increased surveillance in the workplace actually force conflict?
Source: iStockphoto

Collinson's approach to resistance can be applied to these findings. For example, the changing levels of motivation and stress can be interpreted as representing a form of resistance. This might be turned inwards in the form of stress or loss of psychological commitment to the organization, but it is still apparent. Both motivation and stress are, of course, also the roots of more outward resistance, which could lead to expression in the form of political action (say, becoming more active in an employee association or union), industrial action or, at its most individualist level, sabotage or simply resigning from the organization.

Self-esteem is seen to be an important variable, but how does it come to be established? Mann's goal of identifying 'overlapping socio-spatial networks of power' might offer us some help in this context. Likewise, the work of Richard Sennett provides an accessible exploration of how deep wounds to self-esteem are inflicted in the form of 'hidden injuries'[35] and a 'corrosion of character'.[36] These writers help to show how visible symptoms have ideological, social and even political roots. To what degree could Giddens' interest in exploring the power of 'surveillance' be brought to play in looking at how stress develops in relation to perceived power issues? Might increased surveillance in the workplace actually force conflict inward to produce these effects?

If surveillance and control are more often something that the powerful do to the less powerful, it makes some sense to highlight briefly the study of the choice, contingencies and organizational politics involved when those with less power respond. The last of these is particular difficult to study, albeit widely recognized. As Morgan and Kristensen note, organizations can be seen as highly complex configurations of ongoing micro-political power conflicts at different levels, in which strategizing social actors/groups inside and outside the firm interact with each other and create temporary balances of power that shape how formal organizational relationships and processes actually work in practice.[37]

In such complex organizational settings, what does the research tell us about how low-power actors, groups or units respond? According to a recent study by Bouquet and Birkinshaw,[38] 'low-power actors' gain influence in either or both of two ways:

- by adopting creative strategies to effectively challenge the status quo in an organization (or one's position within the status quo of an organization)
- by engaging in **political gaming** within their organization to push their agendas through existing circuits of power.

The first method refers to strategies such as attempting to build one's profile in a company, building relationships with supervisors or managers within the existing power structure of an organization, taking the initiative or, more radically, challenging the way in which business is done and breaking with established norms by working around the standard practices. The second method, political gaming, refers to recognizing and acting on and through existing factions, coalitions and cliques that make up any organization – in other words, engaging in intentional acts of influence to enhance or protect oneself, one's group or one's department.

Ultimately, however, there are a limited set of options for employees to exercise in organizations. One way of understanding these choices is through what has been referred to as the issue of **exit and voice**. Research exploring these types of choice has long been a subject of debate in industrial sociology, and it may be useful here to read the work of Ailon[2] in relation to the classic 'exit or voice' choice since these are only two of the options available to employees when conflict arises. We touch on it above, and it is dealt with in the organizational behaviour tradition by the researchers Mayes and Ganster.[39] In a rich and detailed look at the responses of public service workers to questions posed in questionnaires and interviews, these authors detail the relationship between 'voice' (or 'political action') and 'exit' behaviours on the one hand, and job stress on the other. Importantly, this analysis builds from observations that can be roughly aligned with Collinson's model of alternative, countervailing sources of power.

In Mayes and Ganster's terms, the countervailing source lies outside the bounds of the employee's formal, legitimate role in the organization. For these authors, what is at the heart of the matter is the fit between the employee and the environment. They note that when employees sense 'ambiguity' in their role in the organization, this is an immobilizing factor: it prevents their achieving 'voice' via political action in the workplace. This sense of ambiguity is found, Mayes and Ganster add, despite high levels of organizational commitment.

How can we understand variables such as worker–organization 'fit' and 'commitment' in relation to our opening set of theoretical discussions? Certainly, Foucault's and Gramsci's discussion of domination and consent as two sides of the same 'power coin' is useful here. Commitment, for example, is the side of power that Foucault speaks of when he describes 'induce[ing] pleasure, form[ing] knowledge, produce[ing] discourse. It needs to be considered as a productive network' (ref. 14, p. 119). That is, commitment is what comes out when power works in a positive and productive way.

We could also tentatively link this to Lukes' distinction between power in the context of 'conflicts of interest', which may or may not be apparent. When conflicts of interest are evident, power is reflected as coercion, force and manipulation, whereas when they are not, it is expressed as inducement and encouragement. It is not hard to see that stress, resistance, exit and voice flow from the former a good deal more often than from the latter.

One of the most fascinating and recent sets of exchanges on the matter of 'power' in the organizational behaviour tradition is to be found in a special issue of the

political gaming: a common practice in organizations, which has proven challenging to research, that involves recognition and organizational action based on existing factions, coalitions and cliques that make up any organization in order to engage in intentional acts of influence to enhance or protect oneself or one's group or department

exit and voice: a concept referring to the basic choice that defines an important part of employees' experience at work: they can either exit (leave) or exercise their 'voice' (have a say) in how the workplace is run

Journal of Organizational Behavior Management.[40] At the centre of the debate is the work of Sonia Goltz and Amy Hietapelto, and the question of resistance to organizational change.[41] Goltz and Hietapelto's operant and strategic contingency models of power are based on the behavioural approach, as the concept of 'operant' might suggest. They are linked to the founder of this psychological tradition (B. F. Skinner), to the management of stimulus response, and in some sense to punishment and reward. Despite its classical behaviourialist stance, this model includes some form of relational analysis. To extend this, we might say that it focuses on the relations of the distribution of authority over the application of consequences. Built on well-established operant principles, Goltz and Hietapelto's model states that 'the power an individual has' is based on:

- how many reinforcing and aversive stimuli the power holder controls
- which important dimensions of these stimuli, such as magnitude, delay and frequency, the power holder controls
- which particular combinations and dimensions of the reinforcing and aversive stimuli the power holder controls
- for how many people the power holder controls these stimuli.

If we set aside the obvious major shortcoming of this model (the suggestion that people 'have' power – see our discussion of Foucault above), we can see that it marshals a range of valuable evidence, including that power is subject to both intentional and unintentional results. We might compare this with, for example, Wrong's model outlined above. One very interesting component of the model, which fits into the broad perspective on power introduced here, is that both those who lead and those who follow are subject to this leadership experience, and behave in ways consistent with notions of 'resistance' in organizations. The authors also insist that a central unit of analysis for power and resistance is the change to pre-existing relationships of action and consequence.

The special issue of the *Journal of Organizational Behavior* also includes a range of articles that provide critiques of Goltz and Hietapelto, and constructively extend or challenge their thinking. Quite separate from each author's critique of Goltz and Hietapelto, we can also apply many of the basic conceptual observations we have developed over the course of this chapter. In Boyce's contribution, for example, we might note that there is a need for conceptual clarity.[42] Boyce's work raises some questions when seen in the light of Collinson's observations, for example how is 'resistance' related to power, and from whose perspective is power and resistance defined?

Another contributor, Malott, takes Goltz and Hietapelto to task for their presumptuous leaps from laboratory findings to real-world applications,[43] while Geller extends the discussions further.[44] The consequences someone controls and/or is subject to in any organizational structure are shown to be an expression of organizational power. In support of the Goltz and Hietapelto model, Geller goes on to show that power can, in fact, be measured in terms of quality and quantity of control over consequences.

To conclude this section, we can briefly look back at the work of Mann and others in posing the question, 'How on earth can students of organizational behaviour see the linkages between practice in workplaces and such broad ideological, military and political-economic sources?' To accomplish this intellectual jump, you first need, as we have seen, to move from individual to relational perspectives on power.

It is not difficult to understand how broader national ideologies or local ideological cultures surrounding particular workplaces are implicated in 'power'. Of course, it should be obvious that political economic factors, such as market dynamics, industrial relations

weblink
Visit the following interactive website for additional perspectives on power that will further enhance your understanding of ideas in this area: www. educationforum.co.uk/ sociology_2/power2.htm

and employment law, and trade policy, all deeply affect the phenomenon of power. However, even in highly developed capitalist countries, the military (including the police) provide an important foundation to the industrial relations legal regime. In many cases in history in North America and Europe, the police and even the army have been called out to intervene in workplace-based conflicts. They do this whenever worker–managerial conflict reaches levels, or is concerned with issues, that those in power judge to be unacceptable to the principles of the economic system. These principles include challenges to the private ownership of economic resources (such as factories or even forests).

OB and globalization   Under pressure: the rise of workplace bullying in trying economic times

In an increasingly globalized world, an economic downturn can have far-reaching effects. Compounding regional and national impacts of recession are the impacts associated with global forces, such as the outsourcing of manufacturing and information technology jobs, which can put additional stresses on workers by further limiting job openings. In such an economic climate, workers can find themselves competing against dozens of equally qualified applicants for a single position. Those who are employed may worry about job security.

One manifestation of these economic pressures is the rise of bullying, also called mobbing or psychological harassment, within the workplace. Workplace bullies target fellow workers and use tactics such as verbal abuse, intimidation, rumour, belittlement and embarrassment to force their colleagues out of a job or to prevent them from advancing within the organization. Often, the victims do not report this abuse out of fear of losing their jobs. Recent studies of workplace bullying have found that it is a phenomenon that happens in many countries around the world, and within many different types of organizations. Espinosa (2009) describes how workplace bullying has become more common in Chilean organizations, mirroring the recent rise in unemployment and shrinking job market in that country:

> The lack of job security and stability has forced workers to tolerate increasingly poor working conditions and even outright mistreatment and abuse. While some of these abuses are tangibly evident, there are also more subtle forms of emotional or psychological harassment which are equally damaging.

Espinosa also notes that workplace bullies disproportionately target workers they deem to be most vulnerable, including 'women, sexual and ethnic minorities and people with HIV/AIDS'.

According to lawyer Adriana Muñoz, who advocates for organizational policies and legal penalties against workplace bullies, this behaviour is 'largely intangible' and often 'hidden in the subtleties of daily interactions between people. It can take the form of words, gestures, actions or attitudes that do not constitute physical abuse and are therefore extremely difficult to quantify' (Espinosa, 2009). The results of workplace bullying can include lowered morale, decreased productivity, a decline in workplace attendance and even an increase in on-the-job accidents. In short, the economic stresses that can precipitate psychological harassment in the workplace can, in turn, create additional economic and social troubles for organizations.

Economist and organizational management specialist Denise Salin has written about management techniques to address and quell workplace bullying. She explains that organizations at the greatest risk of harbouring and enabling workplace bullies are most often those with a laissez-faire approach management where expectations about work roles and appropriate behaviours are undefined, where bullies do not expect to face consequences for their actions, and where they are successful in achieving their desired ends. Salin (2008, p. 223) asserts, 'If bullying is to be prevented, it is thus important both to raise the cost, i.e. the risk of being discovered and reprimanded, and to reduce the incentives.'

In a study of how a number of human resources managers addressed workplace bullying in Finland, Salin (2008, p. 228) found that the most effective antibullying measures included widely publicized workplace policies against bullying and the institution of 'sophisticated' human resource management techniques such as performance-based pay, regular performance appraisals and frequent employee 'attitude surveys'. In an economic climate where instability – real or perceived – can give rise to workplace bullying, managers who can recognize and put a stop to these destructive behaviours are well positioned to help their employees and organizations weather tough times in the shifting global economy.

stop!   Imagine that you are a manager of an organization and a worker comes to you claiming that he or she is being bullied by some co-workers. What approaches would you take to address the situation?

Espinosa links workplace bullying to economic uncertainty. Can you think of other cultural, social or structural attributes of organizations that might also enable bullying in the workplace (for example, an organizational culture that condones sexist or racist jokes)?

Sources and further information

Espinosa, M. C. (2009) 'Chile: working with the enemy', Inter Press Service News Agency. Available at: http://ipsnews.net/news.asp?idnews=29934.

Rayner, C., Hoel, H. and Cooper, C. L. (2002) *Workplace Bullying: What We Know, Who Is To Blame, and What Can We Do?* London: Taylor & Francis.

Salin, D (2003) 'Ways of explaining workplace bullying: a review of enabling, motivating and precipitating structures and processes in the work environment', *Human Relations*, 56(10), pp. 1213–32..

Salin, D. (2008) 'The prevention of workplace bullying as a question of human resource management: measures adopted and underlying organizational factors', *Scandinavian Journal of Management*, 24, pp. 221–31.

The Devil Wears Prada (2006): This film pays particular attention to how bullying workplace relationships affect the characters' work and personal lives.

www.workplacebullying.org provides more information and resources on workplace bullying.

Note: This feature was written by Gretchen Fox, PhD, Anthropologist, Timberline Natural Resource Group, Canada

CHAPTER SUMMARY

- In this chapter, we began with broad theory, to provide a basis for a better appreciation of grounded research at the work organization level. Common-sense views of power were outlined to explore the half-truths in them. Power appears to us to be 'embodied' in individuals, as something they possess and exert. However, macro theories of power show that there are many deep social roots or 'sources' of power systems, including the influences of ideology, military, politics and economics. Gramsci and Foucault outlined perhaps the most extensive theories of power, noting that it is anywhere and everywhere, because it constitutes the very way we talk and think about ourselves, let alone our organizational surroundings. Importantly, these two authors argue that power is a coin with two sides: on the one, consent, accommodation and domination; on the other, lack of commitment, stress, resistance, political action and 'voice'.

- This knowledge was then applied to a critical look at key examples of work organization research. Collinson is a representative example of the new social analysis of organization, which links old industrial sociology with labour process theory and the contemporary analysis of meaning and identity in the workplace. We then explored some key examples of organizational behaviour research that deal directly with the concept of 'power'. The organizational behaviour field has hardly seen a flood of research on the topic of 'power', and when it does consider this, it usually adds the prefix 'perceived', further limiting the strength of its analysis. Nevertheless, some fascinating and provocative findings and debates were detailed.

- Clearly, not all power, authority and influence is bad. Good parenting, teaching, policing, political advocacy and, in a certain sense management, can be understood as positive influences. The question of legitimacy, which in turn evokes questions of larger political and economic systems, comes into play as we recognize that there are two main justifications for disobedience to authority. One is when a subject is commanded to do something outside the legitimate range of the commanding authority, and the other is when the history of acquiring the commanding authority is no longer considered to be legitimate or acceptable (which includes being an unjust burden).

- These types of challenge to authority, building from the Gramscian and possibly the Foucauldian models above, start with recognizing people's complicity in the taken-for-granted nature of systems of power, or rather hegemonic blocs of assumptions. Challengers dare to articulate these taken-for-granted assumptions in order to engage in a rational analysis of legitimacy. What some refer to as a crisis in organizational commitment or loyalty may be the thin edge of this kind of wedge. Underlying it are frequently the types of challenge to the status quo or political gaming, for example. That is, it represents the removal of blind obedience, an erosion of the 'other side' of the power coin, consent and complicity. Managers as well as workers (and students of organizational behaviour!) have a right to think through and question the sources of legitimacy. Mahatma Gandhi, Martin Luther King and others operated on the principle of removal of consent, which for our purposes relates directly to a broad, social perspective on power.

KEY CONCEPTS

authority
hegemony
influence
micropolitics of power
power/motivation/stress relations
relational perspective on power
sources of countervailing power
sources of social power

VOCAB CHECKLIST FOR ESL STUDENTS

- Authority, authorize
- Conflict of interest
- Exit and voice
- Game theory
- Hegemony
- Ideology, idealize, ideological
- Influence, influential
- Legitimacy, legitimize, legitimate
- Micropolitics
- Power
- Structuration
- Will to power

CHAPTER REVIEW QUESTIONS

1 What is the substance of the different social theoretic models of Mann, Giddens, Foucault, Weber, Lukes and Gramsci?
2 What is the difference between power and authority?
3 What is the relationship between power and resistance?
4 What is meant by the phrases 'power is relational' and 'power is not possessed, it is exercised'?
5 What are the strengths and weaknesses in current conceptualizations of 'power' in organizational behaviour research?

CHAPTER RESEARCH QUESTIONS

1   Early in the chapter, you will remember a basic definition of power provided by Robert Dahl ('A has power over B to the extent that he can get B to do something that B would not otherwise do'). You will have also seen that another definition of power (from Michel Foucault) suggested that it is not enough to simply understand power's ability to 'say no' (as it also 'says yes'). Now take a moment to discuss some examples of 'power' in your organizational life (whether this is in terms of past work experiences, or even in your school life) in both of these terms. Which are easiest to identify? Why might this be? And what is the significance of forms of power that are particularly difficult to identify? Might there be a special role for such forms of hidden power in the establishment of instances described in this chapter as 'hegemony'?

2   A valuable addition to how one can begin looking into power in organizational behaviour relates to what some researchers have called 'organizational misbehaviour'. A book by Stephen Ackroyd and Paul Thompson entitled *Organizational Misbehaviour* (published by Sage in 1999) summarises this notion very well. Review the introductory descriptions of organizational misbehaviour in this book with special attention to the summary diagram on page 25. Now use these ideas to speak to family or friends about their work experiences (or think of some examples from your own work life) in order to generate a list of at least three examples of organizational misbehaviour. If you choose to read further in the book, you will find more specific discussions of the role of absenteeism, sexual harassment, 'soldiering' and humour that may provide further help. Once compiled, share these examples in discussion with your fellow students, and then discuss how these examples speak to the concepts of power, politics and conflict presented in this chapter.

3   As a final research question for this chapter, we take its ideas a step further by looking at the role of something so fundamental to our work lives that it is virtually always taken for granted, and as such is both invisible and extremely 'powerful' in its invisibility: this is the question of the relationship between power, organizations and *space*. How does space – this most basic element of our behaviour – relate to power, politics and conflict in organizational life? Take a moment to consider this on your own, and then discuss it with a fellow student. Do you find it difficult to imagine that 'space' can play a role in creating and recreating forms of power? If you do, you are not alone. Luckily for us, a recent book by Dale and Burrell called *The Spaces of Organization and the Organization of Space: Power, Identity and Materiality at Work* (published by Palgrave, 2008) provides us with important resources for thinking in this area. Review the introduction of the book (and other chapters if you like) and see if their discussion provides you with some new ways of thinking about these relationships. For example, do things like the architecture of workplaces have a relationship to how we think about ourselves (i.e. our identity) and others, or the corporate culture of a workplace – and if so how may these teach us something about power, politics and conflict?

FURTHER READING

Clegg, S. (1989) *Frameworks of Power*, London: Sage.

Foucault, M. (1980) *Power/Knowledge*, edited by C. Gordon, New York: Pantheon.

Lukes, S. (1974) *Power: A Radical View*, Basingstoke: Macmillan.

French, J. R. P. and Raven, B. H. (1959) 'The bases of social power', pp. 150–67 in D. Cartwright (ed.), *Studies of Social Power*, AnnArbor, MI: Institute for Social Research.

Sennett, R. (1980) *Authority*, London: Faber & Faber.

Case Study   Aiming for a paperless world

Setting

In their book, *The Myth of the Paperless Office*, authors Abigail Sellen and Richard Harper note that office paper use makes up 30–40 per cent of total paper consumption in the USA and Britain, with the average American worker using an estimated 10,000 sheets of paper every year. Although it was originally believed that the use of computers would decrease the reliance on paper, the implementation of networked access to the Internet and company intranets typically results in more documents being printed. The introduction of an e-mail system alone can cause a 40 per cent increase in paper use.

Despite this, organizations have increasingly striven to become 'paperless' in the hope of not only reducing the costs directly associated with paper, but also achieving greater efficiency, 'moving forward' and motivating change. However, Sellen and Harper caution that concentrating on a goal to eliminate paper can prevent organizations from identifying organizational work practices and value systems that really should be the focus of change.

The problem

FACTS Inc., a medium-sized accounting firm located in Basingstoke in south-east England, had gone through tremendous changes in the past year: a merger with another company, a new CEO and lay-offs caused by a decline in the local economy. Many of those affected by the lay-offs had been with FACTS for most of their career, and their abrupt departure caused fear and distrust among the employees who had remained. Absenteeism due to stress leaves suddenly became commonplace. Staff morale was only worsened by the announcement at a recent shareholder meeting that several senior executives would be receiving large bonuses at the end of that fiscal year.

At that same meeting, the company's new CEO, Frank Webster, introduced himself to the audience as an 'environmental champion'. Downplaying the bonuses, he instead focused the meeting on the 'green' strategies he intended to implement during his first year with the company, proclaiming that 'accounting firms are the "watchdog" of the business world and we need to set an example by demonstrating environmentally friendly practices'. He laid out a corporate programme targeted at saving energy and conserving resources, with an initial focus on eliminating paper use. FACTS, he said, would be a paperless organization within 2 years.

The first step was to establish a paperless task force, which would identify key areas of the business and key processes involving the most paper use. When a call to the workforce failed to recruit volunteers, the CEO simply assigned management employees to the task force. Foremost on the task force's agenda was the implementation of an electronic records retention system to reduce paper usage, followed by the roll-out of a new corporate policy allowing only double-sided printing for company documents. Photocopiers and printers were adjusted to default to this setting.

Such policies and attempts to implement the new 'green' initiatives were quickly met with cynicism and scepticism on the part of the workers. Jokes about the next policy mandating 'paperless toilets' began to circulate throughout the offices. Returning to work after a holiday weekend, several managers found their office floors covered in hundreds of documents, with single-sided printing, produced by photocopiers that had been left to run continuously until depleted of paper.

Frank Webster, shocked at the workplace response, quickly assembled his management team for an urgent meeting to review why the new corporate programme had failed to gain acceptance by the employees.

Tasks

Reflect on Collinson's research regarding power in the workplace. As a manager at the review meeting, consider how you would answer the following questions:

1 How might the rise in staff absenteeism have been an indication of how the workers would react to the new 'green' strategies?

2 How did the workers' technical knowledge assist them in using a 'resistance by distance' strategy in dealing with the 'paperless policy'?

Essential reading

Ackroyd, S. and Thompson, P. (1999) *Organizational Misbehaviour*, London: Sage.

Sellen, A. and Harper, R. (2002) *The Myth of the Paperless Office*, Massachusetts: Massachusetts Institute of Technology.

Thompson, P. and McHugh, D. (2002) 'Power, conflict and resistance', Chapter 9 in *Work Organizations*, New York: Palgrave.

Note

This case study was written by Lori Rilkoff, MSc, CHRP, Senior Human Resources Manager at the City of Kamloops, and lecturer in HRM at Thompson Rivers University, BC, Canada.

Case Study   Las Vegas general strike

Visit www.palgrave.com/business/brattonob2e to view this case study

WEB-BASED ASSIGNMENT

The discussion in this chapter provided the basis for a comparison of different theories of power. Take some time to obtain (either online or in your library) and read the discussion of power in the special 2002 issue of *Journal of Organizational Behavior Management*.[40] Further background reading on the concept of power can be found at: www.experiencefestival.com/power_sociology/articleindex.

After reviewing the material, do as we began to do in the last section of this chapter: test the assumptions of the conceptualizations of power in this issue against the broader social theories of power we outlined in the first half of the chapter.

OB IN FILM

One of the best environments for looking at power, influence, authority and conflict is in the political environment. A particularly good example of this is the film, *Milk* (2008), which tracks the rise of gay rights campaigner Harvey Milk to political power in San Francisco. He was the first openly gay person to achieve public office in the USA.

The film is very good in capturing different ways in which Milk is effective in working for the rights of his community. In addition, the film depicts how those opposing his movement use power and influence against him. As you watch the film, try to map the changes in Milk's power, influence and authority. In doing so, assess how effective each is. To what extent is Milk more effective when holding an elected post, that is, in power, compared with his campaigning prior to being elected?

Note: This feature was written by Professor Jon Billsberry, Senior Research Fellow, Open University Business School, UK.

BONUS OB IN FILM FEATURE

Visit www.palgrave.com/business/brattonob2e to see how *Oleanna* (1994) can be considered in relation to the subject of leadership.

REFERENCES

1. Sivanathan, N., Pillutla, M. and Murnighan, J. K. (2008) 'Power gained, power lost', *Organizational Behavior and Human Decision Processes*, **105**, pp. 135–46.

2. Ailon, G. (2006) 'What B would otherwise do: a critique of conceptualizations of "power" in organizational theory', *Organization*, **13**(6), pp. 771–800.

3. Crane, A., Knights, D. and Starkey, K. (2008) 'The conditions of our freedom: Foucault, organization, and ethics', *Business Ethics Quarterly*, **18**(3), pp. 299–320.

4. Austin, J. (2002) 'Editorial', *Journal of Organizational Behavior Management*, **22**(3), pp. 1–2.

5. Dahl, R. A. (1957) 'On the concept of power', *Behavioral Science*, **2**, pp. 201–15.

6. French, J. P. R. Jr. and Raven, B. (1960) 'The bases of social power', pp. 607–23 in D. Cartwright and A. Zander (eds), *Group Dynamics*, New York: Harper & Row.

7. Warren, D. I. (1968) 'Power, visibility, and conformity in formal organizations', *American Sociological Review*, **6**, pp. 951–70.

8. Genovese, E. (1972) *Roll Jordan Roll: The World the Slaves Made*, New York: Vintage Books.

9. Mann, M. (1986) *Sources of Social Power*, Cambridge: Cambridge University Press.

10. Giddens, A. (1985) *A Contemporary Critique of Historical Materialism*, Volume 2: *The Nation State and Violence*, Cambridge: Polity Press.

11. Wrong, D. H. (1979) *Power: Its Forms, Bases, and Uses*, Oxford: Wiley-Blackwell.

12. Lukes, S. (1974) *Power: A Radical View*, Basingstoke: Macmillan.

13. Foucault, M. (1977) *Discipline and Punish: The Birth of the Prison,* New York: Pantheon.

14. Foucault, M. (1980) *Power/Knowledge*, ed. C. Gordon, New York: Pantheon.

15. Astley, W. and Sachdeva, P. (1984) 'Structural sources of intraorganizational power: a theoretical synthesis', *Academy of Management Review*, **9**(1), pp. 104–13.

16. Gramsci, A. (1971) *Selections from the Prison Notebooks*, London: Lawrence & Wishart.

17. Williams, R. (1977) *Marxism and Literature*, Oxford: Oxford University Press.

18. Roscigno, V. and Hodson, R. (2004) 'The organizational and social foundations of worker resistance', *American Sociological Review*, **69**(1), pp. 14–39.

19. Coleman, A. and Fararo, T. (eds) (1991) *Rational Choice Theory*, Berkeley, CA: University of California Press.

20. Krippendorff, K. (1995) 'Undoing power', *Critical Studies in Mass Communication*, **12**(2), pp. 101–32.

21. Goffman, E. (1959) *The Presentation of Self in Everyday Life*, New York: Anchor.

22. Finkelstein, J. (1995) *The Fashioned Self*, Cambridge: Polity Press.

23. Marks, M. (2008) 'Looking different, acting different: struggles for equality within the South African Police Service', *Public Administration*, **86**(3), pp. 643–58.

24. Rubenstein, R. (2001) *Dress Codes: Meaning and Messages in American Culture,* Boulder, CO: Westview Press.

25. Krahn, H. and Lowe, G. (2002) *Work, Industry and Canadian Society* (4th edn), Toronto: Thomson Nelson.

26. Collinson, D. (1994) 'Strategies of resistance: power, knowledge and subjectivity in the workplace', pp. 25–68 in J. Jermier, D. Knights and W. Nord (eds), *Resistance and Power in Organizations*, New York: Routledge.

27. Aligisakis, M. (1997) 'Labour disputes in Western Europe: typology and tendencies', *International Labour Review*, **136**(1), pp. 73–94.

28. Braverman, H. (1974) *Labor and Monopoly Capitalism: The Degradation of Work in the Twentieth Century*, New York: Monthly Review Press.

29. Clegg, S. (1989) *Frameworks of Power*, London: Sage.

30. Burawoy, M. (1979) *Manufacturing Consent*, Chicago: University of Chicago Press.

31. Kondo, D. (1990) *Crafting Selves: Power, Discourse and Identity in a Japanese Factory*, Chicago: University of Chicago Press.

32. Elangovan, A. R. and Xie, J. L. (1999) 'Effects of perceived power of supervisor on subordinate stress and motivation: the moderating role of subordinate characteristics', *Journal of Organizational Behavior*, **20**(3), pp. 359–74.

33. Overbeck, J. and Park, B. (2006) 'Powerful perceivers, powerless objects: flexibility of powerholders' social attention', *Organizational Behaviour and Human Decision Processes*, **99**(2), pp. 227–44.

34. Raghubir, P. and Valenzuela, A. (2006) 'Centers-of-inattention: position biases in decision-making', *Organizational Behaviour and Human Decision Processes*, **99**(1), pp. 66–80.

35. Sennett, R. and Cobb, J. (1972) *Hidden Injuries of Class*, New York: Anchor.

36. Sennett, R. (1998) *The Corrosion of Character*, New York: Norton.

37. Morgan, G. and Kristensen, P. (2006) 'The contested space of multinationals: varieties of institutionalism, varieties of capitalism', *Human Relations*, **59**(11), pp. 1467–90.

38. Bouquet, C. and Birkinshaw, J. (2008) 'Managing power in the multinational corporation: how low-power actors gain influence', *Journal of Management*, **34**(3), pp. 477–508.

39. Mayes, B. and Ganster, D. (1988) 'Exit and voice: a test of hypotheses based on the fight/flight response to job stress', *Journal of Organizational Behavior*, **9**(3), pp. 99–117.

40. *Journal of Organizational Behaviour* (1982) Volume 22, Number 3.

41. Goltz, S. and Hietapelto, A. (2002) 'Using the operant and strategic contingencies models of power to understand resistance to change', *Journal of Organizational Behavior Management*, **22**(3), pp. 3–22.

42. Boyce, T. (2002) 'The power is in parsimony: commentary on Goltz's operant analysis of power interpretation of resistance to change', *Journal of Organizational Behavior Management*, **22**(3), pp. 23–7.

43. Malott, R. (2002) 'Power in organizations', *Journal of Organizational Behavior Management*, **22**(3), pp. 51–60.

44. Geller, E. S. (2002) 'Leadership to overcome resistance to change: it takes more than consequence control', *Journal of Organizational Behavior Management*, **22**(3), pp. 29–49.

WHAT IS WORK SOCIOLOGY?

CHAPTER AIM

To assess why people work, with particular emphasis on the economic and moral dimensions of work.

KEY CONCEPTS

- economic necessity to work
- moral necessity to work
- extrinsic rewards
- intrinsic rewards
- consumption
- post-materialism
- the work ethic
- disciplined compliance
- conscientious endeavour
- work centrality
- work obligation/duty
- post-industrial society
- leisure society
- the psychological contract

LEARNING OUTCOMES

After reading and thinking about the material in this chapter, you will be able to:

1 Evaluate the importance of the economic need to work.
2 Assess the economic commitment to employment drawing on survey evidence.
3 Explain the meaning of the work ethic.
4 Analyse four key themes of the work ethic:
   a. work as an obligation;
   b. work as a central life activity;
   c. work as conscientious endeavour;
   d. work as disciplined compliance.
5 Outline and evaluate theoretical perspectives that explain the change in the work ethic.
6 Explain how changes in the work ethic might be linked to changes in the psychological contract.

INTRODUCTION

Paid work is one of the principal means by which we evaluate others. In this chapter we explore the concept of work, and assess why so much emphasis is placed upon what a person does for a living. Our main concern is to analyse the reasons why people work (see Extract 14.1).

We assess the meaning of work in terms of two features: the economic necessity to work and the moral necessity to work. In relation to the economic necessity, we explore the material reasons for working, and ask whether people would carry on some form of work even if they had no financial need to do so. In terms of the moral necessity we introduce the concept of a 'work ethic', which supposedly encourages people to work irrespective of any economic necessity. In the remaining sections of the chapter, we reflect on how contemporary changes might be affecting the work ethic, in particular the issues of the development of the post-industrial society, of greater leisure and of changes in the psychological contract.

Extract 14.1

Reasons for working

The following are all direct quotes from people about their work. They illustrate how the meaning of work differs between individuals and they highlight some of the key issues this chapter explores. Read the quotes and then try Exercise 14.1.

I enjoy being in work to a certain extent. I don't enjoy the work. But I actually enjoy being here. There are a lot of friends in work…. It's merely a means to an end to get the money at the end of the month and that's all it is. My home life is far more important than my work life. I know I have to have the job. I have to do the work. But I value the home life far more than I do the work life. (Male)

I'm happy working, it does quite a lot for my, sort of self-confidence I think. It's probably very important, you know…. I can't see me being the type of person who would be just happy being at home…. I don't think I'm that type of person. (Female)

It's my duty isn't it as, like, a father to actually go to work and provide for my kids. (Male)

I enjoy being with people you know, I do enjoy working with people like. I don't think I would if I had to – I don't think I would give up work…. I used to think when I had my first daughter I'd love to give up but no. I don't think I could be in the house all day. (Female)

I've never, ever not worked because I've never taken any time off for maternity or anything like that. So I've always worked and it is important to me…. Work, the job I'm actually doing now is a big part of my life […] I take a lot of it home even if it's not carring it home, it's in my mind. I don't switch off. (Female)

If I didn't work, I'd probably end up going sort of stupid…. I think working is one of the most important things in the world, if you want to survive and better yourself you've got to have money. And it means working. (Male)

I don't enjoy being home. I get the buzz. I enjoy working with people. I enjoy the customers. And now I enjoy the authority…sad but there I am. But I do enjoy the job. (Female)

I like working. It gets you out of the house. You socialise, you've got friends…. I'd hate to be unemployed. I like to be active. I just love, well I don't love work, nobody loves work, that's a stupid thing to say. But it's what makes the world go round at the end of the day. (Male)

I am enjoying my life so much because…I'm enjoying my work. Even Saturday or Sunday, all right, I would read work related stuff. I'm not a nerd, I also go out to watch movies and that sort of thing, but I enjoy it so much that I don't really take it as a job. I take it as part of my life and I do that anyway. Like if I'm not getting paid I would still study that sort of thing. I would read it in my leisure time anyway and making it a part of my job I make money from it. So it is a paradise. Heaven. (Male)

Sources: The final quote is from Barrett (2004: 789); the other quotes are from Charles and James (2003: 247–51).

Exercise 14.1

What do you think?

1 Identify the key reasons for working that emerge from the quotes in Extract 14.1.
2 What factors might you expect to influence the attitudes to work shown in the quotes?
3 Compare the quotes from the men with those from the women. What did you find?

THE ECONOMIC NECESSITY TO WORK

Working to live

Intuitively, we know people work in order to earn money to live; it is through paid work that basic needs are satisfied because it provides money for subsistence (food, housing, clothes and so on). However, there is a major problem with accepting this argument as it stands. Can we really talk about the need to work for the purpose of subsistence when most societies provide a welfare system that (in theory at least) prevents people from falling below a basic level of subsistence? Social welfare provision in the form of unemployment benefit, housing allowances and free medical care were specifically designed to act as a safety net, preventing people from becoming destitute. It is the prime example of the state's intervention to stop its citizens being left totally at the mercy of market forces.

Both right-wing and left-wing politicians have argued that the state benefit/welfare system can act as a deterrent to work because it provides a supposedly satisfactory standard of living. The issue arises because in some situations someone could undertake a week's work in a low-paid job and receive comparable income to someone claiming welfare benefits. Moreover, when people take a low-paid job after being on unemployment benefit, they often lose their entitlement to other allowances (such as housing). As a consequence they find themselves financially worse off. This is the classic poverty trap – where the welfare system can act as a financial disincentive to work, even though the person may be keen to be employed.

Some governments have recognised this problem of financial disincentives and have introduced a range of 'in work' benefits: means-tested allowances that can be claimed while in employment. Critics of this policy argue that it exacerbates the problem by effectively subsidising employers who pay low wages. Indeed, it actively discourages them from increasing wages as the employee would lose benefit, and the employer would have to take up the supplement currently funded by the taxpayer. There are two alternative policy solutions which both focus on increasing the differentials between paid work and benefit, although they differ dramatically in their approach:

1 Lower state benefits: this approach considers that benefits are the problem, suggesting the need to lower unemployment allowances and other welfare payments to increase the incentive to work for low wages, thus making unemployment seem 'less attractive'.
2 Raise low wages: this approach is aimed at increasing low wages, typically through setting a national minimum wage, which would similarly increase the differential between those who were in work and out of work, but which would be aimed at making low-paid work 'more attractive'.

Working to consume

As this discussion suggests, in developed capitalist economies it is not just that people need to work to subsist; rather, people work to earn money to acquire consumer power. Money is the means to the goal of consumption, whether that is commodity consumption (smart phones, designer clothes, cars and so forth) or service consumption (drinking, gambling, eating out, using the gym and holidaying). The central, distinguishing feature between those people in work and those who are unemployed is that the former have much higher (although varied) levels of consumer power, and consequently more choice about their lifestyles. This rise of consumption has been one of the fundamental developments of the twentieth century (Ransome, 2005), and some commentators suggest that the nature of consumption has changed in recent years, from mass to niche markets (Piore and Sabel, 1984). This has helped to sustain consumption as one of the defining features of our identity. Moreover, others argue that consumption has become so important that the experience of shopping can be seen as a leisure activity in its own right (Featherstone, 1990).

Given the importance of the link between work and spending power, it is hardly surprising that when asked, most people will say that earning money is the prime reason they go to work (or want to work in the case of the unemployed). This unremarkable observation was verified in the UK by researchers working on a major project entitled the Social Change and Economic Life Initiative (SCELI). We refer to this several times in this book. The researchers questioned people about their reasons for wanting a job, and from analysis of over 5000 responses they found that the majority (68%) worked for the money, either to provide for basic essentials, or in the case of 27 per cent to buy extra things and enjoy some economic independence from the primary earner in the household.

Perhaps the most surprising aspect of this finding is that the figure is not higher than 68 per cent. To uphold the (intuitive) assumption that people work simply for extrinsic reward (money), we might have predicted the figure to be 95 per cent or more. However, an astonishing 26 per cent said that they did not work for the money, but for 'expressive' reasons, in other words for the intrinsic rewards work can bring, such as enjoyment, satisfaction and a sense of achievement. Moreover the percentage of people indicating these expressive reasons remained very similar irrespective of the gender or employment status of the respondent. (See Table 14.1 for a summary, and Rose, 1994, for a comprehensive analysis of the SCELI data.)

Post-materialism

The fact that a significant minority of people say they work for intrinsic reward leads some commentators to argue that materialist values in advanced capitalist societies are waning. Inglehart (1997) suggests people are increasingly opting for interesting and meaningful work, rather than high salaries. This reflects a 'post-materialist' orientation to work, emphasising quality of life. The term 'downshifting' is sometimes used to describe people who have given up high-flying careers and large salaries for a less work-focused, less-materialist way of living (see also Hamilton, 2003). While this post-materialist lifestyle is undoubtedly adopted by some people, the key question is,

Table 14.1 – Summary of the SCELI findings on the reasons for working

	Full-time		Part-time		Self-employed		Unemployed		Housewife returners	Totals
	Men	Women	Men	Women	Men	Women	Men	Women		
Sample size	1786	1026	21	802	248	118	457	272	480	5210
Monetary reasons	75%	69%	77%	66%	69%	60%	69%	65%	65%	68%
Expressive reasons	26%	27%	28%	21%	29%	34%	25%	25%	21%	26%
Other reasons	1%	7%	3%	14%	2%	7%	4%	10%	14%	6%

Source: Adapted from Rose (1994: 294).

how widespread has it become? Is it the start of a new trend, or merely the response of a small minority of people to the increasingly stressful nature of work?

An analysis of this hypothesised increase in post-materialism was undertaken by Russell (1998) using data from the International Social Survey Programme. Her analysis focused on a comparison between three European countries (Britain, West Germany and Italy) in two periods of time, 1989 and 1997. The survey measured a range of attitudes to work which generated an overall score for extrinsic and intrinsic work attitudes in each country. The post-materialist thesis predicts that, compared with 1989, the score in 1997 for the extrinsic value of work will have decreased while the score for the intrinsic value will have increased. The results (see Table 14.2) reveal a mixed picture, which led Russell to conclude that while there is some evidence of post-materialist values, the overall thesis is not borne out by the data. To explore how this conclusion might have been reached, try Exercise 14.2. We return to the issue of downshifting, and other responses that individuals can make to achieve a better 'work–life balance', .

THE COMMITMENT TO EMPLOYMENT

International evidence

One of the most comprehensive international comparative studies is the *Meaning of Working* survey (MOW, 1987) which analyses evidence from eight countries. Respondents from these countries were asked what they would do about work if they acquired a large sum of money and could live comfortably for the rest of their lives without working. This is known as the 'lottery question', and it is frequently used by social researchers in order to get a general view about a person's commitment to employment.

The responses to the lottery question are presented in Table 14.3, ranked according to country. Although the majority of people in each country would continue to work, the table suggests that it is in Britain and Germany where the greatest proportion of people indicated they would stop working. These proportions are noticeably higher than the next ranked country, Belgium (around 30% for Britain and Germany, compared with 16% for Belgium). When looking at proportions of people who would continue in the same job or who would want to work under different conditions are examined, the ranking is almost reversed. Respondents from Japan and Yugoslavia (and to a lesser degree, Israel) demonstrate the highest commitment to their existing

Table 14.2 – Comparison of extrinsic and intrinsic work values

	Britain		Western Germany		Italy	
	1989	1997	1989	1997	1989	1997
Overall extrinsic value score	3.2	3.1	3.2	3.1	3.2	3.2
Overall intrinsic value score	3.3	3.2	3.4	3.4	3.3	3.2
No. of respondents	750	604	703	722	611	530

Notes: Respondents were asked 'How important do you personally think the following items are in a job?': high income; job security; good opportunities for advancement; an interesting job; a job that allows someone to work independently. Their responses were scored on a scale of 0 to 4 – the higher the score, the higher adherence to the particular item being considered. An extrinsic value score for each respondent was calculated by averaging the first three items. An intrinsic value score was based on the last two items. The overall score for extrinsic and intrinsic value is the average across all respondents.
Source: Adapted from Russell (1998: 92).

Table 14.3 – Responses to the lottery question from the Meaning of Working survey

Percentage of respondents who, if they were financially secure, said they would:					
	Stop working		Continue working in the same job		Continue working but under different conditions
Ranking					
1	Britain	31	Japan	66	Britain	53
2	Germany	30	Yugoslavia	62	USA	49
3	Belgium	16	Israel	50	Belgium	47
4	Netherlands	14	Netherlands	42	Netherlands	44
5	USA	12	USA	39	Germany	39
6	Israel	12	Belgium	37	Israel	37
7	Japan	7	Germany	31	Yugoslavia	34
8	Yugoslavia	4	Britain	16	Japan	27

Source: Adapted from MOW International Research Team (1987).

employment. In contrast, respondents from Britain are the least inclined to want to remain in their existing job. Similarly, for the United States, Belgium, Germany and the Netherlands a greater proportion of people would want to continue to work under different conditions than remain in the same job, although the differences between the proportions are much smaller than those in Britain. Taken overall, the MOW data suggests people generally have a commitment to employment (although not necessarily to their current job), and that this is affected by national setting as well as age, occupation, individual differences and life experiences.

British evidence

A survey of employment in Britain (Gallie and White, 1993) assessed the attitudes of 3855 people in 1992 regarding a wide range of issues concerned with work. When asked the lottery question, 67 per cent of people indicated they would continue to work, and there was very little difference in the replies of men and women (68% compared with 67%). Assuming this sample is representative, it suggests the majority of people derive more from work than their salary.

It could be argued that intrinsic satisfaction depends on the nature of the job being done, and that professional workers might be more inclined to stay at work than semi-skilled manual workers, regardless of financial security. Gallie and White (1993) took this into consideration in their analysis and found that the majority of people in all job categories would continue to work even if there was no financial need, although the proportions increased, the higher the job levels of the respondents. In addition, the survey revealed that employment commitment was highest among people in their early 20s and declined with age.

The general picture is that most survey respondents were committed to the principle of being employed, but it is important to note the following points:

- They were not necessarily committed to their particular jobs.
- They were not committed to working full-time, but rather stated a preference for a working week of between 16 and 30 hours.

⊙ They did not necessarily want to maintain their existing conditions of employment, such as work environment and location.

A further point to think about is that the respondents may have been reflecting the socially desirable norm of being 'in work' rather than demonstrating an individual commitment to employment. We return to this issue later in the chapter when we consider the moral necessity to work, but for now let us assume that the respondents are committed to employment. This prompts an additional question: 'What causes individual commitment to work?'

From their analysis of further questions asked in the survey, Gallie and White (1993: 67–9) isolate seven influences on employment commitment. To summarise their argument, we can say that employment commitment will be stronger:

⊙ the more qualifications the person has;
⊙ the greater their feeling of having been successful in their career;
⊙ the higher they value 'hard work';
⊙ the more they feel they have personal control over their destiny;
⊙ the higher their preference for their current job;
⊙ the lower their preference for 'an easy life';
⊙ the higher their attachment to their current organisation.

Of course, this does not mean all these influences have to be present before a person feels committed to employment, but it indicates the possible range of influential factors.

TO SUM UP

The evidence suggests it is not enough simply to argue that people work for extrinsic rewards. Clearly, income beyond the subsistence level is an important reason for working, but surveys reveal that a substantial minority of people work for reasons other than money (the expressive needs, noted above), and that a majority of people say they would continue to work even if there was no financial need to do so. It seems that other factors influence attitudes to work; factors which, some have argued, include a moral necessity to work.

Exercise 14.2

What do you think?

If you currently have a job (part-time or full-time), try this next time you are at work.
○ Ask your co-workers the lottery question.
○ Encourage them to explain their answers.

Write down a few notes to remind yourself of their opinions, then later on answer the following questions:
1 How similar or different are their responses from each other?
2 How might you explain any differences of response?
3 How do their responses compare with those from the research reported in this chapter?

THE MORAL NECESSITY TO WORK

Implicit in much of the discussion in the previous section is the idea that work is 'good': a virtuous, dignified and worthy activity for people to engage in. In other words, there is a moral dimension to work, commonly accepted by society, which values endeavour and enterprise through employment above leisure. Being 'in work' becomes morally desirable irrespective of any financial or social benefit to the individual. This moral dimension to work is usually called 'the work ethic', and it has traditionally been associated with characteristics such as diligence, punctuality, obedience, honesty and sobriety. So, where does this moral dimension to work come from? And what relevance does it have for understanding contemporary orientations to employment?

One of the best accounts of the development of the work ethic in the UK is provided by Anthony (1977). Drawing on Weber (1930), he traces the work ethic from the roots of Protestantism in the seventeenth century, which defined work as a religious calling, through either the Lutheran belief that a state of grace could be achieved through endeavour, or the Calvinist doctrine of predestination whereby work became part of a lifestyle demonstrating one's salvation. The Protestant work ethic became the foundation upon which the ideology of work associated with industrialisation and capitalism was built. As Anthony (1977: 44) argues:

> Work had every advantage. It was good in itself. It satisfied the selfish economic interest of the growing number of small employers or self-employed. It was a social duty, it contributed to social order in society and to moral worth in the individual. It contributed to a good reputation among one's fellows and to an assured position in the eyes of God.

Similarly, in his consideration of the work ethic in the United States, Rodgers (1978: 14) argues:

> The central premise of the work ethic was that work was the core of moral life. Work made men useful in a world of economic scarcity. It staved off the doubts and temptations that preyed on idleness, it opened the way to deserved wealth and status, it allowed one to put the impress of mind and skill on the material world.

Other commentators have noted how the work ethic seems to be a feature of a wide range of societies and have suggested that it seems to be a universal human value (see Extract 14.2).

Extract 14.2

The work ethic: a universal concept?

The work ethic is often referred to as the Protestant work ethic in the UK and Australia, and in the United States as the Judeo-Christian ethic. These religious labels have sometimes been used to imply there are distinct features to the work ethic that make it prevalent only in Protestant-dominated countries. As we note in the main text, these usually emphasise the value and importance of duty, commitment, effort and obedience. However, commentators have suggested that these features of the work ethic can be found in many cultures and among many nationalities, so it is not uniquely Protestant. To illustrate this point, consider the quotes below.

The Islamic work ethic

The concept of the Islamic work ethic (IWE) has its origin in the Quran, the sayings and practice of Prophet Mohammed, who preached that hard work caused sins to be absolved and that 'no one eats better food than that which he eats out of his work'. For instance, the Quran often speaks about honesty and justice in trade, and it calls for an equitable and fair distribution of wealth in the society. The Quran encourages humans to acquire skills and technology, and highly praises those who strive in order to earn a living. The Quran is against laziness and waste of time by either remaining idle or engaging oneself in unproductive activity.... The Islamic work ethic views dedication to work as a virtue. Sufficient effort should go into one's work, which is seen as obligatory for a capable individual.

In addition, work is considered to be a source of independence and a means of fostering personal growth, self-respect, satisfaction and self-fulfilment. The IWE stresses creative work as a source of happiness and accomplishment.

Hard work is seen as a virtue, and those who work hard are more likely to get ahead in life. Conversely, not working hard is seen to cause failure in life.

(Ali, 1988)

In brief, the Islamic work ethic argues that life without work has no meaning and engagement in economic activities is an obligation.

(Yousef, 2001: 153)

The Buddhist work ethic

Reading from interpretations of Buddha's teaching on the ethics of material progress (Nanayakkara, 1992)...Buddha encouraged the proper utilization of human resources to develop the economy. Therefore he presented a very effective work ethic to motivate the workforce. But this work ethic encouraged teamwork and in its widest connotation meant an appropriate attitude toward work. Religion seems to play a major role in this and it is argued that contrary to popular belief that Buddhism is pessimistic in outlook, there is abundant textual evidence that Buddha formulated a work ethic that encouraged workers to put forth their best effort. Buddha singled out laziness as a cause of the downfall of men and nations and urged that everyone should put forth effort. He stressed that one should be one's own master. He encouraged qualities such as initiative, striving, persistence, etc.

(Niles, 1999: 858)

The Catholic work ethic

Roman Catholic bishops will instruct their flocks that manual work can be a remedy for self-indulgence, dishonesty and individualism. A paper, 'The Spirituality of Work', by a committee set up by the bishops of England and Wales, states that going out to work does not guarantee salvation, but it helps. However, the paper also issues a warning of one danger of work: 'It is a prime way of creating wealth, and so presents the risk of serving only to fill the human horizon with a lust for wealth and possessions.' The committee of Catholic laity and workers sets out a list of prayers, hymns and meditation for use in the workplace. They should be used while giving 'proper attention to safety at work', the paper advises. The concept of the 'work ethic' as promoted by St Paul, traditionally thought of as a Protestant ideal, is embraced. 'Mother Teresa of Calcutta understood that all people were called to holiness – even journalists' the paper states. The committee cites the suggestion in St Paul's letter to the Ephesians 'that manual work, or labour, is a suitable remedy for individualist, self-indulgent and dishonest styles of life'.

(*The Times*, 16 January 2001)

Although the notion of the work ethic is appealing, it presents us with an analytical problem: how do we disentangle the notion of a moral commitment to work from that of an economic need to work? Can we really argue that there was a general acceptance of a work ethic in industrialising nations before the birth of social welfare systems? And even after the emergence of decent wages, is the moral dimension to work any easier to pin down?

To answer these questions, four key themes associated with the work ethic need to be examined:

1 Work as an obligation (emphasising duty).
2 Work as the central life activity (emphasising commitment).
3 Work as conscientious endeavour (emphasising effort).
4 Work as disciplined compliance (emphasising obedience).

Each of these will be considered in turn, although as the discussion reveals, in practice there is an overlap and merging of the themes.

Work as an obligation

This theme reflects the importance of doing your utmost to seek paid employment rather than remaining 'idle'. Studies of the attitudes of the unemployed reveal there is a widespread desire not to be perceived as 'lazy'. This might encourage work even if levels of pay are only marginally higher than unemployment benefit (see, for example, Turner, Bostyn and Wight, 1985). To a large extent this may be the result of the desire to be a 'good provider' for one's family. A study of basic life values conducted in the mid-1960s (Yankelovich, 1973) revealed that 80 per cent of US adults linked the importance of being the breadwinner to masculinity. So, being 'in work' not only conferred economic power on the individual, but it also helped to forge a masculine identity – a man who was unemployed was not only unable to provide for his family, he was also less of a man. Other studies have echoed the association between employment and male identify. For instance, McKee and Bell (1986: 141) comment:

> The loss of the male economic provider struck deep chords among both wives and husbands and a passionate defence of men's right to provide was invariably raised.... Fundamental emotions concerning self-esteem, self-image, pride, views of masculinity, respectability and authority resounded in the expressions of both men and women.

Alternatively, it could be argued that the growth of unemployment in Western capitalist societies means the perception that work is the way to becoming a 'breadwinner' is being eroded. It is a forceful argument, particularly when there has been an abandonment of the political commitment to achieving full employment. This means some of the responsibility for this chance lies with the government for failing to provide enough jobs. In other words, as Offe (1985: 142–3) puts it:

> [As] the experience (or the anticipation) of unemployment, or involuntary retirement from working life increases, the more the effect of moral stigmatisation and self-stigmatisation generated by unemployment probably wears off because, beyond a certain threshold (and especially if unemployment is concentrated in certain regions or in certain industries), it can no longer be accounted for plausibly in terms of individual failure or guilt.

But the opposite might also be the case. When work is in short supply, the value placed on it (its scarcity value) rises. This can help to explain why most of the unemployed continue to search for work even when economic conditions offer little hope of secure, long-term, full-time employment. In a further twist to the argument, it may be suggested that when people are faced with unemployment, they are likely to cope much better (in terms of their mental health) if they do not see work as a duty (Warr, 1987). In other words, a strong work ethic might help motivate some people to hunt for work, but it might have a detrimental effect on their ability to cope if they are unable to find a suitable job. On the other hand, a weak work ethic may help some people accept being unemployed, but in so doing it could also inhibit their motivation to gain employment.

An attempt to assess the pervasiveness of 'work as a duty' was undertaken in the international survey on the *Meaning of Working* (MOW, 1987). The researchers examined two issues:

- *obligation to work*: the view that everyone must work to the best of their ability and thereby contribute to society;
- *entitlement to work*: the view that everyone should have the right to a meaningful and interesting job with proper training.

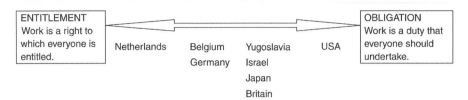

Figure 14.1 – National comparisons in attitudes to work entitlement and obligation

These are two separate dimensions, and so an individual's orientation to both can be measured. The MOW researchers were able to plot the responses from each country to demonstrate how the orientation to (1) obligation to work (duties) and (2) entitlement to work (rights) can vary in different national settings. The important aspect to consider from these findings is the overall balance exhibited by respondents from each country – these differences are illustrated in Figure 14.1.

Work as a central life activity

This theme stresses that paid work is the most important part of life, coming before all non-work activities. Some of the most revealing empirical evidence can again be found in the *Meaning of Working* survey (ibid: 79–93). The researchers defined work centrality as 'the degree of general importance that working has in the life of an individual at any given point in time' (ibid: 81). They developed a method of measuring work centrality that involved asking people to assess working against four other important aspects of their lives: family, community, religion and leisure. Overall, the analysis revealed that in terms of importance and significance, respondents judged work second only to family. In the combined national samples, 40 per cent placed family as most important, while 27 per cent placed working as most important among these five key life roles (ibid: 252). Of additional interest are the effects of three variables: age, nationality and gender. The first two we shall deal with briefly, but the third warrants more detailed comment.

Effect of age

A person's work centrality tends to increase with age. The finding is perhaps not surprising given that people may be promoted or take on more responsibility within an organisation the older they get. This is coupled with the tendency for a person's social life to 'slow down' with age (though family is likely to take a more central role).

Effect of nationality

Work centrality varies according to national differences. The MOW survey data suggested that respondents from Japan were considerably more work-centred than other countries; in Britain, respondents displayed the lowest degree of work centrality.

Effect of gender

Men typically have higher work centrality than women. Caution should be exercised in interpreting this finding, however, because it does not necessarily mean that women are innately less interested in work; rather it might reflect the different roles widely expected of men and women. It is still the case that domestic obligations (particularly cleaning, cooking and childcare) are disproportionately undertaken by women. This not only requires them to be less work-centred (more time and thought must be devoted to the family) but also provides an alternative focus to their lives from which they might derive a sense of fulfilment. As Hakim points out, there has been a failure to recognise how the female labour force is composed of at least two distinct groups that differ dramatically in work orientations: those who choose full-time work, and those who choose the homemaker role. She states:

> [The first] group has work commitment similar to that of men, leading to long-term workplans and almost continuous full-time work, often in jobs with higher status and earnings than are typical for women. The second group has little or no commitment to paid work and a clear preference for the homemaker role; paid employment is a secondary activity, usually undertaken to earn a supplementary wage rather than as primary breadwinner, and is in low-skilled, low-paid, part-time, casual and temporary jobs more often than in skilled, permanent full-time jobs.
>
> (Hakim, 1991: 113)

Of course, it is debatable whether women are really as free to choose their roles as Hakim suggests. Patriarchy (rule by a male elite) constrains these 'choices' (for analysis of the key debates see Crompton, 2002; McRae, 2003; Walby, 1986, 1990, 1997). Nevertheless, for men, the choice of being homemaker is still not widely accepted by society. In that sense, the moral obligation to be work-centred is more imposed on men than women. The general expectation by employers is that a man will want a full-time job, whereas a woman may settle for part-time work.

In addition to domestic obligations, there may be structural reasons for the lower work centrality reported by women. As we note throughout the book, women more frequently have jobs with lower pay and benefits, lower status, less autonomy, less responsibility and less job security. Also, these poor-quality terms and conditions are frequently a feature of part-time jobs, the majority of which are undertaken by women. This is perpetuated because of a widely held assumption that women (in general) have low work centrality. This means a woman in a full-time job is frequently faced with male managers and co-workers who assume she is less committed to a career in the organisation because she may leave to start a family (supposedly deferring to her family-centred values):

> Managers' perceptions of job requirements and procedures for assessing merit have been shown to be saturated with gendered assumptions. ... Feminists can argue (as they have for years) that not all women get pregnant, but it seems unlikely that this will stop managers thinking 'yes, but no men will'.
>
> (Liff and Wajcman, 1996: 89)

Finally, it is worth noting how these possible reasons for lower work centrality can link together. The imbalance of domestic responsibilities means that many women find part-time work more convenient, and consequently find themselves in jobs which are both intrinsically and extrinsically poorly rewarded. In this instance, employment becomes de-centred, yet is endured to provide either an adequate income for the family or an independent income for the women. So among women working part-time, or women not in paid employment, it would not be surprising to find lower work centrality. The proper way to assess whether gender affects work orientation would be to compare like with like: men and women in full-time jobs with similar status and terms and conditions. In practice, this is an extremely difficult comparison to make given the horizontal (in terms of occupation) and vertical (in terms of seniority) segregation of labour by gender. Many occupations are horizontally segregated – occupations such as nursing and hairdressing are predominantly female, while engineering and the building trades are dominated by men. Occupations are also often vertically segregated – most senior positions are held by men. An analysis comparing men and women with similar qualifications suggests gender differences have changed. Evaluating the findings from UK surveys carried out between the mid-1980s and the early 2000s, Rose (2005) argues there has been a convergence between male and female attitudes. More women say they look on work to provide necessities, independence and money rewards over the long term. Also, fewer men say they see themselves as the natural breadwinner.

Irrespective of gender, Moorhouse (1984) challenges the view that for most people work is a central life activity in any sense other than occupying the majority of their waking hours. He argues there is a need to distinguish between what people find important (qualitatively central) from what occupies large amounts of their time (quantitatively central). It is only the former, he argues, that offers any sociological insight into working lives. The MOW (1987) research revealed a high work centrality on both measures: people found work important and it occupied large amounts of their time. But, like all the surveys of this type, it still leaves us with the conundrum of whether people find work important because it occupies large amounts of their time – in other words, to use Moorhouse's terms, whether its quantitative centrality determines its qualitative centrality. In addition, such an approach fails to broach an arguably more interesting question: whether people think work ought to be so central (both qualitatively and quantitatively). In part we can address this issue by examining the third theme of the work ethic: conscientious endeavour.

Work as conscientious endeavour

This theme of the work ethic emphasises the importance of doing a job diligently. No matter how menial the task, the individual is encouraged to put effort and care into it in order to produce the best outcome. It is summed up in the maxim: 'If a job's worth doing, it's worth doing well.'

A contemporary expression of this can be seen in the management rhetoric of 'customer care'. Typically, these are initiatives requiring employees not only to show great respect but also to make customers feel as though they are being individually looked after. This increasingly requires employees to manage their own emotions to elicit a good feeling in the minds of the customers. This 'emotion work' is being recognised as so important for the competitiveness of contemporary organisations that even people in low-paid, low-status jobs such as shop work are required to be increasingly diligent in this aspect of their work.

The theme of conscientious endeavour also implies activity, whether this is physical or mental. The extent of activity of course varies from job to job and task to task. People may place different value on different forms of activity – in particular the difference between manual and non-manual work. Those who value the former tend to invoke the idea of dignity in physical labour, and sometimes suggest that a person has not really done 'a fair day's work' unless they have 'got their hands dirty'. The stress on the virtue of practical rather than knowledge- or emotion-based activity has often been used to differentiate work supposedly suited to men from that supposedly suited to women. In effect this has supported gender divisions at work by creating an artificial, gendered notion of what constitutes skilled work. It has increasingly defined customer contact jobs as emotion based, and therefore more suited to women. The importance of the physicality of work for men is neatly summed up in the following quotes from male printer workers in Cockburn's study of technological change in the printing industry:

> I like to do a man's job. And this means physical labour and getting dirty, you understand…working brings dignity to people I think, they are doing something useful, they are working with these [he demonstrated his hands] that have been provided for that. That's what it is all about. Craftsmanship.
>
> (Quoted in Cockburn, 1983: 52)

> People have to work and get their hands dirty, you get more satisfaction out of it than those people that sit there, you know, like a tailor's dummy at an office desk.
>
> (Ibid: 108)

The roots of this notion of work lie deep and are particularly evident in working-class culture, especially among men (see, for example, Collinson, 1992). This is vividly illustrated by Willis's classic study of a group of working-class 'lads' which reveals how a counter-school culture constructs and reinforces the value of physical labour over mental work:

> Manual labour is outside the domain of school and carries with it…the aura of the real adult world. Mental work demands too much, and encroaches – just as the school does – too far upon those areas which are increasingly adopted as their own, as private and independent…. Thus physical labouring comes to stand for and express, most importantly, a kind of masculinity and also an opposition to authority…. It expresses aggressiveness; a degree of sharpness and wit; an irreverence that cannot be found in words; an obvious kind of solidarity. It provides the wherewithal for adult tastes, and demonstrates a potential mastery over, as well as an immediate attractiveness to women: a kind of machismo.
>
> (Willis, 1977: 103–4)

A further element of conscientious endeavour is the idea that work has some purpose. In other words it is a productive activity that is valued by others. This is important because considerable effort may go into activities for which people do not get paid. Indeed, Moorhouse (1987) has argued that people are as productively active (if not more so) in leisure pursuits as they are in their work. The effort that goes into activities as varied as gardening, DIY, creating your own website, sport, gaming and amateur dramatics confirms this point. Similarly, a huge proportion of highly productive activity is unpaid – notably domestic and voluntary work. Also the informal economy (from e-bay to drug dealing) is a sizable part of productive (and paid) activity that is rarely acknowledged by wider society.

Although productive activity is possible in a variety of spheres, it is key to work centrality – the theme above of the work ethic – and as a consequence is identified with employment. As Jahoda (1979: 313) argues, people might contribute to the community in a variety of ways, but work roles 'are the most central roles and consequently people deprived of the opportunity to work often feel useless and report that they lack a sense of purpose'. This is conveyed by the comments of an unemployed miner in a study by Parry (2003: 240):

> I was unemployed, on the dole, first time for a lot more years than I care to remember…where you had targets before and you're working and had goals to go for, once you're on the dole you stay up late at night, why bother getting up in the morning? Nothing to aim for, to go for. It certainly shook me up, definitely, definitely. I found out how easy it was to get into that position.

The unemployed are not only deprived of the economic rewards derived through work, but they are also denied the moral approval of their conscientious endeavour if they use their initiative to find paid work unofficially (e.g. cash-in-hand jobs) or fill their spare time with non-paid productive (and self-rewarding) activities like voluntary work, gardening, writing poetry and so on.

Work as disciplined compliance

This fourth theme of the work ethic is particularly important *because* it underlines two components essential to capitalist production: (i) the acceptance of the management prerogative and (ii) obedience to time structures.

The management prerogative

The 'management prerogative' refers to the right of managers to direct the workforce as they deem fit, based on their 'expertise'. It can be associated with a style of management that stresses the unitary nature of the employment relationship: that is, the absence of any major conflict of interest and the position of management as the sole legitimate authority. This concept of unitarism, originally defined by Fox (1966), received particular attention during the 1980s with the emergence of a new rhetoric of human resource management (HRM). This emphasises the common goals of employees and managers in organisations. HRM ignores any plurality of interests and imbalance of power in organisations and invokes the idea of organisational commitment and cooperation to secure efficient and effective performance directed towards strategically designed corporate goals. These are often expressed in a waffle-filled mission statement. The employees' disciplined compliance with the values and goals of the organisation is perpetuated by management through the development of employment policies and a corporate culture that stresses individualism. This either marginalises or completely removes any collective representation through trade unions. (For a full discussion of the multifaceted nature of HRM, see Legge, 2005.)

Obedience to time structures

The second element is disciplined compliance with the time structures imposed by management. The working day provides a time structure which clearly differentiates periods of work and leisure. Traditionally, the Monday to Friday '9 to 5' pattern of working hours provided structure not only to the working day but also to the whole of working (and waking) lives. However, these time patterns are undergoing substantial change in contemporary society. Nevertheless, the majority of people still have a structure imposed by the time routines of their paid work. The importance of this structure is often not evident until people are faced with its removal, particularly through the loss of their jobs. One of the foremost researchers on the effects of unemployment sums it up succinctly:

> Everybody living in an industrialised society is used to firm time structures – and to complaining about them. But when this structure is removed, as it is in unemployment, its absence presents a major psychological burden. Days stretch long when there is nothing that has to be done; boredom and waste of time become the rule.

(Jahoda, 1982: 22)

For people out of work, the problem becomes how to fill the unstructured days, and how to create new structures to take the place of the one they have lost. It is well

illustrated by the following quotes from two different studies of unemployment –
one in Scotland, the other in England. The first quote is by an unemployed woman
in her mid-30s, and the second by an unemployed male steelworker of the same
age:

> I used to think it'd be great not to work … when I was working … I'd 'imagine
> having a day off' – it was a treat. Now, I've got every day, and every week, and
> every month … and maybe every year to do *nothing*. There never used to be
> enough hours in the day for me when I was working … now, I know what an
> hour is … it just drags round.
>
> (Quoted in Turner, Bostyn and Wight, 1985: 485,
> emphasis in original)

> When you're employed you make use of all your time. You come home
> from work, have a quick bite to eat, a cup of tea, and get stuck into some
> job you've got to do. You know you've only got a set time. But when you're
> unemployed you've got all the time in the world and you think, ah, I won't
> do that today, I'll do that tomorrow. You take a slap-dash attitude, which is
> wrong.
>
> (Quoted in Wallace and Pahl, 1986: 121)

TO SUM UP

If all four themes are put together, the work ethic can be described as the belief
that it is the duty of everyone to treat productive work as their central life activity
and to perform it with diligence and punctuality under the direction and control
of managers. It is rare that complete submission to the work ethic would be
expressed by an individual, but elements of the four themes are reflected in attitudes to work, as has been illustrated by the research quoted above. The general
point emerging from the discussion so far is that work is seen by many people as
a worthy activity in its own right, over and above the economic rewards it brings.
This leads us to the question whether the moral dimension to work is changing;
more specifically, whether as a result of changes in the structure and nature of
paid employment the work ethic is in terminal decline and is ceasing to have any
contemporary relevance.

Extract 14.3

Polish workers have a terrific attitude to work

Nick Warner, who runs a business supplying workers to pack boxes for supermarkets, said that 95 per cent of the 400
people on his books were Polish or Portuguese.

Poles were the most reliable and displayed a 'terrific attitude', he added … . 'You can ask them to work tomorrow and
they will be waiting for you to pick them up in the morning.'

'The average English guy we are looking for has given up on the work ethic, there is just no incentive to find employment.' Mr Warner, group general manager of Central London-based Good People Recruitment, added: 'We work very
closely with job centres to get people off Jobseekers Allowance and into fulltime employment.'

'But we have found that, with the other benefits they are often on, such as housing benefit and child support payments,
they can earn more sitting on their backsides doing nothing than they can working 40 hours a week for us.'

'We have a great problem motivating these people.'

Quote from *Daily Mail*, 'Workshy British force boss to recruit Poles', 9 February 2005.

Exercise 14.3

THE DEMISE OF THE WORK ETHIC?

As already noted, survey evidence about why people work is inconclusive. On the one hand, it suggests that most people say economic need urges them to work. Yet, on the other hand, most say they would continue to work even if there was no economic necessity for them to do so. Despite this ambiguous evidence, some politicians and academics argue that people are increasingly instrumental in their attitudes to work and suggest that there has been a steady deterioration in the work ethic. Within this perspective, it is possible to identify two explanations that account for the demise of the work ethic. They each suggest a fundamental shift has occurred in the economic context: either to (1) a post-industrial society, or to (2) a leisure society.

A shift towards a post-industrial society?

This explanation stresses the impact of economic developments and argues that the work ethic is in decline because of structural changes in society, which has meant that we have moved from an era of industrialisation to a 'post-industrial' age. The argument contends that while the work ethic was an appropriate basis upon which to build industries, it no longer has relevance in a post-industrial society. This approach is most closely associated with Bell (1973, 1976), who argues that advanced industrial economies are undergoing a shift to become post-industrial societies. This is occurring through changes in the social structure including a transformation in the economic base from manufacturing to services, which leads not only to increasing numbers of people being involved in the delivery of services but also increasing demand for, and consumption of, services: from tourism to participative sports; from psychotherapy to massage parlours. Concomitant with this structural change is an increasing importance on information-handling activities which means more white-collar jobs requiring higher levels of education and training, and the emergence of professionals as the dominant group, deriving influence through specialist theoretical knowledge.

If we apply Bell's thesis, it challenges the notion of the work ethic in two ways:

- First, it means that a work ethic developed for an age of industrial production is no longer relevant for a structurally different society: one based on the increasing consumption of services.
- Second, it suggests that the work ethic will cease to have any moral influence. There will no longer be a moral necessity to work because the post-industrial society is shaped by technological advances, increased efficiency and greater theoretical knowledge, so the cultural realm will have diminishing influence compared with the economic realm.

Critics of Bell (e.g. Webster, 1995: 30–51) would argue his whole notion of a post-industrial society is mistaken because it creates a false dichotomy (an either-or) between manufacturing and services. This is a false dichotomy because in practice the two are interdependent (Gershuny and Miles, 1983). The service sector is helping to sustain the manufacturing sector through 'producer services' (Browning and Singelmann, 1978) such as banking, insurance, marketing and distribution. What is more, there is an increasing expansion not only of service work but also of service products, so the move may be towards a 'self-service' economy (Gershuny, 1978). For example, people drive cars rather than use public transport, and buy washing machines and vacuum cleaners rather than use laundry and cleaning services. This more complex picture of social and sectoral change suggests there is a continuity of economic development rather than a dramatic structural shift. So it follows that the work ethic might similarly adapt to reflect these changes in patterns of production and consumption. It also brings into question Bell's assumption that the social structure can be separated from the realm of culture – if there is no structural shift, then similarly there is a question mark over the supposed break with culture (even if one accepts such a separation as feasible in the first place).

A shift towards a leisure society?

Gorz (1982, 1985) argues the work ethic has ceased to have relevance because of the emergence of increased leisure time, which is 'liberating' people from work. He suggests technological change has led to labour-saving work processes and the creation of a post-industrial age in which leisure and productive activity outside work are increasingly important. Work ceases to be central in people's lives in terms of hours spent working. Gorz (1985: 40–1) projects a future scenario where people will be engaged in work sharing, with the equivalent of no more than ten years of full-time work during their life.

Similarly, it is envisaged that income would not be based on having a job or the amount of work performed; instead, everyone would be guaranteed a minimum income in exchange for a right to work (and an obligation to perform socially necessary work). Demand for goods and services would be stimulated by the guaranteed minimum income for all, but consumption would only be one side of the equation, because the liberating factor for Gorz is the contraction of economic and market activity, and the 'expansion of activities performed for their own sake – for love, pleasure or satisfaction, following personal passions, preferences and vocations' (1985: 53). This 'autonomous activity' could take any form, providing it stemmed from individual choice, and so, for some, this would involve competitive, free enterprise for financial gain. In other words, the purpose of life is self-fulfilment, which will differ from person to person, so with less work time and more free time people can be allowed to pursue fulfilment in whatever manner they choose.

To summarise two volumes of work into a single paragraph does Gorz an injustice. His vision of the future is so at odds with capitalism that it may seem a dream. Certainly there are many aspects of Gorz's thesis that can be criticised, but the discussion here will be confined to three main problems with the notion of leisure replacing work, and hence representing evidence of the demise of the work ethic.

First, there is the difficulty of what 'leisure' means. There is a range of activities, from housework to volunteering, for which people do not get paid yet which fills up their time. It is questionable whether they all could be described as leisure, since most involve (unpaid) effort and many are obligations (especially to the family) rather than free choice. Indeed, perhaps these activities equally demonstrate a work ethic. If a type of work ethic is evident in leisure activities, the move to a leisure society will not dilute the work ethic so much as refocus it.

Second, there is a problem with the location of the work ethic. Even if it is assumed that more leisure time will encourage the majority of people to relinquish any commitment to the moral necessity of work, this does not automatically lead to the demise of the work ethic. As Veal argues, and as expressed in our criticism of Bell's thesis, the work ethic is a cultural phenomenon and as such will not be dislocated easily. On the contrary, the resilience of the work ethic might act as a barrier to the type of leisure society that Gorz envisages:

> The possibility remains…that the work ethic exists within the culture – not necessarily in the hearts and minds of the workers, but among the media, educationalists, the ruling classes, and so on. Thus it has an official existence, rather like an established religion, without being embraced by the population as a whole. In that case, it could be hindering progress towards a more 'leisured' society.
>
> (Veal, 1989: 268)

Third, theories of a leisure society fail to stand up against empirical evidence. Many people in work are working longer and more intensely. This means it is false to suggest that the work ethic is under threat because of people having more leisure time and shifting the balance of their lives away from work towards leisure activities.

TO SUM UP

The conclusion to be drawn from Bell and Gorz is that the traditional work ethic must be abandoned because it is dysfunctional in contemporary society: it is not suited to the changing patterns of employment which emphasise the service sector and force a redefinition of the roles of work and leisure. While there is evidence to support each writer's analysis of the structural change, it does not necessarily signal the demise of the work ethic. Instead, what may be occurring is a realignment of the components of the work ethic to match contemporary economic circumstances. Before reading the next section, read Extract 14.4 and then attempt Exercise 14.4.

Extract 14.4

Overwork – the new work ethic?

In a book entitled *Willing Slaves*, journalist Madeleine Bunting laments the effects of the overwork culture on contemporary society. Far from there being a demise of the work ethic, she argues that it is a strong force, particularly among white-collar professionals, and that it is driven by both consumption and a search for status. She argues as follows:

If someone complains about having to work too hard, sooner or later they'll say that they have 'no choice'. Probe a little further and what becomes clear is that, for much of the workforce living well above the poverty line, the connection between pay and overwork is about aspiration to particular patterns of consumption. This is murky territory, where one person's 'needs' are another's 'desires'.

But money, and the consumer goods we can buy with it, don't tell the whole story of why some people in the high-skill, high-income bracket are working harder. Once the upper-middle-class desired leisure and scorned anything that looked like trying too hard; now they are rarely parted from their mobiles or Blackberry handhelds. They look exhausted, complain of too much work, yet do nothing about reducing their burden.

Part of this is the hangover of a period of high unemployment, when predictions of 'the end of work' made having lots of work a status symbol. But more important is the emergence of a new form of elitism in the labour market: work as vocation and work as pleasure. In a society that places a high premium on self-expression and fulfilment, to have a lot of interesting work is a status symbol.

The new work ethic has been astonishingly successful at exploiting the insecurities of employees and disciplining them to work harder than their parents or grandparents probably ever did – and with zero job security. The feat has been remarkable, particularly in corporate America, where hundreds of thousands of white-collar workers throughout the early to mid-1990s were made redundant, yet managed no collective protest. Instead, they redoubled their efforts – hours of work lengthened significantly over the same period – to devote most of their waking hours to those same corporations. The new work ethic tantalises the white-collar worker with the possibility of satisfactions that are just out of reach, thus heading off potential challenges to the way work is organised, and continually throwing the problem back on to the individual to resolve.

As far back as the 1950s, the great US sociologist, C. Wright Mills, worried that white-collar workers sold not just their time and energy, but also their personalities to their employer. He believed that work took up too much of people's time, and shaped them in such a way as to destroy meaningful life outside work. The overwork culture makes his fears as real as ever.

Source: Extracts from Bunting (2004).

Exercise 14.4

What do you think?

Compare the views of Bunting (see Extract 14.4) with those of three theses that you have already encountered.
1 The post-materialism thesis (from the section on the economic necessity to work).
2 The post-industrial society thesis (Bell).
3 The leisure society thesis (Gorz).

THE WORK ETHIC AND THE PSYCHOLOGICAL CONTRACT

It can be argued that the work ethic is being challenged because of changes in workplace employment practices that put different demands and obligations on employees – changes that have occurred because of the greater intensity and dynamism of the competitive environment. Much of this change, where, in particular, we noted the impact of globalisation. One of the concepts used by some commentators to assess the impact of these broad structural and economic changes is the 'psychological contract' between employees and employers (for a recent review see Conway and Briner, 2009; for earlier influential work see Grant, 1999; Herriot, Manning and Kidd, 1997; Rousseau, 1995; Sparrow, 1996). It is necessary to define this concept before looking at how it is supposedly changing workplace values and thereby affecting the work ethic.

There are various definitions of the psychological contract from different authors, but it can be described as:

> The beliefs of each of the parties involved in the employment relationship about what the individual offers and what the organization offers. For example, an individual employee might be willing to offer loyalty to the organization and in return expects to get security of employment. Unlike the employment contract, the psychological contract is not written down and changes over time as new expectations emerge about what the employee should offer and what they can expect to get back in return.

(Heery and Noon, 2001: 288)

In reviewing the research that has been undertaken into changes in the psychological contract, Martin, Staines and Pate (1998) suggest that two contrasting views exist about the effect on employees: the pessimistic view and the optimistic view.

The pessimistic view concludes that competitive market pressures have led to changes in the structure and processes of organisations (such as delayering, lean production, flexibility and team working) and an obsessive focus on the customer. This results in:

- work intensification,
- reduced job security,
- neglect of employee welfare and satisfaction,
- fewer career opportunities,
- less training and development.

The consequence is that employees feel let down by employers as their expectations of 'the deal on offer' are no longer being met. The psychological contract has been broken.

The optimistic view concludes that despite these competitive pressures, 'the traditional psychological contract built around job security and a career is still alive and surprisingly well' (Guest, Conway, Briner and Dickman, 1996: 1). There is:

- greater employability,
- more demand by employees for training and development,
- greater functional flexibility among employees,
- more mobility between organisations.

Consequently the psychological contract is intact in some organisations and being 'redrafted' in others to accommodate the new competitive conditions.

Both the pessimistic and optimistic perspectives might be valid. For some employees the psychological contract has been breached and they resent this, while for others a change in the psychological contract might be welcomed. Indeed, Herriot (1998: 107) questions the notion of the psychological contract and argues that 'different individuals will have different perceptions of their psychological contract; there will be no universal notion of what "the deal" is in any one organisation'. This is an important point for two reasons. First, it reminds us there is diversity in any workforce regarding their values and orientations to work (thereby emphasising the importance of a pluralist perspective). Second, it alerts us to the possibility that the idea of 'the psychological contract' is a misconception – so perhaps the same can be said about 'the work ethic'.

It is possible to argue that a supposed 'demise in the work ethic' is without foundation because it is based on the false assumption that a work ethic was generally held by people in the first place. There can be no overall demise, if there was never any general acceptance of a work ethic. As Rose (1985: 16) states:

> A possibility is that some sections of the working population did in the past hold work values approximating to a work ethic…while many others were affected in lesser degree by public doctrines about work deriving from it.

Essentially this is an argument for diversity; it suggests that there are, and always have been, numerous orientations to work and that the notion of a monolithic work ethic misrepresents this diversity. This does not preclude the possibility of changes in work values, but it rejects the view that a general shift has occurred. This emphasis on diversity is argued by Moorhouse, who stresses the importance of gender, class and ethnicity upon work values:

> The meanings of work are not likely to be neat and simple, or form some uncomplicated 'ethic', but are rather likely to be jumbled and variegated, so

that any individual has a whole range of types and levels of meanings on which to draw, and with which to understand or appreciate the labour they are doing at any particular moment.

(Moorhouse, 1987: 241)

We have considerable sympathy with this view, especially since one of our starting points is to demonstrate the plurality and subjectivity of work experiences. Often, people use 'work ethic' to mean a positive attitude to work, even though, as has been shown above, it reflects a number of things. Not all of these will be adhered to by those claiming to have a strong work ethic. Our analysis suggests it is probably a gross oversimplification to write and talk about a single work ethic because the term has a variety of meanings which can easily lead to confusion or ambiguity in interpretation – a type of problem we will also encounter in dealing with other concepts in the study of work, such as skill. However, when any of the themes associated with the 'traditional work ethic' are in evidence in contemporary society, we can use the plural 'work ethics' to show the importance of a moral dimension to employment beyond economic need.

CONCLUSION

Throughout, this chapter has been addressing a fundamental question: why work? The evidence indicates that economic need remains an important feature of work, but this does not explain the entire picture. The majority of people say that they would continue to work even if there was no economic compulsion to do so, which suggests that work may also be fulfilling other needs. Aside from earning money (an extrinsic need), people are likely to cite a variety of intrinsic needs that work helps to satisfy. Many of these reflect the moral dimension to work: for example, the search for achievement, creativity and fulfilment, or a sense of worth, purpose or duty. In other words, work is perceived as the proper sort of activity in which to be engaged, a message that is powerfully reinforced through a shared culture in capitalist societies, and most typically expressed as a work ethic. As has been noted, the work ethic concept has a variety of meanings, but in so far as it characterises a moral dimension to work, it remains an important feature of work orientations, and talk of its demise is premature.

Clearly, work provides an opportunity to socialise with people outside of the family and virtually all work involves interaction with other people – co-workers, managers, subordinates, customers, clients and/or the public. We can speculate, therefore, that work fulfils an important social need in people. As Jahoda (1982: 24) argues:

Outside the nuclear family it is employment that provides for most people this social context and demonstrates in daily experience that 'no man is an island, entire of itself': that the purposes of a collectivity transcend the purposes of an individual. Deprived of this daily demonstration, the unemployed suffer from lack of purpose, exclusion from the larger society and relative isolation.

This reality of work playing an important role in social identity continues to be evidence in studies where workers are interviewed. For example, Doherty (2009: 97) concludes from his case study evidence from the private and public sectors 'that work does still fulfil for people important personal and social needs and that the workplace remains an important locus of social relations'.

The research evidence suggests that people rarely express social factors as a reason for working:

- how time and skills can be socially constructed;
- how social interaction helps people to get through the working day;
- the social phenomenon of discrimination;
- the social dependency that drives some employees to seek collective representation;
- the social isolation that characterises some aspects of hidden work.

For most people work is a place to socialise, and complex social systems develop within the workplace which often spill over into leisure time. Moreover, whole communities may be socially linked through the workplace where there is a single major employer within a locality – for example, a manufacturing plant, a hospital, a large retail store or a call centre.

Similarly, organisations are often seeking to establish and reinforce their own corporate culture which encourages identity with the organisation through social interaction. In short, work is an important source of social interaction, but for the majority of people the meaning of work lies more in its economic and moral contribution to the human condition.

SCIENTIFIC MANAGEMENT AND FORDISM

CHAPTER AIM

To explain the dominant forms of work organisation and explore competing theories of skill change.

KEY CONCEPTS

- Taylorism
- Fordism
- deskilling
- labour process
- upskilling
- human capital
- offshoring
- flexible specialisation
- polarisation of skills
- compensatory theory of skill
- automating and informating
- range of work
- discretion in work
- work organisation paradigms

LEARNING OUTCOMES

After reading and understanding the material in this chapter you will be able to:

1 Describe the main features of Taylorism and assess their relevance to contemporary work.
2 Describe the methods and application of Fordism.
3 Explain the theory behind the deskilling thesis.
4 Outline and evaluate the main criticisms of the deskilling thesis.
5 Explain the theory behind the upskilling thesis.
6 Outline and evaluate the main criticisms of the upskilling thesis.
7 Describe alternative approaches to examining skill change.
8 Use the work categorisation framework to analyse jobs.
9 Explain the relationship between skill change and work organisation paradigms.

INTRODUCTION

This chapter addresses a puzzle that has occupied the minds of researchers and theorists for decades: whether the fundamental shifts that have been occurring in the nature of work are causing people to experience either deskilling and degrading, or upskilling and enrichment, in their working lives. We have previously noted some of the structural changes occurring in patterns of employment, but here we assess the impact of these broader employment dynamics by focusing on the nature of work tasks.

To explore these issues, the chapter is divided into five sections. The first examines two dominant traditions in work organisation – Taylorism and Fordism – using contemporary examples to illustrate the central principles of each. This provides the basis for the next three sections, each of which examines a different perspective on how work is changing: the deskilling thesis, the upskilling antithesis and the attempts to synthesise these contrasting approaches. The fifth section of the chapter develops a conceptual framework to integrate the analysis.

DOMINANT TRADITIONS OF WORK ORGANISATION – TAYLORISM AND FORDISM

Routine work in the service sector – burgers and Taylor

Imagine the scene: you are visiting a city for the first time. It is lunchtime and you are feeling hungry, you do not have much money to spend on food, and you only have 30 minutes before your train leaves. As you look along the busy, unfamiliar street you recognise a sign in the distance: a large yellow letter 'M'. A sense of relief overwhelms you as you head for the home of American pulp cuisine, McDonald's. Any uncertainty and anxiety has been replaced by the predictability of the McDonald's experience: no matter where you are, you will get the standard-tasting burger, covered with the same relish, lodged in the same bun, served in the same packaging for consumption in the familiar decor of the restaurant.

Consistency is McDonald's strong selling point – if you are one of the company's 50 million daily customers, you will know exactly what you are going to get when you order your Big Mac and large fries, in any one of McDonald's 31,000 outlets in 119 countries. Of course, to guarantee such a standardised product, the work processes as well as the food have all been standardised. So leaving aside the issue of the product itself, how can we characterise and understand work at organisations such as McDonald's?

If we use a metaphor, we can describe McDonald's as a well-maintained machine in almost every aspect of its operations, from the customer interface to the centralised planning and financial control (Morgan, 1986). Employees at McDonald's (or 'crew members' as they are called) are treated as components of this machine. Each receives simple training to perform a number of tasks, which require little judgement and leave limited room for discretion. Crew members are given precise instructions on what to say, what to do and how to do it. They are the necessary 'living' labour joining the precisely timed computer-controlled equipment that cooks the burgers, fries the potatoes, dispenses the drinks, heats the pies, records the order and calculates the customer's change:

> Much of the food prepared at McDonald's arrives at the restaurant pre-formed, pre-cut, pre-sliced and pre-prepared, often by non-human technologies. This

serves to drastically limit what employees need to do…. McDonald's has developed a variety of machines to control its employees. When a worker must decide when a glass is full and the soft-drink dispenser needs to be shut off, there is always the risk that the worker may be distracted and allow the glass to overflow. Thus a sensor has been developed that automatically shuts off the soft-drink dispenser when the glass is full.

(Ritzer, 1993: 105–6)

This logic of automation is extended to all the processes, with the consequence that the employees push buttons, respond to beeps and buzzers and repeat stock phrases to customers like subjects in a bizarre Pavlovian experiment. The dehumanising effects can often be seen in the glazed expressions of the young people who serve you. But the most poignant, if not ironic, aspect of all this is that one of the world's most successful multinational corporations at the beginning of the twenty-first century relies on labour management techniques that were developed at the beginning of the twentieth century. Indeed, the pioneer of 'scientific management', F. W. Taylor, would have certainly recognised and endorsed the principles upon which McDonald's is organised.

Exercise 15.1

McJobs are good for some people

Some young people are well suited to boring jobs. That was one of the conclusions reached by Gould (2010) in a study of McDonald's restaurants across Australia. In an interesting piece of research, Gould distributed a questionnaire to managers and crew members in 50 restaurants with the approval of the McDonald's corporation. Responses were received from 812 crew members and 102 managers (the total Australian McDonald's workforce is about 55,000, based in 733 outlets). The findings confirmed that the work is organised around Tayloristic principles: 'crew overwhelmingly perceive their duties as comprised of a limited range of non-complex tasks which, by implication, should be done in a prescribed way' (Gould, 2010: 799). However, Gould argues that this has less of a negative effect on employees than often assumed by McDonald's critics (e.g. Leidner 1993, Royle 2000 and Schlosser 2002). The benefits of working at McDonald's include job security, the possibility of a career and flexible working hours.

Most notable, Gould's survey data leads him to conclude that it is important to take a person-specific perspective on fast food work – so looking at individual differences to explain attitudes to the work. In particular, there seems to be an age-related effect:

Compared with their older peers, crew work may be more suitable and offer greater benefits to younger teenagers who mostly appear relatively content. As they get older, crew indicate that they find the work easier and more repetitive and, in these respects, less attractive. Such trends are statistically significant. Older crew are also more inclined to assert their rights at work, a tendency which may be less compatible with a fast-food work environment. (Gould, 2010: 797)

Gould concludes that those who are satisfied with working at McDonald's are not in the minority and have not been indoctrinated. They work there because they are not looking for a complex job and the flexibility suits their lifestyles.

1   What issues do Gould's findings raise about how we should consider routine jobs?
2   What else would you need to know in order to evaluate these findings thoroughly?

F. W. TAYLOR'S GUIDING PRINCIPLES

The ideas of Taylor have been well documented elsewhere (see, for example, Kelly, 1982; Littler, 1982; Rose, 1988), so it is only necessary here to restate the central principles to see how closely aligned the contemporary work processes at McDonald's are to concepts that were originally published in 1911. Efficiency was Taylor's guiding obsession. His own work experience as an engineer led him to believe there was an optimum way of performing any job: the 'one best way'. It was the task of management to discover this through the application of rigorous scientific testing, which involved breaking all activities down into their smallest components and systematically analysing each step. No activity was too complex or too mundane to be subjected to this scientific analysis, argued Taylor (see Extract 15.1).

Extract 15.1

Applying scientific management

Taylor illustrates his theory with the example of managing pig-iron handling and shovelling.

Probably the most important element in the science of shoveling is this: There must be some shovel load at which a first-class shoveler will do his biggest day's work. What is that load? ... Under scientific management the answer to this question is not a matter of anyone's opinion; it is a question for accurate, careful, scientific investigation. Under the old system you would call in a first-rate shoveler and say, 'See here, Pat, how much ought you to take on at one shovel load?' And if a couple of fellows agreed, you would say that's about the right load and let it go at that. But under scientific management absolutely every element in the work of every man in your establishment, sooner or later, becomes the subject of exact, precise, scientific investigation and knowledge to replace the old, 'I believe so,' and 'I guess so.' Every motion, every small fact becomes the subject of careful, scientific investigation.

(ibid: 51–2)

Now one of the very first requirements for a man who is fit to handle pig iron as a regular occupation is that he shall be so stupid and so phlegmatic that he more nearly resembles in his mental make-up the ox than any other type. The man who is mentally alert and intelligent is for this reason entirely unsuited to what would, for him, be the grinding monotony of work of this character. Therefore the workman who is best suited to handling pig iron is unable to understand the real science of doing this class of work. He is so stupid that the word 'percentage' has no meaning to him, and he must consequently be trained by a man more intelligent than himself into the habit of working in accordance with the laws of this science before he can be successful.

(Taylor, ibid: 59)

Having discovered the 'one best way' of performing a task, management's responsibility was to allocate tasks to employees, attempting to fit the right person to each job. The employee should have the requisite skills, acquired through systematic training, to complete the task at hand, and no more than those required by the job.

Emerging from Taylor's principles of organising the work process is a distinctive managerial ideology in which four themes dominate:

- *Division of labour*: this involves the separation of manual work (the doing) from mental work (the thinking). By removing from the employee any discretion over the organisation and execution of work, managers are able to secure control over the method and pace of working. As we shall see, this can have important consequences for determining the skill definition of a work activity.
- *Planning*: managers play an important role in planning each activity to ensure that it is in line with business objectives. In pursuit of these objectives, employees are to be used dispassionately, along with capital equipment and raw materials, in the search for greater efficiency, productivity and profitability. As a consequence, rigorous selection and training of people (to instil required behaviours) become a critical management function.
- *Surveillance*: based on the assumption that people cannot be trusted to perform their jobs diligently, there needs to be control through close supervision and monitoring of all work activities. Hierarchies of authority are constructed giving legitimacy to surveillance and simultaneously constructing a 'division of management' (Littler, 1982: 53).
- *Performance-related pay*: Taylor's deeply entrenched belief was that people were essentially instrumental, and so money could be used as a powerful motivator

providing it was linked directly to the productivity of the individual: a linkage achieved by piece-rate payment systems.

While the logic of Taylorism is impeccable, the conditions of work it produces are often dehumanising and bleak: a set of highly segmented work activities, with no opportunity for employees to use their discretion and a system of close supervision to monitor their work performance. However, the practice of Taylorism has not necessarily followed the theory as closely as its original protagonist would have wished, leading some commentators (notably Edwards, 1979; Palmer, 1975) to argue that Taylor's influence has been overstated because the practical impact of his ideas was limited – not least because of the collective resistance exerted by employees through trade unions.

Certainly, in Taylor's own lifetime the diffusion of the principles of scientific management was modest. Many managers remained unconvinced about the possibility of planning and measuring activities sufficiently accurately to enable the 'science' to work. There were also competing ideas about the nature of job design from the human relations movement (starting with the famous Hawthorne experiments in the 1920s) which brought out the importance of the social factors at work and challenged the economic assumptions underlying Taylor's theory of work design (Schein, 1965).

Notwithstanding these reservations, Taylor's ideas have made (and continue to make) a crucial impact on the thinking about job design and the division of labour. Indeed, as Littler (1982) argues, we must be cautious of assuming a linear progression of management theory where each set of ideas neatly supersedes the previous ones. The persistence of Taylorist principles in contemporary organisations is testimony to the resilience of Taylorism (e.g. see the discussions by Bain, Watson, Mulvey, Taylor and Gall, 2002; Jones, 2000; Nyland, 1995). Of particular importance is the way that service sector organisations such as McDonald's can use features of 'classic' Taylorism in a similar way to the manufacturing industry. Indeed, we might ask whether shovelling chips into a cardboard carton is the twenty-first century equivalent of shovelling pig iron into a furnace, which Taylor studied a century earlier.

The widespread effects of Tayloristic division of labour in the expanding service sector was noted by Ritzer (1993). He contends that McDonald's represents the archetypal rational organisation in search of four goals: efficiency, calculability, predictability and control. McDonald's is a contemporary symbol of a relentless process of rationalisation, where the employee is simply treated as a factor of production. Ritzer's thesis (rather pessimistically) is that both theoretically and empirically this constitutes a general process of 'McDonaldisation' which extends beyond work into the culture of society (Ritzer, 1998). His conclusion suggests there is an inevitable tendency towards a dehumanisation of work – a theme that echoes the work of the deskilling theorists, whose ideas are explored after considering a second key actor in the design of jobs in the twentieth century.

Exercise 15.2

What do you think?

Taylor was obsessed with finding the ultimate solution to the problem of organising work. He believed that by analysing and measuring work activities it was possible to find the optimum method of performing every task. In effect, he was suggesting that by careful, scientific, logical analysis, using his guiding principles, managers can find the best way of managing.

1 What is your opinion about Taylor's theory? What are your reasons for agreeing or disagreeing with him?
2 Why do some organisations follow his methods, whilst others reject them?
3 Consider your own work experiences. Would you describe the work as Tayloristic? If not, does it have elements that reflect Taylor's principles of work organisation?
4 Are some jobs impossible to Taylorise? Use examples to explain why/why not.

Routine work on the assembly line – chickens and Ford

If asked to visualise an assembly line, many people would probably have an image of a car plant, with a steady procession of partly finished vehicles passing groups of workers (or robots) who are rapidly attaching windscreens, wheels, spraying paint and so on. This has been the stereotypical image of assembly line work, not least because its innovative form was originally developed and exploited by the Ford Motor Company – an issue that we return to below.

Let us imagine a different contemporary work setting. You are in a massive room dominated by the sound of humming and churning machinery, though you can occasionally hear the voices of an all-women workforce. The room is cool and the air heavy with the smell of blood. Overhead, weaving around the factory is a conveyor from which hooks are suspended; hanging from each hook is the carcass of a dead bird. It is a chicken factory, made up of a variety of 'assembly lines' that convert live birds into the packets of meat displayed in supermarkets.

The work is Tayloristic in the sense it is segmented into simple, repetitive operations. For example, 'packing' involves four distinct tasks each performed by different employees: inserting the giblets (internal organs) and tucking the legs in, bagging the chicken, weighing it and securing the top of the bag. Not only are these and similar tasks around the factory simple and repetitive, but the pace of the work is also relentless. This is vividly portrayed by an employee carrying out 'inspection' in such a chicken factory, interviewed for a television programme, 'Dangerous Lives':

Employee: The line was coming round with about four and a half thousand birds an hour and you used to have to check the chickens for livers, hearts or anything, by putting your hand in the backside of a chicken, feeling around and then bringing anything out, dropping it in the bin, and then going on to the next. Used to be, sort of, every other chicken.

Interviewer: You were doing two chickens at a time?

Employee: Yes, both hands in chickens together. You hadn't got time to wipe your nose or do anything really.

Interviewer: Did that line ever stop?

Employee: Only if they had a breakdown, you know, a pin went in the line, or there was a breakdown or anything.

Interviewer: So you were doing over 2000 chickens an hour?

Employee: Yes.

Interviewer: 14,000 chickens a day?

Employee: Yes.

Interviewer: What did you think about that?

Employee: Hard work. Real hard work!

Similar experiences of unremitting 'hard work' have been found by researchers studying the harsh realities of factory life in different industries: for example, Pollert (1981) in the tobacco industry, Westwood (1984) in hosiery (legwear), Cavendish (1982) in motor components, Beynon (1973) and Linhart (1981) in cars and Delbridge (1998) in auto components and consumer electronics. The experiences of employees are explored in closer detail, but for now, the emphasis is on the work organisation principles which give rise to the assembly line.

Henry Ford's methods

The name most commonly associated with the development of the assembly line is Henry Ford. His unique contribution was in adapting Taylorist principles to a factory setting geared to the mass production of standardised products. Ford established a production method benchmark against which assembly line work has since been assessed, and the term 'Fordist' has come to be used to describe the combination of linear work sequencing, the interdependence of tasks, a moving assembly line, the use and refinement of dedicated machinery and specialised machine tools (for a detailed discussion, see Meyer, 1981). It has been argued that Fordism is distinguishable from Taylorism because it is a form of work organisation specifically designed for efficient mass production (Wood, 1989).

The success of Ford as mass *production* can only be fully appreciated if seen as part of a system of industrial organisation that also sought to create, perpetuate and satisfy mass *consumption*. The development of mass markets provided the demand for large numbers of rapidly produced standardised products. This was shown best by the output at the Highland Park factory which rose from 13,941 Model-T Fords in 1909 to 585,400 by 1916 (Williams, Haslam and Williams, 1992: 550). This volume of mass production was only possible because of the development of capital equipment capable of producing on a large scale, and the creation of an efficient electricity supply to drive the machinery. In other words, mass production, mass consumption, technological innovation and segmented work organisation were ingredients in Ford's recipe for success. Consequently, as Littler (1985) has argued, Fordism came to be the preferred form of organising work for mass production. It was adopted by Ford's main competitor in the United States, General Motors, and then by Ford's European rivals – Austin, Morris and Citroen. Fordism also transferred to other, newer industries such as electrical engineering and chemicals.

A widely accepted view is that Fordism is synonymous with mass production, rigidity and standardisation, and that the impact of the ideas pioneered by Ford has been widespread. However, there are some voices of dissent. Williams and colleagues (1987, 1992) argue that Fordism has become a stereotype, distorted over time by British and US academics who are keen to attribute failing industrial performance to the persistence of an outdated form of production. In a detailed analysis of Ford's production operations at Highland Park (1909–19), Williams et al (1992) reveal a picture of greater flexibility and less standardisation of the product than most texts on the subject would suggest. Overall, however, such findings do little to dispel the picture of an authoritarian work regime with closely monitored, machine-paced, short-cycle and unremitting tasks.

As the chicken factory example illustrates, Fordist principles persist in contemporary work settings, and these are not restricted to factory work. One can argue that his assembly line can be found in other work settings (see Extract 15.2). McDonald's shows Fordist elements in terms of its mass production of standardised products for mass consumption. Similarly, the supermarket in general, and checkout operations in particular, embody a Fordist approach to retailing: the customer's items pass along the conveyor and are swept across the barcode reader by an operator who carries out a series of repetitive actions. The flow-line, the dedicated machinery and the segmented work tasks are evidence of Fordist principles of work organisation. Similarly the chicken, as an object for consumption, is typically reared through (Ford-like) battery farming, slaughtered and processed in a Fordist factory, and sold through a Fordist retail outlet (the supermarket) or even consumed as chicken pieces in a Fordist restaurant.

Extract 15.2

The white-collar assembly line?

Researchers undertaking an extensive study of call centres in Scotland have come to the conclusion that although not all call centres are identical, the majority of them can justifiably be seen as 'white-collar factories' because employees are subjected to Tayloristic management techniques and the type of routinised, repetitive work normally associated with the assembly line (Taylor and Bain, 1999; Taylor, Hyman, Mulvey and Bain, 2002). The following is a quote from their study:

> The typical call centre operator is young, female and works in a large, open plan office or fabricated building.... Although, probably full-time, she is increasingly likely to be a part-time permanent employee, working complex shift patterns which correspond to the peaks of customer demand. Promotion prospects and career advancement are limited so that the attraction of better pay and conditions in another call centre may prove irresistible. In all probability, work consists of an uninterrupted and endless sequence of similar conversations with customers she never meets. She has to concentrate hard on what is being said, jump from page to page on a screen, making sure that the details entered are accurate and that she has said the right things in a pleasant manner. The conversation ends and as she tidies up the loose ends there is another voice in her headset. The pressure is intense because she knows her work is being measured, her speech monitored, and it often leaves her mentally, physically and emotionally exhausted.... There is no question that the integration of telephone and computer technologies, which defines the call centre, has produced new developments in the Taylorisation of white-collar work.

> (Taylor and Bain, 1999: 115)

An alternative perspective is taken by Korczynski, Shire, Frenkel and Tam (1996) in their detailed analysis of three call centres (two in Australia and one in Japan). They argue that while the customer service representatives have routine aspects to their work, it is misleading to equate their jobs with the sort of routine work typically found in factories. This is because service work relies on the extensive use of social skills when dealing with customers, which can provide a source of creativity for employees. In short, they are cautious not to equate service work with routinisation or deskilling, yet also suggest that there is little evidence of substantial upskilling taking place, even though there were some opportunities for it to occur in their case study companies.

TO SUM UP

The significance of Taylor, Ford and mass production for the way work has been organised is profound. These principles and methods changed the work process by introducing greater amounts of rigidity and regulation, which in turn had important consequences for the skill content of jobs. In particular, this raises the question of whether work, in general, is becoming less or more skilled. The evaluation of the different attempts to answer this question begins with the deskilling thesis.

THESIS – THE DESKILLING OF WORK

The year 1974 saw the publication of one of the most influential books concerned with the study of work: Braverman's *Labor and Monopoly Capital*. Braverman's thesis is that there is an inevitable tendency towards degradation and deskilling of work as capitalists search for profits in increasingly competitive economic environments. His contribution to the study of work must not be underestimated. Although his thesis has since been subjected to a great deal of criticism, in the 1970s, it injected adrenaline into the tired discipline of industrial sociology, and it continues to have an impact on how work is analysed. Indeed the book was republished in 1998. The discussion below explains the central argument of this 'deskilling thesis' and identifies the main criticisms.

Braverman's argument

At the risk of oversimplifying, Braverman's argument is this. Managers perpetually seek to control the process by which a workforce's labour power (its ability to work) is directed towards the production of commodities (goods and services) that can be sold for a profit. The control of this labour process is essential because profit is accumulated through two stages: first, through the extraction of the surplus value of labour (the price of a commodity has to be greater than the costs incurred in its production); and second, through the realisation of that value when the commodities are actually sold. These two stages are frequently referred to as 'valorisation' (a process where value is realised). In other words, managers seek to control the way work is organised, the pace of work and the duration of work, because these affect profitability. Control of labour is the link between the purchase of labour power and valorisation. In Braverman's analysis the managerial obsession with labour control is the key to understanding capitalism, and it leads managers to seek ways of reducing the discretion exercised by the workforce in performing their jobs. In order to exert their own control over the workforce and limit the control and influence of employees, managers pursue a general strategy of deskilling which, according to Braverman, can be identified in two forms: organisational and technological.

Organisational deskilling

Organisational deskilling is embedded in the Tayloristic principle of the separation of the conception and execution of work. The conceptual tasks (the more challenging and interesting parts of the job, such as planning, diagnosing problems and developing new working methods) are transferred to technical and managerial staff, while the execution of the work (often the mundane, less-challenging part of the job) remains in the hands of shopfloor workers. Theoretically, this process allows managers to limit the discretion of the shopfloor workers and to secure a monopoly over technical knowledge about the work. This can be used to exercise greater direct control over the activities of the workforce:

> A necessary consequence of the separation of conception and execution is that the labor process is now divided between separate sites and separate bodies of workers. In one location, the physical processes of production are executed. In another are concentrated the design, planning, calculation and record-keeping.... The physical processes of production are now carried out more or less blindly, not only by the workers who perform them, but often by lower ranks of supervisory employees as well. The production units operate like a hand, watched, corrected, and controlled by a distant brain.
>
> (Braverman, 1974: 124–5)

Technological deskilling

Technological deskilling occurs when automation is used to transfer discretion and autonomy from the shopfloor to the office (from blue-collar to white-collar workers) and to eliminate the need for some direct labour. Braverman focuses on the example of the operation of machines by numerical control (NC) – the latest technology at the time he was writing and before the invention of the microchip – which allowed the planning and programming of the machines to be undertaken away from the shopfloor by technical staff, who prepared punched paper tapes that contained the information for the machine to run automatically. Prior to NC, the machinists would use their own judgement and discretion to set and operate the machines, but they were subsequently left only with the relatively simple tasks of loading and switching the machines. In other words, a technological development (NC – and then later on computer numerical control) allowed the separation of task conception from task execution. This sort of new technology does not inevitably lead to a deskilling of work, but Braverman argues that managers selectively use automation to this end, in order to secure their central objective of exerting control over labour. He writes:

> In reality, machinery embraces a host of possibilities, many of which are systematically thwarted, rather than developed, by capital. An automatic system of machinery opens up the possibility of the true control over a highly productive factory by a relatively small corps of workers, providing these workers attain the level of mastery over the machinery offered by engineering knowledge, and providing they then share out among themselves the routines of the operation, from the most technically advanced to the most routine…. [But such a possibility] is frustrated by the capitalist effort to reconstitute and even deepen the division of labor in all its worst aspects, despite the fact that this division of labor becomes more archaic with every passing day…. The 'progress' of capitalism seems only to deepen the gulf between workers and machine and to subordinate the worker ever more decisively to the yoke of the machine…. The chief advantage of the industrial assembly-line is the control it affords over the pace of labor, and as such it is supremely useful to owners and managers whose interests are at loggerheads with those of their workers.
>
> (Braverman, 1974: 230–2)

There have been plenty of writers willing to comment on Braverman's work. McLoughlin and Clark (1994) divide these into 'sympathisers' and 'agnostics' (see Table 15.1). If you want to explore the issues in more detail, a good starting point is Thompson (1989) followed by the chapters in the edited collection by Knights and Willmott (1990). There is also a thorough and persuasive defence of the value of Braverman's thesis by Tinker (2002), who particularly takes to task the more recent postmodern criticisms of Braverman's analysis of the labour process (e.g. O'Doherty and Willmott, 2001). The main criticisms of and revisions to Braverman's thesis are summarised in the next section, but before reading this, attempt Exercise 15.3.

Exercise 15.3

What do you think?

Interview someone who has been employed in the same organisation for about ten years and ask them about the changes they have experienced. The interview need not be long, but you should structure it in such a way to ensure that you find out about the type of changes introduced and the effect they have had on work.

   You must then use this information to assess whether this helps to substantiate or refute Braverman's deskilling thesis and produce a written or verbal report. Remember there were two components to Braverman's argument, organisational deskilling and technological deskilling, so your interview should be designed in such a way as to elicit information on both these aspects of change. Your report should make explicit reference to these.

Six common criticisms of the deskilling thesis

Criticism 1: the deskilling thesis ignores alternative management strategies

Friedman (1977a, 1977b, 1990) argues that it is false to assume a single trend towards deskilling, since this fails to acknowledge the occasions when it is in the interest of managers to leave some discretion in the hands of employees. He calls this a strategy of 'responsible autonomy' and contrasts it with the 'direct control' which Braverman described. Friedman had in mind job enrichment and quality circles,

Table 15.1 – The key critics of Braverman's thesis

Sympathisers Accept the general approach but offer some refinement	Agnostics Acknowledge some value in the approach, but consider it inadequate
Friedman, 1977a,b, 1990	Littler, 1982
Burawoy, 1979	Wood, 1982
Edwards, 1979	Littler and Salaman, 1982
Zimbalist, 1979	Knights, Willmott and Collinson, 1985
Armstrong, 1988	Knights and Willmott, 1986, 1990
Rose, 1988	Watson, 1986
Thompson, 1989	

Source: Based on McLoughlin and Clark (1994).

but a contemporary expression of responsible autonomy is the notion of 'empowerment', whereby individual employees are expected to take responsibility for their own actions and initiate improvements in the way they work for the benefit of the organisation as a whole. Under responsible autonomy, employees are not deskilled but management continue to control the labour process. Thus, the argument here is that there is a wider choice in the mechanisms employed by management for the accumulation of capital than Braverman suggests.

Criticism 2: the deskilling thesis overstates management's objective of controlling labour

The control of the labour process is not an end in itself, but a means to achieve profit. To concentrate solely on labour control objectives ignores the importance of valorisation:

> It is not simply the *extraction* of surplus value in the labour process which is problematic for capital, but the *realisation* of that surplus through the sale of commodities in markets…. In other words we need to consider the *full circuit* of industrial capital as the starting point for analyses of changes in the division of labour: purchase of labour power; extraction of surplus value within the labour process; realisation of surplus value within product markets. There is no sound theoretical reason for privileging one moment in this circuit – the labour-capital relation within the labour process – if our objective is to account for changes (or variations) in the division of labour.
>
> (Kelly, 1985: 32, emphasis in original)

Moreover, the assumption that labour issues (rather than, for example, product development, marketing or investment) are the central concern of management during strategy formation is highly questionable (Purcell, 1989, 1995). Thus, as Littler and Salaman (1982: 257) contend, the process of capital accumulation acts beyond the labour process:

> The firm is primarily a capital fund with a legal corporate personality, linked to a production process…. While the production process results in a flow of income to the firm, this does not preclude alternative sources playing a major role or even a predominant one e.g. currency speculation, cumulative

acquisition and asset stripping, commodity speculation, and credit manipulation of various kinds.

Child (1972, 1984, 1985) has highlighted the importance of political manoeuvring by managers in an organisation who, as key decision makers, are making 'strategic choices' that reflect their own values and vested interests. The argument here is that internal politics have a greater impact on deciding how work is organised, and on skill requirements, than Braverman implies. The logic of capitalist accumulation may remain the overarching tendency, but this can be mitigated by managers at all levels who are defending their vested interests.

As a consequence, the criticism is that Braverman's thesis underestimates the diversity and complexity of management objectives. The assumption that there is a single shared objective by management – that of labour control – ignores the plurality of interests within management and the diverse, and sometimes competing, objectives (Batstone, Gourlay, Levie and Moore, 1987; Buchanan, 1986; Buchanan and Boddy, 1983; Child, 1985). For example, in research into technological change in the UK provincial newspaper industry undertaken by one of the authors (Noon, 1994), it was found that when managers were questioned about the objectives for introducing new technology, they stressed different reasons which seemed to reflect their own functional responsibilities. In other words, the objective of increased control over labour was not the primary focus for most managers. Instead, they said technological change provided new opportunities in terms of product quality, product development, production control, efficiency and flexibility, together with a reduction in labour cost. This suggests that while labour control objectives may be relevant, they must be placed within the context of broader business objectives. As Armstrong (1989, 1995) argues, the pervasive influence of management accountants at board level in UK companies tends to lead to more strategic thinking based on financial concerns rather than human resource matters.

Criticism 3: the deskilling thesis treats labour as passive

Employees have not been very compliant and have resisted change towards deskilling through both trade union collective action and individual action. Indeed, Edwards (1979) argues that management has sought more sophisticated forms of control as a direct response to (and as a way to suppress) worker resistance. He argues there has been a shifting reliance from the 'simple control' typified by the methods of direct supervision that Taylor advocated, to the 'technical control' of the mechanised assembly line (and more recent developments in computer technology) and the 'bureaucratic control' of workplace rules, procedures and a regulated internal labour market.

Criticism 4: the deskilling thesis understates the degree of consent and accommodation by employees

The work of Burawoy (1979) stands as an important counterpoint to Braverman in that it explores the extent to which the workforce consents to its own subordination. In part, this contrasts also with the previous criticism because it suggests that, rather than challenging management control of the labour process, the workforce may develop an informal culture that offers alternative definitions of the work situation and provides the opportunity for meaningful activity. The labour process is thereby redefined as a type of game through which the employees can derive satisfaction (e.g. by beating the clock, outwitting the supervisor or manipulating the rules). These games act as powerful means of social regulation (self-control) among the work groups and obscure the exploitative nature of the labour process. In so doing, they unwittingly provide alternative additional sources of control for management. Such a brief summary hardly does justice to the subtleties of Burawoy's work

Criticism 5: the deskilling thesis ignores gender

Beechey (1982) has argued that several problems emerge from the gender-blind nature of Braverman's argument. First, he fails to appreciate the importance of women's distinct role as domestic labourers because of his 'conceptual isolation of the family from the labour process and of both the family and the labour process from an analysis of the capitalist mode of production as a whole' (Beechey, 1982: 71). Second, his discussion of the pre-industrial family can be criticised for romanticising the past and ignoring the existence of patriarchal structures. Third, his concept of skill fails to explore gender dimensions, where it was noted that the social construction of skill is particularly important in creating 'gendered jobs', resulting in the undervaluation of women's labour power and skills.

Criticism 6: the deskilling thesis overlooks skill transfer possibilities

The failure of Braverman to recognise that deskilling in one area of work may be compensated by upskilling in another is most forcefully argued by Penn (1983, 1990), whose ideas are examined in some detail later. However, it might be argued that this constitutes one of the most unfair criticisms of Braverman. As Armstrong (1988) points out, Braverman explicitly recognised that change would occur unevenly across industries, and that in some instances new skills and technical specialities might be temporarily created within the workforce.

A defence of Braverman's thesis

A persuasive defence of Braverman comes from Armstrong, who argues that:

> any sensitive reading of his work should reveal that Braverman actually regarded the deskilling tendencies of technical change as a system-wide dynamic or 'law of motion' in capitalist economies which could, temporarily and locally, be interrupted or reversed by a variety of factors, many of which have been rediscovered by his critics as supposed refutations.
>
> (Armstrong, 1988: 157)

This is an important point because, like all meta-theory (i.e. theory about theory), Braverman's thesis will never be able to explain all contingencies, yet this does not necessarily mean its analytical insight is worthless. Indeed, as Armstrong suggests, many of the 'critics' are in practice offering revisions and amendments to the theory, rather than rejecting it.

Another defender of Braverman, Spencer (2000), suggests that the constant revisions and modifications to Braverman's original ideas by subsequent labour process theorists (academic commentators and researchers) show they have lost sight of the subversive intent of Braverman's original text and have become obsessed with the social relations of the workplace, rather than the broader critique of capitalism. In short, Spencer laments the way that Braverman's ideas have been brought into the mainstream, and now run the risk of aiding rather than tormenting capitalism.

Braverman has also been defended against the attacks from academics of a post-modern leaning by Tinker (2002), who suggests that such attacks are deficient for a host of reasons, which he elaborates in detail. One of his main arguments is that the political aims and impact of Braverman's work are under-appreciated (not least the wide reading of the text by non-academics), and that postmodernist analysis:

> is blind to the social and historical specificity of Braverman's political task; exposing 'skill upgrading via education' as an ideology that obfuscates economic decline, recession and deindustrialization.
>
> (Tinker, 2002: 251)

He is also scathing about the philosophical position of postmodernists, which leaves them resorting to philosophies of indecision and able to offer only frivolous, condescending and politically timorous advice to working people (ibid: 273). In contrast, for Tinker, the abiding value of Braverman's analysis is that 'It debunks academic dogmas of management, popular nostrums about skill upgrading via education, and the tacit promises to restore a "golden past" (ibid: 274).

While some commentators (e.g. Lewis, 1995) remain unconvinced by defenders of Braverman, a re-reading of the original text reveals that Braverman had a less deterministic approach than is frequently attributed to him. Therefore, the deskilling thesis needs to be seen as an overall tendency, rather than a universal law applying in all cases:

> Braverman does *not* propound a universal law of deskilling. What he *does* claim is that there exists a general tendency for deskilling to occur in capitalist economies which will become actual where products and processes make this possible and where its effects are not masked by initiatives aimed at changing technology for other reasons.
>
> (Armstrong, 1988: 147, emphasis in original)

If Braverman's thesis is to be countered, it should be challenged on comparable terms: rather than a tendency towards deskilling, there is an opposite trend towards upskilling occurring within capitalist economies. It is to this antithesis that the discussion now turns.

ANTITHESIS – THE UPSKILLING OF WORK

Whereas the deskilling thesis drew from Marxist economic theory and the crisis of capitalism in industrial societies, the upskilling thesis tends to be based on the economics of human capital theory concerning a supposedly new stage of capitalism: the post-industrial society. Human capital theorists (Becker, 1964; Fuchs, 1968) suggest that, increasingly, firms are investing in their workforces through greater training provision, thus shifting the emphasis to 'human capital' as a central means of accumulating profit. One argument for this is that rapid advances in technology require a more educated, better-trained workforce in order to cope with the increasing complexity of work tasks (Blauner, 1964; Kerr, Dunlop, Harbison and Myers, 1960). In turn, this is linked to an ever-reducing demand for manual/physical labour as Western capitalist economies undergo a structural shift away from manufacturing towards service sector activities (Fuchs, 1968).

This shift in the economic base of advanced industrial societies is considered by commentators such as Daniel Bell to signal a fundamental transformation to the post-industrial society, in which theoretical knowledge becomes 'the axis around which new technology, economic growth and the stratification of society will be organized' (Bell, 1973: 112). In other words, the upskilling thesis suggests that the general tendency is towards more complex work requiring higher levels of skill. As a consequence, the shift in the pattern of work organisation will not be towards degradation (as Braverman suggested) but to an enrichment of work. Extract 15.3 provides survey evidence about upskilling patterns in Europe.

The upskilling thesis found expression in Piore and Sabel's (1984) concept of 'flexible specialisation'. They argue that the crisis of accumulation under capitalism is leading to an important shift away from Fordism towards more craft-based, flexible, innovation-led and customer-focused work organisation. So, just as the move from traditional craft production to mass production was 'the first industrial divide', the move from mass production to flexible specialisation is described by Piore and Sabel as 'the second industrial divide'.

The new emphasis is on flexible production systems, which can meet the demands for customised products in increasingly diversified markets. In particular, developments in microelectronic technology allow for more flexibility in the use of capital equipment: machinery no longer needs to be dedicated to specific tasks but can be reprogrammed to perform a variety of tasks. Traditional production methods typically involve long set-up times for the machinery, which mean large production runs are necessary to recover the cost; short production runs for small batches are an inefficient use of the equipment. In contrast, computerised machinery requires shorter set-up times, enabling greater diversity of (small batch) production without incurring the inefficiencies. In other words, economies of scale now have to be considered alongside economies of scope. This is important because customers are supposed to be increasingly discerning and wanting a greater variety of goods which allow them to express their individual identity (Sabel, 1982). Economies of scope become a necessity in a dynamic, competitive market where customers want variety and choice. Computerised production and information-processing capabilities provide the technological infrastructure and (according to the upskilling thesis) bring a demand for highly qualified rather than deskilled labour.

Coupled with this are changes in work organisation that mean employees are expected to work in different ways. Principal among these is teamworking, which is seen as a move away from the individualised, segmented work processes to flexible teams of employees who are multiskilled and take greater responsibility for their work through increased task discretion (control over the work methods, time and quality). It is argued that working in this fashion requires employees to develop and use a wide range of skills. In particular this has been associated with various supposedly post-Fordist production techniques in manufacturing, such as lean production (Womack, Jones and Roos, 1990) and business process re-engineering (Hammer and Champy, 1993).

Extract 15.3

Skill change in Europe

Gallie (2005) assessed the impact of skill change in 15 EU countries by analysing the results of two surveys of employees – one conducted in 1996, the other in 2001. Skill change was measured by asking people whether or not their jobs have become more skilled, evaluating the amount of training received, and assessing the extent to which employees considered they had control over their work (the first two are measures of complexity, the third is a measure of discretion).

Among Gallie's findings are the following:

○ The dominant trend is upskilling.
○ The pace of upskilling slowed down after the mid-1990s.
○ Women are less likely than men to have experienced increases in skill.

○ The decline in the pace of upskilling has affected women and men in similar ways.

○ The reduction in the pace of upskilling is evident in 12 of the 15 countries in Europe surveyed.

○ The decline in the pace of upskilling is statistically significant only in Finland, Germany, Great Britain, Greece, Ireland, the Netherlands and Spain.

One particular aspect of skill that showed clear evidence of decline was job control (the measure of discretion). Employees were asked questions about whether they have a say in what happens in their jobs. Gallie found the following:

○ There is a significant decline in job control between the two periods.

○ Women were typically in jobs with lower opportunities for control than men in both 1996 and 2001, but the decline in job control was similar for both sexes.

○ Job control scores declined in nine of the 15 countries, although the trend reached statistical significance in only seven countries: Belgium, France, Great Britain, Italy, the Netherlands, Spain and Sweden.

○ Only in Denmark was there evidence of an increase in control over jobs.

Source: Summarised from Gallie (2005).

Five criticisms of the upskilling thesis

Criticism 1: the upskilling thesis falsely assumes that the growth of the service sector will create skilled jobs

The growth of the service sector and the increasing importance of considering the customer can give the impression that all white-collar workers are now engaged with handling customer interactions, and that the traditional routinised factory work associated with manufacturing has given way to more varied, expressive forms of work involving customer interaction. It is certainly the case that customer-facing work involves the use of skills that require the management of emotions, but much of the new service work is as monotonous and dull as work on an assembly line.

Korczynski (2004) analysed the work of back-office staff in an insurance company and two banks in Australia. He found that work tended to be routinised with little scope for discretion in how the tasks were performed (particularly in the case of the insurance company). This was reinforced through performance-monitoring systems which set targets (e.g. processing a set number of applications per day) and measured work quality. There was no customer interaction, staff were not required to have (or learn) customer-oriented skills, and on a day-to-day basis they referred to customers in an impersonal way. Echoing the findings of earlier case studies (Crompton and Jones, 1984; Sturdy, 1992), the conclusion Korczynski drew is that back-office work in financial services resembles the formalised, routinised and regulated processes consistent with traditional bureaucratic forms of work organisation. This makes back-office, service work very similar to Fordist production work.

Front-line service work – where the majority of the working day involves dealing with customers either face to face or over the phone – tends to be organised in ways that are slightly less rigid, because of the variation in customer interaction requiring social skills and elements of emotional labour. Even so, front-line service employees are typically faced with a huge amount of routine and repetitive activity. (See Extract 15.2 for two perspectives on call centre workers.) Korczynski (2002) uses the term 'customer-oriented bureaucracy' to suggest that the essential features of bureaucracy are present (e.g. hierarchies, rules and procedures) but that the customer is cared for in the process:

> The concept of the customer-oriented bureaucracy captures the requirement
> for the organisation to be both formally rational, to respond to competitive

> pressures to appeal to customers' wishes for efficiency, and to be formally irrational, to enchant, responding to the customers' desire for pleasure, particularly through the perpetuation of the enchanting myth of customer sovereignty [the myth that the customer is 'King' or always right].
>
> (Korczynski, 2002: 64)

This means employees have to work within clearly defined rules and follow procedures and protocols, while ensuring that customers feel satisfied about the service they are receiving and gain the impression that they are in control (the myth of customer sovereignty). This may require employees to use a range of skills to manage their own emotions and those of the customers.

Criticism 2: the upskilling thesis overstates the extent to which advanced technology requires higher skill levels

The upskilling thesis is as vulnerable as the deskilling thesis to the criticism that there are numerous managerial objectives which reflect vested interests and politics – so the design of work will be based on these just as much as 'technical' decisions about skill requirements. In the 1980s, research revealed that managers could choose to implement technology in different ways that have variable skill consequences for employees. In their study of United Biscuits, Buchanan and Boddy (1983) show that even within one company there can be a mixture of skill changes associated with the introduction of advanced technology which makes any generalisation about upskilling or deskilling difficult to substantiate. Similarly, Sorge, Hartman, Warner and Nicholas (1983) reveal how computer numerical control (CNC) technology was used by British managers to deskill shopfloor workers and turn them into mere machine minders. In contrast, in Germany, the same technology was implemented in such a way as to integrate the (skilled) programming into the work of the operators, and in doing so enhancing their skill (also relevant here is Zuboff's (1988) dual impact theory of technology, which is discussed later in this chapter).

Criticism 3: the upskilling thesis overstates the extent of change

Generally, theorists who support the upskilling thesis, and those who support flexible specialisation in particular, assume a radical break with Fordism is taking place. However, this understates the resilience of mass production for mass markets. For example, the almost insatiable demand for consumer electronics has typically been met by the supply of goods manufactured using production systems that are labour intensive and low skilled (see, for example, Delbridge, Turnbull and Wilkinson, 1992; Sewell and Wilkinson, 1992a). Similarly, the flexible specialisation thesis overstates the extent to which small batch production will create upskilled and multiskilled workers. As Pollert (1991) and Smith (1989) point out, small batch production can and has adopted low-skilled, short-cycle assembly line techniques. So the criticism here is that the upskilling thesis relies on a false dichotomy between mass and craft production (see, for example, Hyman, 1991; Williams, Cutler, Williams and Haslam, 1987; Wood, 1989).

Criticism 4: the upskilling thesis overstates the skill-enhancing impact of new working methods

Employees have not experienced an enhancement of their skills through teamworking to the extent that the upskilling thesis suggests. In an analysis of survey data covering the period from 1996 to 2001, Gallie, Felstead and Green (2004) found that teamworking in the UK was on the increase, but this was accompanied by a decline in task discretion (measured by asking people how much influence they had over how hard they worked, what tasks they did, how they did the tasks and quality standards). This means that although an increasing proportion of the workforce is working in teams, these are not the semi-autonomous teams envisaged by the upskilling thesis.

A survey of ten European countries (Benders, Huijen and Pekruhl, 2001) revealed that forms of team or group working existed in 24 per cent of the workplaces. However, in the majority of these only a minority of core employees were covered, or else the groups had a very restricted range of decision-making rights (mainly concerning the regulation of day-to-day tasks, such as scheduling the work and improving the work processes). Issues such as controlling absence or organising job rotation were least likely to be delegated, and in only 4 per cent of organisations were the majority of core workers in what might be described as semi-autonomous teams. There was also notable variation between countries, with organisations in Sweden and the Netherlands being the most likely to have work groups and also the most likely to have groups who possessed real decision-making authority. Italy and Ireland were the countries with organisations least likely to have adopted group working. The authors of this European survey purposely used the term 'group working' rather than 'teamworking', because they argue it more accurately captures the range of forms or working arrangements – only some of which require upskilling.

Other studies confirm that the term 'teamworking' can mean a variety of things (Procter and Mueller, 2000). In the case of service sector work, it has been shown that 'team' often signifies nothing more than a group of workers who share one supervisor (Frenkel, Korczynski, Shire and Tam, 1999); as such, teamworking cannot be equated with upskilling.

Case studies can be useful in revealing how changes, such as increased flexibility and teamworking, do not result in enhancing skills so much as increase the volume of work at the same skill level. For example, commenting on the impact of multiskilling in a case study of a bank, Grimshaw, Beynon, Rubery and Ward (2002: 105) note that 'multi-skilling was introduced with limited employee discretion over how to vary and control and the timing and division of tasks…. Expansion in the range of job content was associated with increased pressure and a strong loss of autonomy'. Equally, in their case study of a telecommunications call centre these authors found that team-working did not involve multiskilling or job rotation but was a form of teambuilding based on social activities during work time, representing an attempt by managers to break the monotony of the routinised work of employees.

Criticism 5: the upskilling thesis needs to be put into a global perspective

With the rise of the multinational organisation, it is no longer sufficient to consider change simply in a national context. The reduction in demand for low-skilled work in one country might be accompanied by increased demand in another country. As a result, it becomes problematic to try to interpret a fall in the demand for low-skilled labour in one national context as a sign of general upskilling. It may indicate a global redistribution of demand for skills, reflecting the mobility of capital in the search for lower labour costs and the pursuit of greater profitability.

A good illustration of this point is the tendency for large organisations in advanced capitalist economies to outsource parts of their customer services and back-office data processing to countries where labour is considerably cheaper. Typically, Australian companies are outsourcing to India and Indonesia, UK companies to India, US companies to the Philippines and Costa Rica and French companies to Morocco. This process, known as 'offshoring', means that when customers make an inquiry to their bank, insurance company, phone company or rail network they are likely to find themselves talking to an employee in a call centre in another country. Service sector organisations can now use information and communication technology (allowing real-time interaction with customers) to relocate parts of their operation anywhere that can provide an equivalent but cheaper service. In addition to voice services, paper-based operations (e.g. customer complaints, application forms, financial transactions) can take place in remote locations without it affecting the quality of service. This global shift in the location of customer service work means that skill increase in one location may be matched with a decline in other locations, as organisations find new means of sustaining and accumulating profit – and, of course, this is not at all surprising to supporters of the deskilling thesis.

Extract 15.4

Cyber coolies in India?

A research institute funded by the Indian government has produced a damning report on the working conditions inside call centres. It has labelled the educated, intelligent graduates who work there as 'cyber coolies', and claims that they are wasting their talents on undertaking mindless, repetitive work for Western organisations.

According to *The Observer* newspaper, the study claims that the call centre workers are employed under constant surveillance, in an atmosphere similar to that in 'nineteenth century prisons or Roman slave ships'. Despite the relatively high salaries, and modern working environments, the study concludes that 'most of these youngsters are in fact burning out their formative years as cyber coolies' doing low-end jobs.

The true monotony of the work is disguised by 'camouflaging work as fun' – introducing cafes, popcorn booths and ping-pong tables into the offices. Meanwhile, quotas for calls or emails successfully attended to are often fixed at such a high level 'that the agent has to burn out to fulfil it', the report claims.

With employees working through the night to cater for clients in different time zones, the work requires staff 'to live as Indian by day and Westerner after sundown' and takes a 'heavy toll' on agents' physical and mental health, the study states. But more importantly, call centre work 'leads to a wastage of human resources and de-skilling of workers' which will have a high impact on Indian industry in the long-term.

Source: The Observer (2005) 'Painful truth of the call centre cyber coolies', 30 October.

Exercise 15.4

What do you think?

Consider criticism number 5 of the upskilling thesis and read Extract 15.5.

1 What limitations might there be to offshoring that could mean some skilled jobs in the service sector could not be transferred to places such as India?
2 To what extent is technology playing a role in the offshoring process?
3 Have the so-called cyber coolies been upskilled or deskilled by the offshoring? Explain your reasoning.
4 Who are the winners and losers in the case of offshoring to India?

TO SUM UP

The upskilling thesis is as ambitious as the deskilling thesis in attempting to arrive at a theoretical framework that reflects a general tendency of skill change. However, in both cases the unidirectional argument needs to be qualified, as the various criticisms have shown. It is highly problematic to answer whether the dynamics of skill change can be simplified in such a way. A more robust theoretical approach might be to hypothesise multidirectional change within different sectors, industries, occupations and tasks. Three approaches which address such a synthesis are examined in the next section.

SYNTHESES – POLARISATION, COMPENSATION AND THE DUAL IMPACT OF AUTOMATING AND INFORMATING

There have been various attempts to synthesise the perspectives of deskilling and upskilling by arguing that both are occurring, with some people being upskilled while others are deskilled. This section reviews three different approaches to explain how and why this might occur: polarisation, compensation and the dual impact of technology. There is some common ground between the three approaches, and they should not be seen as competing theories but rather as complementary explanations of the effects of upskilling and deskilling.

The polarisation of skills

The polarisation of skills perspective argues that different segments of the workforce will be affected in different ways. For instance, higher occupational groups such as professionals and managers might see their skill levels increase, while those lower in the occupational hierarchy, such as operatives, might experience a diminution in skill. Similarly, those workers on permanent, full-time contracts might be upskilled while their co-workers on part-time or fixed-term contracts (and other non-standard arrangements) might find they are given fewer opportunities to increase their skill levels. Polarisation approaches might also argue that the differences could be linked to structural features, such as the sector or industry, or argue that other contingencies, such as whether or not employees can exert influence through trade unions, will affect the likelihood of being upskilled or deskilled.

Research in the Netherlands (see Extract 15.5) and the United States reveals the differential impact of technological and organisational change on the work of different employees. Milkman's (1997) case study of the General Motors' plant in Linden, New Jersey, depicts a complex picture of work transformation, but it reveals how skilled workers were given opportunities to acquire new skills and retrain, while their semi-skilled counterparts on the production line were denied such opportunities. Similarly, in an entirely different industry (case studies of software and data processing) in a different country (the UK), the same pattern was found whereby changes in skill requirements had the effect of advantaging those already highly skilled 'depriving others of not only the few skills they have but also any hope of a route out of a low skills, low income trap' (Grugulis and Vincent, 2009). The common feature across these case studies is the consequence of upskilling for one group and deskilling for the other: a polarisation effect.

Extract 15.5

Skill polarisation in the Netherlands

As part of a research programme examining the effects of automation on job content, de Witte and Steijn (2000) analysed the responses of 1022 Dutch employees to a questionnaire. The respondents were asked about:

○ the amount of autonomy (freedom or control) they had in their work;
○ the complexity of their jobs;
○ the extent of automation in their work.
○ From analysis of the responses to these and other background questions, de Witte and Steijn, conclude:
○ There is a general trend in upskilling associated with increasing automation.
○ Professionals and white-collar workers experience the most upskilling.
○ Blue-collar workers are least likely to experience upskilling.
○ Some blue-collar workers experience substantial deskilling.

To explain deskilling amongst blue-collar workers, de Witte and Steijn suggest that 'internal differentiation' is occurring. This term means that automation leads to an *increase* in the complexity of the job *but not* the autonomy of the job. However, this internal differentiation is less likely to occur amongst the professional and white-collar workers; for them automation brings an increase in both complexity *and* autonomy.

The compensatory theory of skill

The argument put forward by proponents of the compensatory theory (Penn, 1990; Penn, Gasteen, Scattergood and Sewel, 1994; Penn and Scattergood, 1985) is that the general theories of both upskilling and deskilling are inadequate to explain the complexity of skill change. Instead, 'middle-range' explanations based on actual data offer a better way forward. This is because technological change generates both deskilling and upskilling, and in different forms. First, the effects are international: 'the shift of routine manufacturing from advanced, core economies to less developed, peripheral economies, and the increasing internationalisation of the capital goods (machinery) industry' (Penn, 1990: 25). Second, the effects differ between and within occupations: some groups are advantaged by having a more skilled and central role, while others find themselves deskilled and marginalised. More specifically:

> technological changes tend to deskill *direct productive roles* but put an increased premium on a range of *ancillary skilled tasks* that are associated with the installation, maintenance and programming of automated machinery. This is because modern machinery incorporating micro-electronics tends to simplify many production skills but renders maintenance work far more complex…. [However] within maintenance work itself…there is a far greater need for new electronic based maintenance skills than for traditional mechanical maintenance skills.
>
> (Ibid, emphasis in original)

This position highlights the importance of a broader picture of skill change across occupational groups, industries and national contexts.

Automating and informating – the dual impact on skill change

The important role of advanced technology in reconfiguring skills is explored in detail by Zuboff (1988). She argues that a distinction must be drawn between the processes of automating and informating, since they have impacted upon skills in different ways. Automating work operations involves replacing people with technology and so it is characterised by a deskilling of work and a reassertion of management control over the work process. However, technological developments also provide opportunities to generate detailed information about work operations. These could, if systematically gathered and analysed, increase the visibility of the productive and administrative work undertaken in an organisation. In other words, technology is informating the work process, and that data requires interpretation using cognitive ability. This constitutes an upskilling of work and provides 'a deeper level of transparency to activities that had been either partially or completely opaque' (Zuboff, 1988: 9).

Taken together, the processes of automating and informating lead to a reduction in action-centred skills (doing), but an increase in intellective skills (analysing). At the same time:

> these dual capacities of information technology are not opposites; they are hierarchically integrated. Informating derives from and builds upon

automation. Automation is a necessary but not sufficient condition for informating.

(Ibid: 11)

Zuboff also argues that although automating displaces people, it is not yet clear what the full effects of informating are. While managers can choose either to exploit or to ignore the informating process, her own case study evidence suggests that the tendency has been for managers to stress the automating process and ignore the informating potential. This is not surprising because the informating capacities of advanced technology force managers to rethink traditional structures, work organisation and forms of control:

> The shifting grounds of knowledge invite managers to recognize the emergent demands for intellective skills and develop a learning environment in which such skills can develop. That very recognition contains a threat to managerial authority, which depends in part upon control over the organization's knowledge.... Managers who must prove and defend their own legitimacy do not easily share knowledge or engage in inquiry. Workers who feel the requirements of subordination are not enthusiastic learners.... Techniques of control that are meant to safeguard authority create suspicion and animosity, which is particularly dysfunctional when an organization needs to apply its human energies to inventing an alternative form of work organization better suited to the new technological context.

(Ibid: 391–2)

The analysis presented by Zuboff is detailed, so this summary cannot really do justice to the subtlety of her argument. Still, it illustrates how both the deskilling and upskilling theses are inadequate as single explanations of skill change. While the former concentrates on the process of automating, the latter is focused on the process of informating. As a result, both approaches overlook the dual impact of advanced technology.

TO SUM UP

The syntheses above are more firmly based on empirical research than either the deskilling or the upskilling thesis. All three syntheses identify the possibility of deskilling and upskilling occurring simultaneously, and therefore they reject the notion of an overall general tendency in one direction only. In moving away from general theorising to context-specific understanding of skill change, they can more easily take account of the diversity of empirical evidence. These syntheses also converge in concluding that the overall picture is one of differing experiences of skill change.

DISCUSSION

Possible trends in work transformation, as represented by the various approaches above, can be depicted using a simple framework. As with any model that seeks to simplify the complexities embedded in work organisation, this is limited, but it does allow us to make some important analytical distinctions. The framework draws on

Fox (1974), Friedmann (1961) and Littler (1982) by proposing that work can be described as varying along two dimensions:

○ *The range of work.* Work can vary according to the range of tasks that the employee performs. At one extreme, an employee will perform a very narrow range of tasks, while at the other extreme the employee will be expected to perform a wide range of different tasks.

○ *The discretion in work.* This refers to the extent to which employees have the ability to exercise choice over how the work is performed, deciding such aspects as the pace, quality, quantity and scheduling of work. At one extreme there will be very little opportunity for employees to use their discretion in this way, while at the other extreme work will require employees to use discretion constantly.

By combining these two dimensions as in Figure 15.1, it is possible to visualise the way jobs may vary and to plot four ideal-type (abstract) cases:

1 *Specialist work*: high discretion over a narrow range of work.
2 *Specialised work*: a narrow range of prescribed tasks.
3 *Generalised work*: a wide range of prescribed tasks.
4 *Generalist work*: high discretion over a wide range of work.

A good way to illustrate this typology is to look at a single work setting and assess how different jobs within that setting can be placed in one of these four categories. In a hospital, the paramedics and nurses are undertaking generalised work, the doctors perform generalist work, the porters do specialised work and the surgeons are responsible for specialist work. To take another example, in a nightclub the manager is doing generalist work, the DJ is doing specialist work, the bar staff are doing generalised work and the bouncers are doing specialised work. This type of categorisation can be undertaken for any workplace. Of course not all jobs will fit neatly into one category (some nurses are specialists and have a great deal of discretion, for instance), but that is always a limitation of such frameworks. However, if a job does not fit neatly into

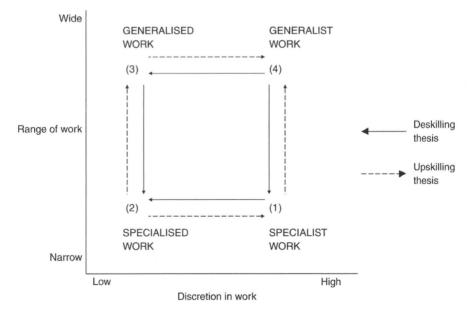

Figure 15.1 – Work categorisation framework and trends in skill change

a category it may indicate that the work is undergoing a transition – the sort of skill change that we discussed above and elaborate below.

Exercise 15.5

What do you think?

Think of a workplace with which you are familiar, list the main jobs and attempt to categorise them using the work catego-risation framework. Remember, this framework cannot tell us about the importance of the work. It does not indicate the value of the work, but it helps us to classify the nature of the work.

Now take several of these jobs and speculate how they could change along the two dimensions (range and discretion) in line with the two theses. You will need to think about the specific tasks required by the jobs.

Mapping the skill changes

In addition to classifying the nature of jobs, the work categorisation framework can be used to show the trends proposed by the skill change theses:

- The deskilling thesis is based on the idea that there is a general trend towards low-discretion jobs comprising a narrow range of tasks. This reveals itself in the form of a degradation of work along the 'discretion' dimension. In other words, discretion is removed from generalist work (making it more generalised) or from specialist work (making it more specialised). Similarly the deskilling thesis suggests a simplification of work along the 'range' dimension, so the work would entail a narrower range of tasks. This would turn generalised work into specialised work, and generalist work initially into specialist work, and then into specialised work through the degradation process. These trends are represented by the solid arrows in Figure 15.1.

- The upskilling thesis identifies an opposite trend towards high-discretion jobs comprising a wide range of tasks. There is an enrichment of work along the 'discre-tion' dimension: by increasing the extent of discretion, specialised work becomes increasingly specialist and generalised work becomes increasingly generalist. In addition, the upskilling thesis suggests that multi-tasking is becoming a feature of all work, so there are changes along the 'range' dimension. Specialised work is becoming more generalised and specialist work is becoming more generalist. The broken arrows in Figure 15.1 show these trends.

- Those researchers who reject a general tendency of either deskilling or upskilling would argue that a mixed pattern emerges. This means that change could occur along any of the paths represented by the arrows, and such changes are likely to vary greatly both between and within countries, sectors, industries, occupations, workplaces and workgroups.

CONCLUSION – MAPPING SKILL CHANGE ONTO WORK ORGANISATION PARADIGMS

Finally, we can return to the issue of work organisation with which we began the chapter. We argued that Taylorist and Fordist methods have had a dominant influ-ence on work organisation, so how do these relate to the different theories of skill change? In Figure 15.2, the work categorisation framework is drawn again, but this time we have mapped onto it the dominant forms of work organisation that can be associated with each work category. The term 'paradigm' – which here means a

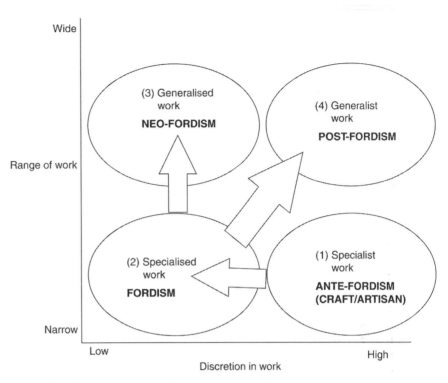

Figure 15.2 – Work categorisation framework and paradigms of work organisation

distinctive pattern or approach – can describe these forms of work organisation. So we can refer to the Fordist paradigm (a pattern of work similar to that developed by Ford). What do these paradigm terms mean, and how do they relate to the theories of skill change?

The word 'Fordism' appears in all the paradigms. This is no accident because the Fordist paradigm had a massive impact on how work was organised during the twentieth century. That is why we discussed it so much at the beginning of this chapter. Because of its impact, other paradigms of work organisation can be defined in relation to Fordism. So:

- Post-Fordism: means 'after Fordism' and refers to types of work organisation that do not rely on the principles of Taylor or the methods of Ford.
- Neo-Fordism: means 'new Fordism' and refers to types of work organisation that have adopted many of the basic methods of Ford but have adapted them – particularly through more flexible working practices – to fit contemporary circumstances.
- Ante-Fordism: means 'before Fordism' and refers to types of work organisation that rely on craft-based skills, often associated with the independent, self-employed artisan (craft worker).

The deskilling and upskilling theses both accept that (in general terms) craft/artisan production in the nineteenth century gave way to Fordism, which dominated the majority of the twentieth century. However, they offer contrasting interpretations of how work organisation is now changing. The upskilling thesis suggests a dramatic change has taken place in advanced capitalist economies in recent decades. This 'paradigm shift' to post-Fordism is based on new concepts of work organisation (incorporating multiskilled workers, self-managed teams, networked organisations and teleworking), an increasingly dominant service-based economy, and frequently characterised as the post-industrial society in which knowledge workers dominate.

In contrast, the deskilling thesis suggests that Fordism is continually being renewed as the dominant mode of work organisation, so there has been no paradigm shift. The consequence is specialised work comprising a narrow range of low-discretion tasks. A variant of this deskilling approach comes from commentators who suggest that Fordism has evolved into neo-Fordism (e.g. Harvey, 1989). This perspective suggests that multi-tasking, new management techniques (such as just-in-time, lean production and business process re-engineering) and increasingly automated and internationalised production processes have revitalised Fordism. Proponents of this view (e.g. Aglietta, 1979) stress the importance of continuity with the past, rather than characterising change as a quantum leap into a new dimension of capitalism. From this perspective, new forms of work organisation continue to reproduce traditional divisions of labour and essentially dispiriting and alienating experiences for employees. Employees cope with these in the best way they can, and sometimes join for collective support to make their voices heard.

SKILLS

CHAPTER AIM

To explore the concept of skill and critically evaluate three different approaches to its definition and measurement.

KEY CONCEPTS

- skill in the person
- skill in the job
- skill in the setting
- complexity and discretion
- tacit skill
- social closure
- ideological, political and material processes of social closure
- social regulation
- social construction of skill
- gender and skill

LEARNING OUTCOMES

After reading and thinking about the material in this chapter, you will be able to:

1 Identify three approaches to evaluating skill.
2 Explain how to assess skill in the person and identify the limitations of this approach.
3 Explain how to assess skill in the job using:
   a the concept of complexity,
   b the concept of discretion.
4 Explain how to assess skill in the setting using the concept of social closure.
5 Explain how skill can be seen as (i) a socially constructed phenomenon that has (ii) disadvantaged women through ideological, political and material processes.

EXPLORING THE CONCEPT OF SKILL

Of all the concepts we encounter when studying the realities of work, 'skill' stands out as the most difficult to pin down. Yet, strangely enough, it is perhaps one of the few topics that most people might claim to have an understanding about. If you ask someone about a job, they would more than likely be able to tell you whether it is skilled or not, and they would probably be able to give a reasonable explanation as to why they considered it skilled. The problem, however, is that we all stress different aspects of a job in evaluating whether it is skilled or not. In extreme cases, the lack of consensus over what constitutes a skilled job is less important because the job attributes are diverse enough for people to reach general, if not specific, agreement. For example, most people would probably agree that the surgeon's job is more skilled than the hospital porter's job, or that the teacher is more skilled than the school care-taker – but some comparisons are far more problematic. To illustrate this, complete Exercise 16.1.

Exercise 16.1

What do you think?

For each of the pairs of jobs listed below, decide which is the most skilled and justify your decision. In other words, explain the criteria you are using to decide how skill should be evaluated.

1 The hotel receptionist compared with the security guard.
2 The computer games software programmer and the paramedic.
3 The cleaner and the car-park attendant.
4 The insurance broker and the travel agent.
5 The police officer and the social worker.

To reach an agreement on comparisons such as those in Exercise 16.1, it is necessary to achieve consensus on what is meant by the term 'skill'. This is not an easy task because skill is a definitional minefield. However, in the rest of the chapter we will enter this dangerous territory!

First we must ask, why worry about defining skill at all? This is a reasonable question, and the answer, as explained below, is that skill is fundamental to the status that people attach to different occupations, and it is frequently linked to pay. Moreover, skill is a key factor in determining the structure of employment, most notably in the way it acts to reinforce gender divisions relating to labour in society.

LOCATING SKILL

The first puzzle that needs to be solved is the problem of where skill resides. Is it part of:

- the person?
- the job?
- the setting?

Cockburn (1983: 113) suggests all three aspects need to be taken into account. In her study of (male) print workers she argues that:

> There is the skill that resides in the man himself, accumulated over time, each new experience adding something to a total ability. There is the skill demanded by the job – which may or may not match the skill in the worker. And there is the political definition of skill: that which a group of workers or a trade union can successfully defend against the challenge of employers and other groups of workers.

A closer consideration of Cockburn's research will be undertaken later in the chapter, but it is worth pausing to give some thought to her three categories because each suggests a different approach to examining skill:

1 *Skill in the person*. Any analysis that concentrates on the person is likely to attempt to identify individual attributes and qualities and seek to measure these through, for example, an aptitude test under experimental conditions. Typically, this approach has been informed by the work of psychologists. Similarly, a questionnaire might be administered to assess a person's education, training and experience, which could then be used as a proxy for (i.e. an indicator of) skill – a method frequently adopted by economists.

2 *Skill in the job*. If the analytical focus is the job, then the concern is less with the person performing the task than with the requirements embedded in the task itself. In this case, attention would be turned towards the complexity of the tasks required to perform the job competently – an approach typically taken by management theorists. It would also include the extent of discretion over the work – an issue of particular interest to industrial–employment relations theorists.

3 *Skill in the setting*. If the focus is on the political and historical setting, an analysis would be assessing the way skill has developed over time and has been 'constructed' by different interest groups, rather than being a feature of the person or the job. This way of looking at skill is an approach pursued by some sociologists (particularly gender theorists) and social historians.

These differences in approach to analysing skill are summarised in Table 16.1. It illustrates how the focus tends to be associated with different methods of analysis and shows how academic disciplines have tended to address different aspects of skill.

TO SUM UP

It is possible for several theorists to arrive at contrasting conclusions about skilled work because they are focusing on different features and are using different methods of analysis.

Now we have charted the terrain, it is necessary to explore each of these areas in closer detail. To do this the rest of the chapter has been divided into three sections,

Table 16.1 – Approaches to the analysis of skill

Focus	Principal area of concern	Typical approach taken	Typically adopted by
Person	Individual attributes acquired through: ⊙ education ⊙ training ⊙ experience	Questionnaire surveys Use of proxy measures (e.g. qualifications, number of years of training) Aptitude tests/experiments	Economists Psychologists
Job	Task requirements ⊙ complexity ⊙ discretion	Job analysis Job evaluation	Occupational psychologists Management theorists Industrial/employment relations theorists
Setting	Social relations	Case studies of industries and occupations Ethnographic studies of workplaces	Social historians Sociologists Gender theorists

each analysing a different aspect of skill: the person, the job and the setting. Each section draws out the strengths and weaknesses of the particular approaches, thereby demonstrating that there is no simple way of assessing skill. Following this, a final section illustrates the contemporary importance of the concept of skill by examining how it can perpetuate gender divisions in relation to labour.

SKILL IN THE PERSON

In this first approach, skill is generally considered a quality possessed by the individual. It can take numerous forms – for example, knowledge, dexterity, judgement and linguistic ability – but the assumption is that it is gained by a person during education, training and experience. At first sight, this is an attractive conception of skill because it is relatively easy to measure and produces quantifiable data that can be incorporated into statistical analyses. For example, people can be asked to complete a questionnaire listing their years in formal education, their number of qualifications, the amount of training they have undertaken and their on-the-job experience.

It is not surprising, therefore, that many labour economists are satisfied with these measures as a proxy for skill. This is typified by the approach of human capital theorists (e.g. Becker, 1964), who argue that in a market economy, a person's human capital will determine his or her value as an employee. From this perspective it is argued that people can choose, as individuals, to increase their human capital through taking advantage of educational opportunities and training. Conversely, they can choose to ignore these opportunities, with the consequence of lowering their relative value in the labour market. For human capital theorists, responsibility for success in work clearly lies with the individual; they call on the notion of a meritocratic society, where individual endeavour is rewarded.

Problems with the human capital approach

Inequality of opportunity

This approach is simplistic if it assumes that everyone has the same opportunity of access to the activities that improve human capital. This is clearly not the case. For example, private education generally provides children with better facilities, smaller class sizes and a more intense learning environment, but such education is available only to the minority of children whose parents can afford it, together with a small number who are awarded scholarships. Similarly, take the example of experience: in order to gain work experience, a person has to be offered a job, but when there are high rates of unemployment allowing employers to pick and choose, a person with no work experience is less likely to be offered a job and hence is unable to gain work experience. Opportunities to get work experience as an intern may also depend on family contacts, for example. These examples illustrate the fundamental problem that people do not compete on equal terms because there is not a level playing field.

Validity of the skill measures

A more general problem is whether the variables of education, training and experience are valid measures of skill. The number of years a person spends in formal education is linked to qualifications attained, but even then it does not necessarily mean that the skills learned will be appropriate or transferable to work. Similarly, while the measurement of training may be a better indicator of industry-specific knowledge and aptitude, it does not take into account the applicability of the training to a specific context.

Use value of the skill

Should measurement include only those attributes that have a current value – in other words, the measurement of 'skills in use' rather than skills possessed? For example, if a person learns to speak Welsh and gains a qualification proving his/her competence, does this constitute a skill? If it has some market value, human capital theorists would say 'yes', but if few employers require Welsh speakers, its value is severely reduced. In other words, a particular skill can be seen as an asset based on its market value. In this sense, all knowledge and abilities can be seen as potential skills, but it is the demand for them and their supply that give them value. Therefore, measuring the skills possessed by the person can be misleading without exploring the labour market context (see Extract 16.1).

Extract 16.1

The supply of and demand for skills – measuring qualifications

In an analysis of the United States and Canada, Livingstone (1998) found considerable discrepancies between the skills people possess and the skills they are expected to use at work. He describes this as the education–jobs gap, and argues that the rise in educational qualifications and work-related knowledge has outpaced the development of jobs where people can put this knowledge to use.

Similarly, in the UK, an analysis of qualifications by Felstead, Gallie and Green (2002) revealed that the proportion of over-qualified workers has increased from 30 per cent in 1986 to 37 per cent in 2001 ('over-qualified' means that the person doing the job has higher qualifications than are required by the job). In particular, at the bottom of the skills hierarchy, the demand for workers with no qualifications greatly outstrips supply: an estimated 6.4 million jobs required no qualifications but there were only 2.8 million people in the labour force with no qualifications. In other words, speaking somewhat simplistically, for every unqualified person there were more than two potential jobs). This contrasts with 1986, when the estimates of numbers of jobs requiring no qualifications and people without qualifications were broadly matched at around just under 8 million (Felstead et al, 2004: 154–8). Of course cynics might question whether the marked increase in those with qualifications between 1986 and 2001 represents a real skills increase. Instead it could reflect an increasing tendency to give formal accreditation to attributes that were once not considered skills. This means it could actually be a sign of declining standards.

The evidence from both studies suggests there is 'underemployment' of the skills available in the labour market. One problem that this raises is so-called 'credentialism'. This is the tendency for employers to ask for higher qualifications for a job without changing the job content, to make use of the improved skills of job holders. The likely consequence for employees is that they feel dissatisfied because they are not using their skills and may consider the job insufficiently challenging.

A broader definition of 'skill in the person'

The limitations noted above mean that the skills a person has may be wider than those captured in measures such as formal qualifications. As a consequence we may need a broader definition of individual skills. This need not simply look at formally recognised achievements. Indeed, it has been argued by some commentators that there is a growing tendency to broaden the definition of skill in the person by labelling certain personal characteristics as skills. For example, Grugulis, Warhurst and Keep (2004) note that attitudes, character traits and predispositions (tendencies to certain moods) are being described by employers as required skills (and also as typically lacking in the labour market). Some commentators use the term 'soft skills' to mean a range of these behavioural and attitudinal qualities that workers can (or should) be able to offer (e.g. Moss and Tilly, 1996).

This broadening of the definition might be explained to some extent by the changing demands of work. It is also the case that internal restructuring can lead to new forms of work organisation and therefore different qualities are demanded – for instance, the ability to work in teams. This being the case, it would seem appropriate that additional qualities need to be assessed, hence broader definitions of skill need to be considered. However, there are at least three objections to such an approach:

- The first objection is that these new qualities should not be considered skills at all. Lafer (2004) argues that a skill is a quality learned or developed by individuals that will secure them a living. Many of the new 'skills' (punctuality, appearance, manners, and so forth) are not skills in this sense because, alone, they cannot secure a living wage, although they might be a prerequisite for getting a job in the first instance, and they are often also qualities required to remain in employment. In Lafer's (2004: 117) words, 'Traits such as discipline, loyalty and punctuality are not "skills" that one either possesses or lacks; they are measures of commitment that one chooses to give or withhold based on the conditions of work offered'. The consequence of broadening the definition of skill in such a way means that the concept of skill in the person becomes increasingly meaningless, and therefore useless (Grugulis, 2007; Lloyd and Payne, 2009; Payne, 2009).

- The second objection comes from commentators who see the broadening definition as being a move by employers to shift responsibility to others for developing qualities such as punctuality, conscientiousness, teamworking, respect for authority and so forth. The objection is not with the meaningfulness of the concept of skill – indeed, a broader definition is considered useful, particularly if this involves recognising previously undervalued skills and especially those associated with jobs in which women predominate (see the discussion later in this chapter). Instead, the objection is with the implications of incorporating the 'new skills'. As Grugulis, Warhurst and Keep (2004: 12) state:

  > By changing the meaning of skill to embrace attitudes and behavioural traits or by increasing the emphasis placed upon the possession of such characteristics, employers have been able to shift responsibility for the creation or reinforcement of some of these attitudes and traits away from their roles as managers and motivators of their employees and onto the education and training system.

- A third objection is that there might be a political motivation behind accrediting a greater range of abilities and attributes as skills. Through the process of redefining skill and issuing certificates to prove the attainment of skills, a government can more easily claim that the skill base of the workforce is increasing – even though many of the now certified skills may have been possessed and used by the workforce in previous periods without formal recognition. This does not detract from the importance of recognising lower-level skills, but caution must be taken in assuming either that this represents a step increase in the skills base for the workforce, or that employers will pay the individual any premium for these certified skills when they are so widely held.

TO SUM UP

The approach of assessing skill in the person tends to view skill as an attribute possessed by an individual, and sometimes described as a person's human capital. While this appears to be a relatively simple way of assessing skill, the problems lie in the methods of measurement and then putting these into practice.

Exercise 16.2

What do you think?

Below is a list of individual qualities that might be required by an employee who deals with customers face-to-face. Which of them would you describe as skills? Explain your reasoning:

o punctuality,
o a friendly manner,
o ability to calm down an irate customer,
o a positive attitude to work,
o a sound knowledge of the company products/services,
o good standard of numeracy,
o good verbal communication.

SKILL IN THE JOB

In this section the analysis focuses on assessing the skill required by the job, rather than the skills possessed by the person doing the job. Of course, in an ideal situation the two would match, but the reality is that some people are more skilled than their job requires, while others are insufficiently skilled. By focusing on the job rather than the person, this potential mismatch is removed from the analysis, thereby allowing us to explore skill by looking at the complexity of the job and the extent of discretion in the job.

Assessing the complexity of jobs

It seems reasonable to suppose there is an association between the complexity of the tasks required by the job and the overall level of skill: the more complex the tasks, the more skilled the job can be said to be. This also suggests that if the extent of complexity in a particular job is measured it should be possible to arrive at a skill level. For instance, in their skills survey, Felstead, Gallie and Green (2004) ask questions about the qualifications required to get the job; the length of training required for the type of work; the time it takes to learn to do the work well; and the importance of 36 different activities that the work might involve (such as caring for others, working with computers, dealing with people, physical stamina, writing reports). The assumption behind such an approach is that it is possible to derive an objective measure of complexity. This is an appealing idea because it means that different jobs could be compared and ranked according to their complexity. This ranking could be reflected in systems of status and remuneration (typically taking the form of job evaluation schemes). Although it seems a feasible and logical exercise, in practice it is notoriously difficult to do because evaluating job content has a subjective element. Two main difficulties are encountered.

The difficulty of observing

Imagine being in the position of observing a job and assessing its complexity. The job might appear complex if it is unfamiliar. For example, to the observer who cannot drive, driving is likely to seem a very complex activity involving physical coordination, spatial awareness, concentration and quick decision making. Yet for the seasoned driver it might not be viewed as a complex skill at all, not least because it is a widely shared ability. This presents a paradox: a fair evaluation would mean the observer having familiarity with the task, but this familiarity may lead the observer to undervalue the task. In other words, there are problems with relying on observation because of the subjectivity of the observer.

The difficulty of asking

A possible alternative approach is to ask the person doing the job to identify its complexity. But this also poses problems for similar reasons: familiarity and adeptness may lead a person to undervalue a task. As Attewell (1990: 430) argues:

> [Mundane activities] become socially invisible to both the actors performing them and to observers familiar with them .... They become buried within their practitioners – either psychologically in the form of habits and non-conscious information-processing or somatically [in the body] in muscles and neurons (knack, deftness and cunning).

This suggests that both observation and self-assessment would lead to a general conclusion that much of human activity in work (as well as outside) is not complex and, by implication, requires little skill. As Attewell points out, this is particularly ironic because when a person achieves a high level of competence, they internalise procedures and routines so the task can be accomplished 'without thinking'. For the novice, each situation and each problem is unique and uncertain and so they must apply conscious thought, but 'the maestro has been there before and has more (nonconscious) routines to apply' (Attewell, 1990: 433). To put this in another way, beginners rely on abstract rules which have been derived by others, and they use these to guide their progress and accumulate experience; experts rely on context-bound knowledge that they have developed through experience and are therefore less conscious of the decision-rules they are using.

Similarly, Manwaring and Wood (1985) identify the importance of considering 'tacit skills' (based upon the analysis of Polanyi and Prosch, 1975; Koestler, 1976; Kusterer, 1978) to suggest that work necessarily involves the internalisation of learning. This means tasks can be performed successfully by drawing on unconscious thought, and that different degrees of awareness are required both within and between jobs. The more frequent unfamiliar situations are, the less likely it is that existing routines are effective, and so this requires greater awareness. From this perspective, it might be argued that skill is embedded in all jobs but tacit skills are taken for granted rather than being formally recognised.

Some of the most undervalued tacit skills are the social skills required in many jobs. Such skills are central to many jobs where customer interaction is key. Research into the work of customer service representatives (CSRs) in the financial services sector in Australia and Japan has revealed the increasing importance and recognition of social skills. Korczynski, Shire, Frenkel and Tam (1996) explored the everyday work of front-line staff dealing with telephone queries from customers. They found that the social skills played a vital role in:

⊚ establishing a rapport with the customer;
⊚ assessing the attitude of the customer;
⊚ persuading the customer to purchase a product.

In fact at two of the three organisations studied, management recognised that social skills were so vital that they changed their recruitment policy – no longer selecting graduates but instead employing a range of people with social skills. Similarly, a study by Darr (2004) of technical salespeople selling cutting-edge technologies (part of the workforce sometimes labelled 'knowledge workers') revealed that technical skills are most valuable to employers only when accompanied by social skills. The 'geek' with a huge amount of technical knowledge but no social skills is not an asset when it comes to sales or after-sales service.

In addition to the social skills required in service sector work, Hampson and Junor (2010) have identified further hidden skills that employees use. Their analysis of the day-to-day activities of public service, education and health employees in New Zealand leads them to identify the importance of the process skills of 'awareness shaping' and 'co-ordinating'. Awareness shaping takes the form of employees being able to sense contexts or situations, monitor and guide the reactions of others and make judgements about the impact of their actions. Co-ordinating involves employees sequencing and combining their activities, interweaving them with the work of others and maintaining the workflow. The complexity of these activities even for low-level personal service jobs is well illustrated by the comments of an Occupational Therapy Assistant that Hampson and Junor interviewed:

> Time management [is]…something I've been working on with the team leader…because I cover different areas, I'm learning to say no, and work in with the other therapists. [They] ask you to do different things, because there's only a certain amount of time that you have in the day and being able to say 'No, I can't do that now, but I can do it at such and such a time'. So you're planning all the time and then being able to adjust your day – because there're little emergencies and things that pop up all the time, so you've got to fit those in.
>
> (Hampson and Junor, 2010: 537)

The increasing requirement for customer service work has led some researchers to argue that many of the service sector jobs require the skilled control and manipulation of emotions (e.g. Bolton, 2004, 2005; Bolton and Houlihan, 2007; Korczynski, 2005). In complete contrast, Lloyd and Payne (2009) point out that some of the skill claims are overstated. They argue that broadening the definition of skill considerably reduces its conceptual value. It can lead, they argue, to the assumption that all routinised service work is skilled even though, as they show through their interviews of call centre employees, the workers themselves do not consider their jobs as skilled. In particular, comments from their interviewees reveal the lack of complexity in the job, the mundanity of the tasks and the lack of challenge in the work. The comments of the call centre workers also show they have relatively little influence over the way they do their tasks; this is an aspect that traditionally has been considered an important indicator of skill, as the next section explains.

Assessing the extent of discretion in jobs

Another way of assessing skill is to examine it in relation to the discretion that employees can exercise when undertaking their jobs and hence the amount of control they have over their work.

The amount of discretion

Discretion is the ability to choose between alternative courses of action. Other things being equal, the greater the number of decisions required by an activity, the greater the level of skill required in exercising discretion. So the more an employee is able to exercise his/her judgement, the more skilled a task may be said to be. In this way skill levels might be assessed by examining the amount of rules employees are obliged to follow. Assuming the rules are comprehensive and clear then the more rules, the less scope there is for discretion and the lower their skill will be judged to be. This distinction between prescribed (rule-dominated) and discretionary (choice-dominated) work was first conceptualised by Jaques (1956, 1967). While it is a useful schema, it must be treated with caution, as Fox (1974: 19–20) points out:

> It is easy to accept…that no work role can be totally discretionary. The occupant of the most elevated post has to operate within prescribed limits, usually a great many. It may be more difficult, however, to accept that all jobs contain discretionary as well as prescriptive elements. Surely many jobs in our kind of industrial society are totally prescribed; totally without discretion? Such a view cannot be sustained. However elaborate the external controlling structure of mechanical, administrative, technical or policy prescriptions, some residual element of discretion always remains.

This resonates with our earlier discussion about tacit skills, which argued that all jobs require discretion, even though such discretion may not be identified by the job description or acknowledged in the reward system. The problem of using discretion as an indicator of skill is that we are focusing on the visible when many of the choices and judgements exercised in the work process remain invisible.

The time-span of discretion

A second concept identified by Jaques (1967) is the 'time-span of discretion'. This is the length of time that a person is allowed to exercise discretion free from surveillance by superiors: the longer a person's period of autonomy, the higher their skill level. Again, however, this is somewhat limited in its usefulness as far as defining skill is concerned. A major problem with the concept of time-span of discretion is that it fails to take into account the significance of the task and the consequences of making a mistake. For example, a gardener may be allocated a patch of land to tend and be left completely alone for long periods. He has few rules to follow and could work incompetently for weeks before it came to anyone's notice. Conversely, the anaesthetist exercises her judgement within a strict framework of rules, and even a slight error of judgement will come to the attention of her work colleagues within minutes.

Discretion is also a misleading indicator because it fails to take into account the interdependence of many modern jobs. The notion of discretion tends to suggest an image of a romanticised past associated with the craft worker, which is really inappropriate when thinking about current jobs. As Attewell (1990: 443) argues:

> The ideal of the artisan conceiving an object, choosing tools and procedures unconstrained by external rules or routines, and fabricating the object from first to last step is so at odds with the reality of modern work that everyone today, from managers down, appears deskilled.

TO SUM UP

The common theme that links the two notions of 'skill as complexity' and 'skill as discretion' is that both approaches emphasise skill as being principally about the requirements of the job. From this perspective, skill is seen as an objective feature of work and therefore can be measured through an analysis of job content in terms of both technical complexity and discretionary requirements. Consequently, researchers tend to view skill as consisting of sub-components, each of which can be measured. A good example of this approach can be seen in Extract 16.2 – read it and then attempt Exercise 16.3 to test your understanding of this section.

Extract 16.2

Measuring skill in the job – perception mismatches

One of the problems of measuring the skill required by the job is that there can be different perceptions depending upon who is doing the evaluating. Most notably, there might be stark differences between the views of employees – who might wish to overstate the skills they need in order to argue for higher remuneration or status, and managers – who might be inclined to understate the skills required to hold down wages and increase status differentials.

This potential perceptual mismatch has been explored by Green and James (2003), who designed a research experiment that allowed them to get the opinions of 110 job holders and their line managers about the skills involved in performing their jobs. The technique of matching pairs of employees and line managers means that it is possible to look at the differences in ratings between each employee and his or her manager, and then draw conclusions about the extent and cause of any differences. To do this they used a statistical analysis that took account of differences in gender, age and job tenure (time employed in a job). To measure the skills involved, the job-holders and their line managers were asked to rate various aspects of the jobs using the same answer scales (allowing overall scores and means to be calculated and compared).

The complexity of the job was assessed by asking about:

○ four specific groups of job skills (verbal, physical, problem solving, planning);
○ the qualifications needed to undertake the job.

The extent of discretion was assessed by asking about:

○ the choice over how the job is done;
○ the closeness of supervision;
○ the freedom to decide how hard to work.

Green and James arrive at three main conclusions from their analysis:

○ There is a good match between the perceptions of the job-holder and the line manager concerning the specific skills (verbal, physical, problem solving and planning) and the level of qualifications needed. However, there is a marked difference of opinion in terms of the discretion element: the job-holder generally judges the job to entail more discretion than the manager believes.
○ Employees tend to rate the skills needed to undertake their job slightly higher on average than their line managers.
○ Gender differences between the employee and line manager have an effect. When the manager is male and the employee is female there is a tendency for the difference between their estimates of the skill level of the job to be greater than with other gender combinations.

In respect of the third finding, Green and James are careful to point out that their data alone do not allow them to conclude that male managers are understating the value of female employees (since there is no independent measure of skill in their research). However, such a finding would not be surprising to those who argue that the skills of women have traditionally been undervalued by male managers – an issue explored in the section on the social construction of skill.

Source: Based on Green and James (2003).

Exercise 16.3

What do you think?

Apply the measures of complexity and discretion used by Green and James (Extract 16.2) to analyse the jobs that you were asked to compare in Exercise 16.1 at the beginning of the chapter. They are listed again below. Of course, you might have to make an informed guess about some of the measures because you will not possess detailed information about the jobs:

○ the hotel receptionist compared with the security guard;
○ the computer games software writer and the paramedic;
○ the cleaner and the car-park attendant;
○ the insurance broker and the travel agent;
○ the police officer and the social worker.

Now consider these questions:

1 Have you arrived at different conclusions than your previous assessment of these jobs?
2 Were the measures of complexity and discretion helpful? Explain why or why not.
3 Were there any problems in applying them?
4 Do you have a systematic and defensible set of conclusions about the comparative skill levels of the jobs? Explain why or why not.

SKILL IN THE SETTING

An assumption underpinning both the 'skill in the job' and the 'skill in the person' approach is that the concept of skill can be objectively defined. But both approaches can be criticised for being overly rational because they often ignore the historical development of skill. Conceptions of skill are not dispassionately developed on blank pieces of paper; they are negotiated socially and politically over time, and they reflect the power and influence of diverse interest groups. This has been the case because skill is considered a measure of worth (both social and economic). As Sadler (1970: 23) has observed, skill is:

> to a considerable extent determined by social factors present in the work situation and in the occupational culture at large … [so includes] the evaluations placed on particular kinds of activity and on particular classes of individual and the actions of organised pressure groups directed at safeguarding the earnings and job security of particular trades and professions.

Consequently, to understand skill it is important to examine the setting in which the valuation of skill is negotiated.

As a starting point of the analysis, it is vital to consider one of the fundamental concepts of sociology as defined by Weber (1947) and elaborated by Parkin (1979) and Kreckel (1980). This is the notion of 'social closure', whereby people with a shared interest protect themselves by acting collectively to form a group that is in some way demarcated. Entry to the group is regulated by the existing members, thus they may choose to exclude or include outsiders depending on whether it serves their interests. Weber argues as follows:

> Whether a relationship is open or closed may be determined traditionally, affectually or rationally in terms of values or expediency. It is especially likely to be closed, for rational reasons, in the following type of situation. A social relationship may provide the parties to it with opportunities for the satisfaction of various interests, whether the satisfactions be spiritual or material, whether the interest be in the end of the relationship as such or in some ulterior consequence of participation, or whether it is achieved through cooperative action or by a compromise of interests. If the participants expect that the admission of others will lead to an improvement of their situation, and improvement in degree, in kind, in the security or the value of the satisfaction, their interest will be in keeping the relationship open. If, on the other hand, their expectations are of improving their position by monopolistic tactics, their interest will be in a closed relationship.

(Weber, 1947: 127–8)

In the case of an occupational group, social closure provides the means of establishing a position at least partially autonomous of labour market competition. Instead of being exposed to the vagaries of the free market, the group is united by a 'consciousness of difference' (ibid: 127), and a willingness to act to regulate itself and influence market forces. This process of achieving occupational social closure is vital in establishing skilled status, and the next section explores it in more detail.

Social closure and skilled status

The overall process of occupational social closure is composed of three interacting sub-processes:

- *An ideological process*: where individuals recognise a shared set of values and beliefs, and reinforce these symbolically.
- *A political process*: where group members act collectively, combining their resources in pursuit of common goals. There will remain a plurality of interests within the group, but they have a mutual interest in combining and institutionalising their relationship (e.g. in the membership of a trade union).
- *A material process*: where members of the group seek to take ownership of the tools and technology of the work process and to control, or at least to influence, the organisation of work.

These three processes are represented by a diagram (see Figure 16.1), and each is described in more detail below.

The ideological process

A key component of social closure is the shared beliefs and values of the occupational group. In this respect the group can be characterised as a subculture seeking

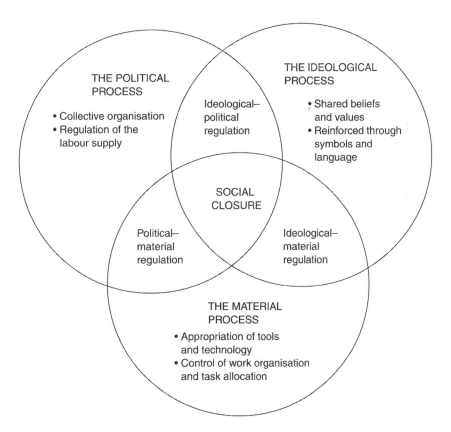

Figure 16.1 – The processes of social closure

to establish and ring-fence its separate identity (Turner, 1971). One of the most important ways the group maintains this distinct identity is through the manipulation of occupational language and symbols. For a group wishing to lay claim to skilled status, it allows opportunity to mystify the work by obscuring the mundane activities and portraying an image of complexity. Language acts as a particularly important regulatory device because it can be used to both exclude and include. In this sense it demarcates the in-group from the out-group – it draws a line between 'us' and 'them'. Being able to use occupation specific jargon or highly technical language symbolises membership of the group. It identifies those who have gained enough experience and familiarity with the occupation to speak and understand the exclusive language. For example, many people have heard the technospeak of computer technicians – an impenetrable jargon that is meaningful to them but bemuses others. Perhaps the clearest examples of this are in medicine – for instance, the title of this recent editorial in the *Annals of Neurology*, 'Systemic inflammation, oligodendroglial maturation, and the encephalopathy of prematurity' (Volpe, 2011).

New entrants to an occupation are quickly reminded by the language that surrounds them that they are on the edge of things. For example, newcomers in an engineering plant might – as a practical joke – be sent for the 'long stand', the 'long weight' (wait), the left-handed screwdriver or the 'glass hammer' – thereby exposing their naivety and lack of familiarity with the setting. Symbolic regulation is also established by rituals, rites of passage, initiation ceremonies, humour and other forms of social control (see also Extract 16.3).

The political process

As well as the shared values and beliefs leading to a collective identity, a group can reinforce this through its own representative body that allows members to organise and act collectively. Typically, it has been trade unions and professional associations that have performed this role. Such organisations demonstrate that the occupational group has a collective interest that is different from, and separate to, the interests of the organisation where members of the occupation are employed. In other words, it suggests that in some instances employees have a dual commitment: to the employing organisation and to the body that represents their occupation (the trade union or professional association). There are occasions when this poses particular dilemmas. For example, a hospital doctor may wish to prescribe a particular drug or treatment because it is in the best interests of the patient, but might also be conscious of the high financial cost to the hospital of doing so, with the resultant loss of treatment for other patients. The doctor's professional commitment (to provide the best care for the particular patient) conflicts with his/her organisational commitment (to use hospital resources effectively to care for patients in general).

An occupation's representative body also plays a key role in regulating the supply of labour. This is important if the members of an occupational group wish to establish and maintain a premium price for their work. In normal circumstances the scarcity of appropriately 'skilled' employees will push up the wage that an employer is willing to pay. Restricting the availability of labour is therefore in the interest of an occupational group. The control of supply has traditionally occurred through the regulation of entry into the occupation. To regulate entry, for example, a trade union typically sought in the past to establish a 'closed shop' (also known as a 'union shop' in the United States), which obliged employers to offer work only to workers who held union cards and were therefore deemed appropriately skilled to be able to accomplish the work safely and with competence. By limiting membership to those who were appropriately qualified, the union could influence the labour supply. It could also impose sanctions on members who broke union rules or acted against the interests of co-workers, by suspending their membership and consequently preventing their continued employment. Similarly, professional groups such as lawyers, doctors and accountants also operate a type of 'closed shop' (although they do not use this term), because to work in these professions one has to have passed the exams regulated by the professional body and be a member of the relevant professional association.

Overall, control over the supply of labour helps to build skilled status by restricting the size of the occupation and thereby implying that only those with special ability can do the job. Coupled with this is the increased price of labour which suggests work of special value, thus further reinforcing the status of the job.

The material process

In addition to controlling entry, occupational groups also need to control or exert influence over the way the work is accomplished. This can be achieved through two means. The first involves influencing the organisation of the work and the allocation of tasks. This requires regulating which person is allowed to undertake particular jobs, and traditionally this has encouraged demarcation where specific employees are limited to certain tasks according to their level of training and seniority. The second means of controlling the material process requires taking control of the tools and technology associated with the work. The workgroup seeks to control how the technology is put to use and to prevent access to it by other groups. Penn (1985: 121) expresses it as follows:

> Skilled manual workers in mechanised factory milieux [environments] are defined by their high degree of social control over the operation and utilisation of machinery. These exclusive controls involve a double exclusion, both of the management from the direct or complete control over the labour process and of other workers who offer a potential threat to such controls.

In other instances appropriation involves redefining the tools or technology (see Extract 16.3 for a good example). However, where organisations require employees to undertake a wider variety of tasks (functional flexibility) then the material process of social closure is potentially undermined because such flexibility broadens the access to particular tasks among the existing workforce. Nevertheless, employees find creative ways to reassert their influence over work processes, so control of the material process continues to be a relevant tactic.

TO SUM UP

In order for an occupational group to lay claim to skilled status it must establish its separateness and distinctiveness. It can achieve this through engaging in the three processes of social closure outlined above: ideological, political and material. These three processes operate at the same time and are mutually reinforcing, but social closure is achieved only when all three processes are carried out.

Extract 16.3

The symbols of skill in everyday occupations

There is symbolism embedded in the 'tools of the trade' which helps to differentiate an occupational group and allows its members to claim skilled status. This is particularly well illustrated by the case of construction workers discussed by Steiger (1993). Combining his findings with the work of Riemer (1977) and Applebaum (1981), he argues that owning the 'tools of the trade', and being able to use them properly is an important feature of defining skill. This is not least because the tools – and by definition the skills one possesses – are in full view. Common tools, such as the shovel used by the labourer, are looked down upon, whereas more specialised tools carry skill status. 'Rarity is important because...only "rare" specialised tools are emblematic of skill. That rarity is important should be of no surprise in a capitalist economy' (Steiger, 1993: 555).

Interestingly, Steiger also cites the example of plumbers, for whom technological advances (such as the advent of plastic piping) have reduced the need for specialist tools. The plumbers' response has been to shift the emphasis away from the tools on to their ingenuity and ability to improvise. In this sense, their occupational closure has become symbolised not through the visibility of tools (which are readily available to anyone) but through the invisible 'know-how' which only the 'skilled' plumber has acquired. This is particularly noteworthy because it takes us back to our earlier discussion of tacit skills. The plumbers are elevating the importance of their embedded knowledge that cannot be appropriated by others, or replaced by new technologies.

In the past few years, plumbers in the UK have consolidated their position further because apprenticeships have declined and fewer young people have entered the trade. The consequent shortfall in the supply of plumbers means that the price of their labour has increased. One particular consequence of the sorts of shortfalls in trades such as plumbing is that workers from overseas (particularly Eastern European countries such as Poland) are increasingly being brought in by construction firms to work on their projects. In part this is the result of skill shortages, but it is also because of the price of labour – the overseas workers may be just as skilled as UK workers, but are often willing to work for less money. In response, UK tradespeople such as plumbers and electricians may claim that overseas workers do not possess the correct knowledge about health and safety regulations – again illustrating how skill is very much a social construction.

Social closure or social regulation?

An important point to note is that social closure is an ongoing process that changes over time. Just as groups can build upon the ideological, political and material processes to create closure, they can also lose closure by neglecting or undermining one or more of the processes. Groups may display forms of social regulation which fall short of social closure. We suggest this can be illustrated by the intersections in Figure 16.1, and they constitute three different types:

- *Political-material regulation*: a group has a representative body that influences the labour supply, the organisation of work and the use of technology in the workplace but does not share a collective identity through a common set of values.
- *Ideological-material regulation*: a group shares an identity through a common set of values, influences the organisation of work and the use of technology in the workplace, but has no representative body and cannot control the supply of labour.
- *Ideological-political regulation*: a group shares an identity, and has a representative body that influences the labour supply, but cannot influence the organisation of work and the use of technology within the workplace.

The introduction of new technology is typically seen as a development that can affect all three of the processes. It can challenge the ideological process by breaking down traditional lines of demarcation between tasks: blurring the boundaries between occupational groups and their separate identities. It can influence the political process by forcing a reappraisal of the qualifications and training needed to undertake the work (thereby affecting the labour supply). And it can reconfigure the material process by redesigning the jobs and requiring the use of different equipment and tools.

A group has the strongest claim to skilled status if it has full social closure. However social regulation provides opportunities for creating differences on which claims to a skilled identity can be built.

Exercise 16.4

What do you think?

Choose an occupation from the list below and assess the extent to which it has achieved social closure. Use Figure 16.1 as a guide.

If the occupation has not achieved full social closure, which type of social regulation has it achieved?

o accountant,
o school teacher,
o fruit picker,
o journalist,
o firefighter,
o hotel receptionist,
o heart surgeon,
o website designer,
o personnel/human resource manager,
o refuse collector,
o minister of religion,
o nanny,
o taxi driver,
o actor.

You might want to repeat this exercise to see differences between occupational groups. You could also try it out on any other occupation or job with which you are familiar.

So far, the discussion has focused on how skill definitions are constructed by occupational groups. However, there is a far more widespread impact of social construction and it raises some serious issues concerning fairness and equality.

GENDER AND SKILL – THE SOCIAL CONSTRUCTION OF DISADVANTAGE

It is possible to argue that a form of social closure exists which centres not on occupational group, but on gender. The evidence suggests that just as an occupational group may seek to construct a notion of skill in its own interest, so too, men have acted as a social group. They have constructed skill in such a way as to benefit their own gender and to disadvantage women. To illustrate how this occurs, consider this example of a law firm.

Suchman (1996) describes the use of image-processing technology for the document management systems of a large law firm. The definitions of skill and work there were gendered. Most lawyers in the firm were males, but the support staff were not, and the latter's work, although vital, was devalued. The process, called 'litigation support', entailed the creation of a database index that guided access to a very large number of documents. Orderly access to and structured retrieval from files was vital to assembling arguments for cases. The males described the document coding as 'mindless' labour, potentially a target for automation or offshore placement. In fact, document coding was a highly knowledge-intensive activity, involving considerable discretion and independent judgement, so that documents that were separated from each other were cross-referenced and 'linked' (articulated) for later structured retrieval (Suchman, 1996: 415–17). This articulation work, a form of knowledge work, had been rendered invisible by the gendered definitions of skill employed by the males who dominated the workplace (Hampson and Junor, 2005: 170).

A considerable amount of evidence like this explores how jobs come to be 'gendered' and how this disadvantages women (Bradley, 1989; Walby, 1986). As a framework for discussion about this, we can use the three interlinking processes discussed above: the ideological, political and material processes of social closure.

Gender and the ideological process

Underpinning the concept of skill is an ideology of gender which labels some attitudes and forms of behaviour as masculine and others as feminine. These identities are not just found in the workplace, but throughout society – they may vary slightly from culture to culture. They result in stereotypes about what being a man or woman means. As Matthaei (1982: 194) found, 'a basic force behind sex-typing of jobs was the workers' desires to assert and reaffirm their manhood or womanhood and hence their difference from the opposite sex'.

Jobs can be associated with gender stereotypes which reflect (and reinforce) dominant cultural beliefs about male and female. For example, jobs requiring physical strength, stamina or logical thought have traditionally been considered masculine, because these are attributes supposedly possessed more by men. On the other hand, women, allegedly being innately sensitive, patient and dextrous, have been associated with caring, repetitive and intricate work.

The source of this belief is the view that a work role is a reflection of a 'natural' ability: in other words, determined by and constrained by biology. For example, in Cockburn's study of print workers (1983: 171–90), the men argued that their job was not suitable for a woman and offered a number of commonly held views why women could not and should not do their work:

- women lacked the strength;
- there was too much standing involved;
- they lacked the mental ability;
- they did not have the right temperament (aversion to technical work);
- they were too temperamental (emotional, bursting into tears);
- they were unreliable (because they had periods);
- they would be exposed to bad moral influences (such as swearing, practical jokes, vulgarity);
- they would force men to behave differently.

For the print workers, women represented a threat because their entry into the occupation challenged the ideology of what constituted male work:

> It's man's work. If you hear of a man secretary, a lot of people raise a few eyebrows. Well, it's the same with a woman working alongside a man doing *his* job ... if I said to my mates I was working with a woman, they would feel, say, oh, he's doing a woman's job – because they can see that a woman *can* do it.
>
> (A print worker quoted by Cockburn, 1983: 180, emphasis in original)

Similarly, a Transport and General Workers Union shop steward at an electrical components factory is quoted by Charles (1986: 163):

> There's been a great increase in humdrum jobs like the jobs here, that you wouldn't get a man doing.... But the women can sit at a bench eight hours and pick up little fiddly screws and put them in. I think it's fantastic, and they can go for week in week out, you know – but you'll never get a man doing it, so that's why you need ... women working.

Such opinions are not exclusive to men. Consider, for example, the views of these women quoted by Pollert (1981: 99) in her study of a tobacco factory:

| Kate (stripping room): | I can't imagine a man doing my work. It's too boring for a man. Women have much more patience. |
| Gale: | Men'd go mad. It'd kill them with boredom! Girls are expected to do that kind of thing. Girls are thought to be the weaker sex. |

In white-collar work, there is similar evidence of sex stereotyping of skill. A vivid example of this is provided by Collinson and Knights (1986), whose case study of an insurance company reveals how the male managers manipulated the setting (the work organisation), the recruitment process, selection criteria and rationale for promotion to segregate the office according to gender, and to justify this in terms of business rationale. The effect is to relegate women to a position of inferiority. This subordination is then used against women and explained as being a product of their gender. To illustrate this, consider the quotes below (taken from Collinson and Knights, 1986: 155, 158, 162, 165):

Branch manager:	Women aren't taken seriously in the insurance world. It can be a soul-destroying job. Inspectors have to advise our professional clients who recommend insurance and pensions to their clients, and we want them to recommend us. Yes, it can be a soul-destroying job, and women are either not hard-bitten enough to ride off insults or those that can are pretty unpleasant people.
Office manager:	My job is to keep them [the female clerical staff] as busy as possible…. You can't keep all six happy at the same time. With some you can tell their monthly changes, even the other girls say so. Sometimes when they're having a good chunner [moan] about the inspectors I have to impress on the girls that if it was not for the men, there'd be no jobs for them, if the blokes don't go out and sell insurance.
Personnel officer, Head Office:	The door is always open to move into the career structure, but we've found by and large, they're girls who are not particularly ambitious, looking forward to getting married, leaving and having a family and that's about the measure of it.
Senior pensions clerk:	I'm very temperamental, you see. This is another thing Mr Brown [the branch manager] drew to my attention. I can get annoyed very easily and I also get strong moods. He said, 'There's no way you could go out to a broker with some of the moods you have.'

The assumption frequently made is that work is not a central life interest for women. Suggests this is a false assumption when comparing work orientations of men and women in full-time work. However, the view persists that the central life interest for all women is the family (either their existing one or the prospect of one), and so they are considered more willing to tolerate boring, repetitive jobs with low career prospects and little responsibility. But this argument may be circular. Are women given boring work because they are perceived to have a lower work orientation, or might it be they have a lower work orientation because they only have access to boring, repetitive, low-paid, undervalued jobs? It could also be that stereotyping men's and women's work limits the type of jobs available to either gender; but in addition it also disadvantages women because it fixes an idea of what is 'women's work'. The argument is summed up by Jenson (1989), who identifies the way work performed by women tends to be seen as involving some natural female 'talent', whereas work done by men is viewed as involving a learned skill.

Extract 16.4

Gender and skill

The critical importance of gender in defining skill was first explored in a keynote article by Phillips and Taylor (1986). They conclude, 'it is the sex of those who do the work, rather than its content, which leads to its identification as skilled or unskilled' (1986: 63). In arriving at this position they bring out two important issues which help to identify the importance of the ideological process of social closure:

○ Where men and women work in similar processes, doing jobs of similar content, men are more likely to achieve skilled status. The research of Rubery and Wilkinson (1979) into box and carton manufacture is used to illustrate this point. The production of cartons and paper boxes involves a similar process except that while box production involves exclusively female labour, carton manufacture is undertaken by men and women. The latter is recognised as semi-skilled; the former as unskilled. Similarly, Spradley and Mann (1975) reveal that the work of waitresses is equally as demanding of a range of abilities as the work of bartenders, yet unlike the (male) bartenders, the waitresses do not enjoy skilled status.

○ Where new work processes were introduced allowing employers to deem some jobs 'female' from the outset, the work tended to be classified as low-skilled, 'not simply by virtue of the skills required for it but by virtue of the "inferior" status of the women who came to perform it' (Phillips and Taylor, 1986: 61).

In an excellent analysis of women's work in a range of industries, Bradley (1989) argues that the hosiery industry (mainly making tights) provides the best example of the feminisation of an occupation. Feminisation can mean women are brought in not directly to take over the work of men, but to work on newly reorganised and degraded work processes. Thus, women are at a disadvantage from the outset: 'The work of women is often deemed inferior simply because it is women who do it. Women workers carry into the workplace their status as subordinate individuals, and this status comes to define the value of the work they do' (Phillips and Taylor, 1986: 55).

The picture then is of a general undervaluation of jobs where women predominate. This disadvantage is frequently institutionalised and consolidated by job evaluation schemes that either fail to recognise all the attributes of jobs mainly performed by women, or value these attributes lower than comparable work mainly performed by men (Horrell, Rubery and Burchell, 1994; Neathey, 1992; Steinberg, 1990). The overall effect is a relatively lower pay rate for jobs where women predominate. For example, job evaluation schemes typically rate fiscal responsibility (such as devising budgets or counting cash) more highly than social responsibility (such as caring for the sick or minding young children). Indeed, we will explore later how social skills are often taken for granted and frequently undervalued by employers. Another example is that physical strength (a supposed male natural ability) is often rated higher than dexterity (a supposed female natural ability). The danger is that the evaluation process is widely considered fair because it is seen as an objective measure of skill – but, as noted earlier in this chapter, such an assumption is naive. In Steinberg's words:

> job evaluation systems … have been constructed to embed cultural assumptions about what constitutes skilled and responsible work in a way

that significantly benefits men through the work they have historically performed.

(Steinberg, 1990: 454)

They institutionalise and perpetuate the ideology of masculine and feminine work, and in this way assist in the ideological process of social closure.

Gender and the political process

In many settings men have been proactive in seeking to protect and differentiate their skills from those of women. The situation is summed up well by Steinberg (1990: 476):

> Skill determinations are socially constructed in highly political contexts, in which males – whether employers or employees – exert considerably more power to maintain their definitions of skill.... Struggles over the meaning of skill between employers and (primarily male) employees have been frequent, bitter, and hard fought. When employees have won, males have maintained their skill designations and wage rates, even in the face of the deterioration of job content. When employees have lost ... skill designations are lowered, wage rates deteriorate, and male employees exit to be replaced by women.

As work processes have changed, men have sought to hold on to their skilled status. Often this has been to the detriment of women (as we explain in more detail below) so that 'skill has been increasingly defined against women – skilled work is work that women don't do' (Phillips and Taylor, 1986: 63).

Trade unions have played an important role in this political process, providing the means by which male workers can organise and exclude women from their trades (Hartmann, 1979). The historical analysis of gender relations in employment by Walby (1986: 244) leads her to conclude that:

> from the last quarter of the nineteenth century an increasing proportion of trade unions used grading and segregation as their response to women's employment, rather than the exclusionary strategy .... It is almost never the case that a union which included men did not follow one of these two patriarchal strategies.

According to this, the political process of organising through trade unions has disadvantaged women in terms of both (i) access to 'skilled' work, and (ii) the attainment of skilled status for jobs where women predominate. In addition, research shows that the domination of the male agenda persists within trade unions, and that 'a wide gap exists between what the unions claim for women and what they deliver, but more to the point, between what they claim and what they *attempt* to deliver' (Cunnison and Stageman, 1995: 237–8).

Gender and the material process

Cockburn (1983, 1985, 1986) explores the importance of material aspects of male domination. Through this she is able to identify the way that men take control and ownership of tools and technology. This gives them an advantage in developing notions of what counts as skilled work. Her argument is based on the importance of two related concepts: physical effectivity and technical effectivity.

Physical effectivity

The first part of Cockburn's argument is that the physical differences between men and women are often exaggerated to the benefit of men. Obviously, there are biological differences between men and women, but these limit each gender in only a very small range of tasks – most of which are not work based. Similarly, there are physical differences in average height and body weight, but again these are not necessarily relevant in most jobs. Gender differences are encouraged through childhood and socialisation – with men being more expected to participate in physical activities. As a consequence, men, on average, attain physical effectivity to a greater extent than women.

Technical effectivity

The second part of Cockburn's argument concerns technical effectivity: familiarity with and control over machinery and tools. As noted above, such control is important in constructing a skill identity. Cockburn argues that men have historically acquired control over the design of technology and work processes, and as a consequence this perpetuates existing patterns of dominance. As Wajcman (1991: 41) puts it, 'men selectively design tools and machinery to match their technical skills. Machinery is designed by men with men in mind. Industrial technology thus reflects male power as well as capitalist domination'. This does not necessarily imply an organised conspiracy by men against women, but it certainly reflects a gender-centricity resulting in some machinery and tools being too bulky or heavy for the 'average' woman. There are exceptions to this which prove that alternative approaches are available. Clarke (1989), for example, shows how the increased availability of female labour in Sweden prompted Volvo to invest in the design of tools ergonomically suited for the 'average' woman. For instance, they developed hydraulic lifting devices to lessen the physical requirements of vehicle assembly. But such examples remain rare.

Generally, technical effectivity is sustained through an ideology that perpetuates the notion that men are technically more competent than women. Nowhere is this more evident than the division of labour in the home (see, for example, Oakley, 1974, 1982; Pahl, 1984). Cockburn vividly portrays this in a chapter entitled 'The kitchen, the tool shed' (1985: 198–224). She illustrates how men not only acquire technical effectivity through work but can use this to improve their social standing in the community, through, for example, being the person who can fix cars or do some rewiring. Women, on the other hand, are discouraged from transporting any technical skills into the home. A woman may use pliers, screwdrivers, Allen keys and a soldering iron at work, but at home these are almost invariably kept for the exclusive use of men and are locked in the tool shed. Acutely aware of how technical effectivity can construct advantage, men jealously guard their knowledge:

> Men's know-how is seldom passed by men to women as a cost-free gift, taught in a serious, generous and genuine way. Often it is hoarded behind a cachet of professional knowledge or craft skill and handed out sparingly, reluctantly. Sometimes it is dispensed from a great height and purposefully used to put women down.
>
> (Cockburn, 1985: 202–3)

The two components of physical and technical effectivity support of the exercise of male power. As Cockburn (1986: 97–8) argues, 'the process ... involves several converging practices: accumulation of bodily capabilities, the definition of tasks to match them and the selective design of tools and machines'. This shows how the material power base, constructed historically, is maintained for the benefit of men.

TO SUM UP

Through exploring ideological, political and material processes, it is possible to see how skill has been constructed in a way that advantages men. In particular, the work of Cockburn demonstrates the way men have, in some occupations, taken control of technology through ideological, political and material means and used it to define their own work as skilled and women's work as unskilled. In this sense, there is an ongoing process of gendered social closure. This is embedded in the power of occupational groups and their institutions and the patriarchal structures of management.

Exercise 16.5

What do you think?

1 Consider each of the jobs listed below and note down whether the image that comes into your mind is of a man or a woman:
   o nursery care worker,
   o nightclub bouncer,
   o midwife,
   o beauty therapist,
   o electrician,
   o librarian,
   o financial advisor,
   o train driver.
2 The likelihood is that your gender assignment to these jobs reflects whether they are currently more likely to be undertaken by men or women. Now consider why this gendered image is dominant. To do this, take two jobs that you have 'assigned' to a gender and explore why they seem to be male or female. You will need to reflect on the points made in the previous section about the gendered nature of the ideological, political and material processes.
3 Now reflect on your own point of view: do you think the jobs ought to be gendered in this way? Explain and justify your reasoning.

CONCLUSION

The controversy surrounding skill is likely to continue as long as there remain different theoretical perspectives from which to look at what skill is, and how (or if) it can be measured. Once again, it demonstrates the importance of acknowledging the plurality of approaches to a particular problem. By exploring the diversity of meanings, this chapter has been able to explain the principal competing interpretations of skill. Instead of suggesting there is one way of looking, the analysis has explored different angles and produced a more complex picture with greater depth. As the different viewpoints have been brought into focus, so new aspects of the notion of skill have come into sharp relief.

As has been shown, the social construction of skill can be used to integrate the different approaches because it provides a framework for understanding both technical (objective) measures and social (subjective) meanings of skill. In other words, 'skill' is constructed by drawing on meanings that incorporate all three elements explored above: the person, the job and the setting. These provide the resources that allow the claim to skilled status to be made. However, making this claim depends on successful social closure, in terms of political, ideological and material processes.

The concept of skill is important because it has important consequences. It can be used by different interest groups to lay claim to status, special treatment and higher rewards. This has impacted on the gender division of labour with a dramatic under-valuing of the work of women.

A further issue remains unanswered: to what extent might there be a general historical shift in the nature of skill? Might skill be hard to define because work is continually changing and demanding different abilities? And if such a change can be detected, in which direction is it heading? Are people becoming less skilled or more skilled?

WHAT IS ER?

HISTORICAL ROOTS

The empirical roots of employee relations enquiry lie in the coincidence at the end of the nineteenth century of the two faces of the 'labour question': the issues of social welfare and social control (Hyman, 1989a:3). The theoretical roots of the subject can be traced principally to the clash between Marxian political economy and the emergent neo-classical economics at around the same time (Marsden, 1982:236–8). In terms of empirical enquiry, the problematic nature of the 'labour question' was epitomised at this time by two significant disputes: the Match Girls' strike of 1888 and the Great London Dock Strike of 1889. At that time, being a match girl 'rated somewhere practically below prostitution in the social scale' (McCarthy, 1988:57–8), their conditions of work were dangerous and unpleasant, their pay meagre. The match girls' victory in the 1888 dispute, however, secured with public opinion on their side, had a significance beyond the strike itself. It 'turned a new leaf in Trade Union annals ... It was a new experience for the weak to succeed ... [and] ... The lesson was not lost on other workers' (Sidney and Beatrice Webb, quoted by Stafford, 1961:79). The following year, the social convulsion sparked by the match girls at Bryant & May's reached the River Thames and the men who worked on the docks and wharves. The dockers' strike became the 'symbol of new unionism' that emerged at the end of the nineteenth century (Clegg *et al.*, 1964:55), not only a great victory for the dockers but a dispute that 'changed the whole face of the Trade Union world' (Webb and Webb, 1920:401). For radicals such as Henry Champion, one of the leaders of the strike, the dispute was won 'despite our socialism' (quoted by McCarthy, 1988:50), but for others such as Frederick Engels, lifelong companion of Karl Marx, the strike was,

> the movement of the greatest promise we have had for years ... If these poor downtrodden men, the dregs of the proletariat, these odds and ends of all trades, fighting every morning at the dock gates for an engagement, if *they* can combine, and terrify by their resolution the mighty Dock Companies, truly then we need not despair of any section of the working class ... If the dockers get organised, all other sections will follow ... It is a glorious movement. (Marx and Engels, 1975:399, original emphasis)

The dockers, like the match girls, had attracted widespread public sympathy, and substantial financial donations, due partly to their own efforts during the strike itself but also to the work of social reformers such as Beatrice Potter (later Webb) and Charles Booth whose *Life and Labour of the People in London* demonstrated to the public and ruling classes alike not only the problems of poverty and degradation among casual workers such as the dockers, but also the wider threat to the stability of society from an 'underclass' deprived of a basic standard of life. The question of social welfare, it appeared, was inseparable from that of social control. Or more precisely, the latter appeared to be largely dependent on the former.

The theoretical origins of the subject can be traced to the 'Achilles Heel' of the emergent neo-classical economics, namely the analysis of labour and labour markets in general and the theory of wage determination in particular. The break between classical economic thought or political economy and neo-classical economics was marked by very different questions being asked about what constituted the subject matter of economics. Classical political economy was concerned, first and foremost, with the conditions that make possible the creation of an economic surplus (or as Adam Smith put it with *The Wealth of Nations*), and in particular how society had been transformed from a situation of subsistence to one of accumulation. Neo-classical economics, in contrast, is concerned with the allocation of scarce resources between competing ends, with the questions of supply and demand, pricing and allocation. As a result, the focus of economics shifted from the production of wealth to its consumption, from the division of labour and social relations between classes to the market mechanism and individual decision-making.

On the question of wages, classical economists such as David Ricardo (1817) had developed 'subsistence' theories to explain the remuneration of human labour. Wages would tend to remain at a level which sustained and reproduced human labour but did not provide that labour with any degree of affluence. Thus, although Ricardo allowed for the influence of 'custom and habit', such that the subsistence wage might increase to reflect what is deemed 'customary' or 'necessary' at any given time (the 'standard of living'), the theory nonetheless presented a rather bleak future for the financial well-being of the working class. Similarly, Marx (1976) also proposed a subsistence theory of wages, but with the added twist of the analysis being grounded explicitly in a theory of capitalism, wherein the wage labourer was subject to exploitation by the employer. Furthermore, even though the subsistence wage might increase over time, Marx put forward the notion of 'absolute impoverishment' for the working class, reflecting the progressive 'de-skilling' and 'alienation' of labour. For Marx, workers under capitalism would gradually, but inexorably, lose control over the process of production as greater division of labour created not only unskilled but highly fragmented work, with workers becoming, as a result, more and more estranged from the product of their labour. At the risk of over-simplification, the working class would thus cease to be a passive class *in itself* and become mobilised into a class *for itself*, ultimately seeking to overthrow capitalism and replace it with socialism.

But what has all this got to do with employee relations? Simply put, neo-classical economics sought to take the 'political' out of political economy by developing a theory of wage determination and income distribution based not on the social relations between classes but on the concepts of marginal productivity and individual choice. According to this new economics, wages were not determined by a (political) power struggle between classes but by the marginal productivity of the worker. To explain the theory, imagine a situation where capital (buildings, machinery and so on) is in fixed supply and the firm increases the number of workers employed. As more and more workers are engaged, there will be less capital per worker, and consequently the output of each additional worker will be less than that of the original workforce. In other words, the productivity of each successive employee to be hired (output per worker) will be lower. What matters is not whether total output is increasing but what the *marginal* increase to output is, because, according to neo-classical economics, it is the productivity of the final worker to be hired which determines the wage. To be sure, the last worker to be engaged adds less output than that created by the original workforce, but more than any future or potential workers because of declining marginal productivity. So, if any of the original workforce demanded a higher wage the employer could sack them and engage the marginal worker in their stead. Each and every worker is therefore worth to the employer only what the last (marginal) worker engaged can produce, and so the employer will continue to employ additional workers only up to the point where their cost (wage) is equal to the value of their marginal product. As each and every worker receives a wage equivalent to the amount of wealth he or she creates, there can be no exploitation. In short, the politics has been taken out of political economy, and the socialist movement theoretically defused.

Unfortunately for the new economists, as Alfred Marshall pointed out in his *Principles of Economics*, first published in 1890, marginal productivity is an incomplete theory of wages. In fact, it is not a theory of wages at all. Rather it is a theory of labour demand. It tells us how many workers an employer will hire at a given wage in order to maximise profits (suggesting that the higher the wage, the fewer the number of workers that will be employed, and vice versa). But what determines the actual wage that prevails? To complete the picture, the theory of wage determination requires an explanation of the supply side. Again, the theory is based on individual decision-making, this time the choices made by individual workers between income and leisure. Higher wages, up to a point, will induce workers to work longer hours (or sacrifice more hours of leisure), or alternatively will induce more people of working age to offer themselves for employment. The result is an upward sloping labour supply curve which intersects the downward sloping labour demand curve at what neo-classical economists call the 'market clearing wage' (that is, the wage at which there are neither shortages nor surpluses in the labour market, the wage which every individual who wants to work can in fact find a job). The problem of wage determination has thus been solved without even a whiff of exploitation or a whisper of power. Or has it?

Even neo-classical economists, for all their heroic assumptions about the labour market, cannot ignore the presence of monopoly, combination and collective action on the part of both employers and employees. If the firm is a monopsonist (single buyer) in the labour market or if business organisations combine to form an employers' association, then neo-classical theory predicts that the firm will pay a lower wage than would prevail in a competitive market. On the other hand, if a trade union is a monopoly (single seller) in the labour market then it will seek a wage above the market clearing rate by restricting the supply of labour. Thus, in a situation of bilateral monopoly there will be no unique 'solution' to the problem of wage determination but rather a *range of indeterminacy* between what the union demands and what the employer is prepared to pay (for a formal exposition see Sapsford, 1981:102–4). In Marshall's words, 'if the employers in any trade act together and so do the employed, the solution to the problem of wages becomes indeterminate ... there is nothing but bargaining to decide the exact shares in which this [surplus] should go to employers and employed' (1930:627–8). For some neo-classical economists, such as Edgeworth (1881:20), the fact that 'contract without competition is indeterminate' meant that such matters were beyond the scope of economics. Not only had the 'politics' been removed from 'political economy' but the analysis of production, labour relations and social relations more widely were now matters to be left to other disciplines or specialist areas of social science research.

One such specialism was industrial relations, arguably founded by Beatrice and Sidney Webb. The Webbs have been credited with being the first to coin the phrase 'collective bargaining' (see Lyddon, 2003:97), for many years the central subject matter of industrial relations. The term itself, however, was clearly derived from Marshall, with whom they agreed 'absolutely in economics' (Marsden, 1982:237). Theoretically, therefore, the analysis and study of industrial relations largely grew out of a concern to explain the supply and sale of labour: 'The concern with collective bargaining did not materialize out of thin air, it was given by economics' (Marsden, 1982:238; see also Clegg, 1979:447). But henceforth it was to be an area of study largely *separate* from economics. As Hugh Clegg (1979:34) put it, there is 'not much to be gained by looking to economics for a theory of industrial relations if economists have to go outside economics to find an explanation for wage determination'. This separation not only narrowed the field of economics, it effectively forestalled the development of any political economy of industrial relations. Unfortunately, in this separation of industrial relations from economics, the work of the earlier classical economists and that of Marx was also ignored, arguably to the detriment of both economics and industrial relations (see Brown and Nolan, 1988; Gall, 2003a; and Kelly, 1998). A consequence of this was that one of the first explicit 'theories' of industrial relations, developed by the American labour economist John Dunlop (1958), centred on a (largely self-contained) 'system' of industrial relations which was *not* part of a society's economic system but a distinctive sub-system of its own, only partially overlapping the economic and political decision-making systems with which it interacts. The three sub-systems themselves were seen to be contained within an overall 'social system'.

THE INDUSTRIAL RELATIONS SYSTEM

For Dunlop, heavily influenced by the functionalism of Talcot Parsons (1952) and the core Parsonian question of how the elements of society interacted to produce social continuity, the industrial relations system is seen to be 'comprised of certain actors, certain contexts, an ideology which binds the industrial relations system together and a body of rules created to govern the actors at the workplace' (Dunlop, 1958:7). The actors include a hierarchy of management and their representatives, a hierarchy of non-management employees (workers) and their representatives, and specialised third party agencies such as governmental bodies. The environmental contexts which influence the decisions and actions of the actors include the technological characteristics of the workplace and the nature of the work community, market or budgetary constraints, and the locus and distribution of power in the larger society. Interaction between the parties within different environmental contexts is governed, in large part, by an ideology or common set of beliefs that 'defines the role and place of each actor and that defines the ideas which each actor holds towards the place and function of others in the system' (ibid:16). But the definition of industrial relations as 'the complex of interrelations among managers, workers and agencies of government' (ibid:v), as Marsden (1982:239) notes, was quickly and quietly switched to the formation and maintenance of the *rules* of the system: 'The central task of a theory of industrial relations is to explain why particular rules are established in particular industrial relations systems and how and why they change in response to changes affecting this system' (Dunlop, 1958:ix). Moreover, it was the *joint* determination of rules that commanded Dunlop's attention – his text contains virtually no reference to non-union employers or the philosophy and practice of management (see Kaufman, 2003:214–15).

At one level, systems theory might be viewed as a useful means of classifying variables relevant to industrial relations, but it is hardly an explanatory approach in its own right. If anything, it is 'more a set of questions than a theoretical statement' (Strauss and Feuille, 1978:267). Indeed, both theoretical and substantive criticisms of Dunlop's model abound (for a review, see Poole, 1981). As Poole (1988:13) in a later discussion argues, the relationship between variables in the framework are assumed to be interlocking and interactive, which runs counter to genuine explanatory analysis: it is very difficult to disentangle central from peripheral variables, to identify causal sequences, to isolate independent variables, and to attach explanatory weights to such variables. At best, systems analysis is a *description* of industrial relations, not a theory, an abstraction from the 'known facts' arranged into a coherent model or system (Marsden, 1982:239). More importantly, the very notion of a 'system' of industrial relations implies a functional integration of component institutions (Hyman, 1992:7), especially when a common ideology amongst the actors is assumed. When combined with a focus on rules, the implication is that 'what industrial relations is all about is the maintenance of stability and regularity in industry' (Hyman, 1975:11).

Subsequent expositions of systems theory (e.g. Craig, 1986) have considerably elaborated Dunlop's original schema and sought to introduce a far more extensive range of variables and a greater awareness of feedback relationships between variables over time. For example, management, unions and the state might be conceptualised as 'primary' or 'direct' actors while other actors not originally considered by Dunlop, such as consumers or other 'end users' of various goods and services, can be incorporated into the model as 'secondary' or 'indirect' actors. These end users might be involved in the industrial relations system as 'co-producers' or 'co-designers' (e.g. disabled groups who work with transport companies to facilitate access to vehicles, both in terms of vehicle design and route networks) or they may act as 'co-supervisors' of the employee's work (e.g. customer complaints or satisfaction surveys that are used increasingly in the service sector) (see Bellemare, 2000:390–8; and Heery, 1993). Thus, end users might influence day-to-day work routines, personnel policies such as supervision and discipline, and even collective bargaining strategies (e.g. legal action by customers in the event of a strike) (Bellemare, 2000:398). Expanding Dunlop's model in this way, however, calls into question his idea of industrial relations as a largely separate (sub)system (ibid:400). At the theoretical level, therefore, the model cannot accommodate a more diverse range of actors, which is tantamount to saying that the model cannot accommodate change or the emergence of new actors in industrial relations. As a result, the emphasis on order and stability remains.

The influence of Dunlop's systems analysis and the focus on stability and order in the study of industrial and employee relations is clearly evident in the work of prominent British academics in the field, most notably Allan Flanders, Hugh Clegg and (the early work of) Alan Fox, often referred to collectively as the 'Oxford School':

> Economics deals with a system of markets, politics with a system of government ... a system of industrial relations is a system of rules. These rules appear in different guises: in legislation and in statutory orders; in trade union regulations; in collective agreements and in arbitration awards; in

social conventions; in management decisions; and in accepted 'custom and practice'. This list is by no means exhaustive, but 'rules' is the only generic description that can be given to these various instruments of regulation. In other words, the subject deals with certain regulated or institutionalised relationships in industry. (Flanders, 1965:9–10)

Similarly, Clegg (1979:1) argues that industrial relations 'is the study of the rules governing employment, together with the ways in which the rules are made and changed, interpreted and administered'. The rules themselves 'cannot be understood apart from the organizations that take part in the process', namely trade unions, employers' associations and government/public bodies, and 'each of these organizations has its own sources of authority' (ibid:1). As a result, rules can be made jointly (through collective bargaining or custom and practice) or unilaterally (through managerial prerogative, trade union regulation or statutory imposition). But to define industrial relations as 'a study of the institutions of job regulation' (Flanders, 1965:10) is to conceive the subject in terms of relationships between agencies rather than between people, to ignore the real, active men and women whose activities *are* industrial and employee relations (Hyman, 1975:13; and Nichols, 1980:12). And there remains the over-riding concern with the 'problem of order', diverting attention away from the structures of power within the workplace and beyond. In sum, such a focus has relegated the problem of social welfare to the periphery, 'while the preoccupation with job regulation brought the problem of control to the centre of the agenda' (Hyman, 1989a:8).

Unsurprisingly, industrial relations became problem-focused, issue-driven, and policy-orientated (see Strauss and Feuille, 1978). In the UK, this was reinforced by governments in the 1960s identifying industrial relations as a 'problem', contributing to low productivity and increasing strike activity. This placed an emphasis on the practical need to study industrial relations institutions in order to recommend policy reform. The role of industrial relations academics in this was epitomised by many of the contributions to the Royal Commission on Trade Unions and Employers' Associations (Donovan, 1968), and in particular in most of the research papers written to inform that Commission.

Research on the subject was thus predominantly empirical, characterised by the aphorism attributed to the Oxford School of 'a pound of facts and an ounce of theory' (Cappelli, 1985:91). To study industrial relations was to be a detective, for as Sir Arthur Conan Doyle wrote in *The Memoirs of Sherlock Holmes*, 'it is a capital mistake to theorize before one has data'. Hugh Clegg made this orientation quite clear in his book on *The Changing System of Industrial Relations in Great Britain*. Having described 'what appear to be the main elements of, and developments in, British industrial relations', it is 'only after that have explanations been offered – where they were available, and as they seemed to fit in' (1979:446).

Methodologically, the approach of the Oxford School, and indeed industrial relations research dating from the Webbs (Brown and Wright, 1994:155–8), can be characterised as essentially one of induction, where 'theories or rules are suggested by behaviour in specific examples and are used to make inferences about the general case' (Cappelli, 1985:91; see also Whitfield and Strauss, 1998 and 2000). The classic example of this approach was Allan Flanders's (1964) investigation of *The Fawley Productivity Agreements*, a single case study which suggested that the structure of collective bargaining could have a powerful influence on the conduct of industrial relations at the plant level, and on the behaviour of management and trade unions. This analysis, and the prescription that followed, was then extended to much of British industry in the form of 'productivity bargaining'. But as Cappelli warns, the inferences generated by induction do not follow logically or necessarily from the phenomena to be explained. They are 'at best probable explanations that must be supported by empirical arguments in order to be judged reasonable' (1985:91). Empiricism is therefore perpetuated, but more importantly there is a tendency for any general laws to come from the same level of analysis that is employed, which in turn is largely determined by the questions being asked. Put differently, if the focus is 'the institutions of job regulation', an inductive theory will place a heavy emphasis on institutional detail, frequently to the detriment of other levels of analysis or explanatory variables, consequently leading to an emphasis on order rather than disorder in employee relations.

An important illustration of the shortcomings of this approach was the work of the Donovan Commission (Donovan, 1968) which, as already noted, was heavily influenced by the Oxford School. Prior to the Royal Commission it was widely believed that Britain had only a single system of industrial relations, based on a formal system of collective bargaining between trade unions and employers' associations, conducted largely at the national level (see, for example, Flanders and Clegg, 1954). Reality proved to be somewhat different, but rather than abandon the idea of an industrial relations system the Royal Commission's approach was to describe an additional one, an informal system of negotiations involving workers, shop stewards and management at the workplace level. The prognosis was that the informal system was in conflict with the formal system, or more precisely the former had undermined the stability of the latter. But to say that the formal and informal systems were in conflict was 'equivalent to saying that systems theory cannot explain reality, fact is in conflict with reality' (Marsden, 1982:242). In order to maintain the integrity of the system, Lord Donovan's prescription was inevitably to bring about a closer integration of component institutions in order to curtail 'disorder'. More elaborate, formalised, systematic procedures at the local level were deemed necessary, as were stronger industrial relations management and a closer integration of shop stewards into (official) trade union structures. These recommendations not only reflected the failure of systems theory to adequately explain the problems of British industrial relations, but also highlighted the hold which the pluralist perspective, as propounded by the members of the Oxford School, had gained.

PLURALISM AND INDUSTRIAL RELATIONS ORTHODOXY

Pluralism is far from being a homogeneous body of analysis and prescription (see Hyman, 1978 for a discussion), but the central tenets of the dominant influence in British industrial relations enquiry – what might be termed 'institutional pluralism' – can be briefly stated. Organisations are viewed as 'a miniature democratic state composed of sectional groups with divergent interests over which the government tries to maintain some kind of dynamic equilibrium' (Fox, 1966:2). Today, these ideas find expression through the discourse of 'stake-holding', with the organisation and its managers presumed to be accountable to the workforce, customers, suppliers, environmental groups, and the general public, rather than just the owners or shareholders. A recent large-scale survey of members of the Institute of Management certainly indicates that many managers subscribe to this view: 'modern managers do now perceive their organisations in terms of a variety of stakeholders having a legitimate stake in the goals and objectives of their organisations' (Poole et al., 2001:29). What, then, are the implications of this approach?

Recognising the reality of separate interests within industry and society, and the legitimacy of their organised expression, pluralists argue that a stable 'negotiated order' will develop from the organisation of competing interests. In other words, conflict is accepted as both inevitable and legitimate within any organisation, but the dominant preoccupation of pluralists is with establishing structures and procedures within which those legitimate conflicts of interest can be contained and prevented from damaging the interests of all. As Brown (1988:49) notes, this 'institutionalisation of conflict' requires a recognition of both the existence and legitimacy of conflicting interests; the effective representation of those interests; some flexibility of objectives and central direction of policy; a climate where sectional interests can be realised; a semblance of power balance between the parties; and, as a second line of institutional defence, a system of mediation and arbitration. In short, not only must management be prepared to *recognise* and *accept* a conflict of interests with their workforce, but be prepared to *negotiate* with independent trade unions in a climate of 'give-and-take'.

Pluralism is usually contrasted with unitarism, where the organisation is viewed as a team 'unified by a common purpose' (Fox, 1966:2), namely the success of the organisation. With a single source of authority (management) and all participants sharing the same goal, harmony and co-operation are the predicted outcomes. For unitarists, conflict is not inevitable but pathological, the outcome of misunderstanding or mischief. Either management has failed to communicate its goals effectively, causing temporary friction until the message 'gets home', or there must be troublemakers deliberately stirring up problems where none would otherwise exist. Writing in the mid-1960s, Fox held that the unitary approach 'has long since been abandoned by most social scientists as incongruent with reality and useless for the purpose of analysis' (1966:4), but the view is still widely held by many British managers (Poole *et al.*, 1981:82–3; and Poole and Mansfield, 1992 and 1993) and underpins many of the recent developments encapsulated in the term 'human resource management' (see Blyton and Turnbull, 1992; Legge, 1995; Redman and Wilkinson, 2001; and Storey, 2001). Consequently, the unitary view of organisations and employment relationships 'is not simply to be dismissed. It is important to try to understand why practitioners hold the views that they do instead of treating them as wrong' (Edwards, 1986:20–1). But then we must treat unitarism as a *perspective* rather than a theory. The same can be said of pluralism.

Although pluralists recognise that there is an imbalance of power within organisations, and that no single interest group will be able to dominate totally all other interest groups, when it comes to employee relations where there are essentially only two main parties (management and labour) there is nonetheless a tendency to assume (at least implicitly, if not explicitly) that an approximate balance of power exists, with the state acting as a neutral referee. As a result, many pluralists very quickly move from a statement that conflict is natural, rational and inevitable to an assessment of how conflict is organised, channelled and ultimately 'managed'. In other words, a pluralist approach 'does not tackle the problem of the nature or the basis of conflict, and merely concentrates on what happens when organizational expressions of conflict have already been articulated' (Edwards, 1986:24). Hence, the focus is on the *resolution* of conflict rather than its *generation*, or in the words of the pluralist on 'the institutions of job regulation'. This in turn 'encourages a segregation of industrial relations as an area of analysis from the underlying social relations of production, and hence facilitates an uncritical orientation towards managerial priorities of cost-effectiveness and technical rationality' (Hyman, 1978:35). Thus, issues of social control tend to predominate over those of social welfare.

Furthermore, by asserting the autonomy of industrial relations (Hyman, 1978:20) and rejecting existing theories derived from the social sciences in preference for an inductive approach (Bain and Clegg, 1974:107), pluralist industrial relations has simply replicated many of the problems of systems analysis. There cannot be a coherent theory of industrial relations when almost every situation is believed or portrayed to be a 'special case', to a greater or lesser extent, inexplicable by existing laws and therefore requiring detailed empirical, institutional analysis. For it is a truism, not a theory, that conflict is inevitable. Pluralism offers no comprehensive explanation for such conflicts, beyond acknowledging that different interests prevail in the workplace. In fact, by failing to elaborate the bases of conflict within organisations, pluralism serves more to mystify than to illuminate. As Richard Hyman has argued,

> understanding would be better assisted by a radically different approach: a sensitivity to the contradictory dynamics of capitalist production, the antagonistic structure of material interests within the labour market and the labour process, and the consequent and persistent generation of conflict and disorder within the very institutions and procedures designed to bring order and stability to employer-employee relationships. (1978:35)

Hyman is one of a number of Marxist theorists who have posed broader questions about the nature of the employment relationship, and in doing so have rejected the accepted orthodoxy of British industrial relations and its tacit support for the *status quo*.

MARXISM AND THE ISSUES OF CONTROL AND RESISTANCE

Just as there is no homogeneous body of pluralist thought, the same is true of Marxist analysis. In particular, because Marxism became a movement, there has been a tendency to focus on the political agenda derived from Marx's writings, rather than what he contributed to our understanding of society. As capitalism has not been superseded by socialism, many writers assume this to be sufficient to dismiss Marxist thought outright. Thus, Farnham and Pimlott (1990:16–17) write,

> To Marxists, industrial relations are essentially politicized and part of the class struggle ... the Marxist stress on the inevitable and polarized class struggle in industry and society between capitalist and proletariat, whilst probably a valid interpretation of nineteenth-century Victorian capitalism, does little to explain the complex, economic and social conflicts of late twentieth-century Britain.

However, this is to miss the point and to ignore the insights that can be derived from Marx's analysis of the nature of capitalism and how these illuminate aspects of the relationship between employers and employed. To focus on the Marxist *movement* rather than Marxist *thought*, and to reject the theory out of hand (as Farnham and Pimlott seem to advocate), is to throw the baby out with the bath water. If nothing else,

> the major contribution of Marxists has been as much in the questions asked as in the answers given or the methods of their attainment. It is the framework of what is taken for granted or what is regarded as problematic that most clearly differentiates Marxists from conventional 'industrial relations' analysts. (Hyman, 1989a:128)

For Marxists, industrial and employee relations can *only* be understood as part of a broader analysis of (capitalist) society, in particular the social relations of production and the dynamics of capital accumulation (Hyman, 1994:171). That is why there can be no such thing, strictly speaking, as a Marxist 'theory' of industrial relations: the project is a contradiction in terms (Marsden, 1982:245). As Hyman notes, for Marxists, 'the activities of employers and unions are to be construed in terms of such concepts as relations of production and class struggle; the term industrial relations is at worst vacuous and at best incoherent' (1989a:124). What Marxian analysis offers is a different perspective to understand society, a theoretical approach which emphasises totality, change, contradiction and practice (Hyman, 1975:4). Totality reflects the idea that all social phenomena are inter-related, and that no one area can be analysed satisfactorily in isolation. Unlike systems analysis, however, Marxists not only seek to construct a political economy of industrial relations, in which industrial relations are *integrated with* and not *separated from* the political and economic spheres, but also to assign causal priority to the social relations of production – that is, 'the way in which economic activity is organised in any society' (Hyman, 1975:4). In other words, the material, productive base of society will shape political institutions, legislation, modes of thought, even the nature of the family. As Marx himself put it, 'the mode of production in material life determines the general character of the social, political and spiritual processes of life' (1972:11).

An emphasis on stability is rejected by Marxists in favour of change and contradiction. Social relations are judged to be not only dynamic but characterised by the opposing interests of different classes. These contradictions present opportunities for change, but actual changes reflect the choices made by the different actors – what Marx refers to as *praxis*. In Marxist analysis, the material features of social life, especially the economics of production, limit the possibilities available for the organisation of human existence, but do not determine behaviour. A dialectical, not a deterministic process takes place.

It is this broader approach to the study of employment relations that most usefully distinguishes Marxism from systems theory, pluralism and unitarism, and it is through this approach that Marxists have sought to dig beneath the surface elements of employee relations such as collective bargaining, management decision-making, legislation, trade union regulations and workplace custom and practice. It is important to emphasise that this is not simply a question of different 'levels of analysis' – the 'individual' or 'unified organisation' in unitarist analysis, the 'sub-system' in the functionalist analysis of pluralism, or the 'system as a whole' in Marxist analysis – but rather how we conceptualise employment relationships (see Martin, 1999:1213–14). Thus, in contrast to any implicit or explicit assumptions about a balance of power in industry, Marxists emphasise the *asymmetry* of power between employer and employee, derived primarily from the ownership or non-ownership of capital. That is, at the most basic level, an employer is able to survive longer without labour than the employee can survive without work. Of course, the employee has a degree of freedom to choose the employer for whom he or she wishes to work but, as Marglin (1974:37) points out, 'it is a strange logic of choice that places its entire emphasis on the absence of legal compulsion'. The employee, by definition, must sell her or his ability to work in order to subsist.

Ownership acts as a source of power and control, bestowing on employers not only the 'right' to hire and fire labour but also to direct that labour in the process of production. Moreover, if employers can convince employees that they not only have a legitimate (property) right to control certain decisions but a moral right or duty, they exercise not only power but authority (see Gospel and Palmer, 1993:189–97). For Marxists, the exercise of power and the achievement of authority is a key dynamic in all employment relationships, because the employer can never secure total control or achieve complete authority. The capacity to work may be bought and sold in a (labour) market like any other commodity, but the object that is sold (the physical, mental and emotional capabilities of individuals) cannot be separated from the subject of the actual exchange (the individuals themselves). When the employee agrees to work for so many hours per week at a given wage, that is not the end of the matter but the start. Unlike other 'factors of production', the precise nature of the labour input, or more accurately the precise tasks the worker is expected to perform, both in a quantitative and qualitative sense, can never be perfectly specified in advance by the employer. The labour input involves 'a continuous bargain every day and hour, renewed either in the prices that are to be paid or the amount of product that the worker turns out' (Commons, 1919:24). The 'wage-effort bargain' is therefore contended and in a continuous state of flux, 'an invisible frontier of control ... which is defined and redefined in a *continuous* process of pressure and counterpressure, conflict and accommodation, overt and tacit struggle' (Hyman, 1975:26, original emphasis). For Marxists, then, the 'negotiation of order' is an unceasing power struggle between capital and labour: the frontier of control, at any point of time, 'represents a compromise unsatisfactory to *both* parties' (ibid:27, original emphasis).

Since first elaborated against the backcloth of nineteenth century capitalism, many subsequent events have challenged aspects of Marx's anticipated development of capitalist society. For example, the growth of a substantial proportion of the labour force occupying 'intermediate' positions in the occupational structure – administrative, middle managerial and professional positions, for example – is not easy to square with Marx's prediction of the general polarisation of the two principal classes within capitalism. Moreover, because much of Marx's analysis was directed at the societal level – identifying the basic nature of capitalism and the sources of its instability – the concepts which he developed often prove in practice somewhat blunt instruments for analysts seeking to understand the nature of employment relations within different work contexts. For example, to what extent, and to what effect, do power relations within organisations display a degree of autonomy from wider social class relationships? Marxism tends to deal with individuals only as bearers of economic class, such as 'labour' (workers or employees) and 'capital' (owners or managers), and the theory fails to provide adequate tools for understanding how 'alienated social relations' are subjectively experienced and acted on by the individual (Thompson and McHugh, 2002:383; see also Martin, 2003:173). There is certainly evidence to suggest that many UK workers *are* alienated from the system (e.g. BSAS data reported by Kelly, 1998) but it is unclear how this affects their behaviour (see Martin, 1999:1212). As Korczynski (2002:155) points out, 'it is conceptually inappropriate to draw conclusions about the subjective experience of work from arguments about the objective nature of labour in capitalism'.

Nevertheless, it is the questions which the Marxian analysis poses, and the situating of employee relations within a broader conceptual framework, that represents its significance to contemporary enquiry. With its emphasis on the 'unceasing power struggle' between capital and labour, it follows that 'industrial relations is the study of *processes of control over work relations*' (Hyman, 1975:12, original emphasis), both inside the workplace and beyond. But the distinctiveness of this definition, and that of the Marxist approach to the subject, is often lost. Clegg (1979:450–2), for example, tries to play down the differences between Marxism and pluralism in both a literary and theoretical sense. By contrasting the definitions of Flanders ('the institutions of job regulation') and Hyman ('the processes of control over work relations'), Clegg concludes that:

> 'Job regulation' is to be preferred *for its greater elegance and precision*, but if students of industrial relations had to rub along with 'processes of control over work relations' they would probably manage fairly well. (1979:452, emphasis added)

In terms of their theoretical approach, Clegg suggests that since both are concerned with conflict and stability, and as both regard conflict as inevitable and seek to explain how it is contained, students adopting either approach 'will come to much the same conclusions at the end of the day' (ibid:452). The divergence, if any, is 'to be found mainly in their attitudes' (ibid:455). Here again, therefore, we are back to a focus on Marxism as a movement rather than a theory. Not only is this a misrepresentation of the different theoretical approaches to the subject, it presents a persistent and significant source of confusion for students. This confusion is compounded by tendencies to draw on different elements of the various perspectives in a generally *ad hoc* manner, resulting in a lack of theoretical coherence and clarity. Such coherence is critical if we are to traverse successfully the 'mountains of facts' and penetrate beneath the surface of the day-to-day activities that make up the practice of industrial and employee relations.

A THEORY OF EMPLOYEE RELATIONS

Industrial relations has always been a specialist area of study. From its origins in the late nineteenth century it has been studied predominantly as a separate, autonomous area of material life. But as the industrial relations 'system' in the UK was seen to disintegrate in the 1960s it was necessary to cast the subject's net more widely, to incorporate the informal as well as formal processes of industrial relations. Pluralists suggested that the UK had two systems of industrial relations, but following the dramatic changes of the 1980s and 1990s very few commentators would insist that there are two identifiable systems in the UK today, let alone one. The traditional focus on male, manual workers is equally unsustainable (Wajcman, 2000), as is the failure of many scholars to look at how life 'beyond the factory gates' and 'office doors' has influenced industrial relations (Ackers, 2002). These issues are addressed throughout this text.

Just as the boundaries and content of the subject have changed in response to events and circumstances, it also responded to theoretical criticism. John Kelly (1998) for example, has drawn attention to the theoretical neglect of workers' interests and power relations in industrial relations. By focusing on 'injustice' and how workers mobilise their interests through collective action, Kelly has considerably deepened our understanding of some of the key questions in industrial relations (for example, whether employees are now less 'collectivist' and more 'individualistic' in orientation, how and why union power has declined in recent years, and by how much, and to what extent this decline can be attributed to the different actors in industrial relations). Yet despite new empirical lines of enquiry and important theoretical developments, the very term 'industrial relations' has been brought into question, as have the underlying assumptions that inform much of the research and teaching in the area (see, for example, Ackers and Wilkinson, 2003b; and Edwards, 1995a:40). Work organisations and corporate managers increasingly use the term 'human resource management' instead of industrial relations, the government displays a preference for 'employment relations' (e.g. www.dti.org.uk), and even those who stick to the title of 'industrial relations' admit that 'employment relations' might be the best label if we were starting from scratch (Edwards, 2003a:1).

Using terms such as employee relations rather than industrial relations reflects part of the redefinition of the boundaries of the subject to include *all* employment relationships, rather than ones only involving unionised male manual workers, but also the underlying assumptions that now inform theoretical perspectives on the subject. Thus, it is possible to discern a growing tendency to focus on, and define the distinctive characteristics of, the *employment relationship*; to locate that relationship within the *broader nature of economic activity*; to analyse the *structural bases* of conflict and accommodation between employer and employee; to consider the influence of the *wider society*; and to develop an *inter-disciplinary approach* using concepts and ideas derived from sociology, economics, psychology, history and political science.

It has become commonplace, for example, for academics in the field to argue that the jurisdiction of industrial and employee relations embraces 'all aspects of the employment relationship' (Strauss and Feuille, 1978:275; see also Fells, 1989; and Kaufman, 1993). Strauss and Feuille (1978:275) go on to argue, however, that

> this is much too broad because the 'employment relationship' encompasses such diverse fields as selection and testing, health and safety, equal employment rules, career paths, government labor market programs, and the entire field of organizational behavior. Pulling this conglomeration together under a single head would be intellectually meaningless.

But this would only be the case if research followed the traditionally empirical, inductive approach of earlier generations of writers. As it is impossible to ignore these diverse factors, the question becomes how to order, prioritise and understand such a complex range of variables, rather than how to limit the subject to a manageable range of analysis. In other words, having defined the boundaries of the subject, it is necessary to assign priority to particular variables or relationships, to identify causal links and to produce (testable) hypotheses. On the latter point we concur with Thompson and McHugh (2002:19) who argue that, 'any critical theory not testing its ideas through empirical investigation or practical intervention is ultimately arid'.

To focus on the employment relationship has the advantage of homing-in on the (material) basis of the interaction between employer and employee, and the relationship from which all other aspects of employee relations stem. As already noted, to focus on a system of rules or the institutions of job regulation is to ignore the foundations underpinning such rules and regulations in the sphere of production, to run before learning to walk (and without an adequate map of which direction to run). So what is the nature of the employment relationship? What do management and workers seek from such a relationship? And how does each party attempt to achieve its goals?

At its most basic level, every employment relationship is an *economic exchange*, an agreement between employer and employee over the sale of the latter's capacity to work (commonly known as labour power). But the employment relationship is also a *power relationship* as the worker, by definition of being an employee, agrees to submit to the authority and direction of the employer. The exchange of labour power is therefore unlike that of any other 'commodity'. As Brown (1988:55–7) points out, the employment relationship is a *continuous relationship*, not a 'one off' exchange; the employment contract itself is *open-ended*, in that the wage might be agreed in advance but effort is not, and cannot be, specified explicitly or exactly; the employment relationship is necessarily an *authority relationship* between super- and sub-ordinates, where the employee agrees to accept and follow the 'reasonable' instructions of those in positions of authority; the parties are *interdependent*, creating patterns of both conflict and co-operation; but the employer is in possession of greater power resources than the employee, creating an *asymmetrical* relationship between the parties. Each of these points warrants further elaboration as they provide the foundations upon which a theory of employee relations can be built.

The demand for labour, to borrow a term from economics, is a 'derived demand' because the employer is not interested in labour *per se* but in the contribution of the employee to the production of goods and services. In other words, the employer has no commitment towards the talents and needs of the employee except, and unless, they are useful in the process of production or the delivery of services. But what the employer purchases in the labour market is the *capacity* of men and women to work (labour power), whereas what the employer is actually interested in is the *performance* of work (physical, mental and in many cases emotional labour). As Edwards (1986:35) notes, 'in the labour contract what the employer wants is not a capacity but its exercise'. This creates an on-going relationship between the parties, but also a pattern of conflict and accommodation because while the wage may be agreed the level of effort is not. Even if workers are paid by the piece or for every sale they complete, their diligence and/or the quality of the product/service is invariably difficult, if not impossible, to specify precisely in the contract of employment. As Mike Emmott (2001a:vii) of the Chartered Institute of Personnel and Development (CIPD) has pointed out, 'few organisations seek to define in advance what is a reasonable level of effort or application'.

In a capitalist economy the emphasis will inevitably fall on the economic aspects of the employment relationship, but there are also important social and ethical issues to consider (Ackers, 2002:12). In fact, all employment relationships reflect a tension between the economic and the social, or between contract and status (see Hyman, 2001a). Conflict will thus emerge from the 'exploitation' of labour, but as Edwards (1986:31–2) argues, exploitation does not exist solely because the employer takes part of the product but also because of the way the product is actually produced. The 'right to manage' must be exercised in a 'reasonable' manner, which in large part will be determined by 'customary' and 'socially acceptable' standards of behaviour. To reiterate, employment relationships are not just 'economic contracts' – there is also a 'psychological contract' between the parties, which for employees involves 'a form of evaluation ... of management policy and practice with particular reference to fairness, trust and delivery of promises' (Guest, 2001:110).

As already noted, the employer hires the mental and physical attributes of employees, not the employees themselves. In effect, therefore, labour bears no market price, because it is *labour time* and not work itself that is purchased. Put differently, paid working time is not necessarily equivalent to time worked. What determines efficiency (and profitability) is not simply the (technical) combination of different 'factors of production' but also the degree of congruence between potential and performed labour. Since the latter depends, in large part, on the power and authority of the employer over the employee, firms can be expected to organise work in a way that reproduces the authority and control of capital over labour (Bowles, 1985; Gordon, 1976; and Marglin, 1974). This may result in, for example, improvements in productivity being sought via changes that involve work intensification, the sub-division of operations, the de-skilling of jobs and outright job losses, all of which are likely to invoke worker and/or trade union opposition (Turnbull, 1991b:141). Employees may submit to the authority of the employer but will always retain a very strong interest in the (ab)use of their labour. Indeed, the study of work group behaviour shows how workers combine and co-operate with each other not only to bargain over wages and working conditions but also to control or influence the pace of work, to create meaning in otherwise alienating work processes, and to protect themselves not just from 'overwork' but particularly from 'unremunerated overwork' (Turnbull, 1988a:101). As Marsden (1999:3) points out, '[t]he key to the employment relationship is that is enables management to decide detailed work assignments after workers have been hired … however, few workers would agree to giving their employer unlimited powers over work assignments'.

Clearly, the use of labour power within the process of production encapsulates within it important sources of potential conflict (see Edwards, 1986:35). The task of management in this process is not to hope or assume that worker and union interests coincide with those of their own, but rather to structure workplace relations in a manner most conducive to the attainment of higher productivity, lower unit costs and improved profitability (Turnbull, 1991b:141). Those holding a unitary perspective of work relations simply assume that the only goal of the employee is furthering the profits of the firm, such that management need only apprise the worker of the 'needs' of the organisation to elicit worker co-operation and optimum performance. This approach characterises much of the recent writing on HRM (see Lewin, 2001). Pluralist writing, which continues to dominate mainstream industrial relations research, accepts a 'conflict of interests' between the parties but rarely explores the material base of those conflicts, preferring instead to focus on the resolution of conflict. Instead, the reality faced by management is how to reconcile the two problems of securing workers' co-operation and a surplus product (Nolan, 1983:303).

It is in this respect that the concept of interdependence plays a crucial role. The interests of capital may dominate the organisation of work, and employers will hold the balance of power in any employment relationship by virtue of their ownership of capital and the authority this imparts. But, ultimately, it is the workforce that actually performs the detailed activities of the work process. Service workers, for example, often play well-defined roles and follow carefully scripted lines but they still hold the power to 'fluff' those lines and reveal the inauthentic nature of the service encounter (see Korczynski, 2002; and Sturdy et al., 2001). Likewise, even unskilled manual workers hold the power to frustrate the efficiency and profitability of the organisation by failing to co-operate actively in the work process (see Delbridge, 1998; and Scott, 1994). The required level of co-operation needs to go beyond mere compliance with rules if work is to be performed efficiently. Indeed, a common form of worker insubordination is 'working to rules', whereby employees are able to undermine the work process merely by doing exactly and precisely as they are required, rather than exercising a level of discretion not covered by the rules. Consider, for example, a service industry setting where employees work 'without enthusiasm' or simply refuse to smile 'genuinely' at the customer – such action might well dull the corporate message of 'service quality' and 'customer care'. Essentially, then, management want workers to follow the spirit, not the letter of the rules. Employers cannot rely on coercion or even compliance to secure high performance; they also need to secure active employee consent and co-operation.

Power is typically understood as the ability of one party to compel another party to do something which they otherwise would not undertake of their own volition. In the employment relationship, employers seek to enjoin *and entice* workers to comply with their demands and co-operate with their instructions. To do otherwise would run the risk of overt conflict between capital and labour. For their part, one reason why workers do not simply resist management control is that they identify with, and define themselves in relation to their work: indeed, the majority of British workers have long-term commitments to their organisation, even though they may be not be particularly satisfied with their work (Diamond and Freeman, 2001). The fact that many people seek intrinsic reward from their work indicates that there is likely to be at least a latent degree of co-operation with management. The nature of the employment relationship, then, is not simply one of (management) control *versus* (worker) resistance, but a more problematic mix of dissent and accommodation, conflict and co-operation. In the past, one of the major criticisms of industrial relations research, and in particular the juxtaposition between pluralism and Marxism, was that 'industrial relations writings, overall, seems polarized around the two problematics of how is order achieved and why is disorder not rampant' (Guille, 1984:486). But in reality,

> It is not a matter of employers gaining what workers lose, or vice versa, but of the coming together of the two sides in a relationship which is inherently contradictory: employers need workers' creative capacities, but cannot give them free rein because of the need to secure a surplus and to maintain a degree of general control; and workers, although subordinate, do not simply resist the application of managerial control. (Edwards, 1986:6)

It is these features of the employment relationship – *the creation of an economic surplus, the co-existence of conflict and co-operation, the indeterminate nature of the exchange relationship, and the asymmetry of power* – not the institutions of trade unions, employers' associations or government agencies, that makes the subject matter of employee relations distinctive. The activities of institutions, such as collective bargaining or other 'rule-making' processes, in fact *arise from* the employment relationship and cannot be understood in isolation from it. Thus, trade union activity, first and foremost, is the organised expression of the grievances, deprivations and wider interests of employees that arise from their (subordinate) role in the process of goods production or service provision. Given the asymmetry of power that exists, collective action is invariably necessary if employee interests are to be represented effectively (see Kelly, 1998). Likewise, the need for management control derives from the tensions that exist between employer and employee within the employment relationship, giving rise to the development of a variety of control strategies. These activities can be grounded in a theory of the employment relationship, which has the added advantage of accommodating both sides of the labour question, namely the achievement of social welfare on the one hand, and social control on the other.

Having emphasised the distinct nature of the employment relationship and the process of creating surplus value, it is also important to acknowledge that the employment relationship does not take place in a vacuum: work organisations are not islands, workers are not automatons. What occurs in the workplace is also influenced by the wider society. Indeed, it is a maxim of industrial sociology that to understand what goes on inside the workplace it is also necessary to look at what goes on outside it, to consider such factors as the structure of power in society, the nature of communities and the degree of occupational solidarities (Lockwood, 1966). The labour forthcoming from a worker depends, in addition to biology and skills, on such factors as states of consciousness, degrees of solidarity with other workers, labour market conditions, and other societal influences such as schooling, welfare provisions and family life (see Gintis, 1976; and Lazonick, 1978). Thus, workers 'learn to labour' (Willis, 1977) and generally enter the workplace with a 'work ethic', a respect for private property, and a general willingness to accept authority:

> explaining the nature of the employment relationship necessarily involves considering the culture, the values and norms of the wider society and the institutional arrangements which ensure that appropriate normative obligations are internalized, and developed and reinforced by each generation. (Brown, 1988:61)

In a modern-day 'consumer society', for example, management increasingly adopts the role of 'champion' for the customer, enjoining workers to internalise the demands and desires of the customer (e.g. 'treat the customer as you yourself would like to be treated', 'the customer is always right'). The consumer is a source of authority in contemporary society. Some commentators go so far as to suggest that people now define themselves by what they consume rather than what they produce, such that a 'consumer discourse' in the workplace can provide management with an important source of legitimacy for their actions (see Korczynski, 2002). Appeals to the 'imperatives of the market', 'competition from rivals', or the ubiquitous forces of 'globalisation' can all provide an equally powerful source of authority for management and the state. The discourse of 'modern business needs' plays an integral, not an accidental role in shaping the relationship between employers and employees.

This framework of analysis is set out in a simplified form in Figure 17.1. As illustrated, the core of our analysis is the employment relationship. At the most general level, the nature of economic activity has a direct bearing on the essential structure of this relationship: the ownership or non-ownership of capital gives rise to an authority relationship characterised by hierarchy and control. But this cannot be achieved simply by using the coercive power that ownership imparts. Thus, in order for management to achieve their objectives they must secure the co-operation and consent of the workforce. The outcome is one of contest and accommodation, as those employed seek to improve the wages and general conditions of their employment. The end result is the many and varied employment relationships that we observe in the real world. Again, however, interaction is a dialectic rather than a deterministic process, as indicated by the influences (arrows) in Figure 17.1 flowing out from, as well as into, the employment relationship.

Rather than attempt to illustrate all the possible influences on the employment relationship in Figure 17.1, we have sought to portray only the central elements of our framework. What should be apparent from our discussion thus far, however, is that any political economy of employee relations must be holistic (i.e. involving a systematic analysis of the workings of the economy as a whole). In addition, this approach:

- takes social and economic structures and relations as its starting point, thereby placing emphasis upon class and stratification more generally (the economy is 'embedded' in society and the polity)
- brings notions of power and conflict to the fore, how they are forged and how they are exercised, not least through the state
- explains systemic tendencies and processes, such as globalisation and uneven development, primarily on the basis of the imperatives of profitability and capital accumulation (see Fine, 2002:197).

While these are generic features of the political economy of capitalism, there is still the question of any specific British characteristics of employee relations that deserve particular attention. After all, the very study of industrial relations as a *separate* field

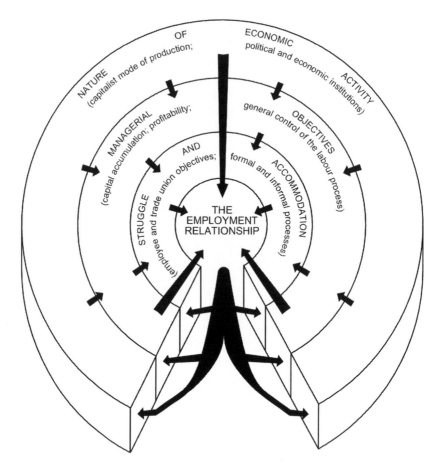

Figure 17.1 – A framework of employee relations analysis

divorced from political economy is an anglophone peculiarity, largely the result of employment regulation in the first part of the twentieth century having developed in the absence of direct and systematic intervention by the state (Hyman, 2003).

EMPLOYEE RELATIONS AND VARIETIES OF CAPITALISM

All employment relationships are 'embedded' in a particular social system of production and bear the imprint of specific national institutional forms (see Hollingsworth and Boyer, 1997). These institutional forms are heavily influenced by the state, especially as the state plays a major role in determining, and enforcing, the 'rules of the game'. For example, the state protects private property rights, upon which all employment relationships are ultimately founded; manipulates fiscal and monetary policy, thereby establishing the general economic context of employee relations; and may engage directly, to a greater or lesser extent, in production and exchange relations (ibid:13; see also Hall and Soskice, 2001:15). In an historical context, the principal characteristic of the British state was seen to be the 'insignificance' of its role in employee relations (e.g. Kahn-Freund, 1954:44). However, what was unique about the British system was not the absence of state intervention but the form of state regulation in key areas such as employment legislation (Ewing, 2003:141). At this point it is more important to highlight the British state's historic reliance on markets rather than institutions. This reliance was heightened by the neo-liberal policies that defined Thatcherism.

Over the past 20 years or more, in the UK and many other advanced industrialised economies, the political and economic consensus was that markets are the most efficient method for co-ordinating business activities, with any public intervention more likely to cause harm than do good. According to neo-liberals, the role of the state is to ensure free and unfettered competition in product, financial and labour markets. Thus, the clarion call of Thatcherism was 'competition where possible, regulation only when necessary'. However, one of the basic features of modern economies is the growing importance, and arguably greater effectiveness, of co-ordinating mechanisms *alternative to* the market (see Gerlach, 1992; and Hamilton and Biggart, 1988). The market might be efficient when it comes to impersonal forms of contractual exchange, where prices provide sufficient information for all parties. Yet many relationships in business and employee relations depend on co-operation rather than competition, trust rather than opportunism, equity as well as efficiency, altruism rather than self-interest, reciprocity instead of indifference. Moreover, at some threshold, as the UK has discovered, 'the domination of the market rationale tends to challenge the viability of other institutional arrangements: the values of community, the family, and other authority systems can be eroded under the pursuit of private interests by each individual' (Boyer and Hollingsworth, 1997:445–7).

It was the failure of Thatcherism that led New Labour to seek a 'Third Way' between the 'invisible hand' of the market and the 'heavy hand' of the state. Nonetheless, there are still far fewer 'constraints' on business and the market in the UK in comparison with most other advanced industrialised economies and the Labour Government is still wedded to the idea that '[e]ffective markets and competition are the best means of ensuring that the economy's resources are allocated effectively' (HM Treasury, 2000:28). As a result, the UK is typically characterised as a 'liberal market economy' (LME), along with the USA, Canada, Australia and Ireland, in contrast to the 'co-ordinated market economies' (CME) of continental Europe (e.g. Austria, Belgium, Germany and the Netherlands), Scandinavia (Denmark, Finland, Norway and Sweden) and Japan. The key difference between these economies is the extent to which firms in a LME rely on the market mechanism (e.g. relative prices) to co-ordinate their endeavours, as opposed to forms of institutional intervention or non-market mechanisms in CMEs (see Hall and Soskice, 2001:33). The latter might include business associations, trade unions and (multi-employer) collective bargaining, cross-shareholding (firms holding shares in their suppliers), industry-wide vocational training programmes, and 'deliberative institutions' such as company-based works councils or national (tripartite) consultation bodies. Such institutions are designed to reduce uncertainty and build credible commitments between various stakeholders, thereby increasing the capacity of firms to develop long-term (strategic) behaviour. This contrasts sharply with the short-term (maximising) behaviour of firms in LMEs (ibid). The implications for employee relations are both manifold and profound. At this point we highlight just one issue by way of illustration, namely job insecurity.

In a business system where firms are (over)reliant on capital markets to finance their activities, as in the UK, they will invariably seek to maintain profits (rather than market share, for example) as this will influence the firm's future access to capital and its ability to resist hostile takeover bids. If revenue or profitability decline, firms will seek to lay off workers, in part to appease the City and bolster the share price as the following, not untypical, report from the *Financial Times* (20 December 1993) bears witness: 'Fisons, the troubled pharmaceuticals and scientific equipment group, is planning plant closures and large scale redundancies *in a bid to restore confidence in the company*' (quoted by Beaumont, 1995:103, emphasis added). It is no coincidence that UK workers enjoy, or rather endure, much weaker statutory employment protection than their European counterparts: firms in a LME demand such 'flexibility' (see Estevez-Abe *et al.*, 2001:163–7; Morgan *et al.*, 2001; OECD, 1999; Purcell *et al.*, 1999:1; and Turnbull and Wass, 2000). In a CME such as Germany, in contrast, firms can sustain a decline in returns because the financial system provides them with access to capital independent of current profitability. Moreover, one reason why German firms seek to retain market share is because labour market regulations demand a social as well as an economic case for any restructuring, making it difficult for firms to shed labour in the short run simply to maximise profits (see Bosch, 1990; and Casey, 1992:428–9). It is hardly surprising, therefore, that UK workers report a much stronger sense of insecurity than their European counterparts (see Burchell *et al.*, 1999; Heery and Salmon, 2000; and ISR, 1996).

Moving from a (somewhat abstract) discussion of the capitalist employment relationship to the specific national context of employee relations represents the first step towards more concrete levels of analysis that enable us to understand the reality, variety and dynamics of employee relations. More importantly, we combine macro (national) level analysis with the meso (industry) and micro (organisation) levels in each of these chapters. Thus, we discuss the case of British Airways in the context of both UK employee relations and broader developments in the domestic, European and global civil aviation industry; we focus on the organising activities of the GMB and T&GWU in different industrial sectors, drawing on evidence from specific firms and relating these to broader developments in both unions and the trade union movement as a whole; and we discuss the proposed privatisation of the Port of Belfast in relation to the port's function as a maritime, industrial and distribution area, as well as in relation to local and national political developments.

Each case represents an example of the varied nature of employee relations and patterns of interaction with wider society. We start with this level of analysis as it is the most immediate and most accessible. However, a deeper understanding of the issues and processes covered in each of these chapters can only be derived from the higher, more abstract levels of analysis which have been identified in this chapter, and which underpin our approach throughout the remainder of the book.

COLLECTIVE BARGAINING

RE-CASTING EMPLOYEE RELATIONS IN CORUS PLC

An industry transformed

Back in 1978, annual crude steel production in the UK stood at just under 21 million tonnes. Most of the 165000 employees involved in producing that steel worked for the nationalised British Steel Corporation (BSC). In that year it took BSC 15.3 man hours to produce each tonne of liquid steel. A decade later in 1988, the output of the UK steel industry was just over 19 million tonnes, 8 per cent lower than the 1978 level. Employment in the industry, however, had been cut by a massive 67 per cent to a little over 55000. BSC's productivity levels had correspondingly risen dramatically (to 5 man hours per tonne) and as a result BSC had gone from being a comparatively high cost producer of bulk steel to one of the world's lowest-cost producers.

After 1988, the year BSC was privatised and renamed British Steel plc (BS), rationalisation continued as management made further cuts and concentrated activity at the most efficient works. During the 1990s, these trends continued; in 1999, the company's output of crude steel was just under 17 million tonnes and its overall productivity levels had improved further to below 4 man hours per tonne. Employment costs, which had been 30 per cent or more of total costs in the late 1970s, had fallen to 21 per cent by the end of 1999. This fall in labour costs during the 1990s, coupled with other factors such as investment in newer and larger-scale technology, was increasingly reflected in the company's profits, which rose to over £1 billion in 1995–6. After this date, however, increasingly difficult trading conditions in the world steel sector resulted in the company experiencing several years of losses: the £1 billion profit of 1995–6 turned into a £1 billion loss in 2000. By this time, British Steel had merged with the Dutch steelmaker Hoogovens to form Corus plc. In response to the losses, job cuts in recent years have been severe, particularly in the UK operations, with the closure of entire plants (such as the Ebbw Vale works in South Wales) and the radical slimming down of other plants (such as the Llanwern works, also in South Wales). By the end of 2002 the Corus Group as a whole employed 50,900 people, but of these only 25,400 were in the UK (Corus, 2002).

Behind these bare statistics lies the story of an industry transformed, and continuing to transform, not to mention the severe impact wrought on numerous steel communities and tens of thousands of people formerly dependent on the industry for their livelihood. Inside the industry, the process of steel-making, little altered for over half a century, has undergone radical changes in scale and technology. A notable feature, too, is the way the process of transformation has been inextricably linked with major changes in work organisation and the structure and process of collective relations between management and trade unions. Given the stability of employee relations structures in the steel industry up to 1980, the extent and pace of developments thereafter beg a series of questions: What factors were central in the change process? What have been the major aspects of employee relations change? Why did the changes apparently occur so rapidly compared to what had gone before? And what have been the main implications of the changes for the different parties involved?

In order to understand contemporary employee relations developments in the steel industry, it is necessary to look back to the late 1970s and a critical period of change focused on the 'Slimline' plan. The problems facing BSC at this time were clear: principally, large-scale obsolescence due to inadequate investment and a failure to modernise over several decades, coupled with enormous over-capacity due both to a stagnant world market for steel and declining competitiveness in the domestic market. It is true that in response to these problems some rationalisation of the Corporation had already taken place during the 1970s. BSC had closed entire plants, as well as shutting down parts of plants, in order to concentrate bulk steelmaking activity and other processes on fewer sites. In the face of mounting economic crisis and financial losses, however, the extent and pace of this rationalisation programme was seriously inadequate. The upshot was both a new rationalisation programme announced in 1979 and moves to alter fundamentally the character of employee relations. The latter was to be achieved, in large part, through the re-casting of collective bargaining arrangements in the industry.

As with the rationalisation of plant and production processes, some attempts at reforming the character of employee relations had been made in the 1960s and 1970s, principally through forms of productivity bargaining (see Blyton, 1993; and Owen Smith, 1971). Negotiations in BSC at this time were characterised by a substantial degree of centralisation; pay rates in the industry were negotiated nationally and separately with each union, while other terms and conditions (for example, hours and holidays, shift and overtime premiums) were negotiated nationally between BSC and a combined union committee comprising the main production union, the Iron and Steel Trades Confederation (ISTC), together with the various craft and general unions with members in the industry. With this national structure in place, the secondary role of local bargaining was to supplement national agreements in such aspects as tonnage bonuses and 'abnormal conditions' payments connected to working in conditions which were, for example, unduly hot or dusty.

Attempts at employee relations reform before 1980 marginally increased labour productivity via agreed redundancies and locally agreed changes in working practices involving increased flexibility both among and between production and craft tasks. The overall extent of work reform, however, was limited. Inter-union differences, rigid demarcations, a lack of monitoring of change and the varied nature of craft work proved significant obstacles to the development of new work practices. Given the slow pace at which rationalisation had been proceeding before the late 1970s, and the degree to which the structure of negotiations and pattern of work organisation were resilient to change, the twelve months from late 1979 were thus all the more remarkable for the developments that occurred and the ways these laid the basis for a refashioning of employment relations in steel on a scale hitherto unknown in the history of the industry, and one that continues to be reflected in those relations today.

'Slimline' and the national strike

In 1979, BSC published its emergency Slimline plan against the background of mounting economic crisis and the newly-elected Conservative government's instruction to stem losses and reach break-even by 1980–1. The plan was based on a cut in output by a quarter to be achieved by total and partial plant closures, and concentrating activity at more efficient works (see Blyton, 1992 and 1993 for more details). The most visible outcome over the next three years was a scale of redundancies unprecedented in the European steel industry (Harris, 1988; and Houseman, 1991).

At the same time, BSC also announced its intention to reduce the prominence of national pay bargaining and increase the degree to which earnings were tied more directly to local performance. This was consistent with the Thatcher government's economic policy, an important part of which was based on cash limits to the public sector and the requirement for pay awards to be self-financing. The first outcome of this was the BSC management's 1980 pay offer which was one based on local performance bonuses with no provision for a national, across-the-board increase. This refusal to make a national offer, coupled with job insecurity surrounding possible further plant closures, culminated in a protracted national strike in 1980, the first official national strike in the industry since 1926 (for accounts of the strike itself, see Docherty, 1983; and Hartley *et al.*, 1983).

The outcomes of the thirteen-week strike, involving almost one hundred thousand workers, are far from easy to quantify, not least because the effects on management and worker attitudes continued to be felt in the industry long after the dispute was over. In several ways the strike acted as a watershed. As one manager put it, 'while the strike was on, we [the managers] sat down and said what we are not going to stand for when it was over' (interview notes). From the unions' perspective, the strike failed either to shift government policy on the funding of the industry, or bring about any reconsideration by BSC of its closure programme. In terms of the wage settlement, a Committee of Inquiry (the Lever Committee), set up under the auspices of ACAS, recommended an improved pay offer which was accepted. A significant part of this increase, however, was to be made up of local bonus payments negotiated at district level.

The move to local negotiations

In the aftermath of the strike, the centre of gravity of employee relations shifted down to the local level. Though national negotiations continued, their role and significance were increasingly circumscribed. Rather than negotiating basic pay rises, the national bargaining machinery came predominantly to function as the mechanism for reaching framework agreements for local negotiations and for consolidating elements of previous local bonuses into basic rates.

Central to the development of local union-management relations was the introduction of a works lump sum bonus (LSB) scheme which tied a significant element of potential earnings (initially up to 18 per cent) to the achievement not only of plant performance targets (including output and quality levels) but also to the acceptance of change by the workforce, including manpower reductions, the introduction of sub-contractors, alterations to work practices, and technical change. By putting a monetary value on co-operation, the LSB scheme, based on multi-union committees at works level, was to play a crucial role in assisting management to fulfil its rationalisation programme in the coming years.

Worker co-operation took three main forms. First, by making job cuts one of the LSB targets, management were able to define job losses as essentially local issues, outside the remit of national industrial relations machinery. The offer of comparatively good severance terms for those made redundant, coupled with tying reduced manning levels to bonus payments for those remaining, combined to diffuse much local union opposition to the redundancy programme. At the same time, national unions were effectively excluded by what they saw as this 'divide and rule' policy by BSC, executed through local employee relations. This exclusion also reflected the unions' diminished power due to membership losses and the difficulties of remounting campaigns against closures so soon after the national strike.

Second, the financial incentive of the LSB payments reduced opposition to other changes which in the past had been resisted by trade unions both locally and nationally. The most significant of these changes was the increased use of sub-contract labour to undertake a wider range of activities within the steelworks (see Fevre, 1987). In addition were specific agreements on technological change and job enlargement involving not only craft and production workers but also non-manual staff. Through job enlargement and increased sub-contracting, coupled with increased automation, BSC management sought to cover the huge reductions in manpower which occurred at sites which continued in production (reductions of more than two-thirds of total employment were implemented at major plants such as Teesside in the North-East, and Port Talbot and Llanwern in South Wales).

Third, tying bonus payments partly to achieved performance acted to stifle any oppositional activity which might affect output. With high levels of inflation prevailing in the early 1980s, securing increases in income was a high priority for those remaining in work. With the LSB potentially worth almost one-fifth of earnings, this was an important source of income for those still employed in the industry. Moreover, the significance of the LSB was further strengthened from 1984 onwards when BSC management made the payment of any national increases conditional on the successful conclusion of local LSB negotiations within a six-week 'window' from the signing of a national agreement (Avis, 1990). Thus, both local and national pay improvements were made to hinge on the acceptance of manpower change and performance improvements at local level.

Privatisation of BSC in 1988 exerted a further pressure on the decentralisation of employee relations. The establishment of four separate business divisions within the privatised British Steel (General Steels, Strip Products, Stainless and Diversified) led to the termination of any remaining national bargaining and its replacement by business level and increasingly local level negotiation machinery. In this way, BS mirrored the creation of strategic business units involving the devolution of financial responsibility to the individual businesses, through the devolution of employee relations machinery (Avis, 1990).

The Future Employment Package and teamworking

Throughout the 1980s and much of the 1990s, LSB negotiations remained a crucial element in the company's relations with its workforce. Only in the late 1990s did the emphasis change again, partly reflecting the impact of declining profits on the scale of bonus payments. In its place, management introduced a twin bargaining approach, much of this again focused at local level. First, in 1998 management and unions agreed what became known as the British Steel Future Employment Package (FEP) which contained two core elements: (i) conditions of employment would be harmonised between manual and non-manual grades, improving manual workers' sick pay entitlement, their holidays, removing clocking on/off for manual grades and introducing a 36.5 hour working week for all grades, and (ii) these changes would be introduced on a stepped basis, once certain 'milestones of improvement' had been agreed. The milestones for implementing the FEP were directed at local level change and included performance improvement targets and particularly the conclusion of local teamworking agreements, followed by the full operation of teamworking practices. Following the merger with Hoogovens, the local (works and departmental-level) negotiating of teamworking has been the main focus of employee relations in the majority of Corus's UK plants.

The importance given to teamworking is part of a longer standing emphasis in the company on changing working practices and progressively eliminating the distinctive occupational categories of 'craft maintenance' and 'production' workers, replacing these, where possible, with single categories of team members comprised of both former production and former craft workers. An important step towards this was the introduction in the 1990s of craft restructuring, under which the former complex craft structure was simplified into two general craft disciplines (broadly covering the mechanical and electrical areas) thereby reducing or eliminating many of the traditional demarcations surrounding particular skills (Blyton and Bacon, 1997).

Teamworking involves a number of fundamental changes to work organisation, including: termination of the seniority system of promotion for production workers (under which the longest serving employees obtained the most senior positions in work crews) and its replacement by managerial selection of team leaders; the integration of former production and craft workers into single teams; a reform of pay and grading structures in the move to teams; and widespread changes in job responsibilities and patterns of work allocation. Levels of work effort and work pace have also risen significantly though this reflects not simply teamworking but also the widespread employment reductions that have accompanied the introduction of teamworking (Bacon and Blyton, 2003a). The extent and detail of the changes – in employment levels, working practices, pay and working time systems, selection and promotion criteria and so on – coupled with the very different conditions prevailing in the different parts of steel works (for example around a blast furnace compared to a rolling mill or a dispatch area), and the need for commitment to the teamworking model (with its various training and work re-organisation implications) meant that the new system required detailed local negotiations.

In Corus's Constructional and Industrial Steel business, for example, centred on its Scunthorpe and Teesside plants, the introduction of teamworking initially involved two plant-level 'enabling' (framework) agreements signed in 1998. These established the 'principles and framework' within which local teamworking negotiations would take place. These enabling agreements set out the principles of five shift working to accompany teamworking, the selection criteria for team members and team leaders, and the general principles of pay structures within teams. These agreements also included an early retirement programme with a full pension from 55 years of age. This was central to departmental managers meeting a requirement from corporate management that the introduction of teamworking should also deliver a 20 per cent manning reduction in each department, to cut costs.

The plant-wide enabling agreements were followed by 22 separate departmental agreements, some of which were negotiated quickly and with high levels of co-operation, whereas others were much more protracted and gave rise to a much greater degree of conflict (Bacon and Blyton, 2003a). Departmental negotiations agreed precise team composition (for example, the mix of former craft workers in different production teams), the nature of the five shift system (some departments opting for 12–hour shifts, others maintaining an 8–hour pattern); and the specific pay levels for team leaders and team members (see Bacon and Blyton, 2003b).

The outcomes of decentralised bargaining

Through this process of local bargaining, management have achieved several of their aims with respect to reducing employment levels and increasing efficiency. Other desired outcomes, however, such as the creation of fully flexible teams with a high degree of job rotation, remain more elusive. Though the types of teamworking that have been introduced vary significantly, with some approaching more advanced, 'high road' forms of semi-autonomous teams, the more typical are somewhat restricted, 'low road' forms of teamworking where levels of discretion, flexibility and autonomy are relatively low (Bacon and Blyton, 2000). These differences have significant effects on team performance.

More generally, the latest wave of local teamworking agreements demonstrates the marked shift in emphasis in the conduct of employee relations in British Steel (now Corus) during the past two decades. Although elements of change were visible earlier, the conjunction of several factors in the 1980s and thereafter fuelled both the depth and pace of change. Market pressures, government policies and the outcome of the national strike combined to create a context in which management were not only forced into making substantial changes to the industry's operations, but were also provided with the conditions conducive to a refashioning of employee relations. In particular, this involved a diminution of centralised bargaining machinery and national trade union influence, and an increase in the significance of local agreements. The upshot was the creation of a system that has proved highly amenable to the pursuit of a managerially-defined agenda for change. Unlike the earlier experiments with productivity bargaining, the LSB scheme allowed management to assert greater control over labour in a context in which the latter was generally weakened by broader labour market conditions, and specifically weakened by the market conditions for steel and the failure of the national strike to bring about any reversal in state or employer policy towards employment in the industry. From management's point of view, greater control has continued to be exercised by maintaining decentralised employee relations and tying improvements in terms and conditions to fundamental changes in work organisation such as the introduction of teamworking. At one level, the result has been a widespread acceptance of change with little organised resistance and a closer linking of earnings to local performance. Yet, while the change to more localised employee relations has helped management to keep the focus on a performance-specific *agenda*, this has not automatically meant that management have achieved all the desired *outcomes* that they have sought from that agenda. Whatever their weakened position, steel unions have still been able to *negotiate*, rather than simply *accept* change and in so doing, win important changes and concessions from management.

THE PATTERN OF COLLECTIVE BARGAINING

In Corus, as in various other sectors of industry, collective bargaining and negotiated agreements remain important features of contemporary employee relations. Historically, for a large part of the post-1945 period, collective bargaining has acted as the principal mechanism for the determination of pay rates and other basic terms and conditions for the majority of the workforce, and more generally has represented a key arena for the conduct of collective relations between managers and managed. By the early 1970s, collective agreements covered over 80 per cent of all male and over 70 per cent of all female manual workers in the UK, and over 60 per cent of the non-manual labour force (both male and female).

Developments since the mid 1980s (set out in more detail below) however, have raised important questions about the future role and significance of collective bargaining in the UK. While for several million employees, collective bargaining remains the principal mechanism by which their trade union representatives exert influence over terms and conditions of employment, for many other workers this mechanism has been far less significant over the past two decades. In fact, the majority of workers are no longer covered by collective agreements and for those workers, any impact is therefore marginal and indirect (e.g. union wage agreements might establish the 'going rate' or act as a 'benchmark' for non-union workers). This contraction of collective bargaining coverage could be read by some as a signal of the ultimate demise of collectivism and negotiated agreements as mechanisms for determining changes in terms and conditions of employment (pay, working hours, holiday entitlement, and so on). Indeed, it is one of the key indicators marking the transformation of employee relations in recent years. But it is too early to write off collective bargaining and other forms of joint regulation as core elements in future employee relations. The recent stabilisation of union density levels in the UK, the introduction of statutory instruments to support union recognition procedures, as well as the priority given by trade unions to collective bargaining activity, are all testament to the continuing importance of collective bargaining and joint regulation. Moreover, in some sectors of the economy, most notably the public sector and significant parts of manufacturing, collective bargaining still occupies centre stage in management-union relations.

Of greater concern, however, is the drift from joint regulation to managerial prerogative. Collective bargaining has not been supplanted by individual negotiation – skilled and articulate workers negotiating a pay and benefits package that best suits their personal needs and career aspirations, ensuring high levels of motivation, commitment to the organisation and maximum productivity – but by managerial fiat (see Brown et al., 2000:615). As we have already noted, and as we demonstrate in the case of non-union workers, management have failed to replace collective bargaining and joint regulation with sophisticated forms of human resource management (in fact, HRM is more often found in unionised workplaces). This is one reason why the UK economy continues to under-perform. As with so many other aspects of employee relations, the UK is again 'out of step' with much of Europe, where collective bargaining coverage is typically over 80 per cent (despite very low levels of union membership in countries such as France and Spain or comparable levels of density in countries such as Germany and the Netherlands). Many firms in co-ordinated market economies (CMEs) employ production systems or service strategies that rely on a highly skilled workforce given substantial autonomy and encouraged to share any information acquired from the work process with management (e.g. potential quality improvements or customer feedback). This approach carries risks, however, for management and workers.

In a CME, the firm is vulnerable because workers may withdraw co-operation in order to back up demands for higher pay or improved benefits, and skilled workers might be 'poached' by rival firms. For employees, sharing the information they gain at work with management exposes them to potential exploitation (i.e.

unremunerated effort). As Hall and Soskice (2001:24–5) point out, CMEs need employee relations institutions capable of resolving these problems. These include multi-employer (national and/or industry-based) collective bargaining which stand-ardise pay, benefits, training provision and the like, thereby reducing the incentives for firms to poach labour; and company-based systems of co-determination (e.g. works councils composed of elected employee representatives endowed with considerable influence over employment policies within the firm) which provide both the mechanisms and security that workers need to share information with management. In this chapter we explore the benefits (and costs) of multi-employer bargaining, which previously played an important role in collective relations between management and labour in the UK, the impact of decentralisation where firms have retained collective bargaining, and the implications for employee rela-tions arising from the recent demise of collective bargaining for the majority of the UK's workforce.

A necessary, but by no means sufficient condition for a 'knowledge-based' or 'learn-ing economy' founded on high skills, high productivity and high wages is a supportive institutional framework for the determination of pay and other conditions of employment (most notably training provision). We therefore begin by considering the nature of collective bargaining in more detail, together with some of the salient features of its historical development. Contextualising recent developments histori-cally and internationally highlights both the scale of the 'representation gap' in the UK (Towers, 1997b) and the deleterious consequences of recent developments for industrial democracy, social justice and economic performance.

WHAT IS COLLECTIVE BARGAINING?

John Goodman (1984:145) succinctly describes collective bargaining as 'a process through which representatives of employers and employee organisations act as the joint creators of the substantive and procedural rules regulating employment'. 'Substantive' rules relate to aspects of the *substance* of the employment relationship, such as the wage rate, the length of the working day or week, holiday entitlement, sick pay and the like. 'Procedural' rules, on the other hand, establish the *procedure* by which, or how, substantive agreements are to be reached (how negotiations are to be conducted, by whom, how any disputes which may arise should be handled, and so on). In other words, collective bargaining is not only a *market* process, affecting the sale of labour power, but also a *political* process which, as a rule-making activ-ity that involves power relations between the parties, serves to define rights, duties and obligations (Flanders, 1975:220). In the words of Slichter (1941:1), collective bargaining is a system of 'industrial jurisprudence' or, as Flanders (1975:236) put it, 'an institution for regulating labour management as well as labour markets'. In this respect, collective bargaining can be regarded as a form of 'industrial government' and a means to 'industrial democracy' (ibid).

Others have argued that the outcomes of collective bargaining can usefully be seen as not just a set of substantive and procedural agreements, but more generally as a means of management control (i.e. a managerial process). At first sight this argument may seem curious, since one of the defining features of collective bargaining is that it is a process in which issues are subjected to *joint* control. So how can it act to augment management's control? The argument here relates both to the consequences of trade unions participating in collective bargaining activity, and the possible repercussions of the absence of bargaining relations. On the former, the joint establishment of the basic terms on which labour is sold will conceivably vest those terms with greater legitimacy in the eyes of the workforce (and are thus less likely to be challenged by that workforce) than where the terms are set unilaterally by the employer:

> There are numerous ways in which a positive acceptance of the union, an effort to integrate it into the administrative structure of the enterprise instead of treating it as a thing apart, can contribute to efficient management ... This sort of relationship, in which union and management officials not only accept each other's existence but support each other's objectives, is frequently referred to as 'mature collective bargaining'. (Reynolds, 1956:176–7)

The establishment of legitimacy is part of a broader issue, however. As Sisson (1987) argues, by entering into a collective bargaining relationship with employers over some aspects of the employment relationship, employee representatives not only demonstrate their willingness to reach compromises with employers over those aspects, but by implication also signal a broader acceptance of managerial rights in other areas and, more generally, the respective roles of management and labour within the status quo. Thus, in the historical development of the rule-making process that constitutes collective bargaining,

> relatively few of these rules were (or have become) the subject of joint regulation; in most cases only a framework of minimum pay and conditions was involved. In fact much more important was the legitimacy that trade union involvement in the rule-making process gave to the employers' right to manage. For collective bargaining involves *mutual* recognition. In agreeing to make some rules subject to joint regulation, employers were requiring that trade unions should recognize the employers' right to make other rules unilaterally. In a number of cases ... this trade-off was explicit ... the exercise of managerial prerogative [was] the *quid pro quo* for the employers' willingness to negotiate over pay and other conditions of employment. (Sisson, 1987:12, original emphasis)

No wonder Harbison (1954, quoted by Jackson, 1991:162) has called collective bargaining 'one of the major bulwarks of the capitalist system'. By entering bargaining relations with trade unions, employers simultaneously 'gained an additional source of supervision over worker behaviour and an institutionalised means of pay settlement' (Ursell and Blyton, 1988:94). In addition, there are areas of workplace activity where, if anything, control rests with the work group rather than with management. Hence, for management, collective bargaining may represent an attempt to establish a degree of joint control where formerly they did not even have that. This strategy underpins much of the development of productivity bargaining in the 1960s and flexibility bargaining in the 1980s and 1990s, in which management sought to gain a greater degree of influence over 'job control' issues such as demarcation, the organisation of work and overtime hours.

As well as according legitimacy to both the specific areas of joint agreement and, following the argument above, to wider areas of managerial action, collective bargaining also represents a potential source of managerial control in the way in which it institutionalises conflict by channelling the power of organised labour into a mechanism which, while acknowledging that power, at the same time circumscribes it and gives it a greater predictability. 'By collective bargaining,' wrote Dahrendorf (1956:260), 'the frozen fronts of industrial conflict are thawed.' Thus, while collective bargaining clearly does not lead to a *cessation* of industrial conflict, the existence of negotiation machinery will tend to act to *temper* that conflict and reduce the chances of it fundamentally threatening the basic existence of the enterprise. Thus in the case of Corus prior to 1980, for example, the extensive national bargaining structures acted as an important contributor to the absence of large-scale strikes in the industry.

This is not to suggest that employers have welcomed collective bargaining with open arms or (as we discuss below) have not sought to diminish its role when given the opportunity to do so. Evidence suggests that, recent legislation notwithstanding, it has become harder than ever for unions to gain recognition in new companies, new sites, or in those industries where recognition has always been difficult to achieve (Brown *et al.*, 1995:140–1; Gall, 2003b; Gall and McKay, 1999 and 2001; and Millward *et al.*, 2000:95–108). There are strong historical precedents for such resistance. The early period of trade unionism in the UK and elsewhere is replete with examples of embryonic unions fighting for recognition with employers highly averse to conceding *any* part of their prerogative to joint control. Faced with growing craft union organisation within the workplace, however, together with increased militancy among the newer unions of semi-skilled and unskilled workers, employers found themselves in a position where yielding to collective bargaining over basic pay and conditions was the lesser of two evils. In so doing, employers ensured that much of the conflict between capital and labour became institutionalised, the basic legitimacy of the system was tacitly acknowledged and union power became accommodated within the broad status quo.

Sisson (1987) and others have pointed to specific historical incidents, such as the industrial unrest in the iron and steel industry in the 1860s and the 1897–8 strike and lock-out over a shorter working day in the engineering industry, as critical events in the formation of particular bargaining arrangements. It is also important, however, to avoid treating these events in isolation. Part of the broader explanation of why employers in the UK did not demonstrate more concerted opposition to the growth of trade unionism, for example, and why they ceded recognition rights relatively early, may lie in the apparent complacency which gripped many employers in the late nineteenth century (see Gospel, 1992). Easy access to colonial materials and markets lowered competitive pressures which might otherwise have fuelled a stronger employer zeal to minimise labour costs by destroying union organisations (Ursell and Blyton, 1988:94). Moreover, the nature of early trade union growth in the UK among the 'labour aristocracy' of craft workers – a unionisation designed to maintain a separateness from, rather than a solidarity with, the growing class of semi-skilled and unskilled workers – meant that employers were 'anxious to avoid giving succour to a more militant unionism by rejecting the extant version' (ibid:94). Thus, in extending recognition and joint regulation to a union movement initially dominated by skilled workers, employers were seeking to accommodate a brand of unionism which shared many of the individualist values of *laissez-faire* capitalism. As we discuss below, the state also came to share this view that the institutionalisation of conflict within collective bargaining accorded a greater degree of stability. As a result, for more than half a century, the state both directly and indirectly supported the development of collective bargaining arrangements (see Ewing, 1998).

Though often discussed as if it were a homogeneous and comparatively simple entity, in practice collective bargaining is both a complex and diverse process. Walton and McKersie (1965) have observed that bargaining encapsulates negotiations occurring within, as well as between, the major parties, and incorporates attempts to structure attitudes as well as establish agreements over the terms of the employment relationship. In addition, collective bargaining exhibits considerable variation in:

- the *level(s)* at which bargaining activity takes place and the linkages between different levels
- the *coverage* of bargaining across different work groups, usually referred to as the bargaining *unit*, which may be few or many, wide or narrow
- the range or *scope* of topics subject to joint regulation
- the *processes* which constitute collective bargaining
- the extent or *depth* of union influence within bargaining activity, and the degree to which union representatives and managers become involved in the interpretation and application of rules and practices
- the *forms* which bargained agreements take, whether they are written or unwritten, formal or informal, precise or flexible (see, for example, Clegg, 1979:115; and McCarthy *et al.*, 1971:3–5).

It is clear that in the recent period significant changes have occurred along several of these dimensions. It is to a consideration of these changes, and the consequences for the parties involved, that we now turn, for it is evident that the type of changes evidenced in the Corus case are far from unique. And, as the steel example illustrates, these changes, such as in the level of bargaining and the nature of representation, can have a significant bearing on the kinds of issues included in (and excluded from) collective bargaining and the resulting outcomes stemming from that bargaining activity.

To this end, the remainder of the chapter examines changes occurring in patterns of bargaining and assesses the extent to which workers have 'lost their voice' at work. Following an historical review, the significance of the period since 1979 is emphasised. One issue of note is the fact that despite a tradition of 'free collective bargaining' in the UK, the outcomes of the bargaining process were foreclosed on numerous occasions in the past as a result of incomes policies. In contrast, the past two and a half decades represent one of the longest sustained periods of 'free' collective bargaining in the post-war years. This recent period has also witnessed many significant changes in the structure and content of collective relations between employer and employees, not least the historically unprecedented withdrawal from collective agreements by many companies in general, and the decline of multi-employer collective bargaining in particular. These developments have permitted a marked increase in wage inequality and a decline in perceived 'fairness' at work (see Brown *et al.*, 2003:210; and Millward *et al.*, 2000:137). It is not only industrial democracy and social justice that suffers as a result but also economic performance.

THE HISTORICAL DEVELOPMENT OF COLLECTIVE BARGAINING STRUCTURES

Early collective bargaining activity tended to be local in character, as individual or neighbouring groups of employers struck bargains with the representatives of local work groups. In the UK, both early trade unions and employer bodies organised on the basis of individual localities or districts: for both parties, national organisation only came later, and in some industries, only much later. To continue our iron and steel example, employers' associations in the industry maintained their regional organisation until comparatively recently; in 1925, twenty-five separate employers' associations were functioning, and by the time of the 1967 nationalisation, ten iron and steel employers' associations remained in existence (Owen Smith, 1971:39). In industries such as engineering and shipbuilding, the localised character of collective bargaining was reinforced by the early development of shop steward organisation before and after the First World War (Hinton, 1973).

In the early decades of the twentieth century, however, local arrangements for collective bargaining became increasingly overlaid by national, industry-wide collective bargaining arrangements involving (by now, nationally-organised) trade union organisations and national industry associations of large numbers of employers. The upshot was the growth of industry-wide agreements on pay and other basic terms and conditions (covering issues such as hours, holidays and overtime rates). Where industries comprised many employers, pay agreements tended to establish *minimum* or 'standard' pay rates, while in the public sector, national pay determination involved setting *actual* rates and scales.

Various factors contributed to the growth of industry-wide bargaining. First, in different ways it served the interests of all the parties to concentrate their bargaining activity at the national level. For employers, this meant a more concerted response to growing trade union organisation, particularly as unions began to expand significantly among semi-skilled and unskilled workers, became more militant (e.g. strike waves in 1912 and 1921) and developed as national organisations. As Traxler (1999:345) notes, '[h]istorically, employer organisations emerged no earlier than in response to the spread of unions which had acquired so much power that collective action in the labour market became an unavoidable ingredient of employer strategies.' Under national or industry-wide bargaining arrangements, individual employers in particular districts and localities became less vulnerable to trade union pressure in the form of 'whipsawing' whereby unions play off one employer against another (e.g. seeking to extend concessions wrought from more vulnerable employers to other employers in the same industry or locality on the basis of 'comparability'). National bargaining also allowed small employers to reduce the amount of time and resources they devoted to negotiating with trade unions. More significantly, perhaps, it kept unions out of the workplace, or at least neutralised their impact (Sisson, 1987:188).

For the expanding trade unions, national bargaining arrangements allowed them to rationalise their bargaining activity and marshal their meagre finances to service more effectively a small cadre of negotiators. It also underlined the role of trade unions within an industry, improving their possibilities for recognition and increasing membership growth (see Bain, 1970; Bain and Elsheikh, 1980). In addition, national bargaining provided some protection against whipsawing by employers (i.e. a 'race to the bottom' in respect of pay and conditions of employment as one employer after another demands concessions to match those secured by their rivals) and enabled unions to wield the 'sword of justice' (standardisation is one route to fairness and greater equality).

Finally, for the state, the extension of collective bargaining represented an important institutionalisation of conflict and both an important counter to bouts of industrial unrest and a mechanism for promoting industrial co-operation, especially during wartime and economic crises. During the First World War, for example, the introduction of industry arbitration under the terms of a Treasury Agreement (subsequently incorporated into the 1915 Munitions of War Act), coupled with the taking of certain industries directly under state control for the period of the war, encouraged a centralisation of employee relations. More generally, the importance of state support for co-ordinated, multi-employer bargaining should not be underestimated as there is always an (economic) incentive for employers to renege on these agreements or their membership of the employers' association. This is because the employer's greatest power resources (e.g. investment decisions) are exercised *outside* its association, unlike workers whose power resources are most effectively mobilised *within* the trade union, such that the individual employer will always perceive some advantage to non-co-operative behaviour, for example setting wages just below the agreed industry rate in order to secure a cost advantage (many UK employers' associations formally recognise this problem through a 'non-conforming member' category which frees the individual employer from certain obligations of ordinary members) (see Traxler, 1999:345–6). More important for the state is the fact that individual employers are unlikely to take account of any 'negative externalities' in terms of the impact of their wage agreements on price inflation or unemployment, as their individual settlement is unlikely to have any noticeable impact on the economy as a whole. In combination, however, a succession of individual (inflationary) wage agreements, with each settlement higher than the last, can have serious economic repercussions in terms of (un)employment, interest rates and growth. As Traxler (2003:198) points out,

> Effective macrocoordination is beyond the capacity of formal institutions based on the principle of free collective bargaining. As an implication, the two sides of industry can arrive at such coordination only when receiving support from a third party. There is no possible party other than the state which can provide this support due to its imperative role in society.

In combination, these factors resulted in the progressive extension of national and/or industry-wide bargaining during the twentieth century in most industrialised economies. In the UK, national bargaining covered at least a third of the employed labour force and over half the total trade union membership by 1917 (Clegg, 1985:168). In that year the government established a Committee of Inquiry (under the chairmanship of the deputy-speaker, J.H. Whitley), and in a total of five reports issued over the next two years the Whitley Committee recommended the establishment of industry-wide collective machinery for all industries, centred on national Joint Standing Industrial Councils (JICs) supported by joint committees at district and works levels. The national committees were rapidly established in many industries and in the public sector; by 1921 seventy-four JICs had been set up (Ursell and Blyton, 1988:115). Though many fell into decay during the recessionary years of the 1930s, there was a revival of interest in industry-wide collective bargaining during the Second World War, again stimulated by government taking direct control of some industries and looking to secure peaceful industrial relations and co-operation with wartime production requirements in others. The upshot was that by the end of the war, 15.5 million employees out of a total workforce of 17.5 million were covered by some form of national bargaining machinery (Jackson, 1991). This proportion rose further as the nationalisation Acts of the late 1940s brought hitherto unorganised groups (particularly non-manual workers) within the scope of national collective agreements.

Throughout this period, a degree of local bargaining activity continued, in some industries more than others, concerned with the application of national agreements, the supplementing of those agreements in particular areas and the establishment of local work rules. The Whitley model also advocated the establishment of works committees to discuss local issues. While these always remained less prominent than the national JICs, they became well established in certain industries, particularly in the growing public sector. Further, during the Second World War, the government promoted the establishment of factory-wide Joint Production Committees: by mid 1943 there were over 4000 of these in the engineering industry alone, dealing with a range of issues from technical matters to levels of absenteeism and the application of 'dilution' agreements (the introduction of workers into skilled jobs who had not completed the normal apprenticeship) (Clegg and Chester, 1954:338; and Currie, 1979:156). Similar committees were established in shipbuilding, mining and construction. While the emphasis was on consultation rather than negotiation, these and similar committees nevertheless contributed to the maintenance of local collective relations at a time when most attention was being given to the development of joint machinery at national level.

From the mid 1950s onwards, however, there was a reassertion of local bargaining activity in the private sector, which gained further momentum during the 1960s. Industry-wide agreements remained in place but were increasingly subject to elaboration and extension at local level. Following Sisson (1987), local bargaining in large parts of manufacturing moved from 'supplementing' national agreements to 'supplanting' them. The shop steward movement grew from an estimated 90000 in 1961 to between 250000 and 300000 by the late 1970s (see Terry, 1983), as did the degree of job control that work groups exerted over aspects of work pace and effort. Explanations for this growth in workplace bargaining have been sought mainly in labour market and economic conditions. The general argument runs that labour shortages, coupled with improved union organisation within the workplace, provided both a power base and a means for unions and work groups to mobilise that power to force wage concessions. The spread of piecework and bonus schemes are seen to have provided increased opportunities for bargaining to take place over rate-fixing for particular jobs. The general conditions of economic growth are further seen to have encouraged employers to secure local settlements in order to avoid disruptions to production and retain scarce skilled labour. As Boxall and Purcell (2003:177) point out, '[t]he old industrial relations were about control and stability: gaining agreements to keep the production system going and avoiding disruptive conflict.'

Sisson (1987) has analysed the significance of the relative weakness of most industry agreements in the UK, compared to their counterparts elsewhere in western Europe. In Europe, the broader range of substantive issues covered by national agreements resulted in local bargaining activity remaining an essentially administrative activity *vis-à-vis* the national agreements. In the UK, on the other hand, the narrower range of coverage of industry agreements meant that local collective bargaining developed a more substantial and independent role, filling larger gaps left by the national settlements. While national minimum rates were agreed at industry level, negotiations (often informal) at local level increasingly took place over issues such as piecework rates and bonuses, as well as demarcation issues and other working practices such as manning levels (Cliff, 1970). Thus, the relative weakness of national industry agreements in the UK gave trade unions significant room for bargaining at local level, and left individual employers faced with the need to establish rules and agreements in those areas insufficiently covered by the industry agreement. As Ogden (1982:170) notes, the variety and complexity of collective bargaining arrangements at that time were 'generally seen to be unsatisfactory not least because they are highly fragmented, encourage the pursuit of comparisons, breed competitive bargaining, are a major source of disputes, and produce dissatisfaction which fuels inflationary wage claims'.

The overall outcome was that by the time of the review of industrial relations undertaken by the Royal Commission on Trade Unions and Employers' Associations in the mid 1960s, it was not only judged that those relations were operating with a considerable degree of, or more precisely too much, informal workplace bargaining activity, despite the widespread retention of national industry agreements, but also, and of greater importance, that this bargaining was 'ineffective' (Donovan, 1968). The existence of this dual system, and in particular the informality, autonomy and fragmentation displayed by the workplace activity, was judged partly to blame not only for the increased numbers of strikes, well over 90 per cent of which were 'unofficial' (Durcan et al., 1983:109–10), but also the relative decline in productivity and wage drift (that is, earnings substantially exceeding nationally negotiated base rates). The significance of local bargaining on earnings levels by the late 1960s is illustrated by Cliff (1970:39). For example, while the nationally agreed standard rate for engineering fitters in 1968 was under £13 per week, in practice average earnings for fitters at that time, excluding overtime but including local agreements, was almost £23 per week, over 75 per cent higher than the national minimum rate (see also Donovan, 1968:9).

Essentially it was the *form* of collective bargaining in the UK that was identified as the problem. Collective agreements were basically 'gentlemen's agreements', and as such were not legally enforceable. This is in stark contrast to many other countries where there is a substantive agreement on all matters currently subject to joint regulation, the agreement runs for a fixed term, and is legally enforceable. During the period of the contract there is a procedure in operation to settle disputes arising over the interpretation of the agreement, but disputes outside the agreement must await termination of the contract itself, when amendments or extensions may be negotiated. Industrial action is only permitted at the end of the contract as a means of reaching a new agreement. Clegg (1979:116–17) classifies this as the 'statute law' model of collective bargaining, which he contrasts with the 'common law' model which is more reflective of (some areas of) British industry. Under this model there is again a disputes procedure, but *any* dispute can be referred to the procedure. In other words, there is no distinction drawn between disputes of right under the existing agreement, and disputes of interest concerning the terms of a new agreement. Industrial action is allowed whenever a procedure has failed to resolve a dispute. Substantive issues can be regulated by as many agreements as the parties choose to make.

Clegg (1979:117) suggests that the common law model has fitted the public sector reasonably well, but points out that in the private sector in particular, negotiation and administration associated with collective bargaining has often been more noticeable by its absence. Moreover, in some key areas such as disciplinary codes and redundancy arrangements there is often no direct trade union involvement, while formal agreements are often rare. More characteristic were *ad hoc* arrangements, custom and practice and unwritten status quo agreements. This 'primitive' or 'basic' model of collective bargaining, as Clegg (1979:123) labels it, is underpinned by a tacit agreement to disagree and an acceptance that there are areas where joint regulation is unwelcome. Both parties have the right to make rules and take industrial action to impose them on the other side, although agreed rules are made wherever possible to avoid anarchy and disruption. Under such arrangements, the action/reaction of one party will be shaped by expectations about the other party's likely response, leading to what Walton and McKersie (1965) describe as 'attitudinal structuring' and a continuous state of flux in employer-employee relations.

Although workers and local union organisation might gain from this pattern of bargaining, the authority of national union officials was perceived to have been undermined and employers faced ever stronger incentives to withdraw from multi-employer bargaining. The former is an example of what Traxler (2003:196–7) calls the 'vertical problem' of bargaining co-ordination (e.g. securing agreement from all parties within an organisation or interest group, such as trade union leaders, local activists and rank-and-file members) whilst the latter is an example of the 'horizontal problem' of co-ordinated bargaining (e.g. securing the agreement of all employers and trade unions who are signatories to the collective agreement). These problems heightened, and according to some analysts were a root cause of the UK's deteriorating economic performance in the late 1960s (most notably wage/price inflation and poor labour productivity). By the end of the 1960s, both major political parties favoured legal reform of industrial relations via the adoption of something akin to the statute law model.

For Donovan, however, the solution to the shortcomings of the dual system lay not in greater centralisation and co-ordination but in the extension and formalisation of local bargaining arrangements around more comprehensive agreements, drawn up and administered by an enhanced industrial relations management function. In other words, the *form* of collective bargaining was to change, and its *scope* extended. Thus, formal bargaining at the plant or company level was envisaged as expanding beyond its traditional subject areas to encapsulate a wide range of job control issues, such as staffing levels, demarcation and work rate, which had hitherto been determined by 'custom and practice'. In addition, payment-by-results (PBR) was to be replaced by measured day work (MDW) or other payment schemes to reduce wage drift. The introduction of job evaluation would reduce the problems of fragmented bargaining and comparability claims, and new dispute procedures would help to reduce strikes. Underlying these recommendations was the criticism that negotiations had traditionally been 'a one-sided affair' (Donovan, 1968:85) with employers failing even to secure concessions on working practices in return for wage increases. Under the expanded version of collective bargaining, however, wage rises would be *exchanged* for agreements over job control issues.

An influential model informing these recommendations, and much quoted in the Donovan Report itself, was the productivity agreement reached earlier at Esso's Fawley refinery (Flanders, 1964). In this highly detailed, book-length agreement, Esso management sought to regain control over labour costs and secure productivity improvements by entering into an agreement with local trade unions which exchanged a (substantial) pay increase for detailed changes in working arrangements involving, among other things, reduced overtime working, greater job flexibility and a simplification of the pay structure. For members of the Royal Commission and others, Esso's 'Blue Book' agreement, and productivity bargaining more generally, became a model of how collective bargaining might be better organised.

Initial enthusiasm for productivity agreements soon evaporated, not least because most failed to deliver significant increases in productivity, due in part to many being used more as a way to by-pass the government's incomes policies in operation at the time. However, workplace bargaining continued to develop in importance during the 1970s, with shop steward organisation spreading among non-manual groups and beyond manufacturing into public service settings such as local authorities (Nicholson et al., 1980). In the decade after Donovan some formalisation of local bargaining did occur (see, for example, Marsh, 1982), partly as management responded to growing shop steward organisation and an increased number of strikes (see Turner et al., 1977). But on the shopfloor, control over working practices by individual work groups if anything increased, although the extent to which this hindered managerial control has been fiercely debated (see, for example, Hyman and Elger, 1981; and Kilpatrick and Lawson, 1980). The growing influence of shopfloor groups may, in part, have been due to employers' lack of investment in newer technologies at that time, which allowed work groups to retain and reinforce the informal rules devised around older, non-automated equipment (see, for example, Belanger, 1987). More generally, it must be acknowledged that the managerially-led reform of collective bargaining proposed by Donovan not only discounted trade union resistance, but assumed that the 'formalisation of the informal' was in the best interests of *both* parties. As Ogden (1981 and 1982) and others have demonstrated, this was simply not the case. As a result,

> Even though trade unions may not positively challenge managerially deter-mined arrangements regarding the levels at which bargaining takes place, trade union power acts as a significant constraint on what choices manage-ment may make. Consequently, decisions about bargaining structure may represent defensive responses by management as well as offensive initiative.
> (Ogden, 1982:182)

Of equal importance, however, were the shortcomings of management. Under the Donovan proposals, the onus was placed upon management to implement change, albeit by consent and through the process of joint regulation. The prescription, as Ogden (1981:31) notes, was that 'if management accepted their responsibility, embraced the opportunities collective bargaining offered, and took advantage of the techniques available such as job evaluation ... they could regain control where they had lost it and improve efficiency and productivity'. But management failed to carry through the Donovan programme for at least three reasons (in addition to the prob-lems of union or work group opposition).

First, managers valued the informality and flexibility of the existing system. Thus, while there were considerable changes in the nature and conduct of bargaining over *market* relations, there was little change so far as *managerial* relations were concerned (Sisson and Brown, 1983:137). As a result, by the end of the 1970s a dual structure of pay bargaining had developed, with multi-employer, industry-wide agreements still prevalent in industries with a large number of small firms, relatively low capital requirements and ease of entry, while elsewhere there was a move towards a formal, single employer pay bargaining system (Sisson and Brown, 1983:147–8). As for managerial relations, however, the scope of collective bargaining appeared 'as hazy as it ever was. It is massively variable from industry to industry and from workplace to workplace, heavily dependent upon the form of management controls and the rela-tive power of the protagonists' (ibid:149–50).

Secondly, many managers had neither the capacity nor the expertise to exercise sufficient (formal) control over industrial relations at the plant or company level (Ogden, 1981:39 and 1982:181). As Michael Edwardes, former Chairman of British Leyland (now Rover) made clear in his autobiography *Back From the Brink*, ten years of vacillation by plant management in employee relations had left them with little cred-ibility or authority (1983:78). But as Nichols (1986:165–6) illustrates, this was not so much a case of workers gaining control as of managers losing it. When combined with the failure of many firms to organise productive activity effectively, this undermined workers' respect for management and led to deterioration in employee relations (Batstone, 1986:41).

Thirdly, in following Allan Flanders's famous dictum that management should 'regain control by sharing it', Donovan not only assumed that management were prepared to share control, but that they would be willing to change their attitude towards trade unions in general and shop stewards in particular. As Ogden (1981:36) notes, however, 'the idea of giving them [shop stewards] more by sharing power was complete anathema to them [management]'. Despite Fox's (1966) critique, most managers still hold a unitarist perspective on employee relations. Not surprisingly, the effort 'to educate management of the need for change in attitudes – from unitary to pluralist frames of reference, from management by prerogatives to joint regulation – deemed essential in the programme of reform has generally met, with some exceptions, little success' (Ogden, 1981:37). In short, management did not seek to share power, but to restore their prerogative.

Thus, by the end of the 1970s, there was still a very complex and varied pattern of collective bargaining in the UK, in terms of each of the various dimensions identified (level, form, scope, depth, and so on). According to Hugh Clegg, the draftsman of the most influential chapter in the Donovan Report, that on collective bargaining,

> the true disciples of the Royal Commission have been those managers of British companies who have carried through a reconstruction of their industrial relations at workplace level along much the same lines as the Commission's report had recommended, with considerable increases in productivity and a substantial decline in strike activity. (1990:6)

But the more widely accepted view, and certainly that of the incoming Thatcher government, was that the Donovan prescription had failed, certainly in its intentions to deliver a higher rate of productivity growth which would reverse the relative economic decline of the UK economy (for an exposition of this view see Metcalf, 1989). Not surprisingly, then, the 1980s and 1990s were to witness more dramatic change, as the experience of Corus and many other organisations clearly illustrates.

DECENTRALISATION AND DECLINE OF COLLECTIVE BARGAINING

Since the early 1980s to the present, the pattern of collective bargaining in the UK has exhibited three main trends: (i) a substantial reduction in the proportion of employees covered by collective bargaining arrangements, (ii) a growing tendency for those arrangements to be local rather than national in character, and (iii) a narrowing of the scope of collective agreements. The contraction in coverage and scope of collective bargaining, combined with the decentralisation to lower levels, add up to a fundamental change in the character and conduct of employee relations in the UK over the past two decades.

In the early 1980s, over two-thirds of employees in Britain were covered by collective bargaining arrangements. In only a decade and a half, this slumped to just two-in-five of all employees (Millward *et al.*, 2000:197). What makes the decline in coverage particularly significant is that it is evident across all sectors of employment: public and private sector, manufacturing and service activities (see Figure 18.1). If smaller workplaces were included in these calculations (i.e. those employing fewer than 25 workers) then collective bargaining coverage would be further reduced.

As Figure 18.1 demonstrates, there remain substantial variations between sectors, both in the degree of coverage and in the rate of change. For example, in the 1990s the rate of decline of bargaining coverage in private sector manufacturing was far less than the rate in the public sector, while in private sector services the fall in the 1990s was particularly marked. Similarly, there are variations within sectors with some (such as energy and water, and metal goods and engineering) maintaining similar

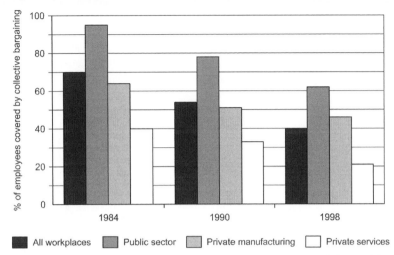

Figure 18.1 – Changes in overall coverage of collective bargaining activity in Britain 1984–98
Source: Millward *et al.* (2000:197).

levels of coverage throughout the 1990s (Millward *et al.*, 2000:198). Overall, however, the picture is one of very substantial decline in bargaining coverage during the 1980s and 1990s. Statistically, this decline reflects two important trends. First, the growing number of workplaces where no unions, and thus no collective bargaining, are present (this trend is not so much attributable to union derecognition, although this has been important in specific industries, rather to the tendency of newly established workplaces not to recognise trade unions). Secondly, even where a trade union has recognition, collective bargaining coverage has declined: in 1998, 69 per cent of employees in workplaces with recognised unions were covered by collective bargaining compared to 90 per cent in 1984. This decline has been particularly evident where union density levels are fairly low, indicating that managers have used low union density as a pretext for withdrawing from collective bargaining for pay determination and other issues, to be replaced by unilateral (i.e. managerially-determined) pay setting. Both trends, of course, are not simply the result of a failure on the part of unions to organise new workplaces or to maintain an active membership where they have recognition, but represent an important shift in management strategy away from joint regulation.

If recent developments are viewed from the perspective of management control, then decentralisation is more readily understood. In many cases, of course, multi-employer agreements have simply been replaced by unilateral pay determination by management (half the workforce now have their pay set by management, a figure that rises to two-thirds in the private sector) (see Brown *et al.*, 2000:615). Where bargaining still takes place, there is a tendency within larger companies for bargaining activity to be devolved to the level of individual divisions, units, establishments and/or profit centres where market forces and internal pressures are more keenly felt. In this way, management seek to diminish the influence of 'comparability', the 'going rate', 'standardisation' or other 'outmoded' concepts of pay determination.

Unfortunately, there is a tendency for some authors to discuss this latter development simply in terms of 'decentralisation', which can be misleading for two reasons. First, many firms and industries were already characterised by highly decentralised workplace and workshop bargaining arrangements (see above). Secondly, and more importantly, in positioning collective bargaining more clearly at the establishment level, what the pattern of change has simultaneously involved has been a decentralisation of bargaining activity from corporate level and an attempt to diminish the role of informal shopfloor bargaining by shifting the focus of local joint regulation from the individual section and department up to more formal activity at establishment level. As a result, 'much of the decentralization that has taken place is an illusion. Things may happen at local level, but they are not decided there' (Storey and Sisson, 1993:212; see also Sisson and Marginson, 1995:105–6). As management retain greater (centralised) control of decentralised bargaining, the resulting bargaining activity at the establishment level is generally of a more formalised nature than that criticised by the Donovan Commission in the 1960s. In the local teamworking agreements at Corus, for example, all aspects relating to the new work structures (grades, pay levels, job responsibilities, working patterns and so on) were formally set out in detail within each departmental agreement. In addition, however, key parameters for those departmental agreements – most importantly, the requirement to reduce employment numbers by a fifth, as part of the move to teamworking – were decisions made by corporate management.

The continued move away from multi-employer to single-employer bargaining has been documented by the series of workplace industrial relations surveys undertaken between 1980 and 1998 (Millward *et al.*, 2000:186–96; see also Brown and Walsh, 1991:49; Gregg and Yates, 1991; Howell, 1995:161–2). In private sector manufacturing, the proportion of workplaces where multi-employer collective bargaining was the dominant mode of pay determination declined from 21 per cent in 1984 to just 6 per cent in 1998. In private sector services the corresponding figures were 17 per cent and 3 per cent (Millward *et al.*, 2000:187–93). As one might expect in the private sector, changes have often been driven by market forces, reflecting the fact that:

> The overwhelming desire by managers has been to get employees to work harder and more efficiently in return for pay increases ... Decentralized bargaining has allowed bargaining over market relations to be linked to bargaining over managerial relations. (Jackson *et al.*, 1993:161–2)

However, unlike the 'productivity bargaining' of the 1960s and 1970s (see McKersie and Hunter, 1973), or the 'flexibility bargaining' of the 1980s (see Dunn and Wright, 1994; Ingram, 1991; and Marsden and Thompson, 1990), 'The usual rules of bargaining no longer apply. For one thing, the items placed on the negotiating table become too numerous, too complex and too interwoven for classic trade-off deals' (Boxall and Purcell, 2003:177).

As bargaining has been decentralised, management have sought to narrow the scope of joint regulation. Survey evidence and case-based research often conflict on this point, reflecting different measures of presence (i.e. where any bargaining takes place) and process (i.e. whether workers or their representatives have any real influence on bargaining outcomes). As the coverage of pay bargaining began its seemingly inexorable decline after 1979, surveys initially indicated a corresponding decline in bargaining over non-pay issues. WIRS90, however, suggested far less change in non-pay bargaining between 1984 and 1990 (Millward *et al.*, 1992:249–53). More detailed case studies, in contrast, identified a more sustained and substantial reduction in the trade unions' bargaining role (e.g. Morris and Wood, 1991), as did a longitudinal case study conducted over a ten-year period (Kinnie, 1992). These findings accord with our own experience at the time of researching in a variety of work contexts including steel, port transport, engineering, electronics, airlines and the automotive industry: unions maintained a bargaining role on certain issues but this was increasingly augmented by management handling work-related changes outside the bargaining framework.

Evidence from case-study research conducted in the mid 1990s suggested not only a continuation of these trends (i.e. a substantial reduction in the scope of collective bargaining in companies that continued to recognise unions) but a narrowing of the bargaining agenda to the point where this was tantamount to 'implicit or partial derecognition' (Brown et al., 1998:iii). By the end of the 1990s, even surveys indicated that the scope of joint negotiation at the workplace was quite modest (Cully et al., 1999:103–4). To be sure, where unions were still well organised and membership levels were high, management were more likely to negotiate (ibid). In these organisations there is evidence of very little change in the scope of bargaining over non-pay issues (see, for example, Millward et al., 2000:167–73). But this should not detract attention from the overall decline in pay bargaining or the much narrower scope of joint regulation at the workplace.

At first sight, one possible exception to these developments might appear to be the public sector, where collective bargaining is still the dominant form of pay determination (see Figure 18.1) with 39 per cent of establishments still covered by multi-employer pay bargaining (Millward et al., 2000:194). Moreover, although this is far fewer than in 1984 when 82 per cent of public sector workplaces were covered by multi-employer bargaining, this decline has been partially offset by two factors: (i) an increase in multi-site, single employer bargaining (unlike the private sector where this form of bargaining has declined in recent years) (ibid:187–96) and (ii) the introduction of pay review bodies (in place of national bargaining) for nurses and midwives (in 1983) and schoolteachers (in 1991) which simultaneously took almost one million employees out of collective bargaining machinery for their pay determination, but at the same time maintained a national system for pay settlement for these groups (Bach and Winchester, 2003:298). Thus, the institutional structure of collective bargaining in the public sector still (potentially) supports an element of standardisation across workplaces.

The dominant trend, however, is still a marked shift away from centralised bargaining systems, reflecting the policy of successive governments, both Conservative and Labour, to 'commercialise' large sections of the public sector and to 'proxy' market forces through compulsory competitive tendering, local management of schools, GP fund-holding, NHS hospital trusts, Next Step agencies in the civil service, and a range of other initiatives. As Bach and Winchester (2003:299) note,

> As managers were given greater responsibility for budgets in which labour costs were the most significant component, the relevance of national pay and conditions arrangements was increasingly questioned. The restructuring and organisational fragmentation of public services, and the growing interest in private sector management 'best practice' added further weight to the arguments in favour of a more decentralized system of pay determination.

As in the private sector, therefore, trade unions are now far less likely to be involved in pay bargaining, and in particular multi-employer pay bargaining, than they were in the past. The same conclusion holds for non-pay bargaining issues such as staffing levels, redeployment, training, physical working conditions, the re-organisation of working hours, and equal opportunities. As the scope of joint regulation has narrowed across the economy, with private and public sector workers alike increasingly subject to market forces and managerial fiat, workers are routinely excluded from decision-making at their place of work. This has deleterious consequences for industrial democracy, social justice and economic performance.

EFFECTS OF CHANGES IN COLLECTIVE BARGAINING

Collective bargaining in the UK, as in other liberal market economies (LMEs) such as the USA, is employer dependent (see Osterman *et al.*, 2001:101; and Turnbull, 2003:508). Without provision for the extension of collective agreements beyond the unionised bargaining unit – either by statutory regulation or more extensive membership of employers' associations (wherein some members of the association apply union-agreed contracts, even though they may be non-union firms or have much lower levels of union density) – then joint regulation is inherently firm-specific.

The UK has always had a 'voluntary' system of industrial relations, but collective bargaining was previously supported by the state, especially in the public sector. Between 1979 and 1997, however, any auxiliary measures to support and encourage collective bargaining were progressively dismantled by successive Conservative governments (e.g. the Fair Wages Resolution, repealed in 1983, which extended the terms of collective bargaining agreements to firms not directly involved in such agreements, and the removal of the duty 'to encourage collective bargaining' from the terms of reference of ACAS in 1993). Concurrently, membership of employers' associations collapsed in the rush to single-employer bargaining (Millward *et al.*, 1992:45–6). Despite some revival in employer association membership during the 1990s (Cully *et al.*, 1999:228) there is no longer a sufficiently robust or extensive membership base through which employers might co-ordinate or standardise collective bargaining in the UK. Even the statutory union recognition procedure introduced by New Labour (Employment Relations Act 1999) is explicitly company, or more precisely bargaining unit specific (50 per cent of employees must vote in favour of recognition, which must represent at least 40 per cent of the relevant bargaining unit). As Towers (1997a:303) points out, 'although effective rights to trade union recognition and a consequent duty for employers to bargain in good faith are important instruments of industrial democracy through collective bargaining, they do nothing for those who are without representation, by choice or circumstance'. Whereas collective bargaining used partly to reflect a national agenda for industrial democracy, income (re)distribution and greater equality, it now more singularly reflects employers' firm-level concerns with productivity and efficiency (see Thelen, 2001:71).

As the Corus case clearly illustrates, changes to the level, scope and processes of collective bargaining, together with the depth of union involvement, have been important instruments driving the restructuring of industry in recent years. When job losses are on the agenda it is much easier for management to secure change, and as we have already noted these job losses have often been associated with work intensification in a process of 'distributive' (win-lose) as opposed to 'integrative' (win-win) bargaining. Employers have certainly been able to secure greater control over staffing levels, demarcation rules, working hours and the like, but this is not always reflected in superior competitiveness. Certainly at the aggregate level, any advantages secured from more decentralised bargaining have been insufficient to close the productivity gap between the UK and other leading industrial economies. Moreover, while for many companies the move away from multi-employer bargaining reflected a desire to shake off the constraints imposed by the annual wage round, cost-of-living increases, and what they saw as 'outmoded' concepts such as 'comparability' and the 'going rate', many of these 'outmoded concepts' of wage setting remain very much in evidence. 'After 15 years, the emphasis on freer markets appears to have left much of the institutional operation of the wage-setting process intact' (Ingram *et al.*, 1999:35).

Unions have always sought to standardise pay across workers, leading to a compression of income distribution and greater equality in society, as well as to increase the pay of their members relative to non-members or the 'market rate' (an increase usually referred to as the union mark-up or wage premium). In the 1980s, the union wage premium held up remarkably well, despite the adverse economic and political climate (Stewart, 1991 and 1995) but by the early 1990s there were clear signs of an erosion of the premium enjoyed by trade unionists (Hildreth, 1999). By the end of the 1990s the wage premium for male trade unionists had all but disappeared (Machin, 2001) and any remaining wage differential was confined to women (ibid) or union members in workplaces with high bargaining density (in excess of 70 per cent) or multi-union recognition (Forth and Millward, 2000; see also Booth and Bryan, 2001). The latter no doubt partly accounts for the decline of multi-union recognition and the move towards 'single-table bargaining' (i.e. all unions negotiating together, rather than in succession as the latter is more likely to encourage competitive pay claims or 'leap-frogging') (see Millward *et al.*, 2000:199–205). As Millward *et al.* (2001) conclude, trade unions now affect the *process* of pay determination in the UK more than the *outcome*.

Decentralisation led to a greater dispersion of pay settlements (Ingram *et al.*, 1999:36–7) and has certainly permitted rising income inequality (Brown *et al.*, 2003:209–10), but employers have been unable to insist on purely internal determinants for pay setting (e.g. profitability, the firm's 'ability to pay', productivity, individual performance and the like). Residual notions of fairness and equity make it difficult for firms to ignore the going rate or cost of living. Failure to account for these variables can serve to heighten the 'trust gap' that exists between management and labour in the UK (see Kessler and Undy, 1996) and undermine employee morale and motivation (BSAS data reveal that approaching half the working population no longer regard their pay as 'reasonable', a similar proportion perceive the gap between high and low incomes at their own place of work to be too large, and almost 90 per cent now believe the gap between high and low incomes within the economy as a whole to be too large). Likewise, comparability, or what is now usually referred to as 'pay benchmarking', also continues to exert an important influence on pay determination. In fact, comparability is inevitable in a decentralised wage-setting system if firms are to recruit good workers or avoid costly labour turnover (see Ingram *et al.*, 1999:41).

Unfortunately, the absence of complementary institutions to support decentralised collective bargaining renders 'high road' production or service strategies unstable. At a minimum, decentralisation requires 'deliberative institutions' to facilitate information sharing, knowledge transfer, trust and co-operation between the parties; and financial institutions that allow the development of long-term business strategies. Without such institutions, employers will more often than not fall back on the 'low road' route of cost-cutting and further deregulation (see Thelen, 2001:74). As a result, attempts to forge greater co-operation with labour, or more precisely the 'core' workforce of the organisation, will usually be based on a strategy of segmentation and strong internal controls (e.g. in-house training and company-based participation schemes) which clashes with trade union principles and national or industry-based collective bargaining structures. Hence, firms prefer to pursue these strategies *without* trade unions, or at least attempt to 'cut off' the local union from the national union where the company retains recognition (ibid:78). But in the process of abandoning centralised pay-setting, employers have also jettisoned any possibility of co-ordinated bargaining (and in doing so have thrown the baby out with the bath water).

Numerous studies have demonstrated the benefits of co-ordinated bargaining, including superior performance in terms of wage moderation, lower unemployment and inflation, and improved international competitiveness (see, *inter alia*, Hall and Soskice, 2001; Soskice, 1990 and 2000; Storper, 1995:155; Traxler and Kittel, 2000; and Traxler *et al.*, 2001). Where collective bargaining is co-ordinated, for example, the union mark-up tends to be lower and a higher level of union membership appears to be less of an obstacle to any employment adjustment (Morgan *et al.*, 2001:65). Union wage policy will more directly affect aggregate employment in economies where collective bargaining coverage is much higher and unions are therefore willing and able to 'exchange' wage restraint for tax and welfare benefits that advance social justice (see Visser, 1998a and 1998b). This is not to deny that markets can, in some instances, improve co-ordination among private sector actors, rather to highlight the fact that employers in the UK have 'missed a trick' by surrendering the ability to co-ordinate collective bargaining and by retreating from more extensive forms of joint regulation that guarantee a higher coverage of more standardised terms and conditions of employment.

It is important at this point not to confuse (or equate) centralisation with co-ordination, where the former refers to the level of collective bargaining and the latter the degree to which bargaining and collective agreements are concerted across the economy (at whatever level) (see Traxler, 2003:195–6). Multi-employer bargaining is generally a precondition for macro-co-ordination and the benefits that ensue, as found in Western Europe, but Japanese companies have reconciled single-employer settlements with co-ordinated bargaining by concentrating all bargaining activity within a very limited time period each year (the 'Spring Wage Offensive' or *shunto*) which is co-ordinated through very strong inter-firm networks (ibid:204 and 207). Even under the UK system of unco-ordinated, single-employer bargaining, joint regulation can still deliver significant benefits. For example, workers are more likely to trust management where their company supports union membership and the union has sufficient power to challenge the employer (Bryson, 2001b and 2001d); management perceptions of the employee relations climate tend to be poorer where unions have higher membership but this relationship does not hold where unions have 100 per cent membership (Bryson, 2001c); and although workplace closures are more likely among unionised manufacturing plants compared to their non-union counterparts, the one exception is plants with a more comprehensive collective bargaining agenda (in particular, where unions are directly involved in negotiation over recruitment and staffing levels, the chances of closure are no different from non-union plants) (Bryson, 2001a; and Millward *et al.*, 2001).

In general, however, the wider benefits of co-ordination rely on the leading role of peak associations or more direct forms of state intervention (see Traxler, 2003; and Traxler *et al.*, 2001). In the UK, neither the CBI nor the TUC is in a position to concert the bargaining activities of its affiliates (ibid; see also Traxler, 1999:350) and the current Labour Government shows little sign of adopting a more supportive or interventionist role in collective bargaining. Somewhat more promising are the forthcoming EU regulations on information and consultation, which will require an employer to set up a works council if a written petition is received from at least 10 per cent of its employees (or 250 of them, whichever is the lower). Notwithstanding this development, however, the assumption that collective bargaining is the most effective way of conducting employee relations no longer runs through public policy (Wood and Godard, 1999:237).

Employer support and state backing for collective bargaining in the UK has always been conditional on its ability successfully to regulate industrial conflict, facilitate industrial restructuring, and deliver higher productivity. Regardless of whether these outcomes ensue, this should not detract from, and certainly should not be allowed to negate the primary democratic role of collective bargaining. As the Donovan Commission (1968:54) pointed out, 'properly conducted, collective bargaining is the most effective means of giving workers the right to representation in decisions affecting their working lives, a right which is or should be the prerogative of every worker in a democratic society'.

CONCLUSION

For much of the twentieth century, collective bargaining was the cornerstone of employee relations in the UK. Collective agreements covered the majority of the workforce and joint regulation was widely regarded as the most effective way to resolve conflicts of interest, manage employment contracts, and involve workers in decisions that directly affected their daily working lives. Today, only 40 per cent of the workforce is covered by collective agreements. More workers now have their pay set by management. The picture with regard to non-pay issues is even more alarming, with very little negotiation (joint regulation) in the majority of workplaces. To be sure, more workers are now 'consulted' or 'informed' about changes to their conditions of employment, training and development, staffing levels, health and safety, performance appraisal and the like, this often falls well short of any real opportunity for workers and their representatives significantly to influence outcomes.

Given the considerable advantages of joint regulation, which are still evident even in the UK context, some commentators admit to being rather puzzled by management's lack of support for trade unions and collective bargaining (Bryson, 2001b:103). After all, the evidence categorically indicates that employees are more likely to trust management, report that the workplace is better managed, and have a more positive view of the firm's employee relations climate where management support union membership and joint regulation (ibid). However, opposition to unionism and collective bargaining appears to make sense, from the employer's perspective, when we recall that positive employee attitudes and effective union voice depend on high levels of union density and the union's ability to challenge managerial authority. Just as employers behave opportunistically in their dealings with labour, unions might use their bargaining power to mark up wages, insist on job demarcation rules, the retention of higher than necessary staffing levels and the like. Employers might be more willing to support collective bargaining if their rival firms would do the same – either via co-ordinated bargaining through an employers' association or statutory requirements enforced by the state – but these conditions do not apply in LMEs (indeed, this is one of the defining characteristics of such economies). As a result, managers know that other firms may choose to reduce costs by cutting back their expenditure on information sharing, management-union meetings, employee involvement and other forms of joint regulation. This in turn will lead many firms to adopt an irrational employee relations strategy (chopping away at the foundations of mutual trust, labour co-operation, and high productivity) for rational reasons (the demands of shareholders for a quick return on their investment, competition with other firms, and traditionally adversarial relationships with employees).

Regardless of the economic arguments for and against different systems of collective bargaining, the democratic role of joint regulation should not be overlooked. As collective bargaining has declined, no effective alternative has yet been implemented to address collective interest representation. Employees want, and deserve, a more effective system of representation at work (see Diamond and Freeman, 2001). The current 'representation gap' is an affront to the principles of a democratic society. Management may have 'regained control', 30 years after the Donovan Report, but in most cases not by sharing it. In the process, the protection of employee rights, the representation of their collective interests and the fair remuneration of their labour have, in many industries and firms, been severely eroded.

Chapter

19

PARTICIPATION AND INVOLVEMENT

MARKS & SPENCER: A MANUFACTURER WITHOUT FACTORIES?

Good jobs and bad jobs

In an industrial town on the outskirts of the Greater Manchester conurbation, Marks & Spencer (M&S) has a well-placed, and invariably busy store. In this respect the town is like many others, as virtually every desirable high street in the country plays host to the UK's most renowned retailer. Every week, 10 million customers pass through the doors of M&S stores, buying the *St Michael* branded goods that have a deserved reputation for quality and value for money (see Kumar, 1997:823). Inside the stores, 67000 employees (70 per cent of whom work part-time) are well looked after. The proverb 'Do as you would be done by' (Sieff, 1990:84) has long been the golden rule of the company's *human* relations policy – so-called because, as the former Chairman Lord Sieff (1984:28) explained, 'we are human beings at work not industrial beings'. Any policy derived from the 'law and the prophets' carries with it a strong moral obligation, as Lord Sieff makes clear (ibid:55 and 118). Indeed, the extensive provision of welfare and medical benefits such as subsidised meals, hairdressing, chiropody and dental check-ups, 'is an act of faith. When asked why the company spends so lavishly on the health of its employees managers reply that it feels right to do so' (*Financial Times*, 30 April 1991). Lord Sieff was always less speculative: 'Good human relations at work pay off; they are of great importance if a business is to be efficiently run' (1990:56). The latter was certainly true of Marks & Spencer, a company hailed by Peter Drucker (1974:98) as one of the most efficient companies in the world, and previously voted Britain's 'best managed company' by a panel of institutional investors, captains of industry and business journalists (*Financial Times*, 19 March 1997).

Less than two miles away from the M&S store is a family-run business, Sew & Son (a pseudonym), making ladies' underwear and nightwear for M&S. Like many of the small and medium sized enterprises (SMEs) who supply clothes and other goods to M&S, the company has 'sold its soul to St Michael', as the *Sunday Times* (6 June 1983) once put it, on the basis of no more than a batch-by-batch contract (see Rainnie, 1984:149). The same could be said of Sew & Son's employees. Although they enjoy a subsidised canteen, conditions of work are almost the opposite of those enjoyed by M&S staff. Lines of sewing machines buzz with continuous activity. Conversation is difficult above the noise, and costly. Payment is by the piece, and the pace of work is intense if the women are to earn a decent wage. On the M&S lines in particular, 'Everything is all speed' (interview notes). As the supervisor elaborated,

> On the M&S work, women either stick it or leave. They're always coming and going. The M&S work can make you ill, it's so fast. It has to be. You only get a few pence for every dozen ... Marks & Spencer tell you how to organise the work. A man from their technical division came in and sorted it all out. And the quality has to be just right. If M&S find even one or two that are not right they send the whole lot back – could be as many as 200 dozen. They turn up any time to check quality. They're like ghosts in the factory – they don't own us, but they're always there. (interview notes)

As another woman commented somewhat ruefully, 'I'd much rather work for Marks & Spencer than make the work for them' (interview notes).

Not surprisingly, Marks & Spencer has been described as a 'manufacturer without factories' (Tse, 1985:4). As such, the relationship between M&S and its factories (suppliers) is of critical importance, not only to the reputation and financial success of M&S but to the continuation of small, low-technology firms in the clothing (and other) industries. Marks & Spencer pays for the welfare benefits of its own employees out of such dependency. In contrast, small textile firms often pay little heed to employee needs or their employment rights.

Who needs a union anyway?

Ever since the late 1960s, the non-union 'Marksist' approach to human relations (Tse, 1985:173–4) (not to be confused with Marxist!) has been popularised as an alternative to the collectivist, institutionalised approach to employee relations based on the Whitley and later the Donovan model, as Lord Sieff (1986:182) points out in his memoirs. When employees are recruited to Marks & Spencer they receive a 'Welcome Pack' which gives information on the company and its principles. These include the company's policy to:

- Sell merchandise of the highest quality and outstanding value
- Provide the highest standard of customer care in an attractive shopping environment
- Improve quality standards continually throughout our operations
- Support British industry
- Pursue mutually rewarding long-term partnerships with suppliers
- Minimise the environmental impact of our operations and merchandise
- Ensure that staff and shareholders share in our success
- Nurture good human relations with customers, staff and the community.

For M&S, 'the newest recruit is in a sense the most important person in the company at any given time since by definition he or she is the least educated and experienced and therefore the most likely to fall below the company's standards' (Sieff, 1990:123). Thus, 'A good firm will make its philosophy of good human relations clear to its employees from the moment they join the company' (ibid:81). A second booklet, 'Facts for New Staff', gives details of employees' conditions of employment. These include competitive rates of pay, non-contributory pensions, profit sharing, and extensive medical care. Female employees, for example, are offered breast and cervical screening, while male employees can view a video and read a company leaflet on testicular self-examination. Everyday health and safety is covered in another booklet, 'The Right Move' (which advises on such matters as the lifting of heavy boxes), while 'Personal Safety' offers employees advice on going to and from work (see Sieff,

1990:81–3). As with other HR policies, the company's recently launched 'work-life balance' package is 'not only about being seen as caring. It makes sound commercial sense to offer policies that attract and retain the best people' (M&S spokesperson, quoted in *People Management*, 27 September 2001).

According to Lord Sieff (1984:28), good human relations is not just about wages and conditions but also moral fortitude and a deeper understanding of employee needs. For this reason, Tse (1985:118) argues that it is a misrepresentation simply to label the 'Marksist' approach to human relations as paternalism (*pace* Turnbull and Wass, 1997b). The company's human relations policy, according to Tse (1985:119), also includes a respect for the individual, attention to the problems of individuals at work, full and frank communications, the recognition of people's effort and contribution, and continuous training and development. In other words, attention is paid not only to those factors which, according to Herzberg (1966), (dis)satisfy employees (wages, amenities, physical working conditions) but also those that motivate employees (achievement, recognition, responsibility, advancement). In the words of Lord Sieff (1990:121 and 176),

> good human relations have a most beneficial effect on the morale of the employees and their performance ... The key fact about a policy of good human relations at work is that it is not *primarily* concerned with the nature of the work which the employee does but with the state of mind, the spirit in which he or she does it. A policy of good human relations at work is not about jobs, it is about people. (original emphasis)

Of course, policy statements and 'good intentions' are one thing, implementation is another. In all organisations there is invariably a 'gap' between aspirations and outcomes, between the espoused management style and the reality of personnel practice (see Purcell and Ahlstrand, 1994:177). An important litmus test of actual policy would of course be employee perceptions, attitudes and experiences of work, but there is a dearth of such information for non-union workers. Management (e.g. Sieff, 1984, 1986 and 1990) and managerialist (e.g. Davies, 1999; and Howells, 1981) accounts of M&S, however, claim that the rhetoric of 'good human relations' is matched by the 'reality' of employees' experience:

> the company not only looks after the staff well, but, more importantly, the staff feel they are being treated as individuals; that they are given opportunities continuously to train and develop themselves; that management is on their side, not against and above them; and that they see very little gap between what top management preaches and what is being practised. (Tse, 1985:118)

Effective implementation is proclaimed to be the result of top management commitment, the importance attached to the personnel function, and the unremitting zeal with which the policy is effected on a day-to-day, day-after-day basis. To quote Lord Sieff again,

> Good human relations cannot be legislated for ... Good human relations develop only if top management believes in and is committed to their implementation and has a genuine respect for the individual. This is not something tackled from time to time but demands continuous action. (1984:29)

In short, 'good human relations owe more to example than precept' (Sieff, 1990:82). The example starts with the personnel function which is heavily staffed and strongly represented on the board of directors. The strategic importance attached to personnel is a key feature of M&S (Tse, 1985:130), but the emphasis is very much on an organic relationship with line management (see Turnbull and Wass, 1997b). In fact, the company's philosophy is that 'good human relations is not something that can be left to the personnel department' (Sieff, 1984:29). Rather, 'personnel work – in the broadest sense of the term – is conceived of not so much as a function but as a way of life, and as such it permeates the entire organization, from the board room to the sales floor' (Tse, 1985:141). Responsibility is therefore delegated to line and store management, who deal directly, and at times generously, with all personnel issues (Sieff, 1986:159). All local managers were told, 'if you are going to make a mistake, err on the side of generosity' (Sieff, 1984:30). Issues that cannot be resolved at this level are taken to the Welfare Committee, first established in the early 1930s, which meets and attempts to resolve issues on a weekly basis. Speed is of the essence.

As far as trade unions are concerned, Marks & Spencer's approach can best be described as 'pre-emptive' (Tse, 1985:122), straightforwardly *non*-union rather than explicitly *anti*-union. Put differently, the approach is one of substitution rather than suppression of union activity (Beaumont, 1987:130). Anybody who works for M&S can join a trade union, but the company 'cannot guarantee an audience' (Sieff, 1990:84). To ensure that an 'audience' does not convene, M&S provides *collective* channels of employee involvement and representation. Thus, in addition to direct communications and employee publications such as 'On Your Marks' that aim to keep individual workers up to date with company developments, M&S also operates business involvement groups (Bigs) at the store, area and national levels. Employees elect representatives to the store Big; there are forty-three area Bigs with representatives drawn from the store Bigs; and the national Big is composed of eight representatives from the area Bigs, two from head office, and one from the company's Burnley Print facility. Like the company's European Works Council, however, Bigs were established largely in (a pre-emptive) response to the European Union's Directive on workplace information and consultation (see Higginbottom, 2003). It is well established that non-union employee representation (NER) systems are more likely to be developed, and to be effective, when there is a real threat of unionisation (Kaufman and Taras, 2000). Otherwise, NER is little more than a 'cosmetic exercise', or as Terry (1999:27) puts it, 'managerial emanations subject to managerial whim'. Union representatives who sit on consultative committees or company councils in unionised firms, for example, will usually be trained in advocacy and negotiating skills whereas 'non-union representatives are less able, trained, expert, or more nervous than their union counterparts (and hence less likely to press management)' (ibid: 25). M&S has provided training for Big representatives, but as the company's Chief Executive has made quite clear, their role is 'making sure that you help your colleagues understand important work issues' (Roger Holmes, quoted in Higginbottom, 2003:33).

Ultimately, union substitution at M&S is based on good pay and conditions of employment, rather than opportunities for employee voice or sophisticated NER (see Turnbull and Wass, 1997b). As the company's former Director of Personnel has pointed out, M&S 'appreciate that in companies that are unwilling or unable to provide more than the basic terms and conditions for their employees, trade unions do have a valuable role to play in negotiating for their members' (Salsbury, 1993:569), but with such care and attention lavished on the promotion of good human relations, 'unionism simply finds it difficult to flourish in St Michael soil' (Tse, 1985:122). As a union official from the building industry commented to an audience of employers after a speech by Lord Sieff at the 1983 annual meeting of the National Federation of Building Trades Employers, 'If you all followed a policy similar to that about which Lord Sieff has spoken I would be out of a job' (quoted by Sieff, 1986:223). As Lord

Sieff himself put it, 'I suppose that so few [M&S employees] join because they feel the management provide them with as much and perhaps more than an active trade union would' (1990:84). The same cannot be said, however, for the management of many of the suppliers who manufacture for Marks & Spencer.

You can't have a union!

At Sew & Son, not all the factory's output was earmarked for *St Michael*. While the majority of the women worked on the underwear section for M&S, a group of sixteen women worked on the ladies outerwear section, producing skirts, jackets, trousers and suits for mail-order catalogue companies. This work was 'make-through', with payment based on ten complete items, and was therefore much more highly skilled. However, 'The boss didn't like outerwear, the make-through section', recalled one woman, 'there was no hum, no buzz. The women liked it. It was well paid and it was interesting work, there was some involvement' (interview notes). But work on this section declined and the women were transferred to M&S work, at first making T-shirts (until this work was transferred to a factory in Cheshire), and then on women's night-dresses. For the women, events had taken a turn for the worse. Under the work system designed by Marks & Spencer for the night-dresses, the garment was broken down into twenty-one separate sections/operations. Not only was the work de-skilled, but the women who had been transferred from outerwear were now earning a third less. At first they were paid an average wage (based on their earnings on the outerwear section) until they had become accustomed to the work, but as the supervisor recalled,

> When they were transferred to the night-dresses they'd already lost heart. When they went on to piece-rates it was too much. Fifteen of them left in the end, all top machinists. So we took on young kids. We'd start ten on Monday morning and there'd only be four left by Friday. But it didn't seem to matter. You didn't have to be skilled, just fast. And young. They wouldn't start any older women. They still had to be trained, but only how to do the job fast. It wasn't a skilled job. (interview notes)

Prior to the transfer onto the M&S work there had been some union recruitment activity in the factory. The women on the outerwear section had been receptive to the idea and nominated one of their number to act as their representative. The response from management, however, was distinctly hostile. The women were called into the owner-manager's office and told outright: 'We don't want a union in here. They only cause trouble' (interview notes). Instead, he suggested promoting the women's representative to the position of supervisor over the outerwear section. This proved to be acceptable to the women, especially as the supervisor kept a close check on the distribution of work between machinists (to ensure equality) and the prices of every item. As she later recalled, 'I always kept the price tickets. With it being catalogue work you got a lot of variety, so I always kept the tickets. When new work came in, management would try to set a lower price, but we wouldn't have any of it. We had the tickets, and they had to pay us' (interview notes). The cut in wages on the M&S work, alongside the de-skilling of the work, therefore proved to be a particularly bitter pill to swallow. Even then, 'If they'd given us a few coppers more we might have got the girls moving, but the money was just too tight' (interview notes). Several women took their case to an Industrial Tribunal, but lost. Shortly after, the supervisor left as well, as did her sister. As for the night-dresses, three months later the section was closed and the work transferred to another factory.

Trouble at t'works?

The constraints imposed on the small textile manufacturer, Sew & Son, by a much larger retail company clearly generated instability in the former's employee relations. Conflict, in this instance, was manifest in the very high levels of labour turnover. Even at Marks & Spencer, however, where the dependency of small firms is used to pay for and protect the conditions of M&S staff, everything is not always 'sweetness and light'. In 1989, for example, the company introduced a telephone 'hotline' to management to enable employees to inform on colleagues suspected of shoplifting. The scheme was widely criticised for being open to abuse by the unscrupulous, and received a negligible response from staff. Both John Lewis and Tesco rejected similar schemes (Hamil, 1993:43). Later, in April 1991, M&S announced 850 redundancies which, in some quarters, was seen to herald 'the end of Marks & Spencer's unofficial commitment to its staff of a job for life' (ibid:41). As Lord Sieff (1990:64–5) makes clear, any such commitment on the part of M&S was always implicit rather than explicit, but the effect on the staff concerned was nonetheless traumatic. 'The Baker Street headquarters in London was gripped by gloom and confusion', wrote the *Financial Times* (30 April 1991), while City analysts predicted 'the transition from a safe, job-for-life type organisation into a meritocracy. To a certain extent, M&S has always been carrying a lot of fat and it is the first time that it has gone on a diet' (ibid).

Marks & Spencer was keen to quash any rumours that the company planned to cut welfare, adopt a less caring approach or change its culture (*Financial Times*, 11 May and 18 May 1991), but in July 1996 the company stopped providing free breakfasts (on the grounds that not all staff enjoyed this 'perk') and the very notion of a full-time employee was abolished (staff are now paid for hours worked rather than a set monthly salary). It must be recognised that M&S has always demonstrated 'a ruthlessness, manifested in a relentless pursuit of corporate objectives, which some commentators have characterised as authoritarian, albeit benevolently so' (Hamil, 1993:43). In other words, benevolence and authoritarian management have never been alternatives but rather part and parcel of the company's human relations policy. The contradictions between these two characteristics, however, have only become apparent in the face of very severe external pressures, most notably the intensification of competition in the mid to late 1990s in both high quality clothing (e.g. from Next, Gap, and Hennes & Mauritz) and discount clothing (e.g. from Primark and Matalan), as well as competition in high quality foods (e.g. from Tesco Finest). M&S was slow to react, believing that its traditional approach would ensure that the company weathered the storm. Indeed, many observers regarded senior management as arrogant and conceited, more concerned with their own position than the fortunes of the company and its workforce (see Eaton, 2001; and Mellahi *et al.*, 2002:23). Sir Richard Greenbury, the company's former Chairman, seemed to dismiss criticism rather than address the company's underlying problems: 'A crisis in women's outerwear? Nonesense. Trouble at t'works council? Balderdash. Too much competition in food? Rubbish' (quoted in Eaton, 2001:187). As a result,

> By the late 1990s ... there were two M&S's. One, as perceived by its management, a world-class retail company with an exemplar management; the other, that seen by outsiders (industry observers and the City) and customers, was a company ill-adapted to the new circumstances and losing its market position and image very quickly. (Mellahi *et al.*, 2002:24)

Inertia led to falling sales and profits. Redundancies inevitably followed, which in their turn created fatalism which fed onto this inertia (ibid:25). One response was to

'Energise' staff through a customer care programme, launched in 1999, 'which teaches teamwork and positivity, [the programme] aims to mould staff thought processes and body language to create a more welcoming environment for customers' (*The Grocer*, 16 June 2001). More importantly, M&S recruited a new Executive Chairman from outside the company to shake up (and rationalise) the inward looking management team. Luc Vandevelde, a Belgian accountant, came to M&S with extensive experience in retail. He echoed the views of the City and industry observers, noting that 'no one here knew what our market share was or what the competition did' (*The Guardian*, 26 May 2001).

Mr Vandevelde's approach to 'human relations' quickly earned him the nickname 'Muscles from Brussels' (older readers might appreciate his other nickname, 'Cruel Hand Luc') (*The Guardian*, 26 May 2001). He acknowledged that morale was extremely low at all levels in the organisation (Vandevelde, 2003:28) but was determined to reduce costs by sourcing from cheaper overseas suppliers, resulting in the indirect loss of thousands of textile jobs in the UK; cutting overtime rates for new recruits; and closing all 38 of the company's Continental European stores along with the company's direct mail operation in Warrington. This resulted in the direct loss of 4400 jobs and led to further doubts about the meaning of 'good human relations'. In particular, the company only informed the employees of the impeding closures 5 minutes before the opening of the London Stock Exchange, which the French courts determined to be illegal (M&S was fined and ordered to withdraw the closure plans until it had properly consulted the workforce) (see Fulton, 2001; and *Labour Research*, October 2001). Unions were recognised at the company's European stores and while they were unable to prevent the closures they did negotiate more favourable redundancy packages or 'social plans' than their non-union UK counterparts (e.g. a 40-year-old worker with 4 years service at M&S received 9 months salary in compensation for job loss in Belgium, 6 months salary in Spain, 3.2 months plus £640 for every dependent child in Germany, and just 10 weeks pay in the UK) (ibid). M&S has now restored its annual turnover to the levels achieved in 1997–98 and profits are climbing once more. The company still proclaims its commitment to people and good human relations, but it seems M&S will no longer err so heavily on the side of generosity.

NON-UNIONISM'S GROWING RANKS

Even using the most flattering (for trade unions) measure of union density (based on civilian employees in employment), less than 30 per cent of the workforce now belong to a trade union. With non-unionism now dominant in the UK, numerically at least, the former labour editor of the *Financial Times* expressed some surprise that this had been all but ignored in texts on industrial relations, although he did suggest a reason why: 'you know how to find the TGWU: it's there, it's tangible. By contrast, non-unionism is amorphous, de-centralised, inaccessible' (Bassett, 1988:45; see also Blackburn and Hart, 2002; McLoughlin, 1996:301; and Terry, 1999). While this may be true of the vast majority of (small) non-union companies, it is certainly not true of them all. Indeed, as Bassett (1988:47) and others (e.g. Legge, 1995:36–7) note, the new role models for British employee relations are no longer Ford or ICI but IBM, Hewlett Packard, and other large multinationals such as Black & Decker, Gillette, Mars, Polaroid, Texas Instruments, Nestlé, and of course Marks & Spencer. Very large non-union companies are the exception rather than the rule (see Bacon, 2001).

Nevertheless, the employment and other policies of these non-union companies are increasingly well-known and more widely publicised. Many are strongly associated with the US 'excellence' literature, for example (Peters and Waterman, 1982), which in turn has informed much of the recent writing on human resource management (see Boxall and Purcell, 2003; Guest, 1990; and Legge, 1995). At the risk of over-generalisation, the generic characteristics of these non-union companies tend to be a sense of caring, combined with carefully chosen plant locations and working environments, market leadership, high growth and healthy profits, employment security, single status, promotion from within, an influential personnel department (and a high ratio of personnel staff to employees), competitive pay and benefit packages, profit sharing, open communications, and the meticulous selection and training of management, particularly at the supervisory level (see, for example, Beaumont, 1987:117–19; and Foulkes, 1981). As with Marks & Spencer, the inevitable question that trade unions confront from employees in such organisations is, 'Why should I join a union?'

Of course, not all large non-union companies are benevolent, and for those which are benevolence is an act of business (to make a profit), not an act of charity. Some large non-union companies, such as McDonald's, are distinctly *anti*-union. Mrs Thatcher once said that 'we must expect that a lot more of our jobs will come from the service sector – from the McDonald's and the Wimpeys', but the neon lights of the hamburger economy 'hides a reality that is more like the slum industries of yesteryear' (Lamb and Percy, 1987:15). Labour costs at McDonald's outlets must not rise above 15 per cent of sales, such that if sales decline then staff numbers are cut back and work intensified. The company employs those with few other opportunities, typically women, ethnic minorities and youths (two-thirds of staff are less than 21 years old), and although annual labour turnover is around 200 per cent, labour is cheap and flexible (three-quarters are part-time) and tasks can be learnt in a day. In fact, workers' skills have effectively been eliminated (there are no chefs), and computerised machines do all the cooking. The more important ingredients are tight labour control and a team grading system that keeps workers smiling for the customers, but at each other's throats (ibid:15–17; see also Goffee and Scase, 1995:123–4; and Royle, 2000).

Clearly, then, not all large non-union companies are alike. Moreover, small non-union companies are different again. More importantly, there is a major discrepancy between the popular image and the reality of working in small firms. The popular image was articulated by a Committee of Enquiry on Small Firms back in the early 1970s:

> In many respects the small firm provides a better environment for the employee than is possible in most large firms. Although physical working conditions may sometimes be inferior in small firms, most people prefer to work in a small group where communications present fewer problems: the employees in the small firm can easily see the relation between what they are doing and the objectives and performance of the firm as a whole. Where management is more direct and flexible, working rules can be varied to suit the individual. (Bolton, 1971:23)

According to this account, employees choose small firms because of the non-economic rewards they offer. Not surprisingly, the predicted outcomes are greater moral involvement, organisational attachment, and of course industrial harmony. As the Conservative Party document *Moving Forward* (1983) claimed,

> One of the advantages that small businesses do, in fact, enjoy is the generally good state of relations between the owners and managers and their

employees. There is a sense of partnership based on the willingness to work for a clearly perceived common purpose from which everyone benefits. (quoted by Goss, 1991:154)

Thus, the 1980s became the decade of 'small business revivalism' and the 'enterprise culture' (Burrows and Curran, 1989:527). Under Mrs Thatcher, the small firm was 'taken up as the articulating principle of right-wing reaction to economic crisis' (Curran and Burrows, 1986:274), and the entrepreneur cast in the role of 'dynamic saviour of a moribund economy' (Rainnie, 1989:1). 'No longer reviled as a tax dodger or exploiter of cheap labour, small business exemplifies most of the [Conservative] Government's ideals, whether small shop (thrift, independence) or fast expanding Thames Valley electronics concern (risk taking, ambitious, profit orientated)' (*Financial Times*, 12 June 1984, quoted by Rainnie, 1985b:141–2). New Labour has continued to promote SMEs, establishing a Small Business Service under the auspices of the DTI to champion the interests of these firms. Mr Blair's government regards entrepreneurship as an important source of efficiency, innovation, opportunity, and even the renewal of the poorest and most marginalized communities and localities in the UK (SBS, 2003b). In short, '[s]mall is supposed to be not only beautiful, but also dynamic, efficient, competitive and perhaps most important, a source of new jobs' (Rainnie, 1989:1).

For both Conservative and Labour governments, then, the promotion of small firms is not only a key element of economic policy but also employee relations policy. The apparent industrial harmony of small firms is usually attributed to the absence of trade unions, minimum state intervention and, as a result, a more direct employer-employee relationship uncontaminated by 'outside' interference (Goss, 1991:152). For many policy makers, '[t]his combination of factors is claimed to reveal the employment relationship as it should be: a relationship between equals in the market (one the buyer and one the seller of labour) with a mutual interest in the success of the enterprise' (ibid). The reality, on *all* counts, however, can be very different. For example, an increasing number of studies have revealed employment relations in SMEs to be more akin to a 'black hole' or 'bleak house', characterised by poor conditions of employment, low pay, the absence of good (or any) personnel practices, little or no opportunity for employee voice, and enforced compliance rather than active employee commitment (see, for example, Guest and Conway, 1999; and Sisson, 1993).

Likewise, there is another side to the employment effects of SMEs. Although the number of small firms has increased in recent years, and although small firms have increased their share of total employment and created a great many new jobs (Dale and Kerr, 1995; and SBS, 2003b), they also contribute more than their fair share to the ranks of the unemployed (Daniel, 1985; and Rainnie, 1989:2 and 23). The death rate of small firms is almost as high as the birth rate (Daly, 1990), with one in ten currently failing in the first 12 months and a third going out of business within 3 years (www.sbs.gov.uk). Self-employed workers in the UK are far less likely to employ additional workers than their counterparts in the EU, with only 29 per cent of the self-employed in the UK hiring employees compared to 51 per cent in Germany, over 47 per cent in Austria, almost 46 per cent in Denmark and well over 40 per cent in Ireland (Cowling, 2003). As a result, micro firms (0–9 employees) often fail to grow into small businesses (10–49 employees) and these firms in particular find it difficult to grow into medium-sized firms (50–249 employees) (see Gallagher *et al.*, 1990:95–6), suggesting that most small businesses are likely to remain small (Hakim, 1989a and 1989b). Such companies find it difficult to change from an informal to a more formal management structure, especially when dealing with employee relations (see Wilkinson, 1999).

The more important deficiency of the popular account of small firms, however, is that size *per se* is not a *necessary* characteristic of an organisation but a *contingent* one (Burrows and Curran, 1989:530). Size is an important variable in employee relations because of the very clear correlation between size and a number of key industrial relations indicators: as establishment size increases, organisations display more elaborate management structures (differentiated hierarchically and functionally), they devote more resources to personnel matters, and they are more likely to have formal management procedures for issues such as discipline and dismissal; bigger establishments are also more likely to recognise a trade union, have shop stewards present and experience strikes (see, for example, Cully *et al.*, 1999; and Millward *et al.*, 2000). But size plays a role in the functioning of an organisation *only* in relation to other factors (Curran, 1990:129). As Rainnie (1991:177) notes, 'to say that smallness *per se* is a characteristic that, alone, will determine the internal operation and external relations of this unit is bizarre'. The more important variables to consider *in relation to size* are industrial sector, technology, locality, labour and product markets (see Wilkinson, 1999:214). In their study of 397 small firms, for example, Scott *et al.* (1989) found it more useful to sub-divide the sample into four broad industrial groups, namely traditional manufacturing, high-tech manufacturing, traditional services and high-tech services. Size, in itself, could not account for the differences between firms.

Thus, 'what constitutes smallness will be very much contextual – dependent upon economic sector, market size and the like' (Burrows and Curran, 1989:530). As the small firm sector extends from the corner shop to the high-tech firms of the M4 corridor and Silicon Glen in Scotland, such a heterogeneous collection of organisations demands, first, a *relational* conceptualisation of their activities, and secondly the identification of those factors which, in general and in combination, determine why a great many firms, and the majority of small firms, are non-union. As in the case of Sew & Son and many other small clothing manufacturers producing *St Michael* branded goods, the (dependent) relationship with its major customer, Marks & Spencer, plays a crucial role in shaping employer-employee relations (see also Barrett and Rainnie, 2002; and Rainnie, 1984 and 1985a). Equally, the structural characteristics of the workplace and the composition of the workforce, the informal nature of employee relations, and the (unitarist) attitude of the owner/manager can combine to produce an environment unconducive to trade union membership. Each of these variables is analysed in turn. Finally, the problems of trade union recruitment, organisation and representation are analysed in more detail. Is it realistic to anticipate that the seeds of trade unions revival can be planted in the 'never unionised' sectors of the economy?

SMALL FIRMS, BIG FIRMS

The nature of employee relations in any organisation can only be fully understood in the context of, and in relation to, wider socio-economic, political and legal structures. Inter-organisational relations play an important part, especially in the case of small firms whose relationship with much bigger firms can have a major bearing on their own labour process characteristics (Rainnie, 1991). Simply put, 'large capital determines not only the field of play, but also the rules of the game that small firms are engaged in' (Rainnie, 1985b:165). For this reason, 'Size *qua* size ... is secondary to the relationship with the wider economy and it is these which determine the organisational and social frameworks of the enterprise' (Curran, 1990:130). In the case of Marks & Spencer, for example, the highly competitive nature of the retail sector, and the uncertainty of market trends and changing fashions, has led to a relationship with suppliers described as 'benevolent dictatorship' (Salmans, 1980:68). Retailers such as M&S did not create a highly competitive, small-scale clothing sector, but they have certainly taken advantage of it. And in doing so they ensured that this situation would continue (Rainnie, 1984:153). In other words, a major reason why the clothing sector is characterised by low technology, ease of entry (and exit), and therefore small, predominantly non-union firms employing cheap female labour is because a dependent small-firm sector is necessary to the continuation of large-scale enterprise in retailing (Curran and Burrows, 1986:274).

> Briefly, the advantages to companies like Marks and Spencer of formally independent, but in reality utterly dependent small suppliers, are enormous and can be summed up as cheap flexibility, crucial at a time of increased competition. The existence of the *individual* small firm is not important, the continued existence of a *number* of them is vital. (Rainnie, 1985b:157, original emphasis)

As early as the mid 1920s, M&S pioneered a relationship with suppliers that allowed the company to decide *what they wanted to sell*, rather than would simply have to buy from what the manufacturers had produced. As Tse (1985:75) notes, 'Marks & Spencer has *dictated* a new type of relationship between the manufacturer and the retailer' (emphasis added). This account is somewhat at odds, however, with the more popular accounts of the harmonious, collaborative relationship that M&S enjoys with its suppliers. Tse (1985:76–7), for example, also talks of the relationship as a 'marriage', while Lord Sieff himself provides details of the technical support that M&S provides and the long-term partnership the company has enjoyed with many suppliers, adding that M&S encourages all its suppliers (who are required to sign a 'code of conduct') to offer similar terms and conditions of employment for their own workers (Sieff, 1986:161). Of particular concern to Lord Sieff was always the condition of the supplier's toilets, which he appeared to regard as a barometer of the state of employee relations at supplier companies (ibid). But the companies that 'Dan, Dan the lavatory man', as he was sometimes called (ibid), discusses are all larger companies with whom Marks & Spencer would have more of a *mutually dependent*, rather than dominant relationship (see, for example, Sieff, 1990:93–111). With smaller companies, such as Sew & Son, M&S has always displayed much less compunction about switching contracts or playing one supplier off against another (see Rainnie, 1984 and 1985b). That said, when competition intensified in the late 1990s and profits fell for the first time in 30 years, M&S revised its 'buy British' policy and its relationship with larger suppliers. Contracts with large clothing companies such as William Baird were cancelled, in this instance ending a 30 year relationship and wiping out 40 per cent of Baird's total business. Whereas M&S used to source almost 90 per cent of its clothing from UK suppliers, by 1999 this was down to 55 per cent and is expected to fall to just 30 per cent (*Financial Times*, 10 March 2001). The company now has 1500 suppliers in over seventy countries.

Although the strategies of large firms play a crucial role in the restructuring of economic relations in general and those with, and within, small firms in particular (e.g. Shutt and Whittington, 1987), this should not divert attention away from the small-firm sector itself. What is often suggested, for example, is that the relationship between small and large firms is simply one of *dependence*, with consequent implications for employee relations. The general argument, as Goss (1991:160) points out, is that 'small firms – directly or indirectly – are generally in a dependent position, a dependence which is frequently reflected in patterns of industrial relations as employers seek to maintain a competitive edge through rigorous exploitation of labour'. In many respects this is undeniably true: the appalling conditions of many (sweat shop) firms bears testament to this (e.g. Byrne, 1986; Hoel, 1982; Phizacklea, 1987; Pond, 1983; Toynbee, 2003; Wills, 2002; and www. nosweat.org.uk). But as Rainnie (1991:187) points out, it is important to consider the relationship between small and large firms more directly and in more detail, since there are at least four very different relationships which can be identified:

- *Dependent* small firms complement and service the activities of larger firms (e. g. sub-contracting). Labour costs must be minimised and flexibility is essential.
- *Dominated* small firms compete with large firms through the more intense exploitation of machinery and especially labour. Hyper-exploitation of labour is not uncommon.
- *Isolated* small firms operate in specialised and/or geographically discrete markets, the niches of demand that are unlikely to be touched by large capital. Living off the crumbs from the large firms' table, however, entails a hand-to-hand existence and invariably sweat shop conditions for the workforce.
- *Innovative* small firms compete in (or even develop) specialised markets, but are always open to the potentially fatal attractions of large firms. Flexibility and innovation are essential, and attractive pay and conditions may be necessary to attract highly skilled workers (see Rainnie, 1989:85 and 1991:188).

In the clothing sector, small firms generally find themselves in a *dependent* relationship with their larger customers, with obvious implications for employee relations. Tight supervision, authoritarian management and payment systems that tie the workers to their machines are just some of the outcomes cited by Rainnie (1985a:218; see also Taplin *et al.*, 2003). These are not universal or inevitable features of the clothing industry *per se*, but rather reflect *the relationship with the customer*. As Ram (1991:607–11 and 1994) demonstrates in a study of clothing firms in the West Midlands where output went to intermediaries rather than direct to the retailers, supervision was not so tight, the workers tended to work at their own pace and controlled effort levels, and there was extensive negotiation, and re-negotiation, over the rate for the job. The difference between the outerwear section and the M&S work at Sew & Son bears out a similar point. At the same time, however, in either case, there appears in practice to be very little room for manoeuvre: the field of play is determined by the customer, and while the *precise* rules of the game may be subject to interpretation (negotiation), the large firm can always move the goalposts or take the ball elsewhere to play.

Among the *dominated* and *isolated* groups of small firms are to be found those which depend largely on second-hand machinery and cheap labour (Rainnie, 1991:188), the 'chaff' of yesterday's harvest rather than the 'green shoots' of future growth. These small firms operate in established markets (e.g. general printing) and/or those now populated by a large number of self-employed people (e.g. craft-related occupations) (see Cowling, 2003). Moule (1998), for example, discusses a small company supplying buttons to clothing manufacturers and large retailers such as M&S. Operating in a niche market, competition was limited but customers demanded very rapid turnaround of orders. While all work was 'urgent', deadlines were especially tight for key customers such as M&S – 'These initials were a byword for URGENT. Workers in all departments recognised their significance' (ibid:642). In this way, even isolated firms, and in particular their workforces, feel the presence of large firms.

Finally, among the *innovative* small firms we at last encounter those businesses that perhaps epitomise the 'enterprise culture' of the 1980s and 1990s, the high-tech firms of the electronics, computer and related sectors (Rainnie, 1991:191–4; and Scase, 2003:483–6). Contrary to popular belief, however, many of these companies are in fact unionised. In a survey of Scottish electronics plants, for example, 70 per cent of employees worked in establishments where trade unions were recognised (Sproull and MacInnes, 1987:335). In a more comprehensive study using data from the second Workplace Industrial Relations Survey (1984), Beaumont and Harris (1988a:833–4) found that the extent of union recognition was actually *higher* in 'high tech' than 'non-high tech' industries for domestically-owned establishments (both for manual and non-manual employees). In the case of foreign-owned companies, however, the reverse was true, especially in relation to manual employees (ibid). In the media, most notably television, unions might seem alien in the new 'virtual world' of freelance engineers, camera crews and other staff who sell their skills and innovative talents to broadcasting companies who are little more than commissioning agents for programmes made by small-scale enterprises (Davis and Scase, 2000; and Scase, 2003:483). But unions such as BECTU have been quite effective in retaining membership among freelance workers and skill shortages have encouraged some broadcasters and programme makers to bring such workers back 'in-house' (see Saundry, 2001). In general, employer responses to union organising activity tends to be more positive when directed at professional as opposed to (skilled) manual workers or machine operatives (Heery and Simms, 2003). Moreover, given that many small, innovative (non-union) companies in high-tech sectors or the media are subject to predatory take-over by larger (unionised) companies, the effect of small-firm/large-firm relationships, over time, is perhaps more likely to result in unionisation among the innovative small-firm sector, rather than a perpetuation of non-union status (as in the previous three groups identified).

While Rainnie's fourfold categorisation of dependent, dominated, isolated and innovative firms allows us to distinguish a greater variety of relationships that SMEs experience, Curran (1990:130) argues that there is still a tendency, overall, for observers to suggest a subordinate or subservient role. Put differently, autonomy may in practice be greater than is often assumed among the small-firm sector (see also Ram, 1991 and 1994). This can be illustrated by the juxtaposing of Atkinson's (1984) model of the 'flexible firm' and Piore and Sabel's (1984) model of 'flexible specialisation'. In the former, small firms are seen as part of the periphery, involved in a dependent relationship with large firms for whom they provide numerical flexibility or lower costs as a result of 'distancing' (the replacement of an employment contract with a commercial contract, possibly via self-employment and labour-only sub-contracting). In the 'flexible specialisation' model, in contrast, small, craft-based firms are presented as a *complement to* or even an *alternative to*, rather than an appendage of, large firms, able to compete with the mass production techniques of large firms through the use of new technology (which lowers minimum efficient scale) and co-operative (network) relations with other small firms in the locality. Thus, a shift from a Fordist to a post-Fordist model of production (purportedly) implies a symbiotic and co-operative relationship between large (buyer) and small (supplier) firms (as opposed to a competitive and dependent relationship) (see Barrett and Rainnie, 2002:421). Although there are both conceptual and empirical problems with both models (see Pollert, 1988), the contrast between the subordinate, peripheral firm (more likely to be non-union) and the craft-based firm (more likely to be unionised) serves to highlight still further the possible roles and relationships that can influence employee relations in small firms. The skills of the workforce, for example, is just one of the characteristics that plays a key role in non-union employee relations (see, for example, Scase, 2003:478).

THE STRUCTURAL CHARACTERISTICS OF NON-UNION FIRMS AND THE COMPOSITION OF THE WORKFORCE

Although 'single shot' pictures taken from cross-sectional surveys are, in many respects, unsatisfactory for the analysis of dynamic and diachronic processes of employee relations, they nevertheless provide a rich source of data on the *general* characteristics of non-union firms. This enables us to say whether, on the whole, non-union firms are more likely to be, for example, large or small, and employ predominantly manual or non-manual workers, men or women, full-time or part-time staff. Data from the Workplace Employee Relations Survey (1998) confirms the results of previous surveys that indicate that, *ceteris paribus*, non-union establishments are more likely to be small, single-plant rather than multi-establishment undertakings, and located in the private sector (and especially private services) rather than the public sector. For example, less than 40 per cent of workplaces with 25–49 employees recognise a trade union compared with 78 per cent of workplaces with 500 or more employees (Cully *et al.*, 1999:92; see also Cully and Woodland, 1996:223; Millward *et al.*, 1992:64; and Scott *et al.*, 1989:17). It is hardly surprising, then, that union membership is extremely low in industries such as clothing where over 50 per cent of firms employ fewer than twenty-five workers and nearly 90 per cent of all firms employ fewer than 125 workers (Rainnie, 1989:89–9). Likewise, in hotels and restaurants only 7 per cent of workplaces recognise a trade union (Cully *et al.*, 1999:92). Data from all three WIRS and WERS98 are presented in Table 19.1. A particularly interesting result from these surveys is that, as expected, older workplaces are more likely to recognise trade unions and have a higher union density (independent of size) but the rate of recognition among new workplaces has been much lower (see Disney *et al.*, 1995), indicating a 'cohort effect' (i.e. new businesses established during the 'Thatcher years' are far less likely to recognise unions) (Cully *et al.*, 1999:24). This effect has persisted, with the likelihood of recognition substantially less in 1998 than in 1990 (Millward *et al.*, 2000:101–3).

Locality also plays an important part in union or non-union status. The latter establishments, for example, are more likely to be located in areas of high unemployment (Millward *et al.*, 1992:63–4). Geographical sub-systems are generally overlooked in the study of industrial and employee relations, although it is often suggested that the decline of major conurbations – the heartland of union organisation and industrial militancy – and the growth of industry in new towns or semi-rural areas (Mason, 1991:74–6) can have a significant impact on employee relations (e.g. Handy, 1984:85; Lane, 1982; Massey, 1984). Bassett (1988:46), for example, notes that in Milton Keynes, the UK's fastest growing town in the mid to late 1980s, two-thirds of the local companies employed fewer than ten workers, two-thirds of all jobs were in the service sector, and around 80 per cent of all companies were non-union, a fact boldly advertised by the town's development corporation. Similarly, in a study of 411 companies in three new towns in Scotland (Glenrothes, Irvine and Livingston), over 86 per cent were non-union, a figure much higher than manufacturing in general (Beaumont and Cairns, 1987:14–15). On a regional basis, there is essentially a North-South divide when it comes to union membership and recognition. In 2002, for example, union

Table 19.1 – Non-unionism by sector and size

(a) Sector – percentage of establishments that do not recognise a trade union for collective bargaining (and percentage of establishments with no union members)

	1980		1984		1990		1998	
All establishments	36	(27)	34	(27)	47	(36)	55	(46)
Private manufacturing	35	(23)	44	(33)	56	(42)	*	(58)
Private services	59	(50)	56	(47)	64	(54)	*	(65)
Public sector	6	(1)	1	(–)	13	(1)	5	(3)

Note: * 75% of all private sector establishments did not recognise a union in 1998

(b) Size: non unionism in private sector establishments (percentage of establishments that do not recognise a trade union)

	1980	1984	1990	1998
Workplace size				
25–49 employees	59	60	70	84
50–99 employees	51	51	60	77
100–199 employees	35	38	52	61
200–499 employees	25	34	31	46
500 or more employees	8	14	25	36

Source: Calculated from Cully *et al*. (1999:68 and 240) and Millward *et al*. (2000:85).

density among full-time employees was 44 per cent in Wales and 43 per cent in the North East compared to just 23 per cent in the South East. If part-time workers are included then density levels fall to 40 per cent in Wales, 38 per cent in the North East and 21 per cent in the South East (*Labour Market Trends*, July 2003). Union recognition is also much higher in the North and lower in the South, and it is no coincidence that London and the South East have more small businesses and more rapid growth in the small business sector (SBS, 2003a).

Workforce characteristics are also notably different between union and non-union firms. The latter are more likely, *ceteris paribus*, to employ relatively fewer manual workers, more women, and a higher proportion of part-time staff (Cully *et al*., 1999:254; and Millward *et al*., 1992:63–4). In the clothing industry, for example, almost 88 per cent of the workforce is female (Rainnie, 1989:90). However, while trade unionism in the 1980s largely reflected a male-dominated labour market and work culture, with male-dominated private sector workplaces more likely to have union members than female-dominated workplaces, union presence in male-dominated workplaces plummeted between 1980 and 1998 whereas in female-dominated workplaces it stayed more or less constant (Millward *et al*., 2000:85–6). In fact, by 1998 the differences between them had reversed in the private sector, with female-dominated workplaces more likely to have union members. As Millward *et al*. (2000:86) observe, 'Workplaces that had formed the bedrock for union membership in earlier decades, male-dominated workplaces, had not just become less common – they had also lost their appetite for unionism'.

Many non-union companies also rely on family or kin, who are often placed in key positions within the company (e.g. Moule, 1998:638; and Ram, 1991:609). In the small firms studied by Scott *et al.* (1989:47), almost half the workforce could be tied by bonds of kinship, thereby constituting a 'core' group of employees that the owner/manager could rely on. Family pressures are often brought to bear on the workers of small firms in a different way:

> Management in the clothing industry feels the necessity, but also the freedom, to impose discipline in their workers, particularly married women, from the word go. Taking advantage of the pressures on women brought to bear in trying to reconcile the dual roles of wife/mother and worker, management rely on this situation making women less likely to leave in response to poor wages and conditions. (Rainnie, 1989:119)

In other SMEs, management deliberately promote a 'family culture' to deter unionisation as well as control the labour process (see, for example, Dundon *et al.*, 1999).

Poor wages and conditions are a principal characteristic of small, non-union firms (McNabb and Whitfield, 2000). The owner/managers of small firms take a *deliberate* decision to pay lower wages (Craig *et al.*, 1985; and Phizacklea, 1987), recognising that there is a trade-off between lower pay and higher labour turnover but reconciling this trade-off through the employment of disadvantaged groups such as married women (e.g. Rainnie, 1989:119), ethnic minorities (e.g. Ram, 1991:605 and 1994:158–9) or young workers (Curran and Stanworth, 1981b:144), who are more stable, in employment terms, at lower levels of pay (due to their limited opportunities elsewhere) (see Cully *et al.*, 1999:254). Goss (1988 and 1991), for example, draws a contrast between non-union instant print shops that employ low-skilled, low-paid, predominantly younger workers, and unionised colour printing where skills are vital and the workforce older. Another important variable that distinguishes different types of small firms is ownership, with small, stand-alone firms more likely to pay low wages than establishments that are part of a larger organisation (small multiples) (see McNabb and Whitfield, 2000). The former are also far less likely to employ a personnel specialist on site, to recognise unions or use formal communication systems (Cully *et al.*, 1999:257–68). More detailed studies of specific industrial sectors confirm these differences. Brown and Crossman (2000:215), for example, found that independently-owned hotels were significantly more likely to follow a short-term, cost minimisation strategy than hotels owned by national or international chains.

The idea, then, that workers deliberately choose to work for non-union companies because 'convenience of location, and generally the non-material satisfactions of working in them, more than outweigh any financial sacrifice involved' (Bolton, 1971:21), begins to appear somewhat suspect. As Curran and Stanworth (1981b:145) note, 'small firm workers did not so much self-select themselves into jobs as a result of possessing certain stable motivational patterns but rather developed a market situation in which their job choices were often highly circumscribed'. Many employees in non-union firms, for example, are unable to develop stable employment patterns when they are forced to work on a casual or seasonal basis, as in the hotel and catering industry (e.g. Macaulay and Wood, 1992:21), or even work 'off the cards' so that the employer can avoid statutory employment laws and national insurance contributions (e.g. Ram, 1991:605–6; and Scott *et al.*, 1989:24–5 and 92). 'Voluntary resignations' are much higher in small private establishments, especially in hotels and restaurants where, on average, almost two-fifths of all employees leave their job every year (Cully *et al.*, 1999:127–8). Self-employment may be the only option available to many seeking employment, and it comes as no surprise that ethnic minorities, married people and women with dependent children are more likely to be self-employed, or that many of the self-employed have a second job as an employee (see Daly, 1991).

All these characteristics of non-union firms and non-union workers are invariably set within a highly informal working environment. Informality begins with recruitment and extends right through the organisation, from communications and grievance handling to pay determination and the highly personalised, day-to-day relations between management and labour (Gilman *et al.*, 2002; and Scott *et al.*, 1989). In a large scale survey of SMEs, for example, Matlay (1999: 288) found that 92 per cent of micro business managers favoured an informal management style compared to 68 per cent of small business managers and just 24 per cent of managers working for medium-sized firms. For management, and of course the advocates of small non-union firms, the absence of bureaucracy is seen as a positive advantage, not least as reflected in very low levels of strike activity. The key advantage lies, however, not in the extent to which informality allows for more direct and flexible arrangements to suit the individual, but in the extent to which such arrangements serve to obscure the conflicts of interest inherent in the employment relationship – not least those prevailing in the small non-union firm. In fact, as Curran (1990:137–8) notes, employer-employee relations in small firms are based on a contradiction likely to lead to *permanent* instability: small firms find themselves in largely dependent relations with big firms and are therefore more susceptible to (i.e. less able to control) the external, competitive environment; yet within the firm, relations tend to be highly personalised such that when change and conflict cannot be contained or handled through such informal relations, 'it erupts with an intensity that is absent in more formal, procedurally regulated relationships' (Scott *et al.*, 1989:61). Is the absence of strike activity, then, an indication of industrial harmony or employee powerlessness in small, non-union firms?

INFORMALITY AND INDUSTRIAL HARMONY IN THE NON-UNION SECTOR

Collective action requires collective organisation (see Kelly, 1998). Working without unions has therefore enabled many large non-union companies to remain 'strike free' (see Bassett, 1986:161; and Sieff, 1990:84). Just as there has been little incentive for workers in companies such as Marks & Spencer, IBM or Hewlett Packard to join a trade union, there is little incentive to strike. But the idea of industrial harmony in non-union firms is associated more directly with smaller firms, where it is assumed that better communications, easier working relations, personal ties, job satisfaction, employee involvement and a greater awareness of individual needs serve to overcome any inherent tension between capital and labour. Low levels of union membership and very few strikes combine to suggest that 'small is beautiful'. As far as small-firm employee relations are concerned, however, this would seem to be a 'modern myth' (Rainnie 1985a:213–16 and 1989) that arises from a confusion of image and reality. The image presented by the Conservative Party, for example, in their pamphlet *Small Firm, Big Future*, is that,

> Working relationships are easier and happier in small companies. Many of the problems that arise in large enterprises are unknown in firms where the owner is known to all his employees. (quoted by Rainnie, 1985b:148)

Unfortunately, there is virtually no empirical evidence to support such claims (Goss, 1988:115; and Scase, 1995), and that which does exist (e.g. Ingham, 1970) is methodologically suspect (Curran and Burrows, 1986; Curran and Stanworth, 1981a; and Rainnie, 1989:156–70). Invariably, the suggestion that the firm is 'one big happy family' is derived from the opinions of owners/managers, rather than from the workforce (Curran and Stanworth, 1981a:14–15; and Goss, 1988:115, and 1991:158). In general, managers express a more positive (i.e. favourable) view on the 'climate' of employee relations in their organisation than either union representatives or employees (see Cully *et al.*, 1999:277; see also Bryson, 2001c). Moreover, managers seem to equate 'good employee relations' with outcomes such as financial performance and higher labour productivity (i.e. where the organisation achieves the latter then managers are more likely to proclaim 'good employee relations') whereas workers are more likely to view employee relations in a positive light if they feel secure, have some influence over their work and are committed to their job, and in particular if they are 'fairly' treated (Cully *et al.*, 1999:277–81). It is well established that union members tend to be less satisfied with their jobs and pay than non-union members, but most of this satisfaction differential can be accounted for by differences in the demographic, job and workplace characteristics of the two groups (Bryson *et al.*, 2002). As Gilman *et al.* (2002:62) discovered, many non-union workers are 'not necessarily satisfied in some absolute sense, but given their skills and labour market options, they had found some consolation'. Thus, quiescence need not imply individual deference, nor does the absence of strike activity imply the eradication of industrial conflict. It is essential, therefore, to delve further into the social relations of production within small, non-union firms, and in particular to elicit the opinions of the workforce.

One of the most striking features of small, non-union firms, as already intimated, is the informality of employee relations. In their study of 397 small firms, for example, Scott *et al.* (1989:16) found that 61 per cent had no regular meetings with workforce representatives, and 44 per cent had no arrangements for informing or consulting employees through informal meetings or internal memos (see also Cully *et al.*, 1999:257–8; Matlay, 1999:288; and Millward *et al.*, 1992:364–5). Informality is, of course, a dynamic rather than a fixed characteristic of small firms (i.e. it is a matter of degree, rather than the total absence of formality) and it is highly context specific (see Cully *et al.*, 1999:272; and Ram *et al.*, 2001:846). Nonetheless, as Gunnigle and Brady (1984:23) conclude from their study of 25 small manufacturing firms, 'there seems to be a dangerous perception of complacency about communications and consultation in small firms. Owner/managers place emphasis on the frequency of employer/employee contact rather than on the quality of such contacts'. If problems arise, these will also be settled informally, as less than a third of the firms studied by Scott *et al.* (1989:16), for example, had a formal, written grievance procedure (see also Millward *et al.*, 1992:364). As expected, larger firms were more likely to have formal procedures, as were those that were unionised (Scott *et al.*, 1989:16–17; see also Earnshaw *et al.*, 2000:63–4). In sum, procedural informality characterises the small, non-union sector to a much greater extent than either the unionised or large, non-union sector. Figure 19.1 summarises the principal differences between union and non-union, large and small firms (see also Millward *et al.*, 1992:236–9).

The notion of small firms being 'one big happy family' is, of course, a cliché, 'and yet as with all clichés it contains a grain of truth' (Scott *et al.*, 1989:51). The significant presence of family members within small firms has already been noted. More generally, personal relations tend to become employee or industrial relations in small firms. In the building industry, for example, where market conditions are highly unstable, employers frequently adopt a *fraternal* strategy with few overtly hierarchical relations.

	UNION		NON-UNION	
	Large	Small	Large	Small
Pay system	Formalised system	Industry agreement	Formalised system	Informal
Differentials	Continuous and extensive pay hierarchy, few on industry minimum	Relatively continuous	Wide differentials, many pay 'industry standard' or above	Discontinuous, narrow differentials, now pay National Minimum Wage
Sick pay/ Pensions	Common, non-discretionary	Pensions uncommon, sick pay mainly for key staff	Common, but often restricted to specific groups	Pensions uncommon, sick pay for key staff
Holidays	Industry standard or better	Industry standard	Industry standard or low minimum entitlement increasing with grade/ service	Low entitlement for all grades, often below industry standard
Job guarantees	Collective agreement at industry or local level	Industry agreement/ statutory measures	None (statutory measures only)	None (statutory measures only)
Staffing agreements	Formal/informal deals	Industry agreement/ informal bargaining	Determined by management prerogative	Determined by management prerogative
Training systems	Formal (linked to state schemes)	Recruit skilled workers externally or formal (linked to state schemes)	Formal (linked to state schemes)	Recruit externally trained or informal/firm-specific training

Figure 19.1 – Pay, benefits and working arrangements in union versus non-union finances
Source: Adapted from Rubery (1987:62-3).

Instead, the employer will adopt an 'all workers together' attitude, for example working alongside his employees on the job (see Goffee and Scase, 1982; and Scase, 1995:587–8). Thus, it is the *particularistic* relations that develop between employer and employee that demand attention. Like family relations, feelings of 'good' and 'ill' tend to be more intensely held in small firms (Holiday, 1995:157; and Scott *et al.*, 1989:42 and 51), as Rainnie (1989:127–8) illustrates:

> Management stress on the 'family' nature of their own firm and relationships within it, not only points to the way in which a particular social formation is used to legitimate power structures (manager-as-father allowed to discipline the children/workers), but also the way that disagreement can be termed pathological. The ideological power of the family is such that attacking this sacred institution is almost unthinkable within the ruling consensus. Likewise, anybody breaking the managerially defined boundaries of decent behaviour in a family firm, by definition steps out of the bounds of acceptable action.

The appearance of industrial harmony thus begins to appear somewhat suspect once the reality of (authority) relations between employer and employee within small, non-union firms is analysed more closely. When workers in small firms are questioned about relations with their employer, for example, they invariably report 'socially distant' relations (Curran and Stanworth, 1981b:148; see also Goss, 1988 and 1991; and Moule, 1998). Relations are often not overtly hostile, but 'it would be wrong to see such relations as necessarily tokening deep and strong affective relations between workers and bosses' (Curran and Stanworth, 1981b:149). Rather, 'friendship' and easy-going relations are simply the easiest way to deal with others in a closed environment. Conflict may therefore be 'submerged' in small firms due to the need to manage inter-group conflicts on a personal basis (Stephenson *et al.*, 1983:33). But herein lies the source of instability: such relations may achieve a degree of integration and a veneer of industrial harmony, but 'if the basis of legitimacy is relationships other than those stemming purely from the employment relationship, their continuance is threatened by change. Change of many types can pull back the veil of obscurity and reveal the unmediated effect of the employment relationship' (Scott *et al.*, 1989:48–9).

Even the 'happy family' owner/manager will change his tune when confronted by external pressures or internal dissent. Scott *et al.* (1989:50), for example, refer to one manager who boasted of his caring, paternalistic approach which he illustrated by reference to two older workers allowed to stay on at the firm beyond their retirement age. At a subsequent interview, however, he referred to these two workers in less affectionate terms. In the interim period, profits had fallen and the company had gone into the red for the first time. The result had been redundancies, including the two older workers who were now described in terms of 'getting rid of the shit'. As this and other examples cited by Scott *et al.* (1989:50) illustrate, it is not uncommon for the advantages of family and affective ties to turn into their opposites, into feelings which can border upon enmity (ibid:52). If an employee is not performing satisfactorily, for example, the owner/manager is initially just as likely to have a word with the employee's friend or a family member in order to put pressure on the offending party. Scott and his colleagues even cite the case of one employer who had a quiet word with an employee's husband at the local pub! If this approach fails, however, the owner/manager may not apply disciplinary action; instead, problems are often left to fester until critical rather than corrective action is taken (i.e. dismissal rather than discipline) (ibid:92; see also Earnshaw *et al.*, 2000). Most small employers are (blissfully) ignorant of workers' individual employment rights – most appear to operate on a 'need to know' basis (e.g. when they need to dismiss a worker or when an employee brings a claim of unfair dismissal) (see Blackburn and Hart, 2002). Disciplinary sanctions and dismissals are much lower in unionised firms compared to non-union firms (Cully *et al.*, 1999:128; Knight and Latreille, 2000; and Millward *et al.*, 1992:364). In 1998, the average workplace in the hotels and restaurant sector had dismissed a quite astonishing 5.9 employees in every 100 during the previous year (compared to the average for all workplaces of 1.5 dismissals per 100 employees and just 0.6 in education) (Cully *et al.*, 1999:128). In many cases, non-union employees in small workplaces are dismissed without statutory notice or even fair grounds (see Dickens *et al.*, 1985; and Earnshaw *et al.*, 2000). The burgeoning number of work-related complaints made to Citizens' Advice Bureaux come predominantly from non-unionists, mainly those employed in small workplaces (see Abbott, 1998:259–60).

For this reason, and of course the generally poorer conditions of work and pay in small, non-union firms, there is a good deal of 'churning' among the workforce (Cully *et al.*, 1999:128; and Scott *et al.*, 1989:30). Numbers may be fairly stable, but there is a high rate of entry and exit. In the clothing industry, for example, labour turnover is high where firms deliberately adopt a 'like it or leave' approach (Rainnie, 1985a). As at Sew & Son, many decide, or are forced, to leave. Many more have little alternative but to stay. Exit and/or silence, then, rather than voice, is the most likely scenario. Most employees in small, non-union firms lack the articulateness and self-confidence to challenge, or even question, the self-assured, and often highly opinionated owner/manager (Cully *et al*, 1999:257–8; and Goss, 1991:165), and even if they do, managers either fail to listen or do nothing about it (Scott *et al.*, 1989:45). Knowing this, many employees see it as pointless to complain. This powerlessness is often combined with enforced compliance which in some companies 'is made an explicit condition of continued employment, and the threat of dismissal kept ever-present' (Goss, 1991:161). As Scott *et al.* (1989:39) note, 'those who did not support management aims and policy were seen not only to be unreasonable, but also as being in some way treacherous'. The language may be strong (non-compliance as treachery), but such views are deeply held by many owners/managers of small businesses.

As a result, conflict is usually manifested in individual, invariably unorganised forms, such as absenteeism or high labour turnover. Edwards and Scullion's (1982:107, and 1984:561–2) account of two clothing firms is a case in point. In some instances, workers' discontent is vented on other individuals, or groups of workers, rather than through direct confrontation with its source, the company or proprietors (see Moule, 1998:645). Such forms of 'displaced resistance' or 'lateral conflict' (Burawoy, 1979) are all the more likely in the absence of collective (trade union) support as individuals are understandably reluctant to challenge management directly (e.g. Goss, 1991:165; and Rainnie, 1985a:219), especially as they will almost inevitably be labelled as 'troublemakers'. Owners/managers blame so-called 'troublemakers' for virtually all their labour ills, ranging from high turnover (unsettling staff), provoking unfair dismissal cases and encouraging absenteeism (Gunnigle and Brady, 1984:22; and Scott *et al.*, 1989:42). More generally,

> The notion of the 'trouble maker' appears far too often to be dismissed merely as an interesting but insignificant feature of management accounts of the nature of their workforce. Rather, the importance of this notion is that it serves as an element within a *conflict neutralisation* technique. (Scott *et al.*, 1989:42, original emphasis)

In other words, the unitary perspective adopted by management serves to *personalise* conflict within the organisation (problems are attributed to individuals, not to inherent antagonisms that exist between management and labour in *all* organisations). While most managers are unitarist in outlook, such views appear to be more deeply held by the owner/managers of small firms. Since they fail to recognise or accept *any* conflicts of interest as being legitimate, such attitudes play an important role in both the determination of management style in non-union firms and the (in) ability of trade unions to organise such companies.

MANAGEMENT STYLE IN NON-UNION FIRMS

One of the problems which besets many discussions of non-union firms and workers is that they tend to be studied predominantly from the perspective of the propensity of workers to unionise and/or the differences in management practice *vis-à-vis* unionised firms. Consequently, 'the very term non-unionism becomes a limiting definition of workplaces' (Guest and Hoque, 1994:2) which tend to 'fall' into one of either two principal 'types': 'traditionalists' who display outright hostility towards trade unions, or 'sophisticated paternalists' whose management policies effectively 'substitute' for union presence (see Turnbull and Wass, 1997b). As Purcell and Sisson (1983:113) point out, sophisticated paternalists might refuse to recognise trade unions, 'but do not take it for granted that their employees accept the company's objectives or automatically legitimise management decision-making; they spend considerable time and resources ensuring that their employees have the right approach'. Sew & Son would obviously be counted as a 'traditionalist' whereas Marks & Spencer is often cited as the archetypical 'sophisticated paternalist'. The distinction between *anti*-union (suppression) and *non*-union (substitution) firms, however, is a somewhat false dichotomy. Sophisticated paternalists display an apparent indifference towards trade unions because, first, they can afford to, and secondly because they rarely face any challenge from organised labour. If they are challenged, however, management are always quick to act and firm in their resolution to remain non-union.

In the IBM recognition vote in the UK in 1977, for example, which Bassett (1986:162–4) cites as evidence of both employee indifference towards trade unions and the effectiveness of the company's employee relations policies, IBM spent £10000 on an advertising campaign to secure a 'NO' vote (Beaumont, 1987:121; see also Oliver and Wilkinson, 1992:125–6), a fact which Bassett fails to acknowledge, or perhaps conveniently overlooked. According to Dickson *et al.* (1988), even IBM employees may not be permanently lost to the trade union movement, a point perhaps reinforced by the company's recent troubles. McDonald's is another case in point (Royle, 1999 and 2000). M&S recently faced an organising campaign by USDAW among warehouse staff following the imposition of a three-year pay freeze. This was to bring the salary of (predominantly female) sales staff into line with those of (predominantly male) warehouse staff (by increasing the former by 26.5 per cent and freezing the latter), following an 'equal pay for work of equal value' case at Sainsbury's in November 1989. M&S accepted the right of warehouse staff to join a union but would not grant recognition, and certainly would not countenance the workers' claim to have their pay freeze cancelled. USDAW has accused M&S of victimising union members in one of its Glasgow depots by introducing 'unworkable shifts', with start times too early for employees to use public transport, an allegation M&S vigorously disputed (Hamil, 1993:43). M&S recognised trade unions in their European stores, however, which the company attributed to employment legislation and industrial relations practices in these countries which 'required' M&S to deal with trade unions (Salsbury, 1993:569). Industrial action at the company's stores in Dublin over pay, shift patterns and consultation procedures, however, suggests that 'internal' rather than purely 'external' factors are at work, illustrating yet again the highly *contingent* nature of management style.

If faced with a challenge, then, sophisticated paternalists can display vehement opposition to union organisation. It is at such times that the asymmetry of the employment relationship is revealed. As Hamil (1993:43) notes, few other companies would have the power to impose the kind of deal implemented at M&S in response to the equal value case, at least not without significant employee opposition. Management policy is clearly directed towards the maintenance of an employee relations system that does not include trade unions, which is one thing that the sophisticated paternalists have in common with the traditionalists. In the case of M&S and other 'sophisticated paternalists', however, management thinking is effectively pluralist to the extent that management recognise the need to manage employee relations *as if* the workforce has divergent interests. In this way, management is able to identify concerns, allay fears, satisfy workers' aspirations *and stay non-union*. Actual policies, of course, are to all intents and purposes unitary in both composition and purpose, but are founded on a deeper management understanding of the employment relationship. At companies such as Sew & Son, in contrast, management thinking is unashamedly unitarist, but employee relations policies are often imposed *against* the express wishes of the workforce. Given that actual policies are often implemented through coercion, it is more appropriate to label the management style as 'authoritarian': if all the organisation's members are on the 'same side' and part of a team, as the unitary perspective holds, then surely management would only need to *inform* employees of its policies, not enforce them.

Such characteristics of management style among small, non-union firms in the clothing industry are not uncommon (Rainnie, 1985a, and 1989:168). Likewise, in hotels and restaurants, management style tends to be highly autocratic and strongly anti-union (Brown and Crossman, 2000; Hoque, 2000; Macaulay and Wood, 1992:21; and Macfarlane, 1982:33–4). Variation obviously exists across different hotels, and in particular between the large chains and smaller independent hotels, but there is a common framework within which different management styles function, namely 'a framework which is reluctant to accept the legitimacy of employees taking any meaningful part in the influence or control of their working conditions or environment' (Macfarlane, 1982:34; see also Millward *et al.*, 1992:365). More general studies of non-union firms confirm management attitudes to be a mixture of unitarism, paternalism and authoritarianism (e.g. Gilman *et al.*, 2002; Gollan, 2001; Gunnigle and Brady, 1984:21–2; Matlay, 1999; Scase, 2003:481; and Scott *et al.*, 1989). Paternalism, as the nomenclature suggests, has traditionally been based on a transfer of family/domestic relations into the workplace, with face-to-face relations between management and labour characterised by deference and indulgency (workers were treated as children to be looked after, rewarded and disciplined by their employer as a parent would a child) (Wray, 1996:702; see also Ackers, 1998). This benevolent form of despotism is typical of many small firms (see Scase, 1995:285; and Wray, 1996:702). To sustain paternalistic relations as firms grow in size, formal consultation and communication procedures are adopted and indulgency is maintained by corporate largesse through profit-sharing schemes and other benefits (at M&S, for example, benefits include subsidised meals, medical care, hairdressing, store discount cards and the like). Sophisticated paternalism thereby remains loyal to the familial culture of traditional paternalism, but only in an attempt to maintain employee subordination (Wray, 1996:703–4). At the heart of all forms of paternalism, in other words, is a over-riding desire to perpetuate managerial authority.

The principal reason for unitarist attitudes and paternalistic and/or autocratic management practices in small firms appears to be possessiveness. Owner-managers in particular regard *their* company as unique and regard themselves as benign, fair, even-handed and reasonable (Scott *et al.*, 1989:36). 'Typically the business is seen as his possession to do as he wishes – and especially where the owner/manager is also the founder. It is important to realise that for many owner/managers the business is essentially an extension of their ego' (ibid:91). Many members of the UK's 'petty bourgeoisie' (broadly defined as those who own small-scale capital which is used for productive purposes in conjunction with the proprietor's and, often, others' labour) (Scase, 1982:148), 'show strong psychological inclinations towards notions of autonomy and independence, and this is often translated into an organisational form to ensure their maximisation' (Curran and Burrows, 1986:270; see also Ford, 1982:45–6). As Cully *et al.* (1999:257–8) found, almost three-quarters of small business managers, and especially owner-managers, strongly believe that 'those at the top are best placed to make decisions about this workplace'. Not surprisingly, these managers are more likely to favour direct forms of control (ibid). In short, owners/ managers not only believe in, but often impose their primacy over the labour process (Scott *et al.*, 1989:93). The implications for employee relations are immediately apparent. Not only will the personality of the owner/manager have a major impact on management style, but the owner's/manager's desire for independence and autonomy 'often result in ill-defined organisational structures with poorly defined roles, a high level of centralised decision-making and little forward planning. For employees the result may be feelings of lack of security and involvement' (Curran, 1990:138).

Generally, management policy in small firms is not formulated in a self-conscious way, relying instead on informal routinisation. This is especially true of labour relations policies, where there is little evidence of pre-planning: 'The dominant approach is one that stresses that as long as the workers are working there is no problem' (Scott *et al.*, 1989:34). There is some evidence that, in hotels at least, some managers have embraced a more strategic approach to HRM (Hoque, 2000) and many more have been compelled by the introduction of a National Minimum Wage (NMW) to think more strategically (Brown and Crossman, 2000:210). However, the dominant response has been one of cost minimisation, combined with numerical flexibility and union avoidance (ibid), and most small firms operate with sufficient indeterminacy to allow them to absorb the costs of the NMW (Arrowsmith *et al.*, 2003; and Gilman *et al.*, 2002:54). This helps to explain the apparent 'paradox' of an increase in wages (via the NMW) resulting in only modest employment effects (ibid).

Differences between small, non-union firms will of course be inevitable. Guest and Hoque (1994), for example, differentiate (newly-established) non-union firms according to whether or not the company has a human resource strategy on the one hand, and the nature of human resource policy and practice, on the other. This gives rise to a four-fold classification of 'good' non-union employers that have a clear human resource strategy and positive human resource management policies; 'lucky' non-union companies that have opportunistically followed the latest 'fads and fashions' of human resource management; 'bad' non-union companies that have no strategy and a low uptake of human resource policies; and the 'ugly' face of non-unionism represented by employers who (strategically) deprive workers of their rights and exploit their labour. In a sample of 122 non-union firms studied by Guest and Hoque, only 8 could be described as 'ugly' whereas 56 were 'good' employers. The comparatively high number of 'good' employers, in marked contrast to the picture suggested by successive WIRS and WERS98, is no doubt partly attributable to the 'self-selecting', rather than representative, nature of the sample. One might expect 'good' non-union firms with more sophisticated employee relations policies to be small 'high tech' firms in the 'innovative' group identified by Rainnie (1989:85, and 1991:188), but in fact most tended to be found in the non-financial service sector rather than manufacturing (Guest and Hoque, 1994:6–7). A major deficiency of this study, however, is that employees were not asked whether their employer was good, bad, or ugly.

In a specific study of high-tech companies, McLoughlin and Gourlay (1992:673–4) consider management style along two different dimensions, namely individualism-collectivism and the extent of 'strategic integration' (essentially the extent to which company policies achieve a 'tight coupling' between strategic intent, management attitudes and actual behaviour or, at the other extreme, are largely informal, idiosyncratic, unco-ordinated or even contradictory). McLoughlin and Gourlay were concerned to establish the extent to which a sophisticated human resource management (HRM) strategy, such as that deemed to characterise companies such as IBM and Hewlett Packard, was pursued by non-union companies in this sector. The picture that emerged from a detailed study that included 23 non-union companies was that the companies most closely approximating to such an approach all employed fewer than 500 workers, employed predominantly non-manual labour (less than 20 per cent were manual workers in 8 of the 10 companies in this group), half had been established since 1979, and the majority were non-assembly/manufacturing plants (ibid:679). Overall, the conclusion was that 'non-union status was likely to be the result of straightforward avoidance or opportunism as any HRM-derived sophisticated substitution strategy designed to obviate a perceived need for union representation on the part of employees' (ibid:685). Put differently, companies such as M&S and IBM are very much the exception rather than the rule among non-union firms: most non-union firms do not *need*, nor could the majority *afford*, to adopt a substitution strategy. Given the market position of most sophisticated paternalists, these companies are improbable 'role models' for most managers. Equally for trade unions in the UK, companies such as M&S and IBM remain an attractive, but unlikely prize. The reality that trade unions must confront, and the problems they must overcome if they want to organise the growing ranks of non-union employees, are those that characterise the more traditional firms such as Sew & Son. Whether such companies are non-union as a result of deliberate avoidance or simply pragmatic opportunism (or indeed lack of attention by union recruiters), the question that remains to be answered is whether employees in such companies would be receptive to unionisation.

ORGANISING THE UNORGANISED

As the debate on the future of trade unionism shifts from analysis of decline to prognosis for growth, attention has focused on the prospects for new union strategies to organise in the expanding service sector of the economy. During the 1980s, the structure of trade unions in the UK was exposed as seemingly inappropriate, or incapable, of dealing with many of the changes thrown up by economic restructuring and recession, government legislation and employer hostility. This was especially so in the service sector, the new towns and the small-firm sector where union organising attempts were often duplicated (and diluted) and where unions were often unable to present potential members with a single, and clearly identifiable 'appropriate' union (Winchester, 1988:509). In hotels and catering, for example, the T&GWU and the Hotel and Catering Workers' Union (HCU) (a specialist union spawned by the GMB in 1980) competed for members. But within the T&GWU, hotels came under the Food, Drink and Tobacco division and officials simply did not know enough about the industry to recruit effectively. The HCU, on the other hand, adopted a 'softly, softly', non-confrontational approach, trying to build up membership by persuasion and establishing some confidence in the union among the management of larger hotel chains (Macaulay and Wood, 1992:22–3; and Macfarlane, 1982:35). Inappropriate structures and an ineffective approach to recruitment have led to the unions' role being characterised as one of 'studied invisibility', and it comes as no surprise that very few employees (only 15 per cent in one study) could even name the appropriate unions involved in the industry (Macaulay and Wood, 1992:23–5).

To recruit non-union members in the vast majority of non-union firms will require what Kelly and Heery (1989:198–9) classify as a 'distant expansion' recruitment strategy. Such firms are not covered by recognition agreements (unlike distribution, for example, where union membership is low but there is at least union recognition in place), and are outside most unions' traditional areas of recruitment (unlike non-union white-collar staff in manufacturing). This presents a much wider, and more difficult, range of problems that unions must overcome if they are to attract new members. Obstacles to expanding membership in new job territories include high rates of labour turnover, the small size of many establishments, their geographical dispersion, and in particular employer opposition (ibid:199; see also Dundon *et al.*, 1999:262; Gall and McKay, 2001; Gollan, 2001; Green, 1992:456; Heery and Simms, 2003; Macaulay and Wood, 1992:27; and Turnbull, 1997 and 2003:505). In hotels and restaurants, for example, employer antipathy puts trade unions 'in a Catch 22 situation where, in order to appear a credible source of representation to employees, they must demonstrate an ability to participate meaningfully in the process of job regulation, but this can only be achieved where the employer has conceded sufficient recognition rights' (Macfarlane, 1982:30). The latter is now regulated by a statutory recognition procedure (see Chapters 5 and 6), but many studies have still found that 'Everything turns … on the orientation of employers' (Colling, 2003:387; see also Heery and Simms, 2003).

Without recognition from the employer, union effectiveness is more difficult (though not impossible) to establish and certainly more costly to maintain. As Willman (1989:263) argues, pre-recognition representation is more expensive as the union is at best only allowed individual representation rights (e.g. in discipline or dismissal cases). Recognition allows some of the representation costs to be shifted on to the employer, which means that unions typically seek to operate in *two* markets, one for members and one for employers. In small firms the market for employers is particularly important since access to employees is more difficult to secure and the union must establish independent workplace organisation (participative self-organisation) if it operates only in the membership market. Invariably, therefore, 'unions will not seek to organise employees where they see no prospect of gaining bargaining rights, since they must deal only with individual issues which are costly' (ibid). Thus, unions seek to offer something to the employer as well as the employee, as Figure 19.2 demonstrates.

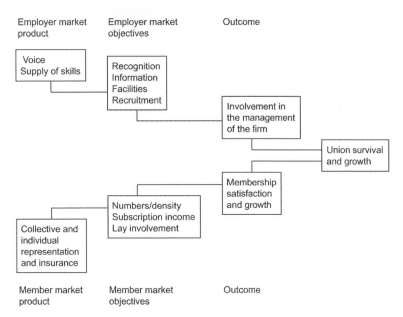

Figure 19.2 – The market for trade unionism
Source: Willman (1989:264).

Willman (1989) argued that 'market share unionism', where unions compete for a declining membership base in already organised sectors, rather than expand their membership in areas such as the private services sector (distant recruitment), was inevitable given the hostility of employers, the costly nature of such recruitment, the financial weakness of most British unions and the absence of legal recognition procedures that unions could use to force recognition on a recalcitrant employer. Even though a statutory union recognition procedure is now in place (Employment Relations Act, 1999), a considerable number of employers continue to resist union organising and recruitment campaigns, and some 'are prepared to resort to nakedly unethical behaviour to prevent workers forming unions' (Heery and Simms, 2003:6). Moreover, employers continue to exploit competition between unions, responding to union organising campaigns by inviting other (more pliant) unions to put forward a counter-proposal (ibid).

Although the 'logic' of market-share trade unionism continues to frustrate union revival, it is, of course, inherently *illogical* for the labour movement as a whole to have destructive competition for membership. This can be overcome, because the 'logic' of market-share unionism rests on two preconditions. The first is an absence of structures, procedures or a central body with sufficient authority to effect co-ordination and co-operation between individual unions. A good illustration of these problems was the Special Review Body (SRB) set up by the TUC in 1987. Under the auspices of the SRB, Congress conducted six pilot studies of local labour markets in order to facilitate new membership recruitment. These studies revealed striking deficiencies in the internal information systems of many unions, limited knowledge of the key organisational and workforce characteristics of non-union firms, and strictly limited attempts to recruit many non-union workers (see Beaumont and Harris, 1990:276). But while the diagnosis of the problem was accepted by the major unions, they were not prepared to accept a more 'intrusive' (proactive or co-ordinating) role on the part of the TUC.

In some respects, the authority of the TUC has declined in recent years (Ackers *et al.*, 1996:27), although the 'relaunch' of the TUC in the mid 1990s has resulted in a more strategic approach to a series of campaigns based on 'partnership' and the building of supporting coalitions. Thus, instead of simply seeking greater control and direction over affiliates, the TUC has become a networking organisation (Heery, 1998:346). Equally important, under the *New Unionism* initiative launched in 1996 an Organising Academy has been established by the TUC to train union organisers in the techniques of the organising model. Dedicated organisers will target non-union workplaces and non-union workers, particularly women, young workers and ethnic minorities, disseminate 'best practice', and above all promote an 'organising culture' where recruitment and organising are regarded by everyone in the labour movement as a key priority. Private service sector workers, where union membership is lowest, are a key target. As Korczynski (2002) points out, there are particular features of service sector work that must be acknowledged and incorporated into the organising model if it is to prove successful, especially for the recruitment of 'front-line' (customer-contact) workers. In particular, the unions' role must not simply be 'anti-employer' as it is often perceived to be when unions follow the organising model, but also 'pro-customer'. As Table 19.2 highlights, unions should seek to civilise production *and* consumption, thereby connecting more directly with the interests of front-line workers (ibid:188–9).

The second precondition for the logic of market-share trade unionism to prevail is a dependence on employers. One of the dilemmas facing all trade unions is that, over time, organisational survival is increasingly separated from, and is largely independent of, the motivation, mobilisation, solidarity and 'willingness to act' of the rank-and-file membership. In effect, the union substitutes external guarantees of survival – employer recognition and check-off arrangements, statutory recognition procedures and strong political ties to social democratic parties – for internal dependence on its members. As Offe and Wiesenthal (1980:107) point out, unions invariably develop

Table 19.2 – Three union approaches to organising front-line service workers

	Partnership approach	**Organising approach**	**Organising on the front line**
Who to organise?	Focus recruitment efforts on core workers in organisations in which unions have a presence	Bring in members from occupations and workplaces with little union presence, target both core and contingent workers	Recognise limited union presence in many service firms, focus on non-union workers and workplaces
What interests to prioritise?	Common interests with management, e.g. pay to hire and keep good workers, training and development	Issues of conflict with management, e.g. low pay, safety, work intensification	Issues of direct concern to front-line workers, e. g. definitions of 'customer care' or 'emotional labour'
How to organise and represent interests?	Representative democracy; relatively passive members with union official engaged in bargaining and 'back-stage' discussions with management	Participative democracy; active role for members at workplace level in mobilising to force concessions from management	Build union organisation around centralised nodes of consumption; use company rhetoric of customer service to mobilise customer support
The ideology of unionism	'Stakeholder' in the organisation and wider society	Class and community organisations	Civilising force in both production and consumption

*Source:*Adapted from Korczynski (2002:179).

bureaucratic structures in order to maximise the independence of the union's officials and their control over internal decision-making on the one hand, and a more 'individualistic' relationship with rank-and-file members on the other, emphasising individual incentives to join (for a review of these developments in the UK, see Heery and Kelly, 1994). The problem which then arises, of course, is that once the relative independence of the organisation from its members' 'willingness to act' has been achieved, 'the organization *no longer has any capacity to resist attempts to withdraw external support* and the externally provided legal and institutional status' (Offe and Wiesenthal, 1980:108, original emphasis). To date, previously non-union employers in the UK appear to have taken their lead from the change in public policy effected by the Employment Relations Act (1999) and have accepted union organising (Heery and Simms, 2003), but it must be acknowledged that statutory provisions can equally be used *against* trade unions. Certification law in the USA, for example, which is very similar to the new recognition procedure in the UK, was likewise passed originally to facilitate union organising and promote collective bargaining, but it frequently has the opposite effect as managers use the provisions of the law to derecognise existing unions or resist new recognition campaigns (see Adams, 2002; Brody, 2001; and HRW, 2000).

Even if unions can avoid or overcome these problems, two important questions still remain: will non-union workers want to join, and will non-union employers surrender their autonomy and authority? The answer to the first question is a resounding 'YES', *but only if unions can make a difference in the workplace*. The answer to the second question is a resounding 'NO'.

Workers in the UK want union representation. Around 40 per cent of non-union employees say they would join a union if one were available at their workplace (CEP, 2002; Charlwood, 2002:464; and TUC, 1996a). Moreover, the demand for union membership is highest in precisely those industries (e.g. wholesale and retail) where union density is lowest (CEP, 2002; see also Gallie, 1996; and Macaulay and Wood, 1992:26). Likewise, many part-timers (Labour Research Department, 1996:17; and Sinclair, 1996) and young people would like to join a union (TUC, 1996b). However, there is a profound lack of awareness of trade unions among many groups of workers, especially young people (ibid; and Roberts, 2003a), due in large part to the fact that they are simply never actively recruited or asked to join a union (see Cully *et al.*, 1999; and Green, 1990). Other workers might be aware of unions and the benefits union membership might bring, but unions lack 'appeal' in terms of their structure, organisation and activities. Women, for example, 'benefit' considerably from union membership in terms of their wage premium (the union-negotiated 'mark-up' over comparable non-union jobs) and other benefits, unlike their male counterparts (Machin, 2001), but unions must do more than 'sell' these benefits to female workers if they are to increase their membership – they must also change their own gendered organisational structures and culture (Colgan and Ledwith, 2002; Cunninson and Stageman, 1995; Heery and Kelly, 1989; and Ledwith and Colgan, 1996). The most important constraint on union revival, however, appears to be workers' uncertainty about whether unions can 'deliver' (see Diamond and Freeman, 2001).

There is a significant difference between 'demand' (an expressed desire for unionism) and 'effective demand' (a 'willingness to pay' for union protection, benefits or services) (see Troy, 2001:254). Employer opposition can heavily weight the cost side of the equation, leaving workers to question whether the union can secure benefits in the face of the hostility of their employer. To be sure, once they become members, workers tend to support their union (see, for example, Diamond and Freeman, 2001:19) and the majority believes that their union does a good job and responds positively to their needs (Bryson, 1999:81). Data from WERS, for example, indicate that 46 per cent of trade unionists in Britain believe that unions 'make a difference to what it is like to work here' (compared to 30 per cent of non-unionists and 26 per cent of ex-unionists) (Cully *et al.*, 1999:212–13) and data from the BSAS reveal that 49 per cent of respondents believe that the removal of union representation at their workplace would make things worse (Bryson, 1999:83). But this counts for nothing if unions cannot persuade workers to unionise or the employer to recognise. Many non-union workers are simply resigned to the fact that, while they might like to join a union, their employer would not 'allow' them.

Many workers continue to face victimisation by their employer when they attempt to form a union (Heery and Simms, 2003). This is a particular problem when unions attempt to organise small, owner-managed firms (ibid; see Rainnie, 1989:219; and Scott *et al.*, 1989:72–3). In the hotel and catering industry, for example, employees are well aware of management hostility towards trade unionism, and 'employees' perception of this hostility has a role in forming apparent psychological barriers to acceptance of the likely benefits of union membership and plays some part in generating a sense of both resignation and of the immutability of hotel and catering workers' lot in life' (Macaulay and Wood, 1992:27). Given the unitary outlook of the owners/managers of small firms, it is hard to imagine that many would voluntarily decide to grant union recognition. The majority would simply not countenance such a challenge to their cherished independence and authority.

Perhaps, however, we should not paint too bleak a picture. There have always been some non-union employers who are more receptive to union organising, if approached (see Abbott, 1993:310), and the Employment Relations Act (1999) does appear to have tempered employer hostility to unionisation (Diamond and Freeman, 2001:2; Heery and Simms, 2003; and Oxenbridge *et al.*, 2003). In many respects, 'small firms and unions each need on the one hand to be far less wary. On the other hand, there might be positive benefits from co-existence' (Scott *et al.*, 1989:83). Handling disciplinary matters and the management of change in small, non-union firms are examples of areas where such firms might benefit from more formal, collectively-determined procedures which provide rights of representation for the workforce (see also Freeman, 1995). As already noted, one reason why small firms do not grow, and therefore do not create the jobs that successive governments have longed for, is their inability to move from an informal employee relations system based on personal relations to a more formalised procedure: a principal reason why owners/managers do not expand their business is precisely because they perceive potential problems with staff. More formal procedures in the internal labour market should not, then, be equated automatically with inefficiency or a lack of flexibility but rather, if anything, their opposite. At the same time, and equally important, an independent organisation can protect and promote employee rights. Unionisation, in other words, need not be a 'zero sum' process for the owner/manager. At present it is not only the non-union employee that suffers from management hostility and the apathy of many trade unions, but also the economy itself wherein small, non-union firms fail to stimulate economic growth.

CONCLUSION

Now that 'non-unionism has come out of the closet' (Flood and Turner, 1993:54), it has been suggested that 'the influence by example of non-union companies of excellence (e.g. IBM, Marks & Spencer) ... may be factors working to bring about changes in management attitudes towards unions through the course of time' (Beaumont, 1986:33). This might account for some of the growing interest in HRM and 'high commitment' management practices, but this is clearly not the situation in the majority of non-union firms. Nonetheless, it is often assumed that all is well in the majority of non-union firms because their small size allows for close working relationships, flexible working practices, and employee satisfaction. This is reflected in public policy, with successive governments seeking to remove unwelcome 'restrictions' (including those imposed by trade unions) on SMEs in order to encourage 'enterprise'. However, instead of being 'burdened by the law', especially employment law, many small firms are genuinely ignorant of their obligations or else deliberately choose to flout the law (see, for example, Blackburn and Hart, 2002; Earnshaw *et al.*, 2000; and Scott *et al.*, 1989:90). Unfortunately, *unorganised* employment is often *unregulated* employment (Dickens and Hall, 1995:271).

New Labour has gone some way towards enhancing the individual employment rights of workers and the rights of employees to collective representation at work, but this has not yet closed the 'representation gap' (Towers, 1997b) which leaves millions of workers in the UK without an effective voice at work. The UK is one of the few exceptions (along with the United States) to the pattern of 'dual representation' (i.e. collective bargaining and statutory works councils) found in most advanced industrialised economies (see Rogers and Streeck, 1994) and there are now far fewer workers covered by collective agreements in the UK than anywhere else in the European Union. Moreover, the 'institutional' (UK and US) approach to workers' right to freedom of association, based on a majority vote in a democratic election, presents an additional hurdle for unions to overcome and a formal opportunity for employers to put their anti-union cards on the table and resist organisation (e.g. by victimising union activists and warning employees of the dangers of 'outside interference' in the affairs of the business). This approach is very different from European practice where employment policy respects the constitutional right of employees to join a union (or refrain from doing so) while at the same time ensuring the human right of all employees to a collective voice at work. The 'prerogative' approach to workers' freedom of association is based on the principle that no majority should have the power to deny a minority from acting collectively (see Leader, 2002:130–1). In contrast, as with collective bargaining and other forms of joint regulation the UK approach encourages a culture of 'minimal compliance' with the law, especially on the part of SMEs, rather than active engagement with a new set of social norms, values and institutions designed to protect and promote workers' rights *as well as* the efficiency of firms.

In liberal market economies, it is widely assumed that any diminution of the 'social constraints' on self-interested rational action will enhance efficiency and entrepreneurial activity. However, as we have already noted, economies that rely excessively on 'free markets' encounter problems of social justice and fairness (see Boyer and Hollingsworth, 1997:440). Moreover, socially institutionalised (and therefore accepted) constraints on firms' behaviour may actually enhance market performance (Streeck, 1997). If nothing else, such constraints would foreclose exploitative forms of cost minimisation that characterise the employee relations of many SMEs. The UK needs a new approach to the statutory regulation of employee relations and a much wider recognition and acceptance of the potential benefits of joint regulation (especially, it must be said, among the owners and managers of small firms). To be sure, not all workers want trade union organisation or even legislated works councils (Diamond and Freeman, 2001:3), but workers should not have to surrender rights they enjoy as citizens as soon as they walk through the office door or factory gates. At the most elementary level, more formalised procedures in SMEs would benefit workers *and* management: it would not only help to stabilise employee relations, but facilitate managed growth. As Scott *et al.* (1989:90) argue, 'it would be useful to dispel the myth that formalised, stable employment relationships ... represent creeping bureaucratisation, the death of enterprise and damage to employment growth'. In sum, many non-union employees need effective collective representation. A great many owners and managers would benefit as well. So too, it must be added, would the economic and social health of the nation.

INDEX

Printed and bound by CPI Group (UK) Ltd, Croydon, CR0 4YY